THE USE OF FOREIGN PRECEDENTS BY CONSTITUTIONAL JUDGES

In 2007 the International Association of Constitutional Law established an Interest Group on the Use of Foreign Precedents by Constitutional Judges to conduct a survey of the use of foreign precedents by Supreme and Constitutional Courts in deciding constitutional cases. Its purpose was to determine—through empirical analysis employing both quantitative and qualitative indicators—the extent to which foreign case law is cited. The survey aimed to test the reliability of studies describing and reporting instances of 'transjudicial communication' between Courts. The research also provides useful insights into the extent to which a progressive constitutional convergence may be taking place between common law and civil law traditions. The present work includes studies by scholars from African, American, Asian, European, Latin American and Oceania countries, representing jurisdictions belonging to both common law and civil law traditions, and countries employing both centralised and decentralised systems of judicial review. The results, published here for the first time, give us the best evidence yet of the existence and limits of a transnational constitutional communication between courts.

Volume 1 in the series Hart Studies in Comparative Public Law

The Use of Foreign Precedents by Constitutional Judges

Edited by
Tania Groppi
and
Marie-Claire Ponthoreau

·HART·
PUBLISHING
OXFORD AND PORTLAND, OREGON
2013

Published in the United Kingdom by Hart Publishing Ltd
16C Worcester Place, Oxford, OX1 2JW
Telephone: +44 (0)1865 517530
Fax: +44 (0)1865 510710
E-mail: mail@hartpub.co.uk
Website: http://www.hartpub.co.uk

Published in North America (US and Canada) by
Hart Publishing
c/o International Specialized Book Services
920 NE 58th Avenue, Suite 300
Portland, OR 97213-3786
USA
Tel: +1 503 287 3093 or toll-free: (1) 800 944 6190
Fax: +1 503 280 8832
E-mail: orders@isbs.com
Website: http://www.isbs.com

© The editors and contributors severally, 2013

The editors and contributors have asserted their right under the Copyright, Designs and Patents Act 1988, to be identified as the authors of this work.

All rights reserved. No part of this publication may be reproduced, stored in a retrieval system, or transmitted, in any form or by any means, without the prior permission of Hart Publishing, or as expressly permitted by law or under the terms agreed with the appropriate reprographic rights organisation. Enquiries concerning reproduction which may not be covered by the above should be addressed to Hart Publishing Ltd at the address above.

British Library Cataloguing in Publication Data
Data Available

ISBN: 978-1-84946-271-6

Typeset by Compuscript Ltd, Shannon
Printed and bound in Great Britain by
TJ International Ltd, Padstow, Cornwall

Contents

Table of Cases vii
Table of Legislation xxv

Introduction. The Methodology of the Research: How to Assess the
Reality of Transjudicial Communication? 1
Tania Groppi and Marie-Claire Ponthoreau

Part I 11

1. Reference to Foreign Precedents by the Australian High Court:
   A Matter of Method 13
   Cheryl Saunders and Adrienne Stone

2. Canada: Protecting Rights in a 'Worldwide Rights Culture'.
   An Empirical Study of the Use of Foreign Precedents by the
   Supreme Court of Canada (1982–2010) 39
   Gianluca Gentili

3. India: A 'Critical' Use of Foreign Precedents in Constitutional
   Adjudication 69
   Valentina Rita Scotti

4. The Supreme Court of Ireland and the Use of Foreign Precedents:
   The Value of Constitutional History 97
   Cristina Fasone

5. Israel: Creating a Constitution—The Use of Foreign Precedents
   by the Supreme Court (1994–2010) 129
   Suzie Navot

6. Namibia: The Supreme Court as a Foreign Law Importer 155
   Irene Spigno

7. South Africa: Teaching an 'Old Dog' New Tricks? An Empirical Study
   of the Use of Foreign Precedents by the South African Constitutional
   Court (1995–2010) 185
   Christa Rautenbach

Part II 211

8. Austria: Non-cosmopolitan, but Europe-friendly—The Constitutional
   Court's Comparative Approach 213
   Anna Gamper

9. Lifting the Constitutional Curtain? The Use of Foreign Precedent by the German Federal Constitutional Court 229
Stefan Martini

10. Hungary: Unsystematic and Incoherent Borrowing of Law. The Use of Foreign Judicial Precedents in the Jurisprudence of the Constitutional Court, 1999–2010 253
Zoltán Szente

11. A Gap between the Apparent and Hidden Attitudes of the Supreme Court of Japan towards Foreign Precedents 273
Akiko Ejima

12. Mexico: Struggling for an Open View In Constitutional Adjudication 301
Eduardo Ferrer Mac-Gregor and Rubén Sánchez Gil

13. Romania: Analogical Reasoning as a Dialectical Instrument 321
Elena Simina Tanasescu and Stefan Deaconu

14. Russia: Foreign Transplants in the Russian Constitution and Invisible Foreign Precedents in Decisions of the Russian Constitutional Court 347
Sergey Belov

15. Judges as Discursive Agent: The Use of Foreign Precedents by the Constitutional Court of Taiwan 373
Wen-Chen Chang and Jiunn-Rong Yeh

16. United States of America: First Cautious Attempts of Judicial Use of Foreign Precedents in the Supreme Court's Jurisprudence 393
Angioletta Sperti

Conclusion. The Use of Foreign Precedents by Constitutional Judges: A Limited Practice, An Uncertain Future 411
Tania Groppi and Marie-Claire Ponthoreau

Table of Cases

INTERNATIONAL

European Court of Human Rights

Baranowski v Poland App no 28358/95 (28 March 2000) 316
Dudgeon v United Kingdom Series A no 45 (1982) 4 EHRR 149 404
Handyside v United Kingdom Series A no 24 (1979–80) 1 EHRR 737 316
Hatton v United Kingdom App no 36022/97 (2003) 37 EHRR 28, 15 BHRC 259 93
Hirst v United Kingdom App no 74025/01 (2006) 42 EHRR 41, 19 BHRC 546 316
Kamasinski v Austria Series A no 168 (1991) 13 EHRR 36 316
Lingens v Austria Series A no 103 (1986) 8 EHRR 407 316
Oberschlick v Austria Series A no 204 (1995) 19 EHRR 389 316
Păduraru v Romania App no 63252/00 (2012) 54 E.H.R.R. 18 326
Refah Partisi (Welfare Party) v Turkey App no 41340/98 (2002) 35 EHRR 3 316
Stanford v United Kingdom App no 16757/90 (23 February 1994) 316
Tripodi v Italy, App no 13743/88 316
Tyrer v United Kingdom Series App no 26 (1979–80) 2 EHRR 1 93

European Court of Justice

Jipa v Ministry of Administration and Interior (C-33/07) 31 July 2008 326

Inter-American Court of Human Rights

Radilla-Pacheco v Mexico, 23 November 2009 .... 304, 305

DOMESTIC

Australia

Al-Kateb v Godwin (2004) 219 CLR 562 .... 24, 25, 32
Amalgamated Society of Engineers v Adelaide Steamship Co Ltd
 (Engineer's case) (1920) 28 CLR 129 18
Austin v Keele (1987) 61 ALJR 605, UKPC 24 17
Australian Capital Television Pty Ltd v Commonwealth (1992) 177 CLR 106 22
Australian Communist Party v Commonwealth (1951) 83 CLR 1 19
Baxter v Commissioners of Taxation (NSW) (1907) 4 CLR 1087 23
Behrooz v Secretary, Department of Immigration and Multicultural and
 Indigenous Affairs (2004) 219 CLR 486 32
Betfair Pty Ltd v Racing New Soth Wales [2012] HCA 12 21
Coleman v Power (2004) 220 CLR 1 32
Cook v Cook (1986) 162 CLR 376 17
Deakin v Webb (1904) 1 CLR 585 (State) 19

viii *Table of Cases*

Dietrich v Ilic Queen [1992] HCA 571 75
Fardon v A-G (Qld) (2004) 223 CLR 575 32
Forge v Australian Securities and Investments Commission (2006) 228 CLR 45 25
Freightlines and Construction Holdings Pty Ltd v New South Wales [1968] AC 625 17
Hogan v Hinch (2011) 243 CLR 506 38
ICM Agriculture v Commonwealth (2009) 240 CLR 140 38
Jago v District Court of New South Wales (1989) 168 CLR 23 14
James v Australia [1936] AC 578, [1936] 2 All ER 1449, (1936) 55 Ll L Rep 291 91
Judiciary and Navigation Acts, Re (19221) 29 CLR 257 19
Kirmani v Captain Cook Cruises (1985) 159 CLR 351 23
Lange v Australian Broadcasting Corp (1997) 189 CLR 520 22
Mabo v Queensland (No 2) (1992) 175 CLR 1 .... 15, 23
McCawley v The King [1920] AC 691 88
Melbourne Corp v Commonwealth (1947) 74 CLR 31 22
Minister for State for the Army v Datziel (1944) 68 CLR 261 89
Minister of State for Immigration and Ethnic Affairs v Teoh (1995) 183 CLR 273 23
Momcilovic v R (2011) 245 CLR 1 .... 14, 20, 21, 38
Mulholland v Australian Electoral Commission (2004) 220 CLR 181 32
New South Wales v Commonwealth (2006) 228 CLR 1 21
Newcrest Mining (WA) Ltd v Commonwealth (1997) 190 CLR 513 23
Ouartermaine v The Queen [1980] HCA 29 175
Pape v Commissioner of Taxation (2009) 238 CLR 1 38
Parker v R (1963) 111 CLR 610 17
Piro v W Foster & Co Ltd (1943) 68 CLR 313 17
Plaintiff S157/2002 v Commonwealth (2003) 211 CLR 476 23
Polites v Commonwealth (1945) 70 CLR 60 23
Public Service Board of New South Wales v Osmond (1986) 159 CLR 656 23
R v Barger (1908) 6 CLR 41 (Commonwealth) 19
R v Kirby; Ex parte Boilermakers' Society of Australia (Boilermaker's case)
    (1956) 94 CLR 254 16
R v Wakin; Ex parte McNally (1999) 198 CLR 511 18
Roach v Electoral Commissioner (2007) 233 CLR 162 .... 25, 26, 423
Singh v Commonwealth (2004) 222 CLR 322 21
Sportsbet Pty Ltd v New South Wales [2012] HCA 13 21
Theophanous v Herald & Weekly Times Ltd (1994) 182 CLR 104 22
Victoria v Commonwealth (1971) 122 CLR 353 18
Viro v R (1978) 141 CLR 88 .... 17, 18
Wainohu v New South Wales (2011) 243 CLR 181 21
Wilde v The Queen [1988] HCA 6, 164 CLR 365 175

Austria

G78/00 221
VfGH Beschluss V 136/94-10 [1995] 264
VfGH 28/06/2003 221
VfSlg 1341/1930 218
VfSlg 1351/1930 218
VfSlg 2455/1952 225
VfSlg 3118/1956 225
VfSlg 7138/1973 218

VfSlg 8981/1980	221
VfSlg 9138/1981	221
VfSlg 9416/1982	221
VfSlg 9446/1982	221
VfSlg 10.291/1984	221
VfSlg 10.809/1986	221
VfSlg 11.260/1987	221
VfSlg 11.402/1987	221
VfSlg 11.483/1987	221
VfSlg 11.651/1988	221
VfSlg 11.774/1988	221
VfSlg 12.103/1989	221
VfSlg 12.568/1990	221, 331
VfSlg 12.645/1991	221
VfSlg 12.660/1991	221
VfSlg 12.940/1991	221
VfSlg 13.036/1992	221
VfSlg 13.038/1992	221
VfSlg 13.661/1993	221
VfSlg 13.704/1994	221
VfSlg 13.785/1994	221
VfSlg13.839/1994	221
VfSlg 14.075/1995	225
VfSlg 14.390/1995	221
VfSlg 15.031/1997	221
VfSlg 15.040/1997	221
VfSlg 15.103/1998	221
VfSlg 15.299/1998	221
VfSlg 15.390/1998	221
VfSlg 15.632/1999	221, 223
VfSlg 15.987/2000	221
VfSlg 16.030/2000	221
VfSlg 16.636/2002	221, 223
VfSlg 17.098/2003	221
VfSlg 17.195/2004	221
VfSlg 17.206/2004	221
VfSlg 17.330/2004	221
VfSlg 17.415/2004	221
VfSlg 17.574/2004	221
VfSlg 17.584/2005	221
VfSlg 17.600/2005	221
VfSlg 17.605/2005	221
VfSlg 17.837/2006	221
VfSlg 17.979/2006	221
VfSlg 18.010/2006	221
VfSlg 18.018/2006	221
VfSlg 18.031/2006	221
VfSlg 18.150/2007	221
VfSlg 18.257/2007	221
VfSlg 18.298/2007	225
VfSlg 18.462/2008	221

x Table of Cases

VfSlg 18.541/2008 .... 221, 223
VfSlg 18.587/2008 221
VfSlg 18.603/2008 226
VfSlg 18.741/2009 .... 218, 221, 223
VfSlg 18.792/2009 221
VfSlg 18.830/2009 226
VfSlg 18.831/2009 .... 221, 226
VfSlg 18.861/2009 .... 218, 221, 223
VfSlg 18.893/2009 .... 221, 223, 224
VfSlg 18.927/2009 221
VfSlg 18.965/2009 221
VfSlg 19.021/2010 221
VfSlg 19.170/2010 221

Belgium

Advocaten voor de Wereld, 128/2007 [2007] 263
Arrêt no 151/2002 de la Cour d'Arbitrage 264

Bulgaria

Decision no 10/22.09.1999 331

Canada

Andrews v Law Society of British Columbia [1989] 1 SCR 143 54
Arsenault-Cameron v Price Edward Island [1999] 3 SCR 851 198
Attorney General of Canada and Dupond v Montreal [1978] 2 SCR 770 42
Bank of Toronto v Lambe (1887) 12 AC 575 PC 61
BC v Imperial Tobacco Canada Ltd [2005] 2 SCR 473 55
Canada (AG) v City of Montreal [1978] 2 SCR 770 44
Canadian Western Bank v Alberta [2007] 2 SCR 3 55
Case no A-463-90 of 1991 331
Charkaoui v Canada (Citizenship and Immigration) [2007] 1 SCR 350 65
Committee for the Commonwealth of Canada v Canada [1991] 1 SCR 139 60
Consolidated Fastrate Inc v Western Canada Council of Teamsters [2009] 3 SCR 407 55
Edwards v Attorney General of Canada [1930] AC 124 49
Egan v Canada (1995) 29 CRR (2nd) 79 198
Ford v Attorney General of Quebec [1988] 2 SCR 712 .... 66, 147
General Motors of Canada Ltd v City National Leasing [1989] 1 SCR 641 55
Hess and Nguyen v R [1990] 2 SCR 906 121
Hill v Church of Scientology of Toronto [1995] 2 SCR 1130 64
Hunter v Southam [1984] 2 SCR 145 63
Irwin Toy v Attorney General of Quebec [1989] 1 SCR 927 264
Lavigne v Ontario Public Service Employees Union [1991] 2 SCR 211 .... 63, 65, 422
Mahe v Alberta [1990] 1 SCR 342 147
McDonald v City of Montréal [1986] 1 SCR 460 147
Miron v Trudel [1995] 2 SCR 418 60
Ontario Film and Video and Ontario Board of Censors, Re (1983) 41 OR (2nd) 583 146
Ontario Hydro v Ontario (Labour Relations Board) [1993] 3 SCR 327 55

Osborne v Canada (Treasury Board) (1991) 82 DLR (4th) 321 180
Ponoka-Calmar Oils Ltd v Earl F Wakefield Co [1959] UKPC 20 46
Queen v Butler [1992] 1 SCR 452 63
Queen v Towne Cinema Theatres Ltd (1985) 18 DLR (4th) 146
R v Bevan [1993] 2 SCR 599 175
R v Big M Drug Mart Ltd [1985] 1 SCR 295 .... 198, 205
R v Butler (1992) 89 DLR (4th) 449 146
R v Drybones [1970] SCR 282 43
R v Edward Books and Art Ltd (1987) 35 DLR 4 180
R v Elshaw [1991] 3 SCR 24 62
R v Kang-Brown [2008] 1 SCR 456 60
R v Keegstra [1990] 3 SCR 697 .... 63, 64
R v Morgentaler [1988] 1 SCR 30 60
R v Oakes (1986) 1 SCR 103 .... 46, 50, 114, 115, 126, 179, 180, 420, 425
R v Rahey [1987] 1 SCR 588 64
R v Ruzic [2001] 1 SCR 687 60
R v Seaboyer [1991] 2 SCR 577 60
R v Simmons [1988] 2 SCR 495 62
R v Sinclair [2010] 2 SCR 310 64
R v Tran [1994] 2 SCR 951 175
R v Zundel (1987) 31 CCC (3d) 97, 35 DLR (4th) 338 .... 178, 180
Reference re Alberta Statutes (Alberta Press Case) [1938] 2 SCR 100 42
Reference re Language Rights Under Manitoba Act, 1870 (1985) DLR (4th) 147
Reference re Persons of Japanese Race [1946] SCR 248 42
Reference re Provincial Electoral Boundaries (Sask) [1991] 2 SCR 158 64
Reference re Public Schools Act (Man) [1993] 1 SCR 839 147
Reference re Remuneration of Judges of the Provincial Court of Prince Edward Island
   [1997] 3 SCR 3 42
Reference re Same-Sex Marriage [2004] 3 SCR 698 50
Reference re Secession of Quebec [1998] 2 SCR 217 .... 50, 55
Reference re Section 94(2) of the British Columbia Motor Vehicles Act [1985] 2
   SCR 486 64
Rodriguez v British Columbia Attorney General [1993] 3 SCR 519 264
Saumur v City of Quebec [1953] 2 SCR 299 42
Singh v Minister of Employment and Immigration [1985] 1 SCR 177 48
Société des Acadiens v Association of Parents [1986] 1 SCR 549 147
Switzman v Elbling [1957] SCR 285 42
Thomson Newspapers Ltd v Canada (Director of Investigation and Research,
   Restrictive Trade Practices Commission) [1990] 1 SCR 425 198
United Food and Commercial Workers Local 1518 v Kmart Can Ltd [1999] 2
   SCR 1083 63
Vriend v Alberta [1998] 1 SCR 493 63

Cyprus

Ap 294/2005 263

Czech Republic

Decision of 10 January 2001 332
Decision of 14 July 2005 332

xii *Table of Cases*

ÚS 53/2000 [2000] 263
ÚS 66/04 [2006] 263
ÚS 19/08 [2008] 263
ÚS 29/09 [2009] 263

France

Arrêt GISTI (CE) 8 December 1978 150
Avis (CE) no 368.282 263
Decision no 91–1141/1142/1143/1144 [1991] 263
Decision no 93-325 DC [1993] 150
Decision no 84-181 DC [1984] 319
Decision no 89-269 DC [1989] 331
Decision no 93–1328/1487 [1993] 263
Decision no 99-412 DC [1999] 331
Decision no 2001-48 DC [2001] 263

Decision no 2004-492 332 DC [2004]
Decision no 2004-496 DC [2004] 263
Decision no 2005-530 DC [2005] 263
Decision no 2006-540 DC [2006] 263
Decision no 10-16 QPC [2010] 332

Germany

Decision nº 1 28 January 1987 331
BGHSt 42, 305 [1996] 264
BVerfGE 1 BvF 1/01 (2002) 262
BVerfGE 1 BvL 83/86 (1991) 262
BVerfGE 1 BvL 24/88 (1991) 262
BVerfGE 2 BvE 2/08 (2009) 263
BVerfGE 2 BvL 37/91 (1995) 263
BVerfGE 2 BvL 42/93 (1998) 263
BVerfG 1 BvR 1995/94 (1998) 262, 263
BverfG 1 BvR 1164/07 (2009) 263
BVerfGE 2 BvR 2194/99 (2006) 263
BverfGE 2 BvR 2236/04 (2005) 263
BVerfGE 2 BvR 1830/06 (2008) 262
BVerfGE 2 BvR 2365/09 (2011) 239
BVerfGE 2 BvR 987/10 (2011) 332
BVerfGE 1, 44 (1950) 243
BVerfGE 1, 97 (1951) 243, 249, 251
BVerfGE 1, 97, 100 (1951) 241
BVerfGE 1, 299 (1951) 239
BVerfGE 2, 1 (1952) 234
BVerfGE 2, 79 (1952) 250
BVerfGE 2, 79, 84 (1952) 233
BVerfGE 5, 85 (1956) 234, 239
BVerfGE 7, 198 (1958)—Lüth 233, 249, 251
BVerfGE 9, 89 (95) 316
BVerfGE 12, 205 (1960)—First German Television 234

BVerfGE 19, 342	311
BVerfGE 26, 66 (1969)—the right to a fair trial	233
BVerfGE 30, 1 (25–26)	313
BVerfGE 30, 173 (1971)	247, 251
BVerfGE 30, 173, 225 (1971)	249
BVerfGE 32, 54 (1971)	249
BVerfGE 33, 23 (1972)—Eidesverweigerung aus Glaubensgründen	263
BVerfGE 34, 269 (1973)—Soraya	262
BVerfGE 37, 271 (1974)	251
BVerfGE 39, 1 (1975)	247, 251
BVerfGE 45, 187 (1987)	251
BVerfGE 45, 187, 259 (1987)	249
BVerfGE 46, 342 (1977)	243
BVerfGE 65, 1 (1985)	234
BVerfGE 73, 1 (1986)—Politische Stiftungen	262
BVerfGE 73, 118 (1986)	319
BVerfGE 74, 358, 370 (1987)	242
BVerfGE 78, 77, 84 (1988)	263
BVerfGE 80, 188 (1989)—Wüppesahl	234
BVerfGE 81, 278 (1990)—Bundesflagge	262
BVerfGE 82, 60 (85–86)	313
BVerfGE 84, 9 (1991)—Ehenamen	262, 263
BVerfGE 89, 155 (1993)—Maastricht	233
BVerfGE 90, 145 (1994)—Cannabis	262, 263
BVerfGE 90, 286 (1994)—out of area permissions	234
BVerfGE 92, 91 (1995)	242
BVerfGE 89, 155 (1993)—Maastricht	233
BVerfGE 93, 266 (1995)—Soldaten sind Mörder	262
BVerfGE 96, 375 (1997)	262
BVerfGE 102, 347, 359 (2000)—Schockwerbung	263
BVerfGE 104, 337, 349 (2002)	249
BVerfGE 105, 197 (2002)—investigation committee	234
BVerfGE 109, 13 (2003)	243, 245
BVerfGE 109, 38 (2003)	243, 245
BVerfGE 111, 307 (2004)—Görgülü	235
BVerfGE 114, 121, 159 (2005)	233
BVerfGE 115, 118, 151 (2006)	238
BVerfGE 116, 69, 90 (2006)	249
BVerfGE 116, 135, 146 (2006)	249
BVerfGE 117, 141 (2006)	243
BVerfGE 118, 79 (2007)	243
BVerfGE 120, 224 (2008)	249, 252
BVerfGE 120, 378, 380 (2008)	249
BVerfGE 123, 267 (2009)—Lisbon	233, 235, 243, 251
BVerfGE 124, 300 (2009)—Wunsiedel	250

Hungary

Decision No 23/1990 (X 31) of the Constitutional Court	265
Decision No 36/1994	331

xiv *Table of Cases*

Decision No 455/B/1995 331
Decision No 277/B/1997 331
Decision No 39/1999 (XII.21) 331
Decision No 14/2000 (V 12) of the Constitutional Court 265
Decision No 36/2000 (X 27) of the Constitutional Court 261
Decision No 57/2001 (XII 5) of the Constitutional Court 261, 263, 264
Decision No 22/2003 (IV 28) of the Constitutional Court 261, 264, 267
Decision No 65/2007 (X 18) of the Constitutional Court 267
Decision No 32/2008 (III 12) of the Constitutional Court 261, 268
Decision No 2/2009 (I.12) 332
Decision No 143/2010 (VII 14) of the Constitutional Court 260

India

Additionl District Magistrate, Jabalpur v Shiv Kant Shuka (Haeas Corpus case)
   (1976) 2 SCC 521 81
Amritsar v Hazara Singh, AIR 1975 83
Bachan Singh v State of Punjab (1938) SCR 145 93
Basheshar Nath v Union of India (1959) SC 149 .... 90, 91
Bengal Immunity co v Bihar, AIR 1955 SC 661 82
BR Kapoor v State of Tamil Nadu (2001) SCC 231 94
Chiranjit Lal v Union of India (1950) 1 SCR 869 89
DG Viswanath v Chief Secretary of the Government of Mysore, AIR 1964 82
Golak Nath v State of Punjab (1967) 2 SCR 762 .... 80, 83, 87, 88, 91, 93, 426
Indian Express Newspaper v Union of India (1986) SC 515 94
Jai Kuer v Sher Singh, AIR 1960 SC 1118 82
JS Jebb v Lefevere and Caroline (Ind Dec, OS, 92) 72
Kansara Tribhovandas Jamnadas v State of Gujarat, AIR 1968 82
Kesavanda Bharati v State of Kerala (1973) 4 SCC 225 .... 80, 91, 93
Keshava Mills v IT Commissioner, AIR 1965 SC 1636 82
Maharashtra v HN Rao, AIR 1970 SC 1157 82
Maneka Gandhi v Union of India (1978) SC 597 94
Muhammad Raza v Abbas Bandi (59 IA 245) 72
RC Cooper v Union of India, AIR 1970 SC 564 82
Romesh Thapar v State of Madras (1950) SC 124 90
Sajjan Singh's case (1964) 4 SCR 630 87
Sankari Prasad's case (1952) SCR 89 87
Sitabati v WB, AIR 1967 SC 945 82
Sri Sankari Prasad Singh Deo v Union of India and State of Bihar (1952) SCR 89 94
Srinath Roy v Dinanbandhu Sen (ILR 42 Calc 1915) 73
State of Travancore-Cochin v Bombay (1952) SC 366 87
Tagore v Tagore (IA Supp 70, 1872) 72
Union of India v Firm Ram Gopal Hukum Chand, AIR 1960 82
Zee Films Ltd v Union of India (2005) SCR 913 93

Ireland

Article 26 and the Housing (Private Rented Dwellings) Bill 1981, re [1983] 1 IR 181 108
Article 26 of the Constitution and in the matter of the Employment Equality Bill,
   1996, in the matter of [1997] 2 IR 321 126

Attorney General v X [1992] ILRM 401, [1992] 1 IR 1 .... 103, 126
Campus Oil Ltd v Minister of Industry & Energy (no 2) [1983] IR 88 105
CC v Ireland [2006] IESC 33 121
Condon v Minister of Labour [1981] IR 62 114
Crotty v An Taoiseach [1987] IR 713 105
Desmond v Glackin (no 2) [1993] 3 IR 67 115
East Donegal Co-Op Ltd v Attorney General [1970] IR 317 113
Fajujonu v Minister of Justice [1990] IR 151 150
Heaney v Ireland [1994] 3 IR 593 .... 114, 115, 425
Macauley v Minister for Posts [1966] IR 345 102
Maguire v Ardagh [2002] 1 IR 385 .... 122, 124
Maher v Attorney General [1973] IR 140 106
McD v L [2009] JIC 1001 104
McGee v Attorney General [1974] IR 284 .... 102, 106
Moore v Attorney General for the Irish Free State [1935] AC 484 100
Murphy v Attorney General [1982] 1 IR 241 .... 106, 120
National Union of Railwaymen v Sullivan [1947] 1 IR 77 118
Norris v Attorney General [1984] IR 36 104
O'B v S [1984] IR 316 .... 114, 125, 426
People (Attorney General) v Edge [1943] 1 IR 115 123
People (DPP) v MS [2003] 1 IR 606 107
People (DPP) v O'Shea [1982] IR 384 114
Pól O Murchú v An Taoiseach [2010] IEHC 26 .... 121, 422
Quinn's Supermarket v Attorney General [1972] IR 1 .... 109, 112
Roche v Roche [2010] 2 IR 321 126
Ryan v Attorney General [1965] IR 294 113
Society for the Protection of Unborn Children (Ireland) Ltd v Coogan [1989]
    IR 734 126
SPUC v Grogan (no 5) [1998] 4 IR 343 126
State (Healy) v O'Donoghue [1985] IR 486 102
State (Lynch) v Cooney [1982] IR 337 110
State (Quinn) v Ryan [1965] IR 70 .... 115, 116
State (Shanahan) v AG [1964] IR 239 106
TD v Minister for Education [2001] 4 IR 259 113
Tormey v Attorney General [1985] ILRM 375 114
Ward of Court, A, re (Withholding Medical Treatment) (no 2) [1996] 1 IR 79 .... 119, 424

Israel

CA 6821/93 United Mizrahi Bank Ltd v Migdal Cooperative Village (Hamizrahi Bank v
    Migdal, Bank Hamizrahi case), 49(4) PD 221 ...... 133, 135, 137, 142, 143, 152, 153, 412
CrA 8823/07 Anon v State of Israel (11 February 2010) 134
HC 4908/10 Knesset Member Bar-On v Israel's Knesset (7 April 2011) 151, 426
HCJ 73/53 Kol Ha'am v Minister of Interior (1953) 7(2) PD 871 132
HCJ 40/70 Beker v Minister of Defence, 24(1) PD (1970) 238 137
HCJ 910/86 Ressler v Minister of Defence, 42(2) PD (1988) 441 137
HCJ 4804/94 Station Films Inc v Israeli Film Council, 50(5) PD 661 .... 145, 146
HCJ 6055/95 Tzemach v Minister of Defence, 53(5) PD 241 (1999) 134
HCJ 1715/97 Investment Managers Chamber in Israel v Minister of Finance,
    51(4) PD 367 (1997) 134

xvi *Table of Cases*

HCJ 1030/99 Oron v Knesset Speaker, 56(3) 640 (2002) 134
HCJ 4112/99 Adalla, the Legal Centre for the Rights of the Arab Minority
  in Israel v Municipality of Tel Aviv-Yafo, 56(5) PD 292 147
HCJ 4128/02 Adam, Teva v'Din an Israeli Association for Environmental Protection v
  Prime Minister, 58(3) PD 503 130
HCJ 316/03 Bakri v Israeli Film Council, 58(1) PD 249 .... 145, 146
HCJ 7052/03 Adallah v Minister of the Interior (14 May 2006) 150
HCJ 2605/05 Human Rights Division v Minister of Finance
  (19 November 2009) 134
HCJ 8276/05 Adallah v Minister of Defence (12 December 2006) 134

Italy

Constitutional Court, Judgment 420/94 319
Sentenza no 149/1995 263
Sentenza no 536/1995 263
Sentenza no 118/1996 263
Sentenza no 34/1996 263

Jamaica

Robinson v Queen, The [1985] AC 956, [1985] 3 WLR 84, [1985] 2 All ER 594,
  [1985] Crim LR 448 175

Japan

Supreme Court (GB), judgment of 30 April 1975, *Minshu* 29-4-572 291
Supreme Court (GB), judgment of 10 September 1975, *Keishu* 29-8-489 292
Supreme Court (GB), judgment of 13 July 1977, *Minshu* 31-4-533 293
Supreme Court (Third Bench), judgment of 18 December 1984, *Keishu* 38-12-3026 296
Supreme Court (Third Bench), judgment of 7 March 1995, *Minshu* 49-3-687 297
Supreme Court (GB), judgment of 5 July 1995, *Minshu* 49-17-89 .... 284, 287
Supreme Court (GB), judgment of 2 April 1997, *Minshu* 51-4-1673 287
Supreme Court (GB), judgment of 2 September 1998, *Minshu* 52-6-1373 285
Supreme Court (GB), judgment of 1 December 1998, *Minshu* 52-9-1761 .... 282, 283
Supreme Court (GB), judgment of 10 November 1999, *Minshu* 53-8-1441 285
Supreme Court (GB), judgment of 10 November 1999, *Minshu* 53-8-1704 286
Supreme Court (GB), judgment of 27 January 2000, *Hanrei Jiho* 1260-6 288
Supreme Court (GB), judgment of 27 January 2000, *Katei Saibansho Geppo*
  52-7-78 289
Supreme Court (GB), judgment of 6 September 2000, *Minshu* 54-7-1997 286
Supreme Court (GB), judgment of 14 January 2004, *Minshu* 58-1-56 286
Supreme Court (GB), judgment of 4 June 2008, *Hanrei Jiho* 2002-13 .... 284, 287

Latvia

Decision no 2009-43-01 of 21 December 2009 331
Decision of 18 January 2010 331

Lithuania

Decision of 12 July 2001 331
Decision 33/06 of 27 March 2009 332

Mexico

Constitutional controversy 140/2006 313
Ruling issued on 26 August 1939 (SJF (5th epoch, vol LXI) 3543) 303
SJFG (August 1992) 44 303
SJFG (March 2003) 312
SJFG (November 2003) 955 312
SJFG (September 2005) 1579 312
SJFG (September 2006) 75 312
SJFG (February 2007) 1396 314
SJFG (March 2007) 151 316
SJFG (March 2007) 334 312
SJFG (May 2007) 104 316
SJFG (September 2007) 553 313
SJFG (December 2007) 8 312
SJFG (April 2008) 175 312
SJFG (June 2008) 439 312
SJFG (December 2008) 1052 306
SJFG (August 2010) 463 306
SJFG (August 2011) 878 .... 317, 318, 423
SJFG (October 2011) 313 .... 305, 306
SUP-AG-2/2007 316
SUP-JDC-037/2001 316
SUP-JDC-393/2005 316
SUP-JDC-20/2007 316
SUP-RAP-31/2006 316
Unconstitutionality action 26/2006 319

Namibia

Alexander v Minister of Justice, 2010 (1) NR 328 (SC) 181, 417
Attorney General, Ex parte, Constitutional Relationship between the
    Attorney General and the Prosecutor General, Re, 1998 NR 282 (SC) 169, 170, 183
Attorney General, Ex parte, Corporal Punishment by Organs of State,
    Re (SA 14/90) [1991] NASC 2, 1991 (3) SALR 76 (NmS)
    (5 April 1991) 167, 169, 170, 172, 176, 177
Chairperson of the Immigration Selection Board v Frank, 2001 NR 107 (SC) 169
Kauesa v Minister of Home Affairs, 1995 NR 175 (SC), 1995 (1)
    SA 51 (NmHC) 169, 173, 178, 179, 181, 182
Malama-Kean v Magistrate, District of Oshakati, 2002 NR 413 (SC) 169
Minister of Defence v Mwandinghi, 1993 NR 63 (SC), (SA 5/91) [1991]
    NASC 5 .... 169, 174
Minister of Home Affairs v Majiedt, 2007 (2) NR 475 (SC) 169, 179
Muller v President of Namibia, 1999 NR 190 (SC) 169

xviii *Table of Cases*

Myburgh v Commercial Bank of Namibia, 2000 NR 255 (SC) 169, 179
Namibia v Sikunda, 2002 NR 203 (SC) 179
Namunjepo v Commanding Officer, Windhoek Prison, 1999 NR 271 (SC) 169
Nationwide Detectives and Professional Practitioners CC v Standard Bank
  of Namibia Ltd (SA 32/2007) [2008] NASC 14 (24 October 2008) 179
S v Gaseb (SA 9/99) [2000] NASC 6, 2000 (1) SACR 438 (NmS)
  (9 August 2000) 176
S v Kandovazu, 1997 NR 1 (SC) 169
S v Luboya, 2007 (1) NR 96 (SC) 169
S v Redondo, 1992 NR 133 (SC), (SA 14/91) [1992] 172, 173
S v Shikunga, 1997 NR 156 (SC), (SA 6/95) [1997] NASC 2 .... 174, 175
S v Tcoeib, 1999 NR 24 (SC), 1996 (1) SACR 390 (NmS) 180
S v Van Wyk (SA 6/91) [1991] NASC 6, 2000 (1) SACR 438 (NmS)
  (9 August 2000) 176, 177

New Zealand

Simpson v Attorney General [1994] 3 NZLR 667 43

Poland

K 21/05 [2006] 263
Minister for Justice, Equality and Law Reform v Rettinger (2010) 7 JIC 2301 120
P 1/05 [2005] 263

Romania

Decision nº 107/1995 .... 331, 332
Decision nº 115/1996 330
Decision nº 140/1996 .... 331, 333
Decision nº 113/1999 .... 331, 333, 340, 341
Decision nº 203/1999 .... 331, 333
Decision nº 22/2000 330
Decision nº 34/2000 330
Decision nº 121/2000 330
Decision nº 124/2001 .... 331, 334
Decision nº 295/2002 330
Decision nº 478/2006 .... 331, 334
Decision nº 334/2007 .... 331, 335
Decision nº 1415/2009 .... 331, 335, 340
Decision nº 872/2010 .... 331, 336
Decision nº 873/2010 .... 331, 336
Decision nº 874/2010 .... 331, 336
Decision nº 53/2011 330
Decision nº 766/2011 .... 332, 337, 340
Decision nº 1470/2011 .... 332, 338
Decision nº 1533/2011 .... 332, 339, 341
Tramways of Bucharest case 1912 326

Russia

Decision of the Constitutional Court of 16 June 1998	360
Decision of the Constitutional Court of 20 February 2006	358
Judgment of the Constitutional Court of 23 January 2001 No 1-P	364
Judgment of the Constitutional Court of 25 April 2001 No 6-P	368
Judgment of the Constitutional Court of 24 May 2001	366
Judgment of the Constitutional Court of 2 April 2002 No 7-P	361
Judgment of the Constitutional Court of 30 October 2003 No 15-P	368
Judgment of the Constitutional Court of 14 July 2005 No 9-P	368
Judgment of the Constitutional Court of 14 November 2005 No 10-P	365, 368
Judgment of the Constitutional Court of 16 June 2006 No 7-P	365, 368
Judgment of the Constitutional Court of 23 January 2007 No 1-P	371
Judgment of the Constitutional Court of 16 May 2007 No 6-P	364, 368
Judgment of the Constitutional Court of 26 February 2010 No 4-P	355
Resolution of Highest Arbitration Court, 14 February 2008, No 14	357
Ruling of the Constitutional Court of 15 February 2005 No 1-O	365
Ruling of the Constitutional Court of 15 February 2005 No 17-O	366
Ruling of the Constitutional Court of 2 November 2006 No 444-O	364
Ruling of the Constitutional Court of 19 November 2009 No 1344-O-R	355

Slovenia

U-I-367/96 [1996]	263
U-I-127/01 [2004]	263
U-I-14/06 [2006]	263

South Africa

Affordable Medicines Trust v Minister of Health [2006] 3 SA 247 (CC)	201
Arma Carpet House (Johannesburg) (Pty) Ltd v Domestic and Commialo Carpet Fittings (Pty) Ltd [1977] 3 SA 448 (W)	179
August v Independent Electoral Commission [1999] 3 SA 1 (CC)	199
Beyers v Elf Regters van die Grondwetlike Hof [2002] 6 SA 630 (CC)	201
Bloem v State President of the RSA [1986] 4 SA 1064 POD	185
Booysen v Minister of Home Affairs, CCT 8/01	150
Christian Education SA v Minister of Education [2000] 4 SA 757 (CC)	201
Coetzee v Government of RSA; Matiso v Commanding Officer, Port Elizabeth Prison [1995] 4 SA 631 (CC)	194, 207
Dawood v Minister of Home Affairs, CCT 35/99	150
Doctors for Life International v Speaker of the National Assembly [2006] 6 SA 416 (CC)	189, 201
Du Plessis v De Klerk [1996] 3 SA 850 (CC)	196, 199, 200, 201, 418
Estate Reid v Goodwin [1920] AD 367	185
Ferreira v Levin; Vryenhoek v Powell [1996] 1 SA 984 (CC)	199, 200
First National Bank of SA Lt t/a Wesbank v Commissioner, SARS; First National Bank of SA Ltd t/a Wesbank v Minister of Finance [2002] 4 SA 768 (CC)	201
Fose v Minister of Safety and Security [1997] 3 SA 786 (CC)	196, 422

Grant v Torstar Corp [2009] SCC 61 199
Harksen v Lane [1998] 1 SA 300 (CC) 198
Khumalo v Holomisa [2002] 5 SA 401 (CC) 201
Knox D'Arcy Ltd v Shaw [1996] 2 SA 651 (W) 179
Magajane v Chairperson North West Gambling Board [2006] 5 SA 250 (CC) 200
Maphahlele v First National Bank of SA Ltd [1999] 1 SACR 373 (CC) 201
Matatiele Municipality v President of the RSA (no 2) [2007] 6 SA 477 (CC) 201
Matiso v Commanding Officer, Port Elizabeth Prison [1994] 3 BCLR 80 (SE) 188, 189
MEC for Education Kwazulu-Natal v Pillay [2008] 1 SA 474 (CC) 201
Mistry v Interim National Medical and Dental Council of South Africa [1998]
    4 SA 1127 (CC) 193
Mohlomi v Minister of Defence [1997] 1 SA 124 (CC) 179
National Coalition for Gay and Lesbian Equality v Minister of Justice [1999]
    1 SA 6 (CC) 208, 422
National Media Ltd v Bogoshi [1998] 4 SA 1196 (SCA) 199
President of the RSA v Hugo [1997] 4 SA (CC) 198
President of the RSA v South African Rugby and Football Union [2002] 2 SA 64 (CC) ... 198
President of the RSA, Ex parte: Constitutionality of the Liquor Bill, re [2000]
    1 SA 732 (CC) 201
Prince v President, Cape Law Society [2002] 2 SA 794 (CC) 205, 206
R v Hall [2002] 3 SCR 309, 2002 SCC 64 199
R v Tebetha [1959] 2 SA 337 (A) 185
S v Blaauw [1980] 1 SA 536 (C) 185
S v Dlamini; S v Dladla; S v Joubert; S v Schietekat [1999] 4 SA 623 (CC) 199
S v Khanyapa [1979] 1 SA 824 (A) 185
S v Lawrence; S v Negal; S v Solberg [1997] 4 SA 1176 (CC) 205
S v Makwanyane [1995] 3 SA 391 (CC) 9, 186–88, 190, 196, 201, 412, 415
S v Naudé [1975] 1 SA 681 (A) 179
S v Zuma [1995] 2 SA 642 (CC) 189, 190
SABC v National Director of Public Prosecutions [2007] 1 SA 523 (CC) 206
Sauvé v Canada (Chief Electoral Officer) [2002] SCC 68, [2002] 3 SCR 519 198
Sonderup v Tondelli [2001] 1 SA 1171 (CC) 200
Union Government (Minister of Mines) v Thompson [1919] AD 404 185

Spain

Constitutional judgment 171/1990, FF.JJ. 4–5 312
ESP-1994-2-025 263
Judgment 12/1982 of the Constitutional Court 316
Sindicato de la Central Sindical Independiente y de Funcionarios
    (CSI-CSIF) c el Servicio Andaluz de Salud [2003] 264
STC 113/1989, FJ 3 313

Taiwan

JY Interpretation No 1 380
JY Interpretation No 165 (12 September 1980) 381, 386
JY Interpretation No 177 (5 November 1982) 378
JY Interpretation No 185 (27 January 1984) 378

JY Interpretation No 261 (21 June 1990)... 387, 423
JY Interpretation No 334 (14 January 1994) 379
JY Interpretation No 342 (8 April 1994)... 381, 387, 388
JY Interpretation No 371 (20 January 1995) 377
JY Interpretation No 392 (22 December 1995) 379, 381, 388, 389
JY Interpretation No 419 (31 December 1996) 379
JY Interpretation No 445 (23 January 1998) 379
JY Interpretation No 499 (24 April 2000)... 374, 381, 382, 389
JY Interpretation No 585 (15 December 2004) 379
JY Interpretation No 603 (28 September 2005) 379
JY Interpretation No 680 .... 380, 381
JY Interpretation No 689 (29 July 2011) 379

United Kingdom

Airedale NHS Trust v Bland [1993] AC 789, [1993] 2 WLR 316, [1993] 1 All ER 821,
  [1993] 1 FLR 1026, [1994] 1 FCR 485, [1993] 4 Med LR 39, (1993) 12 BMLR 64,
  [1993] Fam Law 473, (1993) 143 NLJ 199 119
B v An NHS Hospital [2002] EWHC 429 (Fam), [2002] 2 All ER 449, [2002]
  1 FLR 1090, [2002] 2 FCR 1, [2002] Lloyd's Rep Med 265, (2002) 65 BMLR
  149, [2002] Fam Law 423, (2002) 99(17) LSG 37, (2002) 152 NLJ 470, (2002)
  146 SJLB 83 264
Bidie v General Accident, Fire and Life Assurance Corp [1949] Ch 121, [1948] 2
  All ER 995, 65 TLR 25, (1949) 113 JP 22, 47 LGR 465, [1949] LJR 386,
  (1948) 92 SJ 705 91
Bribery Commissioner v Ranasinghe [1965] AC 172, [1964] 2 WLR 1301, [1964] 2
  All ER 785, (1964) 108 SJ 441 88
DPP v Jones [1999] 2 AC 240, [1999] 2 WLR 625, [1999] 2 All ER 257,
  [1999] 2 Cr App R 348, (1999) 163 JP 285, 6 BHRC 513, [1999]
  Crim LR 672, (1999) 163 JPN 355, [1999] EG 36 (CS), (1999)
  96(13) LSG 31, (1999) 96(11) LSG 71, (1999) 143 SJLB 98, [1999] NPC 31 264
Eyre v Measday [1986] 1 All ER 488, (1986) 136 NLJ 91 264
Gerard v Worth of Paris Ltd [1936] 2 All ER 905 82
Gold v Haringey HA [1988] QB 481, [1987] 3 WLR 649, [1987] 2 All ER 888,
  [1988] 1 FLR 55, [1987] Fam Law 417, (1987) 84 LSG 1812, (1987) 137 NLJ 541.... 264
Howard v Gosset, 116 ER 139, (1845) 10 QB 359... 124
J, Re [1991] Fam 33, [1991] 2 WLR 140, [1990] 3 All ER 930, [1991] 1 FLR 366,
  [1991] FCR 370, [1990] 2 Med LR 67, (1990) 140 NLJ 1533 264
London Street Tramways v London CC [1898] AC 375.. 82
R v Bourne [1939] 1 KB 687, [1938] 3 All ER 615 .... 126, 405
R v Chaytor [2010] EWCA Crim 1910, [2010] 2 Cr App R 34; (2010)
  160 NLJ 1154, (2010) 154(31) SJLB 28 110
R v Secretary of State for the Home Department, Ex parte Brind [1991] 1 AC 696,
  [1991] 2 WLR 588, [1991] 1 All ER 720, (1991) 3 Admin LR 486, (1991)
  141 NLJ 199, (1991) 135 SJ 250... 146
R (on the application of Pretty) v DPP [2001] UKHL 61, [2002] 1 AC 800,
  [2001] 3 WLR 1598, [2002] 1 All ER 1, [2002] 2 Cr App R 1, [2002]
  1 FLR 268, [2002] 1 FCR 1, [2002] HRLR 10, [2002] UKHRR 97, 11 BHRC 589,
  (2002) 63 BMLR 1, [2002] ACD 41, [2002] Fam Law 170, (2001) 151 NLJ 1819........ 264
St Nazaire Co, re (1879) 12 Ch D 88 331

United States

Case	Pages
Abbott v Abbott (Case 08-645) 17 May 2010	200, 397
Abrams v United States, 40 S Ct 17, 250 US 616 (1919)	132, 146
Adamson v California, 332 US 46 (1947)	395
Antelope, The, 23 US (10 Wheat) 66 (1825)	403
Apthekar v Secretary of State, 378 US 500 (1964)	94
Arver v US, 245 US 366 (1918)	396
Atkins v Virginia, 536 US 304 (2002)	2, 406, 408, 425
Baker v Carr, 369 US 186 (1962)	64, 88, 287, 314, 315
Banco Nacional de Cuba v Sabbatino, 376 US 398 (1964)	395
Barbier v Connolly, 113 US 27 (1885)	89
Beauharnais v Illinois, 343 US 250 (1952)	64
Betts v Brady, 316 US 455 (1942)	396
Bigelow v Virginia, 421 US 809 (1975)	263
Bollman, Ex parte, 8 US (4 Cranch) 75 (1807)	403
Bowers v Hardwick, 478 US 186 (1986)	404, 405
Bram v United States, 168 US 532 (1897)	403
Brian Majors v Marsha Abell, 361 F3d 349 (2004)	369
Brown v Board of Education, 347 US 483 (1959)	114
Brown v United States, 12 US (8 Cranch) 110 (1814)	403
Burson v Freeman, 504 US 191 (1992)	396
Calder v Bull, 3 US (3 Dall) 386 (1798)	403
Campbell v Holt, 115 US 620 (1885)	395
Central Hudson Gas and Electricity Corp v Public Service Commission, 447 US 557 (1980)	263
Chaplinsky v New Hampshire, 315 US 568 (1942)	146
Chinese Exclusion Case, The, 130 US 581 (1889)	397
Chisholm v Georgia, 2 US (2 Dall) 419 (1793)	403
Clinton v City of New York, 524 US 417 (1998)	319
Coker v Georgia, 433 US 584 (1977)	396
Coleman v Miller, 307 US 443 (1939)	88, 389
Collin v Smith, 578 F 2d 1197 (1978)	146
Columbian Insurance Co of Alexandria v Ashby, 38 US (13 Pet) 331 (1839)	397
Compassion in Dying v State of Washington, 79 F 3d 790 (1995)	263
Cruzan v Director, Missouri Department of Health, 497 US 261 (1990)	263
Cubbins v Mississippi River Commission, 241 US 351 (1916)	396
Cunnius v Reading Sch Dist, 198 US 458 (1905)	395
Dickerson v United States, 530 US 428 (2000)	331
Dillon v Gloss, 256 US 368 (1921)	88
Dred Scott v Sandford, 60 US (19 How) 393 (1856)	403
Duncan v Louisiana, 391 US 145 (1968)	395
Eisenstadt v Baird, 405 US 438 (1972)	263
Employment Division, Department of Human Resources of Oregon v Smith, 494 US 872 (1990)	206
Enmund v Florida, 458 US 782 (1982)	396
Fiori, re, 652 AR 2d 1350 (1995)	119
Foster v Florida, 537 US 990 (2002)	2
Geer v Connecticut, 161 US 519 (1896)	395
Gilligan v Morgan, 413 US 1 (1973)	315
Goldwater v Carter, 444 US 996 (1979)	315
Graham v Florida, 560 US 130 (2010)	2, 408

Table of Cases   xxiii

Griswold v Connecticut, 381 US 479 (1965) 263
Grutter v Bollinger, 539 US 309 (2003) 396
Gulf, Colorado and Santa Fè Rly v WH Ellis, 165 US 150 (1897) 89
Head Money Cases, The, 112 US 580 (1884) 397
Hilton v Guyot, 159 US 113 (1895) 397
Hollingsworth v Virginia, 3 US 378 (1798) 88
Holmes v Jennison, 39 US 540 (1840) 91
Hovey v Elliott, 167 US 409 (1897) 403
Hurtado v California, 110 US 516 (1884) 395
Hyde v United States, 225 US 347 (1912) 123
Jackson, Ex parte, 96 US 727 (1878) 90
Jackson v The Magnolia, 61 US (20 How) 296 (1857) 397
Johnson v McIntosh, 21 US (8 Wheat) 543 (1823) 403
Jones v United States, 137 US 202 (1890) 397
Juilliard v Greenman, 110 US 421 (1884) 403
Kaplan v California, 93 S Ct 2680 (1973) 146
Katz v United States, 389 US 347 (1967) 63
Kent v Dulles, 357 US 116 (1958) 94
Ker v Illinois, 119 US 436 (1886) 403
Knight v Florida, 528 US 990 (1999) 2, 405, 406
Knowlton v Moore, 178 US 41 (1900) 396
Knox v Lee, 79 US 457 (1870) 396
Kotteakos v United States, 328 US 750 (1945) 176
Lawrence v Texas, 539 US 558 (2003) 2, 70, 394, 398, 404–06, 408, 420, 425
Lemon v Kurtzman, 403 US 602 (1971) 294
Leser v Garnett, 258 US 130 (1922) 88
Lindsley v Natural Carbonic Gas Co, 220 US 61 (1911) 89
Linkletter v Walker, 381 US 618 (1965) 83
Lochner v New York, 198 US 45 (1905) 396
Locke v Davey, 540 US 712 (2004) 396
Lovell v City of Griffin, 303 US 444 (1938) 90
Luther v Borden, 48 US 1 (1849) 88
Marbury v Madison, 5 US 137 (1803) 88, 133
McCabe v Atchison, 235 US 151 (1914) 89
McConnell v Federal Election Commission, 540 US 93 (2003) 369
M'Coul v Lekamp's Administratix, 15 US (2 Wheat) 111 (1817) 403
McCreary County v ACLU, 125 S Ct 2722 (2005) 396
McCulloch v Maryland, 17 US (4 Wheaton) 316 (1819) 303
McGowan v Maryland, 366 US 1101 (1961) 396
McIntyre v Ohio Elections Commission, 514 US 334 (1995) 396
McNeil, Ex parte, 80 US (13 Wall) 236 (1871) 395
Miami Herald Publishing Co v Tornillo, 418 US 241 (1974) 263
Miranda v Arizona, 384 US 436 (1966) 64, 70, 331, 334, 396, 405, 406
Muller v Oregon, 208 US 412 (1907) 396, 408
Murdock v Pennsylvania, 319 US 105 (1943) 316
Murray v Schooner Charming Betsy, 6 US (2 Cranch) 64 (1804) 397
Murray v Vandevander, 522 P 2d 302 (1974) 263
National Socialist Party v Village of Skokie, 432 US 43 (1977) 263
Near v Minnesota, 282 US 607 (1931) 90
Neb Press Ass'n v Stuart, 427 US 539 (1976) 395
New York v United States, 326 US 572 (1946) 396, 405, 406
New York Times Co v Sullivan, 376 US 254 (1964) 263, 316

Table of Cases

Ogden v Saunders, 25 US (12 Wheat) 213 (1827) 403
O'Malley v Woodrough, 307 US 277 (1939) 405, 406
Osborn v Nicholson, 80 US (13 Wall) 654 (1871) 403
Palko v Connecticut, 302 US 319 (1937) 396
Paquete Habana, The, 175 US 677 (1900) 397
Philadelphia Newspapers, Inc v Hepps, 475 US 1134, 106 S Ct 1784 (1986) 263
Place v Norwich and New York Transportation Co, 118 US 468 (1886) 403
Poe v Ullman, 367 US 497 (1961) 395, 397
Printz v United States, 521 US 898 (1997) 2, 403, 408, 409, 422, 423
Providence Bank v Billings, 29 US (4 Peters) 514 (1830) 303
Quill v Koppell, 870 F Supp 78 (SDNY 1994) 263
Quill v Vacco, 521 US 793 (1997) 263
Raines v Byrd, 521 US 811 (1997) 396
Rapid, The, 12 US (8 Cranch) 155 (1814) 397
RAV v City of St Paul, Minnesota, 505 US 377 (1992) 263
Red Lion Broadcasting Co v FCC, 395 US 367 (1969) 263
Reynolds v United States, 98 US 145 (1878) 403
Rochin v California, 342 US 165 (1952) 395
Roe v Wade, 410 US 113 (1973) 126, 405
Romer v Evans, 517 US 620 (1996) 63, 312
Roper v Simmons, 543 US 551 (2004) 2, 406, 408, 409, 425
Rose v Himely, 8 US (4 Cranch) 241 (1808) 403
Schenck v United States, 39 S Ct 247, 249 US 47 (1919) 132, 146, 250, 297
School District of Abington Township v Schempp, 374 US 203 (1963) 112
Skinner v Oklahoma, 316 US 535 (1942) 263
Smith v California, 361 US 147 (1959) 395, 405, 406
Smith v Collin, 439 US 916 (1978) 146
Talbot v Jansen, 3 US (3 Dall) 133 (1795) 397
Texas v White, 74 US 700 (1868) 88
Thompson v Oklahoma, 487 US 815 (1988) 396, 403, 423
Towne v Eisner, 245 US 418 (1918) 91, 123
Trop v Dulles, 356 US 86 (1958) 177, 396
Twining v New Jersey, 211 US 78 (1908) 395
Uhler v AFLCIO, 468 US 1310 (1984) 389
United States v Carolene Products Co, 304 US 144 (1938) 291, 292
United States v Hill, 248 US 420 (1919) 118
United States v Korematsu, 323 US 214 (1944) 150, 151
United States v Perkins, 163 US 625 (1896) 396
United States v Smith, 18 US (5 Wheat) 153 (1820) 403
United States v Then, 56 F3d 464 (1995) 393, 409
United States v Wilson, 32 US (7 Pet) 150 (1833) 395
Virginia v Black, 123 S Ct 1536 (2003) 146, 263
Ware v Hylton, 3 US (3 Dall) 199 (1796) 397
Washington v Glucksberg, 521 US 702 (1997) 263, 405, 406
Watkins v United States, 354 US 178 (1957) 124
Whitney v California, 274 US 357, 47 S Ct 641 (1927) 132, 133
Whitney v Robertson, 124 US 190 (1888) 397
Wilkerson v Utah, 99 US 130 (1879) 395
William v United States, 351 US 97 (1951) 91
Wolf v Colorado, 338 US 25 (1949) 405
Worcester v Georgia, 31 US (6 Pet) 515 (1832) 397
Zadvydas v Davis, 533 US 678 (2001) 397

Table of Legislation

INTERNATIONAL

American Convention on Human Rights, 1969 306
Declaration of the Rights of Man and of the Citizen, 1789 277
European Charter of Regional or Minority Languages, 1992 333
European Convention on Human Rights, 1950 .... 45, 93, 104, 121, 164, 183, 197,
　　　　　　　　　　　　　　　　　　　　　　　　　　215–18, 223, 224, 235, 242, 266,
　　　　　　　　　　　　　　　　　　　　　　　　　　272, 327, 345, 355, 388
　　Art 8 104
　　Art 10 224
　　Protocol 1 355
　　Protocol 4 355
　　Protocol 7 355
　　Protocol 9 355
　　Protocol 10 355
　　Protocol 11 355
　　Protocol 12 215
International Covenant on Civil and Political Rights, 1966 .... 25, 45, 54, 164, 355, 388
International Covenant on Economic, Social and Cultural Rights, 1966 .... 54, 164, 355
League of Nations Covenant, 1919
　　Art 22 157
Statute of the International Court of Justice, 1945
　　Art 38(1)(d) 243
UN Universal Declaration of Human Rights, 1948 .... 45, 76, 77, 92, 161, 164, 231
　　Art 29(2) 45
UN Partition Resolution of November 1947 130

EUROPEAN UNION

Charter of Fundamental Rights of the EU, 2010 .... 215, 256
　　First Protocol 25
Treaty of Lisbon, 2009 .... 260, 261, 417

DOMESTIC

Argentina

Constitution, 1853 62

Australia

Australia Acts, 1986 17
Australian Courts Act, 1828 (Imp)
　　s 24 15

Commonwealth of Australia Constitution Act, 1900 (Imp) 16, 88
Constitution, 1901 .... 14–16, 18, 19, 23–27, 29, 30, 416
    s 71 16
    s 72 19
    s 73 18
    s 74 .... 17, 23
    s 75 .... 18, 19
    s 76 .... 18, 19
        (i) 18, 28
    s 92 21
    ss 106–08 16
    s 128 16
Judiciary Act, 1903 (Cth)
    Pt VII 19
    s 30 18
    s 35 18
    s 35A 18
    s 35AA 18
Privy Council (Appeals from the High Court) Act, 1975 17
Privy Council (Limitation of Appeals) Act, 1968 17
Victorian Charter of Human Rights and Responsibilities Act, 2006 (Vic) 38
    s 32(2) 40

Austria

Basic Law, 1867 215
Bill of Rights, 1849 214
Federal Constitution, 1930 .... 214–16, 218, 219
Federal Constitutional Act, 1920 (B-VG) 214
    Art 138(2) 216
    Art 148(1) 219
    Art 149 214

Bahamas

Constitution, 1973 45

Barbados

Constitution, 1966 45

Belgium

Constitution, 1831 324

Botswana

Constitution, 1966 45

Brazil

Constitution 88

Table of Legislation xxvii

Burma
Constitution 88

Cambodia
Constitution 88

Canada
Alberta Human Rights Act, SA 1966, c 39 43
Bill of Rights, SC 1960, c 44 (CboR) 43, 48
   Pt I 43
   s 1 43
   s 2 43
      (e) 43
   s 5 43
British Columbia Human Rights Act, SBC 1969, c 10 43
British North American Act, 1867 (BNAA) 41–49, 54, 58, 88, 100
   Preamble 42, 44
   ss 91–95 42
   s 92(3) 47
   s 95 47
Canada Act 1982, c 11 44
   s 52(1) 45
   Sch B 40, 45
Canadian Human Rights Act, 1977 (CHRA) 44
Charter of Human Rights and Freedoms, SQ 1975, c 6 43
Charter of Rights and Freedoms, 1982 .... 25, 34, 40–52, 54–56, 58,
                                    61–66, 122, 133, 147, 178, 183, 198, 415, 419, 420
   s 1 .... 45, 46, 60–66, 178, 419
   s 3 64
   s 7 .... 61, 64
   ss 7–15 61
   s 8 63
   s 14 175
   s 15 .... 46, 54
   s 23 61
   s 24(1) 46, 175
   s 25 61
   s 28 61
   s 32(2) 46
   s 33 .... 45, 49, 64
   s 52 64
      (1) 46
Constitution Act, 1867 .... 41, 44, 47, 61
   s 91 47
   s 92 47
   s 101 46
Constitution Act, 1982 .... 41, 44, 45, 47, 55, 192
   Pt I 40, 44
   Pt V 44

s 1 45
s 33(1) 49
s 41 47
s 42 47
s 52(1) 45
Manitoba Human Rights Act, SM 1970, c 104 43
Narcotic Control Act, RSC 1970 46
New Brunswick Human Rights Act, SNB 1967, c 13 43
Newfoundland Human Rights Act, S Nfld 1969, no 75 43
Nova Scotia Human Rights Act, SNS 1963, c 5 43
Ontario Human Rights Code, SO 1961–62 c 93 43
PEI Human Rights Act, S PEI 1968, c 24 43
Saskatchewan Bill of Rights Act, SS 1947, c 35 43
Supreme and Exchequer Courts Act, RS 1900, c 154 (SECA) 46, 47
Supreme Court Act, RSC, 1985, c S-26 47
s 4(1) 47
s 6 47
s 53 47

Czech Republic

Constitutional Act shortening the Tenure of the Parliamentary Chamber
 of Deputies 151
Constitutional Act shortening the Term of Office of the Chamber of Deputies 151

Denmark

Constitution Act 88

Finland

Constitution 88

France

Constitution, 1958 .... 88, 277, 324
Napoleonic Code, 1801 327
 Art 4 327

Germany

Aviation Security Act 238
Civil Code (*Bundesgesetzbuch*) (BGB), 1900 349
Constitution (Basic Law) (*Grundgesetz*) (BL), 1949 .... 88, 192, 200, 216,
                                                                                              230–36, 249, 251, 277
 Art 5 250
 Art 10 232
 Art 13 232
 Art 16a 232
 Art 18 234
 Art 21(2) 234
 Art 23 232

Art 54	235
Art 61	235
Art 67	235
Art 92	232
Art 93	235
(1) No 1	234
No 2	233
No 2a	234
No 3	234
No 4	234
No 4a	233
Art 94	232
(1)	237
(2)	232
Art 95	232
Art 100(1)	233
(2)	243
Art 146	231
Constitution of Frankfurt (Constitution of Paulskirche), 1849	231, 232
§ 126	232
Constitution of the Weimar Republic, 1919	215, 231, 232, 277, 375
Federal Constitutional Court Act (FCCA), 1951	232
§ 1(1)	232
§ 2	237
§ 3	237
(4)	237
§ 4	237
§ 5	237
§ 13	235
No 8a	233
§ 14	232
§ 16	232
§ 31(2)	232
§ 36	234
§ 43	234
§ 46	234
§ 93a	236
Political Parties Act, 1967	226

Greece

Constitution	88

Grenada

Constitution, 1973	45

Honduras

Constitution	88

Hungary

Constitution, 1949 255
    Art 2/A 270
    Art 7(1) 270
Constitution, 1989 .... 254–56, 264
    Art 2/A 270
    Art 7(1) 270
Criminal Code 333
Fundamental Law, 2012 .... 255, 256, 258, 259

India

Act 14 of 1965 87
Arbitration and Conciliation Act, 1996 79
Constitution, 1949 .... 45, 69, 70, 73–77, 78, 80, 83, 84, 86–88, 91, 92, 94, 95, 415
    Preamble 73, 76
    Pt III (Bill of Rights) 76, 91
    Pt IV 76, 79
    Pt XI 75
    Art 15 77
    Art 19 82
    Art 21 94
    Art 23 77
    Art 24 77
    Art 29 77
    Art 30 77
    Art 31(3) 82
    Art 32 .... 78, 87
    Art 124 78
    Art 132(1) 79
    Art 133(1) 79
    Art 134 79
    Art 136 79
    Art 141 82
    Art 143 .... 78, 79
    Art 286 87
    Art 368 91
    Sch 7 75
    Sch 9 87
Constitution (First Amendment) Act, 1951 87
Constitution (Seventeenth Amendment) Act, 1964 87
East India Company Act, 1781 c 70 72
Government of India Act, 1935 73
    s 212 81
Indian Independence Act, 1947 92
Law on Immoral Trafficking in Women and Girls, 1956 77
Mysore Land Reforms Act 87
Punjab Land Reform Act 87
Punjab Security of Land Tenures Act, 1953 87

Ireland

Constitution, 1922	100, 101
Constitution, 1937	76, 77, 98, 101–03, 105–07, 110, 113, 114, 116, 118, 119, 124, 183, 415, 424
Preamble	101
Art 8	121, 122
Art 12.3	109
Art 13.1	106
Art 15.2	104
Art 25.4.1	121, 122
Art 26	108, 109, 110, 125
Art 26.2	113
Art 26.9	104
Art 28.3	109
Art 29.4.10	105
Art 34.1	105
Art 34.2	109
Art 34.3.2	109
Art 34.4	102, 103, 109, 113
Art 35.1	106
Art 40	102
Art 40.3.1	102
Art 40.3.2	119
Art 40.4	109
Art 40.6.2	118
Art 41	102
Art 42	102
Art 43	102
Art 44	102
Art 45	76, 102
Art 46	101, 103, 108
Art 47	101, 103, 108
Art 50	100, 104, 107
Art 51	103
Courts and Court Officers Act, 1995	111
Courts (Establishment and Constitution) Act, 1961	105
Courts (No 2) Act, 1997	110, 111
Courts of Justice Act, 1924	105
Courts (Supplementary Provisions) Act, 1961	105
Criminal Law Amendment Act, 1935	121
European Convention on Human Rights Act, 2003	
s 2	104
Fifth Amendment of the Constitution Act, 1973	103
Governemt of Ireland Act, 1920	100
Ministers and Secretaries Act, 1924	102

Israel

Basic Law: Freedom of Occupation, 1992	133
Basic Law: Human Dignity and Liberty, 1992	133, 144, 415

Basic Law: Jerusalem, the Capital of Israel, 1980 144
Basic Law: The Army, 1976 144
Basic Law: The Government, 1968, replaced 1992 and 2001 144
Basic Law: The Israeli Lands, 1960 144
Basic Law: The Judiciary, 1984 144
Basic Law: The Knesset, 1958 144
Basic Law: The President of the State, 1964 144
Basic Law: The State Budget for 2009 and 2010 (Special Provisions)
  (Temporary Provisions), 2009 144
Basic Law: The State Comptroller, 1986 144
Basic Law: The State Economy, 1975 .... 144, 151
Cinematograph Films Ordinance, 1937 146
Citizenship Act, 2011 150
Civil Wrongs Law, 1952
  s 5(c) 134
Harrari Resolution, 1950 .... 131, 133
Military Justice Law, 1955 134
Palestine Order in Council (League of Nations), 1922
  s 46 129
Prisons Ordinance, Amendment 28 134

Italy

Constitution 88, 324

Jamaica

Constitution, 1962 45

Japan

Civil Code, 1896 .... 284, 285, 288
Communication Interception Law, 1999 283
Constitution, 1947 .... 88, 277, 279, 286–88, 294, 297
  Art 6 280
  Art 14 285
  Art 20 .... 287, 293, 294
  Art 21 .... 292, 296, 297
  Art 22(1) 291
  Art 25 279
  Art 31 292
  Art 35 354
  Art 79 280
  Art 81 274
  Art 89 .... 287, 293
Constitution of the Empire of Japan, 1890 .... 278, 279, 375
Election Law, 1925 .... 285, 289
Nationality Law, 2008 .... 284, 287, 289
Pharmaceutical Affairs Law, 1960 291
Road Traffic Law, 1951 292

Kenya

Constitution, 2010 45

Malawi

Constitution, 1994 65
    s 11(2) 2, 187
        (c) 40

Malta

Constitution, 1964 45

Mauritius

Constitution, 1968 45

Mexico

Amparo Act, 1882
    s 34 302
    s 70 302
Civil Code of Mexico City 316
Constitution, 1824 303
Constitution, 1917 .... 88, 303, 305, 307
    Art 1 .... 305, 312
    Art 4 317
    Art 6 303
    Art 16 312
    Art 25(1) 313
    Art 94 .... 302, 305
    Art 123 313
    Art 133 .... 303, 304
Constitution of the State of Yucatan, 1841 302
Federal Constitution, 1847 302

New Zealand

Bill of Rights Act, 1990 .... 34, 35, 43

Namibia

Constitution, 1990 .... 160, 161–70, 173, 181–83, 415
    Preamble 164
    Ch 1 164
    Ch 3 (Bill of Rights) 164, 165, 415
    Art 1(1) 164
    Art 5 165
    Arts 5–25 .... 164, 165
    Art 6 165

Art 8(2)(b) 165
Art 10 .... 165, 166, 169
Art 12(1)(a) 169
Art 14 169
Art 21 178
   (1)(a) 178
   (2) 169, 178, 182
Art 22 165
Art 23 165
   (3) 165
Art 24(3) 165
Art 25 .... 165, 166
Art 27(3) 163
Arts 27–34 163
Arts 35–43 163
Art 39 163
Art 41 163
Arts 44–67 163
Art 45 163
Art 46 163
Art 57(0) 163
Art 66 162
   (1) 169
Arts 66–77 163
Art 69 163
Art 78 167
   (4) 162, 183
Art 79 167
   (2) 170
   (3) 176
Art 81 167
Art 87(c) 170
Arts 89–94 166
Art 95 165
Art 131 164
Art 138 167
Art 140 173
   (1) 162, 169
Art 141 173
Art 142 173
Art 143 173
Criminal Procedure Act 51 of 1997
   s 217(1)(b)(ii) 174
Interim Constitution, 1978 159
Namibian Nations Act, 1968 157
Police Act 19 of 1990
   s 58(32) 169
Supreme Court Act 15 of 1990 176
   s 13(2) 177

Nigeria

Constitution, 1960 45

Norway

Constitution 88

Pakistan

Constitution 1973 45

Romania

Civil Code, 1865 327
   Art 3 327
Constitution, 1923 324
Constitution, 1965 324
Constitution, 1991 .... 323–25, 333, 338
   Art 1 333
   Art 6 333
   Art 13 333
   Art 24 334
   Art 31 334
   Art 114 333
   Art 135 339
   Art 148 333
Criminal Procedure Code 334, 335
   Art 320 338
Labour Code 330
Law 47/1992 on the Organisation and Functioning of the Constitutional Court
   Art 51 341
   Art 52 341
   Art 59 341
Law 71/2009 for the Approval of the Emergency Ordinance of the Government 339
Moldova and Wallachia Constitution, 1866 324

Russia

Arbitration Procedure Code, 2002
   Art 170(4) 357
Civil Code, 1960 349
Civil Procedure Code, 2002
   Art 336 358
Constitution, 1978 349
Constitution, 1993 .... 88, 348–55, 357–59, 364, 366
   Ch 2 (Bill of Rights) 354, 355
   Art 15(4) 351
   Art 17 351
   Art 39 355

xxxvi   *Table of Legislation*

   Art 40(1) 355
      (3) 355
   Art 41 355
   Art 120 356
   Art 125 360
   Art 126 360
   Art 127 360
Federal Constitutional Law of 3 November 2010 No 7-FKZ 359
Federal Constitutional Law on the Constitutional Court, 1994 .... 358, 360
   Art 74 359
Federal Constitutional Law on the Judicial System, 1996 357
Federal Law of 30 March 1998 No 54-FZ 355
Federal Law of 25 July 2006, amending the Federal Law 'On Basic Guarantees
   of Electoral Rights and Right of Participation in Referendum of Citizens
   of the Russian Federation' No 67-FZ of 12 June 2002 354

Samoa

Constitution, 1960 45

South Africa

Aliens Control Act 96 of 1991 150
Bill of Rights 187, 188, 192, 195, 198, 201–03, 420
Constitution 200 of 1993 (interim Constitution) 186, 188, 189, 192, 199–201
   Preamble 192
   s 33 207
   s 35 194
      (1) 187
   s 231 187
Constitution of 1996 .... 25, 65, 88, 150, 188, 190, 192, 200, 201, 202, 415
   Ch 2 202
   s 2 192
   s 8(1) 192
      (3) 189
   s 33 202
   s 35 203
   s 36 207
   s 39 .... 2, 65, 121, 181, 194, 208, 416
      (1) 40, 186, 187
         (b) 197
         (c) 187, 189, 197, 207, 218
      (2) 189
   s 165(2) 192
   s 166 192
   s 167 .... 189, 192
   s 168 192
   s 173 189
   s 231 187
   s 232 187

s 233.. 187
Criminal Procedure Act 51 of 1977
 s 217.. 189
Development of Self-Government for Native Nations in South West Africa
 Amendment Act 20 of 1973 158

Spain

Constitution 324

Sri Lanka (Ceylon)

Constitution Order in Council, 1946 88

Sweden

Constitution 88

Switzerland

Federal Constitution, 1874 .... 215, 223

Taiwan

Act Regarding the Council of Grand Justices, 1958 .... 374, 377, 378
Constitutional Interpretation Procedure Act, 1993 .... 374, 377, 378
 Art 10 378
 Art 13 379
 Art 14 378
Organic Act of the Judicial Yuan 376
Republic of China Constitution, 1947 .... 374–77, 387
 Ch VII 377
 Additional Articles, Art 5 376

Trinidad and Tobago

Constitution, 1976 45

Turkey

Constitution 88

United Kingdom

Criminal Law Amendment Act, 1865
 s 11 104
Magna Carta, 1215 277
Offences Against the Person Act, 1861 405
 s 61 104
 s 62 104

United States

American Justice for American Citizens Act, HR 4118,
  108th Cong (2004) 394
Bill of Rights, 1791 .... 40, 44, 45, 48, 61–63, 65, 67, 279, 294, 426
Constitution, 1787 .... 16, 27, 41, 61, 62, 88, 101, 178, 200,
                                                276, 277, 282, 288, 354, 393, 394, 399, 402, 419
  Art 1 16
  Art 2 16
  Art 3 16
  Art 6 .... 303, 304
  First Amendment 62, 178, 288, 294
  Fourth Amendment 62
  Fifth Amendment... 62
  Sixth Amendment 62
  Eighth Amendment.. 62, 408
  Fourteenth Amendment 62
Constitution Restoration Act of 2004, HR 3799, 108th Cong (2004) 394
Restatement (third) of the Foreign Relations Law of the US: International Law and
  Agreements as Law of the United States
  § 111 397

Venezuela

Constitution 88

Introduction
The Methodology of the Research: How to Assess the Reality of Transjudicial Communication?

TANIA GROPPI AND MARIE-CLAIRE PONTHOREAU

TABLE OF CONTENTS

I. Origin and Purpose of the Research 1
II. The Selection of the Country Studied 3
III. A Common Methodology 5
   A. The Object of the Research 5
   B. The Constitutional and Legal Context 6
   C. Explicit Citations and Implicit Influences 6
   D. The Quantitative Analysis 7
   E. The Quality-Based Analysis 8
   F. The Time Period 9

I. ORIGIN AND PURPOSE OF THE RESEARCH

IN THE LAST 10 years, literature on so-called 'transjudicial communication'[1] has grown vast, mainly in the English-speaking world, where these studies are long-established and deep-rooted.[2] Prominent scholars have focused on the emergence of a 'global dialogue' bringing judges around the world closer to each other[3] and emphasised that, more often than in the past, courts in performing their adjudicatory functions find inspiration in foreign case law, engaging in a conversation with other judges worldwide.[4]

Among other things, these studies have benefited from the contrasting attitude and impact of two courts, currently under global scrutiny for a different set of reasons.

---

[1] For this expression, see A-M Slaughter, 'A Typology of Transjudicial Communication' (1994) 29 *University of Richmond Law Review* 99.
[2] PK Tripathi, 'Foreign Precedents and Constitutional Law' (1957) 57 *Columbia Law Review* 319.
[3] A-M Slaughter, *A New World Order* (Princeton, Princeton University Press, 2004).
[4] C L'Heureux-Dubé, 'The Importance of Dialogue: Globalization and the International Impact of the Rehnquist Court' (1998) 34 *Tulsa Law Journal* 40.

On one side of the spectrum, attention is focused on the approach—ranging 'from indifferent to hostile'[5]—exhibited by a majority of Justices within the United States (US) Supreme Court with regard to the direct citation of foreign precedents.[6]

At the other end of the spectrum lies the openness of the South African Constitutional Court, also as a result of the interpretative rule codified in Section 39 of that country's Constitution, pursuant to which '[w]hen interpreting the Bill of Rights, a court, tribunal or forum ... may consider foreign law'.[7]

Non-English-speaking commentators have not focused as extensively on this matter.

Indeed, the absence within civilian legal systems of one or more catalysing factor(s), such as prior subjection to the Privy Council, or a single language within a common cultural and legal space, together with the preference for a less articulated form of reasoning, has significantly reduced the incentive to use foreign precedents.

More recently, however, civil law scholars and commentators have also showed a growing interest in this phenomenon, due to a series of reasons, including the aforementioned ongoing debate in English-speaking systems, the process of European integration, and the propensity displayed by some constitutional courts to quote foreign precedents in their decisions.[8]

Most commentators, whether from English-speaking or other countries, have focused extensively on the theoretical aspects of this practice, presenting arguments in favour of or against the use of foreign jurisprudence either as an aid to or as a method of constitutional interpretation, an aspect of the debate that has been widely explored in several jurisdictions, although none has reached the dramatic tones[9] of the United States.

---

[5] SK Harding, 'Comparative Reasoning and Judicial Review' (2003) 28 *Yale Journal of International Law* 409, 417.

[6] See especially *Printz v US*, 521 US 898 (1997), *Knight v Florida*, 528 US 990 (1999), *Atkins v Virginia*, 536 US 304 (2002), *Foster v Florida*, 537 US 990 (2002); *Lawrence v Texas*, 539 US 558 (2003), *Roper v Simmons*, 543 US 551 (2005), *Graham v Florida*, 560 US 130 (2010).

[7] To our knowledge, the only other national Constitution providing a similar (even more specific) clause is the 1994 Constitution of Malawi, whose s 11.2 establishes: 'In interpreting the provisions of this Constitution, a court of law shall ... where applicable, have regard to current norms of public international law and comparable foreign case law'.

[8] In German scholarship, Peter Häberle has addressed this issue in many of his works; among them it is worth citing: P Häberle, *Rechtsvergleichung im Kraftfeld des Verfassungsstaates* (Berlin, Duncker & Humblot GmbH, 1992) 27 (where legal comparison is presented as a new interpretative argument). Within Italian scholarship, see L Pegoraro, *La Corte costituzionale italiana e il diritto comparato: un'analisi comparatistica* (Bologna, CLUEB, 2007), including comprehensive bibliographical references; the former President of the Italian Constitutional Court, Gustavo Zagrebelsky, devoted to this subject the official speech given in April 2006 on the occasion of the 50th anniversary of that Court: G Zagrebelsky, 'Corti costituzionali e diritti universali' (2006) *Rivista trimestrale di diritto pubblico* 297. In France, see M-C Ponthoreau, 'Le recours à l'argument de droit comparé par le juge constitutionnel. Quelques problèmes théoriques et techniques' in F Mélin-Soucramanien (ed), *L'interprétation constitutionnelle* (Paris, Dalloz, 2005) 168.

[9] The word 'dramatic' referred to vis-a-vis the United States is justified in light of the astonishing intensity that the debate has reached there, to the point that two US Supreme Court Justices (Ruth Bader Ginsburg and Sandra Day O'Connor), in several extrajudicial speeches, have publicly showed their favour towards citations of foreign law and received, in turn, not only criticism, but even death threats: see AL Parrish, 'Storm in a Teacup: The US Supreme Court's Use of Foreign Law' (2007) *University of Illinois Law Review* 637, 645.

Only a handful of studies have attempted to catalogue the different approaches adopted by constitutional (or supreme) courts in their use of foreign law and jurisprudence,[10] and even fewer have tried to base their considerations upon effective empirical data, probably discouraged by the practical difficulty and width of this type of research.[11]

The purpose of this book is to address this void, presenting data on 16 different constitutional or supreme courts, organised according to a common methodology including both a quantitative and a qualitative analysis: the goal is to assess, beyond the vast amount of theoretical scholarship, the reality and true extent of transjudicial communication between courts by looking directly at case law.

The book is the result of several years of research, developed within a group of scholars (the 'Interest Group on Cross-Judicial Fertilization. The Use of Foreign Precedents by Constitutional Judges' or Group) established in Athens on 14 June 2007, on the occasion of the VII World Congress of the International Association of Constitutional Law (IACL). Subsequently, the Group has held two intermediate meetings (in November 2008 in London and in April 2010 in Siena) and eventually presented the first results of the research in December 2010 at the VIII World Congress organised by IACL in Mexico City. The Group is composed of both senior and junior constitutional comparative law scholars. While most of the former drafted reports on their own jurisdictions, the majority of the junior scholars—who, during this period were PhD candidates at the University of Siena—wrote reports on countries other than their own and then submitted them to local senior scholars who operated as referees.

The origin of the research, and especially the link with the IACL Interest Group, helps to explain the criteria employed in the selection of the country studied.

II. THE SELECTION OF THE COUNTRY STUDIED

The book has been divided in two parts, addressing, respectively, courts that often resort to foreign precedents (part one) and courts that only rarely cite such precedents (part two).

The jurisdictions covered in the book are (in order of presentation): in part one, the High Court of Australia, the Supreme Court of Canada, the Supreme Court of India, the Supreme Court of Israel, the Supreme Court of Ireland, the Supreme Court of Namibia, the Constitutional Court of South Africa; in part two, the Constitutional Court of Austria, the Constitutional Court of Germany, the Constitutional Court of Hungary, the Supreme Court of Japan, the Supreme

---

[10] See, among others, C McCrudden, 'A Common Law of Human Rights?: Transnational Judicial Conversations on Constitutional Rights' (2000) 20 *Oxford Journal of Legal Studies* 499; S Choudhry, 'Globalization in Search of Justification: Toward a Theory of Comparative Constitutional Interpretation' (1999) 74 *Indiana Law Journal* 819, 834; H Botha, 'Comparative Law and Constitutional Adjudication' (2007) 55 *Jahrbuch des öffentlichen Rechts der Gegenwart* 335; B Markesinis and J Fedtke, 'The Judge as Comparatist' (2005) 80 *Tulane Law Review* 11.

[11] The 'empirical void' has been emphasised by U Bentele, 'Mining for Gold: The Constitutional Court of South Africa's Experience with Comparative Constitutional Law' (2009) 37 *Georgia Journal of International and Comparative Law* 219, 221.

Court of Mexico, the Constitutional Court of Romania, the Constitutional Court of Russia, the Constitutional Court of Taiwan and, finally, the Supreme Court of the United States.

A quite significant factor influencing the structure of this contribution is that this book is co-edited by two professors who originally received their legal education, and currently operate within, the civilian legal tradition. We would like to offer a new perspective, beyond the many studies already existing within common law scholarship. While there is an expectation that in the common law tradition judges often, and more naturally, resort to foreign cases, special attention in the book is purposefully dedicated to civilian jurisdictions.

Actually, among the many possible approaches to the issue of transjudicial communication,[12] the research was mainly aimed at checking, on this specific ground, the reality of the thesis of the convergence of the common law and civil law traditions.

The selection of the countries studied is functional to this purpose, thus, alongside some leading common law or mixed-tradition jurisdictions, the book includes several civilian jurisdictions, representing an important set of diversity, for reasons of geographical repartition (Asia, Europe, America) and longevity of the courts. Intuitively, it was not possible to extend the research to all jurisdictions worldwide: important civil law countries, such as Italy and Spain, are missing. Other countries were excluded mainly due to the form of reasoning of their constitutional judges' decisions that materially leave no room for citations, as in the case of the French Conseil constitutionnel or the courts operating in the 'French space of Africa', which follow the French tradition in terms of legal reasoning.

Other civilian legal jurisdictions of primary interest are not covered in the book, such as those of the Portuguese Constitutional Court, the Brazilian Supreme Court, the Constitutional Court of Colombia and the Argentinean Supreme Court. Although all these jurisdictions belong to the civil legal tradition, for a variety of reasons they present an established practice of explicit citation of foreign case law.[13] Unfortunately, at this stage, it has not been possible to include these countries' reports—currently still under development—in the book. We are aware of the significant impact that this absence has on the research; an absence, however, that leaves room for further studies in the future.

---

[12] Other interesting approaches could have been followed to assess the reality of transjudicial communication on other grounds, such as one-way transmission from more influential countries to less influential ones, according to various standards, such as a country's colonialist past, its influence in international relationships and the size of the country. On these factors see V Jackson, *Constitutional Engagement in a Transnational Era* (Oxford, Oxford University Press, 2009) 95.

[13] See R Orrù, 'La giustizia costituzionale in azione e il paradigma del diritto comparato: l'esperienza portoghese' in GF Ferrari A Gambaro (eds), *Corti nazionali e comparazione giuridica* (Napoli, ESI, 2006) 1 ff; MJ Garcia-Mansilla, 'La Corte Suprema de los Estados Unidos y su debil influencia en Iberoamerica' in P Manili (ed), *Tratado de derecho procesal constitucional*, III (Buenos Aires, La Ley, 2010) 109; VA da Silva, 'Integração e Diálogo Constitucional na América do Sul' in A von Bogdandy, F Piovesan and M Morales Antoniazzi (eds), *Direitos Humanos, Democracia e Integração Jurídica na América do Sul* (Rio de Janeiro, Lúmen Júris, 2010) 530; M Neves, 'Transconstitucionalismo. Breves Considerações com Especial Referência à Experiênica Latino-Americana' in A von Bogdandy, F Piovesan and M Morales Antoniazzi (eds), *Direitos Humanos, Democracia e Integração Jurídica* (Rio de Janeiro, Lumen Juris 2010) 255; M Neves, *Transcontitucionalismo* (São Paulo, WMF Martinsfontes, 2009).

III. A COMMON METHODOLOGY

From the beginning of the research, we realised the importance of, and the need to employ, a common methodology in order to guarantee a high degree of homogeneity (ie comparability) of data and reports. At the same time, we also became immediately aware of the need to integrate this common methodology with a consideration of some specific national features, which determined several derogations to the common guidelines, according to the needs of the authors.

A. The Object of the Research

The 'use of foreign case law by constitutional judges' is the object of this research.

The word 'use' is purposefully employed in a broad fashion, to encompass, as it will soon be further elaborated, both explicit citations and implicit influences in constitutional interpretation, although the main focus of the research is on explicit citations.

'Foreign case law' means judicial decisions of another national jurisdiction, at the constitutional level. In many cases, the word 'precedent' is used synonymously, leaving aside issues related to the different meaning that this word may have depending on the particular legal system.[14]

Since the purpose of our research is not to assess the propensity of the courts towards 'transnational engagement' or the 'migration of constitutional ideas',[15] but, conversely, the reality and extent of transjudicial communication, other extra-systemic materials such as citations of foreign Constitutions, foreign statutes and foreign legal literature have been excluded from consideration, although they may represent an indication of the openness of a court (considered, at any rate, as a contextual element).

The use of international case law has also been excluded from the research:[16] we strongly believe that reference to international case law can divert attention from the optional and purely voluntary horizontal dialogue between courts, by introducing elements of vertical 'compulsory dialogue'.[17]

The only exception to this rule has been made when the country is not a party to a treaty, because in this circumstance no hierarchical relationship exists between national and international or supranational institutions (for example, citations of the European Court of Human Rights (ECtHR) by the US Supreme Court, by the

---

[14] HP Glenn, 'Persuasive Authority' (1987) 32 *McGill Law Journal* 261, 263. See the extensive comparative research presented in E Hondius (ed), *Precedent and the Law* (Bruxelles, Bruylant, 2007).

[15] Citing from the titles of two influential books on this subject: V Jackson, *Constitutional Engagement in a Transnational Era* (Oxford, Oxford University Press, 2009); S Choudhry (ed), *The Migration of Constitutional Ideas* (Cambridge, Cambridge University Press, 2006).

[16] In this, we take a different view to other scholars, such as Vicki Jackson and Giuseppe de Vergottini, who included international case law in the unique category of 'transnational law'. See V Jackson, *Constitutional Engagement in a Transnational Era* (2009); G de Vergottini, *Oltre il dialogo tra le Corti. Giudici, diritto straniero, comparazione* (Bologna, Il Mulino, 2010). We share the approach of C Saunders, 'The Use and Misuse of Comparative Constitutional Law' (2006) 13 *Indiana Journal of Global Legal Studies* 37.

[17] See A-M Slaughter, 'A Typology of Transjudicial Communication' (1994) 29 *University of Richmond Law Review* 99.

High Court of Australia, by the Supreme Court of Mexico or by the Canadian Supreme Court, etc, can still be considered a sort of horizontal, voluntary communication).

A significant issue was raised by citations to Privy Council precedents in common law systems: in this case, we asked authors to exclude from consideration cases decided by the Privy Council or by other English courts during the period when these were binding for the national jurisdiction at issue (as occurred in Australia until 1986, in Canada until 1949 and in Ireland until 1933), since at that time these decisions represented a 'local', rather than a 'foreign', authority.

'Constitutional Judges' means judges in specialised constitutional courts in the countries following the 'Kelsenian model' of judicial review. However, the expression also includes supreme courts which adjudicate constitutional cases in countries following the 'American model' of judicial review. In this latter case, since normally supreme courts are vested with several competences, it was necessary to identify the boundaries between 'constitutional' and 'non-constitutional cases'. We opted for a broad approach, and defined as 'constitutional' any case involving 'constitutional interpretation' and dealing either with 'institutional' or 'human rights' issues. A specially articulated definition of 'constitutional case' was necessary for Israel, in the absence of a complete constitutional text.

The research is based on single-country studies. For each country, we asked the authors to divide the report into two parts: an analysis of the constitutional and legal context and the empirical research.

B. The Constitutional and Legal Context

Regarding the context, each author presented some features of the jurisdiction being studied that can help us to understand better the current legal attitude, such as how the Constitution and the legal system developed (cultural and historical origins; foreign influences on the constitutional text with an emphasis on existing declarations of rights; classification as a common law, civil law or mixed system); the structure and functions of the courts (career of judges; use of precedents and their role; techniques of judicial reasoning, such as presence of dissenting or concurring opinions; propensity towards citation of foreign law or foreign case law by ordinary courts; propensity towards citation of international case law; when present, extrajudicial speeches of the judges on the use of foreign case law); and scholarship (links between legal scholarship and the courts; attention paid by scholars to the influence of foreign case law; existence of a doctrinal debate on the use of foreign case law by the courts).

C. Explicit Citations and Implicit Influences

As for the empirical research, we focused our attention on *explicit* citations.

In taking this view, we are aware that lack of express citations in the decisions of many courts should not be considered to be indicative of a lack of knowledge of foreign case law by the judges. In all honestly, we believe such lack of awareness to be impossible in today's globalised and interconnected world. Modern computer technology, personal connections between justices, developments in legal education, only to name a few factors, have made the 'circulation' of case law easier and more frequent. Unquestionably, foreign jurisprudence exercises a 'hidden' influence on all jurisdictions.[18] One of the most strenuous detractors of citations of foreign jurisprudence, Justice Antonin Scalia of the United States Supreme Court, in the end contradicted himself, and was not able to deny that some knowledge of foreign decisions is ultimately valuable: 'I mean, go ahead and indulge your curiosity! Just don't put it in your opinions!' he reportedly said.[19]

It is our view, therefore, that the frequency with which a court cites foreign case law in its decisions is only a partially reliable measure to assess the extent to which the court actually resorts to and makes use of foreign case law.[20]

We do believe this to be a very important point particularly when courts rarely quote foreign precedents. Nonetheless we are also aware that assessing non-explicit influence requires not only very deep and extended studies, but also significant extra-judicial research, conducted by way of interviews and questionnaires.[21]

D. The Quantitative Analysis

Although focusing mainly on explicit citations, assessing the influence exercised by a foreign court or by one or more foreign judicial decision(s) on another judicial body is a complicated task.

The mere number of explicit references does not represent a meaningful indicator: in fact, this may be dependent on many factors, such as the number of foreign decisions quoted by each single jurisdiction, or the total number of decisions rendered.

---

[18] See P Ridola, 'La giurisprudenza costituzionale e la comparazione' in G Alpa (ed), *Il giudice e l'uso delle sentenze straniere* (Milano, Giuffré, 2006) 15, 24, where the author maintains that the 'hidden' or 'underlying' influence is the real avenue for cross-judicial fertilisation, citing as an example the Italian Constitutional Court; although this Court very rarely cites foreign precedents, since 1995 it has established within its offices a 'Comparative Law Department' composed of young lawyers from many different countries. What is interesting is that, since 1995, the number of foreign citations in the Court's decisions actually decreased. DS Law and W-C Chang, 'The Limits of Global Judicial Dialogue' (2011) 86 *Washington Law Review* 523, 539, indicate that the Constitutional Court of Korea, that only rarely cites foreign case law explicitly, established a research institute staffed by full-time researchers speaking the main western foreign languages as well as Japanese.

[19] Scalia's statement is quoted by AL Parrish, n 6 above at 675.

[20] David S Law and Wen-Chen Chang, 'The Limits of Global Judicial Dialogue' (2011) 86 *Washington Law Review* 523 at 527.

[21] In fact, to our knowledge, only one such study has been published as a book: this is Catherine Dupré's contribution on the influence of German Constitutional Court decisions addressing human dignity issues on the Hungarian Constitutional Court, an influence that is completely non-explicit. See C Dupré, *Importing Law in Post-Communist Transitions* (Oxford, Hart Publishing, 2003). Recently, some articles based on interviews with judges have been published: U Bentele, 'Mining for Gold: The Constitutional Court of South Africa's Experience with Comparative Constitutional Law' (2009) 37 *Georgia Journal of International and Comparative Law* 219; B Flanagan and S Ahern, 'Judicial Decision-Making and Transnational Law: A Survey of Common Law Supreme Court Judges' (2011) 60 *International and Comparative Law Quarterly* 1; E Mak, 'Why Do Dutch and UK Judges Cite Foreign Law?' (2011) 70 *Cambridge Law Journal* 420; DS Law and W-C Chang, 'The Limits of Global Judicial Dialogue', n 18 above, on the Constitutional Court of Taiwan.

A quality-based approach appears therefore to be more significant, although it implies a number of premises in order to set the context to evaluate the influence.

As a first step, we asked all the authors to follow a quantitative approach, that is, to indicate, for the time period analysed, the following data, when possible sorted both in total and per year:

(i) the number of decisions citing foreign case law, out of the total number of decisions, irrespective of the location of the citation;
(ii) the total number of citations;
(iii) the number of citations of the decisions of each foreign jurisdiction cited;
(iv) the number of citations in cases dealing with human rights and in cases dealing with institutional issues;
(v) the number of citations in majority or minority opinions.

The authors were free either to use reliable databases and conduct their research using specific keywords, or to read and select directly the relevant cases citing foreign precedents.

In order to make the data more easily understandable and to emphasise the courts' trends and patterns of behaviour, we also asked the authors to produce charts, tables and graphs, especially on:

(1) the number of decisions citing foreign precedents out of the total per year;
(2) the percentage of citations in institutional and human rights decisions, out of the total number of citations (when a distinction was possible);
(3) the percentage of citations sorted by countries cited, out of the total number of citations;
(4) the percentage of citations in majority, concurring, and/or dissenting opinions, out of the total number of citations.

In addition to these four common charts, authors were left free to include up to two additional charts to better emphasise specific aspects of the jurisdictions they analysed.

Although all the data have not always been detected and mere numbers are not a sufficient indicator, we believe that the data and charts on the 16 countries hereby presented provide an interesting starting point for further theoretical studies on the topic.

E. The Quality-Based Analysis

The most challenging part of the research was the qualitative analysis of the citations.

We asked the authors to assess the courts' 'use' of foreign case law, by investigating the role played by foreign precedents in legal reasoning. We were perfectly aware that a careful study of any single citation would have been almost impossible in countries where hundreds and hundreds of citations could be found, and therefore, in those cases we left the authors free to develop the analysis in a more general way.

The starting point was the consideration, very common in scholarship (and fully confirmed by the research), that no court has treated foreign precedents as having more than persuasive authority: as Justice Chaskalson of the South African

Constitutional Court—one of the most strenuous supporters of citations of foreign case law—wrote in the famous case *S v Makwanyane*[22] on the constitutionality of the death penalty, 'We can derive assistance from public international law and foreign case law, but we are in no way bound to follow it'.

We proposed that authors classified citations in three categories:

(1) Citations used at the very first stage of the interpretative process, when the reasoning must be oriented, to provide a 'guiding horizon'.[23] In those cases, examples of similar judgments decided in other jurisdictions may be used to illustrate the range of potential choices, or rather, the possible consequences of a decision.
(2) Citations used for the purposes of 'probative comparison', that is, with the purpose of proving that 'even there' a certain measure was adopted, which the court intends to adopt 'even here'.
(3) Citations cited as an example not to be followed (*a contrario*), in order to exclude or set aside some of the possible readings of a provision or patterns of hermeneutical development.

We hoped that several aspects of practice would emerge through this, such as the quality of the citations and/or the variety of roles played by them in the reasoning of the courts.

F. The Time Period

After careful consideration, we realised the practical impossibility of establishing a time period for the analysis which was common to all countries. Therefore, the choice of the time period to be covered by the research was left to the authors, in the hope that this would better accommodate the specificities of each country.

At the same time, we were not unaware of the fundamental importance that the time period to be covered represented for the research. For example, many scholars have emphasised the significance of so-called 'formative periods', and the propensity of recently-established courts not supported by an extensive line of precedents or even older courts dealing with the interpretation of a newly enacted constitutional document, to look for inspiration to the case law of older and better established systems of rights protection.[24]

Furthermore, the choice of a longer period of time allows authors to draw comparisons between the different attitudes of the court within the period. Reports on India, Ireland, Namibia, Romania, Russia, South Africa and Taiwan cover the whole period of activity of their respective courts. In many cases practical considerations (such as the high number of decisions or citations, or the existence of

---

[22] *S v Makwanyane* [1995] 3 SA 391 (CC) 39.
[23] We refer to the interpretation 'to know', distinguished from the interpretation 'to decide': see O Pfersman, 'Le sophisme onomastique: changer au lieu de connaître. L'interprétation de la constitution' in F Mélin-Soucramanien (ed), *L'interprétation constitutionnelle* (Paris, Dalloz, 2005) 146.
[24] M-C Ponthoreau, 'Le recours à l'argument de droit comparé par le juge constitutionnel. Quelques problèmes théoriques et techniques' in F Mélin-Soucramanien (ed), *L'interprétation constitutionnelle* (Paris, Dalloz, 2005) 168.

previous studies) drove the authors towards a different selection for the time period, excluding the formative years: a specific explanation of the reasons leading to this choice is found in the specific report.

However, all the reports—with the exception of the Australian and Japanese ones, which stop in 2008—cover the period from 2000 to 2010.

At the end of this five-year project, we would like to thank all the scholars involved in this research, especially those that provided the final report included in this book. They enthusiastically engaged in a very time-consuming empirical analysis and raised several challenging methodological issues, actively contributing to a lively and enriching debate among the Group.

Students of the PhD programme in Comparative Public Law at the University of Siena (2007–10) carried out detailed bibliographical research and implemented a dedicated website: we are grateful to them.

Special thanks are due to the IACL for encouraging the inclusion of the Group in the programme of the VIII World Congress of the Association, held in December 2010 in Mexico City, and especially its former President, Didier Maus, for his support.

It is not possible to list here the names of the many colleagues that provided useful and thoughtful comments during a series of seminars and workshops worldwide: to them we would like to express our deepest and most heartfelt gratitude. We are not sure, based on the outcome of this research that a real global judicial dialogue does exist. What is certain, though, is the existence of a lively global legal community of scholars.

Finally, Professor Groppi would personally like to thank the Max-Plank Institute for Comparative Public Law and International Law in Heidelberg and especially its Director, Professor Armin von Bogdandy, for providing a safe haven of peace and intellectual vivacity where the Introduction and Conclusion of this book were drafted.

Part I

1

Reference to Foreign Precedents by the Australian High Court: A Matter of Method

CHERYL SAUNDERS AND ADRIENNE STONE[*]

TABLE OF CONTENTS

I. Introduction 13
II. The Australian Context 15
   A. Australian Constitution 15
   B. The High Court of Australia 18
III. Citation of Foreign Precedent in Australia 22
   A. Anecdotal Impressions 22
   B. Reactions to the US Debate 24
   C. Previous Australian Studies 26
III. The Data 28
   A. Overview 28
   B. The Data Presented 31
IV. Conclusions 37

I. INTRODUCTION

THIS CHAPTER IS the Australian contribution to a comparative project on the citation of foreign precedents in constitutional adjudication.[1] The project brings together constitutional law scholars from a wide range of states with different legal and constitutional systems to explore some significant questions for comparative constitutional law: the reality of transjudicial dialogue, the convergence of common law and civil law legal systems and the universalism of human rights. As the chapter demonstrates, the citation of foreign precedents in constitutional as well as other cases is common in the Australian apex court, the High Court of Australia. The ways in which such precedents are chosen and used sometimes raise questions

---

[*] Cheryl Saunders is Laureate Professor, Melbourne Law School, Australia. Adrienne Stone is Professor of Law and Director, Centre for Comparative Constitutional Studies, Melbourne Law School, Australia.

[1] The contribution of Martin Clark towards research for this chapter, in particular the organisation and analysis of the data, is acknowledged with much appreciation.

about comparative methods.² The practice is long-established in Australia, however, and its legitimacy is rarely, if ever, raised as a question in its own right.³

As in any other state, Australian practice can be adequately understood only in light of the context in which it occurs. For present purposes, moreover, context not only assists in interpreting the data but has influenced the scope of the study. First, the number of cases in which foreign precedents are cited has caused the period over which data has been collected for this project to be confined to nine years, from 2000–08, although the chapter also refers to empirical analyses for other periods. The choice of this particular period is explained and justified later in the chapter. Secondly, the diverse purposes for which references to foreign precedents are used complicate qualitative analysis of the kind that may be possible elsewhere. While there is some discussion of use in the chapter, therefore, there is no data set that attempts to categorise it by reference to purpose. Third, because the Australian Constitution, exceptionally, does not include a Bill of Rights, it has not been practicable in this study to distinguish cases that cite foreign precedents in the course of determining institutional questions from those that do so in relation to rights. While some Australian constitutional cases in fact raise questions about rights, these are often resolved through an application of institutional provisions dealing either with representative government or the separation of judicial power.⁴ As a further complication, many justiciable rights disputes in Australia do not raise constitutional questions but are determined on the basis of statute or the common law.⁵ Australian courts may well refer to foreign precedents in cases of this kind.⁶ They nevertheless lie beyond the scope of this study, unless the cases in which they arise involve constitutional questions as well.

This chapter begins with an analysis of the context for constitutional adjudication in Australia. To this end, it focuses in particular on the character and scope of the Australian Constitution and the status, jurisdiction and modes of operation of the High Court of Australia. The second substantive part of the chapter deals directly with the citation of foreign law in constitutional cases in Australia by examining the place of the practice within approaches to Australian judicial reasoning, the Australian reaction, such as it was, to the controversy over foreign citations that broke out in the United States in the early years of the twenty-first century; and the links between the data collected for the purposes of this chapter and earlier empirical studies. This part also explains the distinction presently drawn by most Justices of the High Court between references to foreign and international sources. The third part of the chapter presents, analyses, and explains the present data set using a number of tables and graphs. The final part offers some tentative conclusions, together with suggestions for further research.

---

² A Stone, 'Comparativism in Constitutional Interpretation' (2009) *New Zealand Law Review* 45.
³ C Saunders, 'The Use and Misuse of Comparative Constitutional Law' (2006) 13 *Indiana Journal of Global Legal Studies* 37.
⁴ C Saunders, *The Constitution of Australia: A Contextual Analysis* (Oxford, Hart Publishing, 2011) 274–75.
⁵ Ibid, 265–72.
⁶ For an example, see *Jago v District Court of New South Wales* (1989) 168 CLR 23. With the introduction of legislative charters of rights in two Australian sub-national jurisdictions, the Australian Capital Territory and Victoria, there are likely to be even more cases that raise rights questions without engaging the Australian Constitution unless, as occasionally happens, a constitutional challenge is mounted against part of the rights instrument: *Momcilovic v R* (2011) 245 CLR 1.

II. THE AUSTRALIAN CONTEXT

A. Australian Constitution

The Australian Constitution is embedded in a common law legal system. It creates institutions and relies on assumptions that are shared by most other common law states. Australian membership of the common law legal family is a consequence of its settlement by Great Britain, as a series of six colonies, in the late eighteenth and early nineteenth centuries. Because Australia was characterised as *terra nullius*, the common law of England was absorbed into the colonies, on or after their establishment, to fill what in effect was treated as a legal void.[7] Even when this was acknowledged as a fiction and the doctrine of *terra nullius* discredited, the common law foundations of the legal system remained unaffected.[8] The decision in the famous *Mabo* case, in which it was accepted that indigenous rights to land might have survived British settlement, created a form of native title as a doctrine of the common law, rather than recognising its continuing effect as part of a pluralist legal system.[9]

The common law setting for the Australian Constitution is significant for present purposes in at least two ways. First, the history of settlement ensured that the institutions of colonial government, once created, would be broadly similar to those of the Imperial power. The early Australian colonies thus created Parliaments, governments and courts that were modelled on those at Westminster.[10] As long as the Imperial connection remained, they were also subject to the authority of Imperial institutions: the British Parliament, the British Crown and the Judicial Committee of the Privy Council.[11] While there have been major evolutionary changes since then, the principal design choices thus were made. They have particular implications for the role, jurisdiction and operation of courts, which will be taken up in the next section.

Secondly, in such a setting, the sources of law lie in the common law, in the sense of judge-made law, in addition to statutes and any written Constitution. Australia inherited and continued to develop all the precepts of a constitutional kind that were the products of the common law.[12] Relevantly for present purposes, these included a protective attitude towards such rights as freedom of speech, a particular understanding of the scope of executive vis-a-vis legislative power and a dualist approach to international law.[13] Moreover, while the Australians necessarily required written Constitutions to create institutions of government for their new polities they also inherited an assumption that, at the time, they shared with other settler states in the second British Empire, that rights were adequately protected by Parliament and

---

[7] W Blackstone, *Commentaries on the Law of England*, Book 1 (Dublin, Exshaw et al, 1766) 104–05.
[8] *Mabo v Queensland (No 2)* (1992) 175 CLR 1.
[9] M Tehan, 'A Hope Disillusioned, An Opportunity Lost? Reflections on Common Law Native Title and Ten Years of the *Native Title Act*' (2003) 27 *Melbourne University Law Review* 523.
[10] P Finn, *Law and Government in Colonial Australia* (Melbourne, Oxford University Press, 1987).
[11] Saunders, *The Constitution of Australia*, n 4 above, 18–19.
[12] For the Eastern Colonies see Australian Courts Act 1828 (Imp), s 24.
[13] L Zines, 'The Common Law in Australia: Its Nature and Constitutional Significance' (2004) 32 *Federal Law Review* 337.

by independent courts administering the common law. On this view, rights did not require additional constitutional protection.[14]

The Australian Constitution came into effect in 1901 as the framework for a federation that brought together all six of the colonies.[15] These became States, retaining their existing Constitutions, institutions and court systems, subject to the new Constitution.[16] The Constitution also created the institutions for a new sphere of national government, the Commonwealth of Australia. These included a new national court, the High Court of Australia, as the final Australian court of appeal in matters of both Commonwealth and State jurisdiction.[17] To preserve the hard-fought federal bargain the Constitution was heavily entrenched; it was subject to change only when a proposal passed by the Commonwealth Parliament was accepted at referendum by a national majority and by majorities in a majority of States.[18]

This Constitution drew for its inspiration on both of the two major common law constitutional traditions. The institutions of the legislature, executive and, arguably, the courts, continued to be modelled on those of Great Britain. Consistently with the British tradition also, the Constitution made almost no express provision for the protection of rights. However, the model of federalism and the concept of a supreme Constitution itself were adapted from the Constitution of the United States, which also had some influence on other aspects of institutional design.[19] In particular, the first three chapters of the Constitution were devoted respectively to the institutions of the legislature, the executive and the judiciary, along lines that were strikingly similar to the first three Articles of the Constitution of the United States. In due course this encouraged the High Court to conclude that a strict separation of judicial power was constitutionally protected.[20] It was also assumed, although not explicitly stated, that Australian courts, like their United States counterparts, had a power of judicial review that extended to finding that legislation of either sphere of government was invalid if it conflicted with constitutional requirements.

At the time of federation, Australia was not yet fully independent. This was evidenced by the way in which the Constitution was brought into effect, as an Act of the British Parliament, after having been negotiated and drafted in Australia and approved at referendum by a majority in each of the participating colonies. Consistently with Imperial practice, the institutions of both the Commonwealth and the States thus were subject, ultimately, to British authority. Importantly for present purposes, appeals lay to the Judicial Committee of the Privy Council from the Supreme Courts of the States and from the High Court itself, with an exception only for a category of cases that dealt with relations between the Commonwealth and

---

[14] H Moore, *The Constitution of the Australian Commonwealth* (London, John Murray, 1902) 329.
[15] Commonwealth of Australia Constitution Act 1900 (Imp).
[16] Australian Constitution, ss 106–08.
[17] s 71.
[18] s 128.
[19] N Aroney, *The Constitution of a Federal Commonwealth: The Making and Meaning of the Australian Constitution* (Cambridge, Cambridge University Press, 2009).
[20] While the doctrine began to emerge early in the history of federation its contours finally were set in *R v Kirby; ex parte Boilermakers' Society of Australia (Boilermakers' case)*, (1956) 94 CLR 254.

the States *inter se*.[21] Over the course of the rest of the century, Australia achieved independence from what was now the United Kingdom by a slow and gradual evolutionary process, which did not culminate until the passage of the Australia Acts in 1986.[22] Even now, the retention of the Queen as the formal Australian head of state is lingering evidence of Australia's former colonial status.[23]

The story of Australian independence is relevant to an understanding of the citation of foreign precedents by the High Court of Australia in several respects.

Most obviously, it must be taken into account in evaluating High Court citations of decisions of courts based in the United Kingdom in the first half-century after federation. As long as appeals still lay to the Privy Council, it was part of the Australian judicial hierarchy, and its decisions necessarily were not only cited but followed.[24] Acceptance of the dominant role of the House of Lords in development of the common law caused its decisions to be treated as binding as well.[25] This situation continued until the 1960s, long after Australia had become independent in fact. It was made tolerable for a time by changes to the membership of the Privy Council to include judges of the dominions from which appeals lay[26] and by acceptance on the part of the Privy Council that the law in the two countries might develop differently.[27] Appeals to the Privy Council from the High Court were finally severed, in two tranches, in 1968 and 1975.[28] The final avenue of appeal, from State Supreme Courts, was removed by the Australia Acts in 1986. The last constitutional appeal from the High Court to the Privy Council was decided in 1968 and the last appeal from any Australian court was concluded in 1987.[29] In the face of these changes, it fell to the High Court to determine the authoritative status of the decisions of these bodies. In anticipation, it already had decided in 1963 that decisions of the House of Lords were no longer binding.[30] In 1978, decisions of the Privy Council were also held no longer to be binding.[31] To complete the picture, following the passage of the Australia Acts in 1986, the High Court made it clear that no precedents from other legal systems were binding on any Australian courts.[32] The Australian legal system now stood alone, with the High Court at the apex of a system of federal and State courts administering what it soon identified as the common law of Australia.[33]

---

[21] Australian Constitution, s 74.

[22] Saunders, *The Constitution of Australia*, n 4 above, 19–29.

[23] C Saunders, 'Beyond Minimalism' in Sarah Murray (ed), *Constitutional Perspectives on an Australian Republic* (Annandale, Federation Press, 2010) 54.

[24] J Goldring, *The Privy Council and the Australian Constitution* (Hobart, University of Tasmania Press, 1996).

[25] *Piro v W Foster & Co Ltd* (1943) 68 CLR 313.

[26] C Smith, 'An Introduction to the Judicial Committee of the Privy Council', Privy Council Papers Online, www.privycouncilpapers.org/judicial-committee.

[27] M Gleeson, 'The Birth, Life and Death of Section 74', an address to the Samuel Griffith Society, 2002, www.hcourt.gov.au/assets/publications/speeches/former-justices/gleesoncj/cj_griffith2.htm.

[28] Privy Council (Limitation of Appeals) Act 1968; Privy Council (Appeals from the High Court) Act 1975.

[29] *Freightlines and Construction Holdings Pty Ltd v NSW* [1968] AC 625; *Austin v Keele* (1987) 61 ALJR 605, UKPC 24.

[30] *Parker v R* (1963) 111 CLR 610.

[31] *Viro v R* (1978) 141 CLR 88.

[32] *Cook v Cook* (1986) 162 CLR 376.

[33] A Mason, 'Future Developments in Australian Law' (1987) 13 *Monash University Law Review* 149.

The continuing ties of the empire in the early years of Australian federation clearly played some role in the citation of foreign precedents by the High Court during this period, even if decisions of the Privy Council are acknowledged not to have been, strictly speaking, foreign. The Court's attitude towards foreign precedents, however, both before and after independence cannot be explained on this basis alone. From the time of its establishment in 1903 the High Court also cited precedents from the courts of other states, including the Supreme Court of the United States; a natural process, given the genealogical relationship between the two Constitutions.[34] The seminal decision on the interpretative approach to Commonwealth legislative powers, handed down by the High Court in 1920,[35] was in part a contest between the interpretative methods of the Privy Council and the Supreme Court of the United States and, while the former was preferred on that occasion, the choice was influenced by the Court's perception of Australian needs and was by no means a lay down misere.[36] Moreover, in repudiating the binding status of decisions of British courts, the High Court observed that they would continue to be cited as long as their reasoning was 'persuasive'.[37] It is more plausible to ascribe the willingness of Australian courts to cite foreign precedents to an attitude to the 'openness' of a system of law that is a joint legacy of the common law method and the evolution of states in the British constitutional tradition.

B. The High Court of Australia

The High Court of Australia sits at the apex of what is otherwise essentially a dual system of federal and State courts. Matters arising in State jurisdiction are dealt with almost exclusively by State courts, unless they are sufficiently closely linked with a federal matter to fall within the accrued jurisdiction of a federal court.[38] The Constitution identifies nine heads of federal jurisdiction, including matters arising under the Constitution or involving its interpretation, which can be conferred on either federal or State courts or both.[39] The High Court has a sizeable original jurisdiction, which includes constitutional jurisdiction.[40] It also hears appeals from both federal and State courts, on matters for which it is prepared to grant special leave.[41]

---

[34] The contemporary annotated guide to the new Constitution, in 1901, is replete with references to the case law of other jurisdictions, including the United States: J Quick and RR Garran, *Annotated Constitution of the Australian Commonwealth*, 1901 reprint (Sydney, Legal Books, 1976).

[35] *Amalgamated Society of Engineers v Adelaide Steamship Co Ltd* (*Engineers'* case) (1920) 28 CLR 129.

[36] *Victoria v Commonwealth* (1971) 122 CLR 353, 396, Windeyer J.

[37] *Viro v R* (1978) 141 CLR 88, 121, Gibbs J; see more generally Sir Anthony Mason, 'The Break with the Privy Council and the Internationalisation of the Common Law' in Peter Cane (ed), *Centenary Essays for the High Court of Australia* (Australia, Lexisnexis Butterworths, 2004) 66.

[38] *Re Wakim; ex parte McNally* (1999) 198 CLR 511.

[39] ss 75, 76. The constitutional jurisdiction is in s 76(i).

[40] s 76(i); Judiciary Act 1903 (Cth), s 30.

[41] Australian Constitution, s 73; Judiciary Act 1903, ss 35, 35AA, 35A. On special leave applications generally see D Jackson, 'Leave to Appeal' in T Blackshield, M Coper and G Williams (eds), *Oxford Companion to the High Court of Australia* (Sydney, Oxford University Press, 2002) 425–27.

The first appointments to the High Court were made in 1903, two years after the Constitution, formally establishing the Court, came into effect. From the outset the High Court has taken its role as guardian of the Constitution seriously and it enforces constitutional limits against both the Commonwealth and the States.[42] The present Court comprises seven judges, one of whom is the Chief Justice. Section 72 of the Constitution lays out the basic requirements of appointment and tenure. Justices are appointed by the Governor-General in Council, conventionally advised by the Attorney-General, after a decision by the Cabinet. No Justice can be removed from office except by the Governor-General following an address from both Houses of Parliament on the grounds of misbehaviour or incapacity. A Justice's remuneration cannot be diminished during tenure in office, which expires at the age of 70. Typically, Justices have been highly regarded practising barristers in the fields of either commercial or public law. All of the Justices but one of the present Court held office in another superior court at the time of appointment and the majority were appointed at or around the age of 60.

Constitutional review in Australia is diffuse. The High Court deals with cases other than constitutional cases and other courts, both federal and State, can resolve constitutional questions. Constitutional cases can be determined in courts below the level of the High Court, even by the lowest courts in the hierarchy. There are, however, statutory procedures whereby significant constitutional cases can be removed from a lower level court to the High Court and less significant constitutional cases that begin in the original jurisdiction of the High Court can be remitted to a court below.[43] At least in the federal courts, all questions for determination must be concrete, as a consequence of the constitutional form in which federal jurisdiction is described, understood through the lens of the constitutional separation of judicial power.[44] Proceedings are adversarial, involving both written submissions by the parties and open oral hearings. Constitutional questions may be raised in a variety of ways: as the principal substantive issue; as one of a number of substantive issues; or on procedural or jurisdictional points. A case that raises a substantive constitutional issue may be resolved on other grounds, including statutory interpretation or the application of another principle of law.

Consistently with the practice of common law courts elsewhere, the judges of all Australian superior courts, including the High Court, provide full written reasons for their decisions. These explain the orders of the Court and outline the process of reasoning on the part of each judge or group of judges. They are likely to indicate the authorities on which the court relied, those it distinguished and those it rejected. Reasons typically respond to the arguments put to the court by counsel for the parties, which may shape the outcome of a case. While reasons for a judgment perform the important function of helping the parties to understand why they

---

[42] For early cases see *Deakin v Webb* (1904) 1 CLR 585 (State), *R v Barger* (1908) 6 CLR 41 (Commonwealth). In *Australian Communist Party v Commonwealth* (1951) 83 CLR 1, 262, Fullagar J described 'the principle of *Marbury v Madison*' as 'axiomatic' in Australia.

[43] Judiciary Act 1903 (Cth), pt VII.

[44] Each of the heads of federal jurisdiction in sections 75 and 76 of the Constitution are prefaced by a requirement for a 'matter', which has been held to federal courts from being empowered 'to determine abstract questions of law without the right or duty of any body or person being involved', *In Re Judiciary and Navigation Acts* (1921) 29 CLR 257, 267.

won or lost, they also are the source of the principles for which the case stands. When a case is decided at the level of the High Court, these principles bind all other Australian courts, in accordance with the doctrine of precedent, and are generally also followed by the High Court itself in subsequent cases. One Australian scholar has characterised the reasons of the High Court as fulfilling a 'double purpose: to formulate a clear and persuasive basis for decision in the instant case, and to shape and restate the developing body of relevant legal doctrine in a way that is both just and "coherent"'.[45]

In practice, the reasons for decisions of Justices of the High Court are often long and discursive. Further, while the Justices occasionally combine to deliver a single judgment, they more often deliver individual judgments, or judgments in which two or more Justices join. To take one recent, admittedly extreme case, there were six separate judgments in *Momcilovic v R*, only one of which was a joint judgment, and the reasons collectively ran for 226 pages.[46] As *Momcilovic* also demonstrates, cases involving multiple or particularly contentious issues may lead to fragmentation in the reasoning of the respective Justices, complicating neat categorisation. There is no practice in the High Court of clearly identifying the majority reasons as the opinion of the Court. Where there is a judgment in which four Justices join the majority opinion is obvious. In other cases the majority must be divined from the orders and the accumulated sets of reasons. Further, while in many cases it is possible to categorise Justices as forming the majority, or 'concurring' or 'dissenting', in some the categories are less clear cut and the reasons in any event may be disparate. The majority Justices may disagree on some issues or place different emphases on particular considerations. A judgment might agree on the final orders while taking a quite different approach to the legal issues canvassed and relying on different authorities. Dissenting Justices may write reasons that differ significantly from each other. These complexities should be borne in mind in considering the conclusions from this study. At some risk of oversimplification, in the interests of quantitative analysis, we have grouped judgments into only two categories—'majority' or 'minority'—combining concurrences with 'majority opinions' and grouping dissents as 'minority opinions'.

As one of us has argued elsewhere, there are features of the common law methodology of adjudication that assist in explaining the relative willingness of common law courts to cite authorities from other jurisdictions.[47] The first is the typically inductive mode of reasoning, often by way of analogy, by reference to decided cases, whether considered formally binding or merely persuasive. The second is the discursive form that written reasons take as a judge seeks both to explain and persuade, often by reference to existing authority. Thirdly, constitutional review in common law countries tends to be diffuse, in the sense that it is carried out by courts that also decide cases according to the general law in which citation of foreign authority is also established practice. Finally, in the course of the adversarial process the respective

---

[45] T Blackshield, 'Judicial Reasoning' in Blackshield, Coper and Williams (eds), n 41 above.
[46] n 6 above.
[47] C Saunders, 'Judicial Engagement with Comparative Law' in T Ginsburg and R Dixon (eds), *Comparative Constitutional Law* (Cheltenham, Edward Elgar Publishing, 2011) 571.

parties may refer to foreign precedents that support their argument, to which the Court will necessarily respond unless it rejects them out of hand.

Within the common law family, however, the Australian approach to legal reasoning is somewhat distinctive in ways that provide relevant context for the present study. The dominant approach to constitutional interpretation in Australia is often described as 'legalism', understood as possessing particular characteristics.[48] Australian legalism relies extensively on constitutional text, context including historical context and a sometimes creative use of authority, employing what one very influential Chief Justice, Owen Dixon, who held office in the middle, formative years of the twentieth century described as the 'high technique' of the common law.[49] It cannot accurately be equated with either formalism or originalism, although it also has been characterised as 'moderate originalism' by an influential Australian legal theorist.[50] While there are many variants of Australian legalism, depending on the style of particular Justices, all tend to suggest that answers to questions that come before the Court can be derived from legal sources without reference to external values; an approach that, paradoxically, may encourage citation of foreign precedent. In recent years, this has been reinforced by a new twist in the constitutional doctrine of the separation of judicial power, which confines federal judges to the resolution of legal disputes by reference to law, in contradistinction to what in Australia is referred to as the 'merits' of the case.[51]

Despite this apparently restrictive interpretative methodology, constitutional review has been a powerful force in developing the meaning and application of the Australian Constitution, which has proved almost impervious to formal textual change. Through successive decisions of the High Court, for example, the legislative and financial powers of the Commonwealth have been given an extraordinarily broad reach that could not have been anticipated at the time of federation,[52] a doctrine of separation of powers has been developed in considerable detail,[53] the concept of constitutionally protected freedom of interstate trade has been defined and redefined[54] and a notion of Australian citizenship has begun to be elaborated.[55] Significantly, a degree of rights protection has been derived from the institutional provision for representative government and separation of judicial power with implications for the right to vote, freedom of political communication and aspects of due process.[56]

---

[48] L Zines, *The High Court and the Constitution*, 5th edn (Annandale, NSW, The Federation Press, 2008) ch 17.

[49] O Dixon, 'Concerning Judicial Method' (1956) 29 *Australian Law Journal* 468, 469.

[50] J Goldsworthy, 'Constitutional Interpretation' in HP Lee and P Gerangelos, *Constitutional Advancement in a Frozen Continent* (Annandale, NSW, The Federation Press, 2009) 245.

[51] B Selway, 'The Principle Behind Common Law Judicial Review of Executive Action—The Search Continues' (2002) 30 *Federal Law Review* 217.

[52] For the most recent high-water mark in the interpretation of legislative powers see *New South Wales v Commonwealth* (2006) 228 CLR 1. An overview of the more complex story of Commonwealth fiscal dominance can be found in Saunders, *The Constitution of Australia*, n 4 above, 237–43.

[53] Ibid, 191–213. For more recent developments, largely affecting the position of State judiciaries, see *Wainohu v New South Wales* (2011) 243 CLR 181 and *Momcilovic v R*, n 6 above.

[54] The doctrine builds on s 92 of the Constitution; the most recent decisions are *Betfair Pty Ltd v Racing New South Wales* [2012] HCA 12 and *Sportsbet Pty Ltd v New South Wales* [2012] HCA 13.

[55] *Singh v Commonwealth* (2004) 222 CLR 322.

[56] Saunders, *The Australian Constitution*, n 4 above, 136–42, 201–07.

The implication of rights protection from the terms of an instrument without an express Bill of Rights was a controversial development when it began in the 1990s, during the Chief Justiceship of Sir Anthony Mason.[57] The controversy was heightened by a discernible shift away from 'strict' legalism on the part of the Court as Justices occasionally explained their conclusions by reference to extra-legal considerations, in what came to be described as a form of Australian realism.[58] This approach did not last, although the implied rights doctrines survived in a somewhat more limited form.[59] Under Chief Justice Gleeson, whose tenure ran from 1998 to 2008, most Justices explicitly returned to yet another variant of legalism.[60] The period of this study is deliberately chosen not only as one that is relatively recent but as one that coincides with all but the first two years of the Gleeson court.

III. CITATION OF FOREIGN PRECEDENT IN AUSTRALIA

A. Anecdotal Impressions

Even a cursory examination of decisions of the High Court of Australia suggests a long-standing willingness to cite foreign law in both constitutional and other kinds of cases. The extent of the practice varies between different Justices and over time. Nevertheless, it is an established feature of Australian judicial reasoning that has never been controversial merely on the ground of citation of a source from another jurisdiction. Justices have referred unselfconsciously to decisions of courts of the United States and Canada as well as British cases from the time of the establishment of the High Court.[61] At the mid-point of the twentieth century, the influential exponent of Australian legalism, Chief Justice Dixon, cited foreign precedents in his own reasoning and explained recourse to them in extra-judicial writing.[62] References to foreign precedents were common and unremarked on during the years of the Mason Court, despite the controversy that attended other aspects of some of its decisions. Thus every judgment[63] in each of the three most influential early cases on the freedom of political communication cases—*Australian Capital Television Pty Ltd v Commonwealth*,[64] *Theophanous v Herald & Weekly Times Ltd*,[65] and *Lange v Australian Broadcasting Corporation*[66]—referred to foreign law for some purposes, without attracting untoward comment.[67] The practice remained common

---

[57] A Stone, 'Australia's Constitutional Rights and the Problem of Interpretive Disagreement' (2005) 27 *Sydney Law Review* 29.
[58] R Gray, *The Constitutional Jurisprudence and Judicial Method of the High Court of Australia* (Adelaide, SA, Presidian Legal Publications, 2008) 57, 64ff.
[59] *Lange v Australian Broadcasting Corporation* (1997) 189 CLR 520.
[60] AM Gleeson, 'Judicial Legitimacy' (2000) 12 *Judicial Officers Bulletin* 41.
[61] For example, *D'Emden v Pedder* (1904) 1 CLR 91.
[62] *Melbourne Corporation v Commonwealth* (1947) 74 CLR 31, 81–83; O Dixon, 'Concerning Judicial Method' n 49 above, 170–71.
[63] Six judgments were delivered in *Australian Capital Television*; five in *Theophanous*; and a single judgment in *Lange*.
[64] (1992) 177 CLR 106.
[65] (1994) 182 CLR 104.
[66] (1997) 189 CLR 520.
[67] Saunders, 'Use and Misuse', n 3 above, 53.

thereafter. During the period from 2000 to 2008 for which data was collected for this chapter, the High Court cited over 2,800 foreign authorities in a total of 193 constitutional cases.[68]

There is a contrast here with the Court's resistance to international law, which should be noted in passing.[69] While international law may be taken into account indirectly in Australia, for the purposes of statutory interpretation[70] or development of the common law,[71] only Justice Kirby, during his time on the bench, was prepared to use it in constitutional interpretation.[72] No doubt the explanation lies at least in part in the more authoritative status of international law, the forms that it takes and, perhaps, the emphasis that it gives to human rights in relation to a Constitution that does not explicitly protect them.[73] Nevertheless, as some more recent cases considered later in this section demonstrate, it is an additional complication in examining the citation of foreign law in Australian courts.

With a necessary exception for decisions of the Privy Council and other British courts during the period when these were regarded as binding, the High Court has never treated foreign precedents as having more than persuasive value. On the contrary, from the time of its establishment the High Court has been jealous of its own role as arbiter of the limits of the Australian Constitution. In the early years of federation it discouraged recourse to the Privy Council as far as it was able to do so.[74] High Court Justices took the opportunity to sit on the Privy Council when dealing with Australian cases when this became a possibility. Once the jurisdiction of the Privy Council was brought to an end, the High Court was quick to assume that it was now the guardian not only of the Constitution but also of a discrete Australian common law.[75]

Citation of foreign precedents may play a variety of roles at various points in the reasoning of Justices of the High Court. Foreign precedents may help to identify or throw a different light on a legal issue, may suggest options for judicial development of a particular legal doctrine, may be used empirically, to illustrate the consequences of a certain course of action; may support or confirm a conclusion that a Justice

---

[68] See below for an explanation of the methodology for determining whether a case is classified as 'constitutional'.

[69] The foundation case is still *Polites v Commonwealth* (1945) 70 CLR 60, somewhat oddly, in view of the developments in the significance of international law since then.

[70] *Minister of State for Immigration and Ethnic Affairs v Teoh* (1995) 183 CLR 273, 187, Mason CJ and Deane J; compare *Plaintiff S157/2002 v Commonwealth* (2003) 211 CLR 476, 492.

[71] *Mabo v Queensland*, n 8 above.

[72] He raised the point regularly after his initial observations on the subject in *Newcrest Mining (WA) Ltd v Commonwealth* (1997) 190 CLR 513. He retired from the High Court in 2009.

[73] The rationales for the High Court's position are briefly explored in Stone, 'Comparativism in Constitutional Interpretation', n 2 above, 46.

[74] *Baxter v Commissioners of Taxation (NSW)* (1907) 4 CLR 1087, 1111–12, Griffith CJ; see also the discussion in Gleeson, 'The Birth, Life and Death of Section 74', n 27 above. Although s 74 of the Constitution enables the High Court to certify that an 'inter se' question is one that should be determined by the Privy Council it did so only once, in 1914, and made it clear in *Kirmani v Captain Cook Cruises* (1985) 159 CLR 351 that it would not do so again.

[75] The term 'common law of Australia' was used occasionally before 1986, generally when a question arose about whether a particular English common law rule had been absorbed into Australian law. In 1986 the term was used in *Public Service Board of New South Wales v Osmond* (1986) 159 CLR 656 to refer to the Australian common law as distinctive. It has become commonplace since.

already was minded to reach; or may be not much more than a rhetorical flourish.[76] By definition, a foreign precedent raised before the Court in argument may be cited by the Court only to reject it. And, as an anecdotal impression of Australian practice, even where a foreign precedent is regarded as persuasive it is unlikely simply to be followed rather than incorporated as a supporting factor in a more complex legal argument.

There is much more to be said than is possible here about the methodology of judicial citation of foreign law. Questions about the selection of appropriate comparators are complicated by the adversarial system and by the extent of the Court's reliance on the arguments put to it by the parties. Questions about understanding of the context in which a foreign precedent is set may arise whether the precedent is followed or not. A shallow contextual understanding of a foreign precedent that is applied may expose the reasoning of the court to criticism. Too ready rejection of the relevance of a precedent may also be a cause for criticism, however, particularly if it appears to be a subterfuge for refusing to consider foreign law. As Australian public law becomes increasingly distinctive there are some early signs that particular Justices may be distancing themselves from foreign precedents by this means, particularly in human rights cases. This also is no more than an impression at this stage, however, based on several high profile cases to which attention is drawn in the next section.[77] It awaits both closer analysis and further developments.

B. Reactions to the US Debate

Once the debate broke out in the United States about the propriety of references to foreign law in constitutional cases there was a question about whether and, if so, to what extent, the American debate might have an impact on Australian practice. While the constitutional discourse is very different in the two countries it is not unusual for constitutional preoccupations in the United States to have some resonance in Australia. In the case of the debate on foreign law, its links with originalism as an interpretative method, which had also attracted some attention in Australia,[78] made the question more pressing still.

The signs to date are that there has been some impact although so far it is ambiguous and relatively slight. The ambiguity stems from the different approaches taken by the High Court to the citation of foreign and international law, to which reference was made earlier. A famously sharp exchange between two Justices of the High Court in 2004 on one view muddled the two. In *Al-Kateb v Godwin*[79] the applicant contested his continued immigration detention on constitutional grounds for which he sought support from both foreign and international law. One of the majority Justices, McHugh J, took issue with the suggestion that the Constitution

---

[76] Some of the variety of usages in a small handful of cases is examined in Saunders, 'The Use and Misuse of Comparative Constitutional Law', n 3 above.
[77] Two of the principal cases are analysed in Stone, 'Comparativism in Constitutional Interpretation', n 2 above.
[78] J Kirk, 'Constitutional Interpretation and a Theory of Evolutionary Originalism' (1999) 27 *Federal Law Review* 323.
[79] (2004) 219 CLR 562.

could be interpreted by reference to international law, pointing in part to the extent of the development of international law since the Constitution came into effect.[80] McHugh J was not persuaded by the arguments from foreign law either; elsewhere in his reasons, however, he distinguished these from the case in hand on the grounds of contextual difference, rather than repudiating them altogether.[81] By contrast Kirby J, dissenting, combined a rebuttal of both sets of McHugh J's arguments in a section pressing the interpretative claims of international law, encouraging an understanding of the exchange as an antipodean version of the divisions in the United States.[82]

In subsequent cases, however, it appears to have emerged that at least one member of the current Court objects also to the citation of foreign law, at least when it involves the application of constitutional human rights instruments that postdate the Australian Constitution. There are overtones in his reasoning of the rationale offered by McHugh J for the rejection of the relevance of international law in *Al-Kateb*. Nevertheless in 2006, in *Forge*,[83] in dealing with the implications of the Australian separation of judicial power for the appointment of acting judges, Heydon J observed that:

> Considerable reliance was placed upon cases on the European Convention for the Protection of Human Rights and Fundamental Freedoms, Art 6; the *Canadian Charter of Rights and Freedoms*, s 11(d) and the Bill of Rights of the Constitution of the Republic of South Africa, s 34. These documents all post-dated Ch III ... Accordingly, no assistance is to be obtained from cases on these documents in construing Ch III and evaluating its impact on State laws.[84]

The same judge took up the theme again in 2007, in *Roach*,[85] in which the Court was faced with a challenge to the validity of legislation removing the franchise from all prisoners. In a dissent from the majority ruling partially upholding the challenge Heydon J repudiated reliance on comparative materials that included decisions of the Supreme Court of Canada based on the Canadian Charter of Rights and Freedoms:

> [T]hese instruments[86] can have nothing whatever to do with the construction of the Australian Constitution. These instruments did not influence the framers of the Constitution, for they all postdate it by many years ... The language they employ is radically different [from the Constitution] ... [T]he fact is that our law does not permit recourse to these materials.[87]

For the moment, at least, Heydon J is alone in this position, the precise scope of which is, in any event, unclear. Other Justices in both *Forge* and *Roach* referred to

---

[80] [62]–[71].
[81] [51]–[54].
[82] [152]–[176].
[83] *Forge v Australian Securities and Investments Commission* (2006) 228 CLR 45.
[84] At 139–40.
[85] *Roach v Electoral Commissioner* (2007) 233 CLR 162.
[86] Other instruments to which he referred were the International Covenant on Civil and Political Rights, the First Protocol of the European Charter of Rights and Freedoms and the Constitution of South Africa.
[87] At 224–25.

foreign precedents without raising objections in principle to their use. Even Hayne J, who also dissented in *Roach* and who declined to rely on foreign precedents based his rejection on methodological arguments rather than dismissing them out of hand.[88] As the analysis of the data in the next section shows, there was also some decline in the proportion of foreign precedents in individual judgments during the period from 2000 to 2008, which includes these cases. Even so, the implications of this development should, therefore, not be overstated. During this same period, as a reaction to the debate in the United States, there have been repeated reaffirmations of Australian practice, often by judges of superior courts themselves.[89] Even on the likely assumption that Heydon J maintains his originalist objection to the citation of some foreign law there are no signs that other Justices will follow suit. For the moment a greater threat to established practice seems likely to lie in the development canvassed in the previous section: a growing willingness on the part of at least some Justices to distinguish foreign precedents by reference to what they claim to be relevant points of contextual difference.

C. Previous Australian Studies

There have been previous Australian empirical studies that confirm the existence of a long-standing practice of citation of foreign law by Australian courts which give some idea of its extent in the past. The most recent deal with foreign law citation practices in the various Australian State Supreme Courts.[90] While State courts also can interpret and apply the Constitution, however, constitutional cases form a much smaller proportion of their case load and they are constrained by High Court authority. The findings of these studies are therefore of marginal relevance for present purposes and they are not pursued further here.

---

[88] 'Any appeal to the decisions of other courts about the operation of other constitutional instruments or general statements of rights and freedoms is an appeal that calls for the strongest consideration of whether there are any relevant similarities between the instruments that were examined and applied in those decisions and the particular provisions that this court must consider': at 221. For a critique, which also expresses misgivings about the comparative method in the joint judgment of Gummow, Kirby and Crennan JJ see Stone 'Comparativism in Constitutional Interpretation', n 2 above, 64–68.

[89] See, eg, the Hon John Basten of the New South Wales Court of Appeal:'[i]t is almost impossible to resist the conclusion that Australian courts are generally entirely comfortable with reliance upon overseas authority and do not have much difficulty in placing reliance appropriately. Although we are not unique in this regard, we are likely to succumb neither to grandiose views of Australian exceptionalism, nor to unbecoming servility' in 'International Influences on Domestic Law: Neither Jingoistic Exceptionalism nor Blind Servility', New South Wales Bar Association Lecture Series, 11 May 2010.

[90] See, eg, R Smyth, 'Citations of Foreign Decisions in Australian State Supreme Courts over the Course of the Twentieth Century: An Empirical Analysis' (2008) 22 *Temple International and Comparative Law Journal* 409; R Smyth, 'Trends in the Citation Practice of the Supreme Court of Queensland over the Course of the Twentieth Century' (2009) 28 *University of Queensland Law Journal* 39; I Neilsen and R Smyth, 'One Hundred Years of Citation of Authority on the Supreme Court of New South Wales' (2008) 31 *University of New South Wales Law Journal* 189; D Fausten, I Neilsen and R Smyth, 'A Century of Citation Practice on the Supreme Court of Victoria' (2007) 31 *Melbourne University Law Review* 733.

Two previous studies, however, focus specifically on the citation of foreign law in the High Court of Australia.[91] The first is an examination by Von Nessen of High Court citation of decisions of the Supreme Court of the United States, across all fields of law, from the establishment of the Court to 2002. A first study, completed in 1992,[92] was revised and expanded further in 2006.[93] A central conclusion of this work is that United States authorities have been cited by the High Court in constitutional and public law cases 'far more frequently than in any other area of law'. Von Nessen attributes this to the influence of the United States Constitution on the drafters of the Australian Constitution, resulting in similarities in the constitutional issues facing both Courts.[94] He further concludes that the High Court began to use United States authority more widely, in cases beyond the sphere of public law, during the 1990s and early 2000s, following the cessation of appeals to the Privy Council.[95] Von Nessen's methodology involved a simple count of citations. He did not examine how United States authority was used or whether the Australian court applied it or not.[96] By definition, his study is limited also to citations of decisions of the Supreme Court of the United States. Its survey period ends shortly after the commencement of the present study.

The second major study of High Court citation practice is an inquiry by Opeskin into the 'global' aspects of the High Court's thinking, parts of which are supported by empirical research.[97] In the course of this inquiry, Opeskin investigated the citation of foreign law in judgments of the High Court. To this end, he constructed a sample for the period from federation to 2000, by taking the first five 'constitutional cases' reported in the *Commonwealth Law Reports* at the beginning of each decade. This gave him a total of 55 cases and over 1,400 separate citations. Opeskin deemed a case to be 'constitutional' if it was identified in the headnote as 'addressing a significant constitutional question, even if other issues (such as statutory interpretation) arose in the case'.[98] Obviously, his data set selected only a few cases from each decade which, as he noted, represented only one-tenth of the average of five

---

[91] In addition, there are two short entries with some empirical data on High Court citation of foreign law practice in the *Oxford Companion to the High Court of Australia*: see B Topperwein, 'Foreign Precedents' in M Coper, T Blackshield and G Williams (eds), *Oxford Companion to the High Court of Australia* (South Melbourne, Vic, Oxford University Press, 2007) 280–82 (examining various foreign jurisdictions often cited by the Court) and R Smyth, 'Citations by Court' in M Coper, T Blackshield and G Williams (eds), *Oxford Companion to the High Court of Australia* (South Melbourne, Vic, Oxford University Press, 2007) 98–99 (examining particular courts and jurisdictions cited by the High Court over the last century).
[92] P von Nessen, 'The Use of American Precedents by the High Court of Australia, 1901–1987' (1992) 14 *Adelaide Law Review* 181.
[93] P von Nessen, 'Is There Anything to Fear in Transnationalist Development of Law? The Australian Experience' (2006) 33 *Pepperdine Law Review* 883, which updates the original study with data from the period from 1987–October 2002, collected using the same methodology as the earlier study.
[94] Ibid, 905–06.
[95] Ibid, 909–12, 914.
[96] Ibid, 893–96.
[97] B Opeskin, 'Australian Constitutional Law in a Global Era' in R French, G Lindell, C Saunders (eds), *Reflections on the Australian Constitution* (Federation Press, 2003) 171.
[98] Ibid, 183. Opeskin does not expand on what might constitute a 'significant' constitutional issue. Headnotes in the *Commonwealth Law Reports* generally quite clearly indicate the number and gravity of constitutional issues raised by a case, however. As is indicated below, our own approach to identifying a case as 'constitutional' cast the net somewhat more broadly than this.

Full Court constitutional decisions per year during the 1990s.[99] Given his desire to cover a century of judicial decision, the large number of constitutional judgments, and the typical length and complexity of each, his approach is understandable. Its limitations, nevertheless, must be taken into account in evaluating the results.

Opeskin's conclusions offer insights into broad trends over the century in the citation of foreign law in constitutional cases. His data suggests that the citation of foreign authority was extensive after federation but gradually decreased over the following 80 years as the High Court's own constitutional jurisprudence developed.[100] Opeskin notes, however, that from the 1980s onwards there was some resurgence in the citation of foreign materials reaching, on his figures, 29 per cent of total citations in 2000. Comparing the citation of particular jurisdictions in the decades from 1900–1910 and 1990–2000 respectively, Opeskin also notes that, on his data, US citations stayed steady at around 30 per cent, UK citations increased slightly from 50 per cent to 54 per cent, whilst Canadian citations dropped sharply from 19 per cent to 4 per cent.[101] Our own data shows that these are indeed the three jurisdictions most likely to be cited, and in this order, although it lowers the proportion of UK cases cited and raises that for the United States and Canada.

III. THE DATA

A. Overview

With the data set in this study we analysed all decisions of the High Court from 2000 to 2008. The number and length of the judgments, combined with the prolific foreign citation practices of Justices of the High Court, made it impracticable to expand the data set beyond this nine-year period. This time span has the further advantages of being recent and of coinciding with the whole of the latter years of the Gleeson High Court, during which most Justices relied on interpretative techniques generally associated with Australian legalism and that might be taken as 'typical' to this extent. This section further explains the methodology employed in selecting the data set, and justifies departures from the template necessitated by the exigencies of the Australian legal system.

The High Court's status as the apex court of appeal on all questions of Australian law required us to identify the boundaries between 'constitutional' and 'non-constitutional cases'. As described earlier, the High Court resolves any case that comes before it in either its original or appellate jurisdiction by reference to all applicable sources of law, including the Constitution. It is generally not necessary in the Australian legal system for a case to be definitively classified as constitutional or not.[102] We have taken a broad approach to this question, defining as 'constitutional'

---

[99] High Court of Australia, *Annual Report 1999–2000*, Table 14, p 69, cited in Opeskin, n 97 above, 183.
[100] See Opeskin, n 97 above, 183–86.
[101] Ibid, 184.
[102] This might occur, however, if the only basis for commencing a claim in the original jurisdiction of the High Court relied on the constitutional jurisdiction in section 76(i).

any case in which the High Court has considered a provision of the Constitution. This approach has the potential to include in the data set cases in which the Court refers to the Constitution only for the purpose of verifying its own jurisdiction. On balance, however, we are comfortable with this approach. Significant constitutional questions are sometimes raised as ancillary issues. The only alternative would have been to assess qualitatively the weight of the constitutional issues in each case, which would introduce an element of arbitrariness into the analysis that we were anxious to avoid. And the outcome also seems unremarkable. During the period from 2000 to 2008, the High Court handed down 616 decisions that were reported in the authorised *Commonwealth Law Reports*. Of these, only 193 were identified as 'constitutional' cases on our approach, 99 of which contained references to foreign law. On this basis, less than one third of High Court decisions over the period of the study involved constitutional issues in accordance with our definition and only half of these included citations of foreign law. Our impression, which we have not sought to verify quantitatively, is that many of the cases that were classified as constitutional but in which foreign law was not cited referred to the Constitution only briefly or tangentially.

Analysis of 99 lengthy cases, many of which comprise multiple judgments and multiple citations of foreign law, nevertheless is a formidable task. It is made more formidable still by the wide variety of ways in which foreign citations are used in constitutional analysis in Australia, as described earlier in this chapter. In these circumstances, it has not been practicable to attempt to quantify the number of citations indicating respectively that a foreign case should be followed, modified, rejected, or merely noted. Nor would it be possible to do so with any degree of accuracy. For similar reasons of practicality, we have not attempted to investigate whether a citation of foreign law was in support of a constitutional or non-constitutional argument in each of these cases or whether the cited cases themselves might be characterised as 'constitutional' in nature. It follows that at least some of the more than 2,800 foreign citations in these 193 constitutional cases are likely to be raised in the context of determining legal questions that are not of a constitutional kind.

Once the set of constitutional cases was identified, we examined the text and footnotes of all judgments in each, counting all foreign law citations and grouping citations by jurisdiction of origin.[103] We used only cases in the authorised *Commonwealth Law Reports* for this purpose. Unreported judgments, which almost entirely comprise orders relating to special leave applications, are not included in the data set, regardless of whether they touch upon constitutional issues.[104] Although the *Commonwealth Law Reports* are available in a full-text, searchable electronic format, the range of overseas courts cited necessitated a manual reading

---

[103] This 'simple count method' was also employed by von Nessen in his empirical study of the High Court's citation of US case law: see von Nessen, 'Is There Anything to Fear', n 93 above.

[104] Unreported transcripts of the proceedings of the High Court can be found at www.austlii.edu.au/au/other/HCATrans. These documents are selected and provided by the Court, and include special leave hearings and decisions on special leave. As special leave applications relate to appeals from lower courts, orders allowing or dismissing the application usually focus specifically upon the grounds for appeal, and rarely involve extensive citation of cases. We were unable to find any record of references to foreign law among special leave transcripts or orders.

of each judgment. The resulting figures were then tallied to produce the tables from which the graphs that follow were drawn. We have not 'weighted' joint judgments by multiplying each foreign law citation by the number of judges subscribing to the judgment as some other studies have done.[105]

We have included in our data set all citations from foreign domestic courts, at any level. We have also included citations to the European Court of Human Rights (ECtHR) and the European Court of Justice (ECJ). While these are supranational or international courts for European jurisdictions, Australia is not part of these judicial hierarchies and from an Australian perspective both can be considered foreign courts. We have however excluded the occasional citations to international courts and tribunals, including the International Court of Justice, United Nations Human Rights treaty bodies and the various Ad Hoc International Criminal Tribunals in order to avoid the complications presented by the Australian distinction between citation of foreign and international law for the purposes of constitutional interpretation.

Two further aspects of the character of Australian constitutional adjudication can usefully be reiterated here, to explain the charts that follow. First, the absence of a clear category of constitutional rights cases in Australia has made it necessary to omit a chart that distinguishes between 'institutional' and 'rights' cases. Rights do not arise as constitutional issues in Australia in the same way that they arise elsewhere. While this is partly because the Constitution has few explicit rights provisions it is also because, when rights questions are raised in constitutional arguments, they generally draw on institutional arrangements. As the interpretation of the Constitution has evolved, a limited rights-protecting function has emerged from the provisions dealing with responsible and representative government and the separation of federal judicial power exercised by independent federal and State courts. It is not possible in these circumstances to draw a neat distinction between constitutional cases dealing with institutions and with rights.

Secondly, our charts distinguish only between citations of foreign authority in majority and minority judgments and do not include a distinct count for 'concurring' opinions. As explained earlier, the High Court of Australia does not authoritatively identify an 'opinion' of the Court. The majority opinion thus must be constituted by the reader from the judgments that are handed down. While this is relatively straightforward when there is a judgment in which four or more Justices join, the configuration of judgments does not take this form in all or even in most cases. Where a majority must be constructed from two or more judgments, identifying others as 'concurring' would, inevitably, be arbitrary. In Figures 5 and 6, which deal with this question, we have included in the category of the majority all judgments that are in agreement with the final order, counting in the minority any judgment that is not in agreement with the order. While this approach overlooks more nuanced degrees of difference on legal issues between the judgments themselves, it offers a relatively clear distinction that is useful enough for present purposes.

---

[105] See Smyth, 'Trends in the Citation Practice of the Supreme Court of Queensland over the Course of the Twentieth Century', n 90 above, 49–50.

B. The Data Presented

Figure 1 identifies the total number of reported constitutional cases and constitutional cases citing foreign law over the nine-year period from 2000 to 2008. The general trends are clear. The total number of cases involving constitutional issues gradually decreased during this period, while the total number of constitutional cases citing foreign law remained largely constant. The decrease in constitutional cases is likely to be due to the less adventurous character of the constitutional jurisprudence of the Gleeson Court, which for a period discouraged litigants from raising new constitutional points. One consequence of the trend for present purposes, however, is an increase in the proportion of constitutional cases which cite foreign law. In the years from 2006 to 2008, almost every constitutional case included references to foreign law.

Figure 2 picks up the theme of Figure 1, to demonstrate that there has been a steady overall increase in the proportion of constitutional cases which include citations to

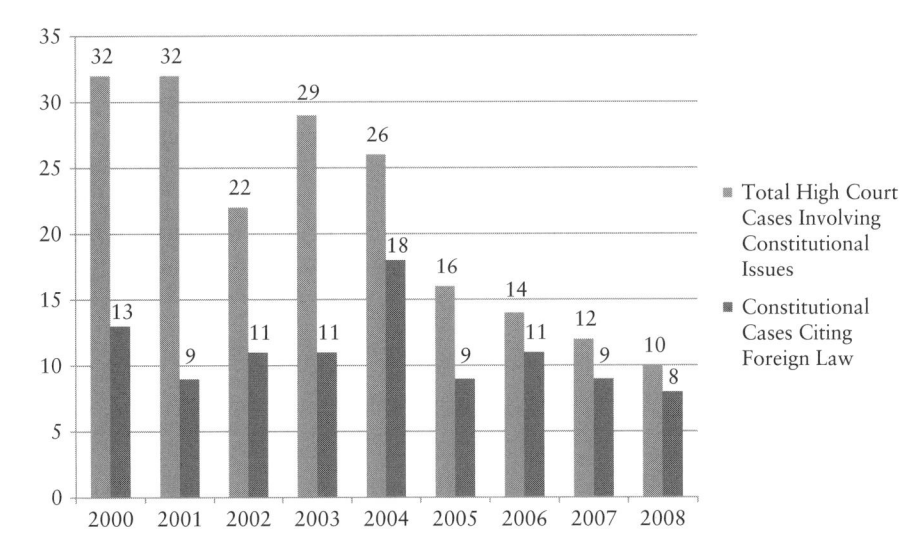

Figure 1: Constitutional Cases which Cite Foreign Law of Total Constitutional Cases

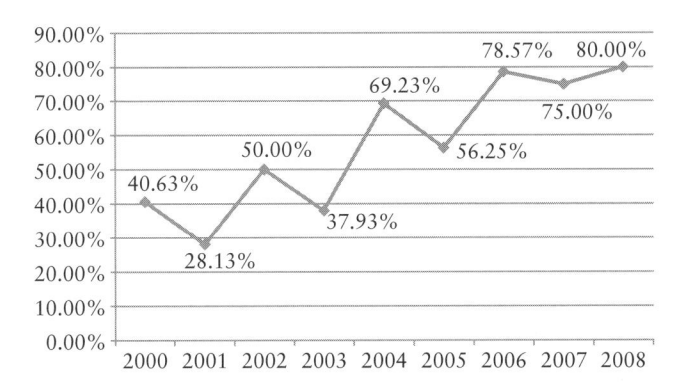

Figure 2: Percentage of Constitutional Cases Citing Foreign Law, by Year

foreign law. Interestingly, this increase has not been constant, but rather has proceeded in fits and starts: each increase was followed by a drop throughout the 2000–08 period. It is difficult to determine what might be causing this pattern (if indeed there is a logical explanation at all). It is likely to be no more than a chance consequence of the types of cases coming before the court each year and is highly unlikely to reflect changing attitudes to the citation of foreign authority from year to year. When this data is read in conjunction with Figure 1, however, it becomes apparent that there has not necessarily been any overall increase in the aggregate number of cases citing foreign law.

Figure 3 shows the total number of foreign law citations per year, in a form that also indicates the total number of constitutional cases and separate reasons for judgment within constitutional cases each year. Beneath each year, the first figure in round brackets indicates the total number of judgments in the constitutional cases handed down that year and the second indicates the number of constitutional cases: (<judgments>/<cases>). The figure in square brackets gives the average number of citations to foreign sources per judgment in the year in question.

As the Figure shows, aside from a sharp spike in 2004, and a small relative recovery in 2006 and 2007, the overall number of foreign law citations declined substantially between 2000 and 2008. The 2004 spike is easy to explain. Five significant and contentious constitutional cases were decided that year, dealing with detention and with the implied freedom of political communication.[106] Two of them were also used as vehicles for the debate between Justices on the relevance of international law to constitutional interpretation. Between them these five cases account for 217 of the 523 foreign citations in the 18 constitutional cases decided in 2004 that cited foreign law.

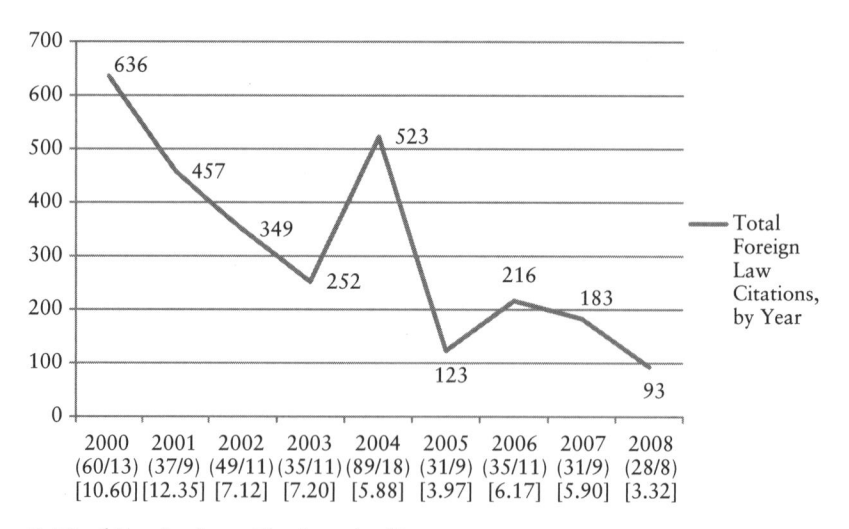

Figure 3: Total Foreign Law Citations, by Year

---

[106] The detention cases are *Behrooz v Secretary, Department of Immigration and Multicultural and Indigenous Affairs* (2004) 219 CLR 486 (48 citations); *Al-Kateb v Godwin* (2004) 219 CLR 562 (102 citations) and *Fardon v A-G (Qld)* (2004) 223 CLR 575 (50 citations). Two other cases raised aspects of the implied freedom of political communication: *Coleman v Power* (2004) 220 CLR 1 (51 citations); *Mulholland v Australian Electoral Commission* (2004) 220 CLR 181 (66 citations).

Most Justices also chose to write individual judgments in these cases, contributing to the larger than usual number of 89 judgments in 18 constitutional cases in 2004. Relevantly, however, the average number of foreign law citations per judgment that year is the third lowest in the data set. This Figure shows a steady decline in the average number of foreign law citations by judgment from 2001 (12.35) to the lowest point in 2008 (3.32), with a short recovery in 2006 (6.17, up from 3.97 in 2005) and 2007 (5.90).

It is possible to speculate about the reasons for the overall decline in the number of foreign law citations over this period, although a more definitive explanation requires further work. This would involve both a qualitative analysis of the cases in this data set and comparison with citation numbers in the periods immediately before and after this one. As noted earlier, this was not an adventurous period in the constitutional jurisprudence of the High Court and cases dealing with relatively settled questions are generally determined by reference to Australian authorities alone. The spike in 2004 lends some support to this hypothesis. It may also be, however, that the decline over this period indicates some reaction to the controversy in the United States, at least on the part of particular members of the Court.

Figure 4 and Table 1 show that the High Court overwhelmingly cites UK and US authority, in that order of frequency. In numerical terms, Canadian jurisprudence is a strong third source of foreign citations, with New Zealand decisions come fourth. After that, the number of citations per jurisdiction diminishes markedly. Relevantly, the overwhelming majority of jurisdictions cited, including the top seven, publish their decisions in English.

None of this is particularly surprising. The long historical links between the law and the courts of Australia and the UK have been noted already. Some instances of the citation of UK precedents undoubtedly also involve the resolution of common law issues in the context of a constitutional case. The Constitution of the United States was used as a model for parts of the Australian Constitution, and Supreme Court decisions have been cited in Australia since federation. There are

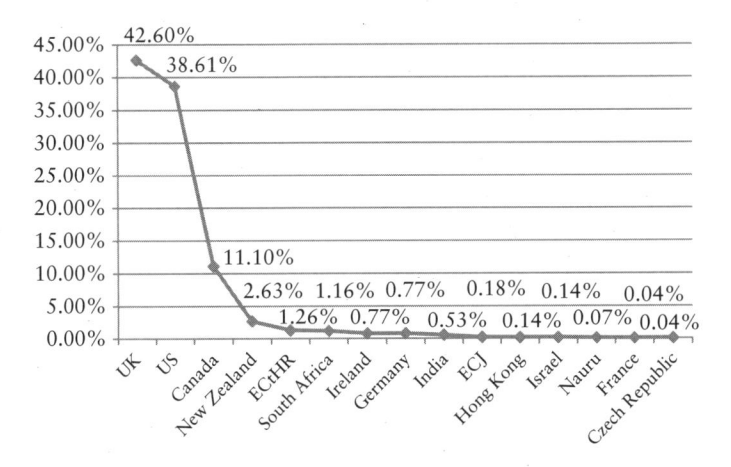

Figure 4: Total Foreign Precedent Citation, arranged by Country

Table 1: Total Foreign Precedent Citation, arranged by Country

Jurisdiction	Total Citation Count (2000–08)	Percentage of Total Foreign Law Citations
UK	1217	42.60%
US	1103	38.61%
Canada	317	11.10%
New Zealand	75	2.63%
ECtHR	36	1.26%
South Africa	33	1.16%
Ireland	22	0.77%
Germany	22	0.77%
India	15	0.53%
ECJ	5	0.18%
Hong Kong	4	0.14%
Israel	4	0.14%
Nauru	2	0.07%
France	1	0.04%
Czech Republic	1	0.04%
Total	2857	100.00%

many similarities between the constitutional arrangements of Canada and Australia, deriving from their shared history as colonies within the second British empire with Constitutions originally enacted by the Imperial Parliament, their federal systems of government superimposed on Westminster institutions, and the design of their apex courts as general courts of appeal on questions in both federal and sub-national jurisdictions. The New Zealand legal system also shares many commonalities with Australia; most of the citations to New Zealand, also, are likely to come in the context of deciding a question of general law. The principal point of interest in relation to the rest of the citations lies not in their relatively low numbers (less than 40 out of a total of 2,800) but in the fact that these jurisdictions are cited at all. We suspect that the diversity of jurisdictions cited is a relatively recent phenomenon, although it is not possible to verify this from this data set. If this hypothesis is correct, it is indicative of a gradually more inclusive dissemination of ideas between the constitutional courts of the world, made possible by information technology and, perhaps, by the increasing availability of decisions in English.

Reflection on the principal jurisdictions cited, however, also suggests the potential for the practice of citing foreign precedents in constitutional cases to enter a new phase. The legal and constitutional systems of Australia on the one hand and the United Kingdom, Canada and New Zealand on the other are gradually diversifying through, for example, the influence of European law in the United Kingdom, the impact of the Canadian Charter of Rights and Freedoms on Canadian constitutional jurisprudence and implications of the New Zealand Bill of Rights Act

1990 on aspects of New Zealand law. As diversification occurs, the opportunities to distinguish foreign precedents by reference to context and relevance expand, for judges minded to take them. Retention of the advantages of recourse to foreign legal experience in resolving constitutional questions may now require a more sophisticated comparative method, in order to continue to derive value from foreign decisions at a level at which it is appropriate to do so.

Figures 5 and 6 illustrate the position of foreign law citations in either majority or minority opinions. For reasons that were explained earlier, we have analysed citations by reference to these two categories only, without attempting to create a third category for concurrences. The Figures draw on the data in Table 2 below, which is conveniently explained first.

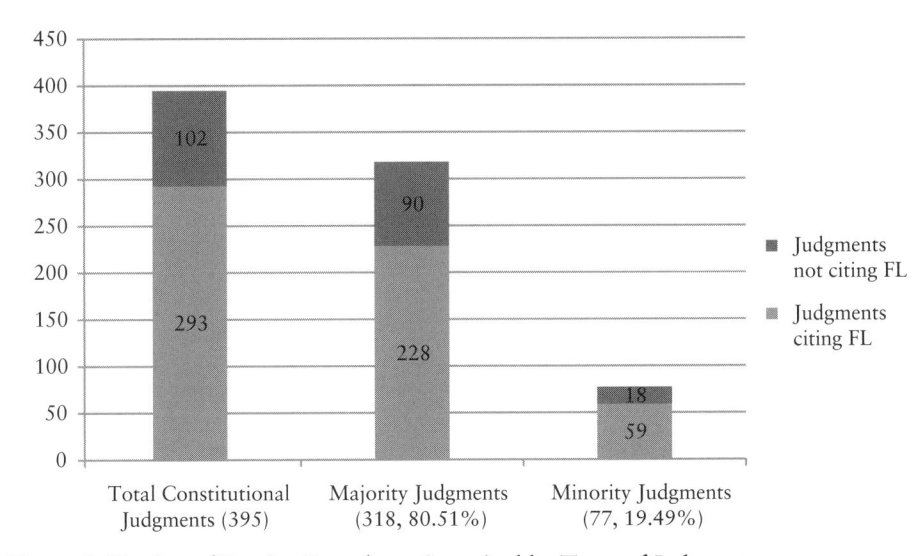

Figure 5: Citation of Foreign Precedents Organised by Types of Judgment

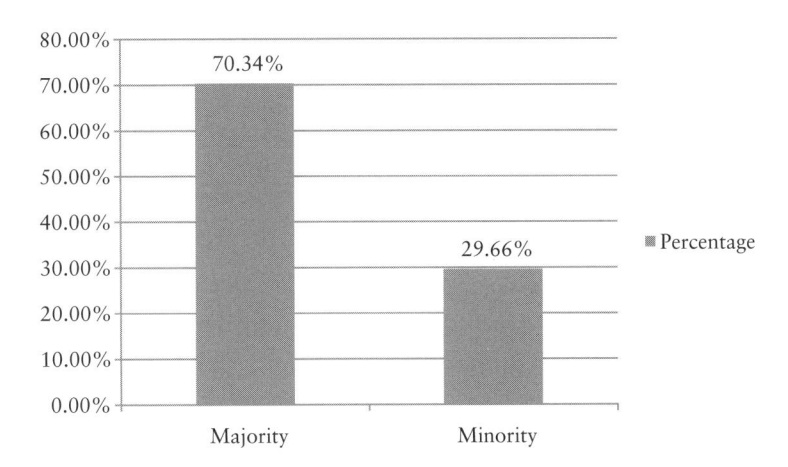

Figure 6: Percentage of Citations According to Majority or Minority Opinions

Table 2: Number of citations to Foreign Precedents by Type of Judgment

Year	Con Cases	FL CCs	Total CC Js	Total FP Js	Total CCFL Cites	Maj Js	Maj FL Js	Maj Cites	Min Js	Min FL Js	Min Cites
2000	32	13	60	48	636	48	40	475	12	7	161
2001	32	9	37	29	457	31	25	338	6	4	119
2002	22	11	49	42	349	42	35	306	7	6	43
2003	29	11	35	21	252	29	17	158	6	5	94
2004	26	18	89	67	523	68	48	330	21	16	193
2005	16	9	31	25	123	26	19	82	5	5	41
2006	14	11	35	24	216	25	15	118	10	8	98
2007	12	9	31	23	183	23	17	106	8	6	77
2008	10	8	28	14	93	26	12	79	2	2	14
Total	193	99	395	293	2832	318	228	1992	77	59	840
%s		51.30%		74.18%		80.51%	71.70%	70.34%	19.49%	76.62%	29.66%

By way of explanation, this data shows that during the period from 2000–08, the High Court of Australia adjudicated 193 constitutional cases in 99 of which, representing 51.30 per cent, foreign precedents were cited. There was a total of 395 separate judgments in these 99 cases, with an average of 3.99 judgments per case. Of these, 318 were majority opinions (80.51 per cent), 228 (70.81 per cent) of which contained foreign law citations (1992 foreign citations in total). The remaining 77 judgments are classified as minority opinions, amounting to 19.49 per cent of the total. Of these, 59 (76.62 per cent) contained citations of foreign precedents (840 foreign citations in total). In aggregate, 2,832 foreign precedents were cited in the 395 judgments over the eight-year period from 2000–08.

As Figures 5 and 6 show, more than 70 per cent of foreign law citations appear in majority judgments of the High Court, and the remainder in minority opinions. Given the differences in the number of judgments in each category, however, this means that minority judges are marginally more likely to cite foreign law than those in the majority. Although minority judgments account for less than 20 per cent of the total judgments, they contain almost 30 per cent of the foreign law citations, and over 75 per cent of minority judgments included references to foreign law. In contrast, majority judgments, though constituting over 80 per cent of the judgments, provided only 70 per cent of the citations to foreign law, and cited foreign law at a rate of 71.7 per cent. What is perhaps surprising is that these figures are roughly the same: on a purely quantitative level, minority judges do not cite foreign law at a substantially higher rate than those in the majority.

Although this study has not qualitatively assessed the level of reliance placed upon a citation, or the influence of a particular reference, on the basis of Australian practice it does not seem likely that minority judges use foreign citations to bolster their arguments to any greater extent than majority judges. In this connection, it should be recalled that foreign citations may serve a variety of purposes in Australian constitutional reasoning, and need not necessarily be used to support any particular side of the argument. In any event, whatever the reliance placed upon a citation, there is no substantial difference between minority and majority judges in the High Court of Australia. On the basis of this data set, Justices of the Australian High Court cite broadly similar numbers of foreign precedents whether they are in the majority or minority.

IV. CONCLUSIONS

There have of course been changes in the composition of the High Court of Australia since 2008. A new Chief Justice, Robert French AC, was appointed towards the end of 2008 on the retirement of Chief Justice Gleeson. Two new Justices have been appointed to fill vacancies caused by retirements and one further Justice will retire over the next two years. Changes of this kind in the membership of the Court may have some effect at the margins on the rate and purpose of citation of foreign law in constitutional cases.

A cursory examination of recent constitutional decisions shows that the practice of citing foreign law continues, for a variety of purposes and on a variety of constitutional issues.[107] In *Momcilovic v R*[108] Chief Justice French also specifically affirmed that Australian courts were free to consider decisions of foreign courts in interpreting statutory provisions 'where they have logical or analogical relevance' to the interpretative question before them.[109] While this observation was made in the context of statutory rather than constitutional interpretation, there is no qualifier in the statement with reference to cases of the latter kind. On the other hand, while other judgments in *Momcilovic* cited foreign law extensively, their purpose often was to distinguish it from the case in hand.[110] *Momcilovic* has further seeded the suspicion, identified earlier in this chapter, that the basis on which the High Court distinguishes foreign precedents on human rights questions may bear closer examination.

In terms of the goals of the volume as a whole, the insights from the Australian case are relatively clear. First, the Australian High Court undoubtedly is, and has been, party to a transjudicial dialogue although the typically one-sided character of judicial citation of foreign precedents makes the more neutral terminology of 'engagement' more suitable.[111] If anything, in Australia, the sources from which precedents are drawn are diversifying, in the face of the possibilities offered by information technology. Secondly, Australia remains a resolutely common law jurisdiction although, as this study suggests, as the common law legal family fragments, the methodology of foreign citation practice may change. It may be possible to extrapolate from this presently minor and inchoate development some tendency for the civil and common law systems to converge. Finally, whatever the conclusion reached about the universality of human rights, the Australian case presently appears to demonstrate some reluctance to embrace foreign authority in determining rights questions on the grounds of difference in constitutional context, despite what often appear to be similar human rights goals.

---

[107] For examples, see *Pape v Commissioner of Taxation* (2009) 238 CLR 1; *ICM Agriculture v The Commonwealth* (2009) 240 CLR 140; *Hogan v Hinch* (2011) 243 CLR 506.

[108] n 6 above.

[109] At [18]. His observation was made in the context of examining the authority to consider international and foreign law in the Victorian Charter of Human Rights and Responsibilities Act 2006 (Vic), which he identified as, in effect, unnecessary.

[110] See for example, Gummow J: 'The human rights systems established in the United Kingdom, Canada, South Africa, New Zealand and Hong Kong provide only limited assistance in construing the Charter. They present imperfect analogues': at [146].

[111] V Jackson, *Constitutional Engagement in a Transnational Era* (Oxford, Oxford University Press, 2010).

2

Canada: Protecting Rights in a 'Worldwide Rights Culture'. An Empirical Study of the Use of Foreign Precedents by the Supreme Court of Canada (1982–2010)

GIANLUCA GENTILI[*]

TABLE OF CONTENTS

I. Introduction.. 39
II. The Context.. 41
    A. Canada's Constitutional Origins: The *British North America Act, 1867* 41
    B. Enhancing Protection of Fundamental Rights 42
    C. The *Charter of Rights and Freedom*.. 44
    D. The Supreme Court of Canada 46
III. The Empirical Research 49
    A. Methodology.. 49
    B. Quantitative and Qualitative Results 51
    C. Use of United States Precedents... 60
    D. The Role Played by Section 1 of the *Charter* 65
IV. Conclusions 66

I. INTRODUCTION

THE 'MIGRATION OF constitutional ideas'[1] represents a distinctive feature of contemporary constitutionalism. This expression[2] captures the increased exchange of legal ideas that has occurred between constitutional systems

---

[*] PhD, Comparative Public Law, University of Siena. I wish to thank Professors Tania Groppi, Marie-Claire Ponthoreau, Cheryl Saunders, Jean-François Gaudreault-DesBiens and Richard Kay for helpful discussions and comments on previous drafts of this article. The author holds the responsibility for remaining errors and inaccuracies. Comments are welcome: gianluca.gentili@unisi.it.

[1] S Choudhry (ed), *The Migration of Constitutional Ideas* (Cambridge, Cambridge University Press, 2006).

[2] This concept has also been described as 'importation of constitutional law': C Dupré, 'The Importation of Law: A New Comparative Perspective and the Hungarian Constitutional Court' in A Harding and E Orocu (eds), *Comparative Law in the 21st Century* (The Hague, Kluwer, 2002);

since the end of the twentieth century, when a new wave of constitution-making endeavours prompted the adoption of a new generation of national charters of rights.[3] One declination of this exchange is the practice of judges citing foreign precedents when interpreting national Constitutions, a trend variously referred to as 'judicial dialogue',[4] 'judicial internationalization', 'trans-judicialism', 'judicial cosmopolitanism', 'judicial globalisation',[5] or 'judicial engagement with foreign law'.[6] While a handful of fundamental charters worldwide expressly allow this engagement,[7] the majority remains silent on a practice that has grown controversial. A view indeed holds that Constitutions—which, since the rise of the nation-state, have been understood as the product of a given ethos—should be interpreted exclusively on the basis of domestic, rather than foreign, legal materials. The topic has received uneven scholarly attention: studies have focused extensively on the theoretical aspects of this practice (legitimacy and methodology), while empirical analyses on the frequency and meaning of citations remain generally still rare.

Since the adoption of the 1982 *Charter of Rights and Freedoms*[8] (*Charter*), the Supreme Court of Canada (SCC or Court) has established itself as one of the most progressive constitutional judges worldwide. Expressly endowing the Court with powers of judicial review for the protection of constitutionally-entrenched rights, this constitutional Bill of Rights changed the Court's role and hermeneutic approach, in a system rooted in the British tradition of parliamentary supremacy.[9] The *Charter*—inspired by the United States *Bill of Rights* and several other international human rights documents—fostered an openness to foreign legal sources typical of a common law high court, and prompted the Court to refer to an even broader range of foreign jurisdictions.

This chapter presents an empirical analysis of the Court's decisions issued between 1982 and 2010. Our research will show that the SCC, in deciding constitutional cases and interpreting the newly enacted *Charter* has consistently considered other jurisdictions. Our goal is to achieve a better understanding of the decision-making process informing the Court's activity in today's globalised legal context and of the

---

'constitutional borrowing': B Friedman and C Saunders, 'Editor's Introduction' (2003) 1 *International Journal of Constitutional Law* 177; 'cross-constitutional influence': KL Scheppele, 'Aspirational and Aversive Constitutionalism: The Case for Studying Cross-Constitutional Influence through Negative Models' (2003) 1 *International Journal of Constitutional Law* 296.

[3] J Elster, 'Forces and Mechanisms in the Constitution-Making Process' (1995) 45 *Duke Law Journal* 364, 368. Cheryl Saunders notes that, worldwide, '91 new constitutions or constitutional-type instruments for states and other distinct polities have come into force since 1990': C Saunders, 'Judicial Engagement with Comparative Law' in T Ginsburg and R Dixon (eds), *Comparative Constitutional Law* (Cheltenham, Edward Elgar, 2011) 574, fn 22.

[4] S Harding, 'Comparative Reasoning and Judicial Review' (2003) 28 *Yale Journal of International Law* 409.

[5] S Muller and S Richards (eds), *Highest Courts and Globalisation* (The Hague, Asser Press, 2010) 4.

[6] V Jackson, *Constitutional Engagement in a Transnational Era* (New York, Oxford University Press, 2010).

[7] s 11(2)(c) of the Constitution of the Republic of Mali, 1994; s 39(1) of the Constitution of South Africa, 1996; s 32(2) of the *Charter of Human Rights and Responsibilities Act 2006* (Victoria).

[8] *Charter of Rights and Freedoms*, Part I of the *Constitution Act, 1982* being Schedule B to the *Canada Act 1982* (UK), 1982, c 11.

[9] In a legal system based on this principle, no constraints are imposed upon what Parliament can do, because it is thought that Parliament represents the best place to draw the appropriate balance between individual freedoms and a broader public interest.

role played by the *Charter* in this process. Referring to cases decided by British, American, European and Australian courts, the Court has, over the years, established its *Charter* jurisprudence by drawing critical inspiration from foreign judicial decisions and adapting their legal principles to the unique features of Canada's legal system and society.

Section II will provide an overview of Canada's constitutional and institutional history since the country's foundation as a member of the British Commonwealth. Section III will focus on the empirical study, its methodology, qualitative and quantitative results, detailing the Court's use of foreign precedents in constitutional cases, both in general and with specific regard to United States precedents.

II. THE CONTEXT

A. Canada's Constitutional Origins: The *British North America Act, 1867*

Canada as a political entity came into being in 1867, when several North American political systems north of the United States (US) united into a Federation. The *British North America Act* of 1867 (BNAA or *Act*)—the main document that served as Canada's constitution until 1982—created the Dominion of Canada out of three separate entities and established the framework for admission of other colonies and territories in the future.[10] Since none of the then existing Canadian entities was independent, this process was overseen by the British Foreign Office, with the BNAA enacted as ordinary legislation by the United Kingdom (UK) Parliament. The *Act* did not terminate the relationship with the UK—independence was not sought at that time—and the new Dominion remained a British colony. For the same reason, the BNAA contained no provision for a domestic amendment procedure: Canada, therefore, was required to resort to the UK Parliament for constitutional change.

While representing one of the key components of Canada's constitution, care should be taken to distinguish the BNAA and 'the constitution' of Canada.[11] The nineteenth-century Canadian constitution, in fact, was traditionally understood as an instrument of government wider in scope than the BNAA,[12] and could not be found in one single, written document. Following the British political tradition, it was formed by a heterogeneous set of materials including a compendium of Acts and

---

[10] The original three Provinces were New Brunswick, Nova Scotia and the United Province of Canada, comprising present-day Ontario and Quebec. Between 1867 and 1949, six more Provinces joined (British Columbia, Prince Edward Island, and Newfoundland) or were created from federal territories (Manitoba, Saskatchewan, and Alberta). Now Canada has ten Provinces and three federal territories (Yukon, Northwestern Territories, and Nunavut).

[11] Throughout this work, the Canadian 'constitution' will not be capitalised, while the US 'Constitution' will be. Indeed, in the case of the US, usage refers to a distinctive document, whereas with regard to Canada the term refers to a collection of documents (including, but not limited to, the *Constitution Act, 1867* and the *Constitution Act, 1982*) along with a substantial unwritten constitution.

[12] Drafters of the BNAA had a limited purpose: creating a governmental structure ('the Dominion of Canada') for the three English colonies in North America. Accordingly, it did not include a Bill of Rights. Under that system, the Provinces retained considerable autonomy, and the Dominion as a whole was under the authority of the English Crown. MC McKenna, 'Introduction: A Legacy of Questions' in MC McKenna (ed), *The Canadian and American Constitutions in Comparative Perspective* (Calgary, Calgary University Press, 1993) XV.

statutes along with common law decisions and customary practices ('constitutional conventions'[13]) that together organised the political life of the nation and prescribed how the government was to operate.[14]

Despite just being a part of the Canadian constitution, the BNAA was a significant one nonetheless. The *Act* defined the basic institutional framework of the new Federal government and provided for the distribution of legislative powers between the Federal Parliament and the legislatures of the Provinces.[15] Furthermore, its Preamble contained an important interpretative statement to determine Canada's form of government, prescribing for Canada 'a Constitution similar in Principle to that of the United Kingdom'.[16]

B. Enhancing Protection of Fundamental Rights

Before the adoption of the *Charter* in 1982, the legislative powers of the Federal and Provincial parliaments were subject to very few limits. Cases raising civil liberties issues were addressed under the BNAA provisions outlining the division of power between the Federal and Provincial governments.[17]

One of the first attempts to develop limits to the governments' powers, with a view to protecting fundamental rights, saw Canadian courts resorting to the idea of an 'implied bill of rights'. In the *Alberta Press* case,[18] Chief Justice Duff found that limitations to governmental actions could be found in the idea that citizens' rights and freedoms were necessary to the proper functioning of a 'responsible government'. Although the theory received some support, it was never endorsed by a majority of the SCC, and was eventually rejected.[19]

After the Second World War, more articulate attempts were made—both at the Federal and Provincial levels—to ensure fundamental rights protection.

---

[13] Albert Venn Dicey maintained that political actors and institutions were bound by two sets of rules, the first being 'laws' in the strict sense, and the second defined as 'conventions, understandings, habits, or practices which, though they may regulate the conduct of the several members of the sovereign power, of the Ministry, or of other officials', are not 'laws' and hence not enforceable by courts: AV Dicey, *An Introduction to the Study of the Law of the Constitution*, 10th edn (Macmillan, 1960) 23.

[14] For the sources of Canadian constitutional law, see PW Hogg, *Constitutional Law of Canada*, 4th edn (Toronto, Carswell, 1997) ch 1.

[15] Arts 91–95 BNAA.

[16] Preamble, BNAA.

[17] In *Saumur v City of Quebec* (1953) 2 SCR 299, the SCC upheld a Jehovah's Witness' challenge to a Quebec law against street distribution of literature without prior police permission. Although the case addressed religious freedom issues, the SCC based its judgment on the federal division of power, ruling that the power to regulate religious practices fell under the purview of national government rather than of the Provinces.

[18] *Reference re Alberta Statutes* [1938] 2 SCR 100 ('*Alberta Press* case'). The implied Bill of Rights theory was invoked mostly before the *Charter*'s enactment (eg *Reference re Persons of Japanese Race* [1946] SCR 248) and received its most explicit articulation in *Switzman v Elbling* [1957] SCR 285.

[19] In 1978, a Court's majority rejected this theory declaring that no civil liberty, including those inherited from the UK, 'is so enshrined in the Constitution as to be beyond the reach of competent legislation': *AG Canada and Dupond v Montreal* [1978] 2 SCR 770, 796. The idea, however, has been revisited in a recent case: *Reference re Remuneration of Judges of the Provincial Court of Prince Edward Island* [1997] 3 SCR 3.

Beginning in 1947, several Provinces adopted human rights statutes, effective within their territories: Saskatchewan, Ontario, Nova Scotia, Alberta, New Brunswick, Prince Edward Island, Newfoundland, British Columbia, Manitoba and Quebec.[20] In 1960 a *Canadian Bill of Rights*[21] (*Bill* or CBoR) was enacted as an ordinary statute by the Canadian Parliament. The *Bill*, still in effect today, is an interpretative Bill of Rights listing a series of fundamental freedoms and providing that all other laws be 'so construed and applied so as not to abrogate, abridge or infringe' any of the rights or freedoms declared in the *Bill* itself.[22] Almost completely superseded by the 1982 *Charter*, it nonetheless contains some guarantees not included in this latter document.[23] The CBoR, however, suffered three main shortcomings: a) it only applied to Federal laws, therefore not affecting Provincial enactments;[24] b) it could be derogated from by a subsequent Act of the Canadian Parliament (with an express declaration that the Act could operate notwithstanding the *Bill*);[25] c) as an ordinary Act of Parliament it was not part of the Canadian constitution, and could be repealed at any time by the Federal Parliament, without recourse to the amending procedure.[26] This latter feature, together with an attitude of deference to the legislator imbued in the judiciary, represents the main reason why, with just one exception,[27] courts have been reluctant to consider the *Bill* as conferring upon the judiciary the authority to invalidate other duly enacted laws; this concept, without an express constitutional grant of power, seemed to Canadian courts to run against the basic rule of parliamentary supremacy.[28] The CBoR has therefore mostly been used by courts as a guide to the interpretation of other statutes, receiving narrow judicial application.

---

[20] *Saskatchewan Bill of Rights Act*, SS 1947, c 35; *Ontario Human Rights Code*, SO 1961–62, c 93; *Nova Scotia Human Rights Act*, SNS 1963, c 5; *Alberta Human Rights Act*, SA 1966, c 39; *New Brunswick Human Rights Act*, SNB 1967, c 13; *PEI Human Rights Act*, S PEI 1968, c 24; *Nfld Human Rights Act*, S Nfld 1969, no 75; *BC Human Rights Act*, SBC 1969, c 10; *Manitoba Human Rights Act*, SM 1970, c 104; *Charter of Human Rights and Freedoms*, SQ 1975, c 6.
[21] *Canadian Bill of Rights*, 'An Act for the Recognition and Protection of Human Rights and Fundamental Freedoms' SC 1960, c 44. For the *Bill*'s legislative history: WS Tarnopolsky, *The Canadian Bill of Rights*, 2nd rev edn (Canada, Carleton University Press, 1978) 11–14.
[22] Pt I, s 2 *Bill*.
[23] Eg s1(a) *Bill* protects the right of property, while s 2(e) *Bill* guarantees everyone 'the right to a fair hearing in accordance with the principles of fundamental justice for the determination of his rights and obligations'. The *Charter* does not protect property rights, and the guarantee to a fair hearing is deemed narrower.
[24] s 5, c 2 *Bill*. This is unlike the *Charter*, which has application to both Federal and Provincial governments. It should be noted that much of the SCC's activity after 1982 has involved challenges to Provincial legislation.
[25] s 2 *Bill*.
[26] The *Charter*, conversely, is a constitutionally entrenched document which expressly overrides inconsistent statutes.
[27] *R v Drybones* [1970] SCR 282.
[28] Other common law courts, however, concluded otherwise. In *Simpson v AG*, 3 NZLR 667, 706 (1994) the New Zealand Court of Appeals, interpreting that country's 1990 (statutory) *Bill of Rights Act*, noted that lack of constitutional status 'makes no difference to the strength of the Bill of Rights where it is to be applied'. In some authors' view 'this and other recent decisions of the Court of Appeals indicate that the [New Zealand] *Bill of Rights*, though unentrenched, may gradually gather sufficient legal authority to allow courts to exercise most of the powers of scrutiny and control they would have had under a system of full-scale judicial review', gaining de facto entrenched status: R Hirschl, 'The Struggle for Hegemony: Understanding Judicial Empowerment Through Constitutionalization in Culturally Divided Polities' (2000) 36 *Stanford Journal of International Law* 73, 110 fn 173.

In 1977, the Federal government enacted the *Canadian Human Rights Act* (CHRA), a statute whose aim is to counter discriminatory practices based on a list of prohibited grounds set out in the document.[29] While the CHRA finds application throughout Canada, it only affects federally regulated activities.

Finally, in 1978, the Supreme Court rejected the idea that fundamental freedoms could be derived from the Preamble to the BNAA.[30]

This being the constitutional landscape at the beginning of the 1980s, in 1982 a major change occurred within the Canadian legal system, due to the enactment of two statutes of the UK Parliament. The first, the *Canada Act, 1982*, terminated the legislative authority of the UK over Canada.[31] The second, the *Constitution Act, 1982*, an annex to the *Canada Act, 1982*, along with declaring a list of 30 Acts and statutes—including the *Constitution Act* itself and the BNAA (renamed the *Constitution Act, 1867*)—to be the supreme law of Canada, contained two Parts relevant for our study. Part V of the *Constitution Act, 1982*, 'patriated' the constitution introducing amending procedures that could be promoted entirely by Canadian institutions. Part I introduced a *Charter of Rights and Freedoms*, a constitutional Bill of Rights entrenching fundamental personal freedoms against legislative and executive action. The *Charter*'s enactment caused the Canadian system to move away from a pure British tradition of parliamentary supremacy, closer to the American concept of judicial supremacy.[32]

C. The *Charter of Rights and Freedoms*

The *Charter* is a constitutional declaration of fundamental rights drawing inspiration from various international human rights covenants and from the 1791 *Bill of Rights* to the US Constitution. The connection between these two declarations of rights is so intense that it could be defined—in the words of a famous scholar—as 'genetic'.[33] Despite being significantly influenced by a document almost two centuries older (the US *Bill of Rights*), the Canadian *Charter* fully participates in the expansive conception of rights characteristic of contemporary constitutionalism, due to the concurrent influence on the *Charter*'s drafters of international human rights treaties and conventions.[34]

---

[29] The CHRA established the Canadian Human Rights Commission, a body investigating claims of discrimination, along with the Canadian Human Rights Tribunal that judges these cases.

[30] *Canada (AG) v City of Montreal*, 2 SCR 770 (1978).

[31] *Canada Act, 1982*, 1982 c 11.

[32] L Weinrib, 'Canada's Constitutional Revolution: From Legislative to Constitutional State' (1999) 33 *Israeli Law Review* 13.

[33] The two documents being 'genetically related'. In Louis Henkin's view, constitutional documents are genetically related if one influenced the framing of the other, or if both were framed under the influence of a third: L Henkin, 'A New Birth of Constitutionalism: Genetic Influences and Genetic Defects' (1993) 14 *Cardozo Law Review* 533, 536–38. On the influence wielded by the US *Bill of Rights* and the US Supreme Court's jurisprudence on the *Charter*'s drafters, see L Weinrib, 'Of Diligence and Dice, Reconstituting Canada's Constitution' (1990) 42 *University of Toronto Law Journal* 207, 220, where the author details the unsuccessful effort, amidst the drafting process, to disengage from consideration of US jurisprudence.

[34] See J Claydon, 'International Human Rights Law and the Interpretation of the Canadian Charter of Rights and Freedoms' (1982) 4 *Supreme Court Law Review* 287, 295–302, noting the influence of the

The *Charter* represented the fulfilment of a project furthered by Pierre Trudeau's Liberal government against the initial objections of most Provinces, concerned that the declaration would increase the judicial power to interfere with the policies of elected governments. To counter these concerns, Conservative and Socialist Provincial governments supported inclusion in the *Charter* of a provision—section 33—allowing Provincial and Federal legislatures to enact laws for a renewable five-year period, notwithstanding the fundamental freedoms and legal rights protected therein.[35] Although seldom resorted to, section 33 represents a defining feature of Canadian constitutionalism.

As an entrenched document, the *Charter* has supremacy over all Federal and Provincial enactments. The power to strike down legislation inconsistent with the *Charter* is expressly codified in section 52(1) of the *Constitution Act, 1982*, which entrenches the Canadian version of the US Supremacy Clause, providing that the constitution, including the *Charter*, is the supreme law of Canada, and mandating that laws that are inconsistent with it are of no force or effect 'to the extent of the inconsistency'.[36] This makes this document a stronger Bill of Rights than the interpretative one enacted in 1960 in Canada and of those in force in New Zealand and the UK.[37] At the same time, the *Charter* differs from the US *Bill of Rights* in that it hosts in its section 1 a general 'salvage' or 'limitations' clause allowing the government to justify reasonable limits on rights,[38] an innovation subsequently adopted in New Zealand and South Africa. Unlike India or Ireland, or under the European Convention on Human Rights (ECHR), the Canadian limitations clause is open-ended and does not prescribe the reasons that legitimately justify limitations of rights.[39] The *Charter* therefore protects fundamental freedoms and rights, subject to the limitation set out in section 1, implicitly acknowledging that no legal system can treat any right as an absolute. This way, courts are permitted to uphold statutes found to infringe *Charter* rights, provided that legislation meets the procedural ('prescribed by law') and substantive ('demonstrably justified in a free and democratic

European Convention on Human Rights (ECHR), the UN Universal Declaration of Human Rights, and other international human rights instruments upon the *Charter*.

[35] *Charter of Rights and Freedoms*, s 33: (1) Parliament or the legislature of a Province may expressly declare in an Act of Parliament or of the legislature, as the case may be, that the act or a provision thereof shall operate notwithstanding a provision included in section 2 or sections 7 to 15 of this Charter ... (3) A declaration made under subsection (1) shall cease to have effect five years after it comes into force or on such earlier date as may be specified in the declaration.

[36] *Constitution Act, 1982* being Schedule B to the *Canada Act, 1982* (UK), 1982, c 11, s 52(1).

[37] For a comparison of the Bills of Rights adopted in Canada, the UK and New Zealand, which, in different forms, accommodate judicial protection of fundamental rights with claims of parliamentary sovereignty, see S Gardbaum, 'The New Commonwealth Model of Constitutionalism' (2001) 49 *American Journal of Comparative Law* 707.

[38] s 1 *Charter* famously states: 'The *Canadian Charter of Rights and Freedoms* guarantees the rights and freedoms set out in it subject only to such reasonable limits prescribed by law as can be demonstrably justified in a free and democratic society'.

[39] This clause derives from some earlier twentieth-century human rights instruments: art 29(2) of the UDHR includes a limitations clause which, in turn, inspired analogous provisions in the ECHR and the ICCPR. Other Constitutions also included similar clauses: Bahamas (1973), Barbados (1966), Botswana (1966), Grenada (1973), India (1949), Jamaica (1962), Kenya (2010), Malta (1964), Mauritius (1968), Nigeria (1960), Pakistan (1973), Samoa (1960), Trinidad and Tobago (1976). See V Jackson, *Constitutional Engagement in a Transnational Era* (2009) 86, fns 89–90.

society') requirements of section 1.[40] Section 24(1) gives the Court the power to devise remedies for those whose *Charter* rights have been violated.[41] A joint reading of sections 52(1) and 24(1) of the *Charter* vests the power of judicial review in the Canadian courts. Finally, section 32(2) of the *Charter* originally provided that the right to equality protected by section 15 would become effective three years after enactment of the document.

D. The Supreme Court of Canada

The BNAA only made a brief reference to the establishment of a national High Court,[42] without detailing the Court's composition, authority, functions and jurisdiction. This silence is explained by the fact that, at the time, appeals from the courts of the British North American colonies could be lodged with the Judicial Committee of the Privy Council (PC or Privy Council), a London-based final court of appeal which, after the creation of the Dominion of Canada in 1867, entertained cases directly from the Provincial courts of appeal.[43]

Pressure for the development of a national High Court led to the adoption, in 1875, of the *Supreme and Exchequer Courts Act* (SECA), an ordinary Act of Parliament, and to the creation of the SCC.[44] The SECA established the Court's jurisdiction over all Provincial and Federal legal issues, common and statutory law. The SCC, however, did not immediately become the Court of last resort for Canada, its decisions remaining subject to appeal to the Privy Council until 1949, when that right was completely terminated. This occurred gradually: criminal appeals to the Privy Council were terminated in 1933 (with a few exceptions) while civil appeals ended in 1949.[45] Until then, the PC had a significant influence upon the evolution

---

[40] In *R v Oakes*, 1 SCR 103 (1986), a case dealing with the constitutionality of a reverse onus provision of the *Narcotic Control Act*, RSC 1970, the SCC developed the test for the application of the balancing mechanism set out in section 1. According to the two-stage '*Oakes* test' courts first need to establish whether there has been an infringement of a *Charter* right. If an infringement is found, and the government action has been authorised by law, the Court then moves to the second step to decide whether the right was legitimately denied under section 1 and the violation—and corresponding law—can be 'demonstrably justified in a free and democratic society', and therefore 'salvaged' from a declaration of unconstitutionality. This second step has three important components, requiring a court to assess whether: 1) 'the measures adopted ... [are] reasonably connected to the objective' (rationality); 2) 'the means ... impair "as little as possible" the right or freedom in question' (minimal impairment); 3) there is 'proportionality between the effects of the measure responsible for limiting the Charter right and the objective which has been identified as of "sufficient importance"' (proportionality as such): *R v Oakes*, 139.

[41] s 24(1) *Charter* provides that '[a]nyone whose rights or freedoms, as guaranteed by this Charter, have been infringed or denied may apply to a court of competent jurisdiction to obtain such remedy as the court considers appropriate and just in the circumstances'.

[42] s 101 *Constitution Act, 1867*, granted power to the Federal Parliament to create a new 'General Court of Appeal for Canada ... and any additional Courts for the better administration of the Law of Canada'.

[43] The Council consisted of English judges, members of the House of Lords. LP Beth, 'The Judicial Committee: Its Development, Organisation and Procedure' (1975) 3 *Public Law* 219, 222–23, 232; ibid, 'The Judicial Committee of the Privy Council and the Development of Judicial Review' (1976) 24 *American Journal of Comparative Law* 22, 22–23.

[44] *Supreme and Exchequer Courts Act*, RS, 1900, c 154, later known as the *Supreme Court Act*.

[45] The last Canadian case was heard by the PC in 1959, as the case had been grandfathered: *Ponoka-Calmar Oils Ltd and anor v Earl F Wakefield Co, and ors* [1959] UKPC 20.

of the Canadian constitution, establishing the principles to be adopted in the interpretation of the BNAA, favouring strict literal interpretation and Provincial powers over those of the Federal government.

Originally composed of six members, the Court's composition grew over the years to reach the current total of nine. According to the *Supreme Court Act*, the Court is composed of one Chief Justice and eight Puisne (Associate) Justices exercising jurisdiction over appeals from Provincial courts in civil and criminal matters.[46] The Court's composition takes into account regional representation, selecting its members among different regions.[47]

In 1975, an amendment to the *Supreme Court Act* abolished most appeals as of right, introducing a leave to appeal mechanism that gave the Court control over its own docket. Since the Court could now select the cases it would review, its docket decreased rapidly, enabling the Court to focus on cases with national relevance. Furthermore, unlike its US counterpart, the Court has the possibility of delivering advisory opinions, so-called 'reference cases', on constitutional or other issues referred by Federal or Provincial governments.[48]

The enactment of the *Constitution Act, 1982*, prompted another momentous change in the Court's status, functions and role. Originally lacking formal recognition in the BNAA, some aspects of the Court came to enjoy entrenched status in the amending formula of sections 41–42.[49] Furthermore, since the beginning of its activity, the Court had reviewed legislation and executive actions to ensure consistency with the BNAA (now *Constitution Act, 1867*). This had consisted, primarily, in enforcing the allocation of legislative competences between Provincial and Federal governments pursuant to sections 91–92 of the *Constitution Act, 1867*.[50] The *Charter*'s enactment endowed the Court with explicit powers of judicial review over now constitutionally entrenched rights, radically transforming the Court's powers. The SCC's docket changed significantly[51] as the Court started to address new issues

---

[46] *Supreme Court Act*, RSC, 1985, c S-26, s 4(1). In 1875 the Supreme Court was composed of six members. The number was raised to seven in 1927 and finally reached the current number of nine in 1949.

[47] Regional representation results from a combination of legislation and conventions. The *Supreme Court Act* requires three judges to come from Quebec: *Supreme Court Act*, RS 1985, c S-26, s 6. Of the Court's remaining seats, conventionally, three are allocated to Ontario, two to the Western Provinces and one to Atlantic Canada.

[48] *Supreme Court Act*, RSC, 1985, c S-26, s 53.

[49] *Constitution Act, 1982*, ss 41 and 42.

[50] The BNAA provides specific lists of 'exclusive' powers for both levels of government. Unless otherwise stated (see ss 92(3) and 95 BNAA), these powers are mutually exclusive, rather than concurrent as in the US. s 91 grants the Federal government exclusive authority over issues of national importance, like 'trade and commerce' and criminal and family law; the BNAA's drafters' purpose was indeed to create a stronger Federal government than the one in the US. s 92, in turn, grants the provincial governments 'exclusive' authority in a number of broadly defined legislative areas, such as natural resources and land management, education, family institutions, property and civil rights, and other matters of a 'merely local or private nature'. It should be noted, however, that despite ss 91–92's textual emphasis on exclusiveness, the current dominant interpretative trend embraces more an overlapping conception of federalism than a 'watertight compartments' approach. Until the *Charter*'s enactment, the SCC was almost exclusively concerned with cases involving the Federal structure.

[51] Since the *Charter*'s enactment, 'cases in the areas of criminal law and civil liberties have increased dramatically while cases dealing with private law and economic interests have fallen significantly': D Songer, *The Transformation of the Supreme Court of Canada: An Empirical Examination* (Toronto, Toronto University Press, 2008) 58–67.

concerning the balance between governmental actions and individual or group freedoms, and developing a rights' jurisprudence.[52] The express judicial obligation to set aside legal provisions conflicting with the *Charter* caused the Court's authority to extend beyond the area of rights protection into areas previously addressed by the legislator, changing the balance of power in favour of the judiciary and eventually moving the system's focus away from the principle of Parliamentary supremacy.[53] Since then, in the effort to protect fundamental rights, reliance has been placed more on adjudication (and strategic litigation) than on the enactment of legislation.

This reliance is also related to the Court's choice of interpretative theories. The Court's most frequently employed hermeneutical approach to the *Charter* is one of 'purposive interpretation', that considers rights likely to change with the passing of time and the varying of circumstances.[54] This hermeneutical approach is consistent with the Court's commitment to the idea of a 'living constitution' and the view of the constitution as a 'living tree', a notion that has deep roots in Canadian constitutional interpretation[55] and whose application to the *Charter* also came as a reaction against the much-criticised judicial self-restraint applied to the 1960 statutory *Canadian Bill of Rights*.[56]

Despite allegations of judicial activism, especially during the first years of the *Charter*'s application,[57] the Court has eventually embraced a more shared approach

---

[52] Unlike the US *Bill of Rights* and the 1960 statutory CBoR, the *Charter* explicitly recognises group rights. It also expressly protects the special status of the French-speaking minority.

[53] A phenomenon termed as 'judicialisation of politics': R Hirschl, 'The New Constitutionalization and the Judicialization of Pure Politics Worldwide' (2006) 75 *Fordham Law Review* 721, 741–42. Frequently cited examples of this trend are the 'Patriation Reference' (*Reference re: Resolution to Amend the Constitution*, 1 SCR 754 (1981)) and the 'Quebec Secession Reference' (*Reference Re: Secession of Quebec*, 2 SCR 217 (1998)) where the Court dealt with fundamental issues like the nature of the Canadian polity, sovereignty, self-determination and the extent of the Court's powers. See S Harding, 'The Supreme Court of Canada' in AAVV, *Annuario di Diritto Comparato e Studi Legislativi* (Napoli, ESI, 2011) 281; PH Russell, 'The Effect of the Charter of Rights on the Policy-Making Role of Canadian Courts' (1982) 25 *Canadian Public Administration* 1.

[54] Harding, 'The Supreme Court of Canada', 288. In Peter Hogg's view this approach allows the Court to go beyond a traditional understanding of rights to embrace an interpretation that fits with the broader goals of the *Charter* and the constitution as a whole: P Hogg, *Constitutional Law of Canada* (2003) 724–25.

[55] The 'living tree' metaphor and subsequent doctrine of constitutional interpretation trace back to Lord Sankey's opinion for the Privy Council in the *'Persons Case'* recognising the right of women to sit in the Canadian Senate: 'The British North America Act planted in Canada a living tree capable of growth and expansion within its natural limits ... Their Lordships do not conceive it to be the duty of this Board ... to cut down the provisions of the Act by a narrow and technical construction, but rather to give it a large and liberal interpretation': *Edward v Canada (AG)*, AC 124 (1930) 136. According to Vicki Jackson, 'the constitution as a "living tree" ... exists in interaction with changing social understanding; ... the metaphor implicitly acknowledges limitations on interpretive evolutions that may arise from the text and (possibly) the need to distinguish between those areas in which meaning can change through interpretation and those in which a formal amendment through constitutionally specified processes is required': V Jackson, 'Constitutional Interpretation in Comparative Perspective', in Ginsburg and Dixon (eds), *Comparative Constitutional Law* (2011) 601; ibid, 'Constitutions as Living Trees? Comparative Constitutional Law and Interpretive Metaphors' (2006) 75 *Fordham Law Review* 921.

[56] Justice Wilson characterised the *Charter* as sending 'a clear message to the courts that the restrictive attitude which at times characterised their approach to the Canadian Bill of Rights ought to be reexamined': *Singh v Minister of Employment & Immigration* [1985] 1 SCR 177.

[57] Scholars noted a rise in activism in the first cases under the *Charter*, followed by a drop in the following years: FL Morton, P Russell & M Withey, 'The Supreme Court's First One Hundred Charter of Rights Decisions: A Statistical Analysis' (1992) 30 *Osgoode Hall Law Journal* 1, 14; C Manfredi,

to decision-making, engaging the legislator in a dialogic process of constitutional interpretation.[58] The 'dialogue' metaphor, in the Canadian context, has a twofold meaning: not only does it describe the shared interpretative responsibilities of the Court and the other democratic institutions within the system;[59] in a second, more structural meaning, it also refers to the possibility, for the National or Provincial legislators—each within their respective areas of competence—to re-enact legislation pursuant to section 33 of the *Charter* most likely in response to a declaration of unconstitutionality.[60] In fact, the Court does not enjoy the final say in constitutional interpretation, and pursuant to the so-called 'notwithstanding clause', legislatures have been granted the power to re-enact a statute notwithstanding the *Charter*'s individual rights provisions, for a renewable five-year period.[61] This mechanism has shaped what has been defined as a 'weak-form' of constitutional review,[62] one that stresses legislative—rather than exclusively judicial—responsibility for adherence to constitutional norms.

III. THE EMPIRICAL RESEARCH

A. Methodology

In light of the complexity of Canada's legal history and constitutional system, our research relied on a few methodological choices. Citations of judgments of some international adjudicatory bodies, like the International Court of Justice or the International Criminal Court were excluded from consideration, with the exception of decisions of the European Court of Human Rights (ECtHR) and the Court of Justice of the European Union (CJEU), since Canada is a signatory to neither of these Treaties and decisions of these two Courts exercise only persuasive, rather than

---

Judicial Power and the Charter: Canada and the Paradox of Liberal Constitutionalism (Oxford, Oxford University Press, 2001).

[58] The 'dialogue' approach is traced back to PW Hogg and A Bushell, 'The Charter Dialogue Between Courts and Legislatures (Or Perhaps the Charter of Rights Isn't Such a Bad Thing after All)' (1997) 35 *Osgoode Hall Law Journal* 75. See also S Choudhry, 'Globalization in Search of Justification: Toward a Theory of Comparative Constitutional Interpretation' (1999) 74 *Indiana Law Journal* 819, exploring the dialogue approach in the Court's attitude to foreign law. A critique of this phenomenon is given in LB Tremblay, 'The Legitimacy of Judicial Review: The Limits of Dialogue between Courts and Legislatures' (2005) 4 *International Journal of Constitutional Law* 617.

[59] K Roach, The Supreme Court on Trial: Judicial Activism or Democratic Dialogue (2001); C Manfredi, 'Life of a Metaphor: Dialogue in the Supreme Court, 1998–2003' (2004) 23 *Supreme Court Law Review (2nd)* 105; R Dixon, 'The Supreme Court of Canada, Charter Dialogue, and Deference' (2009) 47 *Oosgode Hall Law Journal* 235, 240.

[60] *Constitution Act, 1982*, s 33(1).

[61] The clause does not apply to voting and language rights.

[62] As opposed to 'strong' forms of constitutional review, typically represented by the US system of judicial review. According to Mark Tushnet, '[w]eak-form review combines some sort of power in courts to find legislation inconsistent with constitutional norms with some mechanism whereby the enacting legislature can respond to a court decision to that effect': M Tushnet, 'The Rise of Weak-form Judicial Review' in T Ginsburg and R Dixon (eds), *Comparative Constitutional Law* (2011) 322; M Tushnet, 'Judicial Activism and Restraint in a Section 33 World' (2003) 53 *University of Toronto Law Journal* 89; M Tushnet, *Weak Courts, Strong Rights: Judicial Review and Social Welfare Rights in Comparative Constitutional Law* (Princeton, Princeton University Press, 2007).

binding, authority in Canada.[63] More importantly, since 1986[64] and increasingly in the past 20 years, judgments of the ECtHR have represented a fundamental point of reference for the SCC in the effort to enhance protection of fundamental rights domestically. With only this—rather significant—exception, our analysis focused on what has been defined 'horizontal communication' between national courts, to the exclusion of vertical and mixed vertical–horizontal interactions.[65] Citations of sources of law other than case law (ie treaties, foreign statutes or codes, etc) were likewise excluded.

With regard to its functions, the SCC has been frequently called to exercise its advisory jurisdiction and has indeed rendered some of its most important determinations in the form of 'reference' opinions.[66] Despite their precedential value being controversial, our research included these determinations among the Court's acts surveyed for citations to foreign precedents.[67]

Canada's former membership of the British Commonwealth of Nations and its subjection to the jurisdiction of the Privy Council mandated a few additional methodological choices. While in 1933 the right of appeal to the PC was abolished for criminal cases, only in 1949 did a complete abolition of that right (ie, also including civil cases) come into effect. This development carries momentous importance for our study, since, in our opinion, it requires us to consider criminal cases decided and lodged with the PC and other English courts before 1933 and civil cases adjudicated and filed before 1949—whenever cited by the SCC—as 'local', rather than foreign, authority for Canada, and therefore ones that should be excluded from consideration in the quantitative assessment of citations to foreign precedents.[68] Indeed, before the colonies acquired independence, the Privy Council could hardly be considered

---

[63] On the difference between persuasive and binding authority see HP Glenn, 'Persuasive Authority' (1987) 32 *McGill Law Journal* 261, 263, emphasising that persuasive authority is an 'authority which attracts adherence as opposed to obliging it'; M-C Ponthoreau, 'L'argument fondé sur la comparaison dans le raisonnement juridique' in P Legrand (ed), *Comparer les droits, résolument* (Paris, Presses Universitaires de France, 2009) 548.

[64] When in *R v Oakes* [1986] 1 SCR 103, the SCC cited for the first time a decision of the European Commission of Human Rights, a body operating until 1998 as a filter to the ECtHR. See Table 2 below.

[65] See A-M Slaughter, 'A Typology of Transjudicial Communication' (1994) 29 *University of Richmond Law Review* 99. According to the author, horizontal communication occurs between courts of similar status across international borders; vertical communication occurs when there exists a hierarchical relationship between national and international or supranational institutions; mixed vertical–horizontal communication takes place when supranational tribunals serve as a conduit for horizontal communication.

[66] See, eg *Reference re Secession of Quebec*, 2 SCR 217 (1998); *Reference re Same-Sex Marriage*, 3 SCR 698 (2004). All of SCC's determinations (both judgments and reference opinions) are available at scc.lexum.org.

[67] An argument for the exclusion of advisory opinions from this study could also have been made considering that the presumption of constitutionality normally applied by a court when reviewing 'ex post' the constitutionality of statutes, does not find application when that same review is conducted 'a priori', that is, when the statute has not yet been enacted. However, eventually advisory opinions were included in the research in light of their relevance in the general system of rights protection developed by the SCC.

[68] See also R Lefler, 'A Comparison of Comparison: Use of Foreign Case Law as Persuasive Authority by the United States Supreme Court, the Supreme Court of Canada and the High Court of Australia' (2001–02) 11 *Southern California Interdisciplinary Law Journal* 165, 166.

a foreign court.[69] At some point, however, the colonies became independent but continued to accept the jurisdiction of the Privy Council. From this time, and for as long as the colonies still accepted its jurisdiction, the Privy Council operated as a supra-national Court (whose decisions, as seen, are excluded from this research, due to their binding authority on Member States). On this basis, it is our view that only decisions issued by the Privy Council and other English courts in criminal and civil cases lodged, respectively, after 1933 and 1949, can genuinely be considered as foreign precedents for Canada, and legitimately included in the research when cited by the SCC.

Finally, since one of the main purposes of the study is to assess the *Charter*'s impact on the SCC's citation attitude, the study will cover the years from 1982 to 2010.[70] In choosing this time frame, we are aware of the view, expressed by some authors,[71] that a study on the frequency of foreign citations should avoid the uncommonly high number of references to foreign jurisprudence expected during the so-called 'formative period' of domestic jurisprudence, seen as a potentially anomalous phase. Nonetheless, we decided to start our analysis from the year of the *Charter*'s enactment for two reasons: first, because it is our view that a comprehensive study on citations of foreign precedents should also include 'formative periods' to better determine the effects of the new document on the constitutional system as a whole and on the Court's functions and role; and second, due to practical difficulties in defining the temporal limits of the so-called 'formative periods' supposedly to be excluded from the analysis, and in determining a specific moment when the interpretation of the *Charter* would became 'mature'.

B. Quantitative and Qualitative Results

Scholars have identified some general, systemic reasons to help explain the practice of citation of foreign precedents, some of which may also find application to the SCC and the Canadian legal system.

Common law jurisdictions, like Canada, for a variety of reasons[72] appear to be more prone to citing foreign precedents than civil law countries. However, some of

---

[69] This principle applies not just to PC decisions on cases originating from Canada, representing the overwhelming majority of citations, but to all PC judgments; under the then-prevailing doctrine of precedent, 'decisions of the Judicial Committee of the Privy Council bind all colonial courts of whatever status or jurisdiction': TO Elias, 'Colonial Courts and the Doctrine of Judicial Precedent' (1955) 18 *Modern Law Review* 356, 361.
[70] Covering therefore the work of four Chief Justices: Bora Laskin (CJ from 1973–84), Brian Dickson (1984–90), Antonio Lamer (1990–2000) and Beverley McLachlin (2000–10).
[71] Eg B Roy, 'An Empirical Survey of Foreign Jurisprudence and International Instruments in Charter Litigation' (2004) 62 *University of Toronto Faculty Law Review* 99, 103.
[72] Among these, Vicki Jackson includes i) a less deeply positivistic culture than civil law countries, ii) 'familiarity and comfort with the idea that constitutionalism involves principles that exist outside of written legal commitments': Jackson, *Constitutional Engagement in a Transnational Era* (2009) 243. Cheryl Saunders identifies further reasons in: a) the fact that cases in the common law tradition are established by reference to earlier cases (whether domestic or foreign, binding or merely persuasive) considered analogous; b) the form of judicial decisions, requiring written reasons for the judgment and an analysis of how legal authorities are used; c) the fact that constitutional cases are determined by the courts that also administer the rest of the law, promoting interdependence of the constitution with the

these jurisdictions have shown signs of 'discomfort' with this practice, as it is the case with the US, Singapore and Malaysia.[73]

Canada's former membership of the British Commonwealth may prove therefore a more persuasive argument. The use of foreign precedents received stimulus from the Commonwealth practice of considering the common law as a single, unified legal system with a high degree of permeability between jurisprudences.[74] When addressing judicial review issues, under the Constitution of one Commonwealth Member, the Privy Council would refer to cases involving other Members' Constitutions, making comparison a familiar exercise in constitutional adjudication and practice.[75] Canadian legal actors became therefore accustomed to reading cases from the UK, Australia and New Zealand, all English-speaking countries sharing the same Commonwealth history and similar social and economic conditions. While Canada is no longer a member of this system, extra-systemic materials are today resorted to due to perceived membership of a single cultural space which justifies jurisprudential cross-references.

Several other reasons, more specifically related to Canada, have been put forth to explain the SCC's use of foreign precedents.[76] From an institutional standpoint, Canada is a bilingual and bijural country.[77] It is thought that familiarity with more than one language and legal tradition—originating from Quebec's French linguistic heritage and civilian legal tradition—would make Canadian lawyers and judges more accustomed to understanding multiple legal systems, more likely to access and understand foreign legal materials and more prone to include them in their briefs and amici curiae (lawyers) and decisions (judges).[78]

The aforementioned progressive hermeneutical approach of the SCC (the 'living tree' metaphor) also arguably plays a central role in explaining the Court's use of foreign precedents. As pointed out by Vicki Jackson, 'while living constitutionalism need not necessarily embrace consideration of foreign case law, it is more open to them than intentionalists or originalists modes of interpretation'.[79] Furthermore, international covenants and human rights treaties played an important role in the *Charter*'s drafting. It should not come as a surprise, therefore, that in interpreting the *Charter*, the SCC is open to citation of foreign materials coming from the

---

rest of the legal system; d) reliance on adversarial procedure and the fact that foreign experiences enter judicial deliberations through parties and amici briefs, and are in turn expected to be reflected in its reasons: Saunders, 'Judicial Engagement with Comparative Law', 575.

[73] Saunders, 'Judicial Engagement with Comparative Law', 574.

[74] The theory was that there was a single, monolithic body of common law: see WR Lederman, *Continuing Canadian Constitutional Dilemmas* (Toronto, Butterworths, 1981) 68; 'a comprehensive body of doctrine ... uniform throughout the British Empire': Hogg, *Constitutional Law of Canada* (1997) 32.

[75] Jackson, *Constitutional Engagement in a Transnational Era* (2009), 96.

[76] Roy, 'An Empirical Survey of Foreign Jurisprudence'.

[77] J-F Gaudreault-DesBiens, *Les solitudes du bijuridisme canadien. Essai sur les rapports de pouvoir entre les traditions juridiques et la résilience des atavismes identitaires* (Montréal, Thémis, 2007).

[78] However, as Table 2 and Graph 4 will show further below, the citation process is overwhelmingly dominated by decisions from common law countries, that is, from only one of Canada's languages and legal cultures. P McCormick, 'Waiting for Globalization: An Empirical Study of the McLachlin Court's Foreign Judicial Citations' (2009–2010) 41 *Ottawa Law Review* 209.

[79] Jackson, *Constitutional Engagement in a Transnational Era* (2009) 97.

Canada 53

Table 1: Number of Decisions and Citations to Foreign Precedents (CFPs)

Year	- A - Total decisions per year	- B - Cases with CFPs (constitutional & others)	- C - Constitutional cases	- D - Constitutional cases with CFPs (% of total decisions)	- E - Total CFPs per year	- F - Total CFPs in constitutional cases per year
1982	119	39 (32.8%)	15	4 (3.4%)	113	10
1983	90	17 (18.9%)	12	2 (2.2%)	36	4
1984	64	15 (23.4%)	13	3 (4.7%)	112	13
1985	84	31 (36.9%)	28	9 (10.7%)	182	48
1986	76	32 (42.1%)	19	9 (11.8%)	200	97
1987	94	28 (29.8%)	34	12 (12.8%)	178	89
1988	106	31 (29.2%)	32	12 (11.3%)	155	66
1989	133	49 (36.8%)	61	26 (19.5%)	209	122
1990	144	60 (41.7%)	80	33 (22.9%)	327	196
1991	108	29 (26.8%)	38	15 (13.9%)	180	103
1992	109	39 (35.7%)	49	20 (18.3%)	235	57
1993	138	40 (28.9%)	53	21 (15.2%)	204	88
1994	111	33 (29.7%)	41	17 (15.3%)	169	81
1995	108	37 (34.2%)	39	21 (22.7%)	201	122
1996	121	39 (32.2%)	54	23 (19.0%)	136	78
1997	110	43 (39.1%)	33	18 (16.4%)	195	83
1998	90	27 (30.0%)	33	15 (16.7%)	80	37
1999	80	26 (32.5%)	36	13 (16.3%)	163	82
2000	69	21 (30.4%)	20	7 (10.1%)	111	26
2001	94	32 (34.0%)	34	15 (16.0%)	161	90
2002	86	38 (44.2%)	38	21 (24.4%)	184	55
2003	74	21 (28.4%)	27	8 (10.8%)	67	21
2004	83	18 (21.7%)	28	7 (8.4%)	53	26
2005	87	19 (21.8%)	30	8 (9.2%)	59	19
2006	59	20 (33.8%)	18	3 (5.1%)	64	3
2007	55	28 (50.9%)	20	12 (21.8%)	157	77
2008	72	25 (34.7%)	19	7 (9.7%)	110	52
2009	62	19 (30.6%)	18	7 (11.3%)	114	86
2010	67	17 (25.4%)	27	9 (13.4%)	84	66

ECtHR or from other worldwide jurisdictions.[80] Finally, considering the experiences of Hungary and South Africa, extensive revision or enactment of a new constitutional document and corresponding lack of a line of domestic precedents interpreting the new provisions, may promote recourse to foreign precedents.[81]

A comparison of columns B and D and columns E and F of Table 1 illustrates that the SSC's tendency to refer to foreign case law is present not only in constitutional cases, but also in other areas of law, a fact highlighting the SCC's general, favourable attitude towards cross-section citation of foreign precedents. Furthermore, our research shows that reference to foreign precedents follows a distinctive pattern across the various areas of law: the incidence of US and ECtHR decisions is higher in constitutional cases, given the US Supreme Court's extensive experience in constitutional interpretation and the ECtHR's focus on human rights cases; on the other hand, the areas of tort, contract and property law still appear to be very much reserved to British common law rulings.

From a quantitative standpoint, Table 1 shows that the number of cases granted leave to the SCC increased at its maximum between the end of the 1980s and the first half of the 1990s,[82] reaching its peak in 1990 and remaining high at least until 1997: arguably the period when most of the new Charter cases reached the Court.

While the openness to foreign precedents remained unchanged, citation rates of foreign jurisprudence declined between the end of the 1990s and the end of the 2000s (see Table 1, column D),[83] indicating that once the SCC had developed a sufficient domestic jurisprudence, it relied less on foreign sources and more upon its own domestic body of established law.

---

[80] On the *Charter*'s relationship to other international and human rights documents, see AF Bayefsky, 'International Human Rights Law in Canadian Courts' in I Cotler and FP Eliadis (eds), *International Human Rights Law: Theory and Practice* (1992) 115, 125–29. The timing of the adoption of the *Charter* may have reinforced Canadian openness to foreign influences, particularly since the *Charter* was drafted, negotiated and adopted shortly after Canada's 1976 ratifications of the ICCPR and the ICESCR: Jackson, *Constitutional Engagement in a Transnational Era* (2009) 239.

[81] *Charter* claims were qualitatively different from earlier arguments relying on the BNAA in that they were based on direct constitutional protection of civil liberties. This made pre-*Charter* precedent of little help to judges seeking guidance on civil liberties issues. On this, then-Justice McLachlin noted: 'the difficulty is that the Canadian Charter ... is a new experience. We have not had anything like it before. Our judges cannot rely on their own experience to breathe life into the *Charter*; instead they must find that life elsewhere': B McLachlin, 'The Charter of Rights and Freedoms: A Judicial Perspective' (1988–1989) 23 *University of British Columbia Law Review*, 579, 580. The tendency to resort to foreign precedents will eventually decline when a significant line of domestic jurisprudence becomes available.

[82] This is roughly the time when s 15, which took effect in 1985, received its first serious judicial interpretation by the SCC, in *Andrews v Law Society of British Columbia* [1989] 1 SCR 143. Other early equality cases are described, along with US comparison, in JM Pellicciotti, 'The Constitutional Guarantee of Equal Protection in Canada and the United States: Comparative Analysis of the Standards for Determining the Validity of Governmental Action' (1997) 5 *Tulsa Journal of Comparative and International Law* 1.

[83] With the total number of foreign precedents per year in constitutional cases dropping (see Table 1, column F). This is also due to the highly diminished number of cases granted leave to the SCC, which, in the 2000s amounted to 741, that is, 33.8% fewer than the cases reaching the Court in the 1990s (1119).

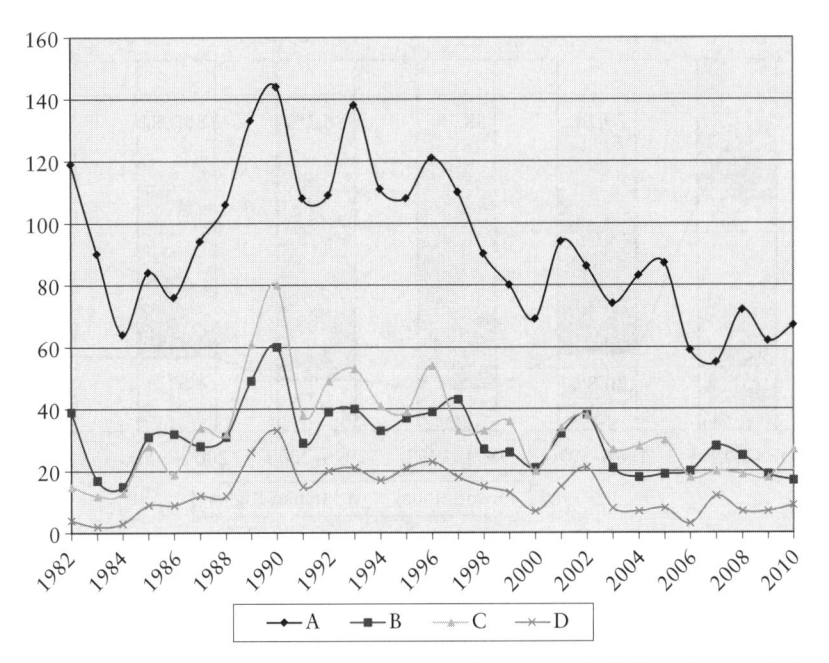

Graph 1: Constitutional Cases Citing Foreign Precedents out of all Constitutional Cases
A: Total number of decisions issued per year by the Court
B: Decisions citing foreign precedents
C: Constitutional cases
D: Constitutional cases citing foreign precedents

The impact of the *Charter*'s enactment on the SCC's docket can also be analysed considering the type of cases—whether dealing with institutional or human rights issues—that the Court addressed in the period under consideration (Graph 2).

With the new functions that the *Constitution Act, 1982* vested with the Court, the vast majority of judicial review cases fell under the *Charter*'s purview, and civil liberties cases rapidly increased in number, bringing Canada closer to the US in the level of rights-based litigation.[84] The majority of these citations are in cases involving questions of individual rights, rather than questions of allocation of powers among the levels of government. However, use of foreign precedents is certainly not reserved only to fundamental rights cases. A small number of significant institutional cases—addressing the boundaries between Federal and Provincial powers—is dealt with each year by the Court.[85]

---

[84] Table 1 shows that the total SCC's caseload increased significantly in the first 10 years under the *Charter*, with constitutional cases accounting for around 50% of the Court's total judgments. However, the caseload rapidly decreased in the second half of the 2000s bringing the SCC even closer to the US Supreme Court in terms of cases adjudicated per year.

[85] See, eg, *General Motors of Canada Ltd v City National Leasing* [1989] 1 SCR 641; *Ontario Hydro v Ontario (Labour Relations Board)* [1993] 3 SCR 327; *Reference re Secession of Quebec* [1998] 2 SCR 217; *BC v Imperial Tobacco Canada Ltd* [2005] 2 SCR 473; *Canadian Western Bank v Alberta* [2007] 2 SCR 3; *Consolidated Fastfrate Inc v Western Canada Council of Teamsters* [2009] 3 SCR 407.

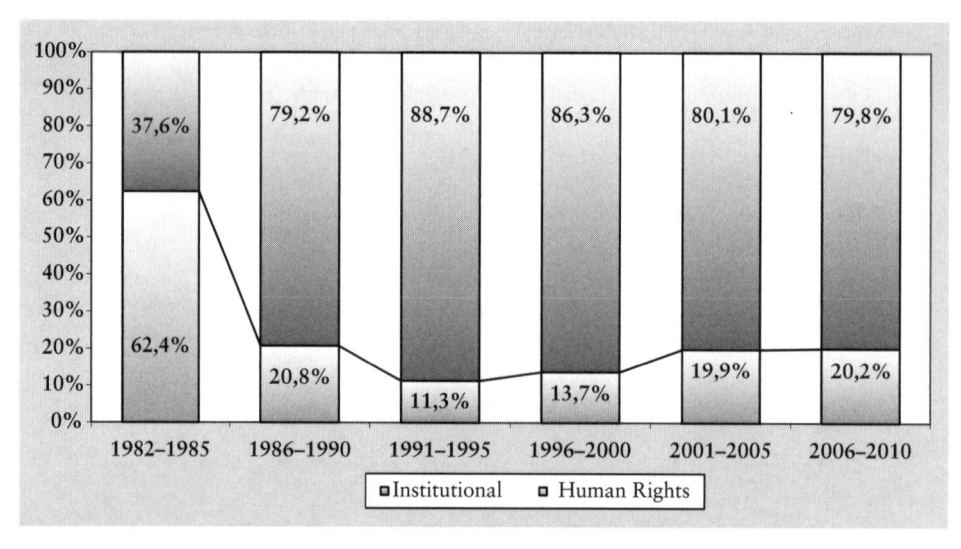

Graph 2: Human Rights or Institutional Cases out of Constitutional Cases
1982–1985: 37.6% HR–62.4% INST.
1986–1990: 79.2% HR–20.8% INST.
1991–1995: 88.7% HR–11.3% INST.
1996–2000: 86.3% HR–13.7% INST.
2001–2005: 80.1% HR–19.9% INST.
2006–2010: 79.8% HR–20.2% INST.

In analysing these two different typologies of cases, a clear pattern emerged: English or domestic cases are cited predominantly for federalism issues while US, Australian, New Zealand and ECtHR precedents are cited for human rights cases. This very limited recourse to US precedents in federalism cases originates in the fact that litigation over the allocation of legislative powers among levels of government represented the main area of constitutional decision-making even before the *Charter*'s enactment and a long line of precedents was already available; also, differences in the constitutional provisions—and corresponding design—of Canadian and US federalism[86] and a peculiar hermeneutical approach of the PC[87] made US precedents unlikely to be considered in recent federalism issues.

This rather interesting dichotomy (UK precedents cited predominantly in institutional cases; US precedents in human rights decisions) helps to explain the data presented in Table 2 and Graphs 3 and 4. Indeed, the steady increase in human rights cases reaching the SCC, combined with the lack of domestic jurisprudence interpreting the *Charter* account for the extensive use of US precedents displayed.

---

[86] See n 50.
[87] See n 94 and corresponding text.

Table 2: Citations of Foreign Precedents in Constitutional Cases per Country

Year	UK	US	AU	ECtHR	NZ	Other Jurisdictions
1982	5	5	-	-	-	-
1983	4	-	-	-	-	-
1984	6	6	1	-	-	-
1985	12	31	-	-	-	Bahamas: 2; Cyprus: 1; Pakistan: 2
1986	12	70	-	4	2	-
1987	18	69	-	1	1	-
1988	22	33	4	7	2	Germany: 1
1989	32	74	5	9	-	Belgium: 1; EU: 1
1990	23	157	2	9	1	India: 2
1991	5	92	2	2	1	Ireland: 1
1992	20	25	1	2	-	-
1993	31	50	2	2	2	-
1994	32	40	11	1	1	Germany: 2; Hong Kong: 1; Israel: 1; South Africa: 1
1995	39	77	3	2	-	-
1996	24	50	1	-	3	-
1997	12	63	6	-	2	-
1998	18	14	2	2	-	France: 1
1999	34	33	5	-	5	EU: 1; India: 1; South Africa: 1
2000	11	15	-	-	-	-
2001	23	51	10	6	-	-
2002	22	24	4	4	-	Israel: 1; South Africa: 1
2003	10	11	-	-	-	-
2004	2	23	-	1	-	-
2005	5	8	-	-	-	EU: 2; France 4
2006	-	3	-	-	-	-
2007	14	40	5	4	2	France: 4; Israel: 4; South Africa: 1
2008	19	24	6	-	2	Hong Kong: 1
2009	26	30	7	3	4	South Africa: 3
2010	19	28	4	8	4	Netherlands: 1; South Africa: 1
Total	502	1144	81	67	32	France: 9; South Africa: 8; Israel: 6; EU: 4; Germany: 3; India: 3; Bahamas: 2; Hong Kong: 2; Pakistan: 2; Belgium: 1; Cyprus: 1; Ireland: 1; The Netherlands: 1.

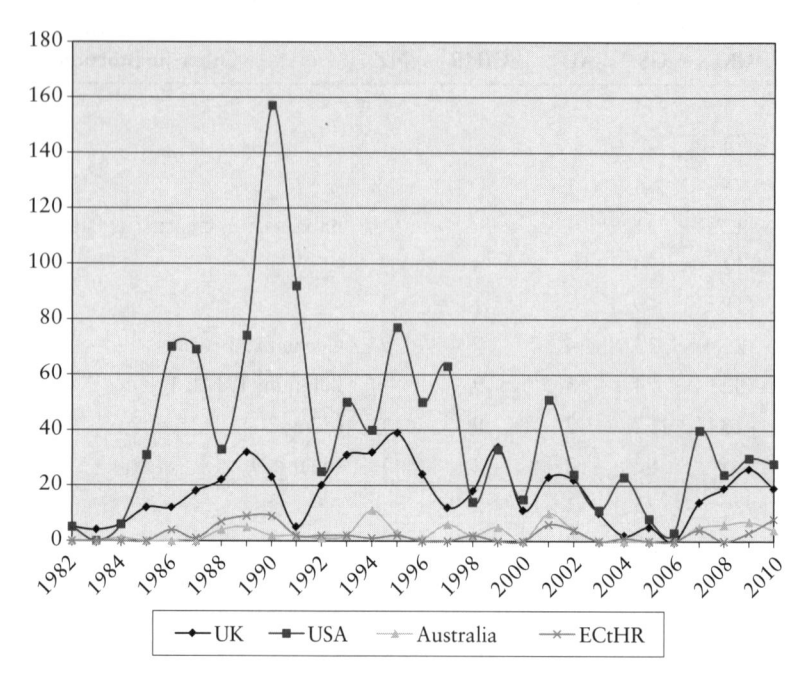

Graph 3: Citations of Foreign Precedents per Country in Constitutional Cases (4 most-often cited Jurisdictions)

Citations of British precedents are not surprising, given the historical ties that existed between the Canadian court system and the UK and Commonwealth systems. The *Charter*'s enactment, however, at least with regard to constitutional cases, soon brought to an end the 'English captivity',[88] determining a rapid decline in institutional cases and a corresponding decrease in the number of UK precedents cited by the SCC. Conversely, the increase in human rights cases reaching the SCC made US precedents valuable resources, extensively resorted to, reaching a peak in the early 1990s. This rise was determined mainly by two reasons: claims of civil rights' violations previously filed under the BNAA's provisions concerning the allocation of legislative competences between the Federation and the Provinces started to be filed under *Charter* provisions; furthermore, the *Charter*'s enactment changed citizens' attitudes towards the protection of fundamental rights. The Parliament was no longer the only appropriate place to protect and advance fundamental rights protection, with courts becoming a privileged locus for this type of claims.

Arguably, language also plays an important role in the choice of the foreign jurisdictions considered. As shown by Graph 4, in the almost 30 years of the SCC's activity surveyed by the research, more than 98 per cent of the SCC's decisions in constitutional cases made reference to six main jurisdictions, either being former

---

[88] B Laskin, 'The Supreme Court of Canada: A Final Court of and for Canadians' (1951) 29 *Canadian Bar Review* 1038, 1045–46.

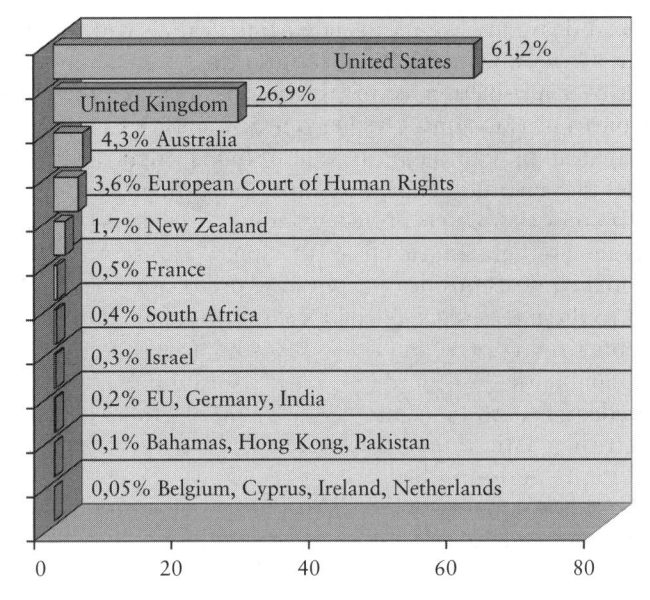

Graph 4: Percentage of Cases using Foreign Precedents, sorted by Countries

Country	%
United States	61,2%
United Kingdom	26,9%
Australia	4,3%
European Court of Human Rights	3,6%
New Zealand	1,7%
France	0,5%
South Africa	0,4%
Israel	0,3%
EU, Germany, India	0,2%
Bahamas, Hong Kong, Pakistan	0,1%
Belgium, Cyprus, Ireland, Netherlands	0,05%

Members of the British Commonwealth or speaking familiar languages (English and French, both official languages in Canada): the US, the UK, Australia, the ECtHR (whose decisions are issued in both English and French), New Zealand, France and South Africa, listed in order of frequency of citations. Citations to US and UK precedents alone account for 88 per cent of the total foreign citations in constitutional cases.

The numerous references to UK, Australian and New Zealand precedents illustrated by Table 2 and Graph 3 can be explained through the so-called 'genealogic interpretation'[89] theory: as mentioned, a common law court may find it useful to resort to precedents of a foreign court of a country belonging (presently or in the past) to the same (cultural or legal) space to address controversial cases, whenever suitable legislative or jurisprudential aids are missing within its own legal system.[90]

Regarding the types of opinion hosting references to foreign precedents, citations are not limited to only one typology—whether majority, concurring or dissenting—but, conversely, are equally present in all different types. While SCC decisions are notable for their high rate of unanimity (around 65 per cent of the total),[91] as Graph 5 shows, the highest numbers of citations of foreign precedents are found in majority and dissenting opinions. This is a sign that the number of foreign precedents cited

---

[89] Choudhry, 'Globalization in Search of Justification', 838ff.
[90] G de Vergottini, *Oltre il dialogo tra le Corti. Giudici, diritto straniero, comparazione* (Bologna, Il Mulino, 2010) 108.
[91] An attitude that has not changed after the *Charter*'s enactment, despite the increase in more controversial cases. D Songer, *The Transformation of the Supreme Court of Canada* (2008).

60 *Gianluca Gentili*

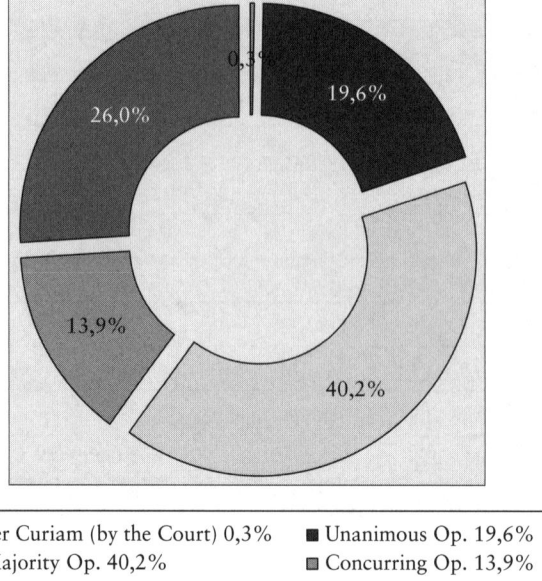

- Per Curiam (by the Court) 0,3%   ■ Unanimous Op. 19,6%
- Majority Op. 40,2%   ■ Concurring Op. 13,9%
- Dissenting Op. 26,0%

Graph 5: Location of Citations to Foreign Precedents in Constitutional Cases

increases along with the level of disagreement on a specific issue and the number of opinions filed. Judges seem to feel compelled to cite a higher number of precedents not only to overcome opposition from colleagues but also to make their decisions more acceptable to the public and to other institutional actors with enforcement powers. Also, on average, judges appear to resort more to foreign precedents when overturning government action than when upholding it.[92]

C. Use of United States Precedents

Together with the aforementioned general features favouring the use of foreign citations, two elements, specific to Canada, deserve more careful consideration: the special value accorded to US precedents and the role of section 1 of the *Charter*.

The use of US precedents has featured in Canadian judicial decision-making since Confederation. Indeed, the first years after 1867 were characterised by references of Canadian courts to US constitutional cases, and by discussions about the similarities and differences between the two constitutional systems.[93] The Privy Council,

---

[92] See, eg, *R v Morgentaler* [1988] 1 SCR 30 (19 foreign precedents); *Committee for the Commonwealth of Canada v Canada* [1991] 1 SCR 139 (20 foreign precedents); *R v Seaboyer* [1991] 2 SCR 577 (18 foreign precedents); *Miron v Trudel* [1995] 2 SCR 418 (14 foreign precedents); *R v Ruzic* [2001] 1 SCR 687 (23 foreign precedents); *R v Kang-Brown* [2008] 1 SCR 456 (13 foreign precedents).

[93] The study of the use of US precedents by Canadian courts has longstanding roots: Lex, 'The Authority of American Decisions in Canadian and English Courts' (1899) 35 *Canada Law Journal* 518;

however, soon established a formalist approach to statutory interpretation and indicated that US decisions bore no relevance in the adjudication of cases arising from Canada.[94] The interpretation of the *Constitution Act, 1867* developed therefore along domestic lines, making foreign precedents of no utility in resolving hermeneutical issues. This situation did not change even in 1949 when the SCC became Canada's highest appellate court.

The *Charter*'s enactment radically changed this landscape: at the outset, the US experience with civil rights jurisprudence was explicitly considered during the *Charter*'s drafting process, when the phrasing of some sections was changed as a result of concerns arising from the US experience.[95]

Then, language similarities with the US *Bill of Rights* made US jurisprudence immediately relevant.[96] Indeed, while, on one hand, the sections dealing with group rights[97] addressed distinctive aspects of Canadian society and the override provision of section 33 reflected concerns of judicial activism and the willingness to safeguard—at least to some extent—the British tradition of parliamentary sovereignty,[98] on the other hand, both the US and Canadian declarations entrench a series of negative rights (substantive and procedural) protecting the individual from State unconstitutional actions, leaving outside of their purview positive or social rights.[99] These rights are included in section 2 and sections 7 to 15 of the *Charter*

JM MacIntyre, 'The Use of American Cases in Canadian Courts' (1964–66) 2 *University of British Columbia Law Review* 478: the articles suggest that, after an initial period of acceptance, a bias emerged against American authorities; SI Bushnell, 'The Use of American Cases' (1986) 35 *University of New Brunswick Law Journal* 157: Bushnell found that the use of American cases declined in the 1920s to re-emerge only in the 1970s. CP Manfredi, 'The Use of United States Decisions by the Supreme Court of Canada under the Charter of Rights and Freedoms' (1990) 23 *Canadian Journal of Political Science* 499: Manfredi notes that between 1949–68 American cases constituted less than 2% of all citations; conversely, between 1969–78 a significant increase in US citations occurred. American jurisprudence therefore influenced Canadian legal doctrine even before 1982, showing that in Canada enhancement of fundamental rights and reference to US cases were connected even before the *Charter*'s enactment.

[94] Early PC case law rejected the view that US authority would be controlling in the interpretation of the Canadian constitution: *Bank of Toronto v Lambe*, 1887 12 AC 575, 587 (PC) (appeal taken from Canada).

[95] The October 1980 draft of s 1 referred to 'reasonable limits ... in a free and democratic society with a parliamentary system of government'. The *Charter*'s drafters eventually removed reference to 'a parliamentary system of government' from s 1 in order not to imply the irrelevance of US jurisprudence in *Charter* adjudication: PW Hogg, *Constitutional Law of Canada*, 2nd edn (Toronto, Carswell, 1985) 679, n 149. On the other hand, provincial concerns about the interpretation given to the expression 'due process' by US courts led to its replacement with 'principles of fundamental justice' in s 7 of the *Charter*: R Romanow, J White and H Leeson, *Canada Notwithstanding: The Making of the Constitution, 1976–1982* (Toronto, Carswell, 1984) 245–46.

[96] For early comparisons between the *Charter* and the US Constitution, see D Stone and FK Walpole, 'The Canadian Constitution Act and the Constitution of the United States: A Comparative Analysis' (1983) 2 *Canadian-American Law Journal* 1; WS Tarnopolsky, 'The New Canadian Charter of Rights and Freedoms as Compared and Contrasted with the American Bill of Rights' (1983) 5 *Human Rights Quarterly* 227; P Bender, 'The Canadian Charter of Rights and Freedoms and the United States Bill of Rights: A Comparison' (1983) 28 *McGill Law Journal* 811.

[97] That is, s 23 (minority language education rights), s 25 (aboriginal rights) and s 28 (affirmative actions), entrenching a distinctive Canadian perspective on multiculturalism, one embracing linguistic and cultural diversity ('ethnic mosaic'). US pluralism tends, conversely, to pursue assimilation to a common national identity ('melting pot').

[98] Other specific Canadian issues were the 'patriation' of the Canadian constitution and the different process of legal consent the *Charter* underwent compared to the US Constitution.

[99] M McKenna (ed), *The Canadian and American Constitutions* (1993).

and are expressed in broad terms analogous to the First, Fourth, Fifth, Sixth, Eighth and Fourteenth Amendments to the US Constitution, subject only to the limitation of section 1. The *Charter*, therefore, brought US and Canadian cultures closer, the latter acquiring a rights-based foundation the former had already experienced for decades, and making US precedents relevant to the interpretation of Canadian laws.[100] It came naturally to the SCC to resort to US precedent interpreting cognate constitutional provisions to those entrenched in the *Charter*.[101] Furthermore, even when the language of the *Charter* differed from the one of the US *Bill of Rights*, US cases represented a useful source of ideas and comparisons, in order to foresee possible, long-term outcomes of certain interpretations.

From a qualitative standpoint, our research shows that while the SCC's use of American precedents in constitutional cases is focused on US cases decided in the latter half of the twentieth century, these are not necessarily recent decisions.[102] Furthermore, the fact that the SCC has cited US rulings coming not only from the US Supreme Court but from across all levels of American courts (including lower US federal and state court judgments), suggests a rather sophisticated understanding of US jurisprudence by Canadian judges. Despite the significant (positive or negative) influence exerted on the Canadian legal system, US precedents have never enjoyed more than mere persuasive authority.[103]

In addition to textual similarities between the two Constitutions, several other elements concurred in making US precedents a suitable resource for Canadian courts and arguably explain the SCC's high rate of citation of US precedents.

Focusing exclusively on legal and institutional features, both countries share a background as former British colonies, although the relationship with the UK was terminated in two rather different ways.[104] They both established their constitutional systems—and federal systems of government—more than a century ago[105]

---

[100] CP Manfredi, 'Adjudication, Policy-Making and the Supreme Court of Canada: Lessons from the Experience of the United States' (1989) 22 *Canadian Journal of Political Science* 313.

[101] CJ Dickson expressed willingness to examine US case law: 'the American courts have the benefit of two hundred years of experience in constitutional interpretation. This wealth of experience may offer guidance to the judiciary in this country', *R v Simmons* [1988] 2 SCR 495, 516. The same spirit is evident in Justice L'Heureux-Dubé's concurring opinion in *R v Elshaw* [1991] 3 SCR 24, 57: 'to reject the American experience out of hand and to refuse to engage in its examination, at least as a comparative exercise, would surely be ... a [great] mistake'. See also C L'Heureux-Dubé, *Two Supreme Courts: A Study in Contrast*, in M McKenna (ed), *The Canadian and American Constitutions in Comparative Perspectives* (Calgary, Calgary University Press, 1993) 163.

[102] The majority of Canadian citations concerns US Supreme Court decisions taken during the Warren and Burger Courts (1953 to 1986). See C L'Heureux-Dubé, 'The Importance of Dialogue: Globalization and the International Impact of the Rehnquist Court' (1998) 34 *Tulsa Law Journal* 15, 29: 'An informal analysis of Canadian Supreme Court decisions since 1986 revealed that the Rehnquist court was cited in fewer than one-half as many cases as the Warren Court, and in just under one-third the number of Burger Court cases'.

[103] Unlike in Argentina, where, due to the influence of the US Constitution on the 1853 Argentine Constitution, for a certain number of years, decisions of the US Supreme Court enjoyed binding authority: see JM Miller, 'The Authority of a Foreign Talisman: A Study of US Constitutional Practice as Authority in Nineteenth Century Argentina and the Argentine Elite's Leap of Faith' (1997) 46 *American University Law Review* 1483.

[104] Canada experienced an incrementalist—rather than revolutionary, as in the US—development from colony to independent sovereign State.

[105] However, as seen, the division of legislative powers is designed differently in the US and Canada: see n 50.

and belong to the same common law legal tradition of British origin that in both cases needed to be adapted to social and geographical circumstances markedly different from those in the UK. Furthermore, Canada followed the US—rather than the British—model of legal education when, in the twentieth century, it established legal education within its universities. Finally, both countries have a 'generalist' Supreme Court with jurisdiction over ordinary and constitutional legal issues.[106]

Another significant reason for frequent use of US precedents lies in the fact that, following the *Charter*'s enactment, Canada developed a system of strategic litigation. In other words, the *Charter* created new ways to further protection and advancement of fundamental rights in which judicial bodies—rather than the legislator, as in the British constitutional tradition—played an influential role, attracting interest groups looking for ways to influence public policy and employing court litigation to promote their objectives, analogous to well-established US dynamics.

Looking beyond one's own borders does not necessarily imply, however, automatic acceptance and adoption of foreign solutions. This represents probably the most striking feature of the Canadian attitude towards citation of US precedents. While there are, certainly, a few instances of endorsement of US interpretations of the *Bill of Right*'s provisions,[107] our research shows that, in the majority of cases, results achieved by US courts have not been followed.[108] The different structure of the *Charter*, especially with regard to its general limitation clause (s 1), represented a starting point for the development of a distinctively Canadian jurisprudence.[109]

The Court is extremely conscious of the risks involved in citing foreign precedents. In *Lavigne v Ontario Public Service Employees Union*,[110] Justice Wilson wrote:

> This Court has consistently stated that even although it may undoubtedly benefit from the experience of American and other courts in adjudicating constitutional issues, it is by no means bound by that experience or the jurisprudence it has generated. The uniqueness of the *Canadian Charter* flows not only from its distinctive structure if compared to the American Bill of Rights but also from the special features of the Canadian cultural, historical, social and political traditions.

---

[106] For these and additional elements, see Jackson, *Constitutional Engagement in a Transnational Era* (2009) 240ff.

[107] Eg, in *Hunter v Southam* [1984] 2 SCR 145, the SCC, in addressing the s 8 *Charter* guarantee of freedom from unreasonable search or seizure, adopted the warrant requirement set forth in *Katz v United States* 389 US 347 (1967), despite the *Charter* making no reference to such requirement. In obscenity cases, the SCC has relied extensively on US case law to develop a similar test for assessing the constitutionality of obscenity statutes: see *The Queen v Butler* [1992] 1 SCR 452. In *United Food & Commercial Workers Local 1518 v Kmart Can Ltd* [1999] 2 SCR 1083, in determining whether different standards apply in reviewing the constitutionality of leafleting and picketing bans, the SCC adopted the distinction between these two activities established in US First Amendment jurisprudence. In *Vriend v Alberta* [1998] 1 SCR 493, the SCC, in dealing with employment discrimination based on sexual orientation, cited with approval the US Supreme Court's decision in *Romer v Evans*, 517 US 620 (1996).

[108] With regard to the outcome of the cases, between 1982 and 2010, out of 268 constitutional cases with citations to US precedents, US solutions have been followed in only 15% of these cases, while being distinguished in 29% of them. The remainder of cases (56%) presents merely informative references to US precedents (neither followed, nor distinguished).

[109] In *R v Keegstra* [1990] 3 SCR 697, 740, Chief Justice Dickson, for the majority, stated: '... applying the *Charter* to the legislation challenged in this appeal reveals important differences between Canadian and American constitutional perspectives. ... Section 1 has no equivalent in the United States, a fact previously alluded to by this Court in selectively utilizing American constitutional jurisprudence'.

[110] *Lavigne v Ontario Public Service Employees Union* [1991] 2 SCR 211.

This is consistent with the view that engagement with foreign law is first and foremost an exercise in self-understanding, which leads to identification of the distinguishing elements of Canadian society. In other words, 'engagement' is a stance 'primarily concerned with the self-reflective elements of constitutional adjudication',[111] rather than a finalistic exercise in comparative reasoning within judicial decision-making. As a result, consideration of US precedents by the SCC is mainly 'aversive' or 'negative'.[112] Our research shows that the Court is willing to be receptive to foreign solutions only when they are compatible with the principles informing Canadian society and its legal system.

The Canadian *'manifesto'* of this aversive attitude was expressed in the early days of *Charter* adjudication by Justice La Forest, who maintained that judges 'should be wary of drawing too ready a parallel between constitutions born to different countries in different ages and in very different circumstances ... American jurisprudence, like the British, *must be viewed as a tool, not as a master*' (emphasis added).[113] A recent example of this stance is found in *R v Sinclair*, a 2010 case dealing with a detainee's right to counsel, where the SCC refused to adopt the guarantee established by the US Supreme Court in *Miranda v Arizona*,[114] indicating: 'We are not persuaded that the (American) Miranda rule should be transplanted in Canadian soil ... Adopting procedural protections from other jurisdictions in a piecemeal fashion risks upsetting the balance that has been struck by Canadian courts and legislatures.'[115]

For those who studied the Court's use of US jurisprudence *before* the enactment of the *Charter*, this is not surprising, and is consistent with 'a fluctuating attitude toward American jurisprudence'.[116] Probably a striking Canadian feature, the awareness of a national and constitutional uniqueness, even more present after the *Charter*'s enactment, suggests a considerate approach to foreign sources. Nowadays, on most *Charter* issues, Canadian law diverges significantly from US law, substantive rights

---

[111] Jackson, *Constitutional Engagement in a Transnational Era* (2009) 71.

[112] CL Ostberg, ME Wetstein and CR Ducat, 'Attitudes, Precedents, and Cultural Change: Explaining the Citation of Foreign Precedents by the Supreme Court of Canada' (2001) 34 *Canadian Journal of Political Science* 377.

[113] *R v Rahey* [1987] 1 SCR 588.

[114] *Miranda v Arizona*, 384 US 436 (1966).

[115] *R v Sinclair* [2010] 2 SCR 310. Other examples of this 'aversive' attitude are: *Reference re Section 94(2) of the British Columbia Motor Vehicles Act* [1985] 2 SCR 486: at issue was the meaning of s 7's 'principles of fundamental justice'; Justice Lamer (as he then was), on the basis of ss 52, 33 and 1 rejected the US distinction between substantive and procedural due process in light of 'fundamental structural differences between the two constitutions': see GV La Forest, 'The Use of International and Foreign Material in the Supreme Court of Canada' (1988) 17 *Canadian Council of International Law* 238; J Cameron, 'The Motor Vehicle Reference and the Relevance of American Doctrine in Charter Adjudication' in R Sharpe (ed), *Charter Litigation* (Toronto, Butterworths, 1987) 69. In *R v Keegstra* [1990] 3 SCR 697, the SCC upheld a statute prohibiting public hate speech directed at vulnerable groups, rejecting the rationale developed in the US First Amendment case *Beauharnais v Illinois*, 343 US 250 (1952); in *Reference re Provincial Electoral Boundaries (Sask)* [1991] 2 SCR 158 the SCC rejected the US principle of 'one man, one vote' from *Baker v Carr* (1962), to embrace a principle of 'effective representation' for the right to vote entrenched in s 3 *Charter*; in *Hill v Church of Scientology of Toronto* [1995] 2 SCR 1130, the SCC considered the consequences of the adoption of the US 'actual malice' standard, concluding that it was undesirable in Canada, due to the consequences it would have determined.

[116] Roy, 'An Empirical Survey of Foreign Jurisprudence' 135, citing Bushnell, *The Use of American Cases* 167.

having usually been interpreted in a broader fashion, before being tested in relation to section 1.

D. The Role Played by Section 1 of the *Charter*

A most important role in furthering the SCC's recourse to foreign precedents has been played by the presence of the general 'salvage' or 'limitations' clause in section 1 of the *Charter*. As an explicit balancing and limiting provision, section 1 acknowledges that even fundamental rights cannot be absolute, and mandates consideration of the people's will in a 'free and democratic society' in the process of reviewing governmental activity allegedly infringing such rights.

Determining what limitations are justified in a 'free and democratic society', however, requires some degree of comparison, since the words 'free and democratic' imply a contrast with societies that are not, and, conversely, commonality with others sharing the same features. It is clear, therefore, that such provision de facto represents 'a directive to engage in comparative exercise and research the position in other jurisdictions' and not to 'blindly [accept] the Canadian experience as the last word on how a free and democratic society ought to conduct itself.'[117] Indeed, in some scholars' view, section 1 represents something analogous to the express authorisation to cite foreign precedents codified in the Constitutions of South Africa and Malawi,[118] and determines in Canada a framework where 'comparative analysis is regarded as internal to the activity of constitutional adjudication'.[119] This view was reaffirmed in Justice Wilson's statement that 'our courts have found the experience in other "free and democratic" societies useful in determining whether means adopted in this country are the best alternative'.[120]

Our research shows that the SCC has been receptive to this invitation, making use of the experience of other free and democratic countries and citing foreign precedents not only in defining the substance of the rights at issue, but also in assessing the constitutionality of limitations.[121]

Furthermore, section 1 probably entrenches the most relevant difference between the *Charter* and the US *Bill of Rights*, one that determines much of the aversive attitude of the SCC toward US precedents. In fact, this provision mandates to the SCC a rather different hermeneutical approach to the one required by the US *Bill of*

---

[117] C L'Heureux-Dubé, 'Two Supreme Courts: A Study in Contrast' in MC McKenna (ed), *The Canadian and American Constitutions* (1993) 164; see also La Forest, 'Use of International and Foreign Material' 236.

[118] See B-O Bryde, 'The Constitutional Judge and the International Constitutionalism Dialogue' in B Markesinis and J Fedtke (eds), *Judicial Recourse to Foreign Law* (New York, Routledge, 2006) 306, where the author suggests that in the case of limitation clauses analogous to s 1 the 'text of the national constitution cannot be understood without comparative analysis'. See also C Saunders, who, comparing s 1 *Charter* to s 39 of the 1996 Constitution of South Africa, emphasises that 'a requirement of the kind in section 1 of the Charter ... anticipates reference to foreign experience': Saunders, 'Judicial Engagement with Comparative Law' (2012) 574. Vicki Jackson looks at this clause as probably requiring comparison: Jackson, *Constitutional Engagement in a Transnational Era* (2009) 73.

[119] L Weinrib, 'Constitutional Conceptions and Constitutional Comparativism' in V Jackson and M Tushnet (eds), *Defining the Field of Comparative Constitutional Law* (2002) 3–4.

[120] *Lavigne v Ontario Public Service Employees Union* [1991] 2 SCR 211, 298 (Can).

[121] Eg *Charkaoui v Canada (Citizenship and Immigration)* [2007] 1 SCR 350.

Rights, where rights are expressed in absolute terms and limitations are developed by judicial interpretation in the very process of defining the substance of rights. Section 1, conversely, allows the SCC to balance the rights and freedoms protected by the *Charter* against other values without limiting the substance of the provisions. It appears clear, therefore, that in most cases the substantive definition of rights determined in the US may appear too narrow to Canadian courts.[122]

IV. CONCLUSIONS

The attitude of the SCC towards citation of foreign case law is still in flux. Confronted with the major demands that the *Charter*'s enactment brought on the Court, the SCC resorted to the example provided by foreign precedents to develop domestic jurisprudence.

External sources, however, have never been dispositive of the outcome of a case before the Court. The SCC, through a principled approach towards citation of foreign precedents, seems to provide evidence that concerns about 'cherry picking'[123] should be, at least to some extent, reconsidered, in light of the numerous aversive citations. More precisely, the SCC shows that comparative reasoning—usually associated with a finalistic approach, aiming to emphasise analogies more than differences—can also be used aversively, in order to reassert differences with other jurisdictions and define the identity of a domestic system.[124]

If the use of comparative law and recourse to foreign precedents is not done with finalistic intents, the utilitarian component of the practice is, conversely, undeniable. When domestic jurisprudence on the interpretation of a newly-enacted document is insufficiently developed, judges resort to foreign solutions in order to foresee possible consequences for the various interpretations of the constitutional provisions theoretically available.[125] This 'dialogical interpretation' helps the Court to become more self-aware and aware of the direction that its own jurisprudence is taking.[126] Foreign precedents can also 'alert [the Court] to some of the theories about which we might want to think'.[127]

---

[122] See eg, *Ford v Attorney General of Quebec* [1988] 2 SCR 712, where the Court indicated that s 1 'permitted the Court to give a large and liberal interpretation to s. 2(b), ... leading to the inclusion of commercial expression within its ambit', something notoriously in contrast with the US Supreme Court's jurisprudence on the issue.

[123] Critics of the use of foreign precedents in constitutional adjudication argue that when judges quote foreign decisions, they would be unable to use these resources in a principled manner and would not resist 'cherry picking', ie citing only foreign decisions supporting their preferred result.

[124] A concept defined by Pierre Legrand as 'prioritization of difference': P Legrand, 'The Same and the Different' in P Legrand and R Munday (eds), *Comparative Legal Studies: Traditions and Transitions* (Cambridge, Cambridge University Press, 2003) 240ff, 292ff; de Vergottini, *Oltre il dialogo tra le Corti* (2010) 35.

[125] SI Smithey, 'A Tool, Not A Master. The Use of Foreign Case Law in Canada and South Africa' (2001) 34 *Comparative Political Studies* 1188.

[126] Choudhry, *Globalization in Search of Justification*, 836; C Saunders, 'Judicial Dialogue in Common Law Countries' in AAVV, *Renouveau du droit constitutionnel. Mélanges en l'honneur de L Favoreau* (Paris, Dalloz, 2007) 423.

[127] M Tushnet, 'The Possibilities of Comparative Constitutional Law' (1999) 108 *Yale Law Journal* 1225.

Along with reasons connected to processes of legal adjudication, citation of foreign precedents may also involve some policy elements. Indeed, in recent times, the political reasons behind citation of foreign precedents have become the subject of relevant consideration. The SCC seems to be aware of the relevant role that its jurisprudence plays on the international arena and the importance to be regarded as a progressive and outward-looking judicial body in the area of fundamental rights protection. By citing civil liberties cases from other countries extensively, Canadian judges have become part of a global debate on the extent of human rights in democratic societies. Openness towards citation of foreign precedents has also been perceived as an invitation to other courts to interact and has encouraged other jurisdictions to cite Canadian precedents in the exercise of their own adjudicatory functions.[128] This has also had an effect on constitution-drafting efforts worldwide, leading some scholars to observe that 'the Canadian Charter of Rights and Freedoms has, in recent years, become a leading alternative' to the US *Bill of Rights* as a model for constitution-making.[129]

In light of this policy component, one may wonder whether the SCC's citations of foreign precedents, in recent years, are still inspirational or have rather taken on a more cosmetic use. After all, 'judges from Canada may experience satisfaction from being regarded as committed to a cooperative transnational project of judging and human rights'.[130]

Regarding this aspect, our research seems to detail a recent trend in citation of foreign precedents. Citation of foreign precedents may be declining due to the development of significant lines of domestic precedents, but the SCC's openness to foreign precedents has not changed, now focusing mostly on cases dealing with previously unaddressed issues. While consideration of political reasons may be unavoidable, to a certain degree, the SCC appears genuinely to perceive itself as operating within a new 'worldwide rights culture'[131] implying a genuine, optimistic view of legal cosmopolitanism and a 'sincere outward-looking interest in the views of other societies'.[132]

---

[128] 'Canadian law serves as a source of inspiration for many countries around the world': A Barak, 'Foreword: A Judge on Judging: The Role of a Supreme Court in a Democracy' (2002) 116 *Harvard Law Review* 19, 114. Recent studies detailed the influence of the SCC's decisions on other jurisdictions' high courts: T Groppi, 'A User-friendly Court. The Influence of Supreme Court of Canada Decisions Since 1982 on Court Decisions in Other Liberal Democracies' (2007) 36 *Supreme Court Law Review* 337.

[129] S Choudhry, 'Globalization in Search of Justification' 822; Anne-Marie Slaughter suggests that Canada and South Africa are 'looking around the world and canvassing the opinions of their fellow constitutional courts, and each is disproportionally influential as a result', A-M Slaughter, 'A Brave New Judicial World' in M Ignatieff (ed), *American Exceptionalism and Human Rights* (Princeton, Princeton University Press, 2005) 289. See also DS Law, M Versteeg, 'The Declining Influence of the United States Constitution' (2012) 87 *New York University Law Review* 762.

[130] Jackson, *Constitutional Engagement in a Transnational Era* (2009) 240.

[131] Remarks of Chief Justice McLachlin on 'The Use of Foreign Law' delivered at the 104th ASIL's Annual Meeting held from 24–27 April 2010 in Washington, DC, USA. Materials available at: www.fora.tv.

[132] G La Forest, 'The Use of American Precedents in Canadian Courts' (1994) 46 *Maine Law Review* 211.

3

India: A 'Critical' Use of Foreign Precedents in Constitutional Adjudication

VALENTINA RITA SCOTTI*

TABLE OF CONTENTS

I. Introduction 69
II. The Union of India and its Supreme Court 70
   A. The General Context: A Stratified Legal Culture and the Influence
      of the British Colonisation 70
   B. The Independent Indian Constitution and Constitutional Borrowing 73
   C. The Supreme Court: Composition and Functioning 77
   D. A Brief Periodisation of the Activism of the Supreme Court 80
III. Case-Study on the Use of Foreign Precedents by the Supreme Court
    of India in its Constitutional Adjudication 84
   A. The Methodology of the Research 84
   B. The Use of Foreign Precedents 85
IV. Conclusion 95

I. INTRODUCTION

A TIRELESS INTERPRETER of a long and detailed Constitution, which combines ideas coming from other constitutional paths and elements that are an inner part of Indian legal culture, the Supreme Court of India has led the country into the so-called world constitutionalism, taking part in transjudicial communication and constitutional borrowing among political and judicial bodies.[1] The case of India can be considered an 'explicator for the broader

---

* PhD in Comparative Public Law at the University of Siena; Research Fellow in Comparative Public Law at the LUISS 'Guido Carli' University of Rome.
[1] On this topic see B Ackerman, 'The Rise of World Constitutionalism' (1997) 83 *Virginia Law Review* 771 ff, AM Slaughter, 'A Typology of Transjudicial Communication' (1994) 29 *University of Richmond Law Review* 99 ff, and Idem, 'Judicial Globalization' (2000) 40 *Virginia Journal of International Law* 1103 ff. Scholars also debate the justifications for this phenomenon: see M Adler, 'Can Constitutional Borrowing be Justified?' (1998) 1 *University of Pennsylvania Journal of Constitutional Law* 350 ff, S Choudhry, 'Globalisation in Search of Justification: Toward a Theory of Comparative Constitutional Interpretation' (1999) 74 *Indiana Law Journal* 819 ff. It cannot be ignored that in the debate raised in the USA some academics support a position definitively contrary to the use of foreign precedents, ibid,

debate'[2] because of its peculiarities concerning the characteristics of the population and the stratification of subsequent legal cultures. Since its independence under the guide of Mahatma Gandhi in 1947, India felt the influence of many external actors and in its constitutional adjudication the Supreme Court often took into account British precedents, soon after joined by American ones and then the supranational Courts' decisions were added. However, the Supreme Court has never been subservient but has adopted a critical approach which often leads to a decision completely different from those of the foreign cases considered.

With the aim of exploring the attitude of the Supreme Court of India to relying on foreign precedents, this essay is divided into two sections. The first one proposes an overview of the Indian legal system, focusing on some aspects of constitutional history and on the content of the Constitution. Furthermore, this section analyses the composition, role and functioning of the Supreme Court as well as the main phases of its activities, as a preface to the empirical research on its use of foreign precedents in constitutional adjudication, which is analysed in the second part. Specifically, the use of foreign precedents is discussed, with the support of graphs and using as explanatory examples some of the prominent decisions the Court issued taking into account foreign precedents.

II. THE UNION OF INDIA AND ITS SUPREME COURT

A. The General Context: A Stratified Legal Culture and the Influence of the British Colonisation

India has more than 5,000 years of history, during which different legal systems overlapped and mixed up. The Hindu period was followed by the Muslim one and then by the British colonisation.

It is generally considered that only the last one left a mark on Indian legal culture, while it must be recognised that the previous legal systems also influenced the current one. The first stage of this pyramidal legal system is composed of the Vedic culture of the Hindu period, where philosophical thinking involved rational laws shaping not only religious beliefs but also institutions and society. As a matter of fact, the four Vedas[3] posed an advanced conception of the State and of some individual and collective rights and duties. However, the basis of this system was the moral constraint which reconnected obedience to the sanctity attached to the source of the laws and not to the sanctions that temporal powers are entitled to

---

R Posner, 'No Thanks, We Already Have Our Own Laws' (2004) 32 *Legal Affairs* 40 ff, and A Scalia, 'Commentary' (1996) 40 *St Louis Law Journal* 1119 ff. Regarding the ideas of Justice Scalia on this topic see also his opinion in *Lawrence v Texas*, 539 US 558 (2003) 558–98 or the debate between Justice Scalia and Justice Breyer in *Miranda vs Arizona*, 384 US 436 (1996).

[2] This is the theory, shared by the author of this essay, elaborated in A Smith, 'Making Itself at Home: Understanding Foreign Law in Domestic Jurisprudence: The Indian Case' (2006) 24 *Berkeley Journal of International Law* 218 ff.

[3] The Vedas are the four canonic texts of the Hindus' religious tradition.

issue.[4] In this context, customary laws also assumed great importance, particularly in the definition of the rules that governed the caste system, a rigid social scheme where each group was composed only of people born into it. It is noteworthy that the Brahmins, the upper caste, were at the same time priests and judges, assisting the King in his function of the administration of justice in the King's Court. Even though justice was always administered in the King's name, some local councils, the so-called *Kulani*, were instituted in villages. They represent the very first ancestors of the *panchayats*, the first level of Courts in modern India.

Since 1206 AD, the Vedic legal culture was joined by the Muslim judicial system. The consolidation of the Sultanate of Delhi, in fact, imposed the Muslim conception that the Quran is the only source of law, and its interpretation, the *shariat*, had to rule every aspect of life.

In this period we find the consolidation of administrative units for land governance, which also represents the base for the judicial system. For example, the *Munsif*, a title still used nowadays, was introduced as a civil judge as well as the practice, in force also during the British Raj, of transferring judicial officers every two or three years.

The legal culture of the Muslim period survived, *mutatis mutandis*, during the Mughal Empire, while it was deeply questioned at the beginning of the British period.

At the origins of the legal system that this colonisation period introduced in India, there were the Charters granted in 1600 and in 1609, by Elizabeth I and James I respectively, to the East India Company (Company), whose powers were enlarged by the 1661 Charter. It allowed the Company to administer justice in its settlements, not only to English people but to every person living in them, in civil or criminal cases, according to British laws. In this way the Company was no more a simple trading agent but became the territorial power which started the transplant of British law into India. This period saw the cohabitation of Mughal laws, mainly based on personal statutes according to which each people had to be judged considering its religious belief, and English laws, applied in English settlements and, because of a specific *firman* (charter) of the Emperor, to every Englishman. The same hybrid application of the laws characterised the administration of justice in the Presidency Towns of Madras, Calcutta and Bombay, which represented the first centres of British power.

This situation lasted until 1683, when Charles II granted a Charter authorising the Company to establish Courts for the application of the British laws in mercantile and maritime cases. These Courts introduced in India the rules of equity and good conscience.[5] However the authority of these Courts emanated from the Company, and it was only with the 1726 Charter of George I that the administration of justice consistently evolved, as the Charter posed all the constituted Courts under the control of the British Crown. Thus, criminal and civil Courts took well defined legal bases and their decisions could be appealed to the Privy Council in England: this was the first step that firmly linked the British legal system and the Indian

---

[4] JCM Vincent, 'Legal Culture and Legal Transplant. The Evolution of the Indian Legal System' 2010 *Reports to the XVIII International Congress of Comparative Law* 4–5, www.isaidat.di.unito.it.
[5] See MP Jain, *Outlines of India Legal and Constitutional History* (Bombay, Tripathi, 2010).

one. Principles of British laws started to be applied in disputes decided by Courts, although in cases concerning inheritances, marriages, castes, debts and contracts Quranic laws continued to be applied for Muslims while Hindus were submitted to their customary laws, as affirmed by the Act of 1781 and also by the Privy Council in the case of *Tagore v Tagore*.[6]

It could be affirmed that during the British period the peculiarities of the Indian legal system in force before the colonisation were deeply understood, as demonstrated by the distinction between British laws approved before and after 1726. For the first group, Courts were entitled to evaluate if they could fit them with local circumstances in order to decide whether to apply them or not, while for the second group, the laws passed after 1726, it was the British Parliament which declared them applicable or not to India. However for the other groups inhabiting the British settlements in India, the aforementioned Act of 1781 did not provide for any reserve, affirming that they were subject to British laws. This is demonstrated, for example, by the decision of the Calcutta Supreme Court in the case of *JS Jebb v Lefevere and Caroline*.[7]

In order to consider how much the British colonisation influenced the legal system of India, one must also make reference to the effort of the Privy Council to define clearly the content of Hindu and Muslim laws. As a matter of fact, if those laws had to be respectively applied to groups of believers, their contents had to be clarified and understood. In this way Hindu law was defined thanks to a case law developed following some fixed principles. First of all the Privy Council referred directly to the literature and, in case of conflict between the ancient writers and the commentators, the latter were preferred. Secondly, the Privy Council tried to make a distinction between mandatory rules and moral rules, giving effect only to the former, using in this effort a reference to customary rules. In a way, the Privy Council recognised a more relevant role for the living rules of Hindu society and finally gave a place of honour to customs in the administration of justice.[8] Similarly, the Privy Council ascertained the Muslim law from ancient sources trying at the same time to introduce notions derived from English notions of equity and law.

On this topic, it would be relevant to point out that, notwithstanding the application of their religious rules to Hindus and Muslims, the introduction of British law into the Indian legal system also meant the progressive recognition among India's Provinces of the maxim 'justice, equity and good conscience' that the Privy Council considered the ultimate test for all provincial Courts in India.[9]

So the elements of the maxim and the customs were both considered as sources for case adjudication until the introduction of the High Courts in 1862. As they were composed of judges trained in British law, they began to base their decisions on it more than on any other source. However, the Privy Council, in its role of ultimate Court of appeal for India, continued to respect the peculiar circumstances of the

---

[6] *Tagore v Tagore* (IA Supp 70, 1872).
[7] *JS Jebb v Lefevere and Caroline* (Ind Dec, OS, 1, 92).
[8] Vincent, Legal Culture, 59.
[9] See *Muhammad Raza v Abbas Bandi* (59 IA 245).

colonised country. In *Srinath Roy v Dinanbandhu Sen*,[10] for example, it affirmed that the application of rules established in one country to another one with vastly different historical, geographical and social circumstances has to take into account all these differences and to provide for an adaptation.

Through these evolutions, principles and doctrines of British law became deeply rooted in India's legal system, in a way that, as we will soon see, is still evident in the decisions of the Supreme Court and in the codification of principles derived from the customs of religious groups.

It is pertinent to highlight, finally, that India's system is also influenced by European continental legal systems, and particularly by the French civil code that is applied in cases concerning the personal status of Renocants, Indian Christians and French nationals domiciled in Pondicherry.

In conclusion, the ethnic, cultural and religious mosaic that is India is reflected in the legal system, which is evidently a kaleidoscope of laws, legal systems and institutions indigenous or imported thanks to centuries of dialogues and confrontations with the populations that progressively inhabited the country.

B. The Independent Indian Constitution and Constitutional Borrowing

In order to better understand the role of the Supreme Court and its attitude towards foreign precedents in constitutional adjudication, it is noteworthy to consider not only the legal system in force before independence but also, and obviously, the one created by the 1950 Constitution.

As a matter of fact, the British Raj and its laws, in particular the 1935 Government of India Act, represent the juridical framework for the Constitution of the Union of India, but it is possible to highlight several other influences of foreign constitutionalism, briefly summarised in Figure 1. Thus, constitutional borrowing can be assumed to be one of the reasons for the choice of specific foreign precedents by the Supreme Court in its constitutional adjudication.

In its current formulation, the Constitution of India consists of a Preamble, 395 Articles, 22 Parts, and 12 Schedules. For its content, this Constitution is one of the longest in the world, characterised by a clear programmatic structure aiming to found, as the Preamble says, a society based on justice, freedom, equality, fraternity and a socialist and secular republic.[11]

i. The Influence of the British Model

From the organisation of powers we can see the influence of foreign models, but also the deep reflection of the framing fathers on the topic. In fact, they rejected the axiom that a federal State must have a presidential government and decided to

---

[10] *Srinath Roy v Dinanbandhu Sen* (ILR 42 Calc 1915).
[11] Regarding the reference to a 'socialist' State, it is important to underline that it does not aim to found a legal order based on socialist doctrine, but simply to stress the character of a State based on social justice.

From UK	— Parliamentary Type of Government — Cabinet System of Ministers — Bicameral Parliament — Lower House more powerful — Council of Ministers responsible to Lower House
From US	— Written Constitution — Executive head of State known as President and his being the Supreme Commander of the Armed Forces — Vice-President as the *ex-officio* Chairman of Rajya Sabha — Bill of Rights — Supreme Court — Provision of States — Independence of Judiciary and judicial review — Preamble — Removal of Supreme court and High court judges
From USSR	— Fundamental Duties — Five Year Plan
From Australia	— Concurrent List — Language of the preamble — Provision regarding trade, commerce and intercourse
From Japan	— Law on which the Supreme Court function
From Weimar Constitution of Germany	— Suspension of Fundamental Rights during the emergency
From Canada	— Scheme of federation with a strong centre — Distribution of powers between the centre and the states and placing residuary powers with the centre
From Ireland	— Concept of Directive Principles of States Policy — Method of election of President — Nomination of members in the *Rajya Sabha* by the President

Source: www.facts-about-india.com

Figure 1: Constitutional Influences on the Constitution of India

create a parliamentary federation based on the Westminster model. Following the model, the legislative power, affirming *mutatis mutandis* the principle of the King in Parliament, is composed of the President of the Union, the House of People (*Lok Sabha*) and the Council of the States (*Rajya Sabha*). Also the executive is structured as in the British model, being based on a cabinet system where the formal guide is attributed to the President of Union but the Prime Minister, who is usually the leader of the party that wins the election, exercises the charge; in his duties, he is supported by the Cabinet and by the Council of Ministers.

ii. The US Model: Considered but Tempered

Though the organisation of powers is strictly related to the Westminster model, there are also huge references to the American model,[12] as it is evident looking at the organisation of the judiciary and at the prevision of a procedure of judicial review. The Constitution has provided for a single integrated system of Courts to administer both Union and State laws. At the apex of the whole judicial system is the Supreme Court of India, below which there are the High Courts of each State or group of States and a hierarchy of Subordinate Courts. Each State is divided into judicial districts which have their own District and Sessions Judge; this is the highest judicial authority in a district and the principal civil Court of original jurisdiction, able to try all offences, including those punishable with death. Below, there are Courts of civil jurisdiction, known in different States as *Munsifs*, civil judges, sub-judges. Similarly, the criminal judiciary comprises the Chief Judicial Magistrates and Judicial Magistrates of First and Second Class. In some States *Panchayats* function under various names, like *Nyaya Panchayat, Panchayat Adalat, Gram Kachheri,* etc, and decide civil and criminal disputes of a local nature.

Notwithstanding the influence of the US model on the structure of justice administration, the definition of the sources of law takes into account India's peculiarities: even if the Constitution provides for a homogeneous organisation of the legal system, the local Hindu, Muslim or tribal juridical experiences derived from the said hegemonic waves continue to be fundamental in the adjudication of cases concerning private law, because local customs and conventions, which are not against statute, morality, etc, are, to a limited extent, recognised and taken into account by Courts while administering justice.

The reasoned and critical reference to the US model is evident in two other cases.

A first example can be found in the federal structure defined in Part XI of the Constitution on 'Relations between the Union and the States'. The choice of a federal system was due to the wish to keep the country together through the attribution of specific powers to local authorities. However, the framers of the Constitution of India decided on a federalism based on the cooperative principle but characterised by strong centripetal trends, more similar to the Canadian example. The idea[13] was to preserve unity despite the different ethnic, linguistic and religious affiliations of the population in an attempt to avoid an excessive fragmentation of the centres of decision-making, as would have happened if they had given space to any specific ethno-cultural realities in the area.[14] For these reasons, the Seventh Schedule affirms that the Indian Parliament legislates on the 97 matters enumerated in the Union List, while State Legislatures are competent to make laws on the 66 matters enumerated

---

[12] AP Blaustein, 'Influence of the United States Constitution Abroad' (1987) 12 *Oklahoma City University Law Review* 456.

[13] See K Navlani, 'National Integration and Dynamics of Coalition and Federalism in India' (2006) 67 *The Indian Journal of Political Science* 119–39.

[14] About the relation between federalism and regionalism in India, see U Baxi, A Jacob and T Singh, *Reconstructing the Republic* (New Delhi, Har-Anand Publications, 1999) 151–52, which underlines how the federal structure helps India to maintain national unity.

in the State List and both the Union and the States have power to legislate on the 47 matters enumerated in the Concurrent List.

The residual clause is the very reason for the centripetal trends, because it attributes to Parliament the power to make laws on matters not included in the State List or the Concurrent List; in the event of conflicts, laws passed by Parliament prevail over laws made by State Legislatures. Moreover, the centripetal trends derive from the prevalence of the central level in issues concerning the budget or, in general, the economy of the Union as well as by the power of the President of the Union to revoke, when the constitutional institutions of a member State cannot work or when there are serious threats to public security, the State government and to use its executive power until the end of the emergency.[15]

Another outstanding example of the influence of US constitutionalism, tempered by the wish to preserve India's own characteristics, is the Bill of Rights. Although strongly inspired by the US one, the Bill of Rights entailed in the Constitution of India shows the interesting and unusual character of this Charter, that is the reference to the protection of disadvantaged people and the acknowledgment of the relevant role of groups and communities inside Indian society. The Bill of Rights, included in Part III of the Constitution, provides not only for the general enumeration of the protected rights, but also a list of remedies to protect them. After the 1976 Amendment, the set of fundamental rights was divided into six parts: the right to equality, rights of freedom, rights against exploitation of the person, rights to religious freedom, cultural rights and education and, finally, the right to constitutional protection.[16]

iii. The Defeat of Discrimination: The Attention Paid to the Irish Constitution and the 1948 UN Declaration

It cannot be ignored that India and Ireland share a long history of strong British domination which moved many Indian nationalists to look at the Irish ones as examples. In the constitutional framing, the influence of this dialogue is evident in Part IV of the Indian Charter, which contains some dispositions called 'Directive Principles of State Policy', clearly recalling the 'Directive Principles of Social Policy' listed in Article 45 of the Irish Constitution.

In theory, these principles are non-justiciable but are used to orient legislative and executive actions, even if the introduction of public interest litigation in some ways seems to circumvent this ban. Through the prevision of those principles, the Constitution of India provides for the protection of almost all the basic rights listed in the 1948 UN Universal Declaration of Human Rights (UN Declaration), whose influence on the constitutional framing is evident since the Preamble.

The attention given to the principles stated in the UN Declaration appears also in the attention paid to equality in the Constitution of India. In Article 14, it specifies both the profiles of formal equality (equality before the law) and of substantial

---

[15] For more information about the cooperative federalism in India, see C Pal, *Centre-State Relations and Cooperative Federalism* (New Delhi, Deep&Deep, 1983) ch 4.

[16] For a general overview of the protection of human rights in India, see S Deshta and P Singh, *Human Rights in India: Enforcement, Protection and Implementation*, Allahabad Law Agency, 2004. See also B Shiva Rao, *The Framing of India's Constitution* (Bombay, Tripathi, 1968).

equality (equal protection of the law), stressing the absolute prohibition on negative discrimination, in contrast with the broad possibility of positive discrimination in favour of certain disadvantaged groups.[17] It is noteworthy that even though some principles were derived from foreign Constitutions, the Indian constitutional framers tailored the rules to the country's own specificities. For example, Article 15 indicates that the non-discrimination principle must be applied with particular reference to free access to shops, restaurants, hotels and entertainment venues open to the public, and to the use of public facilities (roads, wells, etc). The clear intention was to ban any discriminatory practices, including those related to the differences between castes, which have marked the history of India for centuries. On these bases, the Union of India, following the perspicuous example of the Constituent Assembly which elected as its President the 'untouchable' Ambedkar,[18] adopted policies supporting well-defined social groups traditionally affected by important discrimination. Similarly, the aim of reforming those elements of the tradition which led to important discrimination is also evident in Article 23, which prohibits trafficking in human beings (*begar*) and all the forms of forced labour imposed according to the *zemindary* system, a peculiar kind of agricultural organisation.[19] The following Article 24 adds that 'No child below the age of fourteen years shall be employed to work in any factory or mine or engaged in any other hazardous employment'. It is evident how these sections have a high symbolic value but also define important prohibitions to ensure effective protection in the Courts as well as a constitutional basis for some laws in defence of disadvantaged groups, such as the 1956 Law on immoral trafficking in women and girls.[20] Finally, Articles 29 and 30 affirm, together with the rights of minorities to preserve their languages, scripts or cultures also through the establishment of educational institutions, that 'No citizen shall be denied admission into any educational institution maintained by the State or receiving aid out of State funds on grounds only of religion, race, caste, language or any of them'.

C. The Supreme Court: Composition and Functioning

The Supreme Court of India came into being on 28 January 1950. Originally, it was composed of a Chief Justice and seven judges who sat together, but, as the workload increased and cases began to accumulate, the Indian Parliament increased

---

[17] On this topic, see AK Vakil, *Reservation Policy and Scheduled Castes in India* (New Delhi, APH Publishing, 1985) 22.

[18] Untouchability means the social exclusion of an individual because of specific reasons that, in the Indian case, merely relate to the caste into which an individual is born. About the role that Ambedkar had on the definition of a new status for untouchables in the 1949 Constitution, see C Jaffrelot, *Dr Ambedkar and Untouchability: Analyzing and Fighting Caste* (London, C Hurst & Co Publishers, 2005).

[19] For more information about this land tenure system and attempted land reforms in India, see PK Agrawal, *Land Reforms in India: Constitutional and Legal Approach (with Special Reference to Uttar Pradesh)* (Springfield, MD Publications, 1993) chs 1–3; RS Gae, 'Land Law in India: With Special Reference to the Constitution' (1973) 22 *International and Comparative Law Quarterly* 312–28.

[20] See SA Jilani Syed, *Affirmative Actions to Curb Sale and Trafficking of Girls* in TSN Sastry (ed), *India and Human Rights: Reflections* (New Delhi, Concept Publishing Company, 2005) 189–243.

the number of judges according to Article 124[21] and they started sitting in smaller benches of two or three, coming together in larger benches of five or more only when required to do so or to settle a difference of opinion or a controversy. A bench of five or more judges is required for constitutional cases. Members entitled to hear constitutional cases are chosen by the Chief Justice of the Court.[22]

At the present time, the Court comprises a Chief Justice and 25 judges appointed by the President of the Union among those citizens of India which have been, for at least five years, a judge of a High Court or of two or more of such Courts in succession, or an advocate of a High Court or of two or more of such Courts in succession for at least 10 years or that are, in the opinion of the President, a distinguished jurist; provisions exist for the appointment of a judge of a High Court as an *ad hoc* judge of the Supreme Court and for retired judges of the Supreme Court or High Courts to sit and act as judges of those Courts. Supreme Court judges retire when they reach the age of 65.

The Constitution ensures the independence and the impartiality of Supreme Court judges in various ways. They cannot be removed from office except by an order of the President passed after a vote with a specific majority in each House of Parliament on the ground of proved misbehaviour or incapacity. Moreover, a person who has been a judge of the Supreme Court is debarred from practising in any Court or authority in India.

According to the 1966 Supreme Court Rules, the proceedings of the Supreme Court are conducted only in English.

As for its jurisdiction, the Court has original, advisory and appellate jurisdiction.[23] Its exclusive original jurisdiction extends to any dispute between the Government of India and one or more States or between the Government of India and any State or States on one side and one or more States on the other or between two or more States, if and in so far as the dispute involves any question—whether of law or of fact—on which the existence or extent of a legal right depends. In addition, Article 32 of the Constitution gives an extensive original jurisdiction to the Supreme Court with regard to the enforcement of Fundamental Rights.

It is empowered to issue directions, orders or writs, including writs in the nature of *habeas corpus*, *mandamus*, prohibition, *quo warranto* and *certiorari* to enforce them. The Supreme Court has the power to direct or transfer any civil or criminal case from one State High Court to another State High Court or from a Subordinate Court to a State High Court; it may also withdraw a case or cases pending before a High Court or High Courts and dispose of all such cases itself. Under the

---

[21] Accordingly to art 124 of the Constitution, the Parliament is entitled to pass laws to increase the number of judges; specifically, they were increased from eight in 1950 to 11 in 1956, 14 in 1960, 18 in 1978 and 26 in 1986. On this point, see SK Verma and K Kusum, *Fifty Years of the Supreme Court of India: Its Grasp and Reach* (Oxford, Oxford University Press, 2000).

[22] It is interesting to underline that there is not a clear definition of a constitutional case, and it is the Chief Justice who decides if this label fits a specific case and allocates it to the constitutional bench. Generally, these cases concern the interpretation of the Constitution and all matters related to substantial questions of law. Only questions concerning the special advisory jurisdiction to the President of India (art 143) must be allocated to the constitutional bench.

[23] See SR Sharma, *The Supreme Court in the Indian Constitution* (Kolkata, SC Sarkar, 1972) vol 1, ch 3.

1996 Arbitration and Conciliation Act, international commercial arbitration can also be initiated in the Supreme Court.

The Supreme Court has special advisory jurisdiction in matters which may specifically be referred to it by the President of the Union under Article 143 of the Constitution.

The appellate jurisdiction of the Supreme Court can be invoked in respect of any judgment, decree or final order of a High Court, in both civil and criminal cases, involving substantial questions of law as to the interpretation of the Constitution.[24] Appeals also lie to the Supreme Court in civil matters if the High Court concerned certifies that the case involves a substantial question of law of general importance and that the said question needs to be decided by the Supreme Court. In criminal cases, an appeal lies to the Supreme Court if a High Court has sentenced an accused to death or to imprisonment for life or for a period of not less than 10 years or has certified that the case is fit for an appeal to the Supreme Court; Parliament is authorised to confer on the Supreme Court any further powers to hear appeals from any judgment, final order or sentence in a criminal proceeding of a High Court. Finally, the Supreme Court has a very wide appellate jurisdiction over all Courts and Tribunals in India in as much as it may, in its discretion, grant special leave to appeal under Article 136 of the Constitution from any judgment, decree, determination, sentence or order in any cause or matter passed or made by any Court or Tribunal in the territory of India.

People may also directly appeal to the Court through public interest litigation, which allows any individual or group of persons either to file a writ petition at the Filing Counter of the Court or to address a letter to the Chief Justice of India highlighting a question of public importance thereby invoking this jurisdiction. In this kind of action the petitioner can appeal to the Court not only in respect of the violation of fundamental rights, but also for any violation of those rights which derives from an extensive interpretation of the duties of the authorities listed in Part IV of the Constitution. Concerning public interest litigation, finally, it must be said that it is the principal vehicle which allows poor people to access the Courts and find remedies. In evolving this instrument, the Supreme Court diluted the common law requirements, such as *locus standi*, introduced innovative remedies, such as *continuing mandamus* to executive agencies, and relied on the practices which evolved through class action lawsuits in the USA.[25]

It could be interesting to underline that, in order to support specific disadvantaged people, the Supreme Court Legal Aid Committee provides for financial aid,[26] while, to facilitate those petitioners who are in jail or those involved in any

---

[24] See arts 132(1), 133(1) and 134 of the Constitution.

[25] S Meer, 'Litigating Fundamental Rights. Rights Litigation and Social Action Litigation in India: A Lesson for South Africa' (1993) 9 *South African Journal on Human Rights*, 358–72. See also U Baxi, *Taking Human Suffering Seriously: Social Action Litigation Before the Supreme Court of India* in N Tiruchelvan and R Coomaraswamy (eds), *The Role of the Judiciary in Plural Societies* (New York, St Martin's Press, 1987). Finally, on the introduction of Public Interest Litigation in India, with some specific references also to the attitude of the Supreme Court toward foreign precedents in these adjudications, see A Thiruvengadam, 'In Pursuit of "the Common Illumination of Our House": Trans-Judicial Influence and the Origins of PIL in South Asia' (2008) 2 *Indian Journal of Constitutional Law* 67 ff.

[26] On this topic see S Sivakumar, 'Access to Justice: Some Innovative Experiments in India' (2003) 22 *Windsor Year Book of Access to Justice* 239–47.

criminal matters, it is possible to appoint an advocate as amicus curiae; the Court may appoint *amici curiae* also in civil matters if it thinks it is necessary in case of an unrepresented party or in any matter of general public interest.

D. A Brief Periodisation of the Activism of the Supreme Court

The activity of the Supreme Court was deeply influenced by the history of the country and by the attempts of the executive power to strengthen its position at the expense of other institutions, first of all the Supreme Court. Thus, in the first two decades after independence (1950–73) the Court affirmed itself as the guardian of the Constitution and then (1974–77) was constricted to be subservient to the executive after some constitutional amendment and forced election of judges that altered its composition and its ability to resist the authoritarian government during the emergency period. After a brief period of obedience, the balance of power was restored and the Court started to show a strong, but often theoretical, activism.

At the origins of the 'battle' between India's executive and judiciary power there was a strongly-felt perception by the government of Jawaharlal Nehru that the judiciary was not able to meet society's need for a social revolution. In fact, the Government passed a number of laws that, once under the control of constitutionality, obliged the Court to recognise the power of Parliament to amend the Constitution but to affirm the unreviewability of the constitutional provisions concerning fundamental rights. The most important decision on this topic, which will be discussed in the second part, was *Golak Nath v State of Punjab*,[27] held in 1967. After the general election of 1971 the new Prime Minister Indira Gandhi was made to approve by Parliament some changes to the Constitution which clipped the judiciary's wings, overruled *Golak Nath* and started a new programme of nationalisation and economic reform accompanied by vigorous attacks of judges.[28] At this point the Court issued the *Kesavananda Bharati v State of Kerala*[29] decision, which affirmed that even if Parliament's power of constitutional amendment was extensive, any attempt to alter the 'basic structure of the Constitution'[30] would be impermissible.

The reaction which followed *Kesavananda* opened the second period. A few days after the judgment was delivered, the Government announced its decision to

---

[27] *Golak Nath v State of Punjab*, 1967 2 SCR 762.

[28] About the controversial relationship between the Court and Prime Minister Gandhi, see R Chandrasekhara, *Mrs Indira Gandhi and India's Constitutional Structure. An Era of Erosion* in YK Malik, *India: The Years of Indira Gandhi* (Leiden, Brill, 1988) 22–41.

[29] *Kesavananda Bharati v State of Kerala* (1973) 4 SCC 225.

[30] Foreshadowed in the *Golak Nath* case, the content of the 'basic structure of the Constitution' was explained in the *Kesavananda* case. It is composed of: supremacy of the Constitution; republican and democratic form of government; secular character of the Constitution; separation of powers between legislative, executive and judicial; federal character of the Constitution. Although this was the definition contained in the leading case, the Court added or removed elements to the content of the 'basic structure' in several later cases and even now a certain degree of ambiguity is still evident. For a more specific analysis of the 'basic structure' of the Constitution of India, see PB Mehta, *The Inner Conflict of Constitutionalism. Judicial Review and the 'Basic Structure'* in Z Hasan, E Sridharan and R Sudarshan (eds), *India's Living Constitution: Ideas, Practices, Controversies* (London, Anthem Press, 2005) 179–206.

pass over three of the most senior judges for the office of Chief Justice of India, contravening the long-standing and unbroken convention that appointments to the chief justiceships would be based on seniority; the reason of the Government was that it needed a judiciary committed to the principles of social justice. In the same period the Prime Minister decided to advise the President of India to declare a state of nationwide emergency on the ground of 'internal disturbance'. Emblematic of this period was the Supreme Court's judgment in *Additional District Magistrate, Jabalpur v Shiv Kant Shuka*,[31] best known as the *Habeas Corpus* case. In a situation of strong limitations on fundamental rights, nine High Courts held that anyone detained against his will could approach the Courts to have the detention examined for due compliance with the law and for absence of mala fides. The Gandhi Government appealed the decision to the Supreme Court, which reversed the decision and held that during the period in which the presidential order suspending the right to appeal to the Courts for enforcement of fundamental rights was in force, anyone could apply for a writ of *habeas corpus*. In 1976 Justice Ray, continuing the deferential attitude towards the regime, convened a special 13-judge bench in order to reconsider the basic structure doctrine; the bench was dissolved as unilaterally as it was created by Justice Ray after two days of activity.

With the end of the emergency, the Government tried to restore democratic freedoms and the rule of law; the Supreme Court also followed this trend and began to support the protection and the promotion of fundamental rights and rule of law values through an expansive interpretation of the constitutional provisions and the encouragement of public interest litigation.

Even if the commitment of the Court to the protection of fundamental rights cannot be denied, particularly concerning its activism in the consolidation of poor people's rights and for its affirmation of a stable procedure for public interest litigation, it cannot be ignored that the activism may be considered just theoretical because of the incapacity of the Court to deliver speedy justice aggravated by the general perception that an appeal to the Supreme Court is the most effective way to react to unresponsive and corrupt public bodies. This has inevitably led to the judicialisation of a large number of issues normally discussed through administrative channels or procedures.

i. The Supreme Court and the Doctrine of Precedent

As we saw in the preceding paragraphs, India's legal system was deeply influenced by the English one, from whom it also derived the doctrine of precedent.

Section 212 of the 1935 Government of India Act, which confirmed the Privy Council as the supreme judicial authority, stated that laws laid down by a federal Court and any judgment of the Privy Council were binding on all Courts of the British Raj.[32]

---

[31] *Additional District Magistrate, Jabalpur v Shiv Kant Shuka* (1976) 2 SCC 521.
[32] About the role of the Privy Council in India, it could be of some interest to see JP Eddy, 'India and the Privy Council: The Last Appeal' (1950) 66 *Law Quarterly Review* 206–15.

After independence, the same attributes were transferred to the Supreme Court's judgments and so its decisions became binding on all the other Courts (Article 141). Although the Supreme Court is not bound by its own decisions, nor by those issued by Privy Council, the English theory of precedent seemed to inform judges' education. In reality, the compliance with this theory is inspired more by the American doctrine than the original British one, as it accepted that the doctrine of precedent is useful for maintaining the continuity of the law,[33] but can be overcome by the juridical *escamotages* of overruling and distinguishing.

Particularly, in order to maintain the continuity of the law, the Supreme Court affirmed[34] that overruling must be used very carefully and sparingly, although it overruled itself very often. Moreover, when similar questions were decided by different benches, this made some authors think that 'in India the authority of any case may depend on the manner in which a particular bench is instituted'.[35] On the same point we can add that, even if the Court did not follow strictly the *stare decisis* principle, it is very severe in reproving judges of lower Courts which decide to step out of the line of precedents.[36] For instance, in the *Kansara* case[37] the Court interpreted Article 141 of the Constitution in a way that ensured respect for the hierarchical structure of precedent and that confirmed the judicial convention that bound lower Courts to higher Courts' decisions. The binding authority of precedent is excluded in just two cases: when a decision passes *sub silentio*[38] or *per incuriam*.[39]

However, in the absence of a clear statement of Article 141, the discussion arises about the bindingness of the Supreme Court's *obiter dicta*, because, even if judges recognise the role of interpretative authority to the Supreme Court,[40] it must be clarified to what part of the judgment this role can be applied. The Court clarified the question in *DG Viswanath v Chief Secretary of the Government of Mysore*,[41] affirming that though not binding as precedents, the Supreme Court's *obiter dicta* were worthy of respect; furthermore, in *Amritsar v Hazara Singh*, it affirmed that

---

[33] See *Keshava Mills v IT Commissioner*, AIR 1965 SC 1636.

[34] See *Bengal Immunity co v Bihar*, AIR 1955 SC 661.

[35] R Dhavan, *The Supreme Court of India. A Socio-Legal Critique* (Bombay, Tripathi, 1977) 41. As examples of this attitude of the Court it is possible to quote the cases *Maharashtra v HN Rao* (AIR 1970 SC 1157) and *RC Cooper v Union of India* (AIR 1970 SC 564), concerning arts 19 and 31(3) of the Constitution. In both cases the judgment was delivered by Shah Justice, but in *Maharashtra* he respected the previous judgment issued in *Sitabati v WB* (AIR 1967 SC 945), while in *RC Cooper*, rendered by a larger bench, he overruled and distinguished the *Sitabati* case as quickly as possible.

[36] *Jai Kuer v Sher Singh*, AIR 1960 SC 1118.

[37] *Kansara Tribhovandas Jamnadas v The State of Gujarat*, AIR 1968.

[38] A decision passes *sub silentio* when the point of law involved in it was not perceived by the Court. Taking an example, if the Court decides in favour of one part considering point X but does not take into account point Y, although the decision logically implies that to decide in favour of point X point Y must also\be decided in the same way, point Y is passed *sub silentio* and therefore the decision is not binding under it. See *Gerard v Worth of Paris Ltd* (1936) 2 All ER 905.

[39] The exception *per incuriam* happens when the decision is taken ignoring a statute or other binding authority. With this exception the Indian judiciary acknowledges the same principle laid down by the House of Lords in *London Street Tramways v London County Council* (1898) AC 375.

[40] See *Union of India v Firm Ram Gopal Hukum Chand and ors*, AIR 1960.

[41] *DG Viswanath v Chief Secretary of the Government of Mysore*, AIR 1964.

statements on matters other than law—essentially, statements on facts—have no binding force.[42]

In order to overcome the *stare decisis* principle, it is possible to *distinguish* or *overrule*, but a very interesting point concerns the use of the so-called *prospective overruling*. The Supreme Court used this technique for the first time in the *Golak Nath* case that will be discussed in the second part, aiming to affirm that Parliament cannot amend the third part of the Constitution in order to limit or abridge the fundamental rights stated in this part. Conscious that the retrospective application of this decision, based on the idea that the Court merely declares the law, would have affirmed the unconstitutionality of several constitutional amendments and statutes not yet entered in force, the Supreme Court ruled that its judgments would only have prospective effect. Moreover, the Court affirmed that this technique can be used only by the Supreme Court and only concerning constitutional matters. We can find here a clear reference to the American doctrine of the *perspective overruling*, used in *Linkletter v Walker*.[43]

As a conclusion it is possible to affirm that, although theoretically the judiciary of India follows the theory of binding precedent, Courts, and particularly the Supreme Court, have found different ways to overcome the theory, giving a consistent contribution to the evolution of the common law rules on precedent.[44]

The use of precedents by the Supreme Court of India is useful to understand the legal culture of the judges. They grew up in a multicultural legal system that provides for the knowledge of various legal cultures inside the country. Furthermore, as India had been part of the British Empire for a long time, its jurists also became acquainted with the legal cultures of the other colonised countries thanks to the fact that their education was often completed in the UK or in other parts of that vast Empire. After independence, this phenomenon continued, even if the reference is no more just the Commonwealth, but the whole world. Thus, Indian jurists are part of world constitutionalism and many judges of the Supreme Court use foreign precedents.

Aiming to facilitate the study of multiple legal systems particularly through dialogue among academics inside and outside the country—considering also that dialogue among professors coming from different States of the Union of India can help the evolution of the legal culture of the country—Indian institutions provide for specific reforms and for the definition of instruments to allow young scholars to travel abroad for conventions and courses.[45]

The definition of curricula where international and comparative law have a relevant place in the education of future judges could also affect their attitude towards participation in the 'cross-fertilization' phenomenon, considering that those who had direct experience of other legal cultures seem more inclined to consider them when analysing the legal culture of belonging.

---

[42] *Amritsar v Hazara Singh*, AIR 1975.
[43] *Linkletter v Walker*, 381 US 618 (1965).
[44] Dhavan, *The Supreme Court of India* (1977) 56.
[45] JE Schukoske, 'Legal Education Reform in India' (2009) 1 *Jindal Global Law Review* 253.

III. CASE-STUDY ON THE USE OF FOREIGN PRECEDENTS BY THE SUPREME COURT OF INDIA IN ITS CONSTITUTIONAL ADJUDICATION

A. The Methodology of the Research

In order to understand the attitude of the Supreme Court of India in quoting foreign precedents while interpreting the Constitution, it was necessary to define some methodological parameters that take into account the need to design research as much as possible to be empirically reliable. Thus, the first step was to individuate where the adjudications of the Court were published. As the official reporter of the Supreme Court's decisions is the Supreme Court Reports Journal (SCR) we decided to use its electronic database provided by the same Court, though some other private reporters were authorised too, such as the Indian Supreme Court Law Reporter (ISCLR), the All India Reporter (AIR) and the Supreme Court Cases (SCC).

The SCR database groups all the decisions published by the SCR since the foundation of the Court in 1950 and provides for an automatic distinction between cases decided by the constitutional bench and others, so it was easy to individuate constitutional adjudications without using keywords in order to search in the database. All the cases listed in the constitutional bench web page were read during a three-year research period, highlighting the foreign precedents quoted by the Court and then searching for the issuing foreign Court when not directly quoted by the Supreme Court of India in its decisions.

The reference period of the research is from 1 January 1950 to 9 April 2010 and the total number of constitutional cases listed in the database is 1,908; quotations of foreign precedents were searched for among those 1,908 cases.

Some other elements have to be added about the identification of 'foreign' cases. Only judgments of Supreme or Constitutional Courts were analysed, while decisions issued by supranational Courts, such as the European Court of Human Rights (ECtHR), were not considered as foreign precedents of Supreme or Constitutional Courts bearing in mind the aim of mainly discussing dialogues among Courts of equal rank. For this reason, some considerations about the use of ECtHR precedents are conducted separately. The question about inclusion/exclusion arouses also a question on how to consider the judgments of the Judicial Committee of the Privy Council, because of its role as Court of last resort for all the countries of the British Empire, India included. It was considered methodologically helpful to divide the decisions issued by the Privy Council into two categories: those concerning India and issued before its independence and those concerning other commonwealth countries. As for the former, in the first 20 years of activity the Supreme Court of India seemed to use the Privy Council's precedents concerning India as its own precedents, so they were considered to be domestic precedents. As for the latter, they were considered to be foreign precedents issued by the higher Court of another country and so they were added to those issued after the establishment of independent judiciary.

B. The Use of Foreign Precedents

Reading constitutional cases, it seems that at the beginning of its activity the Supreme Court developed a different attitude towards foreign precedents depending on whether it was judging as a constitutional Court or in its role of Court of last resort. Probably the will to affirm its independence from any other model pushed the Court to use foreign precedents more rarely in constitutional adjudication, in clear contrast with its attitude when it judged as a Court of last resort, where the Supreme Court of India extensively quotes foreign precedents and makes references to foreign law, particularly to English and American law. Even in present times the situation is still the same and the attitude towards the citation of foreign precedents is very different if the Court decides as a constitutional bench or as a Court of last resort. Considering the latter case, the Supreme Court of India completely participates in the phenomenon of transjudicial communication[46] that considers reliance on foreign precedents as a commonplace in public law litigation. As said, in this case study, however, the focus will only be on the use of foreign precedents, as defined in the methodological explanation of the previous paragraph, in constitutional adjudication, where the Court seems to maintain a restrictive approach, if the reference is only to the precedents explicitly quoted. One of the reasons for the perpetuation of this attitude could be found in the attacks on judges who are open to the consideration of foreign precedents; as a matter of fact, in India the legal doctrine accused cosmopolitan judges of adjudicating cases relying more on alien standards than on domestic context and case law.[47]

However, the number of constitutional judgments containing references to foreign precedents issued by the Court in the period from 1 January 1950 to 9 April 2010 shows that this Court can be added to the category of those Courts that cite foreign precedents and, moreover, foreign case law.

As Graph 1 shows, numerically, over 1,908 constitutional decisions issued in the period considered and grouped, as said, by the SCR under the constitutional bench web page, the Court explicitly quoted foreign precedents in 179 cases. There is no constancy in the number of decisions issued by the Court, with a maximum number reached in the period from 1960 to 1964, both considering the number of constitutional decisions and constitutional decisions containing foreign precedent quotations, and a minimum number in 2009, when the Court issued only one decision that did not contain such a quotation.

Looking at Graph 2, it is also interesting to see that the Court usually refers to the number of foreign precedents cited in every decision in the range 'from 2 to 5' or even in the range 'more than 5', demonstrating in this way that when judges decide to look at the law of another country, they try to go deeply into the point of view of foreign judges and of the evolution of the jurisprudence of those countries.

---

[46] AM Slaughter, 'The Typology of Transjudicial Communication' (1994) 29 *University of Richmond Law Review* 99–137.

[47] On this point see A Thiruvengadam, *The Use of Foreign Law in Constitutional Cases in India and Singapore: Empirical Trends and Theoretical Concerns*, Working Paper on VII World Congress of the International Association of Constitutional Law, 2010, www.juridicas.unam.mx.

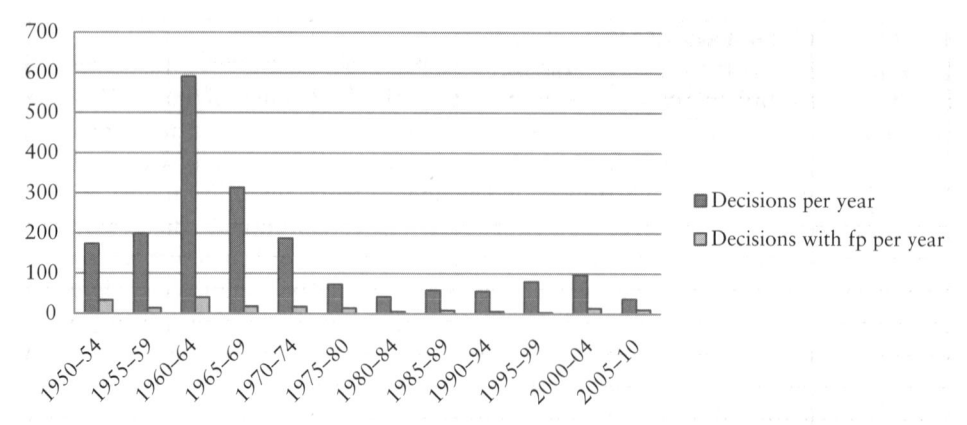

Graph 1: Constitutional Decisions and Citations per Year: Data Summarised in Five-year Periods

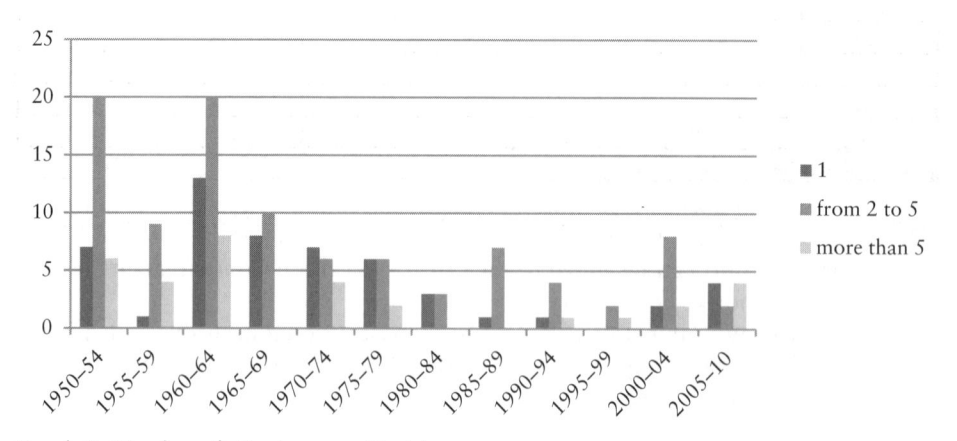

Graph 2: Number of Citations per Decision

Notwithstanding the relevance of the case for matters concerning institutions or the protection of human rights, the Court usually uses foreign precedents in order to support its position, in an approach that can be defined as 'even here–even there'. This is the case for some judgments where the Court discussed foreign precedents in order to 'introduce' into the legal system unnumbered rights or rights not explicitly enumerated in the Constitution.

However, it must be underlined that in the period from 1950 to 1954 the Court often referred to foreign precedents *a contrario*, in order to distinguish itself from other Supreme or constitutional Courts or to highlight that even if India shares some institutional elements with other countries it has its own independence in their interpretation. Here, even if the result is a rejection, the explanation of why it has been distinguished could also be helpful to understand better the Court's reasoning and its position on the constitutional matter discussed.

India 87

As an example, it is possible to quote the case of *State of Travancore-Cochin v Bombay*,[48] where the Court underlines the differences between Article 286 and the principles on interstate commerce elaborated by the US Court. Another case that helps to enucleate the role attributed to foreign precedents by the Supreme Court, and that also shows its great activism which was briefly considered earlier,[49] is the *Golak Nath* case. It originates from the governmental decision to pass a number of laws with the aim of depriving the *zemindars*, typical Indian landowners, of their estate and to amend the Constitution, with the 1964 Constitution (Seventeenth Amendment) Act, aiming to secure the constitutional validity of the acquisition of estates and place land acquisition laws in Schedule 9. These laws were challenged by landowners and several High Courts decided that the laws violated the fundamental right to property because they did not provide for fair compensation. At this point, the Court, despite recognising the power of Parliament to amend the Constitution, refused to accept the unreviewability of individual laws basing its judgment on the adequate compensation of the estate's deprivation. The *Golak Nath v State of Punjab* case occurred in 1967 on a challenge to the Punjab Land Reform Act. In this decision the validity of the 1953 Punjab Security of Land Tenures Act, and of the Mysore Land Reforms Act as amended by Act 14 of 1965 was challenged by the petitioners under Article 32 of the Constitution. Since these Acts were included in Schedule 9 by the 1964 Constitution (Seventeenth) Amendment Act, the validity of the said Amendment Act was also challenged. The Court ruled that Parliament's power to amend the Constitution did not extend to amending any of the fundamental rights listed, even if the majority opinion written by Chief Justice Subba Rao, using a prospective overruling for the first time,[50] saved the constitutionality of the 1964 Constitution (Seventeenth Amendment) Act. Furthermore, this decision represents the first step towards the definition of the theoretical concept of the 'basic structure of the Constitution', that we discussed. In this judgment, as mentioned above, the use of foreign precedents appears to be fundamental. The introduction of the prospective overruling, considered a way that 'enables the court to bring about a smooth transition by correcting its errors without disturbing the impact of those errors on past transactions', was done with the huge support of US Court precedents, even if judges added immediately that 'our Constitution does not ... speak against the doctrine of prospective overruling'. Wishing to harmonise as well as possible the prospective overruling with the Indian legal system and conscious that 'this Court for the first time has been called upon to apply the doctrine evolved in a different country under different circumstances', judges also added that

> the doctrine of prospective overruling can be invoked only in matters arising under our Constitution; it can be applied only by highest court of the country, i.e. the Supreme Court as it has the constitutional jurisdiction to declare law binding on all the Courts as it has

---

[48] *State of Travancore-Cochin v Bombay* (1952) SC 366.
[49] For more information about the periodisation of the activity of the Supreme Court of India, see JK Krishnan, 'Scholarly Discourse and the Cementing of Norms: The Case of the Indian Supreme Court (and a Plea for Research)' (2007) 9 *The Journal of Appellate Practice and Process* 255–89.
[50] This kind of overruling was introduced because the Court in *Sankari Prasad's* case, 1952 SCR 89, and in *Sajjan Singh's* case, 1964 SCR (4) 630, uphold the validity of the 1951 Constitution (First) Amendment Act and of the 1964 Constitution (Seventeenth Amendment Act).

India; the scope of the retrospective operation of the law declared by the supreme Court superseding its earlier decisions is left to its discretion to be moulded in accordance with the justice of the cause or matter before it.

The majority opinion refers to foreign precedents also about the amending power of Parliament, considering, once again, some US precedents[51] to affirm that

> the power of amending the Constitution is however not intended to be used for experiments or as an escape, from restrictions against undue State action enacted in the Constitution itself. Nor is the power of amendment available for the purpose of removing express or implied restrictions against the State.

Interestingly, this opinion also considers some foreign precedents[52] when discussing the fundamental rights protected by the Indian Constitution, but it suddenly affirms that the way this protection is conceived 'makes our Constitution unique and the American or other foreign precedents cannot be of much assistance'.

Also the dissenting opinion considers some foreign, in particular American, precedents in order to explain its position. On the question of the amending power, the dissenting judge Bachawat refers to *Marbury's case*[53] in order to affirm that it is coherent to give to Parliament the power to introduce a new right in the Constitution with an amendment but not to abrogate it with the same procedure.

Although it is not possible to analyse here the whole content of the judgment, it is remarkable to see how judges discussed the role of the Constitution in society, the differences that a choice between a flexible or a rigid Constitution involves, and about the meaning attributed to the Constituent Assembly's debates. Moreover, this judgment shows how some judges, following a line that characterised many decisions of the first years of this Court, were resistant to using and quoting foreign precedents and to taking into account foreign doctrines, as they stated or gave the perception that they were 'uninfluenced by any foreign doctrines' and discussed them only in order to draw a clear difference between the Indian legal system and others. The reliance of some of them on precedents of the Privy Council issued before the independence of India demonstrates, instead, that some judges consider them to be Indian precedents also when they concern other parts of the British Empire.[54]

Though the quotation of foreign precedents is not completely welcomed, the comparative attitude of the Court cannot be ignored; in this judgment the Court proposed a comparison of the dispositions about the constitutional amending procedures in force in many foreign Constitutions.[55] Similarly, it is possible to

---

[51] Those precedents are *Coleman v Miller*, 307 US 443 (1939), *Luther v Borden*, 48 US 1 (1849) and *Baker v Carr*, 369 US 186 (1962).

[52] The references are to *Hollingsworth v Virginia*, 3 US 378 (1798), *Leser v Garnett*, 258 US 130 (1922), *Dillon v Gloss*, 256 US 368 (1921) and *Texas v White*, 74 US 700 (1868).

[53] *Marbury v Madison*, 5 US 137 (1803).

[54] In *Golak Nath*, this is the case of *McCawley v The King* (1920) AC 691, concerning Queensland and *Bribery Commissioner v Pedrick Rana Singhe* (1964) WLR 1301, concerning Ceylon.

[55] Particularly, the Court quotes the precise articles concerning the amending procedure in force in the Constitutions of the United States, Brazil, Union of Burma, French Republic (1958), United States of Mexico, Italy, Greece, Germany, Cambodia, Japan, Norway, Kingdom of Sweden, Finland, Venezuela, Honduras, the USSR and Turkey, as well as in the Ceylon Constitution Order in Council (1946) and in the Commonwealth of Australia Constitution Act, the British North America Act, the South African Act and the Denmark Act.

find a broad quotation of legal doctrine, particularly of the American one, about prospective overruling; in this case, some foreign precedents are quoted through the citation of abstracts of legal issues.

Generally speaking, as the categories presented in Graph 3 demonstrate, it is possible to agree with the four typologies of use defined by Thiruvengadam in his 2010 working paper at the IACL Conference.[56] In the essay, the author considers the case of *Chiranjit Lal v Union of India*[57] as an example of those cases where (1) the Court relies on foreign precedents for guidance on general constitutional principles and when necessary to (2) frame the issue posed for adjudication and/or to formulate evaluative tests and frameworks.

Concerning the use of foreign precedents for guidance, in fact, in *Chiranjit Lal* the Indian Court quotes the US case *McCabe v Atchison*[58] to individuate who is entitled to raise the question of constitutionality, and *Barbier v Connolly*[59] to explain the doctrine of police power, whose basic principles 'are not peculiar to that country [United States], but are recognized *in every modern civilized State*'. This reference to civilised States underlines the wish of Indian judges to affirm the position of India among them through the axiom that if civilised countries agree on principles valid in the United States and India agrees on principles valid in the United States, then India can legitimately be considered to be a civilised country.

In the dissenting opinion of the same decision, Justice Das quotes, among the other foreign precedents,[60] the US cases *Lindsley v Natural Carbonic Gas Company*[61] and *Gulf, Colorado and Santa Fè Railway v WH Ellis*[62] in order to individuate the classes of persons entitled to specific treatments designed to ensure substantial equality.

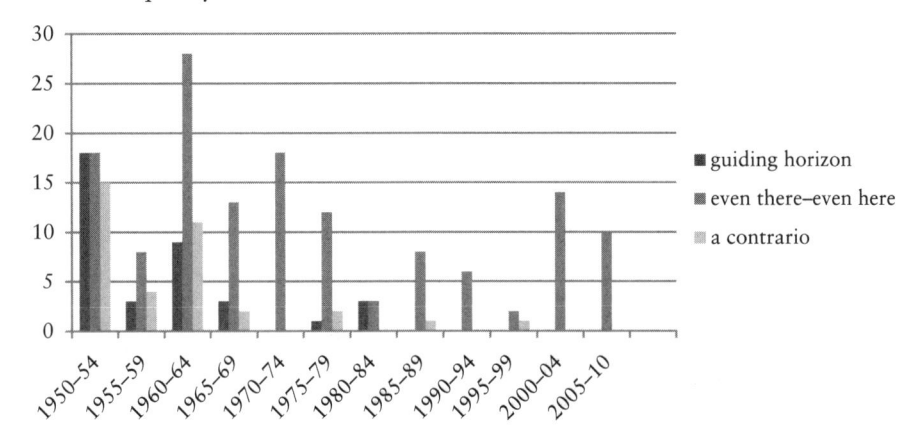

Graph 3: Use of Citations

---

[56] Thiruvengadam, *The Use of Foreign Law in Constitutional Cases in India and Singapore* (2010).
[57] *Chiranjit Lal v Union of India* (1950) 1 SCR 869.
[58] *McCabe v Atchison*, 235 US 151 (1914).
[59] *Barbier v Connolly*, 113 US 27 (1885).
[60] Among the others, the judge quotes also the Australian case *Minister for State for the Army v Datziel* (1944) 68 CLR 261, while discussing the concept of 'property'.
[61] *Lindsley v Natural Carbonic Gas Company*, 220 US 61 (1911).
[62] *Gulf, Colorado and Santa Fè Railway v WH Ellis*, 165 US 150 (1897).

In his analysis Thiruvengadam also recognises, in line with the content of Graph 3, that India's judges often discuss foreign precedents (3) to distinguish the country's context from the foreign one, as the Court did in *Basheshar Nath v Union of India*,[63] or, the direct opposite, (4) to 'read' in the Constitution implied or unenumerated rights, as was the case in *Romesh Thapar v State of Madras*.[64]

As a matter of fact, in *Basheshar Nath* the Court discussed the doctrine of waiver in force in the United States and rejected it firmly stating that

> the doctrine of waiver enunciated by some American Judges in construing the American Constitution cannot be introduced in our Constitution ... We are not for the moment convinced that this theory has any relevancy in construing the fundamental rights conferred by Part III of the Constitution.

On the contrary, in *Romesh Thapar*, the Court completely based its decision to strike down a law restricting the free circulation of newspapers on two US precedents, *Ex parte Jackson*[65] and *Lovell v City of Griffin*,[66] and affirmed that the protection of freedom of expression in India follows the maxim of Madison that the Court transposed from its quotation in *Near v Minnesota*,[67] according to which 'it is better to leave a few of its noxious branches to their luxuriant growth, than, by pruning them away, to injure the vigour of those yielding the proper fruits'.

Another interesting reflexion concerns the position of the citations. Foreign precedents are usually quoted in majority opinions and then considered also in concurring ones, while, generally, dissenting opinions quote those foreign precedents that support their content, though Graph 4 shows a lesser likelihood of using foreign precedents in these opinions.

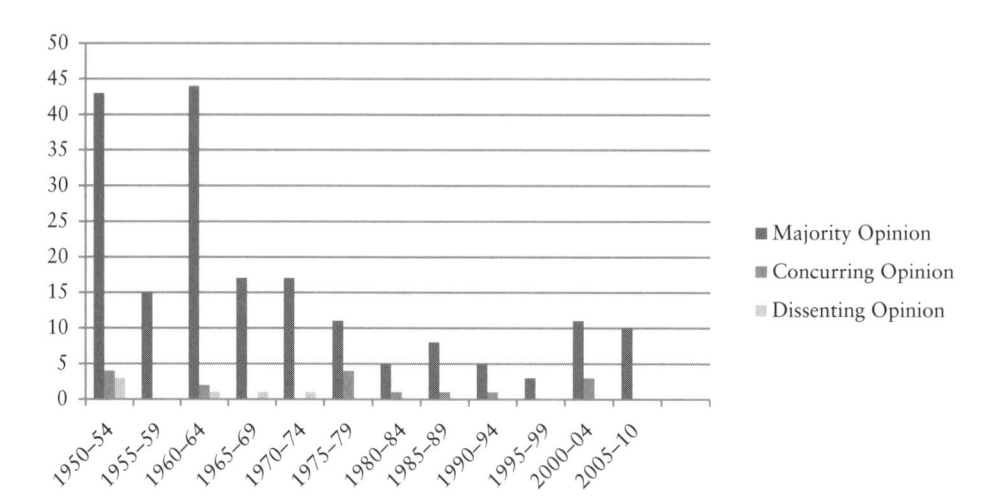

Graph 4: Position of the Citations

---

[63] *Basheshar Nath v Union of India* (1959) SC 149.
[64] *Romesh Thapar v State of Madras* (1950) SC 124.
[65] *Ex parte Jackson*, 96 US 727 (1878).
[66] *Lovell v City of Griffin*, 303 US 444 (1938).
[67] *Near v Minnesota*, 282 US 607 (1931) 717–18.

On this point it is relevant to add that the higher frequency of foreign precedent citations in majority opinions may relate to the fact that judges here discuss all the precedents proposed by the applicants and defendants to support their point of view. The case of *Basheshar Nath v Union of India*, in fact, demonstrates that, even when the Court aims to mark the distinction between India and other countries, the majority opinion deeply discusses the precedents presented. In this case, the Attorney-General proposed several US cases in order to support his idea that the individual had waived his fundamental right so the State was free to proceed against him. It was through a deep analysis of the proposed precedents that Justice Rao affirmed that fundamental rights evolved in different ways in India and the US so that in India a different approach was needed concerning the issue of waiver because the only limitations allowed in respect of rights in India are those listed in Part III of the Constitution.

However, it is worth noting, though difficult to demonstrate empirically, that the foreign precedents directly introduced by the Court often depend on the personal experiences and on the training of the judge who considers them, as noted before.

The role of foreign precedents in a majority opinion is confirmed, as an example, in the decision of *Kesavananda Bharati v State of Kerala*,[68] which clarifies Parliament's power to amend the Constitution.

The Supreme Court affirmed that the legislative power and the constituent power are different, that both powers are bound by constitutional provisions and that Article 368 provides for a special majority in order to amend the Constitution. Even if in these assumptions they partially contrasted with the *Golak Nath* case, judges soon affirmed that, despite this, Parliament's power to amend the Constitution is subject to inherent limitations and that it cannot use this power to damage, emasculate, destroy, abrogate, change or alter the 'basic structure' or framework of the Constitution.

Looking to the use of foreign precedents in this judgment, it is possible to underline that in its majority opinion, Justice Sikri, dealing with the interpretation of Article 368, first of all highlights that

> No other Constitution in the world is like ours. No other Constitution combines under its wings such diverse peoples, numbering now more than 550 millions [sic], with different languages and religions and in different stages of economic development, into one nation, and no other nation is faced with such vast socio-economic problems.

After this premise, however, he accepts, in order to define what an 'amendment' is according to the Indian Constitution, the reasoning of Lord Greene in *Bidie v General Accident, Fire and Life Assurance Corporation*[69] and that of Justice Holmes in *Towne v Eisner*,[70] which affirm that to understand a word it is necessary to understand the context in which it is inserted. To strengthen this, the Indian judge also refers to *James v Commonwealth of Australia*.[71]

---

[68] *Kesavananda Bharati v State of Kerala* (1973) 4 SCC 225.
[69] *Bidie v General Accident, Fire and Life Assurance Corporation* (1948) 2 All ER 995, 998.
[70] *Towne v Eisner*, 245 US 418. Considering the US Supreme Court's precedents, in order to support the theory of interpreting a word in its context, the Indian Court also quotes *Holmes v Jennison*, 39 US 540 (1840) and *William v United States*, 351 US 97 (1951).
[71] *James v Commonwealth of Australia* (1936) AC 578.

Generally speaking, in the whole decision there are many references to Australian, Canadian and American decisions and legal doctrines, probably because the judges wished to base their decision on legal norms, avoiding the fact that the theory of the inherent limitation of the amending power merely had a judicial basis.

Though this does not strictly concern the use of foreign precedents, it is also interesting to see that when judges started to discuss the conception of human rights accepted in the Indian Constitution, they referred to the 1948 UN Declaration on Human Rights, underlining that 'it shows how India understood the nature of Human Rights'. Similarly, judges proposed a broad discussion about how the Indian Independence Act differs from the independence Acts of other countries which were part of the British Empire, with a specific reflection on the constitutional evolution of Ceylon. Interestingly, in the dissenting opinion the idea of fundamental rights accepted in the Indian Constitution is discussed also considering its relation with the Irish one, affirming that

> The words 'fundamental rights' were deliberately omitted from the Irish Constitution (see foot note 9 page 67, The Irish Constitution by Barra O' Briain, 1929). At the same time, there was no question of any guarantee to any religious or other minorities in Ireland.

Finally, Graph 5 allows us to add that precedents quoted relied on the Courts of those countries who also influenced the Constitution-making of India. Indeed, the Supreme Court of India shows an interest in quoting the precedents of those Courts in order to demonstrate that India shares the general principles of constitutional law incorporated in the Constitutions of democratic countries. However, another reason for this comparison with the foreign precedents of those countries, valid particularly for the first decades of the activity of the Supreme Court of India, can be found in the absence of India's own precedents on specific topics.[72]

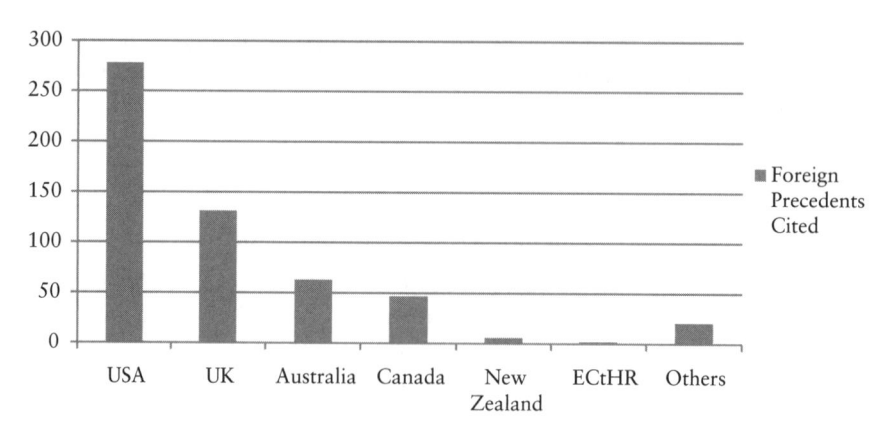

Graph 5: Most Cited Countries

---

[72] Jacobsohn affirms that, in the absence of domestic precedents, the Supreme Court of India was forced to look to foreign case law in order to overcome the gap between the aspirations of Indian people and the rules explicitly enshrined in the Constitution. See G Jacobsohn, *Constitutional Identity* (Cambridge, Harvard University Press, 2010).

Considering these premises, over a total number of 546 citations in the period considered, it is possible to find about 300 quotations of US Supreme Court precedents followed by about 150 quotations of British precedents. Decisions issued by the Supreme Court of Canada and the High Court of Australia number approximately 50. During the 1960s, the Court also tried to open itself to the quotation of some European Courts, citing a Spanish precedent in 1961, a Cypriot one in 1967 and, in the following year, one of the Belgian Cour d'Arbitrage. However, the citations of those precedents are very short and the Court just invites us to 'see also', without any kind of analysis of their content.

Analysing how the Court uses the precedents, it is possible to see that references to US precedents are generally used in cases involving the balance between civil liberties and governmental actions, while in adjudications concerning the relationship between the Union and the States, the Court makes reference to US precedents as well as to those issued by the Supreme Courts of Canada and of Australia. It is interesting to highlight that the Supreme Court of India uses both the precedents issued by federal Supreme Courts and those issued by Supreme Courts of the various States of federations. For example, considering the case of the precedents concerning the United States, it is possible to find some constant quotations of the Wisconsin, Texas, Illinois and Kansas Supreme Courts' precedents.

Some other considerations concern the use of ECtHR precedents. The first time the Supreme Court of India cites Strasbourg is in 1967 in the decision of *Golak Nath* discussed earlier. However in that case the Court just referred to the functioning of the European Commission on Human Rights that, at the time, was the institution charged to control the compliance to the European Convention on Human Rights (ECHR). Similarly, the Supreme Court of India made a general reference to the protection of property rights under the ECHR in the decision of *Kesavananda*, but did not quote any specific precedent. This a trend that the Court still maintains: judges prefer to quote directly the articles of the ECHR rather than their interpretation by the ECtHR. The empirical research shows just two exceptions: in 1982, in the decision of *Bachan Singh and others v State of Punjab*,[73] the Court cited the European case *Tyrer v United Kingdom*;[74] in 2005, the case of *Hatton and others v United Kingdom*[75] was cited in the decision of *Zee Films Limited and others v Union of India and others*.[76]

Concerning the analysis of the quotation of foreign precedents, it is not possible to ignore how often the Indian Court refers to the jurisprudence of foreign Courts without quoting a specific precedent. It is for this reason that the empirical case law analysis demonstrates a low rate of foreign precedent quotes although, reading the decisions of the Supreme Court of India, it is possible to find some references to supranational and foreign jurisdiction decisions. Furthermore, the Court is very attentive to the academic literature of the common law countries, as demonstrated by the numerous decisions in which the Court refers to long passages of academic books or articles concerning the topic it is adjudicating. More specifically, and above

---

[73] Cf *Bachan Singh and ors v State of Punjab* (1983) SCR 145.
[74] *Tyrer v United Kingdom*, no 5856/72 of 1978.
[75] *Hatton and ors v United Kingdom*, no 36022/97 of 2001.
[76] *Zee Films Ltd and ors v Union of India and ors* (2005) SCR 913.

all in the first decade since its establishment, the Court used foreign legal doctrine to affirm the definition of some legal institution not well defined after independence but in the context of Indian legal tradition.[77]

Due to its importance to the interpretation of the Constitution, in order to demonstrate those affirmations, it is possible to quote the *Maneka Gandhi* case,[78] where, even if the Court also makes explicit references to foreign precedents, it is possible also to find generic references to foreign legal doctrine. Maneka Gandhi, the daughter-in-law of the Prime Minister Indira, had her passport impounded 'in the public interest' under an order of the new Janata Government without any reason for its seizure or any hearing and she then appealed the Court for violation of her right to personal liberty. Recognising the reason of the appellant, the Court introduced the concept of substantive due process, holding that the procedure established by law in Article 21 implied a fair and just procedure. In this case the Court demonstrates how it was able to transform itself from a dispute-resolution body to an instrument of social change. Particularly, it evolved from a position which considered that personal liberty may be curtailed as long as there was a legal prescription for the same to a theory of inter-relationship of rights, including in the 'living Constitution' also some rights not explicitly enumerated. In this strategy of rights extension, the Court employed an approach based on the harmonisation of the 'Fundamental Rights' with the 'Directive Principles', which resulted, for instance, in an implementation of women, children and workers' rights. As for the use of foreign precedent, there is reliance on US case law, particularly *Kent v Dulles*[79] and *Apthekar v Secretary of State*[80] but, demonstrating the Court's knowledge of foreign law and academic doctrine, Blackstone's theory of natural law is also quoted and discussed extensively.

In recent years the quotation of academic literature has seemed to be the *escamotages* to consider foreign elements in a decision without explicitly relying on them. In fact, the analysis of constitutional cases demonstrates the rise of a sort of original *vague* that prevents judges from basing their opinions on foreign precedents. As an example, Justice Pattandik in *BR Kapoor v State of Tamil Nadu*[81] says '*I'm tempted to quote* some observations of the US Supreme Court' (emphasis added) and, in his concurring opinion, quotes no more than two precedents of the US Supreme Court. Another way of the Supreme Court of India making implicit reference to foreign precedents is by considering the 'well-known jurisprudence' of this or that country and, in many cases, particularly from the 1990s, it seems that the Court prefers to quote foreign jurisprudence already used in its own case-law or the provisions of the Constitutions of other counties directly,[82] without taking into account any

---

[77] It is possible to find an explicit example in the case of *Sri Sankari Prasad Singh Deo v Union Of India and State Of Bihar and other cases* (1952) SCR 89, which concerns the power to amend the Constitution.
[78] *Maneka Gandhi v Union of India* (1978) SC 597.
[79] *Kent v Dulles*, 357 US 116 (1958).
[80] *Apthekar v Secretary of State*, 378 US 500 (1964).
[81] *BR Kapoor v State of Tamil Nadu* (2001) SCC 231.
[82] An interesting example of this trend of the Court can be found in *Indian Express Newspaper v Union of India* (1986) SC 515 where, discussing the constitutional protection of press expression, the Court quotes the US Constitution, the Federalist Papers, some precedents of the Privy Council and of the US Supreme Court and also various international declarations in order to hold that the imposition of

interpretation that the competent Supreme Court has done of them. Similarly and conclusively, the Court maintains the same attitude towards the decisions of international and supranational Courts, preferring to quote the provisions contained in conventions and treaties directly albeit that this is not so frequent.

IV. CONCLUSION

The analysis of the Supreme Court of India's structure and activism demonstrates how it, as an increasingly political institution, has engaged in some of the most contentious and highly charged 'culture wars' and socio-economic battles that have been fought in the country. In this sense the Court is fully part of the new political order that has been qualified as a 'juristocracy', that is, an order in which there is a 'wholesale transfer to the Courts of some of the most pertinent and polemical political controversies a democratic polity can contemplate'.[83]

It appears clear that the attempt of the Supreme Court of India to ensure constitutional control over the other State powers, in order to improve the confidence of the people in the judicial system and in the Constitution, wishes to convey, in a society where many cleavages continue to divide the population, the message that the rule of law is able to answer critical situations better than violence and extremism. This was also the reason why the Court and the Government were opposed during the land reforms: the Court was not a conservative power contrary to land reform, but it had to ensure respect for the Constitution. For this reason it acted in order to provide a correct balance between the two rights involved, the equality among citizens (that was at the origin of the land redistribution reform), and the proper compensation for expropriation (the absence of which urged the Court to sanction the amendments).

Moreover, the Court strongly defended its power of judicial review. The definition of the aforementioned 'basic structure of the Constitution' had the explicit aim of highlighting governmental responsibilities and to avoid that Parliament, through the inclusion of the most controversial laws in constitutional Schedules, will progressively bend the content of the fundamental rights protected by the Constitution.

Furthermore, in its functioning the Supreme Court of India is not excluded from the world phenomenon of juridical globalisation, though, since its establishment, it has tried to find the Indian way to interpret the Constitution. It is clear that the Court is aware of the case law of some other countries but it prefers implicit or general references to the citation of specific precedents. As a matter of fact, the Supreme Court of India does not have a specific attitude to citing foreign precedents in its constitutional adjudications and, in the limited cases in which the Court decides to quote, it prefers to make reference to countries that were part of the British Empire, such as Australia or New Zealand, or to countries whose history in some ways

---

a tax on publications is not consistent with the right of the freedom of press that, though not explicitly listed in the Constitution, is incorporated in the freedom of expression.

[83] R Hirschl, *Towards Juristocracy: The Origins and Consequences of the New Constitutionalism* (Cambridge, Harvard University Press, 2004).

influenced the Indian one, such as the USA. Furthermore, it must be considered that the Court has its own case law, drafted at a time when even the decision to cite a foreign precedent could lead to discussions about membership of specific ideological doctrines. The Court has indulged such doctrines on very few occasions, preferring, instead, to mark a difference between foreign legal orders which also inspired the founding fathers and the Indian legal system.

4

The Supreme Court of Ireland and the Use of Foreign Precedents: The Value of Constitutional History

CRISTINA FASONE[*]

TABLE OF CONTENTS

I. Introduction: Ireland in the Framework of Transnational Judicial Dialogue 97
II. Foreign Influences upon the Constitutional History of Ireland 99
III. An Outline of the Irish Constitution 101
IV. The Relationship between the Irish Legal System and the European and International Legal Orders 104
V. The Judicial System and the Separation of Powers 105
VI. The System of Constitutional Justice 107
VII. Looking at the Supreme Court as a Constitutional Judge 110
   A. Composition and Background of Justices 110
   B. How the Supreme Court Decides 112
   C. Interpretative Techniques and Tools Used by the Supreme Court and Foreign Influence 113
VIII. The Results of the Empirical Research on the Use of Foreign Precedents 115
   A. Introduction. The Use of Precedents by the Supreme Court and the Place of Foreign Case Law in its Jurisprudence 115
   B. The Research Methodology 116
   C. The Results of the Quantitative Analysis 117
   D. The Results of the Qualitative Analysis 121
IX. Conclusion: The Irish Supreme Court, its Engagement in the Transnational Judicial Dialogue and its Legitimation 127

I. INTRODUCTION: IRELAND IN THE FRAMEWORK OF TRANSNATIONAL JUDICIAL DIALOGUE

UNDOUBTEDLY IN THE last few decades the proliferation of interconnected and interdependent legal orders has led to the increasing openness of national legal systems towards 'external' sources of law (international,

---

[*] PhD in Comparative Public Law, University of Siena (Italy), Post-Doc Fellow in Public Law, Luiss Guido Carli (Italy). I would like to thank Mr James Hamilton for his very insightful comments on the first draft of this chapter, Professor Tania Groppi and Professor Marie-Claire Ponthoreau for their guidance in the research and in drafting the chapter and Mr Tom Daly for having provided me with the basic sources of analysis of the Supreme Court of Ireland's jurisprudence.

supranational and foreign)[1] and to the well-known phenomenon of 'migration of constitutional ideas'.[2]

Transnational dialogue among judges and particularly the 'exchange' of precedents between constitutional judges—which are significant vehicles for the migration of constitutional ideas—seem to take place, according to the taxonomy proposed by Neil Walker, for reasons of 'sympathetic consideration',[3] showing the lowest level of 'connective intimacy and influence'[4] between the 'host' and the 'foreign' system. Therefore a foreign precedent can be used by a constitutional judge simply with a cognitive intent or as if it had a persuasive authority.

Rather than being simply the results of the process of globalisation and of the supranational effects of many policies (such as for environment and immigration), the use of foreign precedents by constitutional judges also depends, in some cases prominently, on other reasons, according to the legal order under scrutiny. For instance, when we look at how Irish constitutional judges manage foreign precedents, as in this chapter, it can be seen that the most important factors affecting the attitude of the Supreme Court derive from the:

(a) common law system;
(b) way the Constitution is drafted and its short catalogue of rights;
(c) powers of the Supreme Court vis-a-vis the Parliament, particularly because of the introduction, for the first time, of the constitutional review of legislation; and
(d) constitutional history of the country (whether it had a colonial past, how independence was obtained, how the Constitution-making process was carried out and to what extent the regime transition led to the abandonment of the previous legal system or its maintenance).

This chapter is focused on the citation of foreign case law by the Supreme Court of Ireland and it is based on empirical research into decisions dealing with constitutional review of legislation and the protection of human rights (between 1937 and 2010). Especially in the first decades after the entry into force of the new Constitution, the Supreme Court proved to have an in-depth knowledge of case law in other common law jurisdictions—namely of the United Kingdom (UK) and the United States (US)—, and quoted them extensively and with full knowledge of the facts that occurred in the 'borrowing jurisdiction'. However, the Supreme Court has progressively decreased the number of foreign citations and quotations as its constitutional jurisprudence and its authority have consolidated, thus limiting the use of foreign case law to when new constitutional issues—ones not yet addressed in domestic jurisdiction—arise.

---

[1] See V Jackson, *Constitutional Engagement in a Transnational Era* (Oxford–New York, Oxford University Press, 2009) 5 ff, who uses the comprehensive adjective 'transnational'.

[2] See S Choudhry, 'Migration as a New Metaphor in Comparative Constitutional Law' in S Choudhry (ed), *The Migration of Constitutional Ideas* (Cambridge, Cambridge University Press, 2006) 1–36.

[3] Indeed, 'sympathetic consideration' is 'to consult a system-external source on the premise that there exists some ground of common understanding or affinity for taking that external source seriously'. Other categories pointed out by Neil Walker are: institutional incorporation, system recognition, normative coordination and environmental overlap. See N Walker, 'Beyond Boundary Disputes and Basic Grids: Mapping the Global Disorder of Normative Orders' (2008) 6 *International Journal of Constitutional Law* 373–96.

[4] See Walker, 'Beyond Boundary Disputes', 384.

II. FOREIGN INFLUENCES UPON THE CONSTITUTIONAL HISTORY OF IRELAND

Irish history has been prominently influenced by the antagonistic relationship with the UK. Although Ireland has tried to move away from its past as a British colony ever since independence, this 'original intent' has sometimes failed in practice and many Irish institutional choices, such as the adoption of the common law system, the form of government and the accession to the European Community, mirror those of the former mother country.[5]

Ireland had been under English rule from the Tudor period, in the fifteenth century. The dominance of the UK over Ireland was sealed by the Act of Union (1800), a response to growing concerns about British security. The Act reserved a consistent number of seats in the Westminster Parliament to the Irish counties and Irish MPs in the House of Commons advocated 'Catholic emancipation, [the] repeal of the Act of Union, land reform and Home Rule'.[6]

However, in parallel with parliamentary activity and the rising of the 'Home Rule movement', in which the Catholic Church played a leading role, the Irish people also began to use a 'strategy of violence' for achieving their purpose. Many private, armed, and mainly secret circles and associations were set up. Most of them benefited from substantive financing by Irish communities in the US which were very active in promoting Irish independence.[7]

At the turn of the nineteenth century, Ireland's struggle for independence changed its nature. Cultural and religious divisions within the island were severe: the 26 counties in the South were predominantly Catholic and anti-British, but contained a Protestant minority; the six Northern counties, which would eventually become Northern Ireland, in the public and political arena were instead dominated by the Protestant population, but contained a very large Catholic majority and were loyal to the British Crown.

Following the 1916 Easter Rising, political and legal struggle and paramilitary activity became strongly interwoven. Indeed, Sinn Féin ('We ourselves' in Gaeilge) started to act as the political counterpart of the Irish Republican Army (IRA). At the 1918 elections, the first universal suffrage elections in the history of the UK, Sinn Féin won almost all seats reserved to Irish constituencies in the Westminster Parliament: it aimed at achieving secession from Britain through 'the withdrawal from Parliament and the setting up of an Irish assembly that would make policy for Ireland'.[8]

Faced with increasing tension, British Prime Minister Lloyd George attempted to negotiate with Sinn Féin leaders, to accommodate Irish claims with the will to assure

---

[5] See G Casey, *Constitutional Law in Ireland* (London, Sweet & Maxwell, 1987).

[6] See RB Finnegan and ET McCarron, *Ireland. Historical Echoes, Contemporary Politics* (London, Westview Press, 2000) 22.

[7] By contrast, in spite of the US' struggle for independence during the eighteenth century, the US Government has not supported the 'Irish cause' in fighting against British oppression. Rather, during the Paris Peace Conference in 1918 the US Government was closely allied with Great Britain. Nonetheless, Irish founding fathers (as well as many Irish judges and scholars to this day) saw the US as a model from which to draw inspiration, from an institutional point of view and most of all as regards the protection of individual rights.

[8] Finnegan and McCarron, *Ireland*, 49.

Northern Ireland (six out of nine counties of Ulster) to the UK. The Westminster Parliament approved the Government of Ireland Act 1920 which allowed for the Home Rule of Ireland.

The negotiation between the British Government and Sinn Féin continued until 1921, when a weak compromise solution was found in the Anglo-Irish Treaty. Ireland became a Dominion within the British Commonwealth. The island was divided into two parts; the boundaries of which were to be defined afterwards with the consent of all factions involved, through a Boundary Commission, composed also of other Commonwealth citizens.

However, the UK maintained control over air and naval bases in Ireland and could recruit Irish soldiers. Irish citizens were allowed freedom of movement and the right to vote in the UK elections, but an oath of allegiance to the British Crown was required from everyone holding a public office. Many people within Sinn Féin strongly criticised the outcome of the negotiations and the irreconcilable divergence between the Irish Government—from which President De Valera resigned—and the national opponents to the Anglo-Irish Treaty led to the civil war of 1922–23. This inherent tension within the Irish people has possibly delegitimised the enactment of the Constitution.

The 1922 Irish Constitution was drafted according to the parameters laid down in the Anglo-Irish Treaty, although the adoption of a written Constitution represented a first point of detachment from the British tradition, as would happen in almost all post-colonial states. With reference to the constituent phase, a Constitutional Commission was appointed which examined 18 different Constitutions (mainly those of other Commonwealth countries) as a source of inspiration. The UK Government and the Irish Government finally agreed on text which was then approved both by the New Irish Parliament (the Dáil Éireann) and Westminster, as happened with the British North America Act in 1867. To this day, scholars have yet to reach an agreement on the nature, Irish or British, of this Act. According to the Judicial Committee of the Privy Council,[9] the highest Court in the Commonwealth system, the Irish Parliament could not amend the Constitution; yet, this obstacle could perhaps be considered as removed after the Statute of Westminster 1931, which allowed Commonwealth dominions to enact laws in contrast with those of the UK Parliament.

The Constitution contained a clause—in Article 50—allowing the adoption of constitutional amendments by ordinary legislation, to be confirmed by a mandatory referendum, for the first eight years after its coming into force (later extended for eight more years). The Free State Constitution became de facto a flexible Constitution. Not only were several constitutional amendments approved between 1933 and 1936,[10] but the courts also concurred in the 'flexibilisation'.[11]

---

[9] See the *Moore* case (1935) AC 472, where the Privy Council stated that the source of validity of the Irish Constitution was the Act of the Parliament of Westminster.

[10] See DG Morgan, *Lineamenti di diritto costituzionale* (Torino, Giappichelli, 1998) 51: the right to appeal decisions by Irish Courts before the Judicial Committee of the Privy Council was repealed, as was the power of the Governor General to intervene in the legislative process; moreover, any reference to the King was expunged, except in the context of foreign policy.

[11] Indeed, the courts substantially overturned their power of judicial review by saying that when an enactment conflicted with the Constitution it was deemed to amend the Constitution itself. See G Whyte and G Hogan, *Kelly: The Irish Constitution*, 4th edn (London, Butterworths, 2003) 2161–62.

III. AN OUTLINE OF THE IRISH CONSTITUTION

One of the most important choices of the Irish 'Founding Fathers' of the 1937 Constitution,[12] in principle, was to perpetuate the legal order inherited from British domination. The Acts of the British Parliament were not repealed: rather, they remained in force provided they were consistent with the new Constitution. In theory, the judicial system was also maintained. When the new Constitution entered into force, all judges in charge continued to hold their position after an oath of allegiance to the Constitution. However a radical departure from the British legal tradition and the principle of parliamentary sovereignty was substantially carried out through the introduction of judicial review and of a rigid Constitution, precluding the problem of prevalence of ordinary legislation witnessed by the 1922 Constitution.

As has become clear since the plebiscite on the Constitution, there was a will to recognise sovereign power as deriving from the people, who had been subjected to the British Crown for so long, thus stressing the notion of popular sovereignty instead of that of parliamentary sovereignty.[13] Several constitutional provisions reaffirmed that: from the Preamble (mirroring that of the US Constitution, except for reference to the 'Most Holy Trinity'),[14] which reads 'We, the people of Éire ... do hereby adopt, enact, and give ourselves this Constitution', to the procedure to amend the Constitution (Articles 46–47). The Supreme Court, too, stated in many of its decisions that sovereignty pertains to the people.[15]

With regard to the protection of fundamental rights, the Irish Constitution shows a great resemblance to that of the US. The US was the only common law country that could have inspired the Irish legal system: at that time the US courts were the only ones to put in place an effective system of judicial review, enforcing a written catalogue of rights, whereas in other common law jurisdictions, such as Australia, Canada, New Zealand and the UK these two elements were not present.[16] 'Ireland has a written Constitution and a set of enumerated personal rights similar to those contained in the first ten amendments to the US Constitution ...':[17]

---

[12] Perhaps the most influential Founding Father upon the 1937 Constitution was De Valera, who was born in the US. Once he took power, in 1932, he decided to abolish the Senate and to summon Dáil Éireann, the Parliament, as a Constituent Assembly. Once the draft Constitution was approved, the plebiscite for the Constitution and the election of the Parliament took place at the same time. De Valera's party, Fianna Fáil, won the majority of the seats in the Dáil and the Constitution was sustained by 38% of the voters, while 29% voted against and almost 31% abstained.

[13] See J Hamilton, *Judicial Activism in Irish Constitutional Law*, Report to the Conference on 'Judicial Activism and Restraint Theory and Practice of Constitutional Rights' (Batumi, Georgia—13–14 July 2010) Strasbourg, Venice Commission, CDL-JU(2010)013, 7 July 2010, 2.

[14] See Whyte and Hogan, *Kelly: The Irish Constitution*, 54–56.

[15] For instance, in Re Article 26 of the Constitution and the Electoral (Amendment) Bill 1983 the Supreme Court explained that the term 'People' only refers to the Irish community of citizens: consequently, it declared the Bill, which granted the right to vote in political elections even to British residents in Ireland, repugnant to the Constitution. However, after the reference, in the same year, the Constitution was amended recognising the right to vote in the Dáil's election to certain non-citizens as well.

[16] See S Ó Tuama, 'Judicial Review under the Irish Constitution: More American than Commonwealth' (2008) 12(2) *Electronic Journal of Comparative Law*, www.ejcl.org/122/art122-2.pdf.

[17] See B Carolan, 'Consideration of Foreign Judgments by the Irish Supreme Court: An Extra-Constitutional Analysis of Several Select Cases' (2005) 12 *Irish Journal of European Law* 115–16.

The Constitutional courts [actually the High Court and the Supreme Court] of Ireland employ the interpretive methods familiar to US lawyers. Ireland, as a former colony, jealously guards its sovereignty. In some ways, Ireland is closer to the legal system of the US than to civil law systems of other Member States of the European Union, which Ireland joined in 1973.[18]

This is probably why the US Supreme Court is the most often cited foreign court in Ireland after the English courts.

If one looks at the catalogue of constitutional rights, regardless of the Supreme Court's jurisprudence, one will notice it is quite limited. In fact, Article 40 deals with the most classic civil and political rights (the right to life—also of the 'unborn', which is the controversial provision inserted in the Constitution in 1983 following a referendum and intended to preclude legalisation of abortion—, the right to equality before the law, the right to freedom of expression, the right to freedom of assembly and association and the guarantee of the inviolability of the dwelling); Article 41 with the rights of the family, which enjoys special recognition in the Irish Constitution;[19] Article 42 with education; Article 43 with private property; Article 44, as amended in 1973 (see below), with religion, and Article 45 with non-justiciable directive principles of social policy. However, as happened in the US, the Irish Supreme Court's case law has devised a set of 'unstated rights' through the doctrine of 'unenumerated rights', found in Article 40.3.1 of the Constitution and, especially, on the State's duty 'to defend and vindicate the personal rights of the citizen'.[20]

Examples include the right to privacy, the right of access to the Court and the right to legal assistance before a Court for indigents. Hence, the right to marital privacy was affirmed in *McGee v AG*,[21] where a woman who had been advised against any further pregnancies challenged the constitutionality of a measure that forbade, amongst the many prohibitions, the importation of contraceptives. In the case of *Macauley v Minister for Posts*,[22] the Supreme Court recognised the right of access to the Court on the basis of Article 34.4 of the Constitution and struck down the provisions of the Ministers and Secretaries Act 1924 according to which the Attorney General had denied authorisation to act against a Minister. In *The State (Healy) v O'Donoghue*,[23] the Court affirmed that when the defendant is not in a condition to pay for legal assistance, he enjoys a constitutional right to have legal aid from the State.

However, even when rights are provided by the Constitution the Supreme Court has often redefined their content. For instance, the right to life of unborn children, introduced only in 1983 in the Constitution, was re-interpreted by the decision of

---

[18] Ibid.
[19] Between the end of the twentieth century and the beginning of the new one the impact of Community and International law on domestic family law has been more and more evident. See G Shannon, 'The internationalisation of Irish family law' (2005) *Judicial Studies Institute Journal* 42 ff.
[20] Carolan, 'Consideration of Foreign Judgments', 119.
[21] *McGee v AG* (1974) IR 284.
[22] *Macauley v Minister for Posts* (1966) IR 345.
[23] *The State (Healy) v O'Donoghue* (1985) IR 486.

the Supreme Court in *Attorney General v X*.[24] The Court stated with a four-to-one majority that, in the case at hand, the practice of abortion was to be considered consistent with the Constitution because a serious and actual peril to the life of the mother (the threat of suicide) had occurred. Subsequently, three constitutional referenda—the last referendum, seeking to reintroduce an absolute ban on abortion in response to the Supreme Court's jurisprudence, was defeated—took place in order to clarify the meaning of the 1983 constitutional amendment on the grounds of this jurisprudence. The outcome was that the amendment could not be understood as limiting the freedom to travel from Ireland to other States in order to have an abortion, nor the opportunity to seek and receive information on medical services available in other States for that purpose.

The issue of the protection of human rights in this country is strictly related to the nature of its Constitution as well as to the role played by the courts. As mentioned above, for the first time in its history, Ireland has a rigid Constitution. Article 34.4 of the Constitution establishes a system of constitutional review of legislation as a guarantee for the protection of the Constitution against any attempt to modify its provisions illegally. According to Articles 46–47 of the Constitution, the Constitution can only be amended through a specific procedure. A Bill to amend the Constitution must be passed by the Dáil and by the Senate, the two Houses of the bicameral system; then it must be submitted to a referendum. The Bill will enter into force if approved by the majority of the votes cast at the referendum. It has been remarked that the Constitution does not require a *quorum* of the electorate to be in favour of constitutional amendments.[25]

Since 1937, 30 constitutional amendments have been approved, but only 28 by means of a referendum. In fact, the first two amendments, in 1939 and 1941, were approved pursuant to the transitory procedure of Article 51 of the Constitution, above all with the purpose of facing the emergency of World War II. Thereafter, the Constitution was not modified until 1972. Some amendments were intended to allow Ireland's participation in the European Community integration process. Indeed, according to the jurisprudence of the Supreme Court (see below), the ratification of the reform Treaties within the European Union has to be anticipated by the approval of an amendment to the Constitution.[26] Others amendments, though, dealt with highly debated and politically sensitive issues. For example, the Fifth Amendment of the Constitution Act 1973 removed from the fundamental law the special position of the Catholic Church and the recognition of other named religions, thus assuring a wider protection of pluralism and of religious freedom.

---

[24] *Attorney General v X* (1992) ILRM 401. In this case a 14-year-old teenager, who had become pregnant as a result of sexual assault, threatened to commit suicide if prohibited from going abroad to terminate her pregnancy.
[25] The 1967 Report of the Committee on the Constitution affirmed that the lack of a *quorum* cannot represent a threat to the solidity of the Constitution, because a constitutional referendum always excites the interest of citizens, thus guaranteeing an adequate voter turnout.
[26] However, other European Treaties, such as accession Treaties, do not, in principle, require a referendum.

IV. THE RELATIONSHIP BETWEEN THE IRISH LEGAL SYSTEM AND THE EUROPEAN AND INTERNATIONAL LEGAL ORDERS

The relationship between the Irish legal order and international law is based on a dualist system of recognition of international law, fundamentally conditioned by Article 15.2 of the Constitution: 'The sole and exclusive power of making laws for the State is hereby vested in the Oireachtas [the Parliament]: no other legislative authority has the power to make laws for the State'; and by Article 26.9 of the Constitution: 'No international agreement shall be part of the domestic law of the State save as may be determined by the Oireachtas'. This provision reveals a certain conception of sovereignty, influenced by centuries of submission to the British Parliament.

However, it also underlines a sort of reluctance to allow courts, mainly the High and the Supreme Court, the power to 'order affirmative injunctive relief, as this would be seen as usurping the legislature's exclusive right to make law'.[27] Neither international treaties nor customary international law are applied in Ireland unless their provisions are incorporated into domestic law.[28] 'A corollary of this view is a limitation on the ability of an individual to rely upon international law in the Irish Courts',[29] with a severe prejudice for human rights protection.

Indeed, though Ireland had already signed it, the European Convention on Human Rights (ECHR) was not applied in Irish courts until 2003, when it was finally incorporated into national law.[30] Under section 2 of the ECHR Act 2003, the courts are now obliged to interpret, in so far as possible, 'any statutory provision or rule of law in a manner compatible with the European Convention on Human Rights'.[31] However, even today the implementation of the ECHR in Ireland does not

---

[27] Carolan, 'Consideration of Foreign Judgments', 121; see also Whyte and Hogan, *JM Kelly: The Irish Constitution*, 110 ff.

[28] The most notable case was that of *Norris v Attorney General* (1984) IR 36. The case involved two Irish people who then gained great prominence: David Norris, later a member of the Senate, as the plaintiff, and Mary Robinson, later President of Ireland, as his counsel. Norris challenged sections 61 and 62 of the Offences Against the Person Act 1861 and section 11 of the Criminal Law Amendment Act 1865. These provisions dated back to British rule, but according to art 50 Constitution they remained in force until declared inconsistent with the Constitution. Norris claimed that these provisions, which punished homosexual acts (even when performed in private) with a maximum sentence of life imprisonment with hard labour, violated his personal dignity and his right to privacy. The Supreme Court dismissed the appeal. Prior to this decision, a quite similar lawsuit against the same provision had been filed before courts in Northern Ireland. The case was finally decided by the European Court of Human Rights (series A) (1981): the Court ruled that the provisions violated art 8 ECHR. The UK therefore amended the Acts, complying with the decision. One may be surprised that the Irish Supreme Court refused the substance of that ECHR judgment in its entirety and generally ignored its other decisions.

[29] Carolan, 'Consideration of Foreign Judgments', 121.

[30] However, even a declaration issued by the Supreme Court on the incompatibility of national legislation with the ECHR is to some extent limited in its effects if there are no practical remedies for the substantive protection of those rights; remedies that should be provided by the Government, which, on the contrary, remains largely inactive. This lack of national regulation can leave room for judicial activism: on this point, see Hamilton, *Judicial Activism in Irish Constitutional Law*, 8, who cites the case of *McD v L* (2009) 12 JIC 1001, on the controversial direct applicability of the ECHR.

[31] See JL Murray (Former Chief Justice of Ireland), 'Judicial Cosmopolitanism' (2008) 2 *Judicial Studies Institute Journal* 1, 14.

come by means of direct incorporation.[32] Moreover, while the Supreme Court often takes foreign case law or the case law of the European Court of Justice (ECJ) into account, this has not happened very frequently with the ECHR so far, but the trend has gradually changed after 2003.[33] In fact, the European Court of Human Rights has been perceived as a court of last instance in the field of human rights, whose decisions are binding also for the courts. The Irish Supreme Court is not inclined to accept external constraints from another Court, as the vertical relationship with the ECHR would determine.

The situation is rather different with regard to the relationship between Irish and EU law. Ireland joined the European Community in 1973; since then it has amended its Constitution every time it has ratified a Reform Treaty. Indeed, in *Crotty v An Taoiseach*[34] the Supreme Court ruled that EC Reform Treaties affecting the sovereign powers of Ireland must be incorporated into domestic law by amending the Constitution. With regard to the enforcement of EU law in Ireland, Article 29.4.10 of the Constitution declares that '[n]o provision of this Constitution invalidates laws enacted, acts done or measures adopted by the State which are necessitated by the obligations of membership of the European Union or of the Communities' nor those Acts adopted by European institutions or bodies within their competence under the Treaty. In *Campus Oil Ltd v Minister of Industry & Energy*,[35] the Supreme Court recognised the supremacy of Community law over Irish law, including the Constitution (in fact, it is usual to talk about the 'European external Constitution' for Ireland).[36] Actually the Supreme Court's deference towards the ECJ and the European legal system seems to go 'beyond what is strictly required under the Irish Constitution and the European Union law'.[37]

V. THE JUDICIAL SYSTEM AND THE SEPARATION OF POWERS

The Constitution of 1937, the Courts (Establishment and Constitution) Act and the Courts (Supplementary Provisions) Act 1961 (as amended) substantially confirmed the existing judicial system, already settled by the Courts of Justice Act 1924.[38] Even under British dominance, the Irish judiciary remained separated from the English judicial system (as well as most Irish laws and legal codes), with the exception of a right to appeal to the House of Lords in London.

Article 34.1 of the Constitution affirms that the judicial function is administered only by courts. The Supreme Court has interpreted this provision as restraining

---

[32] On this issue, see The *Report of the Constitution Review Group* (Dublin, 1996) 216–19.
[33] See Carolan, 'Consideration of Foreign Judgments', 135 f.
[34] *Crotty v An Taoiseach* (1987) IR 713.
[35] *Campus Oil Ltd v Minister of Industry & Energy* (no 2) (1983) IR 88.
[36] By contrast, since 2003 the ECHR has sub-constitutional status in Ireland.
[37] See Carolan, 'Consideration of Foreign Judgments', 126.
[38] See R Keane (former Chief Justice), 'The Irish Court System in the 21st Century: Planning for the Future' (2001) 1 *Judicial Studies Institute Journal*, 1 ff.

the Parliament's power to regulate matters of evidence by statute[39] or to limit the Court's discretion with regard to the entity of punishment. In *State (Shanahan) v AG*,[40] the Supreme Court 'listed' the powers of courts as follows: the power to decide on a point of law or fact, on civil and/or criminal matters; the power to determine the rights of the parties; the power to require and obtain, even through the Executive branch, the attendance of witnesses; the power to make their decisions effective.[41]

Like many common law countries, Ireland is characterised by a high level of judicial activism.[42] In the Irish case, it seems that this feature can be explained above all by the narrow catalogue of rights provided by the Constitution and by some sort of inactivity of Parliament in the last few decades. Many scholars underline that some turning points in the Irish constitutional system's development, particularly concerning the protection of fundamental rights, have derived from decisions of the courts (eg *McGee* or the *Murphy v AG* case), while in the UK the same issues have been addressed by Acts of Parliament.[43] This judicial activism, however, does not contribute to solving present problems, like the delay in dealing with cases, which are due both to inefficiencies and to a lack of information technology or to certain structural features of the Irish judicial system.[44]

Until 1995, the Executive controlled entirely the appointment of judges. Article 35.1 of the Constitution provides that judges in both superior (the High Court and the Supreme Court) and inferior courts (the circuit and the district courts) are appointed by the President, but it is the function of the Executive alone to decide who should be appointed to the courts.[45] In 1995, after a long debate, the Courts and Court Officers Act was adopted. A new body was set up: the Judicial Appointments Advisory Board, chaired by the Chief Justice of the Supreme Court.[46] This body essentially has the power to select and draw up a list of candidates to recommend to the Executive for judicial appointment. To be eligible to become a judge, one is required to have standing for a specified period: academics who have not practised continuously are thus not eligible. 'Character' and 'temperament' (actually very vague criteria) are also taken into account.

---

[39] See *Maher v AG* (1973) IR 140.
[40] *State (Shanahan) v AG* (1964) IR 239.
[41] On the role of judges in Ireland today and, in particular, on their relationship with the media, see T Finlay, 'The Role of the Judge' (2005) *Judicial Studies Institute Journal,* 1 ff.
[42] On the relationship between judicial activism and the doctrine of separation of powers in the Irish legal system, see Hamilton, *Judicial Activism in Irish Constitutional Law*, 6 ff and A Hardiman, 'The Role of the Supreme Court in Our Democracy' in J Mulholland (ed), *Political Choice & Democratic Freedom in Ireland. Forty Leading Irish Thinkers* (MacGill Summer School, 2004) 32.
[43] See Morgan, *Lineamenti di diritto costituzionale*, 39.
[44] In 2001, the Hon Mr Justice Keane, Chief Justice of the Supreme Court, pointed his finger at the presence of a three-tier system of courts of first instance, on the one hand, and at the absence of case management techniques in the High Court, on the other, as the first issues to face in order to modernise the judicial system.
[45] The Executive advises the President of Ireland of its nomination of a candidate for appointment and the President formally makes the appointment (art 13.1 Constitution).
[46] It is composed of the President of the High Court, the President of the Circuit Court, the President of the District Court, the Attorney General, a practising barrister nominated by the Chair of the Council of the Bar of Ireland and a practising solicitor nominated by the President of the Law Society of Ireland, in addition to three lay members, appointed by the Minister of Justice among people with an appropriate knowledge of or experience in public administration, commerce and finance.

When a post becomes vacant, the Board is summoned upon request by the Minister of Justice. The Board then publicly invites interested candidates to apply, but after that its activity is limited to examining the applicants' references, usually without interviewing them. At the end of the day, the process of appointment remains obscure and lacking in transparency. In addition, the appointment of those already holding judicial office to powerful positions (eg the Presidents of each level of court and the Chief Justice) remains a matter for the Executive alone.

Research show that the composition of the Irish judiciary has not changed much since 1969, when 'the Irish judge was white, male, upper middle-class, urban, a barrister, with a background in politics, and a largely conservative approach'.[47] Research conducted in 2004 on superior courts' judges, showed more or less the same picture, except for two differences: since 1969, the percentage of female judges has grown significantly, from the original zero per cent, as well as the figure of respondents reporting no political affiliation—even though it is hard to say that appointees are completely apolitical—, from 12 to 62 per cent.[48] However, in 2008, with a total of 143 Irish judges, only 22.3 per cent were female: Irish women are indeed still affected by a problem of under-representation in comparison with other OECD Countries.

VI. THE SYSTEM OF CONSTITUTIONAL JUSTICE

The opinions about the categorisation of the Irish system of constitutional review of legislation are not unanimous. According to some, the Irish system fits into the category of the diffuse system,[49] but most scholars describe it as 'mixed'.[50] Surely, Article 50 of the Constitution displays some features of the diffuse system, but also others, typical of a centralised system. This is the effect of the constituent choice to guarantee the continuity of the legal system, as the Dominion era drew to an end and that of full independence commenced. It refers to both types of pre-constitutional statutes, that is, those approved by the British Parliament before 1922 and those passed by the Irish Dáil from 1922 to 1937. According to the wording of Article 50 of the Constitution, unless inconsistent with the Constitution, these Acts 'shall continue to be of full force': their consistency can be challenged before any judge, in any proceeding (in theory, even in the district and circuit Courts), according to the traditional American model of judicial review. However, things have changed in the last few years, following a landmark decision of the Supreme Court in *The People (DPP) v MS*:[51] then Chief Justice Keane held that the Constitution precludes a court of local and limited jurisdiction from determining the constitutionality of

---

[47] See D Feenan, 'Judicial Appointments in Ireland in Comparative Perspective' (2008) 1 *Judicial Studies Institute Journal* 37–38 and PC Bartholomew, *The Irish Judiciary* (Dublin, Institute of Public Administration, 1971).
[48] See Feenan, 'Judicial Appointments in Ireland', 38.
[49] See V Tamburrini, 'I Paesi con controllo diffuso di costituzionalità delle leggi' in T Groppi and M Olivetti (eds), *La giustizia costituzionale in Europa* (Milano, Giuffrè, 2003) 375 ff.
[50] See Whyte and Hogan, *JM Kelly: The Irish Constitution*, 421 ff.
[51] *The People (DPP) v MS* (2003) 1IR 606.

a law, whether in the form of a pre-1937 law or a rule of common law.[52] This judgment has strengthened the turn of the Irish system of constitutional adjudication towards a more centralised model of constitutional review of legislation.

Moreover, the original diffuse system has cohabited at length with another system, affecting Bills and post-1937 Acts, which we can consider as centralised or semi-centralised. There are two different ways of accessing this system of review and two different sets of effects. First, the President may refer a Bill passed or deemed to have been passed by both Houses to the Supreme Court (no other judges are involved). This mechanism is 'absolutely' centralised. The President may not refer pursuant to Article 26 of the Constitution money Bills, Bills containing a proposal to amend the Constitution or Bills the time for consideration of which has been abridged by the Senate.

In 75 years of the Constitution's enforcement, the Article 26 procedure has only been used 15 times. According to scholars, a reason for this is that the procedure has an abstract and preventive (to the coming into force of the Bill) character.[53] The Court usually sits in *plenum*, with the judgment being delivered by the Chief Justice. The Court hears the reasons for and against the Bill, as laid out by the Attorney General and by a counsel assigned by the Court. However, because the question is not raised during a dispute among parties, the practical effects of the Bill are only speculated upon. This means that Justices can basically overturn the will of Parliament without testing how it works factually: this option contravenes the general presumption of constitutionality of legislation inherent to the British tradition of a 'strong' Parliament.

In *In re Article 26 and the Housing (Private Rented Dwellings) Bill 1981*[54] the Supreme Court itself expressed some doubts about the reference mechanism, mainly with regard to certain types of Bills. The then Chief Justice O'Higgins stated:

> The Court, therefore, in a case such as this, has to act on abstract materials in order to cope with the social, economic, fiscal and other features that may be crucial to an understanding of the working and the consequences of a referred bill.

The most evident hurdle in the reference mechanism is perhaps its effect.[55] If the Bill is considered invalid, it never comes into force; instead, if the Court decides for its validity, once it becomes an Act it cannot be challenged any more. However, scholars have raised the question as to whether the immunity would be removed where the Bill, as an Act, is subsequently subjected to significant amendments. This general immunity was not in the original text of the Constitution: it was inserted as one of the first constitutional amendments, approved outside the procedure to amend the Constitution under Articles 46–47.[56]

The second model of constitutional review of (post-Constitution) legislation and public authorities' decisions can approximately be called semi-centralised because

---

[52] Ibid, 781–82.
[53] See Casey, *Constitutional Law in Ireland*, 263.
[54] See *In re Article 26 and the Housing (Private Rented Dwellings) Bill 1981* (1983) 1R 181.
[55] See Whyte and Hogan, *JM Kelly: The Irish Constitution*, 218.
[56] Sometimes a Bill, like the Equality Employment Bill 1996, is struck down on narrow grounds, following an art 26 reference procedure, and then re-enacted expunging the offending sections without a further Reference.

it involves two courts: the High Court, as court of first instance,[57] and the Supreme Court as appeal Court (Article 34.4 of the Constitution).[58] The Supreme Court rules on constitutional issues decided upon by the High Court: in fact, most High Court decisions of this type are then appealed before the Supreme Court and this is why the study on the use of foreign precedents focuses on the activity of this latter court.[59]

Both the Supreme Court and the High Court, as constitutional judges of last and of first instance, have assumed the power to review the consistency of all public authorities' decisions with the Constitution, so going beyond the text of the Constitution which provides only for the constitutional review of legislation (Article 34.4 of the Constitution). The constitutional review of legislation also includes statutory instruments, since they are considered 'secondary legislation'; however, the jurisprudence of the Supreme Court has extended constitutional review to any decision of a public authority too.[60]

Nevertheless, there are some exceptions to the constitutional review of legislation. Firstly, due to the supremacy of EU law over domestic law (see above, section IV), the Supreme Court may not challenge the validity of EU regulations, nor that of national Acts incorporating EU law.

Secondly, under Article 28.3 of the Constitution

> Nothing in this Constitution ... shall be invoked to invalidate any law enacted by the Oireachtas which is expressed to be for the purpose of securing the public safety and the preservation of the State in time of war or armed rebellion ...[61]

However, such declaration of immunity from constitutional review applied mostly in the Seventies and is not applied to any provision in force at present, but the Supreme Court held that despite the use of Article 28.3 of the Constitution, it could look behind this declaration, thus further enlarging the *spectrum* of Acts subject to constitutional review.[62]

Thirdly, according to the British model, where courts are not used to interfering with the parliamentary legislative process or questioning how it has been

---

[57] The High Court has 'full original jurisdiction in and power to determine all matters and questions, whether of law or fact, civil or criminal (art 34.4.1 Constitution)'. The Court is composed of 36 judges (maximum), in addition to the President and two added members: the Chief Justice and the President of the Circuit Court. Cases are usually decided by a sole judge, even in the presence of a jury. On the basis of art 40.4 Constitution, the High Court can also grant the writ of *habeas corpus* and it is the court of first instance in the constitutional review of legislation. Indeed, according to art 34.3.2 Constitution, 'no question of validity of any law having regard to the provisions of the Constitution shall be raised ... in any Court ... other than the High Court and the Supreme Court'.

[58] The Supreme Court is the 'Court of final appeal' in Ireland (art 34.2 Constitution), with few exceptions provided for by law. This Court has original jurisdiction in two hypotheses: in determining the *status* of permanent incapacity of the President of Ireland (art 12.3 Constitution) and in deciding on the constitutionality of a Bill referred by the President before its enactment (art 26 Constitution).

[59] In certain hypotheses, such as in the matter of immigration and asylum, the appeal before the Supreme Court is submitted to the endorsement by the High Court which has to authorise it. See Irish Court Service, *Guidelines on the Appeals from the High Court* (Dublin, November 2009) 3.

[60] This extension of the range of Acts submitted to constitutional adjudication was affirmed for the first time in *Quinn's Supermarket v AG* (1965) IR 70, where a regulation allowing kosher shops to be opened in spite of the general requirement for meat shops to be closed on certain days was struck down as a discriminatory measure.

[61] This limit shows a problematic situation, that of the 'conflict' between Ireland and Northern Ireland, which became particularly tense during the period of terrorism in the Seventies.

[62] See the art 26 Constitution Reference in matter of The Emergency Power Bills 1976 (1977) 1IR 159.

carried out, and normally respecting the guarantee of parliamentary sovereignty,[63] in Ireland, notwithstanding the acknowledgment of the constitutional review of legislation, there is a sort of deference towards parliamentary activity, and a presumption of constitutionality is observed, too.[64]

There is no specific procedure to deal with a constitutional issue that can be brought before any judge in any kind of procedure. However, if the plaintiff did not directly appeal to the High Court, then the judge must refer the issue to it; since *State (Lynch) v Cooney*,[65] this has been held true even in *certiorari* proceedings.

Finally, one must take into account the effects of decisions which declare a statute or a public decision unconstitutional, either because it is inconsistent with the Constitution (if enacted before 1937) or because it is invalid (if enacted after 1937). As happens in the US, an unconstitutional statute is disapplied. But is it considered inconsistent or invalid *ab initio* or from the moment the decision was delivered? The Supreme Court's answer was that, if found unconstitutional, statutes in force before the Constitution are considered as not having effect since 1937 and those passed after the Constitution's enactment are regarded likewise as invalid from 1937.

VII. LOOKING AT THE SUPREME COURT AS A CONSTITUTIONAL JUDGE

A. Composition and Background of Justices

The Supreme Court is composed *ex officio* of the Chief Justice of Ireland, presiding member, and of seven other judges, in addition to the President of the High Court. The Constitution does not set the number of members of the Court, but states that on specific occasions it cannot consist of less than five judges. In fact, in the past the Court was 'smaller' than today.

Article 26 of the Constitution references are usually ruled upon by the *plenum* of the Court; constitutional issues concerning the validity of a law must be decided by no less than five judges; cases of considerable complexity or importance will often be decided by five (or even exceptionally, seven) judges; all other matters are often decided by a panel of three judges, including the challenge to the constitutional validity of executive measures. The Chief Justice decides who sits in the judging panel for every case.

Although it is a collegial judge, the Supreme Court is characterised by a formal hierarchy. The Courts (No 2) Act 1997 establishes the order of precedence among judges: the Chief Justice is the highest ranking judge; the President of the High Court is second; former Chief Justices are ranked in the third position; and other judges follow according to the priority of their appointment. Yet, this ranking has no specific effects in terms of decision-making power: for example, in terms of opinions, the Chief Justice often delivers dissenting opinions.

---

[63] However, P Eleftheriadis, 'Parliamentary Sovereignty and the Constitution' (2009) 22 *Canadian Journal of Law and Jurisprudence* 267–90 points out that the 'myth' of the Parliament of Westminster's sovereignty has weakened over time. See the decision of the Supreme Court of the UK in *R v Chaytor & ors* (2010) EWCA Crim 1910 about parliamentary privileges.

[64] See Whyte and Hogan, *JM Kelly: The Irish Constitution*, 449, who underline the self-restraint of the Supreme Court.

[65] *State (Lynch) v Cooney* (1982) IR 337.

Under the Act of 1997, the term of office for a Chief Justice is seven years. The Courts and Court Officers Act 1995 lowered the retirement age for Justices from 72 to 70 years. Besides being a judge, the Chief Justice sits in the Presidential Commission, a body composed also of the Presidents of the two Houses of Parliament, which acts for the President of Ireland in case of his/her absence or incapacity. The Chief Justice is also a lifetime member of the Council of State, a body which aids and counsels the President of Ireland in exercising certain constitutional powers (eg the power to convene a meeting of either or both the Houses of the Parliament).

As affirmed above (section V), the system of appointment of Irish judges is essentially 'political'. Supreme Court judges are no exceptions to this model. They are appointed formally by the President, but their appointment lies substantially in the hands of the Government. Unlike in the US model, there is no provision for hearings by parliamentary committees and since 1995 the Advisory Board has intervened in the early stage of the selection process. This means that, while obviously respecting the independence of the judges' role in relation to other constitutional powers, each Executive tries to appoint judges of some political affinity to it.

In order to become a Justice of the Supreme Court, as well as of the High Court, one is required to have been a legal practitioner for no less than 12 years. Most Supreme Court Justices have been judges of the High Court beforehand. Although most of them are very active in the debate over the role of judiciary and often publish articles in eminent legal journals, they do not usually come from an academic career, due to the need to demonstrate their continuous involvement as a practitioner.

With respect to their background, it is remarkable that many of them, above all the Chief Justices, graduated in Ireland but spent a period studying in the US or in the UK; some have been guest lecturers in Italian, French and Belgian Universities, too.[66] One can also explain the so-called 'deference' to EU law which seems to be implicit in the jurisprudence of the Supreme Court by looking at the judges' prior or subsequent experience. Indeed, several Justices have served as judges or Advocates General at the ECJ. Moreover, their attitude towards foreign law, which they appear to be deftly handling, is confirmed by their membership of several international associations of judges and by their participation in international conferences (mainly in Europe and in the US): there, they probably have the opportunity to talk to and exchange information with colleagues from other jurisdictions. For example, the Hon Justice Nial Fennelly was President of the Fédération internationale de droit européen (FIDE) in 2004 and Former Chief Justice Murray was one of the Vice-Presidents of the Network of the Presidents of the Supreme Judicial Courts of the EU until 2011.

It is well known that personal relationships among judges from different national jurisdictions can influence the use of foreign precedents by Constitutional Courts.[67]

---

[66] Such information has been found in the biographies of the former Chief Justices on the Supreme Court's website: www.supremecourt.ie. The 'openness' towards other jurisdictions has also been fostered by the Irish Court Service among judges of the lower courts. The Irish Courts Service also guarantees administrative and technical support to judges through exchange programmes with foreign jurisdictions. To this end, it promoted 'The Foreign Visit Programme' which facilitates judicial visits from several countries. Visitors can meet Irish judges and attend court hearings. So far, there have been visitors from the UK (including Northern Ireland and Scotland), Spain, Canada, Thailand, Bangladesh, Sweden, Brazil, the US, Norway and Uganda.

[67] On the factors that influence the conduct of the Justices, see JA Segal, 'Judicial Behavior' in KE Whittington, RD Kelemen and GA Caldeira (eds), *The Oxford Handbook of Law and Politics* (Oxford, Oxford University Press, 2008) 19–33.

This was certainly the case in *Quinn's Supermarket v The Attorney General*,[68] a case dealing with religious freedom and discrimination. There, Irish Supreme Court Justice Walsh quoted a number of relevant US Supreme Court decisions. As a matter of fact, he explored at great length the concurring opinion of Justice Brennan (a personal friend of his) in *School District of Abington Township v Schempp*,[69] commenting: 'The words of Mr Justice Brennan are very pertinent to the question issue in this case'.[70] In an article published in the Judicial Studies Institute Journal significantly entitled 'Judicial Cosmopolitanism', the then Chief Justice of the Irish Supreme Court, John L Murray, repeatedly quoted a speech by Gustavo Zagrebelsky, President Emeritus of the Italian Constitutional Court, entitled 'Fifty Years of Activity of the Constitutional Court' (22 April 2006), thanking him for the 'translation kindly provided by author'.[71]

Finally, another important issue to address when considering the openness of the Justices to foreign jurisprudence is the role of judicial research assistants in influencing the content or background of Supreme Court decisions. The Chief Justice is supported by an Executive Legal Officer (ELO) whose task, in addition to providing legal support, is to arrange itineraries and liaison with national, foreign and international State bodies, courts and organisations.[72] However, the Supreme Court's tasks are achieved thanks to additional research assistants. Each year 'the Courts Service employs 10 research assistants on a one year basis, [mainly recent honour graduates of Irish universities] and also appoints a Senior Research Assistant from amongst the previous year's pool to be in charge'.[73] Quite significantly, these assistants are not assigned to individual judges. Rather, they are involved in drafting memoranda or carrying out research on single cases or issues according to their expertise, upon a query of the Justices and on the decision of the Senior Research Assistant. The rapid turnover in the group of research assistants enriches the activity of the Supreme Court with a variety of different contributions: as new and young researchers constantly replace one another, the background of the Court is in constant evolution, all but crystallised.

B. How the Supreme Court Decides

Contrary to judgments not related to constitutional matters and to decisions dealing with constitutional issues—such as human rights—but not affecting the validity of an Act, when the Supreme Court deals with the constitutional review of legislation it must follow the 'one-judgment rule'. This rule was absent in the original constitutional text, but was inserted in 1941.

In other words, whenever the validity of a law has to be ascertained one judge is selected to write a judgment, based on the majority view, and no other opinions

---

[68] *Quinn's Supermarket v The Attorney General* (1972) IR 1.
[69] *School District of Abington Township v Schempp*, 374 US 203 (1963).
[70] See Carolan, 'Consideration of Foreign Judgments', 130.
[71] See Murray, 'Judicial Cosmopolitanism', 10.
[72] See Courts Service Annual Report, *Structure of the Court* (Dublin, 2008) 34.
[73] See G Coonan, 'The Role of Judicial Research Assistants in supporting the Decision-Making Role of the Irish Judiciary' (2006) 1 *Judicial Studies Institute Journal* 188.

(whether concurring or dissenting), or even their existence, can be disclosed: 'no other opinions on such question, whether assenting or dissenting, shall be pronounced nor shall the existence of any such other opinion be disclosed (Articles 26.2 and 34.4 of the Constitution)'. Therefore in this case only the majority opinion counts.

On the contrary, all other 'constitutional decisions' of the Supreme Court are often joined by concurring or dissenting opinions. By '*other* constitutional decisions', as briefly mentioned above, we mean decisions having constitutional relevance, even though they do not strictly concern the consistency of a national law with the Constitution. This is the case, for instance, in the increasing number of judgments on the European arrest warrant, as they concern rights and freedoms and often cite foreign precedents—so that they have been included in the research—, but they do not entail the issue of the validity of statutes.

C. Interpretative Techniques and Tools Used by the Supreme Court and Foreign Influence

First of all, as mentioned above, throughout its jurisprudence the Supreme Court has always confirmed that there is a presumption of constitutionality of statutes.[74] The Court has further assured that it does not intend to replace the Parliament, the only institution with legislative power in Ireland,[75] even though the lack of intervention by the legislature and the Executive in politically sensitive areas (eg social rights) has been one of the causes of the often criticised judicial activism.[76] Obviously, the presumption does not apply to legislation enacted prior to 1937 and in *East Donegal Co-Op Ltd v Attorney General*,[77] the Court underlined that 'this benevolent technique has its limits. If the challenged provision is clear and unambiguous and invalid on that basis it may not be saved by giving it a construction which does violence to its language'.

Having clarified this premise, we can now consider some instances in which the interpretative techniques employed by the Court were influenced by foreign jurisprudence. The first is the case of the principle 'Reach constitutional issues last',

---

[74] The burden of proof to demonstrate unconstitutionality rests on the plaintiff.
[75] See *Ryan v Attorney General* (1965) IR 294.
[76] Judicial activism, however, has been considered as a problem by the Supreme Court itself in *TD v Minister for Education* (2001) 4 IR 259, where the then Chief Justice Keane criticised the attitude of the High Court in determining policies in place of the Executive. See Hamilton, *Judicial Activism in Irish Constitutional Law*, 6. Indeed, judicial activism is connected to the issue of the legitimation of courts (see A Bickel, *The Least Dangerous Branch: The Supreme Court at the Bar of Politics*, 2nd edn (Binghamton-NY, Vail-Ballau Press,1986) 111 ff, who emphasises the importance of the passive virtues of the courts) and can depend on other factors too. See R Hirschl, *Towards Juristocracy. The Origins and Consequences of the New Constitutionalism* (Harvard, Harvard University Press, 2004) 211 ff. In Ireland judicial activism can also derive from the need to react quickly to the huge changes happening within society (economic development, the decrease of the Roman Church's influence, immigration), without waiting for a long time of legislative process and political bargaining. See B Sullivan, 'The Irish Constitution: Some Reflections From Abroad' in E Carolan and O Doyle (eds), *The Irish Constitution: Governance and Values* (Dublin, Round Hall, 2008) 6–7 and D Gwynn Morgan, *The Separation of Powers in the Irish Constitution* (Dublin, Round Hall Sweet & Maxwell, 1997) 254–55, who also compares the relationship between the Courts and Parliament in Ireland with the cases of the US and Australia.
[77] *East Donegal Co-Op Ltd v Attorney General* (1970) IR 317.

which derives from the US experience; according to this principle, 'if the case can be decided on a non-constitutional ground, this course should be taken'[78] (see *O'B v S* (1984) IR 326). The second case is that of the application of the US-derived notion of 'mootness', accepted in *Condon v Minister of Labour* (1981) IR 62; there, the Court abstained from deciding upon a constitutional issue which only implied an academic exercise and was of no practical relevance.

Another example of foreign influence is the Supreme Court's extensive interpretation of the individual rights listed in the Irish Constitution, through the doctrine of 'unenumerated rights' (see above, section II), again modelled on US jurisprudence. Focusing on the issue of the interpretation of constitutional rights, one can explore the options the Supreme Court tends to favour when inferring specific meanings from constitutional provisions and then assess analogies with other constitutional or Supreme Courts.[79]

Although on some occasions the Court has affirmed that the Constitution 'must be interpreted ... according to the words which are used, and these words, where the meaning is plain and unambiguous, must be given their literal meaning (*People (DPP) v O'Shea*)',[80] literal interpretation has given way to other interpretative techniques, such as that of 'harmonious construction'. It means that constitutional provisions must be treated 'as interlocking parts of the general constitutional scheme (*Tormey v Att Gen*)'.[81] The so-called 'historical interpretation' is frequently used as an interpretative standard, but seldom autonomously. Moreover, although the Constitution of 1937 largely builds upon the prior legal order of the Dominion of Ireland, after 1922 'Dáil debates on the draft Constitution have never been cited in judgment ...'.[82] Thus, when interpreting the Constitution, the Supreme Court of Ireland seems 'closer' to the evolutive interpretation of the fundamental law used by the Supreme Court of Canada and its 'living tree doctrine' than to the approach currently followed by some Justices of the US Supreme Court through their deference to the original intent of the Framers.

From this point of view, the resemblance with the Supreme Court of Canada—even though its precedents are not cited very often—is further borne out by the 'borrowing'—or, better, the 'transplant'[83]—of its proportionality test by the Irish High Court, first, and by the Supreme Court, afterwards. Indeed, the test set down in one of the most cited precedents by foreign jurisdictions, the Canadian case of *R v Oakes*,[84] was firstly 'imported' by Justice Costello in *Heaney v Ireland*,[85] a decision subsequently

---

[78] See G Casey, *Constitutional Law in Ireland*, 277.

[79] On the relationship between constitutional comparativism and the interpretative method of constitutional adjudication, see RP Alford, 'In Search of a Theory for Constitutional Comparativism' (2005) 52 *UCLA Law Review* 639 ff.

[80] *People (DPP) v O'Shea* (1982) IR 384.

[81] *Tormey v Att Gen* (1985) ILRM 375.

[82] See G Casey, *Constitutional Law in Ireland*, 301. Similarly, the High Court of Australia has never cited debates of the 1898 constitutional convention. On the contrary, the US Supreme Court is accustomed to making ample reference to conventional debates (see, eg, *Brown v Board of Education* (1959) 347 US 483).

[83] On the notion of 'legal transplant', mainly related to the cross-influence amongst national legislations, see A Watson, *Legal Transplants: An Approach to Comparative Law* (Charlottesville, University Press of Virginia, 1974) 95.

[84] *R v Oakes* (1986) 1 SCR 103. This feature of the decision has been underlined by T Groppi, 'A User-friendly Court. The Influence of Supreme Court of Canada Decisions Since 1982 on Court Decisions in Other Liberal Democracies' (2007) 36 *The Supreme Court Law Review* 337 ff.

[85] *Heaney v Ireland* (1994) 3 IR 593.

confirmed by the Irish Supreme Court's jurisprudence.[86] In that decision, *R v Oakes* is largely quoted and the three-step approach used by the Canadian Supreme Court within the proportionality test to assess the seriousness of the right's violation and to proceed with the balancing is entirely adopted in the Irish legal order.[87]

Finally, since comparison is in itself a method of judicial interpretation,[88] as for some other common law jurisdictions like Canada, the Supreme Court of Ireland relies at great length on it,[89] but almost never without taking into account other interpretative techniques. Comparison is used *ad adiuvandum* besides the main interpretative tool/s.

VIII. THE RESULTS OF THE EMPIRICAL RESEARCH ON THE USE OF FOREIGN PRECEDENTS

A. Introduction. The Use of Precedents by the Supreme Court and the Place of Foreign Case Law in its Jurisprudence

The first significant decision on the use of precedents by the Supreme Court was delivered in *State (Quinn) v Ryan*.[90] There, the Court affirmed that its jurisdiction is of a constitutional nature and that, where necessary, it has the power to depart from its prior decisions in constitutional cases. On that occasion, the Court devised a 'flexible' doctrine of *stare decisis* by stating that 'the stare decisis ... is a policy and not a binding unalterable rule'. However, as subsequently declared, an overruling has to be justified by 'compelling reasons' and cannot occur without any motivation, so that they are not so frequent.[91]

As mentioned above (section II), one of the main problems dealt with in the research concerns the nature of decisions rendered by the Judicial Committee of the Privy Council before 1933 and by the Appellate Committee of the House of Lords mainly before 1922. In light of the choice for the perpetuity of the legal system, are these foreign or national precedents? Our understanding is that, despite the decision

---

[86] See B Foley, 'The Proportionality Test: Present Problems' (2008) *Judicial Studies Institute Journal* 75. For a comparative analysis on proportionality tests and the cross-national influence amongst jurisdictions, see A Stone Sweet and J Mathews, 'Proportionality Balancing and Global Constitutionalism' (2009) 47 *Columbia Journal of Transnational Law* 72–164.

[87] The impugned provision has to '(a) be rationally connected to the objective and not be arbitrary, unfair or based on irrational considerations; (b) impair the right as little as possible, and (c) be such that their effects on rights are proportional to the objective' (*Heaney v Ireland*). Murray, Judicial Cosmopolitanism', 13, highlights that this decision is important also for the citation of US precedents as points of reference in matters of self-incrimination: 'The Court of Criminal Appeal then referred to essentially the same distinction which was adopted by the Supreme Court of the US in Schmerber v California (384 US 757 (1966)), when it considered a citizen's right to silence and privilege against self-incrimination under the Fifth Amendment of the US Constitution'.

[88] In this regard, S Choudry, 'Globalization in Search of Justification: Toward a Theory of Comparative Constitutional Interpretation' (1999) 74 *Indiana Law Journal* 835 talks about the dialogical method of interpretation.

[89] See, recently, B Carolan, The Search for Coherence in the Use of Foreign Court Judgments by the Supreme Court of Ireland (2004–05) 12 *Tulsa Journal of Comparative & International Law* 123–48 and B Flanagan and S Ahern, 'Judicial Decision-making and Transnational Law: A Survey of Common Law Supreme Court Judges' in (2011) 60 *International and Comparative Law Quarterly* 1–28.

[90] *State (Quinn) v Ryan* (1965) IR 70.

[91] Afterwards the Supreme Court seems to have slightly changed its approach, affirming that its precedents are 'helpful, relevant, and generally speaking, binding' (see the decision on *Desmond v Glackin* no 2 (1993) 3 IR 67).

on *State (Quinn) v Ryan* and its objective to legitimise the existence 'of a new Constitutional judge', these can be considered as domestic precedents since when the decisions of these two courts were issued Ireland was substantially under British rule or was a Dominion and then these precedents formed part of the national legal order, being binding upon it.

As underlined in the previous sections, when seeking solutions suitable for the context of Ireland, judges (not only in their judgments, but also in the articles they publish in legal journals),[92] as well as Attorney Generals, parties in legal proceedings and scholars devote significant attention to what happens abroad, mainly in the UK, the US, Australia and Canada. Moreover, they look very often at foreign jurisprudence, legislation, legal articles and textbooks in order to explain how domestic institutions function and, most of all, how rights have to be protected. However, since our analysis focuses on the dialogue among constitutional judges, only foreign case law has been taken into account and all other forms of transnational influence have been excluded.

B. The Research Methodology

Data were collected using a subscription database containing all reported judgments of the High Court and Supreme Court from 1937 onwards aiming to ensure the complete coverage of the decisions from the coming into force of the Constitution until the end of 2010.[93]

The constitutional cases decided by the Supreme Court of Ireland—which are those relevant for the research—have been identified as those concerning the constitutional validity of legislative Acts and decisions issued by public authorities (since the constitutionality of the latter can also be challenged in Ireland), but also those dealing with human rights, like decisions on writs of *habeas corpus*, that only indirectly concern consistency with the Constitution (the first aim, indeed, is to redress a violation of rights). Out of a total of 3,247 Supreme Court decisions, 902 are constitutional cases.

In practice the research on the database has been carried out per year using two keywords, constitution (which assures the coverage of decisions where its derivative nouns and adjectives, such as 'constitutional', are reported), and then its abbreviation 'Const', and right. Around 3,000 judgments have been read to assess whether they can be included in the category of 'constitutional case'. As expected, although the research under the two keywords has mainly led to the same decisions—those mentioning right usually refer also to the Constitution and vice versa—, the margin of error has proved to be higher when using the word 'right' instead of 'constitution' because in the former case on some occasions only minor offences of the Constitution have been put in place or the Constitution is only marginally regarded. Indeed, sometimes these prospective constitutional

---

[92] On extra-judicial comments by Irish judges, see R Kennedy, 'Extra-Judicial Comment by Judges' (2005) 5 *Judicial Studies Institute Journal* 199–212.

[93] The database used is *Justis*, www.justis.com. By contrast, free websites, like www.bailii.org, www.irlii.org or www.courts.ie generally contain only judgments from 2001 onwards.

cases only affect the jurisdiction of the Supreme Court as the court of last resort in criminal matters, and therefore their constitutional nature has been denied.

The search for foreign precedents within the constitutional decisions has required a careful examination of the content since decisions have only recently listed domestic and foreign precedents cited. Moreover, the carrying out of the qualitative analysis has obliged us to read through the whole content of the judgments anyway, aiming at understanding how precedents have been used and for what purpose.

C. The Results of the Quantitative Analysis

From 1937 to 2010 foreign precedents were cited in most Supreme Court decisions on constitutional issues (in nearly 44 per cent of the overall number of constitutional cases). However, while the number of judgments using foreign case law reached its apex in the early Sixties, it has gradually decreased afterwards and more intensely since the Eighties.

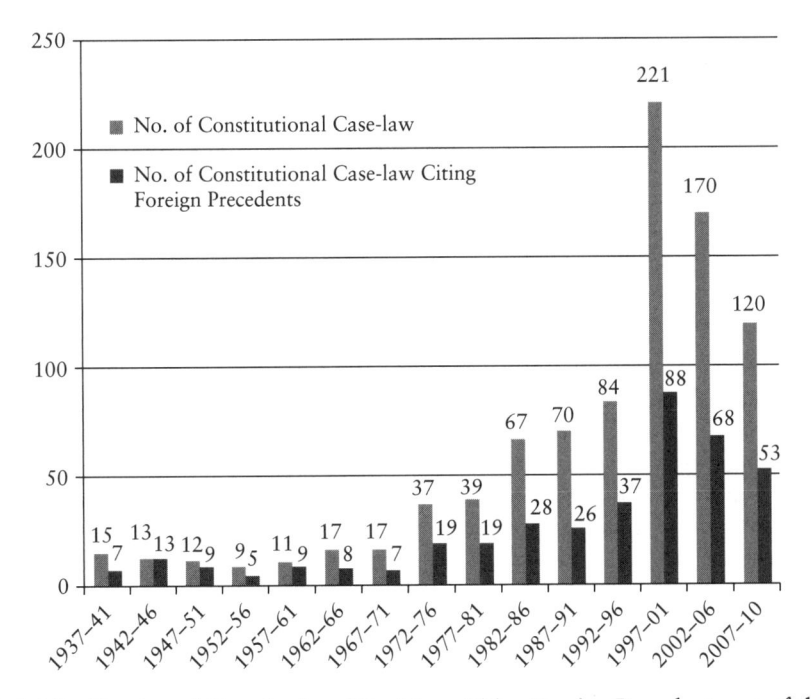

Graph 1: The Number of Constitutional Decisions Citing Foreign Precedents out of the Total per Half-decade[94]

---

[94] Only the period from 2007–10 has been considered, and decisions have been analysed until 31 December 2010.

One possible explanation of this trend relies on the stabilisation of a conspicuous number of precedents within Irish constitutional jurisprudence over the decades, which is particularly important considering that scholars have normally connected democratic transitions, processes of institution-building as well as the achievement of independence—as happened to Ireland—to the attitude of constitutional judges to 'consulting' sources of law coming from other legal orders.[95] By the same token, the more the domestic legal order reaches a certain degree of internal and external acknowledgement and judges acquire their own legitimation,[96] the more courts feel confident to manage national norms without recourse to external ones as additional sources of authority. The reputation of a court is built over the years. At the beginning of its activity or when a new Constitution is enacted, lacking national solutions, it is likely that the courts 'learn' from foreign jurisdictions how similar cases have been solved or how similar provisions have been interpreted. This process of 'emulation', although pursued with accurate weighing, takes place even though national constitutional provisions are definitely the final parameters of constitutional adjudication.

This happened especially during the first years after the entry into force of the 1937 Constitution, when the Supreme Court's Justices also had to become familiar with the new constitutional provisions. In this light, it is instructive to see how Justices examined the wording of the Constitution comparing it with foreign constitutional provisions and with the jurisprudence of foreign courts. For instance, in a famous case decided in 1947, *National Union of Railwaymen and Others v Sullivan and Others*,[97] on the right to associate with trade unions, the Supreme Court cited 12 foreign precedents (mostly from the UK and the US), using them, and especially those of the US Supreme Court, for constructing the correct interpretation of Article 40.6.2 of the Irish Constitution. Although the two national contexts were not held to be particularly dissimilar in terms of the establishment of trade unions, what differed was the phrasing of the two Constitutions: while the constitutional foundation of trade unions in the US is based on the power vested in the Congress to regulate interstate commerce,[98] Article 40.6.2 of the Irish Constitution provides '[t]he right of the citizens to form associations and unions', to be further regulated by law in the public interest of protecting such right. It follows that any limitation to the right of the citizen to join one or more trade unions 'does undoubtedly deprive the citizen of a free choice of the persons with whom he shall associate'. The US Supreme Court case law has been helpful for the Supreme Court of Ireland in understanding what the correct perspective is for looking at the present case: namely, not that of the public authority to dispose the establishment of trade unions, as in the US, but rather that of the citizens' rights. Justice Murnaghan, delivering the opinion of the Court, declared a

---

[95] This thesis is sustained, for instance, by C Dupré, *Importing the Law in Post-Communist Transitions. The Hungarian Constitutional Court and the Right to Human Dignity* (Oxford and Portland, Oregon, Hart Publishing, 2003) 39 ff.
[96] See B Markesinis and J Fedtke, *Judicial Recourse to Foreign Law: A New Source of Inspiration?* (London, UCL, 2006) 110 ff, who list when this transnational judicial dialogue should take place. Amongst the reasons that justify the use of foreign precedents they mention the existence of a legal loophole in the national legal order and the aim to prove that a legal solution could fit well in the legal system because it has already been successful abroad.
[97] *National Union of Railwaymen and ors v Sullivan and ors* (1947) 1 IR 77.
[98] Justice Day, in *United States v Hill*, 248 US 420.

departure from the precedent of the US Supreme Court: 'The analogies would march more closely if our Constitution, instead of declaring a right in the citizens, had given to the Oireachtas, power to regulate the formation of associations and unions'.

However, as Graph 1 shows, constitutional decisions are only a limited part of the total number of the Supreme Court's decisions. As pointed out in section VI, the low figures of constitutional case law are probably due to the observance of the principle '[r]each constitutional issues last', but above all, with regard to the years considered, to the initial exclusion from constitutional review of legislation of statutes and regulations dealing with the security of the State as well as of EU legislation or national norms of execution. The fact that the research is limited to constitutional case law is significant, since Constitutions are usually less amended than other legal norms so they are quite stable in their content throughout the years. This implies that, although the overruling is always admissible, once the jurisprudence upon constitutional provisions has been consolidated over the years, constitutional judges, such as those of the Supreme Court of Ireland, prefer to refer to their own precedents. Nonetheless, when a new sensitive issue arises and there are no precedents, the Supreme Court looks at how the issue has been addressed elsewhere, shaping a sort of teaching function of the foreign precedents vis-a-vis national constitutional judges.[99]

Such a hypothesis occurred in *In re a Ward of Court*,[100] a case concerning, for the first time in Ireland, a decision of the Supreme Court on interrupting medical and nourishment treatments towards a young woman, a ward of the court, in a semi-vegetative state following surgery. This case did not concern the validity of statutes—absent on this matter in Ireland and in the jurisdictions from where precedents were 'borrowed'—but rather whether the request of the mother's ward to withdraw medical treatment could be approved; that is, whether the approval of such request could be found in breach of the right to life under Article 40.3.2 of the Constitution. The majority of the Court followed a UK precedent, *Airedale NHS Trust v Bland*,[101] decided a few years before, and especially Lord Goff's 'best interest test' explained in his opinion on the case and quoted extensively by the Irish Supreme Court's Justices:

> [T]he question is not whether it is in the best interests of the patient that he should die. The question is whether it is in the best interests of the patient that his life should be prolonged by the continuance of this form of medical treatment or care.

Justice O'Flaherty also referred to the then most recent decision of an US appellate State court,[102] *In re Fiori*,[103] also applying the 'best interest analysis'. Therefore the Supreme Court of Ireland held that it was in the best interest of the ward not to prolong her life artificially.

---

[99] See A Barak, 'Response to the Judge as Comparatist: Comparison in Public Law' (2005) 80 *Tulane Law Review* 195–202, who emphasises the usefulness of judges having an extended interpretative field, enriched also by foreign precedents. They can make it easier to opt for the best solution to national problems. The only condition for making this exercise fruitful is that the domestic and the foreign legal orders share a common ideological basis.
[100] *In re a Ward of Court* (Withholding Medical Treatment) (No 2) (1996) 1IR 79.
[101] *Airedale NHS Trust v Bland* (1993) AC 789.
[102] The patient died before the case could be brought to the Supreme Court of Arizona.
[103] *In re Fiori* (1995) 652 AR 2d 1350.

120 *Cristina Fasone*

The Supreme Court's Justices select carefully the jurisdictions whose precedents can be relevant to their opinions or to the judgment. Since 'common legal traditions ... establish basic conditions for dialogue and comparison',[104] common law and Commonwealth jurisdictions are preferred to others, which are considered only in very specific fields like fiscal policy (as was the case with the German Constitutional Court)[105] or the European arrest warrant (as was the case with the Polish Constitutional Court).[106]

Of course, other factors concur to explain why decisions of some jurisdictions are chosen: on the one hand, factors like the effectiveness of the constitutional review of legislation and the equivalent condition of structural lack of constitutional rights move Ireland close to the US; on the other hand, the colonial past, the struggle for independence and the choice of legal continuity influence the citation of UK case law. Precedents have been considered from the Appellate Committee of the House of Lords and the Judicial Committee of the Privy Council, the US Supreme Court (and some State supreme courts), the Supreme Court of Canada, the High Court of Australia (less than other courts on human rights), the Supreme Court of New Zealand, the Constitutional Court of Poland, the German and Italian Constitutional Courts, the Supreme Courts of Cyprus and Israel and the Cour de cassation of Belgium. Instead, 'Indian precedents—potentially so instructive—have been overlooked',[107] as they have been cited only three times, a figure very close to those scored by the Courts of continental Europe.

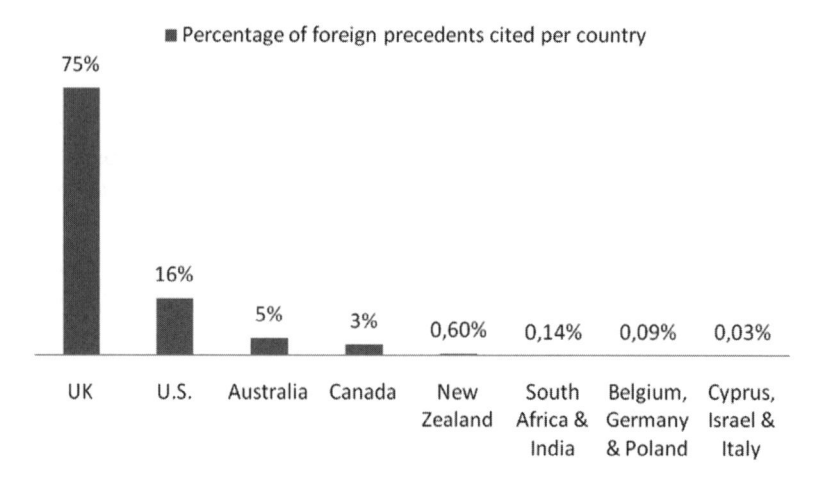

■ Percentage of foreign precedents cited per country

Country	Percentage
UK	75%
U.S.	16%
Australia	5%
Canada	3%
New Zealand	0,60%
South Africa & India	0,14%
Belgium, Germany & Poland	0,09%
Cyprus, Israel & Italy	0,03%

Graph 2: Percentage of Cases using Foreign Precedents, Sorted by Countries

---

[104] See S Cassese, *Legal Comparison by the Courts*, Paper for the Opening Plenary Session of the XVIIIth International Congress of Comparative Law (25 July–1 August 2010) Washington, DC, 11.
[105] See *Murphy v The Attorney General* (1982) 1 IR 241.
[106] See *Minister for Justice, Equality and Law Reform v Rettinger* (2010) 7 JIC 2301. Whyte and Hogan, *JM Kelly: The Irish Constitution*, 430–31, criticise the fact that European jurisdictions are seldom cited, since they have much in common with the Irish legal system.
[107] See G Casey, *Constitutional Law in Ireland*, p 297.

D. The Results of the Qualitative Analysis

From a constitutional point of view, foreign law, including foreign constitutional case law, is not an interpretative standard in Ireland, as it is under Article 39 of the Constitution of South Africa ('[w]hen interpreting the Bill of Rights, a court, tribunal or forum: ... *may* consider foreign law').[108] According to the Irish Constitution, only the national legislature has the power to make laws for the State. This means that 'foreign national law should occupy approximately the same position as international law in the Irish Constitutional order',[109] similarly to what we affirmed above about the *status* of the ECHR before 2003. However, the situation appears to be a little bit different in practice.

First of all, both the parties and the judges seem to be more comfortable with foreign law than with international law, which they refer to less frequently in their arguments. Secondly, the Supreme Court's Justices analyse foreign precedents (essentially from common law countries) in great detail and often quote majority, concurring and dissenting opinions, depending on the case. Most important, when referring to foreign case law, the Irish Supreme Court adopts the same judicial interpretative techniques as it does when manages its own precedents. It tries to justify its arguments both when it reasons by analogy and when it distinguishes the facts and the relevant principle as considered in Ireland compared to foreign countries. This undoubtedly happens in the case of precedents of the Supreme Courts of Canada and of the US. For example, in *CC v Ireland and Others*,[110] the Court referred to the Canadian Supreme Court's decision in *Hess and Nguyen v R*,[111] looking at that case to sustain more or less the same point of view as the Canadian Court, while rejecting the 'foreign' dissenting opinions.[112]

Therefore the Supreme Court of Ireland proves to be an expert comparatist that uses foreign case law with a full understanding of the whole context in which it was defined. At times the Court initially recalls the foreign precedents submitted by the parties involved in the controversy and afterwards carefully considers whether they can be applied in the domestic jurisdiction and the reasons why they should be followed or, on the contrary, disregarded.

Moreover, the Supreme Court is also aware of the risk of using foreign precedents, as was clearly expressed in *Pól O Murchú v An Taoiseach*[113] by Justice Macken delivering the opinion of the Court. In the case at hand the Court had to decide if Articles 8 and 25.4.1 of the Constitution, read together, gave rise to a constitutional obligation to make available a simultaneous translation of an Act of the Oireachtas in Irish where it was signed into law in English (both being official

---

[108] Therefore we cannot consider Ireland as a case of 'relational engagement' with courts of other states, there being absent any kind of relational obligation: see Jackson, *Constitutional Engagement in a Transnational Era*, 78.
[109] See Carolan, 'Consideration of Foreign Judgments', 121.
[110] *CC v Ireland and ors* (2006) IESC 33. The case dealt with the constitutionality of s 1 of the Criminal Law (Amendment) Act 1935 about the crime of felony deriving from sexual intercourse with a person under 15 years.
[111] *Hess and Nguyen v R* (1990) 2 SCR 906.
[112] See Groppi, 'A User-friendly Court', 358.
[113] *Pól O Murchú v An Taoiseach* (2010) IEHC 26.

122 *Cristina Fasone*

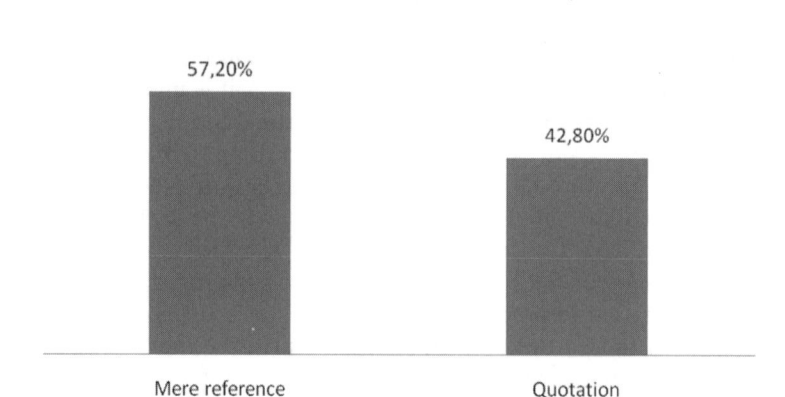

■ Percentage of citations only mentioned or quoted

57,20%   42,80%

Mere reference   Quotation

Graph 3: How are the Citations of Foreign Precedents Made?

languages in Ireland), an option that was finally denied by the Court. The respondent had argued that a constitutional obligation to provide Irish translations of Acts, 'on terms no less favourable' than the provision of the English versions, existed according to Articles 8 and 25.4.1 of the Constitution. The reasoning of Justice Macken started by acknowledging that the phrase 'on terms no less favourable' appeared to be taken from Canadian case law, in the particular context of that country and of its Charter of Rights. In this regard, Macken Justice also affirmed that

> this Court [the Supreme Court of Ireland] finds it of assistance to consider the case law of other jurisdictions as being of use in cases concerning the interpretation of the Constitution, especially where such case law involves closely similar provisions.

However, 'while accepting that this may be an appropriate approach in many cases',—Justice Macken stated:

> I am nevertheless not entirely convinced that the invocation of such case law from other jurisdictions, such as Canada (or indeed from other analogous countries,—as, for example, Belgium or South Africa) is particularly helpful in reaching a view as to the correct interpretation of the particular language requirements or obligations flowing from Article 25.4.4 or Article 8 of the Constitution in this case.

Indeed, it was considered that, in the case of language, the peculiar social, political and historical contexts are too different, also depending on the circumstances when the Constitutions were adopted and because of the constitutional texts themselves.

Consequently, in the first three decades after 1937, because the Supreme Court of Ireland was somewhat committed to demonstrating that it took foreign precedents into account, it showed the different opinions of foreign judges, resulting in some very long constitutional decisions.[114] Almost 60 per cent of foreign precedents are simply mentioned, while a little bit more than 40 per cent are quoted extensively.

---

[114] So far the maximum length was reached in 2002 with 359 pages, in *Maguire v Ardagh* (2002) 1IR 385.

This latter figure is definitely high, if it is considered that the number of mere references is very often raised because 'indirect citations' have been found, that is, mere references to foreign precedents included in citations of paragraphs of other foreign case law. Thus these quotations may contribute to the lengthening of the text of the decisions and can make their reading and understanding less easy.

This problem sometimes occurs when Justices seem to boast of their knowledge of foreign precedents, enriching the content of their opinions or decisions, regardless of the effective need to cite foreign case law for the purpose of coherence and consistency of their legal reasoning. An example of this 'ornamental use' of foreign decisions can be found in *The People (Attorney-General) v Edge*,[115] where, talking about the definition of the 'age of discretion'—ie when a minor is deemed to act with discernment—, Justice Gavan Duffy quoted extensively two opinions of Justice Holmes of the US Supreme Court; one was a dissenting opinion in *Hyde v United States*,[116] whereas the other was the majority opinion in *Towne v Eisner*.[117] Justice Gavan Duffy meant to say that the 'age of discretion' cannot be defined once and for all, but is subject to the passing of time. However no reasons can be found for citing these US precedents in the present case which referred to a completely different subject matter.

The research reveals that most citations of foreign precedents occur in decisions dealing with human rights (72 per cent), compared to 'institutional decisions': indeed, out of the total number of 396 cases where foreign precedents have been cited 285 concern human rights and only 111 institutional matters.

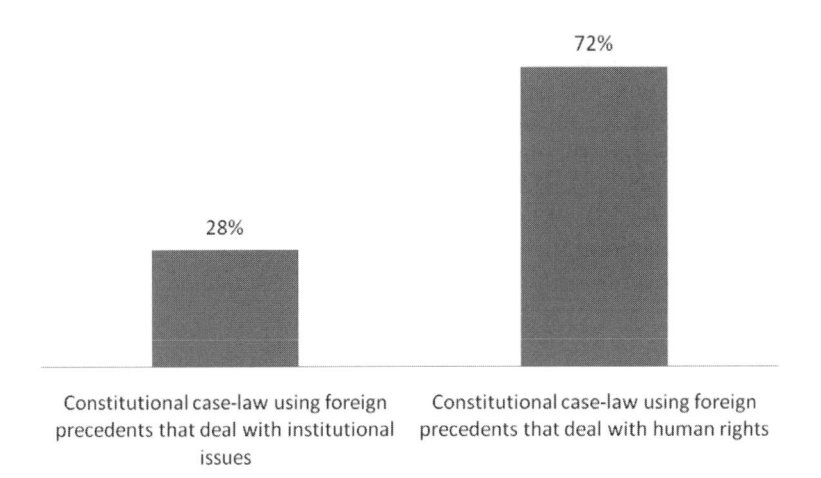

Graph 4: Percentage of Institutional and Human Rights Decisions using Foreign Precedents

---

[115] *The People (Attorney-General) v Edge* (1943) 1IR 115.
[116] *Hyde v United States*, 225 US 347, 391 (1912): 'It is one of the misfortunes of the law that ideas become encysted in phrases and thereafter for a long time cease to provoke further analysis'.
[117] *Towne v Eisner*, 245 US 418 (1918): 'A word is not a crystal, transparent and unchanged; it is the skin of a living thought and may vary greatly in color and content according to the circumstances and time in which it is used'.

By 'institutional decisions' we mean judgments dealing with the Parliament and its members, the Government, the President and the Courts, and also those which involve disputes over jurisdiction, or the relationship between the High Court's and the Supreme Court's jurisdictions. On the contrary, among 'human rights decisions' all cases patently dealing with the protection of human rights are included.[118]

Due to the fact that institutional features, like the form of government, are usually peculiar to each country, foreign precedents abound in decisions affecting human rights, whereas they seldom appear in 'institutional decisions'. The only exception can be represented by decisions dealing with the prerogatives of the Parliament not to be subjected to the interference of the Executive branch and the judiciary. There several precedents from the UK, the US and Australia were used.

At least one landmark decision concerning institutional issues and making use of foreign precedents has to be mentioned, namely *Maguire v Ardagh*,[119] which is a milestone in Irish constitutional jurisprudence about the principle of separation of powers and the relationship between the Parliament, the Government and the judiciary. The case law concerns whether the 1937 Constitution allows Parliament to establish a Joint committee of inquiry (on the killing of a civilian by the police) also creating a sub-committee enjoying fact-finding authority and the power to call witnesses. The majority of the Court held that such power was not provided by the Constitution and that the House of Parliament and its Joint committee and sub-committee acted ultra vires, invading the prerogatives of the courts and possibly jeopardising the rights of citizens. However, in his dissenting opinion, Chief Justice Keane argued the contrary, also relying on precedents of the UK and US courts. He considered *Howard v Gosset*[120] and stated that, according to this precedent and British constitutional theory, the Westminster Parliament itself constituted a 'High Court', something which is arguably applicable per se to the Irish legislature. By contrast, Chief Justice Keane looked at the US Supreme Court decision in *Watkins v United States*[121]—where the power of the Congress to conduct investigations was considered inherent in the legislative process—as if it could provide guidance for the case at hand.[122] The Chief Justice came to acknowledge that he would have substituted without hesitation the word 'Oireachtas' for 'Congress' and 'the executive' for 'the Federal Government', aiming at applying the statement of the US Supreme

---

[118] With regard to 'borderline decisions', such as those involving at the same time the relationship among constitutional powers, the sources of the law and the degree of protection assured to individual rights, we have opted for inclusion in the first or in the second category according to whether the institutional aspects or the human rights dimension prevails.

[119] *Maguire v Ardagh* (2002) 1 IR 785.

[120] *Howard v Gosset* (1845) 10 QB 359.

[121] *Watkins v United States* (1957) 354 US 178.

[122] In *Watkins v United States* (1957) 354 US 178, it was also held that 'power is broad. It encompasses inquiries concerning the administration of existing laws as well as proposed or possibly needed statutes. It includes surveys of defects in our social, economic or political system for the purpose of enabling the Congress to remedy them. It comprehends probes into departments of the Federal Government to expose corruption, inefficiency or waste. But broad as this power of inquiry is, it is not unlimited. There is no general authority to expose the private affairs of individuals without justification in terms of the functions of the Congress. Nor is the Congress a law enforcement or trial agency. These are functions of the executive and judicial departments of government. No inquiry is an end in itself. It must be related to, and in furtherance of, a legitimate task of the Congress. Investigations conducted solely for the personal aggrandizement of the investigators or to "punish" those investigated are indefensible'.

Court within the Irish jurisdiction. According to the Chief Justice, though recognising that 'the English and United States decisions can be of no more than persuasive force' in Ireland,

> they confirm that, in the case of the two states whose parliamentary and legal systems have had by far the greatest influence on ours, it has repeatedly been made clear that their legislators enjoy the inherent power to initiate inquiries of which our legislature is said to be bereft.

The location of the citations, whether they are contained most of all in the majority, in the concurring or in the dissenting opinions of the Supreme Court of Ireland, should not actually be seen as a good marker of the real will of the Justices. Indeed, in the issues dealing with the constitutional review of legislation and in the case of the reference mechanism (Article 26 of the Constitution) Justices are 'forced' to agree, since the one-judgment rule is mandatory. Thus most constitutional decisions of the Supreme Court come out with a unique opinion of the Court, which reflects the will of the majority. Therefore the figures on the location of foreign precedents and the proportion amongst the opinions are somewhat distorted.

For the most part foreign precedents are used as a 'guiding horizon',[123] at the very first stage of the interpretative process, when reasoning must be oriented. All foreign precedents are cited in obiter dicta and scholars unanimously believe that they have persuasive authority only in deciding on a certain case. Even with regard to one of the most cited foreign courts, the Supreme Court of Ireland 'has emphasised that, given the difference in some constitutional provisions between the two States, the United States Supreme Court decisions must be used with care'.[124] However, albeit the percentage is definitely lower, and in spite of the common

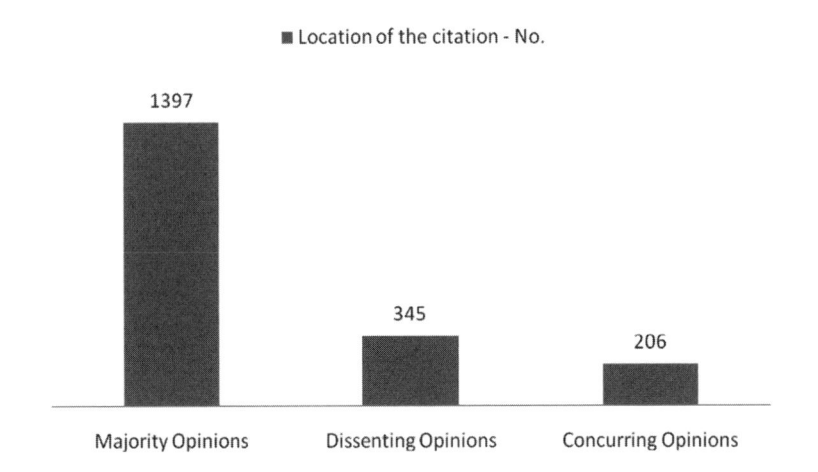

■ Location of the citation - No.

Majority Opinions: 1397
Dissenting Opinions: 345
Concurring Opinions: 206

Graph 5: The Location of the Citations

---

[123] See Groppi, 'A User-friendly Court', 344.
[124] *O'B v S* (1984) IR 316, and see ibid.

126 *Cristina Fasone*

■ Purpose of the citation (percentage)

- 67,80% — Guiding horizon
- 19,90% — Even there, even here
- 12,30% — A contrario

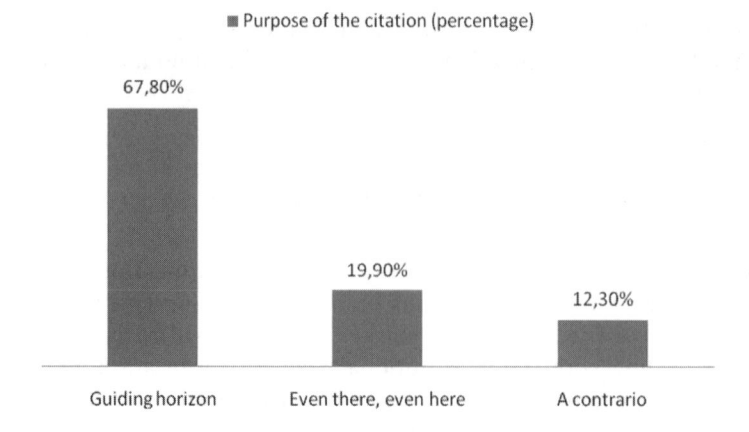

Graph 6: The Purpose of the Use of Foreign Precedents

understanding about the non-binding authority of foreign precedents, nearly 20 per cent of citations (from 1937 to 2010) were used with the purpose 'even there–even here',[125] declaring to accept and to apply a constitutional principle or a specific interpretation of a constitutional clause exactly as done in foreign precedents (this happened only for those coming from the UK, the US, Australia and Canada). In this regard, the most evident example, already mentioned above (see above, section VII), is constituted by the proportionality test defined by the Supreme Court of Canada in *R v Oakes*, which has been substantially 'transplanted' into Irish law by the Supreme Court in *In the matter of Article 26 of the Constitution and in the matter of the Employment Equality Bill, 1996*[126] (after having been used by the High Court).

Finally, the citation of foreign case law *a contrario* is rare. Rather, in those decisions where national constitutional norms underlining the 'uniqueness' of the Irish legal order are applied, as in the judgments on the rights of the unborn,[127] the Supreme Court prefers to ignore foreign case law departing from the 'Irish pattern' (while foreign precedents potentially consistent with the domestic system, such as *Roe v Wade*,[128] are considered a 'guiding horizon'). An exception was the UK precedent *Rex v Bourne*,[129] admitting abortion to preserve the life of a pregnant woman, which was explicitly used *a contrario* by Justice Denham in *Roche v Roche*. She said that *Rex v Bourne* 'was followed in many common law jurisdictions. However, it was never applied to or relied upon in this State. It was no part of our law'.

---

[125] 'Even there' commonly means 'with the purpose to assure a "probative comparison"', as described by Groppi, 'A User-friendly Court', 344, but this idiomatic expression is used in a slightly different manner in this chapter.

[126] *In the matter of Article 26 of the Constitution and in the matter of the Employment Equality Bill, 1996* (1997) 2IR 321.

[127] The most relevant judgments in this regard are: *Society for the Protection of Unborn Children (Ireland) Ltd v Coogan* (1989) IR 734; *Attorney General v X* (1992) 1IR 1; *SPUC v Grogan (No 5)* (1998) 4 IR 343; *Roche v Roche* (2010) 2 IR 321.

[128] *Roe v Wade* (1973) 410 US 113.

[129] *Rex v Bourne* (1939) 1 KB 687.

IX. CONCLUSION: THE IRISH SUPREME COURT, ITS ENGAGEMENT IN THE TRANSNATIONAL JUDICIAL DIALOGUE AND ITS LEGITIMATION

Within the European Union the Supreme Court of Ireland is probably the court of last instance, acting also as constitutional judge, that is used to citing foreign precedents most frequently and in great detail. This is true even though its tendency towards the 'sympathetic consideration'[130] of foreign constitutional judgments seems to have decreased in the last two decades. Ireland can be considered as one of the jurisdictions falling within the model of 'deliberative engagement'[131] in transnational judicial dialogue. Its Supreme Court decides spontaneously to cite foreign precedents—no legal norms bind it—, so that it can autonomously choose to reduce the level of engagement.

The Supreme Court selects foreign precedents, preferably amongst common law jurisdictions, within the Commonwealth. The two most cited Courts are the Appellate Committee of the House of Lords and the US Supreme Court. This depends above all on the constitutional history of Ireland, on its submission to the British jurisdiction and on the decision of 1937 for the continuity between the previous legal order, when the Acts of the United Kingdom were applied, and the following one, that of the independent Republic.

Of course the reasons that explain the consideration of the US Supreme Court's jurisprudence are quite different. Cultural and political influence were exercised by the US over the rising Irish Republic during the constituent phase. At that time, in 1937, the US was the only common law jurisdiction provided with a written and rigid Constitution and with a well-functioning system of constitutional review of legislation: therefore the US constitutional jurisprudence was a sort of obligatory point of reference for the Supreme Court acting as constitutional judge. Finally, the Irish Constitution only contains a very limited catalogue of human rights that has been enriched afterwards by the Supreme Court. The history of the protection of fundamental rights in the US was quite similar, due to their lack in the original text of the Constitution before amendments.

Benefiting as a 'hosting country' from the use of foreign precedents—sometimes also as a persuasive authority[132]—, the contribution of the Supreme Court of Ireland to the 'migration of constitutional ideas' has been significant and basically conditioned by the weight of its constitutional history, as well as its need to fill the legal vacuum caused by the short catalogue of constitutional rights and by social changes and to acquire its own legitimation departing from the era of British dominance.

---

[130] See Walker, 'Beyond Boundary Disputes', 384.
[131] See Jackson, *Constitutional Engagement in a Transnational Era*, 72.
[132] Whyte and Hogan, *JM Kelly: The Irish Constitution*, 430, emphasise the fact that foreign precedents often have persuasive authority upon the Supreme Court's decisions.

5

Israel: Creating a Constitution—The Use of Foreign Precedents by the Supreme Court (1994–2010)

SUZIE NAVOT[*]

TABLE OF CONTENTS

I. Introduction 129
II. Constitutional History and its Influence on the Use of Foreign Law 130
   A. The Early Years 130
   B. The Constitutional Revolution 133
III. The Supreme Court of Israel 136
IV. Empirical Analysis: Figures and Beyond 138
   A. Preliminary Observations 138
   B. Constitutional Cases Citing Foreign Precedents 141
   C. Institutional and Human Rights Decisions Citing Foreign Precedents .. 144
   D. Citing Foreign Precedents—by Country 145
   E. Citations According to Majority, Dissenting, or Separate Judgments ... 148
   F. Some Qualitative Thoughts 151
V. Conclusion 152

I. INTRODUCTION

AS SOON AS the State of Israel was established in 1948, after the British Mandate was terminated, the Israeli Supreme Court (ISC) began engaging in constitutional adjudication even though the new State did not adopt a Constitution. From the beginning, Israeli constitutional adjudication referred to foreign, particularly British, precedents since, though it was already an independent legal entity, it did not sever its linkage with English law.[1] Despite that extensive

---

[*] LLB MA LLD; Professor of Law. The Striks School of Law, Rishon Lezion, Israel. I am grateful to Nofar Asselman, Boris Rogikin, Adi Castro and Chen Avidov for their valuable assistance with the empirical research. Mistakes are mine only.

[1] According to the Palestine Order-in-Council, 1922, s 46 (a section which remained binding after the establishment of Israel and until 1980), British law was a legal source in Israeli law. This section states that when a legal question had no answer in the law, the judges were supposed to rule according to 'the substance of the common law and the doctrines of equity in force in England'. See D Friedman, 'The Effect of Foreign Law on the Law of Israel' (1975) 10 *Israel Law Review* 192 and D Friedman, 'Infusion of the Common Law into the Legal System of Israel' (1975) 10 *Israel Law Review* 324.

application of English precedents during Israel's first years of existence, local studies revealed that the contribution of foreign law to Israeli jurisprudence remained stable for more than 50 years.[2]

Apparently, foreign law has always been extensively used in Israel because of, among other reasons, the great local impact of English law. That trend visibly changed in the early 1980s[3] when American law became a stronger reference source, but use of foreign law as an important comparative source was and remained an inseparable part of Israeli adjudication. Former ISC President Barak said:

> Comparative law—whether international or local—is most important as it expands the interpretative horizon and field of vision. It has the power to instruct the interpreter as to the normative potential of other legal methods. It is limited because every legal system has its own institutions and typical ideology, and the way it treats the individual and the society is unique. Indeed, comparative law is like having an experienced friend. It is good to listen to their sound counsel, but it should not replace one's own decisions.[4]

This analysis focuses on foreign law citations by the ISC, based on empirical research of ISC rulings on constitutional cases. It addresses the background and composition of the ISC which, among other roles, functions as a constitutional court. In the first section, we will try to explain how Israel's constitutional history on the one hand, and the changes that took place in the ISC adjudication on the other, had an impact on the practice of citing foreign law in constitutional cases.

The second section focuses on an empirical study, its methodology, and qualitative and quantitative aspects. The discussion there refers to some of the more prominent verdicts handed down in Israel in recent years, particularly those that will interest comparative constitutionalists.

II. CONSTITUTIONAL HISTORY AND ITS INFLUENCE ON THE USE OF FOREIGN LAW

A. The Early Years

The State of Israel was officially established and proclaimed independent in May 1948, following the UN Partition Resolution of November 1947 and the termination of the British Mandate. Upon the State's establishment, Israel's Declaration of Independence determined that 'the establishment of the elected, regular authorities of the State' shall be 'in accordance with the Constitution, which shall be adopted by the Constituent Assembly...'.[5]

That Constituent Assembly—elected in 1949 and later renamed 'The First Knesset'—conducted extensive debates on the future Constitution. It failed to adopt

---

[2] Y Shachar, 'The Reference Practices of the Israeli Supreme Court 1950–2004' 50 *Hapraklit* (2008) 29, p 42 (in Hebrew). Though that study reviewed all cases of the Supreme Court and not only constitutional cases, it may safely be assumed that the same conclusions apply to it as well. We shall elaborate on this paper below.

[3] Ibid at p 48.

[4] HCJ 4128/02 *Adam, Teva v'Din an Israeli Association for Environmental Protection v the Prime Minister*, 58(3) PD 503, 515–16.

[5] For further reading see S Navot, *The Constitutional Law of Israel* (Kluwer, 2007) 19–20.

a Constitution nonetheless, but before it dispersed, the First Knesset endorsed a 'compromise' that became known as the 'Harrari Resolution'.[6] That resolution stated that the Israeli Parliament (the Knesset) would formulate the Constitution 'chapter by chapter', in stages; that each chapter would be entitled 'Basic Law'; and that in the future, it would unify all the basic laws into an integrated Israeli Constitution. The upshot of the Harrari Resolution was that the initial decision to adopt a complete Constitution for the State of Israel was deferred and replaced by the process of enacting a Constitution chapter by chapter—a process that led to the enactment of 12 basic laws, but was never completed and is yet to produce a full Constitution.[7]

The first important fact for this study on the use of foreign precedents in constitutional cases is that, upon its establishment, the State of Israel lacked a constitutional text to serve as the foundation for constitutional adjudication. That absence had two consequences.

First, it motivated a tight correlation between Israeli and English law, not only in the sense that English law served as a complementary legal source, but also the Israeli regime drew on content from the British regime. Hence, Israel's constitutional regime is based primarily on the constitutional structure of the British regime. Under the powerful influence of the English legacy, Israeli law shares many features with the common law tradition. Until 1980, Israeli courts were bound to follow English judge-made laws. The British system served and continues to serve as the historic source of many arrangements in Israeli constitutional law. The structure of the judiciary, its inner hierarchy, the rules of evidence and procedure, and the status of judges all bear similarities to England and other common law countries. An Israeli judge of the 1950s, therefore, addressed English law because the legislature so ordered, but also and mainly due to the historic linkage between the two states.

Second, the absence of a constitutional text supposedly facilitated judges' references to foreign law and spared them the need to interpret a constitutional text or search for the original intention of the founding fathers. Iddo Porat stated that the absence of a constitutional text:

> [s]ets aside one of the main objections to the use of foreign law in constitutional interpretation—loyalty to the text and original intent. Constitutional interpretation methods based on textualism or on original intent are antithetical to some uses of foreign law, since the way other nations interpret and apply their own constitutions is generally considered irrelevant to the question of the textual content of one's own constitution or of the original intent of its drafters.[8]

Another important historic datum is the fact that since the early years, the ISC developed and defended a series of human rights known as the 'judicial bill of

---

[6] The Harrari Resolution reads: 'The First Knesset charges the Constitution, Law, and Justice Committee with preparing a draft of the State Constitution. The Constitution will consist of separate chapters, each chapter constituting a Basic Law in its own. The chapters will be presented to the Knesset … and all of the chapters shall be consolidated into the State Constitution'.

[7] For further discussion on the process of enacting the Israeli Constitution and on the main problems and defects of the basic laws see, by the same author, in D Oliver and C Fusaro (eds), *How Constitutions Change—A Comparative Study* (Hart Publishing, 2011) 191–209.

[8] I Porat, 'The Use of Foreign Law in Israeli Constitutional Adjudication' (not yet published) (copy with author).

rights', despite the absence of a constitutional text to establish them on. This is directly related to the extensive use of foreign precedents in constitutional adjudication. A 1953 affair demonstrates this well: In *Kol Ha'am v Minister of the Interior*[9] the court addressed a case in which the interior minister decided to close a newspaper because it allegedly carried inciting articles that might have harmed the public's safety. An order dating back to the British Mandate assigns to the government the power to close down a newspaper in Israel. ISC President Agranat,[10] who was the first to establish the special status of the freedom of expression in Israel, determined:

> Israel is a democratic state, and a democratic regime cannot survive if its legal system does not recognize the freedom of expression. Even though it is not possible to judicially review a law that violates the freedom of expression because of the absence of a constitution, the court will prefer an interpretation of the law that is consistent with freedom of expression.

The judge adopted the idea of a 'balancing test' between human rights and other social interests, and held that only the prevention of an 'almost certain'[11] severe violation of public order could justify the infringement on freedom of expression. The decision included citations from classic American free speech cases such as *Schenck v United States* (1918),[12] *Abrams v United States* (1919),[13] *Whitney v California* (1926)[14] and others, as well as citations from American literature and from John Stuart Mill and Blackstone.

The *Kol Ha'am* affair is viewed as the cornerstone of Israel's human rights adjudication, demonstrating how judges turned to foreign precedents to acknowledge the need to defend human rights even in the absence of a Constitution. President Agranat's move is an example of the manner in which human rights evolved in Israel: over the years, almost all of the basic rights were acknowledged in Israel following the freedom of expression example. The court acknowledged them using presumptive and interpretative tools: the presumption that the legislature did not intend to violate human rights; the principle that a statute should be interpreted in the way that best protects human rights; the principle that if a statute violating human rights is introduced, it must be construed restrictively; and the rule for all administrative authorities, whereby the violation of human rights is prohibited unless specifically authorised by law.

The use of interpretative tools made it very easy for the courts to look at foreign sources for comparison, guidance, and inspiration. As we shall see, foreign law and precedents from countries with a long-standing democratic and human-rights orientated tradition served as fertile soil for reference and a natural source of reliance over the years.

---

[9] HCJ 73/53 *Kol Ha'am v Minister of Interior* (1953) 7(2) PD 871.
[10] Shimon Agranat acquired his legal education in the USA.
[11] A balancing test, also known as the 'imminent certainty' or 'close possibility' test; very similar to the American 'clear and present danger' test.
[12] *Schenck v United States*, 39 S Ct 247.
[13] *Abrams v United States*, 40 S Ct 17.
[14] *Whitney v California*, 47 S Ct 641.

B. The Constitutional Revolution

The Harrari Resolution of 1950 was followed by the introduction of basic laws, even though since the first basic law was enacted, in 1958, the legal status of the basic laws remained unclear. By 1992, almost all of the basic laws that dealt with government institutions in Israel had been adopted, but the proposal to pass a basic law dealing with human rights provoked great controversy in the Knesset. Therefore, another political compromise split the Basic Law: Human Rights into a number of separate basic laws. This process made it possible for the Knesset to agree and support the constitutional entrenchment of particular, consensual, human rights, while leaving pending the discussion of 'problematic' rights, such as freedom of religion, speech, conscience, equality, etc.

Following this new 'compromise', two basic laws dealing with human rights were enacted in 1992: Basic Law: Human Dignity and Liberty; and Basic Law: Freedom of Occupation. Both basic laws include a 'limitation' clause, similar to the one found in the Canadian Charter of Rights and Freedoms, an important innovation that will have an impact even on the foreign citations of the Supreme Court.

That 1992 enactment of basic laws changed Israel's constitutional structure and was followed by a crucially important ruling. In 1995, the ISC handed down a monumental decision—that was later known as the 'constitutional revolution'[15]—in which it declared that basic laws in Israel had a 'supra-legal' constitutional status, and that the court was empowered to enforce the limitations they entailed by judicial review of Knesset legislation, even if that power was not specifically mentioned in the basic laws. The ISC legitimised its power to conduct judicial review, without clear textual authorisation, by allusion to foreign law. President Barak referred to the American landmark case of *Marbury v Madison*[16] as a similar case dealing with the authority to conduct judicial review of legislation without explicit constitutional consent. The ISC stated that the new basic laws on human rights embodied the idea of the inherent relativity of human rights. Infringement of human rights is, therefore, permitted in accordance with the rules prescribed in the basic law itself, and it is for the court to declare whether the conditions of the basic law have been fulfilled. Limitations of human rights protected in the basic law may be imposed for worthy purposes and only if they satisfy the conditions stipulated in the limitation clause, including the principle of proportionality.

The adoption of the proportionality principle naturally encouraged the citation of precedents of other states that use that model. For example, Canadian law and German law were cited in many cases where the proportionality test was used

---

[15] The well-known case of *Hamizrahi Bank v Migdal* delivered in 1995 (CA 6821/93 *United Mizrahi Bank Ltd v Migdal Cooperative Village*, 49(4) PD 221). For further reading, in English, see A Barak 'Constitutionalization of the Israeli Legal System as a Result of the Basic Laws and its Effect on Procedural and Substantive Criminal Law' (1997) 31 *Israel Law Review* 3; R Hirsch, 'Israel's Constitutional Revolution: The Legal Interpretation of Entrenched Civil Liberties in an Emerging Neoliberal Economic Order' (1998) 46 *American Journal of Comparative Law* 427; D Kretzmer, 'The New Basic Laws on Human Rights: A Mini Revolution in Israeli Constitutional Law?' (1992) 26 *Israel Law Review* 238; M Mandel 'Democracy and the New Constitutionalism in Israel' (1999) 33 *Israel Law Review* 259; S Navot, n 5.

[16] *Whitney v California*, 137 US (1803).

and applied by the court. Adopting the proportionality test, the ISC joined the ever-growing family of constitutional courts that use it, which made it easier for the court to borrow from and create a dialogue with those systems.[17]

The constitutional revolution started a new era in Israel's constitutional law—a textual period in which there allegedly exists a constitutional text. As even the ISC openly stated, the new basic laws, as well as older ones, form the Israeli Constitution. Indeed, it is not a complete, but rather a lame and restricted Constitution, but a constitutional document was formed that took Israel from the tradition of parliamentary sovereignty to a constitutional model and to the concept of judicial review of laws.

This constitutional change is paramount in terms of judicial-reasoning techniques, particularly regarding the interpretation of laws, and had numerous consequences at the political, as well as the legal, level. The years following the constitutional revolution were characterised by the politicians' growing awareness and internalisation of the special status of basic laws. Judicial review itself has been sparingly employed, but even so, the ISC consistently ruled that judicial review exists in Israel, relying on the supremacy of basic laws.[18] Responding to the constitutional revolution, the Knesset practically and totally abandoned the constitutional enterprise and dropped the task of completing a Constitution. Since 1992, no basic laws were enacted by the Knesset as the constitutional revolution created tremendous tension between the ISC and the Knesset.

This new textual stage of Israeli law did not necessarily change the pattern of references to foreign law. The fact that the Knesset stopped addressing the constitutional process created a new challenge for the ISC: a call for the protection of rights that were not included in the basic laws; and petitions asking for an expansive interpretative approach so as to include new rights that were not explicitly mentioned in existing basic laws.

In summary, a bird's-eye view of the entire Israeli legal system reveals that despite the great influence that British law had on numerous aspects of it, the Israeli contribution to its own system was rather peculiar.

---

[17] I Porat, 'The Use of Foreign Law in Israeli Constitutional Adjudication', n 8 above.

[18] To date, the Supreme Court has struck down about eight laws, or sections of laws, by reason of their violation of human rights anchored in the basic laws, and contrary to the provisions of the limitation clause prescribed therein: HCJ 6055/95 *Tzemach v Minister of Defence*, 53(5) PD 241 (1999) in which the Court declared the invalidity of a section of the Military Justice Law, 1955, which allowed the detention of a solider for up to 96 hours before bringing him before a judge (see English translation at elyon1.court.gov.il/files_eng/95/550/060/I15/95060550.i15.htm); HCJ 1715/97 *Investment Managers Chamber in Israel v Minister of Finance*, 51(4) PD 367 (1997), which invalidated sections of the Management of Investments Law that violated the freedom of occupation of investment managers who had been engaged in the profession before the enactment of the law; HCJ 1030/99 *Oron v Knesset Speaker*, 56(3) 640 (2002), which invalidated sections of the Telecommunications Law; HCJ 8276/05 *Adallah v Minister of Defence* (12.12.06)—invalidation of s 5(c) of the Civil Wrongs Law, which totally denied rights in torts against the state for reasons of security actions by the state (HCJ 2605/05 *Human Rights Division v Minister of Finance* (see English translation at elyon1.court.gov.il/files_eng/05/050/026/n39/05026050.n39.pdf)) where the Court invalidated Amendment 28 of the Prisons Ordinance that anchored the establishment of privately managed prisons in Israel; CrA 8823/07 *Anon v State of Israel* (11.02.10) which invalidated a section of the Criminal Procedure Ordinance that related to extending a detainee's detention in an ex parte hearing.

A great effort was made to build and concisely codify private law, and to codify and reform public law. These branches of law are influenced by different sources: the codification of public law often relied on European legal concepts. The emerging new Constitution was heavily influenced by the reasoning and wisdom of American judges, as we have recently seen in the *Bank Hamizrahi* case, for example, while basic laws that deal with human rights were heavily influenced by the Canadian model. These combined influences created a mixed jurisdiction, though it is presently much closer to the common law family than to continental traditions. The constitutional revolution appears to have been the climax of the departure from the British tradition. The role traditionally played by England was replaced by reliance on the law of constitutional states, primarily the USA, Germany, and Canada.

Israel's historic background and its mixed jurisdiction justify to a large extent the extensive use of foreign law in Israeli cases. The first quantitative study that examined ISC reliance and reference patterns, including foreign adjudication, was conducted in the 1990s.[19] Reviewing ISC verdicts from 1948 to 1994, the study found that, on average, some 21 per cent of ISC citations in verdicts—including references to legislation, adjudication, articles, and literature—came from foreign law.[20] According to the Gross, Haris, and Shachar paper, British references outnumbered references to American law by far, but the latter gained in prominence over the last two years of the database studied (1992–94). The study further pointed at the scarcity of continental references. One interesting finding in Shachar's paper is the fact that references to foreign law in general declined over time. As noted, the database refers to all Israeli adjudications and not only to cases relating to constitutional law. It must be recalled that the citation of precedents gains much importance when the courts hand down groundbreaking or guiding verdicts.[21] Since constitutional adjudication in Israel is different in nature from civil or criminal justice, it is quite hard to reach final conclusions relevant to this paper from the Shachar study, but we believe it is important to show the real picture of the use of foreign law in the entire Israeli justice system ever since the State of Israel was established.

Since the 1980s, Israel as a whole—including its culture, academia, and constitutional revolution—underwent an accelerated Americanisation process.[22] We shall address these changes later on.

---

[19] M Gross, R Haris and Y Shachar, 'References Patterns of the Supreme Court in Israel—Quantitative Analysis' (1996) 26 *Mishpatim* 115 (in Hebrew). See also Y Shachar, M Gross and H Goldsmith, 'One Hundred Leading Precedents of the Supreme Court—A Quantitative Analysis' (2004) 7 *Mishpat U'mimshal* 243 (in Hebrew).

[20] The paper referred to a bank of data collected from 7,147 published verdicts that were randomly selected; ibid, p 152.

[21] Yoram Shachar and Miron Gross conducted a separate study dealing with citation practices in the 100 most cited cases in Israeli law between 1948 and 2000. They found that there were on average 7.8 citations of foreign cases per decision in these 100 cases, which means 8.7 times more than in regular cases. See Chanan Goldschmidt, Miron Gross, and Yoram Shachar, '100 Leading Precedents of the Supreme Court—A Quantitative Analysis', 7 *Haifa University Law Review* 243, 267 (2004) (in Hebrew).

[22] See also Shachar, *The Reference Practices of the Israeli Supreme Court*, n 2 at 48.

III. THE SUPREME COURT OF ISRAEL

One of the striking features of the Israeli system is the ISC's contribution to the development of constitutional law. The ISC plays a decisive role in Israel's public life, covering for the absence of a constitutional court. Historically,[23] disputes between citizens and the State were usually submitted directly to the highest judicial instance—the High Court of Justice (HCJ). Today, it is the ISC sitting in its capacity as the HCJ—which is the first, last, and only judicial instance with jurisdiction in most of the disputes concerning government institutions and state organs, and disputes between citizens and the State.[24]

This chapter addresses the Supreme Court as the comprehensive name for Israel's highest instance. Thus, the ISC serves two functions: it is the highest and last court of appeals in civil and criminal cases,[25] and it serves as Israel's HCJ.

Its authority as the HCJ is broadly and flexibly formulated as seen, for example, in the wording of the law that gives it the power 'to hear matters when it deems it necessary to grant relief for the sake of justice'. The ISC justices use this section extensively to extend the scope of their intervention so as to cover all of the State's authorities. An examination of its rulings over the past few years leads to the conclusion that, at least from the justices' perspective, the 'power' at the disposal of the ISC sitting as the HCJ is practically unlimited.

The ISC presently comprises 15 judges (up from the previous nine-judge panel) who, like all Israeli judges, are appointed by the President of the State,[26] after they are named by a Judges Election Committee, a unique Israeli creation consisting of nine members.[27] Its composition ensures representation for the legislative, executive, and judicial branches. A judicial appointment is 'for life'; practically, until the age of 70. The decisions of the ISC include the opinions of all judges, and every opinion, even dissenting and separate opinions, appears in it. All opinions are officially published, which makes them all significant.

Over the years, the ISC judges came to represent—well, though not perfectly—the Israeli legal community. Most of them had served as district court judges before assuming the high post, while others came from the State Attorney's Office (having

---

[23] During the British Mandate period, judges in the lower courts (Magistrates' and District) were generally locals (Jews and Arabs) whereas Supreme Court justices were British. The policy of the Mandate Government was that in regular civil and criminal matters, local judges would be entitled to adjudicate in regular courts. However if the dispute involved the Mandate Authorities themselves, they preferred that it be heard from beginning to end by judges belonging to the British establishment. The result was the determination that all administrative disputes were under the direct jurisdiction of the Supreme Court. The practical justification for this structure disappeared with the establishment of the State, but the legal situation was never amended accordingly. With the establishment of the State, it was decided in principle that the existing legal and administrative structures of the Mandate would remain intact, and the High Court of Justice therefore continued to operate in the same format, except that its judges were now Jewish. Within a short period, the Supreme Court assumed a central position in the development of the law and almost immediately after the State's establishment, it proceeded to lay down the constitutive principles for a democratic state governed by the rule of law.

[24] Although many administrative issues have been transferred to lower courts.

[25] These cases are referred there by lower instances such as Magistrates' and District Courts.

[26] His role is essentially formal, while the Judges Election Committee makes the real selection.

[27] Two cabinet members (including the Minister of Justice, who also serves as chairperson of the committee), two members of the Knesset (chosen by the Knesset), three Supreme Court justices (including the ISC President), and two advocates, representing the Israel Bar Association.

served as legal advisors to the government or state attorneys), and a few were law professors who came from academia. In that respect, the current (2012) line-up of ISC judges is extraordinary because even though the bench now comprises 15 judges, only one of them is a law professor (recently appointed). This fact is particularly questionable given that the ISC serves as Israel's Constitutional Court as well.

In the early years, the ISC's constitutional adjudication was quite formalistic in nature. Though that period did produce several extraordinary verdicts, particularly on cases pertaining to the acknowledgment of human rights such as the aforementioned *Kol Ha'am* affair, it characteristically provided formalistic interpretations of the law. That tendency can be explained by the prominence of the English tradition: a strict separation of powers in which the judiciary refrains from becoming involved in resolutions by other authorities. Through the 1970s, the ISC mostly employed standing doctrines, refusing to acknowledge *actio popularis* petitions that presented the ISC with issues of political consequence, which the court carefully avoided.[28] Furthermore, until the 1980s, the ISC employed the *non-justiciability* doctrine, which prevents judicial intervention in political questions.

The early 1980s marked a turning point. First, the court lifted some of the traditional barriers of standing and *non-justiciability*, in the wake of which it began to address political issues and petitions against government resolutions.[29] Furthermore, the ISC became increasingly involved in public affairs and started applying tighter supervision to various administrative decisions and even intervened in parliamentary proceedings. A fascinating analysis of that period, which reflected what was called 'the transition from formalism to activism', can be found in Mautners 'The Decline of Formalism and the Rise of Values in Israeli Law'.[30]

That increased judicial activism was supported by the constitutional changes in 1992 which, from the ISC's point of view, climaxed with the *Bank Hamizrahi* affair where the court announced it had the power to conduct a judicial review of laws. The transition to judicial activism was further accompanied by new rules of interpretation and argumentation in the ISC jurisprudence, which became less formalistic. This increased activism was, in part, the result of social processes that gave rise to yet another, more intrusive and invasive, court policy that became known as the judicialisation of the government.[31]

---

[28] A fine example of that approach is found in a statement by Justice Vitkon that was part of a 1970s verdict in which the ISC was asked to determine the legality of the ultra-Orthodox (Yeshiva) students' exemption from military service: 'The court takes caution so as not to be dragged into the general public debate, which is better left to the political echelons ... The issue in this case is of pure political nature and that is the reason for a strict reading of the standing principle': HCJ 40/70 *Beker v Minister of Defence*, 24(1) PD (1970) 238.

[29] See, eg, the statement by Judge Barak, allowing for an appeal which had been dismissed before on grounds of standing: 'When the topic is of grave importance to the community, a "public" petitioner may appeal. Issues of public interest, of constitutional aspects, or concerning serious wrongdoing by any authority have legitimate standing before the High Court of Justice, even if the appellant has no specific interest in it'. See HCJ 910/86 *Ressler v Minister of Defence*, 42(2) PD (1988) 441.

[30] M Mautner, 'The Decline of Formalism and the Rise of Values in Israeli Law' (1993) 17 *Iyunei Mishpat* 503 (in Hebrew).

[31] See A Gal-Nor, 'The Judicialization of the Public Sphere in Israel' (2004) 7 *Mishpat U'Mimshal* 355 (in Hebrew); E Benvenisti, 'Judicially Sponsored Checks and Balances' (2001) 32 *Mishpatim* 797 (in Hebrew).

Additionally, these processes had an impact on constitutional adjudication, its scope, and its reference to foreign law.[32] The transition from the formalistic concept, which characterised Israeli adjudication until the 1980s, to the activist concept, in which the adjudication cites values and discusses moral dilemmas, further explains why English law was abandoned and a new linkage was formed with US law.

Iddo Porat explained:

> Anti-formalism represents an expansion of the notion of legality and of interpretation, and therefore allows and even encourages the use of non-formal legal sources. The more the judiciary steers away from seeing its own function as mechanically applying pre-existing law, and moves toward the role of shaping the law according to considerations of policy and justice, the more it becomes relevant for the judge to look into a variety of sources that deal with similar policy or moral questions, regardless of their formal pedigree.[33]

To summarise this part, it may be stated that the changes in the State of Israel's constitutional regime on the one hand and in ISC adjudication on the other are reflected in the use of foreign law, as we shall see below. Given the historic development and background of the ISC as presented above, we can point at two clear trends: first, like many other common law countries, Israel is characterised by high judicial activism; second, most of the major changes made in the Israeli constitutional regime resulted from ISC rulings.

IV. EMPIRICAL ANALYSIS: FIGURES AND BEYOND

A. Preliminary Observations

This empirical analysis examines the ISC's use of foreign precedents in constitutional adjudication. The data were extracted from reviews of ISC adjudication as published between 1994 and 2010. A database of cases was created that serves as an infrastructure for this study of the ISC's references to foreign law within the framework of its constitutional adjudication. In this context, we shall present data on:

1. The number of constitutional decisions that refer to foreign precedents of the total constitutional decisions handed down each year.
2. The distribution between institutional and human-rights based constitutional adjudication decisions that refer to foreign precedents.
3. Foreign precedents by country of origin.
4. Use of foreign precedents by periods.
5. The location of the references to foreign precedents in the adjudication (ie, part of the majority, the dissenting, or a separate opinion).

---

[32] The above, so it seems, should be coupled with the personal aspect of Professor Aharon Barak—one of Israel's greatest jurists, who served as an ISC judge for nearly 30 years (until 2006), is a Prize of Israel Justice laureate, wrote numerous books including a series on judicial interpretations, and served as Attorney General. He maintains extensive ties with the international legal community. I argue that he made a crucial, unique, and unusual contribution to the use of comparative law.

[33] I Porat, 'The Use of Foreign Law in Israeli Constitutional Adjudication', n 8 above.

This section requires a few preliminary remarks:

i. Publication of Israeli Adjudication

The database this study refers to covers all of the verdicts published between 1994 and 2010. Ever since the State of Israel was established, ISC rulings were published in *Israeli Verdicts* [IVs, *Piskei-Din*] volumes, which generally contained adjudications that the system chose to publish, but not all the decisions that the ISC handed down. Various resolutions and verdicts in which there was no interest were not published at all. Thus, it is particularly problematic to monitor and analyse the total decisions that the court handed down in any given year.

Therefore, the database created for this paper includes only the judgments that were deemed worthy of publication in the IVs, at least until 2005 (namely, only several hundred verdicts). We were unable to use IVs books for later years for the simple reason that they were no longer published in hard copy, and thus our empirical findings were taken out of electronic databases.[34] While these new electronic databases include adjudication from previous years, it turned out that decision numbers there do not correspond with those published in the IVs books. At the same time, the electronic databases contain more decisions because, as noted, the IVs did not cover all judgments, but only those that the editorial board chose to publish. Hence, our distribution into periods is based in part on judgments as published in IVs (1994–2005) and in part on judgments in electronic databases (2006–10). It should be noted that most of the ISC judgments are very brief, include no substantial discussion, and are uploaded to the electronic databases with hardly any kind of screening.[35]

It should also be noted that the data on the number of judgments published are not completely accurate because there are gaps between the number of judgments published in IVs, for example, and the figures that we officially received from the Courts Administration Office.[36]

ii. Identifying Constitutional Cases

Classifying an ISC decision as 'constitutional' is not an easy task in Israel. In the absence of a complete constitutional text and a special instance (such as a constitutional court), the classification of cases as constitutional required special treatment. Addressing conflicts between citizens and government, the ISC serves as both

---

[34] Which are mostly private collections, and do not appear in the ISC online database. We searched the electronic database using mainly keywords such as 'constitution/al' 'human rights/rights'; 'institution/al' law. However, we read them case by case in order to decide whether to include the decision in the study. As for the published IVs books, we used the classification in the indexes of each of the books, but still, we read every case within the classification of constitutional law, human rights and the different constitutional organs of the State, in order to decide whether to include it.

[35] Shachar, *The Reference Practices of the Israeli Supreme Court*, n 2 above at 53.

[36] For example, a letter from the Courts Director dated 15 June 2009 presented us with the number of verdicts the ISC handed down between 2002 and 2007. Below are the official data: 2002: 7,856 verdicts handed down, but IVs for that year contained only 418 verdicts; we worked on the latter; 2003: 9,203 verdicts; IVs carried only 373 verdicts; 2004: 8,570 verdicts; 2005: 8,679 verdicts; 2006: 7,768 verdicts; and 2007: 8,098 verdicts.

an HCJ and as the State's administrative instance, which made it hard to decide whether a given issue was constitutional or administrative in nature. In our process, we used keywords to search the electronic database, and then we read the cases in order to decide whether to include them in our research.

Below, we present the guidelines we employed when classifying the ISC adjudication as constitutional, as well as several problematic examples and the decisions we made regarding their classification:

1. As a rule, we classified cases as constitutional addressing the 'core' of the issue, while offering a restrictive, rather than expanding interpretation of the term 'constitutional adjudication' because in the broad interpretation option, almost any issue can be tagged as constitutional.
2. Even clearly criminal or civil cases contain some reference to constitutional issues. For example, the employment of constitutional tools in the interpretation of contracts is common practice. Almost all the cases that addressed contractual restrictions on an employees' future occupation speak about freedom of occupation, but being 'contractual' in nature, they were not classified as constitutional.
3. Our classification followed the issues that typically characterise constitutional law in the West; thus, when the court addressed issues pertaining to human rights, or the powers of government agencies as defined in the basic laws or inherently 'constitutional' laws, we classified them as constitutional cases.
4. Adjudication that was not viewed as traditionally constitutional was classified as such if the court conducted a particularly extensive discussion on the constitutional aspects of the issue (the 'essence' test).[37]
5. Issues pertaining to Knesset elections were classified as constitutional, while local government elections were not.
6. All cases that addressed Israel's Security Regulations (Emergency Times) and the Emergency Regulations—which assign government agencies with special powers in emergency times—were classified as constitutional only when the issue addressed had some reference to constitutional matters. Administrative detention hearings, for example, were not classified as constitutional.
7. As a rule, reference to the Attorney General (AG)[38] was viewed as institutional and constitutional; decisions that addressed judicial intervention in the AG's resolutions on whether or not to prosecute certain individuals were classified as constitutional; while cases in which the AG represented the public's interest (eg, cases involving minors, wills, etc) were not classified as constitutional.

---

[37] Due to this interpretation approach, our classification of constitutional cases is different from the parallel classification in the IVs, where every verdict that even slightly addressed a constitutional aspect was classified as constitutional.

[38] The Attorney General's Office is one of the most important and influential public offices in Israel. A full and informed understanding of Israel's public life is impossible without reference to this unique institution. The AG is in charge of four principal areas: he/she heads the general prosecution; represents government agencies in judicial forums; acts as the legal consultant of the government and other sovereign authorities, in which capacity he/she is empowered to determine the binding legal policy for the government and its respective branches on a broad range of issues; and is the state official responsible for protecting the public interest and the promotion of the rule of law.

8. All the discussions that pertained to the Knesset and Knesset elections were classified as constitutional, including hearings that addressed political and rotation agreements between political parties and petitions filed by MKs (Members of Knesset).
9. Rulings that were 'administrative' by nature and cases that addressed the powers of cabinet members were not classified as constitutional, with the exception of those meeting the 'essence' test: we examined the essence of discussions of basic laws or constitutional aspects and when they were found to be the core of the verdict, they were classified as constitutional.
10. In principle, cases that addressed extradition, naturalisation, and adoption issues were not classified as constitutional, though there were some exceptions here too, when the discussion was essentially constitutional.

iii. Classification of Institutional and Human Rights Cases

In this study, we classified the constitutional cases in two categories: institutional ones and those pertaining to human rights. The former included clearly institutional issues such as the Knesset, MKs, the government, the AG, the state comptroller, the president, and various ministerial committees. In addition, discussions in which the ISC addressed the constitutionality of laws within the framework of the 'limitation clause' and cases that dealt with the Emergency Regulations and Security Emergency Regulations were classified as institutional as well. Decisions that addressed various human rights, whether or not they were part of Israel's basic laws, were classified as human rights cases.

B. Constitutional Cases Citing Foreign Precedents

Figure 1 below shows the constitutional cases that refer to foreign precedents out of the total constitutional cases each year, between 1994 and 2010.

Figure 1 shows that the number of constitutional adjudications made after the constitutional revolution remained more or less steady. No dramatic increase in constitutional adjudications was noted in recent years.[39] It is further visible that the citation of foreign law in constitutional adjudications remained steady too and has even slightly declined in recent years.

In 1994, we find that one third of the constitutional cases addressed foreign precedents. In 1995, the year of the *Bank Hamizrahi* case, foreign citations were found in some 50 per cent of constitutional cases. Subsequently, (more or less) one in three constitutional adjudications cited foreign precedents, though in 2001 and 2009 their number dropped to 15 per cent of the total.

---

[39] Though the research data show that the number of verdicts the ISC handed down has consistently increased in recent years.

142 *Suzie Navot*

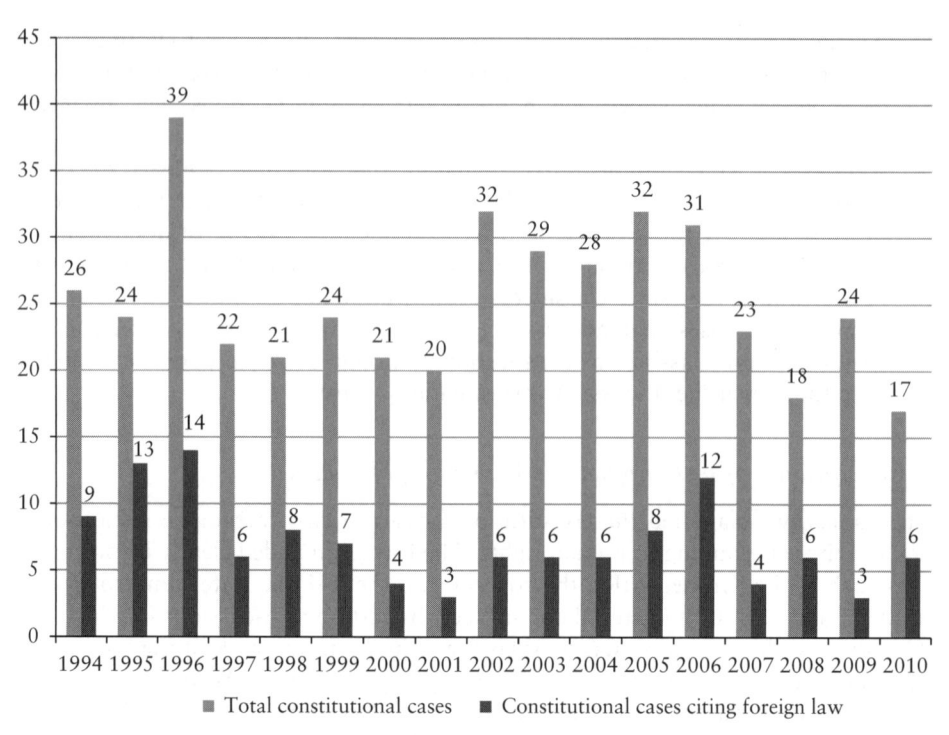

Figure 1: Constitutional Cases Citing Foreign Precedents out of Total Constitutional Cases

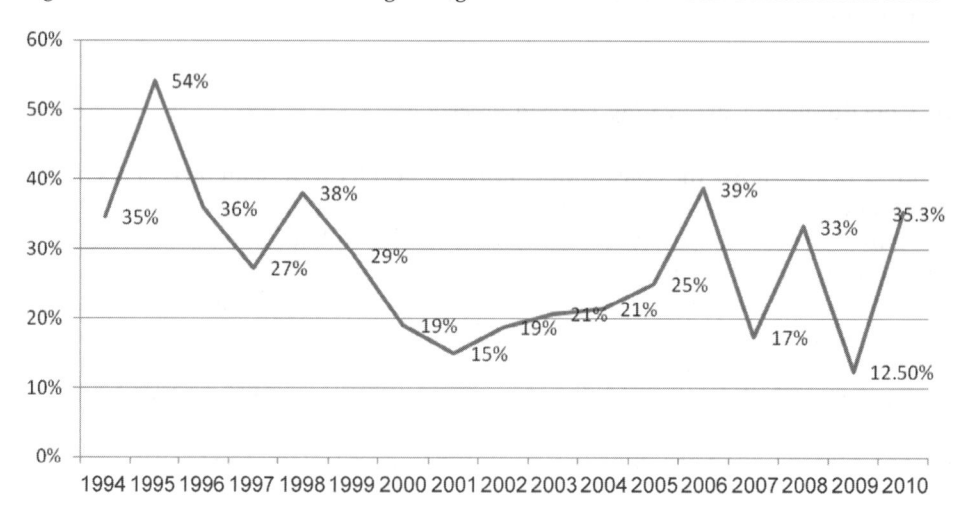

Figure 2: Use of Foreign Precedents in Constitutional Cases per Year (percentage)

Figure 2 shows the percentage of the total constitutional cases citing foreign precedents.

The trend that emerges from Figures 1 and 2 coincides with past studies on the ISC reference patterns, though those studies did not examine only constitutional adjudications.

The first study—conducted by Shachar, Haris, and Gross addressed ISC adjudications between 1948 and 1994—found that some 21 per cent of the total citations on average were from foreign sources.[40] At the time, the study covered all of the ISC cases, including civil and criminal appeals.

It may have been assumed that the position for constitutional adjudications would be the same, but it turns out, from our analysis, that when dealing with constitutional issues, the court cited relatively more foreign sources than in other cases. Interestingly, Shachar, Haris, and Gross also found that the number of foreign law citations remained more or less the same over time, and this conclusion is confirmed in the current analysis too.

In another study, Shachar[41] examined the changing pattern of citation numbers on average per adjudication page (examining some 80 of the long verdicts handed down) between 1950 and 2004, and found a 'surprisingly steady', as he put it, trend of numerous citations (Israeli and foreign) per page over some 50 years of adjudication.

Our study shows that the contribution of foreign law to ISC adjudication over the years of constitutional adjudication in Israel indeed remained more or less steady, though there seem to be 'spikes' here and there. It is worth remembering that it is enough for even very few decisions, albeit long and important, to contain numerous citations to alter the graph. For example, the verdict on the *Bank Hamizrahi* case alone included 116 citations of other cases, of which 35 were from foreign sources.[42]

The conclusion that citations of foreign precedents remained steady should come as no surprise. In the State's early years, most citations came from English law, as explained in the historic background discussion above. Recently, American law has been taking precedence as a reference source, but the number of citations has not changed: English precedents were replaced by American precedents.

Another interesting datum, as seen in Figures 1 and 2, is the relatively high number of cases that include foreign citations. Even if there appears to be a slight trend of using fewer foreign citations, the fact that 15 to 30 per cent of the cases still include them is significant. This may reflect the judges' desire to partake in the international constitutional discourse, to be part of the phenomenon known as 'migration'[43] of constitutional ideas. To a large extent, Israeli judges are open to foreign law, maintain extensive ties with supreme and legislative courts in many countries, and major verdicts by the ISC are published in English. Thus, the use of foreign law is part of ongoing dialogues between judges worldwide.

Additionally, citations of foreign law can be explained by Israel's special need to develop basic principles and basic human rights. The importance of foreign law citations on human rights issues is presented below.

---

[40] That paper referred to a database collected from 7,147 verdicts that were randomly selected and published; n 19 at p 152.

[41] Shachar, 'The Reference Practices of the Israeli Supreme Court 1950–2004', n 2 at p 35.

[42] To wit, of the 35 foreign verdict citations, 17 were American, five were British, three were Australian, three Canadian, two South African, two German, and one was Indian. Another two citations were taken from international verdicts.

[43] S Choudhry, 'Migration as a New Metaphor in Comparative Constitutional Law' in S Choudhry (ed), *The Migration of Constitutional Ideas* (Cambridge University Press, 2006) 1–36.

C. Institutional and Human Rights Decisions Citing Foreign Precedents

Figure 3 shows that, in percentage points, the number of decisions on human rights issues that cite foreign law is nearly twice the number of such citations in institutional cases.

Seemingly, Israel's constitutional history as discussed above could explain the extensive use of foreign law in human rights cases. While the institutional–constitutional law in Israel is, for the most part, organised in the textual framework of basic laws,[44] the Israeli model is textually lacking when dealing with human rights due to the absence of an appropriate Bill of Rights. This means that the role of the ISC in defending human rights was and remains crucial. Even after basic laws on human rights were introduced, and given the fact that the Knesset failed to complete the Constitution enterprise and did not anchor the remaining human rights in a constitutional document, the ISC has been called upon to offer expanding interpretations of existing rights. For example, the right to human dignity—which is protected under the Basic Act: Human Dignity and Liberty—became a source of acknowledgement and protection of rights that were not explicitly stated in writing: for example, additional aspects of the right to equality, freedom of expression, and so on. Throughout the period mentioned, such interpretative moves were accompanied by extensive references to foreign law, as shown in Figure 3 and in examples we shall address below.

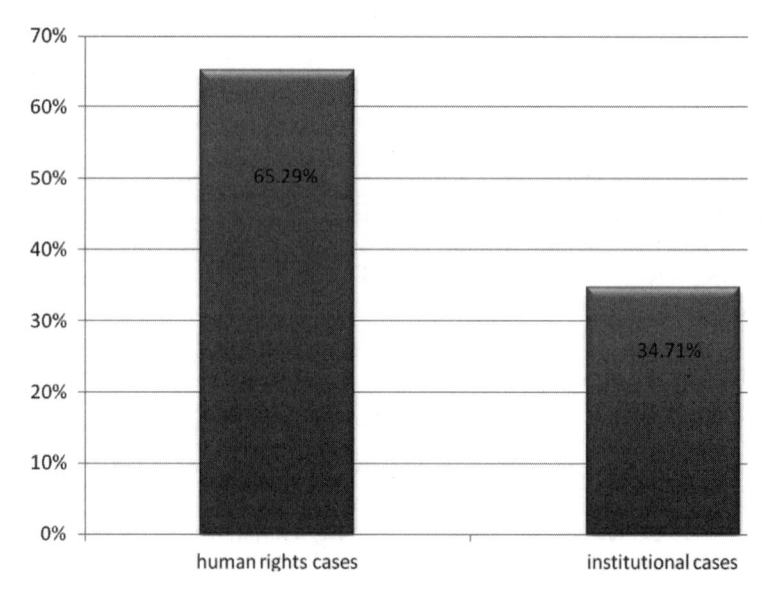

Figure 3: Institutional and Human Rights Decisions Citing Foreign Precedents

---

[44] With the exceptions of two basic laws on human rights, all other 10 basic laws are institutional in nature: Basic Law: The Knesset (1958); Basic Law: The Israeli Lands (1960); Basic Law: The President of the State (1964); Basic Law: The Government (1968, replaced in 1992 and in 2001); Basic Law: The State Economy (1975); Basic Law: The Army (1976); Basic Law: Jerusalem, the Capital of Israel (1980); Basic Law: The Judiciary (1984); Basic Law: The State Comptroller (1986); and Basic Law: The State Budget for 2009 and 2010 (Special Provisions) (Temporary Provision) (2009).

D. Citing Foreign Precedents—by Country

Our study also examined the sources of foreign adjudication that the ISC used. Depicting the citations' origin by country, Figure 4 clearly shows that Israel's constitutional law is undergoing an Americanisation process. English law, which served as the foundation of Israeli law when the State was first established, has been almost completely pushed aside and out of constitutional adjudication in recent years, and replaced by its US counterpart.

Figure 4 further shows that although Israeli law was initially heavily influenced by English references and citations, the number of US citations significantly exceeds the number of English citations in recent years. It may be assumed that this trend follows from the constitutional revolution and its implications, but that is not the only reason. Ever since the 1980s, Israel's law schools have been clearly Americanised: many students travel to the USA for their advanced studies, and most of the academic researchers spend time in American institutions. This is clearly evident in Israeli academic law papers, which mainly aim at the American legal readership, which is just as prominent in ISC adjudication. A fine case in point is the use of American citations when freedom of expression issues are discussed, as can be exemplified in both the *Station Films* affair, published in 1996,[45] and the *Bakri* affair of 2003.[46] The aforementioned *Kol Ha'am* affair of 1953 included numerous citations of US law as well, but at the time it was the exception to the rule.

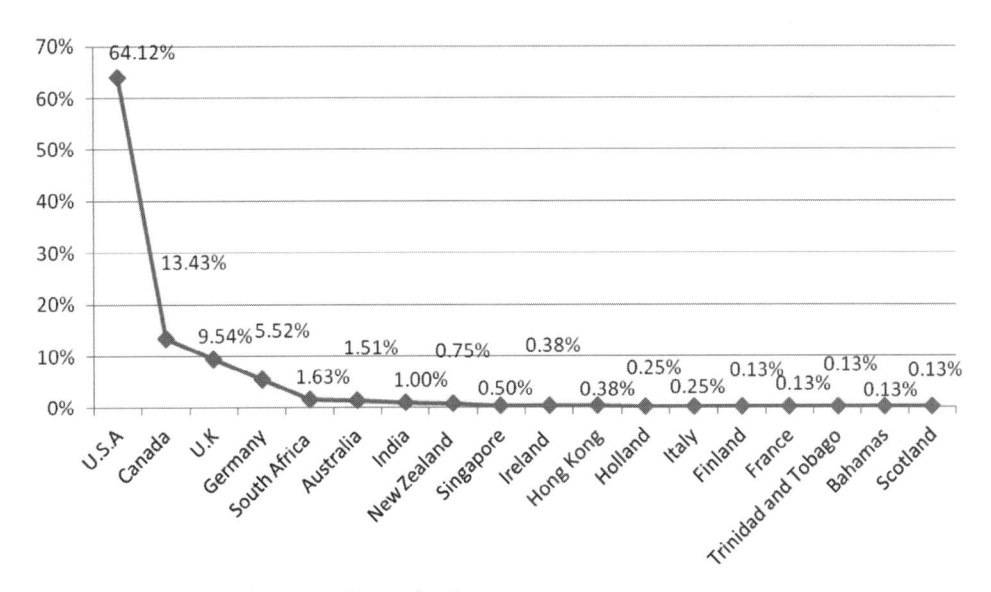

Figure 4: Citing Foreign Precedents—by Country

U.S.A 64.12%, Canada 13.43%, U.K 9.54%, Germany 5.52%, South Africa 1.63%, Australia 1.51%, India 1.00%, New Zealand 0.75%, Singapore 0.50%, Ireland 0.38%, Hong Kong 0.38%, Holland 0.25%, Italy 0.25%, Finland 0.13%, France 0.13%, Trinidad and Tobago 0.13%, Bahamas 0.13%, Scotland 0.13%

---

[45] HCJ 4804/94 *Station Films Inc v the Israeli Film Council* 50(5) PD 661.
[46] HCJ 316/03 *Bakri v the Israeli Film Council* 58(1) PD 249.

The *Station Films* affair was about a petition filed with the ISC against a decision by the Israeli Film Council[47] to allow a film named 'L'empire de sens' to be screened in Israel provided certain pornographic scenes were cut out. The Court decided (by a majority of two judges, one dissenting) to allow the full screening of the original film. The case discussion mainly addressed freedom of expression and its restrictions, and cited 17 foreign sources: 10 from the USA, three from Canada, two from Germany, one from England and one from Ireland. Interestingly, 15 of the 17 citations were found in the majority view as presented by ISC President Barak.[48]

In the *Bakri* affair, film director Muhammad Bakri made a film named 'Jenin, Jenin' in which he purported to present the Palestinian narrative of the battle that took place inside the Jenin refugee camp in April 2002, during IDF Operation Defensive Shield. Bakri intended to present the Palestinian point of view of the events that took place there.[49] The Film Council disqualified the film for public screening in Israel, and Bakri filed an appeal against this decision.[50] Discussing the appeal, the ISC mainly addressed freedom of expression in Israel and reasons to restrict it. In this case too, the HCJ justices reversed the Film Council's decision and allowed the film to be screened. The case included 18 citations: 12 from US sources,[51] four English, and two Australian. This seems to correspond with the trend that emerged from our research findings.

In this context, Professor Yoram Shachar presented interesting findings in his study, where one of his graphs describes how the citation of references switched from English to American between 1950 and 2004, reviewing some 80 ISC verdicts a year.[52] As noted earlier, Shachar's paper reviews all Israeli adjudications, not only constitutional adjudications, and at a certain point he selected 80 long verdicts per year. Professor Shachar found that English references were predominant over the first 50 years, and that this domination was eroded over time, albeit slowly.

---

[47] Israel still maintains a law dating back to the British mandate—the Cinematograph Films Ordinance 1937—under which the screening of a film in public in Israel requires prior approval by a public board established under the Ordinance. It should be noted that over the years, and as freedom of expression gained prominence in Israel, the council's activities have almost totally stopped.

[48] Among the Canadian cases cited: *R v Butler* (1992) 89 DLR (4th) 449; *The Queen v Towne Cinema Theatres Ltd* (1985) 18 DLR (4th) and *Re Ont Film & Video and Ont Bd of Censors* (1983) 41 OR (2nd) 583. The minority opinion, per Judge Cheshin, cited the American case of *Kaplan v California*, 93 S Ct 2680 (1973) on the possible limitations of freedom of expression.

[49] Reacting to a murderous terror attack on Park Hotel in Netanya two days before, the IDF launched Operation Defence Shield on 29 March 2002. On the next day, IDF troops raided the Jenin refugee camp where they engaged in close combat and door-to-door incursions against Palestinians. The bloody battle day left 23 Israeli soldiers dead and 30 injured. According to IDF statistics, 52 Palestinians were killed that day, half of whom were citizens, and Palestinian property sustained heavy damages.

[50] HCJ 316/03 *Bakri v the Israeli Film Council*, n 47 above.

[51] Attempting to establish the argument that, among other things, only severe emotional damage and agony may be cited as reasons to restrict freedom of expression, Justice Dorner cited cases such as: *Virginia v Black* 123 S Ct 1536 (2003); *Collin v Smith* 578 F 2d 1197 (1978); *Smith v Collin* 439 US 916 (1978); and *Chaplinsky v New Hampshire* 315 US 568 (1942). Additionally, to demonstrate that times of national crisis and war—in Israel and in the United States—might be accompanied by a need seriously to restrict freedom of expression so as to protect public order, the court cited *Abrams v United States* 250 US 616 (1919); *Schenk v United States* 249 US 47 (1919); and *British Reg v Home Secretary, ex parte Brind* [1991] 1 AC 696.

[52] Shachar, *The Reference Practices of the Israeli Supreme Court*, n 2 above at 48–50.

Our findings regarding American law are somewhat different, particularly with regard to the speed of the said erosion. It turns out that unlike other fields of the law, and particularly in recent years, American law has taken the lead in all matters concerning constitutional adjudication. English law may have remained embedded in large sections of civil and criminal law even after the linkage with it was severed, but Israeli constitutional law of the period after the constitutional revolution shows—including by the way it uses foreign law—that Israel no longer draws on the English principle of parliamentary sovereignty, but is a 'constitutional' State that practises judicial review, which is a departure from the English tradition. The so-called Americanisation of Israeli constitutional law perfectly coincides with the prevailing judicial trend whereby values rise in prominence while formalistic argumentations decline.

In this context, we would like to add that the important status accorded to Canadian precedents can also be explained by the constitutional revolution in Israel. As noted, the Israeli basic laws on human rights include a limitation clause that is similar to the one in the Canadian Charter. The ISC, however, did not turn to Canada only on that clause, and its constitutional adjudication includes references to Canadian precedents when they are relevant and even uniquely address constitutional issues that emerge in Israel.[53]

Even if we could justify references to American law inasmuch as human rights are concerned, we are quite sceptical about the use of US precedents in the context of institutional–constitutional cases. The Israeli government system is inherently different from the US administration. The Israeli parliamentary system, the multitude of parties, the elections method, and the structure of the government and its branches are much closer to the typical government structure of several European countries than to the American model. Thus, it could theoretically have been assumed that references to countries such as England and other EU members would be more extensive. The minimal number of references to continental courts is even more surprising in view of the fact that several constitutional–institutional issues that the ISC addressed are addressed by European countries as well. An in-depth review of these issues reveals that, in several cases, citations of US precedents were used while avoiding a discussion of the appropriate sources for comparative law on these issues.[54] It seems that language is the main barrier that prevents the 'migration' of legal concepts from certain European countries such as France, Italy, and Spain,

---

[53] For example, when discussing language rights in HCJ 4112/99 *Adalla, the Legal Centre for the Rights of the Arab Minority in Israel v the Municipality of Tel Aviv-Yafo* 56(5) PD 292, the court considered the duty of a municipality to use Arabic in municipal road signs in an area where an Arab minority resides. The verdict included nine references to foreign law, mostly Canadian, and both the majority and minority views used Canadian law, citing the following cases in which the importance of a language as a key element of society was discussed: *Reference Re Language Rights Under Manitoba Act*, 1870 (1985) DLR (4th); *Mahe v Alberta* [1990] 1 SCR 342; *Ford v Quebec* (AG) [1988] 2 SCR 712; *Société des Acadiens v Association of Parents* [549] 1 SCR 549; *McDonald v City of Montréal* [1986] 1 SCR 460; *Reference Re Public Schools Act* (Man) [1993] 1 SCR 839.

[54] These cases include for example MKs' immunity; the status of the MKs' pledge of allegiance; judicial intervention in intra-parliamentarian issues; and the nullification of a law due to a faulty legislation process, to mention but a few. We find references to Anglo–American law on these issues quite troubling.

but the Israeli legal community and its orientation play an important role in these choices too. Iddo Porat described this nicely:

> In the Israeli legal profession, academic prestige is highly dependent on publications abroad, especially in US law reviews. Consequently, Israeli academic researches and papers are oriented towards such areas of law that would be palatable to the American legal audience, so much so that a large number of Israeli academics write more on US law than on Israeli law.[55]

These characteristics of the Israeli legal community explain the Americanisation of constitutional adjudication. At the same time, references from countries rarely seen before in Israeli adjudication—such as Germany, India, and South Africa—periodically appear too.

Regarding German citations, models devised by German lawmakers and the fact that key decisions of the Constitutional Court of Germany are translated into English justify the use and improve the accessibility of these citations. Similarly, there is no language barrier when considering countries such as India or South Africa, where extensive constitutional discussions are held. Another possible reason why new countries began featuring in the ISC's constitutional discourse is the fact that the 'proportionality' concept has been introduced to Israel's basic laws, and it is being increasingly used in constitutional adjudication. Professor Aharon Barak has recently published a book on proportionality and, even though he no longer occupies an ISC seat,[56] it stands to reason that this book too will have a substantive impact on the constitutional cases of the ISC, as his earlier books did. The book offers a fascinating discussion of comparative law in terms of proportionality that includes references to German, European, Canadian, Irish, and English laws, and even a graph reflecting how proportionality laws migrated all over the world.[57]

Whether or not the ISC will address other countries in the future remains to be seen. It seems, however, that as long as the Israeli academic approach remains US-orientated, it will have an impact on ISC constitutional adjudication as well.

E. Citations According to Majority, Dissenting, or Separate Judgments

These two figures reflect the same data, showing who—majority, dissenting, or separate opinions—cited foreign precedents. We decided to present the same data in two separate tables because Figure 5, which includes the number of references to foreign law, offers a comprehensive view of the total foreign-law citations by year—which cannot be seen in any of the previous tables.

Figures 5 and 6 clearly show that the majority (over 70 per cent) of foreign citations are made by judges in the majority opinion. Furthermore, the study found that the vast majority of foreign citations (again, over 70 per cent) were meant to

---

[55] I Porat, 'The Use of Foreign Law in Israeli Constitutional Adjudication', n 8 above.
[56] Justice Barak served some 30 years as an ISC judge, 11 of which (1995–2006) as the court president, and had a crucial impact on Israeli law in general and constitutional law in particular.
[57] A Barak, *Proportionality in Constitutional Rights and their Limitations*, Nevo, 2010, 225–57 (in Hebrew). For the English translation see: *Proportionality: Constitutional Rights and their Limitations* (Cambridge Studies in Constitutional Law) 2012.

Year	Constitutional cases citing foreign law	Total number of citations	dissenting opinion	separate opinion	majority opinion
1994	9	81	7	19	55
1995	13	129	19	7	103
1996	14	71	9	5	57
1997	6	24	9	3	12
1998	8	54	7	0	47
1999	7	19	0	0	19
2000	4	17	0	5	12
2001	3	14	5	0	9
2002	6	31	4	4	23
2003	6	21	0	6	15
2004	6	39	0	1	38
2005	8	36	4	0	32
2006	12	127	50	6	71
2007	4	5	0	2	3
2008	6	36	0	5	31
2009	3	13	2		11
2010	5	80	29	0	51
Total	120	797	145	63	589
percentage			18.19%	7.90%	73.90%

Figure 5: Number of Citations According to Majority, Dissenting, or Separate Judgments

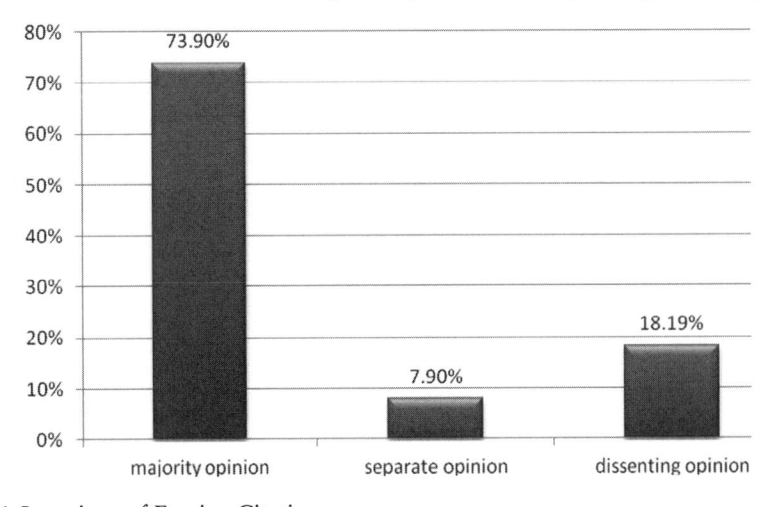

Figure 6: Locations of Foreign Citations

establish the 'even there' claim. Namely, they were meant to bolster the ISC decision with reference to a set of laws that can support it.

We feel that these findings reveal a widespread and well-known situation of foreign-law citations in constitutional adjudication. Constitutional judges wished to establish their rulings on foreign laws, among other things, and the fact that countries of similar judicial values support their judicial conclusions further legitimises them. At the same time, it is often hard to justify the choice of country, legal system, or even the case to be cited. The impression is that often, the various position-holders (majority or dissenting) 'summon' the adjudication that serves their purpose.

The way foreign law was used in the *Adalla* case (on family reunion)[58] demonstrates this well. The affair addressed a disputed question of whether residents of the Palestinian Authority (PA) who marry Israeli citizens (practically, Israeli Arabs) may assume residency or even be naturalised in Israel under what is known as the right to family reunion. The verdict addressed the constitutionality of an amendment to the Citizenship Act, which banned 'family reunions' of Israelis and PA residents.

The case brought to the fore important questions on immigration, citizenship, and residence and, naturally, comparative law was employed to support key arguments. The 281-page verdict that was handed down by a panel of 11 judges in 2006 established (by a majority of 6:5) that the amendment stands and should not be nullified at this stage. The discussion of the ban on family reunions is still pending at the ISC.

That verdict carried some 60 citations of foreign precedents. A fact of particular interest here is the wide scope of countries cited in both the majority and dissenting opinions: they included some 30 US references, six English references, nine Canadian, three German, as well as four South African,[59] one French,[60] and one Irish one.[61] Reference was also made to the European Court of Human Rights. Again, we must point out that, as the main findings of our comparative study show, most of the references addressed US cases, while many fewer English references were used, if at all. For example, both the majority and dissenting opinions carry an extensive and interesting debate on a disputed American affair, the *Korematsu* case.[62] The Israeli

---

[58] HCJ 7052/03 *Adallah v Minister of the Interior* (14.05.06) (see English translation at elyon1.court.gov.il/files_eng/03/520/070/a47/03070520.a47.htm.

[59] In his dissenting opinion, Justice Barak showed that the Constitution of the Republic of South Africa does not explicitly speak about the right to family life. The 'ordinary' law (Aliens Control Act 96 of 1991) imposed restrictions on the entry to the RSA by an alien spouse of an RSA citizen, and the question was raised whether this impairs the right to human dignity, which the Constitutional Court answered in the affirmative (unanimously). See *Dawood v The Minister of Home Affairs*, CCT 35/99 and *Booysen v Minister of Home Affairs*, CCT 8/01.

[60] In 1978, the Conseil d'Etat ruled that an immigration policy that impairs the right of French nationals to live with their spouses in their own country is unconstitutional because it violates the State's pledge to promote the advancement of families (Arret GISTI (CE) 08.12.78). The French Conseil Constitutionnel followed and expanded on that ruling, stating that the constitutional right to a family reunion applies even to individuals who were merely accorded French residency rights (Case 93-325 DC 13.8.1993).

[61] This citation was also part of Justice Barak's dissenting opinion: the Irish court ruled that the constitutional right of a minor Irish citizen to have a family life could obligate the state to grant permanent residency to or even naturalise his parents even if they entered Ireland illegally and resided there without permits (*Fajujonu v The Minister of Justice*, Supreme Court No 387 (1990), Ir 151).

[62] *US v Korematsu*, 323 US 214 (1944). It is worth reminding our readers that during World War 2, when the USA was at war with Japan, American residents and citizens of Japanese origin were excluded and banished to internment camps. While only a few individuals were suspected of disloyalty, the US administration imposed the sanction on an entire population group. In a 6:3 decision the US Supreme Court judges ruled that the exclusion order was constitutional.

judges cited from both the majority opinion and the minority opinion, and from subsequently published articles that criticised the *Korematsu* decision.

One of the most interesting examples of the use of foreign precedents to demonstrate *a contrario*—which is not included in this study because the decision was handed down in 2011[63]—addresses an important constitutional question: may a constitutional amendment be enacted as a 'temporary' provision? Does the ISC have the power to have a judicial review of an unconstitutional amendment?[64] Practically, the issue was whether the doctrine of an 'unconstitutional constitutional amendment' can be applied to this temporary provision. The doctrine of constitutional amendment was discussed extensively by foreign legal systems,[65] but it was the first time it was discussed in Israeli case law.[66] The appeal was dismissed by all seven judges, and the Basic Law that was introduced as a temporary provision remained in force, though it was highly criticised by the ISC.

President Beinisch refers to foreign law, mainly Indian and Turkish law and, for the first time, to the Czech Constitutional Court decision on this matter.[67] Nevertheless, all the references were meant to point out that the situation in Israel is different from the custom in the countries whose cases were cited because the doctrine of the unconstitutional constitutional amendment assumes the existence of a complete Constitution and an amendment made in it, while the Israeli constitutional process is as yet incomplete. The approach of the ISC is that, in the broadest sense, this doctrine of comparative law does not belong in Israel.

That example is a fine demonstration of the way in which the ISC cites foreign law to distinguish the Israeli constitutional legal system from the customary systems of other countries. This is quite an irregular use of foreign law for *a contrario* reasons, but it is interesting because it gives rise to an important constitutional question.

F. Some Qualitative Thoughts

Different reasons were offered for the use of foreign precedents in Israeli constitutional adjudications, such as constitutional history and the bounds of English law;

---

[63] *Knesset Member Bar-On v Israel's Knesset* HC 4908/10 (not yet published, rendered 7 April 2011).
[64] The case dealt with an amendment to the Basic Law: The Economy, according to which the state budget would be passed by the Knesset every other year. The amendment was introduced by a temporary provision for two years, and then extended again, by another temporary provision.
[65] See, eg, GJ Jacobsohn, 'An Unconstitutional Constitution' A Comparative Perspective (2006) 3 *International Journal of Constitutional Law* 460; R O'Connell, 'Guardians of the Constitution: Unconstitutional Constitutional Norms' (1999) 4 *JCL* 48; A Richard, 'Nonconstitutional Amendments' (2009) 22 *Canadian Journal of Law and Jurisprudence* 5. See also K Gözler, *Judicial Review of Constitutional Amendments: A Comparative Study* (2008); A Barak, 'The Unconstitutional Constitutional Amendment' (forthcoming in *Israel Law Review*, 2011). Both of the latter articles were mentioned by the Supreme Court.
[66] Although the idea of supra 'eternal' principles had been recognised in several cases since 1965.
[67] The Czech Constitutional Court addressed the Constitutional Act on shortening the Term of Office of the Chamber of Deputies, in September 2009 (for the English version, see www.concourt.cz/view/pl-27-09) and ruled against a constitutional Act that shortened the tenure of the Parliamentary Chamber of Deputies, which led to early elections there.

the lack of a constitutional text and the need to develop a set of human rights for a democratic state; the need to rely on foreign law in order to construct and expand the constitutional revolution, and in recent years the adoption of a proportionality test and the new global comparative constitutional discourse—including a global judicial dialogue—all of which resulted in the extensive use of foreign citations. It is not always easy to say exactly when those citations are just for comparison, inspiration or guidance and when for legitimacy. The use of foreign adjudication is rich and vast though it has not always been coherent. 'Cherry picking' and sometimes problematic comparisons may be found as well,[68] and that is mainly because judges—when turning to a particular country—do not always explain the reasons for their citing of foreign law.

V. CONCLUSION

One of the issues that this study did not examine, and which definitely deserves further examination, is the use of foreign law in instructive and landmark cases of Israel's constitutional adjudication. A non-empirical review of constitutional cases in recent years—'revolutionary' cases, those which nullified laws for being 'unconstitutional',[69] declared rights that were not included in basic acts as 'constitutional', and ruled on issues associated with the war on terrorism[70]—shows that the ISC verdicts are saturated with foreign citations. Constitutional adjudication is practically undergoing a globalisation process, as numerous recent papers have pointed out.[71] This study on the use of foreign law in Israeli constitutional adjudication indicates that it, too, is involved in the 'migration' process that international constitutional law is experiencing.

To conclude, though the ISC makes extensive use of foreign precedents and references, we feel that Israeli constitutional law is an original Israeli development, based on the unique culture and special nature of the State of Israel as a Jewish and democratic state, and the special circumstances of its existence, including the need to maintain a balance between human rights and the State's security. The fact that ever since the State was established, and regardless of changes it underwent in recent years, citations of foreign law remain stable, indicates that after all, the ISC still establishes its rulings mainly on Israeli law. In the words of President Barak in the *Bank Hamizrahi* case:

---

[68] One of the most interesting examples is the use of American and English precedents in Israeli cases dealing with parliamentary immunities, or judicial review of parliamentary Acts, issues mainly dealt with by European parliamentary states. For a critical discussion, see S Navot, 'Judicial Review of the Legislative Process' (2006) 39(2) *Israel Law Review* 182.

[69] See the *Bank Hamizrahi* affair, the Family Reunion affair, and verdicts that address key human rights such as freedom of expression and the right to legality.

[70] This issue is of particular importance for Israeli constitutional adjudication and calls for a separate discussion which we did not go into in this paper. We would like to mention, however, that adjudications concerning the war on terrorism extensively cited from foreign sources, mainly international law.

[71] See, eg, the chapter on South Africa in this book. Christa Rautenbach mentions that this comparative process has many names and several meanings: 'It has been called "transjudicialism", "transjudicial communication", "constitutionalist dialogue", "judicial globalism", "constitutional cross-fertilisation", "transnational contextualisation", "globalisation of judgment", "globalisation of national courts" and "judicial comparativism"'.

The balance between individual and national [needs] that the Israeli society will introduce will, therefore, reflect the views of the Israeli society, which may differ from perceptions of other societies. Great caution is, therefore, required when using comparative law in this particular field. Indeed, comparative law is very important. It points at options contained in texts. It sheds light on customary arrangements enacted by democratic and constitutional states. It provides judges with the confidence that their interpretation is accepted and works properly in other cases. At the same time, we need to refrain from turning a slave into a master. We must not subjugate ourselves to comparative law. It mainly serves to inspire, and inspiration has limited powers. Indeed, we need to consider the social and cultural variety of the various communities, while considering the special history of the legal system and the unique accentuations it gives to certain issues.[72]

---

[72] In the aforementioned *Bank Hamizrahi* affair, n 15 above at 431–32.

6

Namibia: The Supreme Court as a Foreign Law Importer

IRENE SPIGNO[*]

TABLE OF CONTENTS

I. A Brief Introduction 155
II. Some Hints of Constitutional History: The Road to Independence 156
III. The 1990 Constitution-drafting Process 159
IV. The Constitution of Namibia: Imported or Indigenous Product? 161
    A. The Form of Government 163
    B. The Bill of Rights 164
V. The Administration of Justice and the Supreme Court as Constitutional Judge 166
VI. The Empirical Research: The Methodology 168
    A. The Quantitative Data 170
    B. The Qualitative Data 176
VII. The Use of 'Extra-systemic' Elements in Constitutional Adjudication in Namibia: Some Critical and Conclusive Remarks 180

I. A BRIEF INTRODUCTION

HAUNTED BY PAST experiences with an oppressive racist system of government, Namibian people have been able to overcome social, political, and cultural differences, reaching a strong constitutional agreement[1] approved by the extremely right-wing white people, members of the Democratic Turnhalle Alliance (DTA) and the South West Africa People's Organization (SWAPO), thereby developing one of the most democratic Constitutions in Africa.[2] Since the independence of the

---

[*] PhD in Comparative Public Law, University of Siena. Research Fellow in Comparative Public Law, University of Siena (Italy). A special thanks to the Namibian Supreme Court for giving me assistance during my research there and in particular to Justice Gerhard Maritz for all the information provided and for his kind availability, patience and courtesy in answering all my questions.

[1] In this regard, it has been remarked that 'the Namibian Constitution did not fall out of the sky; it is the product of many years of negotiation and political growth'. See G Carpenter, 'The Namibian Constitution: Ex Africa Aliquid Novi After All?' (1989–1990) 15 *South African Yearbook of International Law* 63.

[2] See A du Pisani, 'Rumours of Rain: Namibia's Post-Independence Experience' (1991) 21 *Africa Insight* 171.

country (formally reached in 1990), the Supreme Court of Namibia has been strongly engaged in the democratic development of the constitutional structure, playing the fundamental role of foreign legal sources importer.

However, a more complete analysis of the use of foreign case law in constitutional adjudication cannot disregard a brief reconstruction of the historical processes that led to independence and the main features of the Namibian constitutional order (with a focus on the catalogue of rights and freedoms and constitutional justice). This is even more true with reference to the Namibian case, where the role played by the Constitution-making process in solving internal as well as external conflicts and in facilitating a peaceful transition to democracy and independence cannot disregard the influence of international and foreign forces.

The purpose of this work is twofold. Firstly, it wants to assess from a quantitative point of view how much the Supreme Court of Namibia, in its constitutional adjudication activity, is engaged in the use of foreign case law. Secondly, its aim is to reflect critically on the outcomes emerging from the empirical survey (qualitative analysis), in order to consider *why* and *to what extent* the Supreme Court of Namibia cites foreign precedents.

Thus, before giving space to the empirical analysis, recent Namibian constitutional history will be put under consideration and a brief description of the constitutional architecture will follow.

II. SOME HINTS OF CONSTITUTIONAL HISTORY: THE ROAD TO INDEPENDENCE

Namibia has a recent constitutional history. After more than a century of foreign control, first by German colonisers and then under the protectorate of South Africa, Namibia celebrated its independence on 21 March 1990.

The whole territory of Namibia, formerly known as South-West Africa, was entrusted to Germany as a protectorate by the Conference of Berlin in 1884–85.[3] During the First World War the troops of South Africa defeated the Germans and occupied the Namibian territory maintaining a similar administrative structure. At the end of the War, the newly established League of Nations officially removed the Namibian territory from the jurisdiction of Germany and gave a Class C mandate to South Africa,[4] according to which the territory should be governed as if it was

---

[3] The German administration did not fully extend over the territory and the northern regions of Ovambo, Kovango, and Caprivi, which did not have settler farms and required limited colonial administration.

[4] See J Dugard, *The SWA/Namibia Dispute* (Lansdowne, Juta, 1973). When the League of Nations was founded three types of mandates were created in order to provide different levels of administration for territories entrusted to nations, acting as 'Mandatories of the League of Nations'. The differences were based on the stage of development of the inhabitants, and other considerations such as economic conditions and geography. Thus, a 'Class A mandate' covered territories that were ready to become independent in a relatively short period of time (they were all territories in the Middle East: Iraq, Palestine, and Transjordan, administered by the UK; and Lebanon and Syria, administered by France). The 'Class B mandate' was assigned to territories for which independence was still a distant prospect (it included African territories, such as the Cameroons and Togoland, each of which was divided between

an integral part of South African territory but always under the supervision of the League of Nations.[5] Due to the fact that the mandate did not include a transfer of sovereignty, South Africa had to give periodical reports to the League's Mandate Commission. Such reports were made regularly only until 1945, when the United Nations (UN) was established. Even if they were not the League of Nation's successor in law, South Africa asked the General Assembly officially to incorporate the mandated territory into the territory of South Africa.

This request was denied and the South-West Africa territory was placed under the supervision of the General Assembly and its Trusteeship Council.[6] South Africa refused to comply with the obligation deriving from the Trusteeship and this refusal led to a long feud in the UN, and one of the worst legal battles in the International Court of Justice (ICJ).[7]

In 1948, the former National Party[8] won the elections and gained control of the South-African Government. The new government decided to interrupt cooperation with the UN, giving birth to a long period of tensions which was in turn aggravated by the introduction of apartheid laws and practices.[9] In 1962 a Commission for South-West Africa was appointed by the South African government. It recommended that the territory be divided into homelands for the different ethnic groups and that they be governed according to the same apartheid policy which applied in South Africa. These recommendations were applied and in 1968 the Namibian Nations Act was approved, entrusting Namibian territories to African ethnic groups; however, no territory was created for coloureds (mixed groups), while the whites, who constituted only 10 per cent of the Namibian population received 60 per cent of the territory.

In the meantime, SWAPO had begun, in September 1965, armed operations along Namibia's northern borders in order to free Namibia from South African control.

British and French administration, Tanganyika, that was under British administration, and Ruanda-Urundi, under Belgian administration). Lastly, territories classified under the 'Class C mandate' virtually had no prospect of self-government (they included South-West Africa, administered by the Union of South Africa; New Guinea, administered by Australia; Western Samoa, administered by New Zealand; Nauru, administered by Australia under a mandate of the British Empire; and some Pacific islands, administered by Japan).

[5] Article 22 of the League of Nations Covenant.

[6] The UN Trusteeship System for Non-Self-Governing Territories was intended to promote progressive development towards self-government or independence in accordance with the wishes freely expressed by the people concerned and to encourage respect for fundamental rights.

[7] M Wiechers, 'Namibia's Long Walk to Freedom. The Role of Constitution Making in the Creation of an Independent Namibia' in LE Miller (ed), *Framing the State in Times of Transition. Case Studies in Constitution Making* (United States Institute of Peace Press, Washington, DC, 2010) 81–110 at 82.

[8] The National Party (*Nasionale Party* in Afrikaans) was the governing party of South Africa from 4 June 1948 until 9 May 1994. Its policies included apartheid, the establishment of a republic, and the promotion of Afrikaner culture. After 1994 it was involved in the implementation of conservative politics and was later renamed the New National Party. In 2006, almost 100 years after its founding, it merged with the African National Congress, considered as its sworn enemy for almost a century. See C Van der Westhuizen, *White Power and the Rise and Fall of the National Party* (Cape Town, Zebra Press, 2007).

[9] For a more detailed description of the construction of the 'Apartheid State' see A du Pisani, 'State and Society under South African Rule' in C Keulder (ed), *State, Society and Democracy. A Reader in Namibian Politics* (Macmillan Education Namibia, 2010) 49–76.

Actually, the UN General Assembly, in its advisory capacity, as well as former member states of the League of Nations (eg Ethiopia and Liberia) had, since 1950, approached the ICJ three times to complain about South Africa's actions.[10] After the ICJ dismissed Ethiopia and Liberia's demands, South Africa continued to govern South-West Africa as one of its own provinces[11] and, by 1966, the UN General Assembly had declared an end to the South African mandate by revoking it.[12] It had then entrusted the territory to UN control,[13] but South Africa refused to acknowledge the UN as the rightful successor of the League of Nations even after an advisory opinion of the ICJ on 21 June 1971.[14] Thus, the South African Government continued to exercise control and also enforced its politics of racial discrimination by strengthening the apartheid regime in Namibia.[15]

---

[10] The perspective held by the international judge was that South Africa was still considered an 'agent' and therefore had no power to change the international status of the territories under mandate; therefore, South Africa's competence was subject to the UN's consent. Ethiopia and Liberia instituted an action against South Africa in 1960, asking the ICJ to declare the forfeiture of the mandate based on the consideration that by applying its apartheid policies, South Africa had betrayed its duty to promote the material and moral wellbeing of territory inhabitants. Although in 1962 the Court declared itself competent to decide the case, four years later it held that the applicants had failed to prove a legal right and interest in the matter and declined to give the judgment.

[11] Actually, the South African Parliament adopted a new Constitution for the territory and Namibia became the fifth South African province, but once again the effective power was handled by the white part of the population.

[12] The mandate revocation had been considered more an act of political offence and outrage than a legally binding decision. See M Wiechers, 'South-West Africa: The Background, Content, and Significance of the Opinion of the World Court of 21 June 1971' (1975) 5 *South Africa Journal of Foreign and Comparative Law* 123–70.

[13] In 1967, the UN Council for Namibia was created with the aim of administering the territory until its independence and 'to promulgate such laws, decrees and administrative regulations as are necessary until a legislative assembly is established following elections conducted on the basis of universal adult suffrage' (General Assembly Resolution 2248). See HG Schermers, 'The Namibia Decree in National Courts' (1977) 26 *The International and Comparative Law Quarterly* pt I, 81–96.

[14] Ibid.

[15] 1971 marks a change in South African politics: during the month of October a new frontier in the war against South Africa's presence in Namibia was opened throughout SWAPO's armed wing that started operating in the Caprivi Strip as well as labour action involving the whole country's mining and commercial sectors, thereby adding a new perspective to the politics of resistance. The political and socio-economic struggle was focused, among other things, on the abolition of the inhuman contract labour system inherited from German colonial times, the freedom to select one's place and type of employment, and permission to reside in the urban areas. As a response, in February 1972 the South African Government introduced an emergency proclamation (Proclamation R 17 GG 3377); thus, unauthorised meetings of more than five persons were prohibited, detention without trial was permitted, and severe restrictions on freedom of political organisation and expression were imposed. The political implications of the 1971–72 strike were profound. Labour-claims-based struggles challenged the essence of the urban/rural division that represented the core of spatial apartheid policy. A period of renewed and stronger repression was ushered in, especially in the region of Owambo, where the South African Defence Force took over control from the South African Police in January 1972. In the attempts to control the process of decolonisation, the South African Government enacted the Development of Self-Government for Native Nations in South West Africa Amendment Act, 1973 (No 20 of 1973), which provided for self-government and independence of the various 'Native Nations', and the establishment of a Prime Minister's Advisory Council for South-West Africa in March of the same year. It was part of a double strategy. On the one hand, it continued to strengthen its policies of ethnic fragmentation and spatial separation, while on the other hand, the Turnhalle Constitutional Conference was established. See du Pisani, 'State and Society under South African Rule', above n 9 at 69.

From this moment onwards, the tensions between South Africa and the UN, as well as the whole international community, continued, producing a mirror image of the conflict internally.

On 1 September 1975, the ruling white authority in Namibia, with the sponsorship of the South African Government,[16] instituted the Turnhalle Constitutional Conference. It was the first time in Namibian history that leaders of the various ethnic groups, excluding SWAPO, were convened in order to debate the political future of their country. The conference's aim was to create an 'internal settlement' for Namibian independence. The conference received strong opposition, first of all from SWAPO, which refused to participate, as well as from the UN which considered the conference's exercise in Constitution-making an unauthorised act of unilateral independence. Regardless of this opposition, the conference represented a landmark in the Namibian constitutional process. Strong foreign influences on the drafting of the Namibian Constitution began at this stage, with conference leaders being taken to the United States, the United Kingdom, and Europe more generally in order to meet members of foreign governments and leaders of political parties.[17]

Towards the beginning of 1978, an interim Constitution was adopted,[18] providing a justiciable Bill of Rights, a parliamentary regime, and a decentralised government with a strong ethnic component. The interim Constitution was expressly refused by both SWAPO and the UN, but the installation of the interim government followed as a result of national elections held the same year with support from 78 per cent of voters. The interim government assisted the abolition of white-only representation for Namibian people in its own parliament and the appointment of an administrator-general with wide legislative and administrative powers, leading to the abolition of some of the most offensive apartheid legislations such as those laws prohibiting mixed marriages and sexual relations between races.

III. THE 1990 CONSTITUTION-DRAFTING PROCESS

All the events described above raised awareness at the international, as well as the UN, level that an agreement on Namibian independence was possible. A 'Western Contact Group' was created: it was an unofficial body of members of the governments of the United States, France, the United Kingdom, Canada, and West Germany which elaborated on an agreement endorsed in 1978 by the UN Security Council as Resolution 435. It has represented the only project which both the South African Government and SWAPO agreed with, consequently forming the basis for political transition to independence.

---

[16] Organised by Dirk Mudge, a white member of the National Party of South Africa and the National Unity Democratic Organisation (NUDO) with South African-sponsorship, the Turnhalle Conference laid the framework for the government of South-West Africa from 1977 to independence in 1989.

[17] During the conference, the DTA was created by the union of 11 ethnic political parties.

[18] The 1978 *interim* Constitution was promulgated as a South African law and its approval followed quite a complicated process. See Wiechers, 'Namibia's Long Walk to Freedom. The Role of Constitution Making in the Creation of an Independent Namibia' above n 7 at 105.

Unfortunately, this agreement was not implemented until 1989[19] as the negotiations were interrupted in 1981 when Ronald Reagan became President of the United States.[20] It was not until 22 December 1988 that a tripartite agreement was signed in New York by South Africa, Angola, and Cuba, whose aim was to break the 10-year impasse and lead to the implementation of Resolution 435 and the independence of Namibia.

Although the UN Resolution prescribed the development of the peace process through the formation of a Constituent Assembly, it did not indicate the nature and the content of the future Namibian Constitution. In 1981, thanks to a United States initiative, the Western Contact Group was successful in reaching an agreement with all of the involved parties, that is, the African states at the border with Namibia, the Organization of African Unity, South Africa, SWAPO, and the internal political parties. This agreement consisted of principles to guide the constitutional process, which were then submitted to the UN. Although it did not formally adopt and incorporate them into Resolution 435, they were considered part of the resolution itself.[21]

The starting point of the constitutional drafting process was based on the 1982 guidelines, according to which the future Constitution would have to define Namibia as a unitary and democratic State, with a constitutional text considered as the supreme law of the country, to which the law was subjected from a substantive as well as a formal point of view. The form of government drawn in the guidelines provided an elected executive branch, a legislative power elected through universal suffrage, and a judicial power entrusted to an independent judiciary responsible for constitutional interpretation and with an aim to assure its superiority. These guidelines also provided for a list of fundamental rights together with the relevant guarantees. More specifically, amongst other things, they recognised freedom of expression, the protection of political parties and private property against abuse and deprivation, and condemnation of all forms of discrimination.

Elections for the Constituent Assembly were held from 7–11 November 1989 and 97 per cent of the population with the right to vote (60 per cent of whom were illiterate) elected 72 members of the Constituent Assembly. The seats were divided between 10 parties according to a proportional basis throughout the country. SWAPO emerged as the winner, obtaining 41 seats (nearly 60 per cent of the vote and almost completely supported by the Ovambo people), while the DTA obtained 21 seats (almost 30 per cent and they defeated SWAPO in many southern districts). The remaining 10 seats were distributed among the other five smaller parties.

---

[19] Resolution 435 entered into force on 1 April 1989. It allowed South Africa to continue administering the Namibian territory and the administrator-general would organise elections, with constant UN supervision.

[20] In fact, as the United States' administration supported the South African government, the Resolution could be implemented only after the Cuban troops' retirement from Angola, where they had been sent to respond to South-African incursions.

[21] The '1982 constitutional guidelines' should have been binding for the future Namibian Constituent Assembly which, according to these indications, would have needed two thirds of its members to approve the Constitution.

The new elected organ had its first meeting on 21 November 1989 in the Tintenpalast, an old building built during the German protectorate's period, and adopted the Constitution on 9 February 1990. It was faced with the hard task of drawing up a Constitution from a multitude of proposals elaborated by the different political parties starting from 1985[22] which needed to accommodate different needs and requests.[23]

A drafting panel of three South African lawyers[24] was appointed and charged with presenting to the assembly a constitutional draft early in 1990. The fact that three South African lawyers were appointed (two of them were Afrikaners,[25] popularly perceived as the original perpetrators of apartheid policies, even if racist policies had already started under British control of South Africa) could be considered problematic; however, the reason behind this choice was quite simple.

According to the dominant idea of that moment, the future Namibian Constitution would have been based on the South African legal system since they shared the same common law as well as similar constitutional laws and traditions. Moreover, it was the same period as the fall of the Berlin Wall and the tumult in Eastern Europe which resulted in a feeling 'that the Namibian Constitution should not be the product of some foreign experiment'.[26]

The final text was drafted by a Standing Committee formed by all Namibian parties, assisted by the three legal experts from South Africa and the Commonwealth Secretariat, and the Constitution was adopted on 21 March 1990.

IV. THE CONSTITUTION OF NAMIBIA: IMPORTED OR INDIGENOUS PRODUCT?

Generally speaking, the Namibian legal system is made up of two components. The so-called western one, and the traditional African one.[27] The western component

---

[22] For a detailed description of the role played by the constitutional council and the analysis of the content of projects presented before the Constituent Assembly was established, see Wiechers, 'Namibia's Long Walk to Freedom. The Role of Constitution Making in the Creation of an Independent Namibia', above n 7 at 86–88. The author underlines how some of the proposals drew their inspiration from the UN Universal Declaration of Human Rights and the European Convention for the Protection of Human Rights and Fundamental Freedoms.

[23] In fact, the political parties that represented the black majority wanted to ensure the fundamental rights so long denied to them, while the white minority did not wish to lose its privileges. In the words of the Namibian President, Sam Nujoma, the result of the work developed by the Constituent assembly was 'one of the most important and memorable acts of self-determination that embodies a very comprehensive bill of human rights to protect the individual from possible abuse of power by organs of state ... [which] should give our people full confidence in the future of our nation'. See *African News*, 2–9 February 1990.

[24] They were Arthur Chaskalson, Gerhard Erasmus and Marinus Wiechers.

[25] Even if the use of the word Afrikaner can sometimes be problematic, in this work, I am referring to the definition in the Oxford English Dictionary online; an Afrikaner is '[a]n Afrikaans-speaking white person in South Africa, especially one descended from the Dutch and Huguenot settlers of the 17th century'.

[26] See Wiechers, 'Namibia's Long Walk to Freedom. The Role of Constitution Making in the Creation of an Independent Namibia', above n 7 at 89.

[27] For a further analysis of the *customary law*, and in particular the role played by local customs within the Namibian legal system see MO Hinz, 'Traditional Governance and African Customary

derives its features from the South African hybrid system, which contains three main elements: Roman, Roman-Dutch and English law.[28]

As a result, in the Namibian experience the expression 'common law' indicates the Roman-Dutch law[29] legal tradition that constitutes the base of Namibian legal system, complemented by statutory law. It is a civil law system later influenced by British common law principles.[30] Actually, references to the original Roman-Dutch sources are very rare in Namibian case law.[31] Civil law principles from the Dutch legal tradition tend to prevail in some areas of substantive law, such as criminal and private law (especially with regard to family law and the protection of human beings in general), while British common law tends to prevail in economic and procedural areas.

Article 66 of the Constitution provides that common law principles as well as customary law traditions existing prior to independence coexist with the new legal order established by the Constitution and the legislation passed by Parliament. However, the purpose the Constituent Assembly wanted to achieve was to ensure legal continuity, not only with common law, but also with customary law provisions in order to emphasise Namibian legal traditions that had been vehemently suppressed during the apartheid regime.

As already mentioned above, one of the features of the drafting process of the 1990 Constitution of Namibia was the influence of foreign legal systems and international forces as a direct consequence of the territory's international status that flowed from the UN mandate system. Analysing both the works developed by the Constituent Assembly, and those that previously led to the '1982 constitutional guidelines' formulation, the strong foreign influence was later transposed into the definitive version of the constitutional text.

Law: Comparative Observations from a Namibian Perspective' in N Horn and A Bösl (eds), *Human Rights and the Rule of Law in Namibia* (Windhoek, Macmillan Namibia, 2008) 59–87. See also MO Hinz, 'Traditional courts in Namibia—Part of the Judiciary? Jurisprudential Challenges of Traditional Justice' in *The Independence of the Judiciary in Namibia* (Konrad-Adenauer Stiftung, Macmillan Education Namibia, 2008) 149–73.

[28] See L Berat, 'The Future of Customary Law in Namibia: A Call for an Integration Model' (1991–1992) 15 *Hastings Internationall & Comparative Law Review* 1.

[29] Roman-Dutch law is a synthesis of Roman law (that entered into the Netherlands between the late thirteenth century and the end of the sixteenth century), Germanic customary law, feudal law, canon law and includes some natural law concepts. See RW Lee, 'The Roman-Dutch Law in South Africa: The Influence of English Law' (1969) 1 *Colombo Law Review* 1.

[30] When the territory of Namibia was taken over by South Africa after World War I, Roman-Dutch law, as applied in the province of the Cape of Good Hope on 1 January 1920, was applicable in Namibia as well. After independence, Roman-Dutch law continues to be applied according to art 140.1 of the Constitution of the Republic of Namibia. See R Zimmermann and D Visser (eds), *South African Law as a Mixed Legal System in Southern Cross: Civil Law and Common Law in South Africa* (Clarendon Press, Oxford, 1996). See also D Carey Miller, 'South Africa: A Mixed System Subject to Transcending Forces, in Esin Ortlci et al (eds), *Studies in Legal Systems: Mixed and Mixing* (Kluwer Law International, 1996) 165–91. See also Berat, 'The Future of Customary Law in Namibia' above n 28, 11–12.

[31] See M Bogdan, 'The First Decade of Namibian Law' (1999) 68 *Nordic Journal of International Law*, 275–91. The author highlights that pursuant to art 78, para 4 of the Constitution, which prescribes the continued application of pre-independence law, many South African statutes enacted prior to 1990 still apply in Namibia. There are many areas in which Namibian law is still identical or nearly identical to South African law, although the degree of similarity depends on whether and to what extent the rules in question have been subjected to changes in both countries.

A. The Form of Government

Actually, the constitutional structure reflects the legal pluralism that permeates the whole legal system. It is based on elements from several constitutional styles, mixing up British influences (individualised as the 'Westminster' model), as the State is unitary, with a quasi-perfect bicameral legislative body of which the Prime Minister and the ministers must be members (both appointed by the President from the members of the National Assembly),[32] and those from the United States constitutional system, in which the President of Namibia is the head of the executive power and is directly elected by the people (thereby reflecting the features of what can be called the 'Washington model'[33]).

The Constitution is notable for its emphasis on Presidential accountability:[34] the President may dissolve the National Assembly, if the cabinet advises the President that the government is unable to govern effectively. In this case the Presidential term of office also automatically expires (Article 57(0)). Of course, it remains open for the President to seek renewed parliamentary support through negotiation.

The cabinet consists of the President, the Prime Minister and other Ministers, all appointed by the President among members of the National Assembly (including nominated members), although Deputy-Ministers may be members of the National Council. The Prime Minister is the leader of government business in Parliament, and is the principal assistant of the President. Ministers' appointments must be terminated by the President if a majority of all members of the National Assembly passes a vote of no confidence (Articles 41 and 39).

The Parliament is composed of two chambers: the National Assembly, which expresses the legislative function; and the National Council, that represents the different regions (two members for each one) and has reduced legislative powers if compared to the National Assembly, being more of a review body.[35] The electoral system is particularly unusual with elected members in the National Assembly being determined by means of proportional representation, while members of the National Council are indirectly elected by the Regional Council (Article 69). The National Assembly consists of 72 popularly elected members and not more than six (non-voting) Presidential appointees selected for their special expertise, status, skill or experience (Article 46). In the performance of their duties, members of the Assembly are to be guided by the objectives of the Constitution, the public interest and by their conscience (Article 45). This

---

[32] See arts 35–43.

[33] See arts 27–34 of the Constitution of Namibia. According to the Constitution of Namibia, the President of the Republic holds the executive power and exercises it through the Cabinet (arts 35–43).

[34] The President, except as otherwise provided, in the exercise of his or her functions, shall 'be obliged to act in consultation' with the cabinet (art 27(3)). On other occasions the President must act on the recommendation of another constitutional body over certain appointments, and with the approval of the National Assembly as regards matters such as the declaration or extension of a state of emergency.

[35] The National Assembly is regulated by arts 44–67 of the Constitution of Namibia and the National Council by arts 68–77. With reference to the legislative and political process and the involvement of civil organisations, see T Bertelsmann Scott, 'Namibia' (2005) 12.1 *South African Journal of International Affairs* 129–46.

implies that a party member is entitled to vote against party policy when moved to do so by his/her conscience.

B. The Bill of Rights

Democratic constitutional values permeate the whole text. Their recognition in the Preamble reflects a democratic political culture, strengthened not only by courts' activity but also by the government upholding constitutional provisions supporting individual and human rights.[36]

If Article 1(1) recognises in general terms the modern Republic of Namibia as a sovereign, secular, democratic, and united State, based on the principles of democracy, the rule of law and justice, Chapter 3 specifically provides the Bill of Rights with a formulation very similar to those found in other contemporary democratic Constitutions and international human rights treaties. In fact, the Namibian Constitution reflects, regarding the structure and the guarantees provided in the catalogue of rights (Articles 5–25), the most important international covenants on human rights, such as the 1948 Universal Declaration of Human Rights, the 1950 Convention on the Protection of Human Rights and Fundamental Freedoms (ECHR), the UN Covenant on Civil and Political Rights and, though to a lesser extent, the UN Covenant on Economic, Social and Cultural Rights. Even if the constitutional drafters have been influenced by international sources of law, the Constitution cannot be considered as a foreign import. Rather, it would be more appropriate to say that it was derived as part of a unique international process that involved political compromise between various external and internal stakeholders.

It is, without doubt, the case that thanks to the significant role played by the UN in bringing out the independence of Namibia, the contents of the document reflect this unique international character.[37] However, it combines elements taken from the individualist vision of democracy (taken from Western liberal democracies) and the acknowledgment of the country's communitarian heritage,[38] including the presence of African customary law.

The way international and Western influences emerge is twofold: firstly, it is evident in a positive approach, in the continuous references to principles such as equality, human dignity and the prohibition of discrimination, all of which are considered fundamental elements in the new constitutional State. Secondly, as provided in Article 131 of the Constitution, the rights and freedoms contained in Chapter 3

---

[36] See, J Forrest 'Namibia—the First Postapartheid Democracy' (1994) 5.3 *Journal of Democracy* 88–100.

[37] See M Sherazi, 'Explaining the Constitution' in N Hishoono, G Hopwood, J Hunter, F Links and M Sherazi (eds), *The Constitution in the 21st Century. Perspectives on the Context and Future of Namibia's Supreme Law* (Namibia Institute for Democracy and the Institute for Public Policy Research, 2011) 20.

[38] For example, while ch 1 indicates English to be the official language, it does not exclude the possibility of using other languages. It can be considered as a fundamental provision considering that Namibia is inhabited by more than 10 ethnic groups speaking 13 languages. See A Wing, 'Communitarianism v Individualism: Constitutionalism in Namibia & South Africa' (1993) 11 *Wisconsin International Law Journal* 295, 329–48.

are entrenched, meaning that these provisions may not be repealed or amended insofar as such repeal or amendment weakens these rights and freedoms. This provision, however, does not stop the legislature from enhancing fundamental rights provisions.

The catalogue of rights (Articles 5–25) includes: protection of life and personal liberty, respect for human dignity, prohibition of slavery and forced labour, the principle of equality and freedom from discrimination, right to due process, and protection of family and children's rights. It also provides for the: right to privacy, right to private property, right to conduct political activity, free expression, and right to culture and education. Furthermore, economic, social and cultural rights are included in the Bill of Rights.

Article 5 is a safeguarding provision which underlines that all organs of government are bound by the fundamental rights and freedoms enshrined in the Constitution, which also places limitations upon those elected to exercise political power in order to prevent them from suspending or changing the Constitution to suit their political agenda.

The entrenchment of fundamental rights is reinforced by Article 25 which prohibits any legislative or executive action in contravention of these rights. Moreover, Article 22 states that wherever the Constitution contemplates a limitation of any fundamental rights, such limitation shall be of general application and not directed at any individual and may 'not negate the essential content thereof'.[39] This is based on the assumption that a right is meaningless when it becomes impossible to exercise it either directly or indirectly. It is also worth noting that under Article 24(3), the majority of these rights cannot be derogated (repealed) or suspended.

The Bill of Rights clearly represents an attempt to break with the past and its apartheid laws. Despite containing a specific provision dedicated to the condemnation of apartheid and to the improvement of affirmative actions (Article 23),[40] detentions without trial, capital punishment, forced labour, and political repression are all prohibited (Articles 6 and 8(2)(b)). The presence of various constitutional provisions that explicitly reject racism and other kinds of human dignity violations is justified according to a general approach that emphasises the principles of equality and freedom from discrimination (Articles 10 and 95). As already mentioned above, Article 23, entitled 'Apartheid and Affirmative Action' provides a detailed regulation against the apartheid legacy and the practice of racial discrimination. Based on the consideration that the majority of Namibian people have suffered the practice and ideology of apartheid for a long time, such practices and their propaganda must be prohibited by the Parliament, which

---

[39] Art 22 of the Namibian Constitution specifies that any law which may validly limit ch 3 rights must be of general application, shall not negate the essential content of those rights, and shall not be aimed at a particular individual. Certain rights are also liable to derogation or abrogation during a period of public emergency.

[40] A special provision is stated for Namibian women in art 23, para 3, according to which in the enactment of 'positive legislation' and in the application of affirmative actions' policies and practices, the legislative body shall take into account the special discrimination traditionally suffered by women in Namibia that justifies the need to encourage and enable them to play a full, equal and effective role in the political, social, economic and cultural life of the nation.

has the constitutional duty to approve regulations rendering them criminally punishable by the Courts. It is also established that the provisions of Article 10 shall not prevent Parliament from enacting legislation providing directly or indirectly for the advancement of persons within Namibia who have been socially, economically, or educationally disadvantaged by past discriminatory laws or practices, or for the implementation of policies and programmes aimed at redressing social, economic or educational imbalances in Namibian society arising out of past discriminatory laws or practices, or for achieving a balanced structuring of the public service, the police force, the defence force, and the prison service, thus justifying specific affirmative actions.

V. THE ADMINISTRATION OF JUSTICE AND THE SUPREME COURT AS CONSTITUTIONAL JUDGE

The administration of justice is entrusted to a three-tier system of independent courts subject only to the Constitution and the law, which is divided into: local courts (lower courts); a High Court with jurisdiction over appeals against decisions of lower courts in civil and criminal cases, including those involving the interpretation, protection, and implementation of constitutional dispositions; and a Supreme Court. Finally, the Ombudsman has specific expertise with reference to the violation of fundamental rights.[41]

In their judicial activity, both the Supreme Court and the High Court have a constitutional duty to interpret and implement the constitutional text, and a relevant part of their interpretation focuses on the protection of fundamental rights and freedoms.[42] Although constitutional adjudication in Namibia is shared, the Supreme Court is at the apex of the judicial hierarchy and is tasked with the constitutional responsibility of hearing and adjudicating appeals from the High Court, including appeals which involve the interpretation, implementation, and upholding of the constitutional text. It is also entrusted to deal with matters referred to for decision by the Attorney-General in his or her fulfilment of the constitutional obligation to take all necessary action for the upholding and protection of the Constitution.[43] The Supreme Court, therefore, functions both as a court of last resort over disputes in all areas of the law as well as the equivalent of a constitutional court.

The Supreme Court was founded on the date of independence and it represents, from a symbolic point of view, the first judicial institution the people of Namibia have had with such extensive jurisdiction and powers. Prior to independence all

---

[41] Arts 89–94 of the Constitution of Namibia.
[42] According to art 25 of the Constitution any person who claims that any fundamental right or freedom has been infringed or threatened may ask the court to enforce or protect such right.
[43] Not only does the Supreme Court of Namibia hear and adjudicate upon appeals emanating from the High Court—including those which involve the interpretation, implementation and upholding of the Constitution and the fundamental rights and freedoms guaranteed thereunder—it also decides matters referred to it by the Attorney-General under the Constitution and such other matters as may be authorised by an Act of Parliament.

appeals against judgments and orders of the Supreme Court of South-West Africa had to be heard and adjudicated by the then Appellate Division of the Supreme Court of South Africa.[44] After independence, the Supreme Court of Namibia inherited the powers which the Supreme Court of South-West Africa had, including the one for regulating its own procedures and making Rules of Court for that purpose. As a consequence, all those appeals pending in front of the Appellate Division of the Supreme Court of South-Africa had been transferred to the Supreme Court of Namibia in order to be prosecuted by this Court.

Decisions issued by the Namibian Supreme Court are binding on all other courts and on all persons in Namibia unless they are reversed by the Supreme Court itself or are contradicted by an Act of Parliament lawfully enacted (Article 81).

According to Articles 78, 79 and 138 of the Constitution, a Chief Justice presides over the Court which is composed of a number of additional judges determined by the President of Namibia. Article 79, in particular, establishes a quorum of three judges. In all probability, the drafters of the Namibian Constitution wanted to leave the possibility of developing its sitting-in divisions in the style of the Indian Supreme Court rather than that of the United States,[45] but it has never developed in that way. In constitutional cases, acting judges of the Supreme Court may be appointed by the President at the request of the Chief Justice on an ad hoc basis where such persons have special knowledge or expertise in such matters.

The Namibian Supreme Court is quite a young court and especially in the first years of its activity its judicial reasoning was strongly influenced by the long period of South African control. Indeed, at the very beginning, the Court in its legal reasoning leans on foreign courts' arguments and case law, for example German ones, to justify its own choices. Moreover, this is the period when the Court cites foreign doctrine the most, with explicit reference to pages and works.[46] All the judges, former and current, have received all or part of their education abroad.[47]

It is important to underline that, as it will emerge from the empirical research, in the first years, the Supreme Court of Namibia tries to find its own style moving away from South African case law.

---

[44] For an overview of the constitutional jurisprudence developed by the Supreme Court of South-West Africa and the Namibian High Court and Supreme Court since 1985, see SK Amoo, 'The Constitutional Jurisprudential Development in Namibia Since 1985' in N Horn and A Bösl (eds), *Human Rights and the Rule of Law in Namibia* (Macmillan Namibia, 2009) 39–57. See also G Coleman and E Schimming-Chase, 'Constitutional Jurisprudence in Namibia Since Independence' in A Bösl, N Horn and A du Pisani (eds), *Constitutional Democracy in Namibia. A Critical Analysis After Two Decades* (Macmillan Education Namibia, 2010) 199–214.

[45] Originally, the Supreme Court was envisaged as mainly an appellate court, it being anticipated that the Attorney-General might refer matters to it under the Constitution. The power the Constitution provides to the Attorney-General is to refer a matter, connected with legislation which the President suggests may be unconstitutional, to 'a competent Court', not specifically to the Supreme Court. See J Cottrell, 'The Constitution of Namibia: an Overview' (1991) 35 1/2 *Journal of African Law*, Recent Constitutional Developments in Africa, 56–78 at 77.

[46] See *Ex parte: Attorney-General, In Re: Corporal Punishment by Organs of State* (SA 14/90) [1991] NASC 2; 1991 (3) SALR 76 (NmS) (5 April 1991).

[47] The information on Supreme Court judges is taken from the Supreme Court website: www.superiorcourts.org.na.

VI. THE EMPIRICAL RESEARCH: THE METHODOLOGY

The data addressed in this article stem from a survey conducted on the entire set of constitutional decisions issued by the Supreme Court of Namibia during the period from 1990 to 2010. As already mentioned above, the choice of 1990 as the chronological starting point of the research is justified by Namibia's independence the same year, its adoption of a Constitution, and the establishment of both the Supreme Court and the High Court.

The research on the use of foreign precedents by the Supreme Court of Namibia has been developed through the analysis of the decisions published in the Namibia Law Reports (NR),[48] starting from the date of independence until 31 December 2010.[49] The data collected have been double checked with those contained in the Supreme Court of Namibia's judgments' database, which I had the opportunity to use for my research during the period of research I spent at the Library of the Supreme Court of Namibia. This double check was necessary because ever since Namibia became an independent State, not all decisions handed down by the Supreme Court have been published in the Namibia Law Reports, but only those considered particularly relevant. However, all of the Supreme Court decisions are available on the Supreme Court internal database (not available to the public and only accessible from the Supreme Court Library).

In the selected period of time, the Supreme Court issued a total number of nearly 150 decisions, including sentences on criminal, civil and constitutional claims.

Within this number, only the cases identified as 'constitutional cases' have been considered, namely 43 decisions. Even though in Namibia the Supreme Court does not only have constitutional jurisdiction but is entrusted with other competences, the identification of the 'constitutional cases' was not a difficult task, mainly thanks to the presence of a constitutional text.

Thus, the selection was based on the summaries contained in the Namibia Law Reports that gave the chance to interpret this expression in a wide sense as involving not only cases in which there was an explicit constitutional challenge, but also those cases in which the Constitution or constitutional rights were involved. Moreover, the keywords 'Constitution', 'Constitutional law', 'Interpretation of the Constitution' and 'Fundamental Rights' were used for the search of the Supreme Court electronic database. The outcomes of the research conducted in this way have led to include within the group of 'constitutional cases' the cases summarised in the three following groups:

1. Firstly, 'constitutional cases' are those cases in which there is a direct constitutional challenge. Obviously, it includes those cases in which the constitutional consistency of legislation is at stake, as happened, for example, with reference to the cases involving the constitutionality of legislative provisions on access to

---

[48] Namibian Law Reports appear in yearly volumes covering cases since 1990. They are published by the Legal Assistance Centre (a non-governmental organisation) in cooperation with JUTA (a South African publishing house). The editor of NR is an advocate, but the editorial board is chaired by a judge of the High Court and includes members coming from, inter alia, the Law Society, the Prosecutor General's Office and the Government Attorney's Office.

[49] Indeed, most of its decisions, the most interesting and important, are also published on two free access websites, available on www.saflii.org and www.superiorcourts.org.na.

courts and their conformity with Article 10 (right to equality) and Article 12(1)(a) (right of access to courts);[50] and the statute[51] that prohibited members of the police force from commenting unfavourably in public upon the administration of the force or other government departments, considered to be against Article 21(2) of the Constitution, being a limitation on the constitutional right of free speech.[52]

2. Even if there is no direct constitutional challenge, those cases in which a constitutional interpretation was at stake have also been included in the 'constitutional case' category. Thus, on the one hand, cases involving the different techniques that should be used in the interpretation of the constitutional text were put under consideration.[53] On the other hand, cases concerning the interpretation of specific constitutional provisions were also considered to be 'constitutional case' (for example, the interpretation of Articles 66(1) and 140(1) of the Constitution that provide respectively that common law and customary law and statutes in force at independence will remain valid unless in conflict with the Constitution and until repealed or declared unconstitutional.[54]

3. A third group includes those cases in which even if there is no constitutional challenge, constitutional rights are at stake (as in civil or criminal cases). Thus, many are decisions issued by the Supreme Court with reference to, for example, the right to a fair trial,[55] the prohibition of discrimination,[56] the prohibition of inhuman and degrading treatment,[57] the right to freedom of speech and expression,[58] respect for human dignity,[59] and the right to family life.[60]

It should be noted that I have also included two decisions handed down by the Supreme Court within its jurisdiction as Court of first instance. In fact, according to

---

[50] See *Minister of Home Affairs v Majiedt and Others* 2007 (2) NR 475 (SC) in which the Court upheld the appeal against the section challenged stating that it should not be amended because of unconstitutionality.

[51] The reference is to section 58(32) of the Police Act 19 of 1990.

[52] See *Kauesa v Minister of Home Affairs and Others* 1995 NR 175 (SC) in which the Supreme Court stated that limitations to constitutional rights should be interpreted strictly and narrowly to be both reasonable and necessary.

[53] *Kauesa v Minister of Home Affairs and Others*, n 52 above. More specifically, according to the Supreme Court of Namibia, a narrow and pedantic interpretation should be avoided, especially when dealing with the Declaration of Fundamental Human Rights in the Namibian Constitution that should be interpreted by applying international human rights norms and given a generous, broad and purposive interpretation (thus in *Minister of Defence v Mwandinghi* 1993 NR 63 (SC)). Also the interpretation of constitutional provisions regarding the relationship between the Attorney-General and the Prosecutor-General has been included in the category of constitutional cases (*Ex parte Attorney-General In Re: The Constitutional Relationship between the Attorney-General and the Prosecutor-General* 1998 NR 282 (SC)).

[54] *Myburgh v Commercial Bank of Namibia* 2000 NR 255 (SC).

[55] See among others *S v Kandovazu* 1997 NR 1 (SC), *Malama—Kean v Magistrate, District of Oshakati, and Another* 2002 NR 413 (SC) and *S v Luboya and Another* 2007 (1) NR 96 (SC).

[56] See *Muller v President of the Republic of Namibia and Another* 1999 NR 190 (SC).

[57] See *Namunjepo and Others v Commanding Officer, Windhoek Prison and Another* 1999 NR 271 (SC).

[58] See *Kauesa v Minister of Home Affairs and Others*, n 52 above.

[59] See *Ex Parte Attorney-General: In re Corporal Punishment by Organs of State* 1991 NR 178 (SC).

[60] See *Chairperson of the Immigration Selection Board v Frank and Another* 2001 NR 107 (SC) in which the Supreme Court stated that according to art 14 of the Constitution, same-sex relationships could not be included in the definition of 'family'.

Articles 79(2) and 87(c) of the Namibian Constitution, the Attorney-General sought to refer to the Supreme Court for the hearing and determining of a constitutional question.[61]

Thus, according to the guidelines provided by the coordinators of the Interest Group, I classified the constitutional cases identified above in two different ontological categories. The first one is the 'human rights' one, which includes the last group (ie the right to dignity and the prohibition of corporal punishment, the right to a fair trial or to legal representation, freedom of expression, the prohibition of racial discrimination, etc). The second one includes the so-called 'institutional cases' (inclusive of groups 1) and 2), that is, those decisions involving the relationship between Parliament and its members, the Government, the President and the Courts, etc).

A. The Quantitative Data

i. Constitutional Cases out of Total Supreme Court Decisions

The number of decisions issued by the Supreme Court is quite constant during the different years under analysis, even if it is possible to notice increasing and decreasing productive fluxes along the different periods.

This first outcome also reflects the Supreme Court's constitutional activity. In fact, it is possible to highlight the fact that there are not huge differences between the different years, meaning that within the Court's general activity there is a homogeneous trend in the number of constitutional cases handed down each year.

The outcomes resulting from the empirical analysis demonstrate that decisions issued by the Namibian Supreme Court on constitutional issues do not represent a substantial part of its general judicial activity, consisting of less than 30 per cent. This data can be explained if we consider that the constitutional jurisdiction is shared between the High Court and the Supreme Court. As already mentioned above, the Supreme Court is entrusted with the constitutional responsibility of hearing and adjudicating appeals from the High Court and has the competence to rule on matters referred to it for a decision by the Attorney-General in his or her fulfilment of the constitutional obligation to take all necessary action for the upholding and protection of the Constitution.

Thus, the number of constitutional cases handed down by the High Court is more relevant (from a quantitative point of view) than the number decided by the Supreme Court.

There was constant growth until the end of the Nineties, a fall in the period between 2000 and 2001, another growth in the following period, and a subsequent drop in 2004 and 2005. Since 2006, the number of decisions issued by the Supreme Court on constitutional matters has had uninterrupted growth.

---

[61] See *Ex Parte Attorney-General: In re Corporal Punishment by Organs of State*, n 59 above, and *Ex parte Attorney-General In Re: The Constitutional Relationship between the Attorney-General and the Prosecutor-General*, n 53 above.

Both data are shown in the following graph.

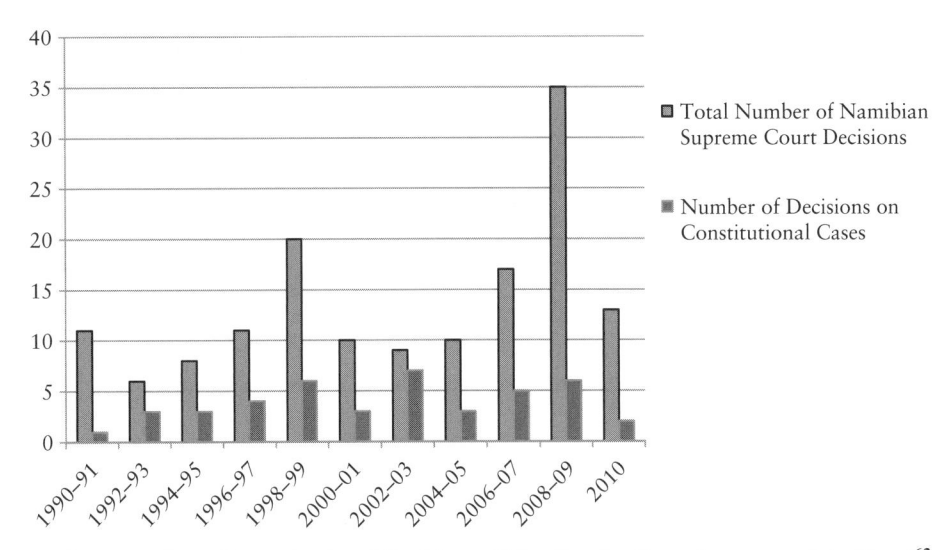

Graph 1: Number of Constitutional Decisions Citing Foreign Precedents out of the Total[62]

ii. Constitutional Cases Citing Foreign Case Law out of Total Constitutional Cases

The number of 'constitutional decisions' in which foreign precedents are cited is 40 (constituting 93 per cent of the total amount) and it represents the most relevant part. On the contrary only three decisions do not include any quotation of foreign decisions. Therefore, the following steps of the empirical analysis have been focused only on the 40 constitutional decisions citing foreign law.

The total number of foreign precedents cited is 554.

The outcomes of the empirical survey show that there has been a variation in the number of foreign precedents cited in the different years covered by the research. In the first period, from 1990 until 1995, there was a more limited use of the citation of foreign precedents (but a high citation of foreign scholarship works) while the number of citations grew in a constant way during the following years, as shown in the following graphs. The only exception is represented by the period from 2008 to 2009, characterised by a considerable number of foreign citations.

---

[62] This data has been collected in two-year periods. Only the year 2010 has been considered individually. It should be noted that the data on the number of judgments handed down for each year are not completely accurate because there are gaps between the decisions published in the Namibian Law Reports and those published in the SC database.

Thus, until 1993 the prevailing number of foreign citations by the Supreme Court refer to South African case law (as in *S v Redondo*[63] or in *Ex Parte Attorney-General: In re Corporal Punishment by Organs of State*[64]), even if in the latter there are also a few references to precedents from the United States and Zimbabwe. This data can probably be explained with reference to Namibia's history: more specifically, during its early years of life, the reference to South African case law or to case law of other African jurisdictions finds its reason in a common cultural and legal background. The increasing reference to other jurisdictions (as will be specified later)—among others England, the United States, Australia and so on and so forth—also produced a rise in the number of citations and of reference sources as well.

iii. Institutional and Human Rights Decisions Citing Foreign Precedents

As already mentioned above, the set of decisions issued by the Supreme Court of Namibia deals with different constitutional topics, distinguishing between 'human rights cases' and 'institutional cases'.

Thus, the total number of 'human rights' decisions is 26, while the sum of 'institutional' decisions is 14. The data are summarised in the following graph.

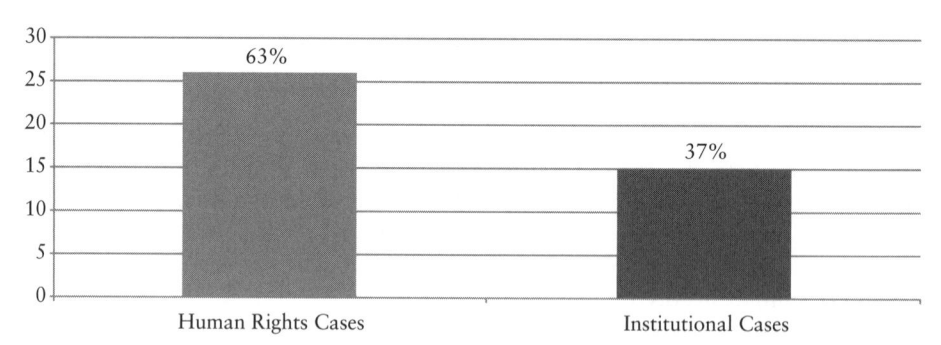

Graph 2: Percentage of Institutional and Human Rights Decisions using Foreign Precedents

Within the total number of 554 foreign decisions quoted, more than 380 foreign precedents have been quoted in human rights cases.

The fact that the number of decisions on human rights issues citing foreign law is higher than the number of decisions on institutional cases can be explained if we consider, once again, Namibian history and the path taken towards independence and the recognition of fundamental human rights.

In particular, the need to strengthen the newly established democracy has pushed the constitutional judge 'to look around' at other democratic constitutional experiences.

---

[63] *S v Redondo* 1992 NR 133 (SC).
[64] *Ex Parte Attorney-General: In re Corporal Punishment by Organs of State*, n 59 above.

This was clearly explained in the High Court decision in *Kauesa v Minister of Home Affairs and Others*.[65] According to the High Court,

> In cases where the provisions of the Namibian Constitution are equivocal or uncertain as to their scope of application, such provisions of the international agreements must at least be given considerable weight in interpreting and defining the scope of a provision contained in the Namibian Constitution. This approach applies particularly to a provision such as art 23(2) relating to the various forms of affirmative action.
>
> When the provisions of s 11(1)(b) read with s 14 of the Racial Discrimination Prohibition Amendment Act 26 of 1991 are seen in the context of the Namibian Constitution, the modern constitutions and/or criminal codes of so-called civilised countries and international treaties and conventions, it can safely be said that s 11(1)(b) clearly falls within the aims and objectives not only of the Namibian Constitution and people, but is also in line with the constitutions and/or penal codes of many other democratic countries and international treaties and conventions.[66]

iv. Citing Foreign Cases—by Country

As has already been highlighted, during the 20 years of its activity, the Supreme Court of Namibia has shown a considerable attitude in citing foreign precedents from several countries. This data can easily be explained if we consider the whole process that led to the independence of the country and, in particular, the role played by international forces and the Western Contact Group, thereby justifying the high number of quotations of decisions issued by, for example, the United States and Canada.

However, many of the foreign decisions quoted have been issued by South African courts. This high number can be explained by the fact that Namibia and South Africa (and also Zimbabwe) have the same common law (deriving from the Dutch-Roman legal tradition).[67] Indeed, upon the date of independence, a lot of South African statutes were still in force in Namibian territory. According to the Namibian Constitution, those rules are still valid, but as statutes of Namibia, until they are repealed by Parliament or declared unconstitutional by courts of law (Articles 140, 141, 142 and 143).[68]

Where a claim is placed before the Namibian courts regarding an issue already decided by South African courts, because South African statutes apply, Namibian judges usually refer to the decisions of the South African courts, making notes of their reasoning without being bound to what those courts decided. Despite strong influence, the Supreme Court itself wants to underline the fact that Namibian case law has developed differently from South African case law; thus, South African judgments must be considered as foreign case law.

Among the countries cited by the Supreme Court, foreign precedents from South Africa (more than 380),[69] Australia (seven decisions are quoted),

---

[65] *Kauesa v Minister of Home Affairs and Others* 1995 (1) SA 51 (NmHC).
[66] Ibid, 150.
[67] See para 4.
[68] See *S v Redondo* 1992 NR 133 (SC) (SA 14/91) [1992], a case involving the interpretation of art 14 of the Constitution and the boundaries of the State, in which all the foreign cases cited were South African.
[69] Due to the high number of South African decisions quoted, we have opted not to include South Africa in Graph 3.

174 *Irene Spigno*

England (68 decisions), United States (30 decisions), Zimbabwe (nine decisions) and Canada (16 decisions) are the more quoted, as can be seen in the following graph.

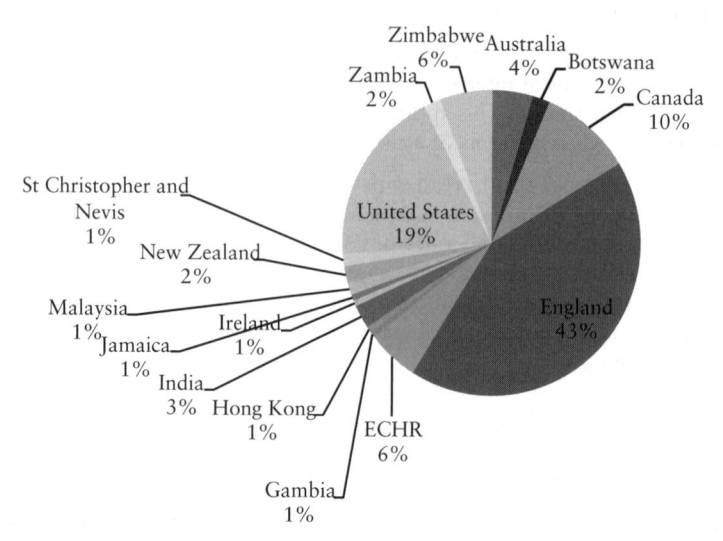

Graph 3: Percentage of Citations, Sorted by Countries

As already mentioned above, the experiences selected for quotation by the Court are those of the countries considered as the most democratic. More specifically, in *Minister of Defence v Mwandinghi*,[70] a case on the interpretative techniques of the constitutional text, the Supreme Court quoted 30 foreign precedents, from six different jurisdictions, including England, Gambia, Jamaica, St Christopher and Nevis, South Africa and Zimbabwe.

Along the same lines, another relevant case is *S v Shikunga*.[71] It was a murder case, in which the constitutional consistency of the presumption provided by section 217(1)(b)(ii) of the Criminal Procedure Act 51 of 1997, permitting a court, under certain circumstances, to convict an accused whose guilt had not been established beyond reasonable doubt, was at stake. In dealing with the case, the supreme judge outlined the tension between two important considerations of public interest and policy. On the one hand, accused persons who are manifestly and demonstrably guilty should not be allowed to escape punishment simply because some constitutional irregularity was committed in the course of the proceedings. This relates to those circumstances which showed clearly that the conviction of the accused would inevitably have followed even if the constitutional irregularity had not been committed. On the other hand, the public interest in the legal system is not confined to the punishment of guilty persons, but extends to the importance of insisting that the procedures adopted in securing such punishments are fair and constitutional.

It is specifically how the courts in various countries have addressed the tensions between these two different considerations that has caught the attention of the

---

[70] *Minister of Defence v Mwandinghi* (SA 5/91) [1991] NASC 5.
[71] *S v Shikunga* 1997 NR 156 (SC) (Sa 6/95) [1997] NASC 2.

Supreme Court. The first reference is to South African authorities,[72] even if with the clarification that the test elaborated by the South African courts was defined prior to the constitutional entrenchment of fundamental rights and freedoms, being a common law test, thereby leading the Court itself to wonder whether the common law test regarding irregularities could be applied to irregularities of a constitutional nature. According to the supreme judge, the approach taken by other jurisdictions in dealing with non-constitutional and constitutional irregularities respectively is instructive as it indicates the methods through which courts in foreign jurisdictions have attempted to distinguish between irregularities of differing natures. For this reason, the Court analyses the approaches adopted in some other jurisdictions as to the effect of constitutional and non-constitutional errors. The countries under consideration are Canada, the United States, Jamaica[73] and Australia.[74]

The citations are detailed, showing that the Court is aware of the foreign precedents cited as well of the legal context in which they have been handed down. Thus, the Canadian approach to non-constitutional errors is considered similar to Namibian common law. The Namibian judge points out that according to the Supreme Court of Canada, where it is found that a trial judge has made an error, the question that is asked is whether there is any reasonable possibility that if the error had not been committed a judge, or a properly instructed jury, would have acquitted the accused. This was the test applied first by Justice Major in *R v Bevan*[75] and later in *R v Tran*,[76] with reference to section 14 of the Canadian Charter according to which the right to the assistance of an interpreter is guaranteed. On that occasion, the Supreme Court of Canada held that the right had been invaded and proceeded to enquire into what was the appropriate remedy in terms of section 24(1) of the Canadian Charter, which in general terms authorises the court to tailor the remedy having regard to the particular circumstances of the case. It distinguished between an interpretation which had prejudiced the accused and which was serious and one which was not. It was held that in that case it was prejudicial to the accused and for this reason the appeal was allowed and a new trial was directed.

As far as the reference to the US approach is concerned, the Namibian supreme judge points out that the US courts make the distinction between the approach to be applied to constitutional and non-constitutional errors respectively. In relation to non-constitutional errors the test that is applied is that 'any error, defect, irregularity

---

[72] The approach adopted by South African courts in assessing the effect of an irregularity in terms of the common law is one that asks essentially whether or not a failure of justice has resulted from the irregularity or defect. To this effect two categories in relation to trial irregularities or defects have been pointed out. A general and an exceptional category have been identified. See *S v Shikunga*, n 71 above at 18.

[73] More specifically the reference is made to the Privy Council decision in *Robinson v The Queen* (163) (19S5) AC—an appeal from the court of appeal of Jamaica.

[74] The Australian courts differentiate between irregularities that constitute a miscarriage of justice per se and irregularities that are less fundamental in nature and only result in a miscarriage of justice if it can be said that as a result of the irregularity the accused lost out on a real chance of acquittal in that it cannot be said that in the absence of the irregularity a jury would inevitably have acquitted (*Wilde v The Queen* (198S) [1988] HCA 6; 164 CLR 365 FC, *Ouartermaine v The Queen* [1980] HCA 29 and *Dietrich v Ilic Queen* [1992] HCA 57).

[75] *R v Bevan* [1993] 2 SCR 599.

[76] *R v Tran* [1994] 2 SCR 951.

or variance which does not affect substantial rights shall be disregarded'.[77] This test was explained, or refined, in *Kotteakos v United States*[78] where the court stated that essentially what this test entails is that:

> If, when all is said and done, the conviction is sure that the error did not influence the jury, or had but very slight effect, the verdict and the judgment should stand, except perhaps where the departure is from a constitutional norm or a specific command of Congress. But if one cannot say, with fair assurance, after pondering all that happened without stripping the erroneous action from the whole, that the judgment was not substantially swayed by the error, it is impossible to conclude that substantial rights were not affected. The inquiry cannot be merely whether there was enough to support the result, apart from the phase affected by the error. It is rather, even so, whether the error itself had substantial influence. If so, or if one is left in grave doubt, the conviction cannot stand.

Actually, despite the high number of citations coming from South African jurisdictions (that can be justified by historical and geographic reasons), in the case of Namibia it is not possible to identify the influence of only one country. As a matter of fact, English sources as well as those of the United States and Canada have all been influential on the development of Namibian constitutional case law.

B. The Qualitative Data

i. Citations According to Majority, Dissenting, or Separate Judgments

The higher number of foreign citations is usually expressed in the majority opinion of the Supreme Court decisions. According to Article 79(3) of the Namibian Constitution, a quorum of three judges is required when the Supreme Court hears and determines appeals, whether criminal or civil, or deals with any other matter referred to in that Article or other matters in terms of the Supreme Court Act.[79]

In general, the Court does not refer to foreign precedents in its dissenting or concurring opinions (mostly because the Court does not use concurring or dissenting opinions that much).

Among the constitutional cases citing foreign precedents, only two decisions cite foreign case law in their concurring opinion. These are *Ex parte: Attorney-General, In Re: Corporal Punishment by Organs of State*[80] and *S v Van Wyk*.[81] The only decision where there is a dissenting opinion is *S v Gaseb and Others*,[82] but no foreign precedent is referred to.

---

[77] See Federal Rules of Criminal Procedure, rule 52, 'Harmless Error and Plain Error'. (a) Harmless error. Any error, defect, irregularity or variance which does not affect substantial rights shall be disregarded and (b) Plain error. Plain errors or defects affecting substantial rights may be noticed although they were not brought to the attention of the court.
[78] *Kotteakos v United States*, 328 US 750 (1945) 764–65.
[79] Supreme Court Act, 15 of 1990.
[80] *Ex parte: Attorney-General, In Re: Corporal Punishment by Organs of State*, n 46 above.
[81] *S v Van Wyk* (SA 6/91) [1991] NASC 6; 1992 (1) SACR 147 (NmS) (29 October 1991).
[82] *S v Gaseb and Others* (SA 9/99) [2000] NASC 6; 2000 (1) SACR 438 (NmS) (9 August 2000).

In *Ex parte: Attorney-General, In Re: Corporal Punishment by Organs of State* only the US decision *Trop v Dulles*[83] is referred to, while in *S v Van Wyk*, no foreign decision is quoted in the concurring opinion.

This outcome might be explained with reference to Article 13(2) of the Supreme Court Act, according to which

> The judgment of the majority of the judges of the Supreme Court shall be the judgment of the court and where there is no judgment to which a majority of such judges agree, the hearing shall be adjourned and commenced *de novo* before a fresh court constituted with the requisite quorum or such larger number of judges as referred to in the proviso to subsection.

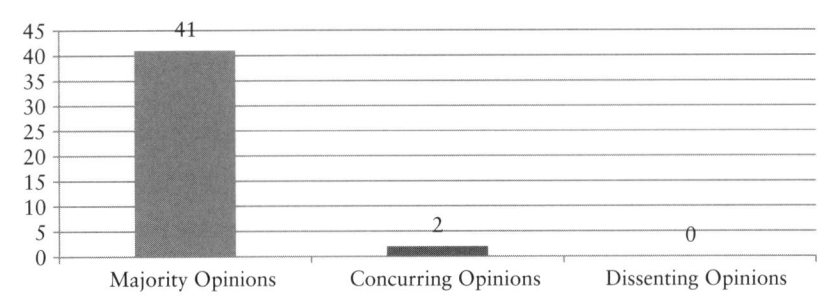

Graph 4: Number of Citations in Majority, Concurring, and/or Dissenting Opinions

- Majority Opinions: 41
- Concurring Opinions: 2
- Dissenting Opinions: 0

iii. Purpose of the Citations: 'Even There, Even Here', Orientation or a Contrario in the Text or in the Footnotes

According to the outcomes of the empirical analysis it is possible to highlight the prevalence of the use of foreign quotations in a positive way, as examples to be followed ('even there, even here', including the categories 'approved, applied followed'), as a guiding horizon (compared, referred or considered). A low percentage of foreign precedents is quoted in a negative way, a contrario, as examples not to be followed.

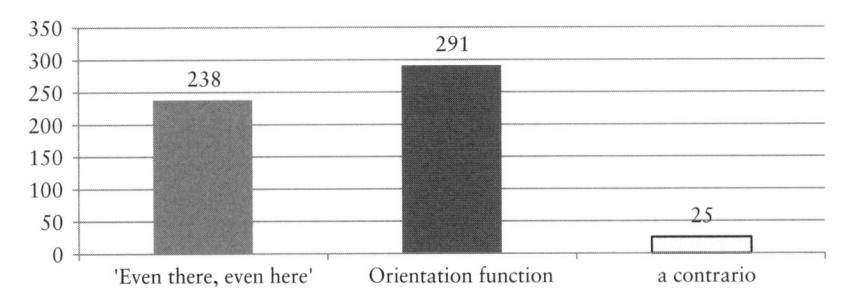

Graph 5: Number of Foreign Decisions Set Up by the Different Purpose

- 'Even there, even here': 238
- Orientation function: 291
- a contrario: 25

---

[83] *Trop v Dulles* 356 US 86 (1958).

In the *Kauesa* case, where the content of the right to free speech and expression provided by Article 21(1)(a) of the Namibian Constitution was at stake, the supreme judge considered the interpretation of the First Amendment of the US Constitution in the following terms:

> The First Amendment does not have exceptions or restrictions. The freedom of speech is expressed as an absolute right. The courts have, however prescribed limits within which freedom of speech is to be exercised. In the First Amendment unrestricted freedom of speech enjoys a high degree of protection. American Courts have over the years held that freedom of speech is not an absolute right. They have identified certain well-defined and limited classes of speech such as obscene or libelous speech or knowingly making false statements and others which are not constitutionally protected (...). *We agree (...) that the criteria developed by the United States Supreme Court to limit the free exercise of the right to free speech does not correspond to and is narrower in its operation than restrictions authorised in more modern Constitutions* (emphasis added by Author).

Moreover, the Supreme Court recalls a Canadian precedent, *R v Zundel*[84] in order to underline the fundamental structural differences between the 1982 Canadian Charter of Rights and Freedoms and the American Constitution, ie the lack in the latter of a provision which corresponds to the general limitation clause of section 1 of the Canadian Charter.

Following the Canadian approach and rejecting the US one, the supreme judge of Namibia stated that

> [t]he First Amendment also differs from Article 21(1)(a) and (2) of the Namibian Constitution in that Sub-Article (2) contains limitations to the exercise of the right to freedom of speech and expression enshrined in Sub-Article (1).[85]

In fact, contrary to the US view according to which the freedoms protected in the First Amendment of the Bill of Rights are perceived as almost absolute,[86] freedoms provided in Article 21 are subject to derogation if necessary in a democratic society in the interests of, inter alia, public security, public safety, public morals or the economic wellbeing of the country.[87]

The provision contained in Article 21 provides a regulation that is quite similar to the one provided by section 1 of the 1982 Canadian Charter of Fundamental Rights and Freedoms. This provision contains the 'general limitation clause' or 'reasonable limits clause' providing that the rights and freedoms set out in the Charter can be subject only to such reasonable limits prescribed by law as can be demonstrably justified in a free and democratic society. This disposition has been interpreted by the Canadian Supreme Court according to the proportionality test developed in

---

[84] See *R v Zundel* (1987) 35 DLR (4th) 338 at 360.
[85] *Kauesa v Minister of Home Affairs and Others*, n 52 above, at 31.
[86] See generally, A Meikeljohn, 'The First Amendment is an Absolute' (1961) *Supp Court Review* 245.
[87] Namibian Constitution, art 21, para 2: 'The fundamental freedoms referred to in Sub-Article (1) hereof shall be exercised subject to the law of Namibia, insofar as such law imposes reasonable restrictions on the exercise of the rights and freedoms conferred by the said Sub-Article, which are necessary in a democratic society and are required in the interests of the sovereignty and integrity of Namibia, national security, public order, decency or morality, or in relation to contempt of court, defamation or incitement to an offence.'

R v Oakes,[88] according to which only limitations on rights and freedoms consistent with the three-step approach are allowed.

We should point out that the majority of the foreign precedents cited a contrario are South African. For example, *Myburgh v Commercial Bank of Namibia*,[89] in dealing with the constitutionality of the institution of marriage in community of property, refers to the South African case *Knox D'Arcy Ltd and Another v Shaw and Another*.[90] This case was quoted by the lower Court in its judgment, stating that women under the common law have a choice and where they decide to marry in community of property they do so voluntarily. However the Supreme Court literally states that

> In my opinion the reliance on the *Knox*-case is inappropriate. In that case it was argued that restraint of trade clauses in contracts were per se unconstitutional as they offend against section 26(1) of the South African Constitution which protected the right to engage freely in economic activity. In the course of his judgment the learned Judge confirmed the right of private persons to contract freely and stated that the Constitution would not, as a matter of policy, protect such persons against their own foolhardy or rash decisions and the Court rejected the application. Although marriage is an institution of private law the interest of the State and the public in the institution is amply illustrated by the many legal rules concerning the contracting of a valid marriage, the proprietary and other rights during the marriage and its dissolution and the effects thereof. To this extent the Constitution itself provides that parties to a marriage shall be entitled to equal rights as to marriage, during marriage and at its dissolution, (Article 14(1)) and the Courts must give effect to this and the other provisions of the Constitution, e.g. Article 10(2). This is also not an instance where meaning and content must still be given to the provisions of the Constitution, as was the case with Article 8 where the Court had to determine the content and meaning of words such as degrading treatment or punishment.[91]

The most relevant part of the foreign precedents cited in the decisions issued by the Supreme Court of Namibia is indicated by a mere reference to the case and not throughout an explicit quotation of part of the foreign sentence. However, the percentage of explicit quotation of entire paragraphs or single sentencesof decisions cited is quite high, representing nearly 24 per cent.

Actually, the two different modalities often coexist in the same decision. For example, in the already-cited *Kauesa* case, the Supreme Court quotes four Canadian

---

[88] *R v Oakes* [1986] 1 SCR 103. According to the Supreme Court of Canada 'First, the measures adopted must be carefully designed to achieve the objective in question. They must not be arbitrary, unfair or based on irrational considerations. In short, they must be rationally connected to the objective. Second, the means, even if rationally connected to the objective in this first sense, should impair "as little as possible" the right or freedom in question. Third, there must be a proportionality between the effects of the measures which are responsible for limiting the Charter right or freedom, and the objective which has been identified as of "sufficient importance"'.

[89] *Myburgh v Commercial Bank of Namibia*, n 54 above. See also, among others, *Government of the Republic of Namibia v Sikunda* 2002 NR 203 (SC), where *S v Naudé* 1975 (1) SA 681 (A) is distinguished; *Minister of Home Affairs v Majiedt and Others*, n 50 above, where *Mohlomi v Minister of Defence* 1997 (1) SA 124 (CC) is distinguished; and *Nationwide Detectives and Professional Practitioners CC v Standard Bank of Namibia Limited* (Sa32/2007) [2008] NASC 14 (24 October 2008), in which *Arma Carpet House (Johannesburg) (Pty) Ltd v Domestic and Commercialo Carpet Fittings (Pty) Ltd and Another* 7 1977 (3) SA 448 (W) is distinguished.

[90] *Knox D'Arcy Ltd and Another v Shaw and Another*1996 (2) SA 651 (W) at p 660 C–D.

[91] *Myburgh*, n 54 above at 276.

180 *Irene Spigno*

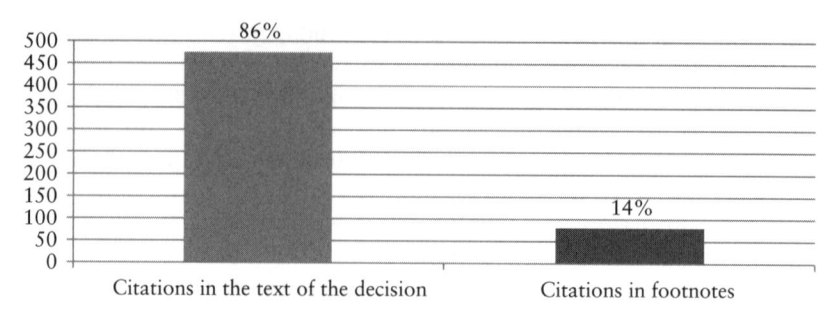

Graph 6: Percentage of Citations in the Text of the Decision or in the Footnotes

precedents. Two of them are quoted explicitly (*Osborne v Canada (Treasury Board)*[92] and *R v Zundel*[93]) while only a short reference is made to *R v Edward Books & Art Ltd*[94] and to *R v Oakes*.[95]

Another relevant outcome is represented by the prevalence of foreign decisions cited in the text of the decision itself: 475 foreign decisions have been cited in the text, while only 80 have been cited in the footnotes. It is necessary to underline that the use of footnotes in Supreme Court decisions is a very recent phenomenon with increasing relevance. In fact, even though the first citations of foreign precedents in the footnotes are found in the 1999 case *S v Tcoeib*,[96] it was not until 2005 that the technique of using footnotes in Supreme Court decisions became more common.

VII. THE USE OF 'EXTRA-SYSTEMIC' ELEMENTS IN CONSTITUTIONAL ADJUDICATION IN NAMIBIA: SOME CRITICAL AND CONCLUSIVE REMARKS

As the outcomes of the research have pointed out, the Namibian constitutional experience represents a valid case study in the use of comparative methodology in the drafting of constitutional text as well as in its interpretation, demonstrating judges' strong commitment to supporting their legal reasoning by the quotation of foreign legal materials, namely, foreign scholarship and foreign case law.

The application of the comparative method in constitutional and legal adjudication involves the use of so-called 'extra-systemic' elements,[97] that is, legal arguments that belong to a foreign legal system. It is a methodology that represents an additional

---

[92] *Osborne v Canada (Treasury Board)* (1991) 82 DLR (4th) 321.
[93] *R v Zundel* (1987) 31 CCC (3d) 97; 35 DLR (4th) 338.
[94] *R v Edward Books & Art Ltd* (1987) 35 DLR at 4.
[95] In the words of the Court '[i]n both the Court *a quo* and in this Court the respondents did not contend that it was incumbent upon the applicant to show that the statutory provision was not a permissible restriction. In fact the onus of proving that a limit or restriction on a right or freedom guaranteed by the Bill of Rights is on the party that alleges that there is a limit or restriction to the right or freedom'. See *R v Oakes* (1986) 26 DLR (4th) 200 at 225.
[96] *S v Tcoeib* 1999 NR 24 (SC) 1996 (1) SACR 390 (NmS).
[97] This expression has been used by Andrea Lollini, 'La circolazione degli argomenti: metodo comparato e parametri interpretativi extra—sistemici nella giurisprudenza costituzionale sudafricana' in *Diritto pubblico comparato ed europeo*, n.1/2007, 479–523.

option,[98] to be used by the interpreter especially with regard to legal systems presenting special features,[99] such as a similar legal tradition or a common culture.

Although the Namibian Constitution does not contain a provision like section 39 of the 1996 Constitution of South Africa, according to which, in the interpretation of the Bill of Rights, courts may consider foreign law, Namibian courts usually make extensive use of comparative methodology, resulting in the quotation of foreign legal doctrine as well as the citation of foreign case law, used by courts as models to follow or reject, depending on the judicial solution they want to achieve.

The justification for this attitude is to be found, according to Justice O'Linn's statement in the High Court's decision in the *Kauesa* case,[100] in the need to find judicial interpretative support. In particular, when the Court, in its interpretative activity, has to interpret a constitutional provision whose meaning is ambiguous and uncertain because of its wording, foreign experiences must be taken into consideration. Although the statement mainly refers to the interpretation of constitutional provisions recognising and protecting fundamental rights, its value can be extended also to the interpretation of other constitutional norms. The key parameter in order to identify which constitutional experiences should be used as models is given by the 'modern Constitutions and/or criminal codes of so-called civilised countries and international treaties and conventions'.[101]

The same idea is expressed in Justice Strydom's words, in the Supreme Court decision *Alexander v Minister of Justice and Others*, according to which

> Because of the international character of human rights, a study of comparable provisions in other jurisdictions, as well as the interpretation thereof, is not only relevant but provides this Court with valuable material which may assist this Court in its own interpretation of a particular Article in its Constitution, always with due regard to any grammatical or contextual differences which may exist between Constitutions used as a comparable study.[102]

Although it was not formally recognised in the constitutional text, the results of the empirical research highlighted how the Supreme Court of Namibia has always expressed a strong willingness to confront constitutional law and jurisprudence developed by other jurisdictions. In fact, the Supreme Court, as well as the High

---

[98] With reference to the use of legal comparison as an interpretative method, see PJ Kozyris, 'Comparative Law for the Twenty-First Century: New Horizons and New Technologies' (1994) 69 *Tulane Law Review*, 165, 167, 'Comparative law not only provides alternative solutions to be used in legal reform but also gives us a better understanding of our existing law. In short, it is an indispensable tool of legal science'.

[99] In particular, the 'transjudicial borrowing' or 'precedent borrowing' among constitutional judges represents a common practice in common law countries: in fact, starting from the nineteenth century, judges in ex-Commonwealth countries were used to refer to case law issued by foreign jurisdictions, generally those issued by British courts as well as those issued by the Privy Council, that, as last resort body, had competence to decide cases from all the countries belonging to the colonial area. Inevitably, its case law has strongly influenced legal development in countries such as Australia, New Zealand, India, South Africa and Canada. See PK Tripathi, 'Foreign Precedents and Constitutional Law' (1957) 57.3 *Columbia Law Review* 319.

[100] N 65 above.

[101] N 52 above at 150.

[102] *Alexander v Minister of Justice and Others* 2010 (1) NR 328 (SC), on the constitutional challenge to s 21 of the Extradition Act (section providing that person to be extradited not entitled to bail once committed pending Minister's decision whether to extradite).

Court, often makes reference to extra-systemic legal parameters, in particular with reference to the protection of fundamental rights and freedoms.

The reasons behind this attitude are many. Among others, a first one can be found in the participation of the Commonwealth of Nations that has created a network of States with a common official language and similar legal systems, thus allowing the circulation of very similar legal principles and jurisprudential models.[103] In fact, the great influence exercised by the British common law on its former colonies—ie India, Canada, Australia and South Africa—together with the role played by the Privy Council, produced a spreading legal effect with reflections also on other countries that were not formerly British colonies, such as Namibia. The common language and the similar legal background constituted the basis for the creation of a solid network of communication between countries that shared a common legal heritage.

Moreover, the influence of the Roman-Dutch legal tradition created a special dialogue between South Africa, Zimbabwe and Namibia, and this data is able to explain the high number of citations from South African jurisdictions (we should consider also the long domination perpetrated by South Africa).

Surely a great influence on the use of foreign precedents by the Supreme Court has been exercised also by individual judges, who entirely or partly received their education abroad, generally in the United Kingdom or in the United States.

The quantitative data that has emerged from the empirical research highlights how a significant number of decisions citing foreign precedents are human rights cases. This data can be understood if we consider that the Namibian Constitution can still be considered a young Constitution. As several scholars who have dealt with this issue point out, judges are more willing to consider foreign materials in their interpretative activity where there is a need to build the basis of a new democratic constitutional order.[104] Due to the absence of their own set of judicial precedents, and in order to accomplish their constitutional duty, judges may be inclined to look to other well established and authoritative Courts' ones, in order to strengthen their own democracy.

Thus, especially in the first years of its implementation, the need to implement and strengthen democratic values emerged. For example, Article 21(2), on fundamental freedoms, establishes the limits the State can provide to the exercise of fundamental freedoms, literally providing that

> The fundamental freedoms referred to in Sub-Article (1) hereof shall be exercised subject to the law of Namibia, in so far as such law imposes reasonable restrictions on the exercise of the rights and freedoms conferred by the said Sub-Article, which are necessary in a democratic society and are required in the interests of the sovereignty and integrity of Namibia, national security, public order, decency or morality, or in relation to contempt of court, defamation or incitement to an offence.

A democratic interpretation of this provision has required a reference to comparative methodology (as in the *Kauesa* case, decided first by the High Court[105] and then

---

[103] See AP Sereni, *Diritto internazionale*, vol 2 (Milano, 1960) 444.

[104] See MC Ponthoreau, 'Le recours à l'argument de droit comparé par le juge contitutionnel. Quelques problèmes théorique et techniques' in F Mélin-Soucramanien (ed), *L'interprétation constitutionnelle* (Paris, Dalloz, 2005) 168.

[105] N 65 above.

by the Supreme Court[106]). Constitutional experiences developed abroad have been considered as fundamental in order to understand how other democratic societies deal with the implementation or limitation of fundamental rights and freedoms. That is also because, as already stated in the previous paragraphs), the drafting process of the Namibian Constitution was influenced by international covenants and other constitutional texts as well, such as the Constitution of India, the 1982 Canadian Charter of Rights and Freedoms, and the 1950 European Convention on Human Rights. Therefore, it sounds natural for Namibian judges to observe and refer to the jurisprudence developed abroad with the purpose of consolidating Namibia's own case law looking at the interpretation given to those dispositions from which the Namibian Constitution took inspiration.

Especially during the early years of its activity, the Court seemed to suffer a little from being a young court, mainly expressed in a double attitude towards South African case law. On one hand it seemed to need to take into account South Africa's jurisprudence with which there was a relationship identifiable in terms of 'identity' or 'continuity', in particular with regard to civil and commercial matters and also some constitutional issues (ie the interpretation of the amplitude of constitutional powers[107]). On the other hand, with reference to the protection of fundamental rights, Namibian supreme judges wanted to separate themselves from South Africa, for a long time identified as the apartheid system perpetrator. Thus, it turned towards the law of others jurisdictions considered to be the most democratic ones at the national level (such as Canada, Australia and the United States) as well as at the jurisprudence developed by the European Court of Human Rights, even if it was not bound by it.

Moreover, at the beginning of its activity the Court, due to the reasons described above, was almost obliged to make reference to South-West African jurisprudence. A specific prevision of the Constitution establishes that:

> The Supreme Court and the High Court shall have the inherent jurisdiction which vested in the Supreme Court of South-West Africa immediately prior to the date of Independence, including the power to regulate their own procedures and to make court rules for that purpose (Article 78(4)).

Thus, South African precedents issued before Namibia's independence continue to be binding in Namibia, while subsequent South African decisions enjoy great persuasive authority. The precedents are supposed to be directly considered or via older precedents based on the Roman-Dutch law.

In conclusion, the reconstruction of the Namibian constitutional process in which foreign influences on the constitutional text have been highlighted, together with the data which emerged from the empirical research on the use of foreign precedents by the Supreme Court, lets us conclude that the Namibian supreme judge is well engaged in the so-called 'transnational judicial dialogue', embodying also a reference position for other jurisdictions.

---

[106] N 52 above.
[107] *Ex parte Attorney-General In Re: The Constitutional Relationship between the Attorney-General and the Prosecutor-General*, n 53 above.

7

South Africa: Teaching an 'Old Dog' New Tricks? An Empirical Study of the Use of Foreign Precedents by the South African Constitutional Court (1995–2010)

CHRISTA RAUTENBACH[*]

TABLE OF CONTENTS

I. Introduction 185
II. Historical and Constitutional Context 191
III. Empirical Analysis: Making Sense of Statistics 192
    A. Methodology 192
    B. Explicit Citations of Foreign Precedents 193
IV. Concluding Remarks 208

I. INTRODUCTION

FOR MANY YEARS the maxim *iudicis est ius dicere sed non dare* (it is the province of a judge to interpret the law and not to make it) relegated the function of judges in South Africa to mere interpreters of the law.[1] In earlier decisions of the South African courts the task of the judiciary was seen as being 'to establish what the law is and then to judge in accordance with the law so found'.[2] Within this framework the South African judiciary has used foreign precedents as extra-textual aids to assist in the process of constitutional interpretation.[3] In doing so, the judges focused mainly on foreign precedents which had historical links with

---

[*] B Iuris LLB LLM LLD Professor of Law, Faculty of Law, North-West University (Potchefstroom Campus), South Africa. I am grateful to the National Research Foundation (South Africa) and the Alexander von Humboldt Foundation (Germany) for their financial assistance whilst conducting this research. Nevertheless, I am solely responsible for my viewpoints and mistakes.

[1] See, eg, *Union Government (Minister of Mines) v Thompson* [1919] AD 404 at 425; *Estate Reid v Goodwin* [1920] AD 367 at 373; *R v Tebetha* [1959] 2 SA 337 (A) 346G; *S v Khanyapa* [1979] 1 SA 824 (A) 835; *S v Blaauw* [1980] 1 SA 536 (C) 537H.

[2] *Bloem v State President of the RSA* [1986] 4 SA 1064 OPD 1075I-J.

[3] The mixed nature of South Africa's legal system necessitated a comparative legal approach to find, develop and make the law, and the South African courts were discreetly doing this behind the scenes. See

the South African legal system.[4] The justification offered for this type of historical comparative interpretation was that there was a relationship of subordination between the country borrowing and the country borrowed from, especially in the case of former colonial countries looking to the colonisers for judicial guidance by comparing foreign situations with domestic ones.[5] This process of 'cross-fertilisation' took the form of a monologue more often than a dialogue.[6] More often than not the colonies borrowed from the colonial powers, and not the other way round.

All indications are, however, that the influence of the colonial powers is fading and that a distinct form of judicial globalisation is gaining momentum, partly as a result of South Africa's new constitutional dispensation and its re-entry into the global community, and partly as a result of the South African judiciary's willingness to engage in global judicial debates. It is trite that South Africa's two Constitutions since 1994[7] have introduced a new constitutional dispensation based on the supremacy of the Constitution and the rule of law. The implication of this transformation is particularly evident when assessing the contemporary role of the judiciary in general, and the techniques of judicial reasoning in particular, especially in the context of foreign case law. Justice Chaskalson's statement in *S v Makwanyane*,[8] which dealt with the constitutionality of the death sentence in South Africa, seems to suggest that the judiciary keeps itself busy with judicial comparativism because it is the right thing to do. He states:[9]

> The international and foreign authorities are of value because they analyse arguments for and against the death sentence and show how courts of other jurisdictions have dealt with this vexed issue. *For that reason alone they require our attention* (emphasis added).

It is believed, seemingly without foundation,[10] that the most important catalyst for judicial comparativism in South Africa today is the unique interpretation clause in the Constitution, viz section 39(1) of the Constitution which reads:

When interpreting the Bill of Rights, a court, tribunal or forum–

(a) must promote the values that underlie an open and democratic society based on human dignity, equality and freedom;
(b) must consider international law; and
(c) *may consider foreign law* (emphasis added).

---

the discussion of LWH Ackermann, 'Constitutional Comparativism in South Africa' (2006) 123 *South African Law Journal* 497, 500.

[4] South Africa was formerly a colony first of the Netherlands and then of the United Kingdom. See overview in s II below.

[5] See the explanation of A Lollini, 'Legal Argumentation Based on Foreign Law: An Example from Case Law of the South African Constitutional Court' (2007) 3 *Utrecht Law Review* 60, 61–62.

[6] HL Buxbaum, 'From Empire to Globalization ... and Back? A Post-Colonial View of Transjudicialism' (2004) 11 *Indiana Journal of Global Legal Studies* 183, 185, 187.

[7] Constitution of the Republic of South Africa 200 of 1993 (the interim Constitution) in operation from 27 April 1994 to 3 February 1997; and the Constitution of the Republic of South Africa 1996 (the Constitution) in operation since 4 February 1997.

[8] *S v Makwanyane* [1995] 3 SA 391 (CC).

[9] Ibid at 34.

[10] Ackermann, 'Constitutional Comparativism' 500 points out: 'I have not the slightest doubt that, because of the comparative law ethos in South Africa, the Court would have placed the same reliance on foreign law even had there been no such provision in the Constitutions'.

Subsections (b) and (c) provide a totally new dimension to comparative interpretation by authorising courts to consider international and foreign law when interpreting the Bill of Rights.[11] There are important differences between these two cues to forms of interpretation in a South African context. The first difference is evident in the dissimilarity of the wording of subsections (b) and (c). In the case of international law the court *must* consider it, and in the case of foreign law the courts *may* consider it. Though there is a clear difference between the two auxiliary verbs 'may' and 'must', both of them are linked with the verb 'consider', which implies nothing more than carefully thinking about or reflecting on something. In the case of international law, the courts are obliged to go through (ie 'must consider') this thinking process, whilst in the case of foreign law there is merely a suggestion that they may think (ie 'may consider') about it.[12] In other words, the courts have the discretion to consider foreign law but an obligation to consider international law.

The second difference between subsections (b) and (c) has to do with the less obvious distinction based on the relationship between South Africa's domestic law and international law. South Africa follows a dualistic approach to the incorporation of international law, which in essence requires the formal transformation of international law into domestic law.[13] South African courts must also prefer an interpretation of legislation consistent with international law.[14] Thus, in addition to section 39(1)(c), international law is connected to South Africa's domestic legal system through ratification procedures[15] and a directive to prefer legislative interpretation in line with international law. In *S v Makwanyane*[16] Justice Chaskalson explained the use of comparative international by pointing out that international law may include binding and non-binding law.[17] Both forms of international law may be used in the interpretation process.[18] On the other hand, there is no similar distinction in respect of foreign law and the statutory permission to consider foreign law during the interpretation process authorises courts only to '"have regard to" such law', and there is 'no injunction to do more than this'.[19]

---

[11] s 11(2) of the Constitution of the Republic of Malawi of 1997 contains a similar provision.
[12] See also *S v Makwanyane*, n 8 above, 37.
[13] J Dugard, *International Law: A South African Perspective* (Landsdowne, Juta, 2005) 47–48.
[14] See s 233 of the Constitution.
[15] The most important procedures are contained in the Constitution in s 231 (international agreements) and s 232 (customary international law).
[16] *S v Makwanyane*, n 8 above, 35. The Court considered the implication of s 35(1) of the interim Constitution, which is almost identical to s 39(1) of the Constitution.
[17] Binding international law will be international law ratified and acceded to in terms of s 231 of the interim Constitution, which is similar to s 231 of the new Constitution. See also s 232 regarding the position of customary international law and s 233, which obliges courts to give preference to international law when alternative interpretation outcomes exist.
[18] For a general discussion of the Constitutional Court's use of international law, see E De Wet, 'The "Friendly but Cautious" Reception of International Law in the Jurisprudence of the South African Constitutional Court: Some Critical Remarks' (2005) 28 *Fordham International Law Review* 1529.
[19] In *S v Makwanyane*, n 8 above, 37.

Other scholars have also recognised the important differences between considering foreign law and considering international law in the South African Constitution. As Lollini[20] explains:

> [M]aking effective international public law norms binding in South Africa has nothing to do with the interpretive procedure based on *extra*-systemic parameters. On the one hand, norms are applied that have been produced by a system outside of the national sphere, but to which South Africa formally belongs. On the other, interpretive solutions created or decreed by foreign constitutional courts may be freely used for interpreting the South African Constitution.

The strategies of considering foreign law and international law are thus poles apart, and one should not lose sight of this fact when assessing the Court's use of foreign precedent.

Contrary to the status of international law in the South African legal system, the status of foreign law is fairly unclear. The use of the words 'comparable foreign law' in the interim Constitution, which might have given us a clue in this regard, were changed in the final Constitution to refer only to 'foreign law'. Does this omission imply that foreign law no longer has to be comparable before it may be considered? There is no clear answer to this question but, in its dealings with foreign law, the Constitutional Court has given some direction as to the factors relevant for the comparison process. For example, in *S v Makwanyane*[21] Justice Chaskalson pointed out that foreign law is important in the early stages of transition where there is 'no developed indigenous [rights] jurisprudence on which to draw' but one should 'appreciate that this will not necessarily offer a safe guide to the interpretation' of the Bill of Rights. In addition, the nature of the South African legal system, its history and circumstances, and the structure and language of the Constitution are important factors to bear in mind when dealing with foreign law.[22]

Another important aspect which must be taken into consideration in a discussion such as this is the difference between constitutional and ordinary statutory interpretation, which is not always readily apparent. Justice Froneman in *Matiso v Commanding Officer, Port Elizabeth Prison*[23] explained the difference as follows:

> The interpretation of the Constitution will be directed at ascertaining the foundational values inherent to the Constitution, whilst the interpretation of the particular legislation will be directed at ascertaining whether that legislation is capable of an interpretation which conforms with the fundamental values or principles of the Constitution. *Constitutional interpretation in this sense is thus primarily concerned with the recognition and application of constitutional values and not with a search to find the literal meaning of statutes.* The values and principles contained in the Constitution are, and could only be, formulated and expressed in wide and general terms, because they are to be of general application. In terms of the Constitution the courts bear the responsibility of giving specific content to those values and principles in any given situation. *In doing so judges will invariably 'create' law* (emphasis added).

---

[20] Lollini, 'Legal Argumentation' 64.
[21] *S v Makwanyane*, n 8 above, 37.
[22] *S v Makwanyane*, n 8 above, 39.
[23] *Matiso v Commanding Officer, Port Elizabeth Prison* [1994] 3 BCLR 80 (SE) 87. *S v Makwanyane*, n 8 above, 87.

Justice Froneman's viewpoint is a clear breakaway from the traditional viewpoint that judges should interpret and not make the law. In the new dispensation of constitutional supremacy, judges are not merely an extended arm of the executive, but reviewers and law-makers in their own sphere (thus a separate segment of government).[24] This notion of judicial law-making is also explained by Justice Froneman as an important function of judicial review which should be based on constitutional supremacy and not take place under the 'guise of simply seeking and giving expression to the will of the majority in Parliament'. He makes it clear that judicial law-making in the form of judicial review differs fundamentally from making law by means of legislation, and says:[25]

> In contrast to legislative law-making the process of judicial review is not partisan in the sense that it is initiated by the law-makers themselves. Judges do not initiate litigation; individual litigants do. And the adjudication process 'creating' law is done by an impartial and independent Judge; not by the majority party who initiates legislation in the legislature.[26]

Since its establishment in 1994 the Constitutional Court, which is regarded as the most authoritative interpreter of the Constitution[27] of South Africa has considered foreign precedents on numerous occasions.[28] The very first judgment the Constitutional Court handed down on 5 April 1995, *S v Zuma*,[29] cited no less than 25[30] foreign precedents of countries such as the United States, the United Kingdom, Canada, Hong Kong, Namibia, China and Botswana. Justice Kentridge, who delivered a unanimous decision, gave no content to the comparable enabling provision in the interim Constitution,[31] but he did caution (by implication) against ignoring 'all the principles of law which have hitherto governed our courts' and neglecting 'the language of the Constitution' in favour of a misguided use of the underlying constitutional values determined, amongst others, by foreign law.[32] Without giving any guidelines as to when and which foreign precedents would be relevant in the comparison process, Justice Kentridge referred to the different solutions of foreign

---

[24] The concept of separation of powers was fully investigated by the Constitutional Court in *Doctors for Life International v Speaker of the National Assembly* [2006] 6 SA 416 (CC).
[25] *Matiso v Commanding Officer*, n 23 above. This viewpoint also accords with the notion that the courts have a developmental function, as expressed in ss 8(3) and 39(2) of the Constitution.
[26] Other authors, such as LM Du Plessis, 'Interpretation of Statutes and the Constitution' in loose-leaf *Bill of Rights Compendium* (Durban, LexisNexis, 2002) 2C50 point out that the maxim *iudices est ius dicere sed non dare* has not disappeared from the scenery in its totality, since it still has a role to play in the realm of statutory interpretation, and it could also act as a restraining mechanism to an interpreter's preferences and prejudices. For that reason Du Plessis proposes the rephrasing of the maxim to read: 'it is the province of the interpreter of an enacted law-text primarily to give the best possible effect to the text as it stands and not to (try and) re-enact (or rewrite) it'.
[27] See s 167 of the Constitution.
[28] The Constitutional Court was formally opened on 14 February 1995. The Court consists of the Chief Justice, the Deputy Chief Justice and nine other judges and is the highest court in all constitutional matters. See ss 167 and 173 of the Constitution.
[29] *S v Zuma* [1995] 2 SA 642 (CC). This case dealt with the constitutionality of the presumption relating to the admissibility of confessions in terms of the former s 217 of the Criminal Procedure Act 51 of 1977.
[30] Some of the foreign cases were referred to more than once, bringing the total citations of foreign cases up to 32.
[31] The provision enabling the use of foreign law in that Constitution was similar to s 39(1)(c) of the new Constitution but referred to 'comparable foreign case law'. The word 'comparable' was discarded from the latter which refers only to 'foreign case law'.
[32] *S v Zuma*, n 29 above, 17.

precedents to the problem of reconciling presumptions of reverse onus simply as 'illuminating',[33] without shedding light on the (un)compelling value of the foreign precedents that he considered.

The Constitutional Court's next judgment, *S v Makwanyane*,[34] which found the death penalty to be unconstitutional, may be considered as the Court's inaugural decision. Every one of the 11 judges on the bench delivered a separate judgment and each one of them considered foreign precedent. Justice Chaskalson earns first place on the podium with 124 foreign case citations and the second place is taken by Justice Ackermann with 33 foreign case citations. In total there were 220 foreign case citations from 11 countries and three supranational courts.[35] To date this record has not been broken and *S v Makwanyane* remains one of the most remarkable judgments delivered by the Constitutional Court in many respects.

Statistics confirm that since its inception in 1994 the Constitutional Court has been considering foreign precedents on an ongoing basis. This may be explained partly by the fact that the newly established Court under a newly adopted Constitution was called upon to develop, through its jurisprudence, a sound foundation for the interpretation and application of that Constitution in the almost complete absence of domestic precedent.[36] This comparative process of referring to foreign case law has many names and several layered meanings and nuances. It has been called 'transjudicialism',[37] 'transjudicial communication',[38] 'constitutionalist dialogue',[39] 'judicial globalism',[40] 'constitutional cross-fertilisation',[41] 'transnational contextualisation',[42] 'globalisation of judgment',[43] 'globalisation of national courts'[44] and 'judicial comparativism'.[45] But there is also another explanation for this phenomenon which has nothing to do with the Court's desire to develop jurisprudence in constitutional issues, and this has to do with the global trend of

---

[33] *S v Zuma*, n 29 above, 19.
[34] *S v Makwanyane*, n 8 above.
[35] Some of the foreign cases were referred to more than once, bringing the total citations of foreign cases up to 220.
[36] See *S v Makwanyane*, n 8 above, 37.
[37] DS Wood, 'In Defence of Transjudicialism' (2005) 44 *Duquesne Law Review* 93.
[38] RC Black and L Epstein, '(Re-)Setting the Scholarly Agenda on Transjudicial Communication' (2007) 32 *Law and Social Inquiry* 789. A valuable contribution to the debate is the scholarly article of AM Slaughter, 'A Typology of Transjudicial Communication' (1994) 29 *University of Richmond Law Review* 99. According to her the overarching term for the process of 'cross-fertilisation' between courts in various jurisdictions is 'transjudicial communication'. This phenomenon takes place within the formal treaty context (references to international law and supra-national courts) and within an informal context (references to foreign law).
[39] B Bryde, 'The Constitutional Judge and the International Constitutionalist Dialogue' (2005) 80 *Tulane Law Review* 203, 213–14. He points out that although the use of foreign law is mostly 'inspirational', it is also used as a genuine legal argument.
[40] Buxbaum, 'From Empire to Globalization' 183.
[41] Buxbaum, 'From Empire to Globalization' 184.
[42] LM Du Plessis, 'Interpretation' in S Woolman, M Bishop and J Brickhill (eds), *Constitutional Law of South Africa* (Kenwyn, Juta, 2010) 32.171.
[43] R Bahdi, 'Globalization of Judgment: Transjudicialism and the Five Faces of International Law in Domestic Courts' (2002) 34 *The George Washington International Law Review* 555.
[44] MJ Tawfik, 'No Longer in Splendid Isolation: The Globalization of National Courts and the Internationalization of Intellectual Property Law' (2007) 32 *Queen's Law Journal* 573.
[45] DC Gray, 'Why Justice Scalia should be a Constitutional Comparativist ... Sometimes' (2007) 59 *Stanford Law Review* 1249. See also Ackermann, 'Constitutional Comparativism' 497.

constitutional judges to communicate with one another. The statistics discussed in Figure 1 point in this direction.[46]

Against this background I have conducted an empirical survey from 1995 to 2010 to establish the use of foreign precedents by the South African Constitutional Court. I commence with a brief overview of South Africa's historical and constitutional context[47] before I set out the methodology that I employed to do this research.[48] Then I focus on the empirical results and the inferences one can draw therefrom.[49] Finally, I conclude this contribution with a few remarks on the propensity of the Constitutional Court to consider foreign law from both a qualitative and a quantitative point of view.[50] The ultimate question is whether the Constitutional Court's use of foreign precedents as a method of constitutional interpretation, especially in the development of human rights jurisprudence, rather than a method of statutory interpretation, boils down to a 'new' form of interpretation, or whether it is merely a matter of teaching an old dog new tricks.

II. HISTORICAL AND CONSTITUTIONAL CONTEXT

The South African Court's tendency to refer to foreign precedents must be understood in its historical and constitutional context.[51] European involvement in South Africa became prominent in 1652 when the Dutch East India Company established a refreshment station in the Cape of Good Hope with permanent settlers. The British seized the Cape in 1795, and then briefly relinquished it back to the Dutch in 1803 before definitively conquering it in 1806, annexing it as a Crown colony. This colony was gradually extended eastwards and northwards by conquest, barter and cession. Furthermore, the interior of Southern Africa was systematically occupied from 1836 onwards by migrating non-British pioneer farmers whose purpose was to break away from British colonial rule. For more than 60 years the country which was later to become South Africa consisted of two British colonies and two sovereign 'Boer' republics.

The Anglo-Boer War of 1899–1902 ended in the annexation of the two 'Boer' republics as new British colonies. On 31 May 1910 the Union of South Africa came into being but it continued to be under British rule. The constitutional dispensation of the Union was typically that of a British *dominion* with a Westminster-type parliament entrusted with legislative sovereignty, which precluded the adoption of a Bill of Rights and substantive judicial review. When the Union was transformed into the Republic of South Africa in 1961, these constitutional characteristics remained in place, making the unfolding of the apartheid system possible.

---

[46] See section a below.
[47] See section II below.
[48] See section A below.
[49] See section B below.
[50] See section IV below.
[51] For a detailed discussion of the constitutional history of South Africa, see S Woolman and J Swanepoel, 'Constitutional History' in S Woolman, M Bishop and J Brickhill (eds), *Constitutional Law of South Africa* (Kenwyn, Juta, 2010) 2.1–2.49.

In 1990 a turning point was reached when the government officially accepted the unavoidability of the introduction of comprehensive democracy and launched a process of negotiating a thoroughly new constitutional dispensation. The main role players in the multi-party constitutional negotiations that produced the interim Constitution were representatives of socialistically-inclined liberation movements on the one hand, and on the other of an order that was established and was functioning under a constitutional dispensation founded in English legal thinking. Nevertheless, as common ground was found in contemporary constitutionalist thinking, the negotiations produced what the first paragraph of the preamble to the interim Constitution referred to as a 'sovereign and democratic constitutional state' and the provisions of the Constitution provided for the realisation of the different elements of the constitutional state. The introduction of a justiciable, supreme Constitution including a Bill of Rights as a key component changed the essence of the system significantly.

The interim Constitution required a 'final constitution' to be drafted, which led to the adoption of the 1996 and final Constitution. This (current) Constitution was largely based on the interim Constitution and preserved the most salient features of the former document, including its human-rights-based dispensation[52] founded upon a supreme basic law[53] of which the Constitutional Court is the authoritative interpreter.[54]

Many comparative insights were incorporated in the Bill of Rights, including other modern Constitutions and international human rights instruments.[55] The two national Constitutions that most strongly influenced the drafting of the final Constitution both in its structural provisions and its Bill of Rights were the German *Grundgesetz* of 1949 and the Canadian Constitution Act of 1982.

III. EMPIRICAL ANALYSIS: MAKING SENSE OF STATISTICS

A. Methodology

The Constitutional Court,[56] the Supreme Court of Appeal[57] and the High Courts of South Africa all have constitutional jurisdiction and may thus use foreign law in their judicial reasoning, but since it would be a mammoth task to survey all of the

---

[52] s 8(1) of the Constitution applies the 'Bill of Rights to all law, and binds the legislature, the executive, the judiciary and all organs of state'.

[53] s 2 of the Constitution confirms the supremacy of the Constitution.

[54] s 165(2) of the Constitution vests judicial authority in the courts and reads: 'The courts are independent and subject only to the Constitution and the law, which they must apply impartially and without fear, favour or prejudice'. s 167 confirms that the Constitutional Court is the highest court in all constitutional matters.

[55] Du Plessis, 'Interpretation' 32.183.

[56] See ss 166 and 167 of the Constitution.

[57] The Supreme Court of Appeal is the highest court of appeal except in constitutional matters. See ss 166 and 168 of the Constitution.

decisions dealing with constitutional issues within these courts this empirical study focuses only on the judgments of the Constitutional Court for the last 16 years.[58]

The empirical survey follows both a quantitative and qualitative approach by counting and evaluating explicit citations of foreign precedents. The qualitative approach entails the collection of empirical information such as the number of foreign precedents cited per year, per judge, per foreign case and per country, as well as by categorising the type of issue dealt with under the headings 'human rights issues', 'institutional issues' or 'other issues'. The quantitative approach makes use of formal and substantive factors to determine the actual or potential influence of the foreign precedents on South African Constitutional Court judges. Formal indicators include the following: whether the judge considering a foreign case delivered a majority, dissenting or separate judgment; whether a reference to the foreign case was merely a reference or a quote; whether the reference was made in the majority or dissenting decision of the foreign case; and whether the foreign case was referred to in the text or footnote of the South African case. The substantive indicators require an analysis of the legal reasoning applied by the judges, and in doing this three categories were used, viz: the reasoning (or argumentative) phase, the 'even there'-approach and the '*a contrario*'-approach.[59]

It is important to point out that the term 'citations' in this contribution does not necessarily refer to the number of foreign precedents considered but the number of times a judge referred to a foreign precedent. In other words, the word 'citations' refers to the number of foreign case citations and not to the number of foreign cases in each constitutional court case.

B. Explicit Citations of Foreign Precedents

i. Quantitative Approach

a. Citations of Foreign Precedents: The Cases

Since the establishment of the South African Constitutional Court, the Court has been handing down judgments that have had a profound impact on the law in South Africa.[60] In *Mistry v Interim National Medical and Dental Council of South Africa*[61] Justice Chaskalson recognised the value of foreign case law and emphasised

---

[58] The empirical results have been captured in a searchable database accessible at www4-win2.p.nwu.ac.za/dbtw-wpd/textbases/ccj.htm. The database is still in a developmental phase and additional data is being uploaded on a regular basis. Preliminary results are available and are discussed in this contribution. Searches can be conducted by means of keywords or empirical results. For more information, see the database.

[59] See section b below for an explanation of the three categories.

[60] Since the rule of precedent or *stare decisis* applies in South Africa, courts will be bound by decisions of certain other high courts, especially the Supreme Court of Appeal and the Constitutional Court, thus obviating the need to re-interpret the law (especially constitutional law) every time by taking foreign precedent into account.

[61] *Mistry v Interim National Medical and Dental Council of South Africa* [1998] 4 SA 1127 (CC). At para 3 the Court said: 'Cases fall to be decided on a principled basis. Each case that is decided adds to the body of South African constitutional law, and establishes principles relevant to the decision of cases which may arise in the future. Particularly where principles have not yet been established, courts may draw on the burgeoning international jurisprudence on constitutional rights'.

that the Constitutional Court will continue to consult foreign law in areas where constitutional principles have not been established. In other words, foreign precedents will be used to 'create' law where there is none. Similar views were expressed by Justice Sachs, giving a dissenting opinion, in *Coetzee v The Government of RSA; Matiso v Commanding Officer, Port Elizabeth Prison*.[62] He agreed that the interpretation clause in the interim Constitution[63] invites judges to have

> regard to international experience where applicable when seeking to interpret provisions relating to fundamental rights. As I understand it, this section requires us to give due attention to such experience *with a view to finding principles rather than to extracting rigid formulae, and to look for rationales rather than rules* (emphasis added).[64]

From 2005 to 2010 the Constitutional Court delivered a total number of 400 judgments with at least 2,742 foreign citations.[65] At least 191 of these judgments do not refer to foreign precedents and at least 52 per cent of the total number of judgments considered foreign precedents in comparison with the 48 per cent which did not consider foreign precedents over the period of 15 years. In other words, the number of judgments citing foreign precedents at the end of 2010 was four per cent more than the number of those which did not cite any foreign precedents. This illustrates the Court's favourable disposition towards foreign precedents, as reflected in Figure 1 below.

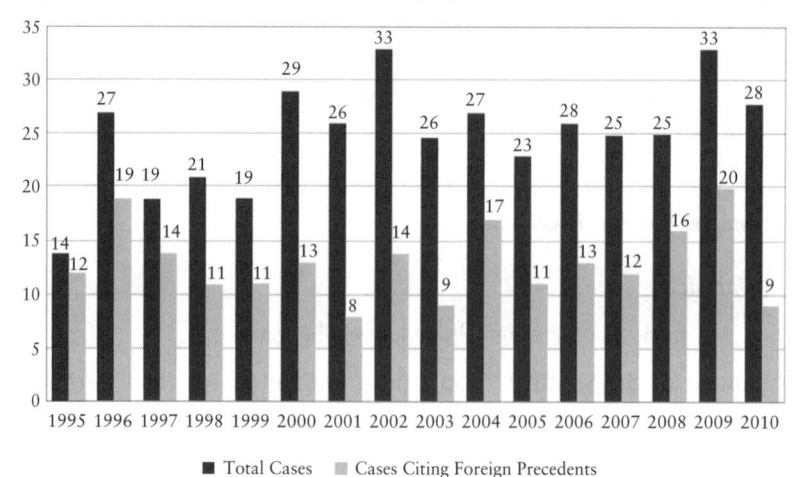

Figure 1: Cases per Year Divided According to those Citing and Total

---

[62] *Coetzee v The Government of RSA; Matiso v Commanding Officer, Port Elizabeth Prison* [1995] 4 SA 631 (CC).

[63] s 35, which is similar in wording to s 39 of the new Constitution.

[64] *Coetzee v The Government of RSA; Matiso v Commanding Officer, Port Elizabeth Prison*, n 62 above, 57.

[65] Not included in this number is the Constitutional Court's citation of other international or supranational institutions. For example, from 1995 to 2010, the judgments from the following institutions have been cited: African Commission on Human and Peoples' Rights (two citations); Benelux Court of Justice (one citation); European Commission of Human Rights (four citations); European Court of Human Rights (138 citations); European Court of Justice (eight citations); Inter-American Commission on Human Rights (two citations); International Court of Justice (14 citations); International Criminal Tribunal for Rwanda (six citations); International Criminal Tribunal for the former Yugoslavia (three citations); International Tribunal for Arbitration (three citations); Iran-United States Claims Tribunal (one citation); UN Human Rights Committee (12 citations); and UK Privy Council (81 citations).

So far the Court has cited foreign precedents quite extensively in its adjudication of constitutional issues, but legal scholars predict a decline in the Constitutional Court's reliance on foreign law in interpreting the Bill of Rights as it begins to develop a jurisprudence of its own.[66] An assessment of the statistics reveals that although there has been a steady decline in the Constitutional Court's citation of foreign precedents since 1995, the rate increased again in 2004 and has since remained more or less consistent, except for 2010, when it declined again. For instance, in 1995, 12 constitutional judgments of a total of 14 (ie 86 per cent) cited foreign precedents, whilst only 11 judgments of a total of 25 (ie 39 per cent) cited foreign judgments in 2003.[67] The citation rate increased again in 2004 to 63 per cent and, except for a slight drop during the next three years (2005–07), the rate hovered around 60 per cent again during 2008 and 2009. In 2010 it dropped again to 32 per cent. The latest drop is perhaps due to the appointment of a number of new judges at the Constitutional Court.

The tendency of the Constitutional Court to keep on citing foreign precedents despite the lack of an obvious motivation for doing so is in line with the argument that South African courts, in particular the South African Constitutional Court, want to keep in step with the global community and thus participate in the global exchange of judicial knowledge on an ongoing basis.[68] Justice Moseneke's receptiveness towards foreign precedents came to the fore in an interview he had with an American legal scholar, Bentele,[69] where he said

> most legal issues are not of exclusive or immediate origin ... Even in this country ... there's been judicial reasoning and adjudication for at least two and a half centuries—and I think as it is helpful to look at domestic jurisprudence, it must surely be helpful to look at what other jurisdictions say ...

Though the Constitutional Court judges show a great openness to foreign jurisprudence, as is evident in the statistics above, the persuasive value of the precedents so cited is less obvious than the number of citations. Or, as another author puts it: '[t]he South African court's engagement with foreign law does not, however, treat such sources [foreign precedents] as "authority", even in the broadest sense of the term'.[70]

b. Citation of Foreign Precedents: The Judges

At this moment,[71] the Constitutional Court has 11 current judges, 11 former judges and has had 12 acting judges. The judges most active in considering foreign precedents are those with permanent appointments and thus include the current and former judges, except for Justice Kentridge, who had an appointment as an acting judge.

---

[66] DM Davis, 'Constitutional Borrowing: The Influence of Legal Culture and Local History in the Reconstruction of Comparative Influence: The South African Experience' (2003) 1 *International Journal of Constitutional Law* 181, 194.
[67] The percentage of cases referring to foreign law increased to 59% in 2004.
[68] Janet McLean, 'From Empire to Globalization: The New Zealand Experience' (2004) 11 *Indiana Journal of Global Legal Studies* 161, 166–69.
[69] Ursula Bentele, 'Mining for Gold: The Constitutional Court of South Africa's Experience with Comparative Constitutional Law' (2009) 37 *Georgia Journal of International and Comparative Law* 219, 222–23.
[70] Bentele, 'Mining for Gold' 226.
[71] As at March 2011.

The statistics reveal that Justice Ackermann has included the most citations during his term of office, viz an average of 55 foreign case citations per year from 1994 to 2004. He is followed by Justice Chaskalson with an average of 46.5 foreign case citations per year during the same period, and in third place is Justice Kentridge with an average of 41.5 foreign case citations during the period from 1995 to 1996.

The high rate of foreign citation by some of the judges reveals that they generally do not shy away from considering foreign law. Nevertheless, an early warning was issued by Justice Chaskalson in *S v Makwanyane*,[72] viz:

> In dealing with comparative law, we must bear in mind that we are required to construe the South African Constitution, and not an international instrument or the constitution of some foreign country, and that this has to be done with due regard to our legal system, our history and circumstances, and the structure and language of our own Constitution. We can derive assistance from public international law and foreign case law, but we are in no way bound to follow it.

The willingness of the judiciary to consider foreign law is illustrated by members' personal views as documented by Bentele in her scholarly work.[73] She refers, amongst others, to the viewpoint of Justice Van der Westhuizen that people (including judges) were eager to become part and parcel of the international community again, and that considering foreign precedents has been a logical consequence of such a desire.[74] Justice Kriegler echoed these sentiments, expressing the people's wish to participate in important international developments.[75] Justices Chaskalson and Goldstone also expressed the opinion that one should be open to learning valuable lessons from jurisdictions other than one's own.[76] In *Du Plessis v De Klerk*[77] Justice Kentridge remarked as follows: '[t]he purpose of this perhaps overlong account of constitutional adjudication elsewhere is to see what guidance it might provide in the interpretation of the South African Constitution'.

Nevertheless, the approach to foreign precedent, albeit friendly, has been cautious in many respects. Justice O'Regan, for instance, in *Fose v Minister of Safety and Security*,[78] pointed out that '[a]s in all exercises in legal comparativism, it is important to be astute not to equate legal institutions which are not, in truth, comparable'. She calls this form of comparativism (where the legal institutions are not comparable) 'shallow comparison' which should be avoided, but indicates that:

> It would seem unduly parochial to consider that no guidance, whether positive or negative, could be drawn from other legal systems' grappling with issues similar to those with which we are confronted. Consideration of the responses of other legal systems may enlighten us in analysing our own law, and assist us in developing it further. It is for this very reason that our Constitution contains an express provision authorising courts to consider the law of other countries when interpreting the Bill of Rights. It is clear that in looking to the jurisprudence of other countries, *all the dangers of shallow comparativism must be avoided. To forbid any comparative review because of those risks, however, would be to deprive our legal system*

---

[72] *S v Makwanyane*, n 8 above, 39.
[73] Bentele, 'Mining for Gold' 229–32.
[74] Ibid 229.
[75] Ibid 230.
[76] Ibid 230–31.
[77] *Du Plessis v De Klerk* [1996] 3 SA 850 (CC) 41.
[78] *Fose v Minister of Safety and Security* [1997] 3 SA 786 (CC) 34.

of the benefits of the learning and wisdom to be found in other jurisdictions. Our courts will look at other jurisdictions for enlightenment and assistance in developing our own law. The question of whether we will find assistance will depend on whether the jurisprudence considered is of itself valuable and persuasive. If it is, the courts and our law will benefit. If it is not, the courts will say so, and no harm will be done (emphasis added).[79]

There is thus, according to her, not much of a danger that 'shallow comparison' would lead to harmful results, because in considering foreign precedents the Court will assess the persuasive value of the foreign precedents and deal with it accordingly.

c. Number of Foreign Precedents: Per Year, Judge and Country

The total number of constitutional cases citing foreign precedents sorted by countries discloses some interesting tendencies. Most evident is the fact that the Court no longer prefers the countries with which South Africa had historical links but also cites, almost haphazardly, other jurisdictions such as Canada, the United States of America (USA) and Germany, as reflected in Figure 2 below.

Although the use of international law has been excluded from my research findings, it is important to point out that there have been circumstances where the Constitutional Court considered the judgments of international or supra-national institutions in a comparative way. One such example is the judgments of the European Court of Human Rights (ECtHR). South Africa is not a member of the Council of Europe and thus not a party to the European Convention on Human Rights (ECHR). Nevertheless, it has cited the judgments of the ECtHR at least 142 times during the period under investigation. It is, however, difficult to determine if these comparisons have been done in the context of 'international law' or 'foreign law' as prescribed by section 39(1)(b) or (c) of the Constitution respectively.

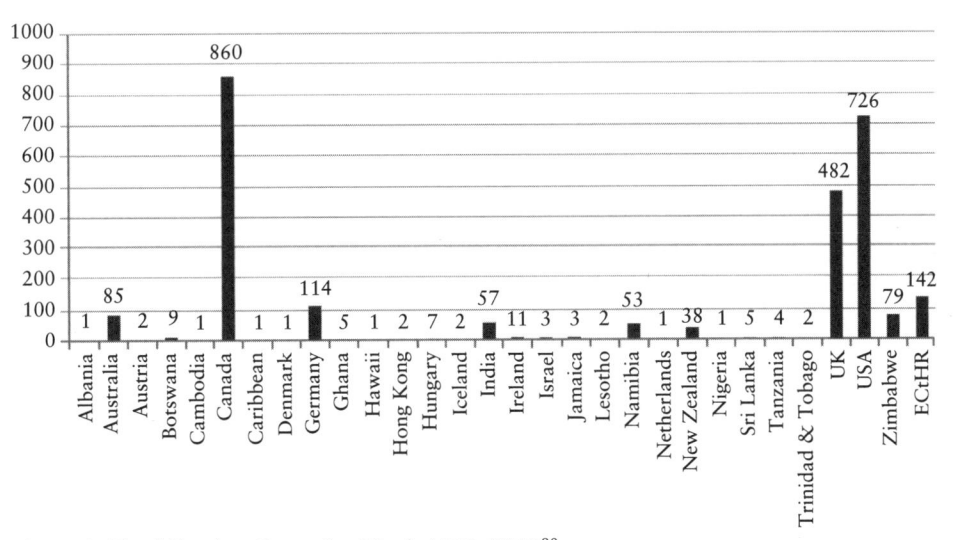

Figure 2: Total Foreign Countries Cited: 1995–2010[80]

---

[79] Ibid 35.
[80] Fig 2 includes the citations of the ECtHR.

The four foreign jurisdictions most cited by the top five judges[81] are, in descending numerical order, Canada and the USA, followed by the United Kingdom (UK) and, finally, Germany.

The overall statistics for foreign countries cited also show that Canadian precedents are the most popular with the South African judges. The popularity of Canadian precedents comes as no surprise and can be attributed mainly to the huge influence that the Canadian Charter of Rights and Freedoms had upon the drafters of the South African Bill of Rights.[82] The top three Canadian precedents cited by the Constitutional Court include *Thomson Newspapers Ltd v Canada (Director of Investigation and Research, Restrictive Trade Practices Commission)*[83] with 50 citations, *R v Big M Drug Mart Ltd*[84] with 31 citations and *Egan v Canada*[85] with 18 citations. All three Canadian cases generally deal with the interpretation of human rights issues and are cited by both the majority and dissenting South African judges, sometimes even in the same case. For instance, the Canadian case *Thomson Newspapers Ltd v Canada (Director of Investigation and Research, Restrictive Trade Practices Commission)*[86] was cited not only by the majority in *Harksen v Lane*[87] but also by the dissenting judge, Kriegler J, in *President of the RSA v Hugo*.[88]

Interestingly enough, there has been some exchange of ideas between the Canadian Supreme Court and the South African Constitutional Court, which accords with the idea that conversations among courts today take the form of a dialogue.[89] A few examples exist where the Canadian Supreme Court has cited South African cases but not nearly as many as the Constitutional Court's citations of Canadian precedents.[90] For example, in *Arsenault-Cameron v Prince Edward Island*,[91] Judge Bastarache applied the Constitutional Court case, *President of the RSA v South African Rugby and Football Union*,[92] in deciding whether a motion for recusal should be allowed or not. Similarly, in *Sauvé v Canada (Chief Electoral Officer)*,[93] McLachlin CJ referred to the Constitutional Court case *August v Independent*

---

[81] By the 'top five judges' I mean those who have referred the most to foreign precedents during the 15 year period, viz Ackermann, Chaskalson, Kriegler, Langa and O'Regan.

[82] The Charter was enacted as Schedule B to the Canada Act 1982, which came into force on 17 April 1982. See also the discussion of D Davis, 'Democracy—Its Influence upon the Process of Constitutional Interpretation' (1994) 10 *South African Journal on Human Rights* 103, 115.

[83] *Thomson Newspapers Ltd v Canada (Director of Investigation and Research, Restrictive Trade Practices Commission)* [1990] 1 SCR 425. At least seven different Constitutional Court judgments cited this case.

[84] *R v Big M Drug Mart Ltd* [1985] 1 SCR 295. At least 12 different Constitutional Court judgments cited this case.

[85] *Egan v Canada* (1995) 29 CRR (2nd) 79. At least nine different Constitutional Court judgments cited this case.

[86] *Thomson Newspapers Ltd v Canada (Director of Investigation and Research, Restrictive Trade Practices Commission)*, n 83 above.

[87] *Harksen v Lane* [1998] 1 SA 300 (CC) 50 and 93.

[88] *President of the RSA v Hugo* [1997] 4 SA (CC) 80. Incidentally, the same Canadian case was also cited by Goldstone and Justice Mokgoro, who delivered the majority judgment (see 41 and 92).

[89] HL Buxbaum, 'From Empire to Globalization' 185, 187.

[90] The author has not performed in-depth research in this regard, and an empirical survey might reveal that there has been more cross-pollination.

[91] *Arsenault-Cameron v Prince Edward Island* [1999] 3 SCR 851 4.

[92] *RSA v South African Rugby and Football Union* [2002] 2 SA 64 (CC).

[93] *Sauvé v Canada (Chief Electoral Officer)* [2002] SCC 68, [2002] 3 SCR 519 35.

Electoral Commission[94] to draw a parallel between a citizen's right to vote and his or her dignity. Two other examples where the Canadian Supreme Court cited South African precedents without much authority include *R v Hall*[95] and *Grant v Torstar Corp*.[96]

USA precedents are statistically the most cited by the top Constitutional Court judges, but generally without attaching much actual authority to them. The reasons for this high citation rate are less obvious than are those of the Canadian precedents, and they are mostly based on the contention that the USA is an 'open and democratic society based on freedom and equality'.[97] Furthermore, citing USA precedents in spite of the absence of a clear connection between South African and USA jurisprudence illustrates a move towards the universality of legal norms in a global community of judges, at least in the case of constitutional adjudication in South Africa. This fact is demonstrated by the words of Justice Ackermann in *Ferreira v Levin; Vryenhoek v Powell*,[98] where he declared as follows:

> [S]ection 35(1)[99] obliges us to promote the values underlying such a society when we interpret Chapter 3 [the Bill of Rights] and encourages us to have regard to comparable case law. In construing and applying our Constitution, *we are dealing with fundamental legal norms which are steadily becoming more universal in character*. When, for example, the United States Supreme Court finds that a statutory provision is or is not in accordance with the 'due process of law' or when the Canadian Supreme Court decides that a deprivation of liberty is not 'in accordance with the principles of fundamental justice' ... we have regard to these findings, not in order to draw direct analogies, but *to identify the underlying reasoning with a view to establishing the norms that apply in other open and democratic societies based on freedom and equality* (emphasis added).

In other words, regarding foreign precedents is more than just comparing for the sake of interpretation; it also means making law by establishing or using norms that apply or exist in other democracies. This paradigm shift from mere interpretation of the law to the making of the law explains why transjudicialism is not limited to comparable foreign jurisdictions but to all foreign jurisdictions which can make a valuable contribution to the law-making process.

Contrary to the Canadian precedents citing South African cases, the relationship between the South African and USA judiciaries is pretty much one-sided. The USA judiciary generally treats foreign precedents with suspicion and very few judgments refer to foreign law.[100] In this context communication between the South African

---

[94] *August v Independent Electoral Commission* [1999] 3 SA 1 (CC).

[95] *R v Hall* [2002] 3 SCR 309, 2002 SCC 64. See para 115, where the Court distinguished the social conditions in *S v Dlamini; S v Dladla; S v Joubert; S v Schietekat* [1999] 4 SA 623 (CC) with the social conditions *in casu*.

[96] *Grant v Torstar Corp* [2009] SCC 61 68. The Court compared the jurisprudence of other common law democracies including South Africa but did nothing more than merely refer to *Du Plessis v De Klerk*, n 77 above, and *National Media Ltd v Bogoshi* [1998] 4 SA 1196 (SCA).

[97] See the words of Ackermann in *Ferreira v Levin; Vryenhoek v Powell* [1996] 1 SA 984 (CC) 72.

[98] Ibid.

[99] Interim Constitution.

[100] USA judges generally fear that transjudicialism might endanger the principles of sovereignty and separation of powers, including the concern that judges might find justification for their subjective viewpoints in foreign precedent. See, eg, where these fears are discussed by Wood, 'In Defence of Transjudicialism' 93; B Markesinis, 'Understanding American Law by Looking at it through Foreign Eyes: Towards a Wider Theory for the Study and Use of Foreign Law' (2006) 81 *Tulane Law Review* 123; and

and USA courts is 'more readily conceptualised as monologue than dialogue'.[101] In spite of huge differences between the USA Constitution and the South African Constitution,[102] USA precedents remain popular with South African judges, although their influence on South African law remains doubtful. Statistics reveal that 700 of the total of 723 citations were referred to by South African judges during the first stage of the interpretative process when they were orientating their judgments.[103] The fact that American interns also work on legal opinions in the Constitutional Court from time to time definitely has an influence on the citation of USA precedents.[104] These judgments are mostly referred to in passing and seem to have no influence on the final conclusion reached by the Court.

The third highest total of foreign cases cited is those of the UK. This phenomenon can probably be attributed to South Africa's historical links with Britain. The latter was a colonial power in South Africa on two occasions, finishing in the 1960s.[105] Although the rationale for the citation of UK precedents was initially based on historical grounds and the subordinate relationship between the UK and South Africa, this is no longer so. Nevertheless, empirical research into the propensity of the UK court to cite South African courts would be needed in order to determine whether the recent equal relationship between these two countries has led to cross-pollination or not.

The Constitutional Court's citing of German precedents is explicable in the light of the fact that the South African Constitution contains some elements of the German Constitution.[106] Although German precedents are inaccessible to most South African judges as a result of the fact that they are expressed in the German language,[107] other factors have helped to develop a sound base for comparison. For example, the practice of appointing German lawyers from time to time as judges' clerks at the Constitutional Court, the availability of English translations, research visits of South African Constitution writers to Germany, and other scholarly contributions from

---

Gray, 'Justice Scalia' 1249. There are, however, a few examples where the USA courts have cited South African cases. A recent example (decided on 17 May 2010) is *Abbott v Abbott* (Case 08-645, accessible at www.supremecourt.gov/opinions/09pdf/08-645.pdf), which cited the South African Constitutional Court case, *Sonderup v Tondelli* [2001] 1 SA 1171 (CC), that deals with the custody of minor children.

[101] See Slaughter, 'A Typology of Transjudicial Communication' 113.

[102] The difference was pointed out by Chaskalson P in *Ferreira v Levin; Vryenhoek v Powell*, n 97 above, 175–76.

[103] See the discussion at B(ii)(b).

[104] In this regard one can refer to the interview with Justice van der Westhuizen documented by Bentele, 'Mining for Gold' 244. He acknowledges the fact that the Harvard Law School intern contributed to the approximately 25 USA citations in *Magajane v Chairperson North West Gambling Board* [2006] 5 SA 250 (CC).

[105] The first British occupation was from 1795 to 1803, and the second from 1806 to 1910. After this date, the Union of South Africa became an independent Dominion within the British Commonwealth and in 1961 South Africa became an independent Republic.

[106] Referred to as the 'German presence' by Du Plessis. He also points out some similarities between the German and South African Constitutions. See L Du Plessis, 'Learned Staatsrecht from the Heartland of the Reichsstaat: Observations on the Significance of South African-German Interaction in Constitutional Scholarship' (2005) 8 *Potchefstroom Electronic Law Journal* 76, 81, 89–91, accessible at www.puk.ac.za/opencms/export/PUK/html/fakulteite/regte/per/issue05v1.html.

[107] See the remark made by Kriegler J in *Du Plessis v De Klerk*, n 77 above, 39: 'The German jurisprudence on this subject is not by any means easy to summarise, especially for one who does not read German'.

German scholars[108] have all contributed to the seepage of German precedent into the Constitutional Court's jurisprudence.[109] For example, the textbook of Kommers[110] on the constitutional jurisprudence of Germany is referred to in quite a number of Constitutional Court cases.[111] Another classic example is the case of *Du Plessis v de Klerk*,[112] where the German principle of 'drittwirkung' in the field of private law was compared with the application of the South African Bill of Rights in private law.[113]

Not all of the judges are comfortable with the consideration of German precedents in the Constitutional Court, especially because of their difficulties with the German language. In this regard, Kriegler's states:[114]

> It [German] is not an easy language, and it's certainly not technically an easy language. And there are writing styles, techniques, [and] mannerisms in legal writing in German, quite apart from always putting the verb in the wrong place. And people blindly concurred with Laurie [Ackermann]'s judgments. I couldn't do that; if I can't get to the guts of what it's about, if I don't understand what they are really saying, what is built on that, I can't go along with it.

However, Justice Kriegler, who indicated his uneasiness with German precedents, made ample use of German law in the *Du Plessis v de Klerk*[115] case, though he made use mainly of secondary sources to find the law. He seems to be comfortable using translations or interpretations of German case law but does not trust the judgments of his own colleagues.

The high citation rate of foreign cases by the South African Constitutional Court also confirms what Lollini[116] calls the 'circulation' of foreign law between

---

[108] Eg, Prof Jochen Frowein (Max Planck Institute for Comparative Public and International Law). Justice Kriegler, because he had difficulties in reading German jurisprudence, referred to the scholarly works of German authors to gain access to the German cases. His conclusions are thus based on secondary information and the inherent danger in such an approach is quite well known.

[109] Ackermann, 'Constitutional Comparativism' 505 refers to two professors, viz Francois Venter (North-West University) and Gerhard Erasmus (Stellenbosch University). See also the discussion of Du Plessis, 'Learned Staatsrecht'.

[110] DP Kommers, *The Constitutional Jurisprudence of the Federal Republic of Germany* (Durham, Duke University Press, 1997).

[111] See *Matatiele Municipality v President of the RSA (No 2)* [2007] 6 SA 477 (CC) at n 11; *Doctors for Life International v Speaker of the National Assembly* [2006] 6 SA 416 (CC) at n 70; *Affordable Medicines Trust v Minister of Health* [2006] 3 SA 247 (CC) at n 53; *First National Bank of SA Ltd t/a Wesbank v Commissioner, SARS; First National Bank of SA Ltd t/a Wesbank v Minister of Finance* [2002] 4 SA 768 (CC) at nn 136 and 139; *Khumalo v Holomisa* [2002] 5 SA 401 (CC) at n 40; *Beyers v Elf Regters van die Grondwetlike Hof* [2002] 6 SA 630 (CC) at para 7; *Ex Parte President of the RSA: In re Constitutionality of the Liquor Bill* [2000] 1 SA 732 (CC) at n 11; *Christian Education SA v Minister of Education* [2000] 4 SA 757 (CC) at n 24; *Maphahlele v First National Bank of SA Ltd* [1999] 1 SACR 373 (CC) at n 10; *Du Plessis v De Klerk*, n 77 above, in the notes at para 104; *S v Makwanyane*, n 8 above, at nn 89 and 164.

[112] *Du Plessis v De Klerk*, n 77 above, 41.

[113] The judgment was delivered when the interim Constitution was still in operation and it is generally accepted that the new Constitution applies directly to private law. See in general the discussion of Stu Woolman, 'Application' in S Woolman, M Bishop and J Brickhill (eds), *Constitutional Law of South Africa* (Kenwyn, Juta, 2008) 31.3–31.161.

[114] His views were expressed during an interview; see Bentele, 'Mining for Gold' 242–43.

[115] *Du Plessis v De Klerk*, n 77 above, 41. He declared: 'In my opinion there is at least one positive lesson to be learnt from the Canadian and German approaches to the problem before us. Both Canada and Germany have developed a strong culture of individual human rights, which finds expression in the decisions of their courts.'

[116] Lollini, 'Legal Argumentation' 60.

constitutional judges or a 'dialogue between judges'. He argues convincingly that the question is no longer whether this phenomenon exists or not. The task rather is to determine and discuss the theories and methods of this form of legal reasoning.[117] Lollini[118] refers to the whole process as one of 'interpretation based on *extrasystemic parameters*' and argues that this process has the potential to transform the interpretative practices of judges into a process where they look to substantiate their normative arguments or viewpoints pertaining to constitutional issues in foreign law. He finally applies his extra-systemic parameters' framework to the South African setting and convincingly comes to the conclusion that there are various reasons why the application of extra-systemic parameters in post-apartheid South Africa is working, namely:[119]

— The express provision in the South African Constitution which allows judges to use extra-systemic parameters (viz foreign precedents).
— South Africa needs to obtain international legitimacy after years of human rights infringements.
— The judiciary needs to search for international principles to aid the interpretation of the South African Constitution, especially the Bill of Rights.
— The judiciary is aware that judicial review in a post-apartheid South Africa would require a period of legal learning which could be provided by the global legal (especially constitutional) arena.

d. Number of Foreign Precedents: Human Rights, Institutional or Other Issues

Each foreign citation was categorised according to the issue it dealt with. Three issues are distinguished, viz 'human rights issues',[120] 'institutional issues'[121] and 'other issues'.[122] A clear division among these three issues is not always possible. For example, a decision by an institution can sometimes also be classified as a human rights issue under the heading 'just administrative action'[123] and thus could fall under both the heading 'institutional issues' and the heading 'human rights issues'. From 1995 to 2010 the Constitutional Court had a total of about 2,152 foreign case citations in the context of human rights issues, approximately 472 foreign case citations dealing with institutional issues, and approximately 2,206 citations which can be classified as other issues.

---

[117] Lollini, 'Legal Argumentation' 61–62.
[118] Lollini, 'Legal Argumentation' 62.
[119] Lollini, 'Legal Argumentation' 63–64.
[120] In order to limit the number of entries the human rights issues are categorised according to the human rights listed in the Bill of Rights. See ch 2 of the Constitution.
[121] Institutional issues may overlap with human rights issues, eg, a decision of a school board may infringe human rights such as equality, freedom of expression and cultural rights but may also be classified as an institutional issue. An example is *MEC for Education Kwazulu-Natal v Pillay* [2008] 1 SA 474 (CC), where the decision of the school board to prohibit a learner from wearing a nose stud can be categorised under both issues.
[122] Other issues include interpretation, constitutional values, the limitation of rights, the rule of law, etc. The other-issues option was also used to refine a particular human right included in the broad categories of human rights listed in Fig 3; eg, the right to a fair trial will be included under other issues but also forms part of the statistics in the category of 'arrested, detained and accused persons' in Fig 3.
[123] See s 33 of the Constitution.

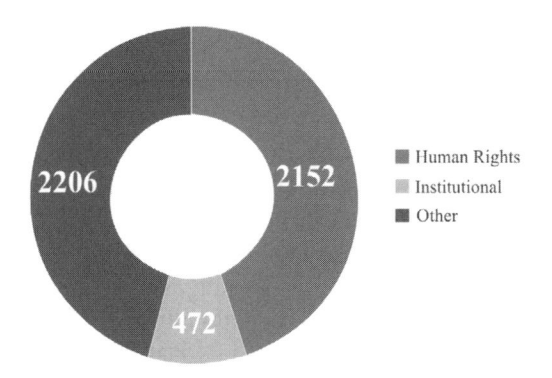

Figure 3: Number of Citations Vis-a-Vis Issues

Furthermore, in order to limit the number of human rights issues involved, the human rights issues have been categorised according to the main provisions in the Bill of Rights. For instance, the right to a fair trial is strictly speaking a right on its own but it is placed in the category 'arrested, detained and accused persons'.[124] In some instances, more information on the particular right falling under the main category is given under the heading 'other issues'. In other words, the right to a fair trial will be categorised as a human rights issue under the heading 'arrested, detained and accused persons' but then simultaneously as a right to a fair trial under the heading 'other issues'. The numbers of citations under 'human rights issues' (as set out in Figure 4 below) and 'institutional issues' are thus fairly accurate at this stage but the number of citations under 'other issues' remains problematic.

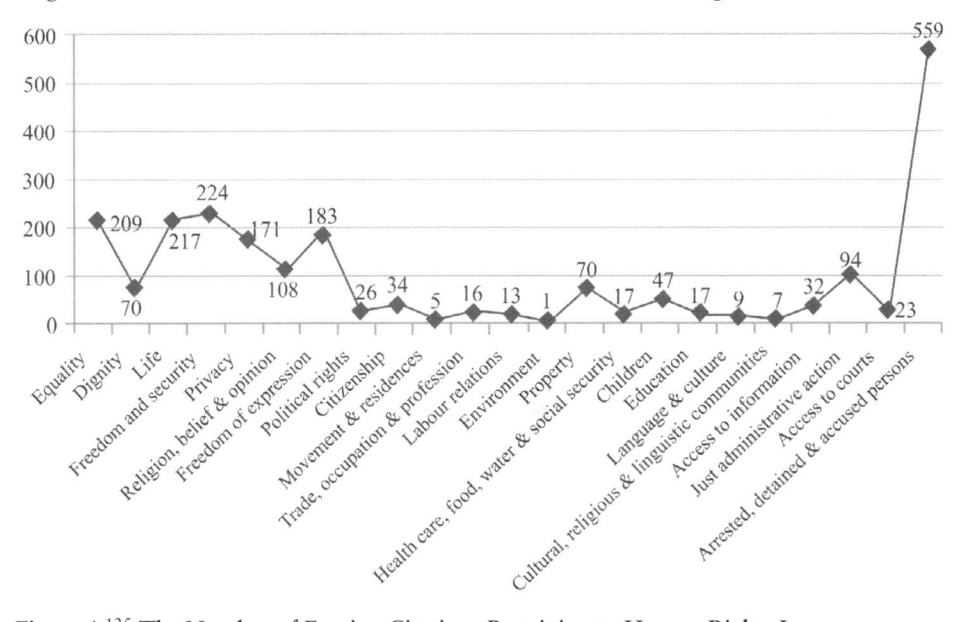

Figure 4:[125] The Number of Foreign Citations Pertaining to Human Rights Issues

---

[124] See s 35 of the Constitution.
[125] Fig 4 illustrates the number and classes of human rights issues most likely to elicit the consideration of foreign precedents by the judges. It is extremely difficult to give exact numbers since a particular

ii. Qualitative Approach

a. Formal Indicators

By using formal indicators one can determine to an extent just how influential foreign cases have been on the South African judiciary. The formal indicators used in the survey are, first and foremost, the mode of citation used by the Court. A citation could be made either in a footnote or in the text, and it could also be a mere reference to or a quote from a foreign case. The second group of formal indicators looks at the question of who is citing whose foreign judgments. The mode of citation does not really tell us what the value of the particular citation for South African law was; a foreign case could be followed by the South African judge but merely referred to in a footnote, or a foreign case could be discussed at length only to be discarded (*a contrario*) at the end.

Mode of Citation

No clear indications as to the authoritative value of a foreign case can be derived from looking at where it was cited in the text of the judgment. It can be cited either in the text or in a footnote and the citation could either be a mere reference to or a quote from the foreign case. According to the statistics, however, it appears that mere references to foreign cases are most common, as are citations in footnotes rather than in the text.

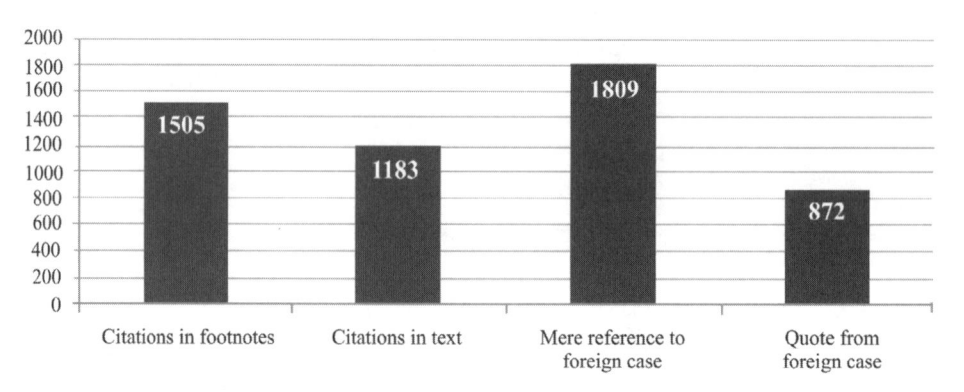

Mode of Citation	Number
Citations in footnotes	1505
Citations in text	1183
Mere reference to foreign case	1809
Quote from foreign case	872

Figure 5: The Number of Citations According to the Mode of Citation

Who is Citing Whom?

As to the question 'who cites foreign precedents', the statistics reveal what we have suspected, which is that judges delivering majority, dissenting and separate judgments all consider foreign precedents. However, as reflected in Figure 6, the vast majority of the Constitutional Court judges citing foreign cases delivered the majority decision and also referred to the majority judgment of the foreign case.

---

foreign precedent might have been cited more than once and also in connection with more than one human right.

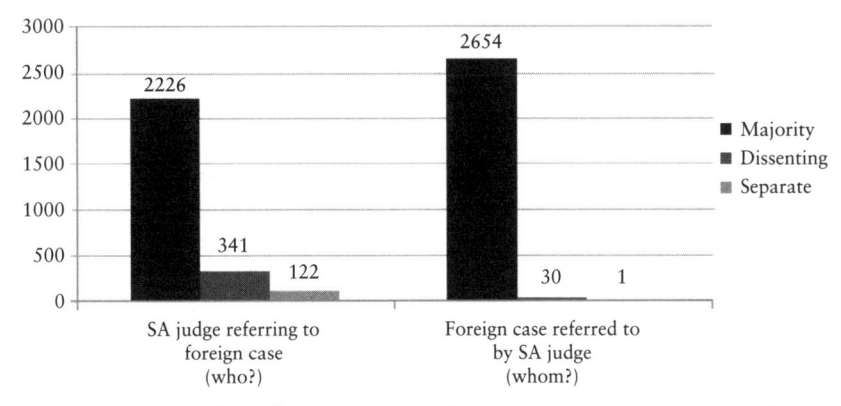

Figure 6: The Number of Citations According to Majority, Dissenting or Separate Judgments

The fact that judges refer to minority judgments in foreign precedents might not be surprising. Interestingly, though, a foreign case is sometimes considered by the judges delivering the majority, dissenting and/or separate judgments, all in one case. For instance, in the well-known case dealing with the constitutionality of legislation prohibiting the selling of liquor on certain days and at certain times, viz *S v Lawrence; S v Negal; S v Solberg*,[126] Justice Chaskalson, delivering the majority judgment, considered the Canadian case, *R v Big M Drug Mart Ltd*[127] and came to the conclusion that it was unnecessary for him to decide whether or not he should follow the Canadian approach to legislation dealing with the selling of liquor on Sundays because of the final decision that he reached.[128] In the same case Justice O'Regan, who delivered a minority judgment, also referred to *R v Big M Drug Mart Ltd*[129] in passing.[130] In a separate but concurring judgment, Justice Sachs too referred to *R v Big M Drug Mart Ltd*[131] but, whilst Justice Chaskalson implicitly stated that he need not follow the Canadian case, Justice Sachs indicated that he endorsed the viewpoint of the latter.[132]

As to the question 'who is cited by the South African judges', the statistics reveal a very interesting phenomenon. Although the majority of foreign case citations (ie 2,654) refer to the majority decisions of foreign precedents, there are also many foreign case citations (ie 30) where the dissenting decisions of the foreign precedents were considered by the South African judges. For example, in *Prince v President, Cape Law Society*,[133] a case dealing with the illegal use of cannabis by Rastafarians,

---

[126] *S v Lawrence; S v Negal; S v Solberg* [1997] 4 SA 1176 (CC) 87, 88, 92, 98 and 104.
[127] *R v Big M Drug Mart Ltd*, n 84 above.
[128] *S v Lawrence; S v Negal; S v Solberg*, n 126 above, 98. He came to the conclusion that Sundays are normally the day that most South Africans do not work and '[a] restriction on the sale of liquor on Sundays is, therefore, likely to be more effective in curtailing the consumption of liquor than a restriction on the sale of liquor on any other day of the week' (see 106).
[129] *R v Big M Drug Mart Ltd*, n 84 above.
[130] Without indicating the weight afforded to the Canadian case, she merely refers to it in a footnote. See *S v Lawrence; S v Negal; S v Solberg*, n 126 above, 126.
[131] *R v Big M Drug Mart Ltd*, n 84 above.
[132] See *S v Lawrence; S v Negal; S v Solberg*, n 126 above, 126 (n 101).
[133] *Prince v President, Cape Law Society* [2002] 2 SA 794 (CC).

the Constitutional Court judges referred 13 times to the USA case *Employment Division, Department of Human Resources of Oregon v Smith*.[134] A break-up of the statistics reveals the following interesting facts:

— Justices Chaskalson, Ackermann and Kriegler delivered the majority judgment and cited the USA case at least nine times. Six times they referred to the majority judgment[135] and the other three times they referred to the dissenting judgment in the USA case.[136] The three justices found the dissenting judgment to be more consistent with the South African Constitution.[137]
— Justice Ngcobo, delivering a dissenting judgment, cited the USA case only once by referring to the dissenting opinion of Judge Blackmun.[138] He did not indicate, however, if the opinion of Judge Blackmun had any influence on his final decision.
— Justice Sachs, who delivered a separate dissenting judgment, referred to the dissenting opinion of Blackmun (which he too favoured) in the USA case at least three times.[139] He recognised the differences between the situation in South Africa (ie a Rastafarian's use of marijuana/dagga) and that of the USA (ie native Americans using peyote) and came to the conclusion that to 'read as a whole his judgment [the dissenting decision of Judge Blackmun] is inconsistent with the granting of a narrowly tailored religious exemption in South Africa for the sacramental use by Rastafari of dagga'.[140]

In all likelihood South African Constitutional Court judges refrain from citing foreign precedents which are not directly to the point or comparable with the facts before the Court. This fact was made clear by Justice Langa in *SABC v National Director of Public Prosecutions*[141] with regard to the foreign precedents referred to by the council for the SABC.

b. Substantial Indicators: Judicial Reasoning

By using substantial indicators it is possible broadly to classify the legal reasoning of the judge citing foreign law into the following three categories:[142]

— Citations used at the very first stage of the process when reasoning must be oriented.[143] In this context, citations of foreign precedents may be useful to illustrate the range of potential choices or consequences. During this stage the influence of a particular foreign precedent is not always clear. In most instances the judges merely refer to the foreign precedents in passing. Using foreign precedents during this stage, without giving consideration to the (potential) value

---

[134] *Employment Division, Department of Human Resources of Oregon v Smith* [1990] 494 US 872.
[135] *Prince v President, Cape Law Society*, n 133 above, 119–21, 123 and 128–29. The majority judgment was delivered by Judge Scalia.
[136] *Prince v President, Cape Law Society*, n 133 above, 122 and 128–29. Judge Blackmun delivered a dissenting opinion and was joined by Judges Brennan and Marchall.
[137] See *Prince v President, Cape Law Society*, n 133 above, 122, 128.
[138] *Prince v President, Cape Law Society*, n 133 above, 47.
[139] *Prince v President, Cape Law Society*, n 133 above, 152, 155, 163.
[140] *Prince v President, Cape Law Society*, n 133 above, 152.
[141] *SABC v National Director of Public Prosecutions* [2007] 1 SA 523 (CC) 56 and 59.
[142] Placing a foreign citation in one of the three categories is not an easy task and this process is still ongoing.
[143] This phase can also be described as the 'inspirational' phase as discussed by Bryde, 'The Constitutional Judge' 213–14.

of a particular foreign case so cited, is also the method disapproved of by some critics. According to the statistics, approximately 2,534 foreign citations fall into this category.

— Citations used with the purpose of proving that 'even there' a certain measure was adopted, which the court intends to adopt 'even here'.[144] An example of where this line of reasoning was applied is *Coetzee v The Government of RSA; Matiso v Commanding Officer, Port Elizabeth Prison*.[145] In this case Justice Sachs, delivering a separate opinion, interpreted the word 'necessary' in the limitation clause[146] and, in doing so, considered foreign case law.[147] He then explained the value of the foreign precedents by saying that the term 'necessary', as indicated by the foreign case citations[148]

> is not made the subject of rigid definition, but rather is regarded as implying a series of inter-related elements in which central place is given to the proportionality of the means used to achieve a pressing and legitimate public purpose. Turning to the South African Constitution, I will not attempt a full definition of the word 'necessary', but, *bearing international experience in mind*, make the following observations (emphasis added).

According to the statistics there are only 147 foreign citations in this category.

— Citations used as an example not to be followed (*a contrario*) in order to set aside some of the potential interpretative readings. Only about 22 foreign case citations fall in this category.

The high rate of foreign case citations during the reasoning phase without any indication of what the explicit influences of the foreign cases are might leave one with some discomfort. If 'considering' foreign law, as authorised by section 39(1)(c) of the Constitution, means nothing more than paying lip service to foreign law, what then is the point of the whole exercise? As explained by Justice Moseneke,[149] Judges 'cherry pick all the time' when they refer to domestic or foreign cases. According to him the process of judicial adjudication

> implies a selection, and a reasoned and rational process to search for the truth by weeding out what's irrelevant and finding what is cohesive and that best answers ... the problem before us.[150]

The dealings of the Constitutional Court judges in citing foreign law during the reasoning phase have been all-encompassing rather than restrictive. The advantage of such a method is, of course, that nobody can blame the Court afterwards for not considering all of the available foreign case law on a particular issue.

---

[144] This phase can also be described as the 'legal argument' phase as described by Bryde, 'The Constitutional Judge' 214–19.
[145] *Coetzee v The Government of RSA; Matiso v Commanding Officer, Port Elizabeth Prison*, n 62 above. This judgment has at least 149 foreign case citations.
[146] As contained in s 33 of the interim Constitution and similar to s 36 in the Constitution.
[147] See *Coetzee v The Government of RSA; Matiso v Commanding Officer, Port Elizabeth Prison*, n 62 above. Justice Sachs has about 30 foreign case citations in his judgment.
[148] *Coetzee v The Government of RSA; Matiso v Commanding Officer, Port Elizabeth Prison*, n 62 above, 60.
[149] See Bentele, 'Mining for Gold' 239.
[150] Quoted in Bentele, 'Mining for Gold' 239.

IV. CONCLUDING REMARKS

Whilst the international community is hotly debating the pros and cons of judicial comparativism, the South African Constitutional Court has been developing, without much ado, an impressive reference list of foreign precedents. Never considering foreign precedents to be binding or persuasive, the Court has been protecting its independence. Justice Ackermann, in a scholarly article, declared as follows:[151]

> [F]oreign law is not in any sense binding on the court that refers to it. There seems to be the fear that in referring to foreign law one is bowing to foreign authority and thereby endangering the national sovereignty of one's own legal system. This is manifestly not so. One may be seeking information, guidance, stimulation, clarification or even enlightenment, but never authority binding on one's own decision. One is doing no more than keeping the judicial mind open to new ideas, problems, arguments, and solutions.

Furthermore, the justices consider primarily open and democratic societies and they are not afraid to recognise the differences and commonalities between the South African legal system and other jurisdictions, or those of the issues before them and the analogous foreign issues. These features, in a nutshell, have been described by Justice Ackermann in *National Coalition for Gay and Lesbian Equality v Minister of Justice*[152] as follows:

> In referring to these [foreign] judgments from the highest courts of other jurisdictions I do not overlook the different nature of their histories, legal systems and constitutional contexts nor that, in the last two cases, the issue was one essentially of statutory construction and not constitutional invalidity. Nevertheless, these judgments give expression to norms and values in other open and democratic societies based on human dignity, equality and freedom which, in my view, give clear expression to the growing concern for, understanding of, and sensitivity towards human diversity in general and to gays and lesbians and their relationships in particular. This is an important source from which to illuminate our understanding of the Constitution and the promotion of its informing norms.

The results of the empirical survey reveal an unprecedented willingness on the part of the Constitutional Court to participate in the constitutional dialogue happening in the global world. It is, nevertheless, dangerous to conclude that the South African Constitution is the main catalyst for the Court's engagement in constitutional comparativism. South African judges have always used foreign precedents in their judicial reasoning and it is quite natural that a newly established court such as the Constitutional Court would continue to do so. In this regard, it might be more truthful to conclude that it is a 'new' dog with 'old' tricks. That being said, it is also true that South Africa did not have a Bill of Rights before, and neither did the foreign jurisdictions that the South African courts used to refer to. For that reason, at least, the section 39-mandate could be seen as a new development enabling the South African courts to refer to foreign case law when interpreting the human rights provisions in the South African Constitution.

---

[151] Ackermann, 'Constitutional Comparativism' 510–13. He also supplies a long list of examples where foreign precedents have proved to be instructive and helpful in the judgments of the Constitutional Court.
[152] *National Coalition for Gay and Lesbian Equality v Minister of Justice* [1999] 1 SA 6 (CC) 48.

Also, although tempting, it is difficult to reach a crystal-clear conclusion that the Constitutional Court's jurisprudence reveals a consistent line of authority that indicates an approach towards foreign precedents which is universally accepted. Such a conclusion could lead to the utopian world of transjudicialism as imagined by Slaughter:[153]

> Imagine a world of regular and interactive transjudicial communication—among ... courts ... It would be a world in which courts perceived themselves independent of, although linked to, their fellow political institutions, open to persuasive authority, and engaged in a common enterprise of interpreting and applying national and international law, protecting individual rights, and ensuring that power is corralled by law. National differences would not obscure common problems nor block the adoption of foreign solutions. Courts would relate to each other in ways that could circumvent and constrain other branches of national governments and that could forge an independent link between national and international institutions. In this conception, the phenomenon of transjudicial communication is a pillar of a compelling vision of global legal relations.

We can all dream about this wonderful world she describes but we all know that the real world does not work this way. At least the statistics of the South African Constitutional Court reveal that the Court does not shy away from judicial globalism but on the contrary is open to dialogue with other jurisdictions—an attitude that is commendable.

---

[153] Slaughter, 'A Typology of Transjudicial Communication' 132.

Part II

8

Austria: Non-cosmopolitan, but Europe-friendly—The Constitutional Court's Comparative Approach

ANNA GAMPER*

TABLE OF CONTENTS

I. The Context 213
   A. Structural Elements of the Austrian Federal Constitution 213
   B. General Aspects of a Foreign-Law-Oriented Methodology in Austria 216
II. The Empirical Research 220
   A. Methodical Remarks 220
   B. The Use of Foreign Precedents in Figures 221
   C. Analysis of the Relevant Case Law 223
III. Implicit Influences of Foreign Case Law? 224
IV. Conclusion 226

I. THE CONTEXT

A. Structural Elements of the Austrian Federal Constitution

THE AUSTRIAN FEDERAL Constitution is a full-fledged member of the 'European family of constitutions'.[1] This is not only due to its historic development and territorial entrenchment in the heart of Europe, but also because Austria joined the Council of Europe in 1956 as well as the EU in 1995. It is a Federal Constitution, at the top of the hierarchy of legal norms of a continental

---

* I am grateful to Dr Mag Veronika Tiefenthaler and Univ-Ass Dr Maria Bertel who kindly assisted me in the research of the Constitutional Court's collection of cases and in footnote references.

[1] See C Grabenwarter, 'Österreich' in A von Bogdandy, P Cruz Villalón and P Huber (eds), *Handbuch Ius Publicum Europaeum, Band II: Offene Staatlichkeit—Wissenschaft vom Verfassungsrecht* (Heidelberg, C F Müller, 2008) 211, 211 ff; for a general view on the European Constitutions, see A von Bogdandy, P Cruz Villalón and P Huber (eds), *Handbuch Ius Publicum Europaeum, Band I: Grundlagen und Grundzüge staatlichen Verfassungsrechts* (Heidelberg, CF Müller, 2007); *Band II: Offene Staatlichkeit—Wissenschaft vom Verfassungsrecht* (Heidelberg, CF Müller, 2008); A von Bogdandy, 'Grundprinzipien' in A von Bogdandy and J Bast (eds), *Europäisches Verfassungsrecht. Theoretische und dogmatische Grundzüge*, 2nd edn (Berlin—Heidelberg, Springer, 2009) 13, 30 ff; P Häberle, *Europäische Verfassungslehre*, 7th edn (Baden-Baden, Nomos, 2011) 53 ff.

European civil-law country and of a federal system.[2] Being the Constitution of a small republic, it has nevertheless been inspired by many elements of the past Austro-Hungarian Empire. It is a particularly flexible Constitution, with an unusually high number of amendments,[3] and it is a fragmented Constitution that, until 2008, consisted of some 1,200 different constitutional norms and is still supposed to consist of several hundred.[4]

The rise of Austrian constitutionalism began in the late forties of the nineteenth century. The era of neo-absolutism, however, prevented the first Austrian Bill of Rights of 1849 from entering into force. It took more than 15 years until the first catalogue of fundamental rights was entrenched formally. Due to Art 149 of the Federal Constitutional Act of 1920 (*Bundes-Verfassungsgesetz*, hence: B-VG), this Basic Law, originally adopted in 1867, is still in force today. In the same year, several other fundamental constitutional laws were adopted, one of which established the *Reichsgericht* which was the forerunner of the republican Constitutional Court (*Verfassungsgerichtshof*).[5]

The end of the Austro-Hungarian monarchy in 1918 and the proclamation of the new Republic of German-Austria (since 1919: Austria) brought a great shift in constitutional terms. The new republic was not the legal successor of the old monarchy. The new Federal Constitution did not continue the former constitutional settings— although it adopted or further developed several previous elements—, but was enacted as the 'historically first' Constitution of the Republic of Austria. For this purpose, the constitutional framers did not only have to bridge deep gaps between the political parties (Christian Socials and Social Democrats), but also between the central government and the constituent *Länder* that took part in the drafting process.[6]

Hans Kelsen, founder of the Viennese School of Legal Positivism, was the leading academic adviser in the constitutional drafting period. In his famous commentary on the Austrian Federal Constitution Kelsen discusses several cases where foreign

---

[2] See generally A Gamper, 'Introduction to the Study of the Law of the Austrian Federal Constitution' (2008) vol 2 *ICL-Journal* 92, 92 ff; recently also, M Stelzer, *The Constitution of the Republic of Austria. A Contextual Analysis* (Oxford—Portland, Hart Publishing, 2011).

[3] 113 amendments have been enacted since 1930, when the B-VG was republished (BGBl 1930/1).

[4] T Öhlinger, *Verfassungsrecht*, 8th edn (Wien, facultas.wuv, 2009) 27 estimates approximately 500 constitutional documents, whereas E Wiederin, 'Verfassungsrevision in Österreich' in M Thaler and H Stolzlechner (eds), *Verfassungsrevision. Überlegungen zu aktuellen Reformbemühungen* (Wien, Sramek, 2008) 17, 25, estimates approximately 300.

[5] H Haller, *Die Prüfung von Gesetzen. Ein Beitrag zur verfassungsgerichtlichen Normenkontrolle* (Wien—New York, Springer, 1979) 39 ff; K Korinek, 'Die Verfassungsgerichtsbarkeit im Gefüge der Staatsfunktionen' (1981) 39 *VVDStRl* 7, 8 ff; G Stourzh, *Wege zur Grundrechtsdemokratie. Studien zur Begriffs- und Institutionengeschichte des liberalen Verfassungsstaates* (Wien—Köln, Böhlau, 1989) 313; T Öhlinger, 'Die Entstehung und Entfaltung des österreichischen Modells der Verfassungsgerichtsbarkeit' in B-C Funk et al (eds), *Der Rechtsstaat vor neuen Herausforderungen—Festschrift Ludwig Adamovich* (Wien, Verlag Österreich, 2002) 581, 589; T Öhlinger, 'The Genesis of the Austrian Model of Constitutional Review of Legislation' (2003) 16 *Ratio Juris* 206, 214; MJ Montoro-Chiner and H Schäffer, 'Die Rezeption des österreichisch-deutschen Modells der Verfassungsgerichtsbarkeit in Spanien' in C Starck (ed), *Fortschritte der Verfassungsgerichtsbarkeit in der Welt—Teil I* (Baden-Baden, Nomos, 2004) 57, 58 f; A Gamper and F Palermo, 'The Constitutional Court of Austria: Modern Profiles of an Archetype of Constitutional Review' (2008) Vol III/2 *Journal of Comparative Law* 64, 64 ff; K Heller, *Der Verfassungsgerichtshof. Die Entwicklung der Verfassungsgerichtsbarkeit in Österreich von den Anfängen bis zur Gegenwart* (Wien, Verlag Österreich, 2010) 74 f.

[6] F Ermacora (ed), *Quellen zum österreichischen Verfassungsrecht (1920). Die Protokolle des Unterausschusses des Verfassungsausschusses samt Verfassungsentwürfen* (Wien, Berger, 1967) 10 ff.

Constitutions had been consulted—in particular, the *Weimarer Reichsverfassung* (Weimar Constitution) and the *Schweizerische Bundesverfassung* of 1874 (Swiss Federal Constitution).[7] These Constitutions were illustrative not only because they were the Constitutions of Weimar Germany and Switzerland—the two countries whose legal traditions most closely resembled the Austrian one—, but also because they were the Constitutions of two federal systems. Whilst the Austrian monarchy had been a decentralised unitary state, the new republic was founded as a federal state. Not least due to the highly controversial political attitudes, Austrian federalism, at least seen from a formal perspective, follows its own (rather centralistic) pattern in many aspects and does not completely mirror either of these two model Constitutions.[8]

It is a peculiar characteristic of the Austrian Federal Constitution that it does not include an incorporated Bill of Rights.[9] Nevertheless, fundamental rights are on the whole protected effectively in Austria, even though they are entrenched in a very fragmented way. The oldest source of human rights is the aforementioned Basic Law of 1867 that was revived as a federal constitutional law in its own right in 1920. Some rights are scattered around the B-VG, whilst others are entrenched in federal constitutional laws and provisions of their own. The most important source in this respect, however, has been the European Convention on Human Rights (ECHR) and its Additional Protocols (which, excluding Protocol No 12, were transformed as part of Austrian federal constitutional law)[10] and, since 2009, the Charter of Fundamental Rights of the EU as far as it is applicable.

On the whole, the Austrian Federal Constitution was not particularly prone to foreign influence as was, for example, the case in many post-colonial or post-communist Constitutions.[11] Its recognition as a 'European' Constitution is mainly due to its historical embedding in the family of continental European legal systems and to the heed that is paid to safeguarding common constitutional values such as democracy, the rule of law, the separation of powers and fundamental rights, upheld by both the Council of Europe and the EU. If foreign constitutional influences are recognisable, this is mostly the case through indirect channels, via the 'common

---

[7] H Kelsen, G Froehlich and A Merkl (eds), *Die Bundesverfassung vom 1 Oktober 1920* (Wien, Verlag Österreich, 2003) 55, 75; E Wiederin, 'Österreich' in A von Bogdandy, P Cruz Villalón and P Huber (eds), *Handbuch Ius Publicum Europaeum, Band I: Grundlagen und Grundzüge staatlichen Verfassungsrechts* (Heidelberg, CF Müller, 2007) 389, 397 ff.

[8] P Pernthaler, *Österreichisches Bundesstaatsrecht* (Wien, Verlag Österreich, 2004) 286; Wiederin, 'Österreich' 401.

[9] M Holoubek, 'Grundrechtskompilation oder Grundrechtsreform? Gedanken zu Zielen und Funktionsbedingungen einer Grundrechtsrevision im Rahmen des "Österreich-Konvents"' in W Berka et al (eds), *Verfassungsreform. Überlegungen zur Arbeit des Österreich-Konvents* (Wien—Graz, NWV, 2004) 31, 31 ff; T Öhlinger, 'Die Grundrechtsreform nach dem Österreich-Konvent' in A Bammer et al (eds), *Rechtsschutz gestern—heute—morgen—Festgabe Rudolf Machacek und Franz Matscher* (Wien—Graz, NWV, 2008) 341, 341 ff; Wiederin, 'Verfassungsrevision' 19 ff; A Gamper, 'A "Bill of Rights" for Austria: Still Unfinished Business' (2010) *Percorsi costituzionali* 211, 212.

[10] T Öhlinger, 'Die rechtliche Bedeutung der Entscheidungen internationaler Menschenrechtsschutzinstanzen, insbesondere des Europäischen Gerichtshofs für Menschenrechte, für die Tätigkeit der Gesetzgebung, Verwaltung und Rechtsprechung' in E Klein (ed), *Gewaltenteilung und Menschenrechte*, 2nd edn (Berlin, Berliner Wissenschaftsverlag, 2010) 233, 248 f; Heller, *Verfassungsgerichtshof* 407 ff.

[11] See, eg, several contributions in J Goldsworthy (ed), *Interpreting Constitutions. A Comparative Study* (Oxford—New York, Oxford University Press, 2007); C Saunders, *The Constitution of Australia. A Contextual Analysis* (Oxford—Portland, Hart Publishing, 2011) 102 ff.

constitutional heritage of Europe' that is frequently appealed to in the European Court of Human Rights' and European Court of Justice's (ECJ's) case law.[12] From a more direct and individual perspective, the German Constitution and constitutional jurisprudence surely are—though still rarely enough—more referred to by the Austrian Constitutional Court than any other national Constitution, because German law is generally seen as the closest 'neighbour' to Austrian law.[13]

B. General Aspects of a Foreign-Law-Oriented Methodology in Austria

i. The Approach of the Constitutional Court

The Austrian legal system is a continental European civil law system. With negligible exceptions, common law—neither judge-made nor customary law—is not recognised as a source of constitutional law.[14] Formally, therefore, the Constitutional Court's decisions are not to be regarded as precedents of a common law system (see, however, Art 138 para 2 B-VG under which the Court may deliver opinions on the constitutional distribution of competences which are binding to the effect of a 'quasi-authentic' interpretation of the Constitution). Nevertheless, the jurisdiction of the Constitutional Court is of paramount importance, especially when it comes to constitutional interpretation. Although the Court in general advocates both a text-based and originalist rather than evolutive method of interpretation, there are cases, particularly in the context of fundamental rights, where the Court approaches what is called an 'open development of law'.[15] The main reason behind this sort of judicial activism is the European case law which instigates the Austrian Constitutional Court to adopt a more dynamic approach.[16]

---

[12] A Gamper, 'Verfassungsvergleichung und "gemeineuropäischer" Verfassungsstaat. Wert und Unwert einer transnationalen Methode unter besonderer Berücksichtigung der verfassungsgerichtlichen Judikatur' (2008) 63 ZÖR 359, 363 ff; A Gamper, 'On the Justiciability and Persuasiveness of Constitutional Comparison in Constitutional Adjudication' (2009) vol 3 ICL-Journal 150, 151. With a European dimension FC Mayer, 'Die Bedeutung von Rechts- und Verfassungsvergleichung im europäischen Verfassungsverbund' in C Calliess (ed), Verfassungswandel im europäischen Staaten- und Verfassungsverbund (Tübingen, Mohr Siebeck, 2007) 167, 172 ff; G de Vergottini, Oltre il dialogo tra le Corti. Giudici, diritto straniero, comparazione (Bologna, Il Mulino, 2010) 45 ff and 173 ff.

[13] M Holoubek, 'Wechselwirkungen zwischen österreichischer und deutscher Verfassungsrechtsprechung' in D Merten (ed), Verfassungsgerichtsbarkeit in Deutschland und Österreich (Berlin, Duncker & Humblot, 2008) 85, 94; Gamper, 'Justiciability' 164.

[14] See H Kelsen, 'Wesen und Entwicklung der Staatsgerichtsbarkeit' (1929) 5 VVDStRL 30, 69 f; However, the Constitutional Court increasingly practises judicial activism under the influence of the ECHR and the EU; T Öhlinger, 'Gesetz und Richter unter dem Einfluss des Gemeinschaftsrechts. Anmerkung zu einem Prozess der "Amerikanisierung" des europäischen Rechts' in P Hänni (ed), Mensch und Staat—Festgabe Thomas Fleiner (Freiburg, Universitätsverlag Freiburg Schweiz, 2003) 721, especially 729 ff.

[15] M Potacs, Auslegung im öffentlichen Recht. Eine vergleichende Untersuchung der Auslegungspraxis des Europäischen Gerichtshofs und der österreichischen Gerichtshöfe des öffentlichen Rechts (Baden-Baden, Nomos, 1994) 285 ff; W Berka, Die Grundrechte. Grundfreiheiten und Menschenrechte in Österreich (Wien, Brauneder, 1999) 83 ff; R Novak, 'Der Verfassungsgerichtshof im Dialog mit dem Europäischen Gerichtshof' in B-C Funk et al (eds), Der Rechtsstaat vor neuen Herausforderungen—Festschrift Ludwig Adamovich (Wien, Verlag Österreich, 2002) 539; Heller, Verfassungsgerichtshof 436 ff. A general overview of the characteristics of the Austrian Constitutional Court's interpretation is given by A Gamper, Regeln der Verfassungsinterpretation (Wien—New York, Springer, 2012) 129 ff.

[16] H Schäffer, 'Die Grundrechte im Spannungsverhältnis von nationaler und europäischer Perspektive' (2007) 62 ZÖR 1, 11 ff; C Grabenwarter, 'Die Auslegung der EMRK im Spannungsverhältnis zwischen Straßburg und Wien' in A Bammer et al (eds), Rechtsschutz gestern—heute—morgen—Festgabe Rudolf Machacek und Franz Matscher (Wien—Graz, NWV, 2008) 129 ff; T Öhlinger, Verfassungsrecht 302.

The Court has a wide range of competences that includes the scrutiny of (constitutional and ordinary) laws, regulations, administrative rulings, state treaties and some other types of legal Acts under the Austrian legal system. The Court is also competent to scrutinise elections, to decide on accusations against supreme executive bodies, and to decide on competence conflicts and financial matters in a subsidiary way. Among the many issues for appeal to the Constitutional Court, complaints against administrative rulings, most of them alleging a violation of fundamental rights, constitute the major part. Although the Constitutional Court has many competences, all of them result in ex-post judicial review. There is only one slight exception, where the Court may exercise ex-ante judicial review, namely with regard to legislative drafts of the federal or *Land* lawmaker respectively, which are submitted to the Court for pre-legislative scrutiny on whether the draft, if it indeed became law, violated the distribution of competences (similarly, with regard to other, non-legislative draft legal Acts).

The structure of judgments delivered by the Constitutional Court—slightly differing, of course, in accordance with the respective competences exercised by the Court—consists of several parts: after a short introductory section that mentions the names of the deciding judges as well as the date and name of the parties, the operative ruling of the judgment follows. Normally, the Court first states the facts of the case and the legal foundation (as well as preliminary remarks in some cases), followed by eventual counter-arguments of the opposing parties. The final part, however, is dedicated to the Court's reasoning, which is always a uniform statement without the possibility of delivering a dissenting or concurring opinion of single judges. The absolute majority of votes regularly decides a case which means that a single judge or a minority of judges can be overruled. The decision is published as a consolidated statement wherefrom it cannot be assessed externally whether all judges were in conformity or not.[17]

In general, the Austrian Constitutional Court is not disposed to cite foreign national law or case law,[18] while European case law (in particular, ECHR cases dealt with by the European Court of Human Rights (ECtHR)) regularly plays an important role in its decisions.[19] This is due to the binding character of both ECHR and EU law, which is lacking in the case of foreign national law or case law, unless

---

[17] The lack of opportunity to give a dissenting opinion is criticised by R Machacek (ed), *Verfahren vor dem Verfassungsgerichtshof und vor dem Verwaltungsgerichtshof. Leitfaden für die Praxis mit Darlegungen auch zu UVS- und EMRK-Beschwerden und zum Asylgerichtshof*, 5th edn (Wien, Manz, 2004) 29, 36.

[18] More openness towards foreign case law is shown by the Supreme Court (*Oberster Gerichtshof*) that deals with civil or criminal law cases in the last instance; see also K Heller, 'Rechtsvergleichung und Verfassungsrecht' in F Matscher and I Seidl-Hohenveldern (eds), *Europa im Aufbruch—Festschrift Fritz Schwind* (Wien, Manz, 1993) 147, 148 f. Having regard to the period between 1 January 1980 and 31 December 2010, 54 out of 62,683 (publicly recorded) decisions of the Austrian Supreme Court include a reference (by the Court or a party) to foreign *constitutional* case law (especially by the German *Bundesverfassungsgericht*), whilst 122 out of 1,561 (publicly recorded) decisions between 1 January 2009 (!) and 31 December 2010 include a reference to foreign law or foreign case law in general; the research was undertaken in accordance with the same search keywords used with regard to the case law of the Constitutional Court.

[19] B Wieser, *Vergleichendes Verfassungsrecht* (Wien—New York, Springer, 2005) 36; Öhlinger, 'Bedeutung' 204 f; Schäffer, 'Grundrechte' 4 and 13 ff; Grabenwarter, 'Österreich' 235 ff; C Grabenwarter, 'Zur Bedeutung der Entscheidungen des EGMR in der Praxis des VfGH' (2007) *RZ* 154, 154 ff; C Fuchs, 'Verfassungsvergleichung durch den Verfassungsgerichtshof' (2010) 18 *JRP* 176, 177. See, with more detail, Gamper, *Regeln* 244 ff.

the ECHR or EU law indirectly demands a comparative approach that considers interpretations of member state courts.

A first reason for the Austrian Constitutional Court's reluctance to use foreign precedents may be that the methodology applied by the Court has for a long time been inspired by the academic influence of the Viennese School of Legal Positivism.[20] Due to the strict normative orientation of this School[21] that does not recognise foreign law (outside the ECHR or EU context) as a source for the interpretation of Austrian law—considering that the Austrian Federal Constitution does not, unlike Article 39 paragraph 1 c of the South African Constitution, refer to any foreign legal authority—, references to foreign law can even today[22] seldom be found in the Court's reasoning and, if used at all, are mainly used in an ancillary way, for underpinning a position that is already based on 'domestic' arguments.[23] Although not hostile to public international and EU law, the Austrian Federal Constitution is neither a particularly 'cosmopolitan'[24] Constitution, nor does the Constitutional Court, though a distinguished archetype of constitutional courts worldwide, traditionally held itself out to be a 'cosmopolitan' court or 'cognate' court as can be found in many Commonwealth countries—not even within the 'family of European constitutional courts', as the link between them is that of European law, but not of a former 'mother' Constitution that they have in common.

A second reason for the Court's reluctance to cite foreign legal sources may be found in Austrian history and legal tradition. Building on earlier elements of constitutionalism, the Federal Constitution was drafted and enacted by a national convention under the aegis of Hans Kelsen and others and was not just copied from another Constitution. It is a Constitution that was 'actually ineffective' during the period of Austro-fascism and during Nazi occupation. After its restoration in 1945, it has thus always been important to highlight the independent character of the Austrian Federal Constitution and not to treat it outside its own context. Until more recently, therefore, both constitutional judges and scholars in Austria were on the whole reluctant to consider issues of comparative law, which, in technical

---

[20] Heller, *Verfassungsgerichtshof* 74 f.

[21] See, eg, R Thienel, 'Der Rechtsbegriff der Reinen Rechtslehre—Eine Standortbestimmung' in Schäffer et al (eds), *Staat—Verfassung—Verwaltung—Festschrift Friedrich Koja* (Wien—New York, Springer, 1998) 161, 177 ff; see, moreover, R Walter, C Jabloner and K Zeleny (eds), *Hans Kelsen anderswo—Hans Kelsen abroad. Der Einfluss der Reinen Rechtslehre auf die Rechtstheorie in verschiedenen Ländern, Teil III* (Wien, Manz, 2010) and the special issue 'The Many Fates of Legal Positivism' of (2011) 12 *German Law Journal* No 2.

[22] In VfSlg 1341/1930 and 1351/1930, the Constitutional Court held that foreign law and foreign precedents were irrelevant, since it was 'obvious' that only Austrian law could be applied by the Court. In 1973, the Constitutional Court remarked shortly that there was no law that *required* an Austrian constitutional provision to be interpreted in accordance with a foreign Constitution (VfSlg 7138/1973). Although, as this paper shows, the Court has since become a little less radical in its refusal to consider foreign precedents, the prevailing methodology allows consideration of foreign precedents only in cases where this confirms the choice from a couple of possible 'national' options. In 2009, moreover, the Constitutional Court stressed that the fact that courts of other states did not require administrative authorities to justify their decisions in the reasons of their rulings to the same extent as this was prescribed by Austrian law could not influence the latter (VfSlg 18.741/2009, similarly VfSlg 18.861/2009).

[23] Gamper, 'Verfassungsvergleichung' 382.

[24] See, eg, M Kumm, 'The Cosmopolitan Turn in Constitutionalism: On the Relationship between Constitutionalism in and beyond the State', in J L Dunoff and J P Trachtman (eds), *Ruling the World? Constitutionalism, International Law, and Global Governance* (Cambridge, Cambridge University Press, 2009) 258 ff and V Perju, 'Cosmopolitanism and Constitutional Self-government' (2010) 8 *ICON* 326 ff.

terms, may also have been due to a limited knowledge of foreign languages and legal training in foreign law. These latter obstacles, however, could be overcome with the increasingly international experience of judges as well as enhanced possibilities to use international networks and internet-based data. Nevertheless, the main reason for the reluctance to use foreign precedents on a grand scale still lies in the methodical approach, as even German case law, of which Austrian constitutional judges have always had a good knowledge, has been cited only in few cases (even though much more often than other foreign precedents).

ii. The Influence of Legal Doctrine

The links between legal scholarship and the Constitutional Court are close. This is the case, of course, because a large number of the judges are professors of constitutional law—a profession which is compatible with the position of a constitutional judge, as expressly provided by the Federal Constitution: according to Art 148 para 1 B-VG, the Court consists of the President, the Vice-President, 12 justices and six substitute justices, who replace the judges if they are temporarily prevented from attending a session. All must have completed the study of law and must have worked for at least 10 years in a legal profession, for which a law degree is a requisite. Although no minimum age is fixed, legal training and professional expertise are thus a precondition for becoming a constitutional judge. In practice, the justices are usually university professors, judges, barristers or senior civil servants working for the public administration (the latter must be released from their normal function as long as they serve as a constitutional judge). Those judges that are proposed for appointment by the Federal Government must be chosen from either civil servants working for the public administration, judges (at other courts) or law professors. The Constitutional Court has no continuing term, but normally meets four times a year (three weeks per session). Not the least due to the inputs of the 'scholar-justices', jurisprudential doctrine and constitutional case law stand in an ongoing process of mutual recognition and further development, although they do not always represent the same legal opinions.[25]

The engagement of Austrian legal scholars with foreign constitutional law or case law has been a significantly increasing phenomenon in recent years. With Austrian EU accession in 1995 and enhanced academic mobility, they have decidedly opened up to comparative constitutional law, which previously had been a field little-known to most Austrian scholars of constitutional law. A serious debate on the use of foreign case law in the Constitutional Court's own case law, however, was, until very recently, neither led by academics nor by the courts.[26]

Where scholars had been involved in international projects or research groups dealing with comparative constitutional law, they had mainly limited their work to describing the Austrian system—as is the case with this paper—, whilst relatively few scholars ventured to undertake a comparison with foreign systems. From the

---

[25] Machacek (ed), *Verfahren* 14, 29.
[26] Gamper, 'Justiciability' 150 ff and Gamper, 'Verfassungsvergleichung' 359 ff. On 3 September 2010, moreover, a conference on 'Constitutional Courts and Constitutional Comparison' took place in Vienna. The conference papers were published in *Journal für Rechtspolitik* 18 (2010): see particularly Fuchs, 'Verfassungsvergleichung' 176 ff; K Lachmayer, 'Verfassungsvergleichung durch Verfassungsgerichte— Funktion und Methode' (2010) 18 *JRP* 166, 166 ff; M Mayrhofer, 'Europäische Verfassungsvergleichung durch den Verfassungsgerichtshof. Ein Kommentar' (2010) 18 *JRP* 188, 188 ff.

perspective of the 'paradigm of textual stages',[27] it has mostly been the text of foreign Constitutions or other Constitution-related Acts and documents rather than foreign case law that has served as a basis of comparative research. This is also due to linguistic problems, as case law is much less translated than the constitutional texts themselves and a profound analysis cannot dispense with a reliable command of both foreign language and legal system.

An important exception to this is the general willingness of Austrian scholars—and, at least to some relative extent, the Constitutional Court as well—to consider German constitutional law and case law, which is not only advantageous for linguistic reasons,[28] but also because German law has the closest links to the Austrian legal system, apart from both countries' membership of the Council of Europe and the EU. The same goes for public international and European law where Austrian legal scholars have gained much expertise.

II. THE EMPIRICAL RESEARCH

A. Methodical Remarks

The time period of the empirical research on the use of foreign precedents by the Constitutional Court dates from 1 January 1980 to 31 December 2010. The data was obtained from the Legal Information System (RIS), a computer-assisted information system on Austrian law, coordinated and operated by the Austrian Federal Chancellery, which contains the Constitutional Court's case law as from 1 January 1980. It should be noted that the number of cases recorded in the database[29] is comparatively low when compared to the actual number of cases[30] that the Constitutional Court deals with according to its annual reports.[31] This discrepancy does not affect the research on the use of foreign case law, however, since the types of decisions that were not recorded are insignificant in this context.

It should be noted that the Constitutional Court's opinions are always uniform, without the possibility of a *votum separatum*, and that the Court does not use footnotes, but inserts 'technical' references in parenthesis. It should also be noted that the research carried out in the Court's electronic collection of cases was organised

---

[27] P Häberle, 'Grundrechtsgeltung und Grundrechtsinterpretation im Verfassungsstaat. Zugleich zur Rechtsvergleichung als "fünfter" Auslegungsmethode' (1989) *JZ* 913, 913 ff. See also K-P Sommermann, 'Die Bedeutung der Rechtsvergleichung für die Fortentwicklung des Staats- und Verwaltungsrechts in Europa' (1999) *DÖV* 1017, 1017 ff; T Öhlinger, 'Vom Sinn und Nutzen der Verfassungsvergleichung' in H Eberhard, K Lachmayer and G Thallinger (eds), *Reflexionen zum Internationalen Verfassungsrecht* (Wien, WUV, 2005) 11; Wieser, *Verfassungsrecht* 27 ff.

[28] Fuchs, 'Verfassungsvergleichung' 176, 177 ff; Lachmayer, 'Verfassungsvergleichung' 166, 170.

[29] 13,251 cases between 1 January 1980 and 31 December 2010.

[30] The Constitutional Court decided 95,111 cases between 1 January 1981 and 31 December 2010 (data on 1980 not available).

[31] Statistical tables on the Constitutional Court's activities are part of the Court's annual report (see, most lately, *Bericht des Verfassungsgerichtshofes über seine Tätigkeit im Jahr 2011*, which can be downloaded at www.vfgh.gv.at).

B. The Use of Foreign Precedents in Figures

In the following, the use of foreign precedents by the Constitutional Court since 1 January 1980 is described in figures and tables. Out of the total number of decisions since that date, there have been only 60 cases where the Constitutional Court's decision includes explicit references to foreign precedents, most (though not all) of which are constitutional precedents (ie decisions taken by constitutional courts).[33] Whereas 58 of these cases deal with human rights issues, only two cases relate to an institutional issue. The cited countries include Belgium, France, Germany, the Netherlands, Switzerland, the United Kingdom and the United States of America. As can be seen from Table 3, however, German precedents—in particular those of the German *Bundesverfassungsgericht*—are cited much more than the precedents of other countries. It is also remarkable to find that, although the total number of decisions varied from year to year, this had no impact on the number of decisions where foreign precedents were cited. According to this survey, the number of such decisions has been slightly increasing in the last two decades, compared to the 1980s, where only 12 decisions explicitly cited foreign precedents during the whole decade. Nevertheless, the number of decisions that cite foreign precedents is even now still on zero level if compared to the total number of decisions that the Court takes each year. The only difference is that such decisions have occurred more regularly, that is, almost annually, in the last two decades, ranging from one to seven cases per year. Moreover, the Constitutional Court itself mentioned a foreign precedent in its reasoning in only 16 out of the 60 cases,[34] whereas, in all other cases, the quotation

---

[32] Such as BGH, Bundesfinanzhof, Bundesverfassungsgericht, BVerfG, BVerfGE, Bundesgericht, Bundesgerichtshof, Conseil Constitutionnel, Corte Costituzionale, Cour constitutionnelle, House of Lords, Privy Council, Conseil d'Etat, Staatsgerichtshof, ausländisch, various country names. Fewer decisions were found by Fuchs, 'Verfassungsvergleichung' 178, even though she extended her search to cases where foreign law (and not just foreign case law) was cited by the Constitutional Court. The following survey, however, does not only include cases where the Constitutional Court itself mentioned a foreign precedent in its legal statement, but also where one of the parties referred to a foreign precedent, provided that this reference is cited in the judgment.

[33] VfSlg 8981/1980, 9138/1981, 9416/1982, 9446/1982, 10.291/1984, 10.809/1986, 11.402/1987, 11.260/1987, 11.483/1987, 11.651/1988, 11.774/1988, 12.103/1989, 12.568/1990, 12.645/1991, 12.660/1991, 12.940/1991, 13.036/1992, 13.038/1992, 13.661/1993, 13.704/1994, 13.785/1994, 13.839/1994, 14.390/1995, 15.031/1997, 15.040/1997, 15.103/1998, 15.299/1998, 15.390/1998, 15.632/1999, 15.987/2000, 16.030/2000, 16.636/2002, VfGH 28/06/2003, G78/00, VfSlg 17.098/2003, 17.195/2004, 17.206/2004, 17.330/2004, 17.415/2004, 17.574/2004, 17.584/2005, 17.600/2005, 17.605/2005, 17.837/2006, 17.979/2006, 18.010/2006, 18.018/2006, 18.031/2006, 18.150/2007, 18.257/2007, 18.462/2008, 18.541/2008, 18.587/2008, 18.741/2009, 18.792/2009, 18.831/2009, (18.861/2009 just includes an indirect reference to 18.741/2009), 18.893/2009, 18.927/2009, 18.965/2009, 19.021/2010, 19.170/2010.

[34] VfSlg 9138/1981, 9416/1982, 9446/1982, 10.291/1984, 11.260/1987, 13.038/1992, 15.632/1999, 15.987/2000, 16.636/2002, VfGH 28/06/2003, G 78/00, VfSlg 17.600/2005, 18.541/2008, 18.741/2009 (18.861/2009 just includes an indirect reference to 18.741/2009), 18.792/2009, 18.893/2009, 18.965/2009. The tables represent the entire 60 cases.

222 Anna Gamper

was only made by one of the parties in the appeal procedure, admitted into that part of the decision where extracts of the parties' statements are reflected under quotation marks.[35] This is the more remarkable, since the Constitutional Court, as mentioned before, very often cites judgments of the ECtHR or the ECJ.

Table 1: The number of decisions of the Austrian Constitutional Court, where foreign case law is cited, out of the total of decisions per year*

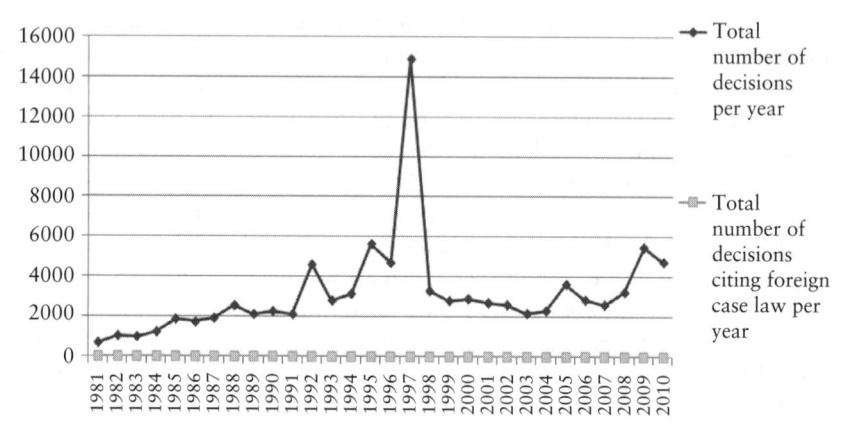

* This graph does not show the decisions of the year 1980 as the constitutional Court's annual report for this year is not available. Due to the low number of decisions using foreign case law in comparison to the overall number of decisions, the first category of decisions appears as a "zero line".

Table 2: Percentage of institutional and human rights decisions, where foreign case law is cited, between 1980 and 2010

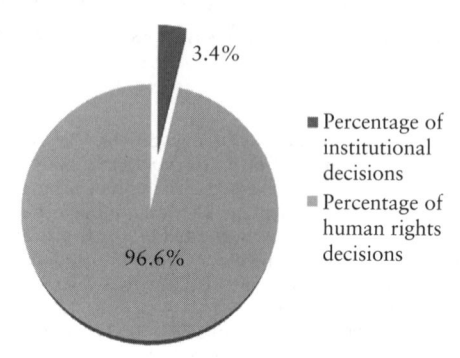

---

[35] However, even in some of the cases where the Constitutional Court explicitly mentioned a foreign precedent, this was only done at external instigation, as the foreign precedent had been mentioned by one of the parties before. Only in about two thirds of the relevant cases were foreign precedents quoted by the Constitutional Court on its own account.

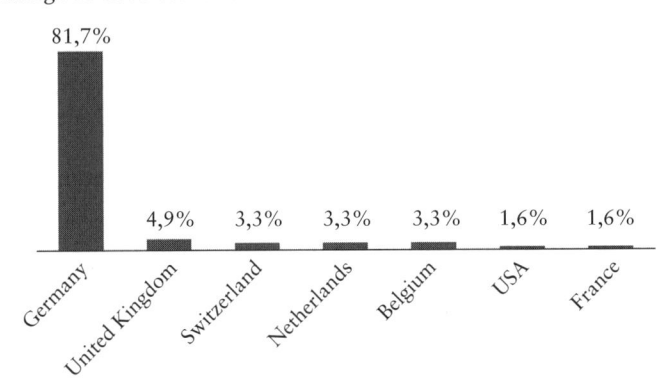

Table 3: Percentage of cited countries between 1980 and 2010

Country	Percentage
Germany	81,7%
United Kingdom	4,9%
Switzerland	3,3%
Netherlands	3,3%
Belgium	3,3%
USA	1,6%
France	1,6%

C. Analysis of the Relevant Case Law

In those few decisions where the Constitutional Court itself referred to a foreign precedent (either at the instigation of one of the parties or on its own account), the citation has mostly been used in order to confirm the decision taken against the background of domestic law. Only in exceptional cases has the Court explicitly referred to such a statement as irrelevant,[36] while there was one case where the Constitutional Court explicitly relativised a foreign precedent mentioned by one of the parties by contextualising it with both the doctrine and another precedent.[37] Where the foreign precedents were mentioned by the Constitutional Court in a positive sense, however, their function was only of a subsidiary nature: they were clearly not decisive for the judgment as such, but just considered to be useful to endorse the arguments brought by the Court on the basis of domestic law. Although this seemingly casts the light of a 'cosmopolitan' attitude on the Court, this would be a strongly blurred picture, as the number of cases where the Court referred to a foreign precedent at all is extremely low. Nevertheless, one may conclude that if the Court cites a foreign precedent on its own account (and not because one of the parties instigated it) it does so with the obvious intention of strengthening its own 'domestic' reasons by comparing them to a similar situation in another legal system (mostly, the German legal system). The foreign precedents thus have a confirming, although not decisive function—whether they originally 'inspired' the Constitutional Court in its decision (which is then based on reasons inherent in the domestic legal system) cannot be derived from the text of the judgments, as the

---

[36] In VfSlg 18.541/2008, the Constitutional Court held the applicant's reference to a German decision to be misguided. In VfSlg 18.741/2009 (indirectly also VfSlg 18.861/2009), the Constitutional Court held the opposing party's references to foreign precedents to be irrelevant. In VfSlg 15.632/1999, the Constitutional Court stated that the Swiss precedent was just based on the Swiss Federal Constitution (which was obviously not considered to be relevant), but not on the ECHR, while case law of the ECtHR or other European constitutional courts was still lacking. However, one may conclude from this latter judgment that foreign precedents on the interpretation of the ECHR could be relevant for the Constitutional Court's own interpretation of the ECHR (see also VfSlg 18.893/2009), as far as these judgments went along with the case law of the ECtHR.
[37] VfSlg 16.636/2002.

quotation does normally not appear at the beginning. If the Constitutional Court cites foreign precedents on its own account it clearly does not do so in order to point out how different the respective legal systems are, but that there are similarities. This is more plausible, as the Constitutional Court could hardly be expected to cite a foreign precedent needlessly—just in order to show that the Austrian legal system differs from another.

Still, the Constitutional Court has reacted negatively with regard to foreign precedents in the majority of the cases where foreign precedents were mentioned only by one of the procedural parties (as far as their statements are related in the judgments). The Court's response was negative insofar as it neither considered nor even alluded to the party's statement on the foreign precedent. In a large number of the cases, moreover, the reaction was also negative in the sense that the Court—apart from neglecting the foreign argument—decided against the party that had, among other reasons, brought this argument, even though on reasons not connected with that argument.

On the whole, the Constitutional Court is not at all prone to citing foreign precedents on its own account and hardly ever takes notice of foreign precedents when they are cited by one of the parties. There is no case where a foreign precedent was both explicitly mentioned and considered to be *the* relevant argument for the decision taken. The furthest degree of 'consideration' that an explicitly mentioned foreign precedent has been entitled to in the prevailing case law is use as a confirming argument which somewhat adds to the rationalisation of the decision, but is needless in a formal legal sense, as the respective decision is already based on a stronghold of domestic reasons.[38] Strongly disinclined to consider foreign precedents explicitly as the Constitutional Court manifests itself according to this survey, it should nonetheless be emphasised once more that the Court has a very different attitude with regard to explicit quotations of European case law (rudimentally, perhaps, even with regard to the case law of national constitutional courts where the ECHR is applied),[39] that there are, moreover, more cases where the Court cites foreign Constitutions, though not foreign precedents, and that some implicit influences of foreign precedents are obvious.

III. IMPLICIT INFLUENCES OF FOREIGN CASE LAW?

It is hardly possible for somebody who is not a constitutional judge to find out if and where the Constitutional Court is implicitly influenced by foreign case law.[40] Still, there are some decisions where implicit foreign influences can be surmised insofar

---

[38] In VfSlg 18.893/2009, it remains unclear whether the German precedent was indeed decisive or whether the Court cited the precedent just in order to confirm its own opinion of the interpretation of Art 10 ECHR.

[39] See the explicit reference made in VfSlg 18.893/2009; there are lots of decisions, moreover, where the Constitutional Court cites a judgment of one of the European 'supreme' Courts which in its turn explicitly or implicitly took account of the decisions of member state courts.

[40] P Häberle, 'Wechselwirkungen zwischen deutschen und außerdeutschen Verfassungen' in D Merten and H-J Papier (eds), *Handbuch der Grundrechte in Deutschland und Europa, Band I. Entwicklung und Grundlagen* (Heidelberg, CF Müller, 2004) 313; Wieser, *Verfassungsrecht* 36; Gamper, 'Verfassungsvergleichung' 372; Gamper, 'Justiciability' 160.

as the lowest common denominator of constitutional law or constitutional case law was applied. In one of its most famous decisions,[41] for instance, the Constitutional Court held that the removal of certain essential elements of federalism 'that could be found in all other federal constitutions' would amount to a 'total revision' of the Constitution. The Court neither explained which Constitutions were actually meant nor referred to any relevant case law.[42] Nevertheless, it is clear that the Court based its arguments on implicit constitutional comparison (less, perhaps, on the comparison of constitutional case law). Another example is the (in recent years less used) application of the 'theory of the essential content'[43] which was developed by the German jurisprudence (the essential content of human rights must not be violated, whatever the reasons are) as well as the 'theory of three stages'[44] which is applied in cases where the freedom of professions is infringed by objective or subjective restrictions: in these cases, the Austrian Constitutional Court obviously followed the German *Bundesverfassungsgericht* without referring to it explicitly.

One species of implicit reasoning affects certain constitutional paradigms or common European principles, such as 'the rule of law', the 'principle of proportionality', 'representative democracy' etc. Whenever the Constitutional Court uses these terms without further explanation, this is not because the Court implicitly argues on the basis of foreign case law using a universalist approach, but because it is influenced by the terminology of general constitutional theory or by standards that were developed at European level, including European case law (even though they themselves may have indirectly emerged from comparison).[45]

As mentioned before, the Constitutional Court has a positivistic attitude and is therefore reluctant to use foreign law as a valid source of interpretation. A fortiori, the implicit use of foreign case law would be even more problematic from the positivistic point of view. As constitutional judges in Austria have traditionally been no experts of foreign law and, according to the relatively few explicit judgments, more or less restricted the comparative method to Germany, it would be inconsistent with this attitude if they made implicit use of foreign precedents, even though the implicit method might be more convenient than the explicit method which requires a precise quotation and rationale.

The former head of the Constitutional Court's department of scientific services and quality management, Univ-Prof Dr Harald Eberhard, professor of public law at the Vienna University of Economics and Business, assesses the use of the implicit method as follows:

> I regard the implicit method as something not at all unknown to the Constitutional Court, although it is difficult to retrace it in detail. In my opinion, the case law of the German *Bundesverfassungsgericht* on the principle of legality (the requirement to determine all

---

[41] VfSlg 2455/1952.
[42] Gamper, 'Verfassungsvergleichung' 377.
[43] Starting with decision VfSlg 3118/1956; see also VfSlg 14.075/1995; 18.298/2007. On the influence of this theory see Berka, *Grundrechte* 153 f; R Walter, H Mayer and G Kucsko-Stadlmayer, *Grundriss des österreichischen Bundesverfassungsrechts*, 10th edn (Wien, Manz, 2007) 633; M Stelzer, *Das Wesensgehaltsargument und der Grundsatz der Verhältnismäßigkeit* (Wien, New York, Springer, 1991).
[44] See BVerfGE 7, 377; Öhlinger, *Verfassungsrecht* 401.
[45] See, with a general view, de Vergottini, *Dialogo* 28 ff.

essential factors by a statute)[46] was crucial to the development of the Austrian principle of legality, even though there had been previous Austrian case law that could be also seen as a starting point.

Another example is the 'theory of the essential content' which had previously been construed by the German *Bundesverfassungsgericht*.[47]

More recently, the Austrian Constitutional Court scrutinised the Carinthian Law on Party Financing, focussing on the factual quality of parties in the political process.[48] It is striking that comparable arguments were used by the German *Bundesverfassungsgericht*[49] with regard to the German Party Act some years ago so that it may well be that the Austrian Constitutional Court was inspired by that decision. I think it also probable that an implicit use of a decision of the German *Bundesverfassungsgericht*[50] led to the—given the fact that the Constitutional Court thereby did not decide *in merito*—unusually lengthy reasoning in the Austrian Constitutional Court's decision on the saving of internet and mobile phone data.[51,52]

IV. CONCLUSION

The Austrian Constitutional Court is still highly reluctant to decide cases on the basis of foreign case law, even though the number of cases where the Court at least has a look at foreign case law has been (very) slowly increasing. Where this is done, it is mostly the German courts that are referred to. Moreover, the Court has never yet really decided a case *on account of* foreign case law. At best, its function is that of a non-binding by-argument in order to support a legal opinion that already derives from applying domestic law. Thus, although an intense transjudicial dialogue exists with regard to the ECtHR's and ECJ's case law, it is hardly so in the case of foreign national constitutional courts. This is, however, not an indicator to show that the Constitutional Court follows a civil law tradition (which it actually does, as shown by other indicators), as the Court shows no reluctance at all to cite decisions taken by the two European 'supreme' courts or by Austrian courts, including the Constitutional Court itself.

In order to evaluate the propensity of a court to consider foreign law (not just case law) or for a legal system to develop from a civil law to a common law system, however, other factors would have to be considered: what is the ratio between foreign law (foreign Constitutions), foreign academic literature and foreign case law that is cited in a decision? How much domestic case law does a constitutional court cite? How much international case law (decisions of the ECtHR and ECJ in particular) does a constitutional court cite? What is the purpose and effect of the quotation? Do constitutional courts feel bound by the case law they cite?

---

[46] BVerfGE 49, 89.
[47] BVerfGE 2, 266.
[48] VfSlg 18.603/2008.
[49] BVerfGE 111, 382.
[50] BVerfGE 113, 348.
[51] VfSlg 18.830/2009 (whilst an explicit reference was made in a related case (VfSlg 18.831/2009)).
[52] My thanks go to Univ-Prof Dr Harald Eberhard for providing me with his written statement for the purposes of this paper.

Apart from the decisions mentioned here, we find decisions where the Austrian Constitutional Court cited foreign Constitutions, other sources of foreign law or foreign doctrine, without, however, mentioning foreign case law. These are channels of foreign influence which must not be undervalued, even though they were not included in the comparative purposes of this book—but they would be well worth another study.

9

Lifting the Constitutional Curtain? The Use of Foreign Precedent by the German Federal Constitutional Court

STEFAN MARTINI*

TABLE OF CONTENTS

I. Introduction 229
II. The GFCC in Context 230
   A. Emergence and Evolution of the Basic Law and the GFCC 230
   B. The GFCC's Jurisdiction 233
   C. The GFCC's Position in the German Political System 235
   D. The GFCC's Style of Reasoning 238
III. Explicit Citation of Foreign Precedent by the GFCC 239
   A. Choices of Method 240
   B. Formal Analysis 241
   C. Substantive Analysis 248
IV. Implicit Influence of Foreign Precedent on the Jurisprudence of the GFCC 250
V. Conclusions 251

I. INTRODUCTION

IT IS WIDELY (and in Germany proudly) held that the German model of constitutional review including the jurisprudence of the German Federal Constitutional Court (hereinafter GFCC) has served as a role model for many 'young' respectively 'revised' democracies.[1] This seeming openness is surprisingly

---

* Research Assistant in Public Law at the University of Münster. I thank Martin Albrecht for his assistance in the data research work.
[1] U Battis, EG Mahrenholz and D Tsatsos (eds), *Das Grundgesetz im internationalen Wirkungszusammenhang der Verfassungen* (Berlin, 1990); A Zimmermann, 'Bürgerliche und politische Rechte in der Verfassungsrechtsprechung mittel- und osteuropäischer Staaten unter besonderer Berücksichtigung der Einflüsse der deutschen Verfassungsgerichtsbarkeit' in JA Frowein and T Marauhn (eds), *Grundfragen der Verfassungsgerichtsbarkeit in Mittel- und Osteuropa* (Berlin, Springer, 1998) 89; J Limbach, 'Das Bundesverfassungsgericht und der Grundrechtsschutz in Europa' (2001) *Neue Juristische Wochenschrift* 2913, 2919; H-P Schneider, 'Das Grundgesetz als Vorbild? Sein Einfluss auf ausländische Verfassungen' in H-P Schneider (ed), *Das Grundgesetz in interdisziplinärer Betrachtung* (Baden-Baden, Nomos, 2001) 159 ff; P Häberle, 'Das GG als "Exportgut" im Wettbewerb der Rechtsordnungen' in C Hillgruber (ed), *60 Jahre Bonner Grundgesetz—eine geglückte Verfassung?* (Göttingen, V&R, 2010) 173; B Pieroth, 'Deutscher Verfassungsexport: das Bundesverfassungsgericht' (2010) *Anwaltsblatt* 8.

mirrored by the also common observation that the GFCC is of a more introverted character,[2] more or less ignoring foreign law and precedent. It is also believed that the rare citations themselves have been declining since the formative period of the GFCC.[3] This contribution will try to validate whether the GFCC is really advancing solely on a one-way street of legal reception by assessing citations of foreign judgments in the jurisprudence of the GFCC (section III) and tracing implicit influence on the GFCC of foreign sources (section IV). Before turning to the figures and their analysis, the overall position of the GFCC in the German political system will be illuminated, taking into account the evolution of the German Basic Law (hereinafter BL), the width of the GFCC's jurisdictional competencies, the careers of the GFCC judges, their links to German legal scholarship, and, moreover, the style of reasoning of the GFCC (section II).

II. THE GFCC IN CONTEXT

A. Emergence and Evolution of the Basic Law and the GFCC

In retrospect, the German constitutional system embodies the feasibility of successful post-conflict transition.[4] Its institutions are stable and trusted; in particular, trust in the GFCC has been established quickly and remains high.[5] After the defeat of the German Army in 1945, which ended World War II and Nazi rule in Europe, nobody could have envisaged this outcome of the occupancy and

---

[2] See U Drobnig, 'Rechtsvergleichung in der Deutschen Rechtsprechung' (1986) 50 *Rabels Zeitschrift für ausländisches und internationales Privatrecht* 610, 623; P Häberle, 'Grundrechtsgeltung und Grundrechtsinterpretation im Verfassungsstaat' (1989) *Juristenzeitung* 913, 916; S Vogenauer, *Die Auslegung von Gesetzen in England und auf dem Kontinent* (Tübingen, Mohr Siebeck, 2001) 43; A Nußberger, 'Wer zitiert wen?—Zur Funktion Zitaten bei der Herausbildung eines gemeineuropäischen Verfassungsrecht' (2006) *Juristenzeitung* 763, 769; A Tschentscher, 'Dialektische Rechtsvergleichung—Zur Methode der Komparatistik im öffentlichen Recht' (2007) *Juristenzeitung* 807, 807 f; P Häberle, *Europäische Verfassungslehre*, 6th edn (Baden-Baden, Nomos, 2009) 474.

[3] K-P Sommermann, 'Funktionen und Methoden der Grundrechtsvergleichung' in D Merten and H-J Papier (eds), *Handbuch der Grundrechte in Deutschland und Europa*, vol 1: *Entwicklung und Grundlagen* (Heidelberg, CF Müller, 2004) 631, para 86; B Markesinis and J Fedtke, *Judicial Recourse to Foreign Law. A New Source of Inspiration?* (London, UCL Press, 2006) 78; A Nußberger, 'Wer zitiert wen?—Zur Funktion Zitaten bei der Herausbildung eines gemeineuropäischen Verfassungsrechts' (2006) *Juristenzeitung* 763, 769.

[4] PE Quint, '60 Years of the Basic Law and its Interpretation: An American Perspective' (2009) 57 *Jahrbuch des öffentlichen Rechts der Gegenwart* 1.

[5] prreport.de/home/gpra-vertrauensindex/februar-2011/; institutional trust in the GFCC is only slightly exceeded by the police and educational institutions; also see U Kranenpohl, 'Die gesellschaftlichen Legitimationsgrundlagen der Verfassungsrechtsprechung, oder: Darum lieben die Deutschen Karlsruhe' (2009) 56 *Zeitschrift für Politik* 436; A Brodocz and H Vorländer, 'Das Vertrauen in das Bundesverfassungsgericht. Ergebnisse einer repräsentativen Umfrage' in H Vorländer (ed), *Die Deutungsmacht der Verfassungsgerichtsbarkeit* (Wiesbaden, VS Verlag, 2006) 259. For an extensive elaboration of this phenomenon, including a discussion of the empirical material and the evaluation of lower acceptance in the 70s and 90s see OW Lembcke, *Über das Ansehen des Bundesverfassungsgerichts. Ansichten und Meinungen in der Öffentlichkeit 1951–2001* (Berlin, Berliner Wissenschafts-Verlag, 2006).

partitioning of Germany. Under the auspices of the occupant nations,[6] corrupted and devastated institutions had to be resurrected in a democratic way, underpinned by a Constitution. Since the German Democratic Republic (East Germany) became part of the Federal Republic of Germany (West Germany) in 1990 and consequently adopted the 'Western' institutional system, the constitutional developments in the Soviet zone, in contrast to those of the US, the UK and France, will be of no interest here.[7] The—originally only West German—Constitution, the 'Basic Law' ('Grundgesetz'), was coined as a provisional solution by a small constituent assembly, the Parliamentary Council ('Parlamentarischer Rat'), between 1948 and 1949, its members appointed by the Parliaments of the Länder (federal states). The work of the Parliamentary Council was formally authorised and substantially governed by the 'Frankfurt documents' of 1 July 1948 of the allied military governors.[8] Beyond that, the actual regulations of the Basic Law were influenced not only by the will to symbolise the renunciation of the Nazi era, but also by external sources, mainly by the liberal German Constitutions of Frankfurt (1849)—never in force—and Weimar (1919); in particular, the phrasing of individual rights appears to be inspired by the predecessors of the Basic Law.[9] Yet, the Parliamentary Council also took into account developments in the international arena such as the Universal Declaration of Human Rights (1948) as well as foreign Constitutions.[10] In particular, the (US) American model of the US Supreme Court and of the enforceability of basic rights served as a point of reference for the framers of the German Constitution.[11] Adopted by the Parliaments of the Länder and approved by the military governors, the Basic Law entered into force on 23 May 1949, erecting the pillars of a state and its institutions for decades to come. Although foreseen by the BL (Art 146 BL), it was not replaced by a new, formal, permanent constitutional document when the German Democratic Republic acceded to the Federal Republic of Germany in 1990—the Basic Law remains in force and incorporates quite numerous amendments.[12] Important amendments have installed a constitutional emergency regime

---

[6] Cf BH Robertson and P Koenig and LD Clay, 'Letter of Approval' in H Wilms (ed), *Ausländische Einwirkungen auf die Entstehung des Grundgesetzes, Dokumente* (Stuttgart, Kohlhammer, 2003) 426.

[7] But see G Brunner, 'Das Staatsrecht der Deutschen Demokratischen Republik' in J Isensee and P Kirchhof (eds), *Handbuch des Staatsrechts*, vol 1, 3rd edn (Heidelberg, CF Müller, 2003) 531.

[8] R Mußgnug, 'Zustandekommen des Grundgesetzes und Entstehen der Bundesrepublik Deutschland' in J Isensee and P Kirchhof (eds), *Handbuch des Staatsrechts*, vol 1, 3rd edn (Heidelberg, CF Müller, 2003) 315 ff.

[9] J-D Kühne, 'Verfassungsvorbilder für das Grundgesetz. Von der Paulskirchenverfassung zum Grundgesetz' in H-P Schneider (ed), *Das Grundgesetz in interdisziplinärer Betrachtung* (Baden-Baden, Nomos, 2001) 57 ff.

[10] T Giegerich, *Europäische Verfassung und deutsche Verfassung im transnationalen Konstitutionalisierungsprozess: Wechselseitige Rezeption, konstitutionelle Evolution und föderale Verflechtung* (Berlin, Springer, 2003) 1125 ff; T Rensmann, *Wertordnung und Verfassung. Das Grundgesetz im Kontext grenzüberschreitender Konstitutionalisierung* (Tübingen, Mohr Siebeck, 2007).

[11] B Pieroth, 'Amerikanischer Verfassungsexport nach Deutschland' (1989) *Neue Juristische Wochenschrift* 1333; H Steinberger, 'American Constitutionalism and German Constitutional Development' in L Henkin and AJ Rosenthal (eds), *Constitutionalism and Rights* (New York, Columbia University Press, 1990) 199, 212 ff; M Kau, *United States Supreme Court und Bundesverfassungsgericht. Die Bedeutung des United States Supreme Court für die Errichtung und Fortentwicklung des Bundesverfassungsgerichts* (Berlin, Springer, 2007).

[12] A constitutional amendment requires a two-thirds vote both in the Federal Parliament ('Bundestag') and the Federal Council ('Bundesrat'), a 'second chamber' composed of representatives of the Länder

(1968), reduced the standard of human rights (Art 10: secrecy of communication, 1968, 13: inviolability of home, 1998, and 16a: right to asylum, 1993), set up detailed provisions for European integration (Art 23 BL, 1992) and reorganised competencies between the federal and state level (2006, 2009).

The roots of the GFCC—as those of the Basic Law in general—reach back to at least the 1849 so-called Constitution of the 'Paulskirche',[13] in which an Imperial Court was envisaged that would have possessed powerful competencies in some way similar to those of the GFCC, including a variant of a constitutional complaint (§ 126).[14] After the failure of republicanism in 1849 the Constitution of the unified German Empire of 1871 did not feature judicial review; constitutional disputes were to be resolved politically. Under the Constitution of the Weimar Republic of 1919, the first valid democratic Constitution in Germany, the State Tribunal possessed the competency to decide institutional and federal issues whereas the Imperial Court had the final word on ordinary cases. The latter even usurped judicial review of federal law by means of judicial interpretation of the Constitution;[15] the consequent jurisprudence does not justify calling it a constitutional court, though.

To overcome the deficiencies of former German federal supreme courts concerning judicial review and, moreover, to install a veto player checking Parliament's and the government's powers to secure individual and minority rights, the framers of the German Basic Law of 1949 invented a specialised and powerful constitutional court. It was designed to be equally part of the judiciary (Art 92 BL) and at the same time independent of all the other judicial branches,[16] exclusively possessing the power of *federal* judicial review: its declarations of (un)constitutionality and nullity share the validity of Acts of Parliament.[17] Since it took almost two years to adopt the necessary Federal Constitutional Court Act (hereinafter FCCA), the GFCC could not commence its work in Karlsruhe, a placid town in the southwest of Germany, until 1951. The GFCC is composed of two senates equally equipped with eight judges, sharing mutual jurisdiction:[18] although originally the first senate was supposed to judge on individual rights issues and the second senate on institutional cases, the workload caused by constitutional complaints has led to a shift in the division of labour over the years of the Court's existence, with more individual rights cases appearing on the docket of the second senate.[19]

---

governments, which has been achieved in the last 60 years by compromises of the big German parties—the two Christian Parties and the Social Democrats. If the Green Party can uphold its electoral approval, it will advance as the fourth player in the amendment game.

[13] The Constitution is named after the Church in which the national assembly sat from 1848 to 1849.

[14] For the following see U Scheuner, 'Die Überlieferung der deutschen Staatsgerichtsbarkeit im 19. und 20. Jahrhundert' in C Starck (ed), *Bundesverfassungsgericht und Grundgesetz. Festgabe aus Anlaß des 25 jährigen Bestehens des Bundesverfassungsgerichts*, vol 1 (Tübingen, Mohr 1976) 1.

[15] RGZ (official case collection of the Imperial Court) 111, 320, 322 f (1925).

[16] Cf arts 94 and 95 BL (www.gesetze-im-internet.de/englisch_gg/index.html) and see § 1(1) Federal Constitutional Court Act (www.iuscomp.org/gla/statutes/BVerfGG.htm).

[17] Art 94(2) BL; § 31(2) FCCA.

[18] In case of conflict between the two senates' jurisprudence the plenary of the Court decides the issue, § 16 FCCA.

[19] See § 14 FCCA and the current allocation of business, www.bundesverfassungsgericht.de/organisation/geschaeftsverteilung_2011.html.

B. The GFCC's Jurisdiction

The jurisdiction of the GFCC covers a wide array of constitutional issues and competencies which the Court itself held unprecedented.[20] In number and impact, the most important proceeding is without a doubt the constitutional complaint. It allows individuals to challenge the constitutionality of individual public acts (mostly court decisions) as well as parliamentary statutes directly by which they have to be affected personally:[21] in both cases the GFCC is competent to nullify an Act of Parliament. Since 1951, the GFCC has decided over 160,000 constitutional complaints; now amounting to about 6,000 decisions per year. Only by a division of labour between the senate and judicial chambers can this workload be mastered. Although less than three per cent of all constitutional complaints lead to a positive result (for the complainants),[22] the jurisprudence triggered by these proceedings has determined and changed the face of the German legal system. In the landmark case 'Lüth', the basic rights guaranteed in the Constitution were made applicable as guiding principles for all activities of the state as well as indirectly in private law cases.[23] Moreover, in the course of 60 years, the GFCC has 'invented' many individual rights not originally enshrined in the Constitution, mainly in the field of personal and procedural rights.[24] It has even established a right—procedurally and substantially—directed against the consent of Germany's institutions to the creation of a transnational state.[25]

Other powerful tools in the hands of the GFCC vis-a-vis Parliament are the proceedings of concrete and abstract judicial review. Through concrete judicial review the GFCC evaluates statutes that are referred to it by a lower court which is convinced that the law it has to apply to decide the pending case is unconstitutional (Art 100 (1) BL). The right to call on the GFCC to decide on the constitutionality of statutes[26] independent of litigation (abstract judicial review) is confined to certain important institutional bodies: the federal government, the federal states' governments and one quarter of the federal Parliament (Art 93 (1) No 2 BL). Thus, a strong political minority in the federal Parliament, which might even be strong enough to govern a federal

---

[20] 'Die Institution des Bundesverfassungsgerichts und der Umfang der Verfassungsgerichtsbarkeit, wie sie durch das Grundgesetz geschaffen worden sind, haben kein Vorbild' (BVerfGE 2, 79, 84 [1952]); see also BVerfGE 114, 121, 159 (2005). R Wahl, 'Das Bundesverfassungsgericht im europäischen und internationalen Umfeld' (B37-38/2001) *Aus Politik und Zeitgeschichte* 45. For an extensive overview in English see EL Barnstedt, 'Judicial Activism in the Practice of the German Federal Constitutional Court: Is the GFCC an Activist Court?' (2007) *Juridica International* 38; DP Kommers and RA Miller, 'Das Bundesverfassungsgericht: Procedure, Practice and Policy of the German Constitutional Court (2008) *The Journal of Comparative Law* 194, 200.
[21] Art 93(1) No 4a BL; § 13 No 8a, 90 ff FCCA. However, since 1969, the proceeding is guaranteed by the Constitution.
[22] Statistics of the GFCC, www.bverfg.de/organisation/gb2010/A-I-1.html.
[23] BVerfGE 7, 198 (1958). See also K Hesse, 'Stufen der Entwicklung der deutschen Verfassungsgerichtsbarkeit' (1998) 46 *Jahrbuch des öffentlichen Rechts der Gegenwart* 1, 7 ff; J Limbach, *The Effects of the Jurisdiction of the German Federal Constitutional Court*, EU Working Paper Law No 99/5 (Badia Fiesolana, San Domenico (FI), European University Institute, 1999) 10 ff.
[24] Eg BVerfGE 65, 1 (1985)—the right to self-determination concerning data processing; BVerfGE 26, 66 (1969)—the right to a fair trial.
[25] BVerfGE 89, 155 (1993)—Maastricht; BVerfGE 123, 267 (2009)—Lisbon.
[26] Not only can the conformity of federal statutes with the Constitution be tested, but also that of federal state law with federal law and federal constitutional law, art 93(1) No 2 BL.

state, can challenge a statute before the GFCC after it has been passed against its will thus handing over the decision of a political conflict—already made—to the court.[27]

Other politically sensitive proceedings are the federal disputes (Art 93 (1) No 2a, 3, 4 BL)—between the federal and state level as well as between states—and disputes between the highest federal institutions, mostly between Parliament and government and between parts of the Parliament and the body itself (Art 93 (1) No 1 BL). The GFCC's jurisprudence has added rights and duties to the text of the Constitution through these proceedings, too. It has, for example, constructed a principle of federal comity between federal and state institutions, obliging them to at least inform respectively to hear the case of other institutions that are affected by their actions or even to coordinate the behaviour of all affected institutions.[28] Before ordering an armed operation by the army, the government has to ask for Parliament's consent, a right of the Parliament unheard of before the decision of the GFCC, partially invoked by a parliamentary group whose party was at the same time a member of the federal government.[29] The GFCC—in deciding institutional disputes—has not only as in this case strengthened the role of the Parliament itself and hence the right of the parliamentary majority, but has also determined minimum rights of individual representatives[30] and minority groups in Parliament, for example, in investigation committees.[31]

In the field of the so-called 'militant' democracy, the Basic Law allows public authorities to fight enemies of constitutional values even with measures severely infringing on individual and political rights. This power is balanced by the institutionalisation of only a few proceedings defining very narrow situations which allow for fighting constitutional enemies, and by concentrating the ultimate decision in the republic's highest judicial body: here also, the GFCC was endowed with exclusive jurisdiction. The proceeding of forfeiture of basic rights (Art 18 BL) can only be invoked by the federal Parliament, the federal or a state government,[32] which has so far occurred four times—pertaining to right wing extremists—although never leading to a forfeiture. Comparatively rarely—eight times—have authorities tried to ban political parties through the proceeding provided by Art 21 para 2 of the BL. The federal Parliament, the federal chamber of Länder governments and the federal government can only file an application at the GFCC claiming that a political party is endangering the constitutional core values and the political system itself and therefore has to be dissolved.[33] Political parties been only twice been declared unconstitutional: the Socialist Reich Party in 1952,[34] and the Communist Party of Germany in 1956.[35]

The Basic Law also regulates the unlikely event that the chiefs of state turn against the Constitution. Although an impeachment may not be directed against the federal chancellor, he or she can be removed by a vote electing a new chancellor

---

[27] DP Kommers, 'The Federal Constitutional Court in the German Political System' (1994) 26 *Comparative Political Studies* 470, 474.
[28] Eg, BVerfGE 12, 205 (1960)—Second German Television.
[29] Eg, BVerfGE 90, 286 (1994)—out of area missions.
[30] Eg, BVerfGE 80, 188 (1989)—Wüppesahl.
[31] Eg, BVerfGE 105, 197 (2002)—investigation committee.
[32] § 36 FCCA.
[33] § 43, 46 FCCA. The GFCC has exclusive competence for political parties. Organisations that are not political parties in the narrow sense may be prohibited by departments of government.
[34] BVerfGE 2, 1.
[35] BVerfGE 5, 85.

(Art 67 BL), the so-called constructive vote of no confidence. However, the federal president, fulfilling mainly representative functions but also endowed with some creative, legislative and emergency competencies (Art 54 ff BL), may be impeached at the GFCC if he or she deliberately breaches the Constitution or federal statutes (Art 61 BL). Since the quorum amounts to a two-thirds vote in both federal chambers and since the office is in general highly esteemed, it comes as no surprise that an impeachment claim has never been made.[36]

C. The GFCC's Position in the German Political System

It has been stated that the BL places the GFCC 'at the epicenter of the Federal Republic's political system'.[37] The wide competencies of the court and also its self-conception indeed make it a strong player in the German political arena—it acts as the ultimate arbitrator of institutional and public conflicts in general;[38] it is the ultimate body to ascertain the constitutionality of Acts of Parliament and, furthermore, constitutional amendment statutes; it has even attained a position where it appears to be the sole interpreter of the Constitution: 'Henceforth, the Basic Law is virtually valid as the German Federal Constitutional Court interprets it',[39] as Rudolf Smend, an important German scholar of the twentieth century, put it. Even where, formally, it does not possess ultimate authority, the GFCC has reserved for itself the power to determine the threshold where the German Constitution takes precedence over transnational law and jurisprudence despite their general primacy.[40]

Taking into account the extrapolations of the constitutional text by the GFCC—often expected by the public and politicians alike—it cannot be denied that the GFCC exerts influence in the political arena.[41] In addition, it needs to be mentioned that the GFCC at times hands out detailed requirements the legislative has to fulfill when not nullifying provisions but rather declaring them incompatible with the

---

[36] Additional competencies of the GFCC not mentioned here can be found in Art 93 BL and § 13 FCCA.
[37] DP Kommers, 'The Federal Constitutional Court in the German Political System' (1994) 26 *Comparative Political Studies* 470, 471.
[38] See only R Scholz, 'Fünfzig Jahre Bundesverfassungsgericht' (B37-38/2001) *Aus Politik und Zeitgeschichte* 6.
[39] 'Das Grundgesetz gilt nunmehr praktisch so, wie das Bundesverfassungsgericht es auslegt', R Smend, 'Das Bundesverfassungsgericht' in R Smend, *Staatsrechtliche Abhandlungen und andere Aufsätze*, 3rd edn (Berlin, Duncker & Humblot, 1994) 581, 582.
[40] ECHR: BVerfGE 111, 307 (2004)—Görgülü; European Law: most recently BVerfGE 123, 267 (2009)—Lisbon. The status of European and European human rights law differs in the German legal system: the latter does not hold constitutional rank; the former supersedes all German law. The conflict of substantial jurisdiction is thus more eminent in the realm of European law.
[41] G Gawron and R Rogowski, *Die Wirkung des Bundesverfassungsgerichtes* (Baden-Baden, Nomos, 2007) 168; A Rinken, 'The Federal Constitutional Court and the German Political System' in T Gawron and R Rogowski (eds), *Constitutional Courts in Comparison. The US Supreme Court and the German Federal Constitutional Court* (New York and Oxford, Berghahn Books, 2002) 55; L Helms, 'The Federal Constitutional Court: Institutionalising Judicial Review in a Semisovereign Democracy in L Helms (ed), *Institutions and Institutional Change in the Federal Republic of Germany* (Basingstoke, Macmillan, 2000) 84. Differentiated theoretical models of influence are advanced and tested by C Landfried, 'Judicial Policy-Making in Germany: The Federal Constitutional Court (1992) 15 *West European Politics* 50; G Vanberg, *The Politics of Constitutional Review in Germany* (Cambridge, Cambridge University Press, 2005).

Constitution and valid until the legislature has produced a constitutional result.[42] This condition explains why the GFCC combines its demands with a fixed time limit for the legislature. The latter sometimes even waits for a GFCC judgment before adopting legal changes and before risking being overruled by the GFCC.[43] There does not exist a *political question* doctrine like that in US constitutionalism; nevertheless, the GFCC exercises judicial restraint in many cases; it is a truism of German constitutional law that the GFCC cannot usurp the position of the legislator.[44] Over the years, the critique of the GFCC has rarely transcended individual cases or a certain line of jurisprudence.[45] The GFCC may regularly expect its judgments to be implemented—often Parliament, when coining new laws, copies sentences out of judgments verbatim.[46] Another meaningful banality is the observation that the GFCC does not set its own agenda: neither can it initiate proceedings nor does it have the power to exercise discretion when selecting cases, comparable to the granting certiorari procedure of the US Supreme Court.[47] In sum, the GFCC may be classified as an activist court when it comes to adherence to the plain words of the Constitution, individual freedoms and parliamentary rights,[48] but nevertheless it defers to the government's assessments in issues of social and economic policy as well as external relations quite regularly.[49]

In recent years, it has been questioned whether the appointment procedure of the GFCC judges still keeps pace with the power the court exercises in the German political system. Half of the judges are elected by an electoral committee of Parliament

---

[42] See T Gawron and R Rogowski, *Die Wirkung des Bundesverfassungsgerichtes* (Baden-Baden, Nomos, 2007) 137 ff; T Gawron and R Rogowski, 'Implementation of German Federal Constitutional Court Decisions. Judicial Orders and the Federal Legislature' in T Gawron and R Rogowski (eds), *Constitutional Courts in Comparison. The US Supreme Court and the German Federal Constitutional Court* (New York and Oxford, Berghahn Books, 2002) 239 ff, also with figures of how many statutes of the German Bundestag are subject to judicial control by the GFCC. L Mammen, 'A Short Note on the German Federal Constitutional Court and its Power to Review Legislation' (2001) *European Human Rights Law Review* 433.

[43] For an example see EL Barnstedt, 'Judicial Activism in the Practice of the German Federal Constitutional Court: Is the GFCC an Activist Court?' (2007) *Juridica Internatonal* 38, 40; J Limbach, *The Effects of the Jurisdiction of the German Federal Constitutional Court*, EU Working Paper Law No 99/5 (Badia Fiesolana, San Domenico (FI), European University Institute, 1999) 19 ff.

[44] See R Scholz, 'Fünfzig Jahre Bundesverfassungsgericht' (B37-38/2001) *Aus Politik und Zeitgeschichte* 6, 13 ff.

[45] GS Schaal, 'Der "Kruzifix-Beschluss" und seine Folgen' in RC van Ooyen and M Möllers (eds), *Das Bundesverfassungsgericht im politischen System* (Wiesbaden, VS Verlag für Sozialwissenschaften, 2006) 175; RC van Ooyen, *Die Staatstheorie des Bundesverfassungsgerichts und Europa. Von Solange über Maastricht zum EU-Haftbefehl*, 2nd edn (Baden-Baden, Nomos, 2008); O Massing, *Politik als Recht—Recht als Politik. Studien zu einer Theorie der Verfassungsgerichtsbarkeit* (Baden-Baden, Nomos, 2005). Recently, M Jestaedt et al, *Das entgrenzte Gericht* (Berlin, Suhrkamp, 2011).

[46] G Gawron and R Rogowski, *Die Wirkung des Bundesverfassungsgerichtes* (Baden-Baden, Nomos, 2007) 51 ff.

[47] But see the—legally framed—admission procedure pertaining to constitutional complaints, § 93a FCCA. W Heun, Access to the German Federal Constitutional Court' in T Gawron and R Rogowski (eds), *Constitutional Courts in Comparison. The US Supreme Court and the German Federal Constitutional Court* (New York and Oxford, Berghahn Books, 2002) 125, 129 ff.

[48] Jarass argues that specialised constitutional courts are activist courts by definition, HD Jarass, 'The Impact of an Active Constitutional Court of the Dimensions or Functions of Fundamental Rights—German Experiences—in G Amato, G Braibant and E Venizelos (eds), *The Constitutional Revision in Today's Europe* (London, Esperia, 2002) 561.

[49] R Scholz, 'Fünfzig Jahre Bundesverfassungsgericht' (B37-38/2001) *Aus Politik und Zeitgeschichte* 6, 10.

and half of them by the second German Chamber, the Federal Council[50]—the necessary two-thirds vote caused the influential political parties to divide up the seats among them and agree on acceptable candidates behind closed doors. The critics call for direct election in the federal Parliament and public hearings of the candidates in order to increase the transparency and henceforth the legitimacy of the appointment procedure.[51] The overall acceptance of both the jurisprudence and the judges of the GFCC has, however, so far hindered the development of any public conviction to change the existing procedure.[52] A certain standard of quality and political independence of the candidates is ensured by a number of requirements:[53] the candidates, who can only be elected for one 12-year term, have to be 40 years of age or older and must have acquired a standard legal education. Furthermore, in each senate, at least three judges have to sit who have formerly served with a federal supreme court for at least three years.

Conspicuously, the remaining seats have often been filled not with practitioners of law—let alone attorneys—but with legal scholars. At present, eight out of 16 judges at the GFCC share a university background; thus, the minimum requirement of three former judges per senate is only exceeded by two judges in the second senate. Conversely, this appointment practice ensures a close link between constitutional justice and public law scholarship which is even furthered by the exception to the incompatibility of the office of a GFCC judge with other professions. This exception allows residing judges to lecture in law.[54] It is not uncommon that judges, especially the presidents of the GFCC, publicly give their opinions on legal issues.[55] German legal scholars have often worked as assistants at the GFCC and pleaded before the Court. They follow the jurisprudence of the GFCC closely which is widely commented on in legal journals[56]—despite disagreements in detail and principle, a sense of community among lawyers dealing with public and constitutional law issues prevails.[57] However, critics have deplored the fact that scholars defer to the interpretations and solutions of the GFCC too easily.[58] This doctrinal deference might not only be caused by the applicative identity of the discipline,[59] but perhaps also by the outlook of one day being considered a candidate for a position on the GFCC bench. Vice versa, the GFCC tends to consider, and sometimes even cite verbatim or discuss the output of (not only)

---

[50] Art 94(1) BL; § 5 ff FCCA.

[51] J Montag, 'Transparenz und Legitimität: notwendige Reform der Wahl der Richterinnen und Richter zum Bundesverfassungsgericht' (2008) 44 *Recht und Politik* 139; C Landfried, 'Es fehlen Frauen und Transparenz' *Frankfurter Allgemeine Zeitung* (27 August 2009) 8.

[52] In favour of the existing procedure B Zypries, 'The Basic Law at 60—Politics and the Federal Constitutional Court' (2010) 11 *German Law Journal* 87, 96 f.

[53] § 2, 3, 4 FCCA.

[54] § 3(4) FCCA.

[55] Eg A Voßkuhle, interview, *Süddeutsche Zeitung* (18.10.2010).

[56] See the collection of P Häberle, *Kommentierte Verfassungsrechtsprechung* (Königstein, Athenäum, 1979).

[57] DP Kommers, 'The Federal Constitutional Court in the German Political System' (1994) 26 *Comparative Political Studies* 470, 484.

[58] B Schlink, 'Die Entthronung der Staatsrechtswissenschaft durch die Verfassungsgerichtsbarkeit' (1989) 28 *Der Staat* 161.

[59] See only A von Arnauld, 'Die Wissenschaft vom Öffentlichen Recht nach einer Öffnung für sozialwissenschaftliche Theorie' in A Funke and J Lüdemann (eds), *Öffentliches Recht und Wissenschaftstheorie* (Tübingen, Mohr Siebeck, 2009) 65.

German scholarship extensively: on average, the GFCC has cited doctrinal sources 10 times per published decision in the last decade. Only its own jurisprudence is referred to more frequently, approximately 40 times per decision in the last 10 years.[60]

D. The GFCC's Style of Reasoning

The high percentage of scholars on the bench has surely influenced the style of reasoning of the GFCC. It is thus consistently and widely acclaimed for its learned, doctrinal and solemn style.[61] Although the judges have had the opportunity to add separate opinions to senate judgments since 1971, they are trying to convey objectivity[62] and clarity although not achieving the Cartesian precision of French judicial reasoning. In contrast, judgments quite often deliver complete lectures on constitutional law and connected issues of political and societal theory, sometimes comprising the size of textbooks.[63] The GFCC does not shy away from extensive *obiter dicta*, the *dictum* in the Aviation Security Act case being a well-known example.[64] The appeal to objectivity is strengthened by the extensive citation of own (established) precedent: the GFCC frequently refers to its 'established jurisprudence'. Thus, the GFCC is able to convey a consistent totality and systematic closure of German constitutional law, its jurisprudence being part and parcel of it.[65] This commitment to objectivity and systematisation is deeply rooted in German idealism and legal culture of the nineteenth century.[66]

Many observers notice an eclectic usage of interpretative tools by the GFCC.[67] This corresponds to statements of former judges that the constitutional arguments applied by the judges follow the peculiarities of the individual case.[68] Since the beginning of its case law the GFCC has emphasised that it construes norms according to the

---

[60] 3,132 and 12,818 hits out of 308 judgments; for the statistical universe see III.A.

[61] See, eg, K Zweigert, 'Duktus der Rechtsprechung des Ersten Senats des Bundesverfassungsgerichts und einige Erinnerungen an seine Anfangszeit' in Bundesverfassungsgericht (ed), *Das Bundesverfassungsgericht: 1951–1971* (Karlsruhe, CF Müller, 1971) 95, 114 f.

[62] Displaying objectivity, at a distance from politics, is one of the resources of the GFCC's acceptance, U Kranenpohl, 'Die gesellschaftlichen Legitimationsgrundlagen der Verfassungsrechtsprechung, oder: Darum lieben die Deutschen Karlsruhe' (2009) 56 *Zeitschrift für Politik* 436, 440 ff.

[63] An extreme example is the judgment on the Communist Party of Germany, BVerfGE 5, 85 (1956), which is more than 300 pages long. See also DP Kommers, 'Germany: Balancing Rights and Duties' in J Goldsworthy (ed), *Interpreting Constitutions: A Comparative Study* (Oxford, Oxford University Press, 2007) 161, 210.

[64] BVerfGE 115, 118, 151 (2006).

[65] DP Kommers, 'Germany: Balancing Rights and Duties' in J Goldsworthy (ed), *Interpreting Constitutions: A Comparative Study* (Oxford, Oxford University Press, 2007) 161, 207 f, traces this orientation to Germany's civil law tradition.

[66] See, eg, P Lerche, 'Stil und Methode der verfassungsrichterlichen Entscheidungspraxis' in P Badura and H Dreier (eds), *Festschrift 50 Jahre Bundesverfassungsgericht* (Tübingen, Mohr Siebeck, 2001) 333.

[67] E-W Böckenförde, 'Die Methoden der Verfassungsinterpretation' (1976) *Neue Juristische Wochenschrift* 2089; P Lerche, 'Stil und Methode der verfassungsrichterlichen Entscheidungspraxis' in P Badura and H Dreier (eds), *Festschrift 50 Jahre Bundesverfassungsgericht* (Tübingen, Mohr Siebeck, 2001) 333.

[68] EG Mahrenholz, 'Probleme der Verfassungsauslegung. Verfassungsinterpretation aus praktischer Sicht' in H-P Schneider et al (eds), *Verfassungsrecht zwischen Wissenschaft und Richterkunst. Konrad Hesse zum 70. Geburtstag* (Heidelberg, Müller Jur Verl, 1990, 53, 60). U Kranenpohl, 'Die Bedeutung von Interpretationsmethoden und Dogmatik in der Entscheidungspraxis des Bundesverfassungsgerichts' (2009) 48 *Der Staat* 385, 392.

objective will of the lawgiver expressed by the wording and context whereas the *travaux préparatoires* only play a supportive role.[69] Although this positioning has paved the way for giving weight to the purpose of a norm when interpreting it in many cases, still, it cannot be stated that the GFCC focuses on certain interpretational ideologies; beyond the fact that recognised legal interpretation methods play a certain role, the picture is rather blurry. The darkness is complete in the field of comparative reasoning: the GFCC has never resolved the status and method of the comparative argument in its jurisprudence. One minor exception can be seen in a recent judgment in which the GFCC adjusted its position on preventive detention in light of the new jurisprudence of the European Court of Human Rights. Here, the GFCC compared the method of importing elements of international law to the method of comparative constitutional interpretation[70] thereby implicitly accepting it as part of constitutional interpretation. Apart from this general commitment, one is forced to look at the practice of comparative reasoning in order to learn more about it.

III. EXPLICIT CITATION OF FOREIGN PRECEDENT BY THE GFCC

Research on the comparative reasoning of the GFCC has occurred rarely in the first decades of the existence of the court.[71] In general, comparative research in Germany tends to concentrate on private law, in any case. Consequently, German scholars have looked more closely at comparative reasoning in private law courts.[72] Yet, the comparative activities by the GFCC appear to raise more interest notably in the course of the last few years;[73] two former judges of the GFCC have even

---

[69] BVerfGE 1, 299 (1951).
[70] Judgment of 5 May 2011, 2 BvR 2365/09, para 92.
[71] B Aubin, 'Die rechtsvergleichende Konkretisierung von Kontrollmaßstäben des Verfassungsrechts und des Kollisionsrechts in der deutschen Rechtsprechung' in E von Caemmerer and K Zweigert (eds), *Deutsche Landesreferate zum VII. Internationalen Kongreß für Rechtsvergleichung in Uppsala 1966* (Berlin, De Gruyter, 1967) 100; B Aubin, 'Die rechtsvergleichende Interpretation autonom-internen Rechts in der deutschen Rechtsprechung' (1970) 34 *RabelsZ* 458, 469; JM Mössner, 'Rechtsvergleichung und Verfassungsrechtsprechung' (1974) 99 *Archiv des öffentlichen Rechts der Gegenwart* 193.
[72] See H Dölle, 'Der Beitrag der Rechtsvergleichung zum deutschen Recht' in E von Caemmerer and E Friesenhahn and R Lange (eds), *Hundert Jahre Deutsches Rechtsleben. Festschrift zum Hundertjährigen Bestehen des Deutschen Juristentages 1860–1960* (Karlsruhe, CF Müller, 1960) 19; B Aubin, 'Die rechtsvergleichende Interpretation autonom-internen Rechts in der deutschen Rechtsprechung' (1970) 34 *Rabels Zeitschrift für ausländisches und internationales Privatrecht* 458ff; B Grossfeld, 'Vom Beitrag der Rechtsvergleichung zum deutschen Recht' (1984) 184 *Archiv der civilistischen Praxis* 289; H Kötz, 'Der Bundesgerichtshof und die Rechtsvergleichung' in Heldrich and Hopt (eds), *50 Jahre Bundesgerichtshof, Festgabe der Wissenschaft*, vol 2 (München, Beck, 2000) 825 ff; J Bornkamm, 'The German Supreme Court: An Actor in the Global Conversation of High Courts' (2004) 39 *Texas International Law Journal* 415; H Unberath, 'Comparative Law in the German Courts' in G Canivet, M Andenas and D Fairgrieve (eds), *Comparative Law before the Courts* (London, BIICL, 2004) 307.
[73] N Oberheiden, *Typologie und Grenzen des richterlichen Verfassungsvergleichs* (Baden-Baden, Nomos, 2011); H Sauer, 'Verfassungsvergleichung durch das Bundesverfassungsgericht' (2010) 18 *Journal für Rechtspolitik* 194; A Kaiser, 'Verfassungsvergleichung durch das Bundesverfassungsgericht' (2010) 18 *Journal für Rechtspolitik* 203; J Schwarze, *Zukunftsaussichten für das Europäische Öffentliche Recht: Analyse im Lichte der jüngeren Rechtsentwicklung in den Mitgliedstaaten und der Europäischen Union* (Baden-Baden, Nomos, 2010) 42 ff; C Walter, 'Decentralised Constitutionalisation in National and International Courts: Reflections on Comparative Law as an Approach to Public Law' in A Halpin and V Roeben (eds), *Theorising the Global Order* (Oxford and Portland, Oregon, Hart, 2009) 253; AM Cárdenas Paulsen, *Über die Rechtsvergleichung am Bundesverfassungsgericht* (Hamburg, Kovač,

published on the issue.[74] Thus, the wave of ongoing international discourse on the intermingling of legal orders slowly but surely reaches German shores. Yet, the 2009 dissertation of Cárdenas Paulsen appears to be the only one applying quantitative methods. Overall, it seems justifiable to redo her 'experiment', firstly because in (empirical) science the validity of results is based on their verifiability. While Cárdenas Paulsen more or less relies on a database keyword scan,[75] I want to present the results of a page by page inquiry. Of course, both methods share vulnerabilities, although opposing ones.[76] Secondly, this study analyses several different and additional parameters missing in Cárdenas Paulsen's study, such as the number of total citations of foreign precedent and the ratio of institutional cases.

A. Choices of Method

The GFCC has issued over 164,000 decisions from its establishment in 1951 up to the end of 2010.[77] Due to accessibility restraints and limitations inherent both in human nature and data processing, this analysis is obviously incapable of tracing and tracking citations of foreign precedent in *all* of these decisions. Thus, one has to pick and choose: since the overwhelming majority of these decisions pertains to chamber decisions,[78] which generally follow established case law, it is even warranted to confine the research data to decisions of the two senates and the plenary of the Court, which still comprise the large number of approximately 7,000 cases from 1951 to 2010. The GFCC has obliged itself to publish (almost) exactly this selection of decisions—including provisional measures—in its official case collection, yet nevertheless allows itself to refrain from publishing decisions on an individual basis.[79] Unpublished decisions are mainly decisions of minor importance. As this study is based on 'manual' research it seems justifiable to rely on the case collection of the GFCC covering 3,105 decisions published in—until 2010—126 volumes of approximately

2009); A Nußberger, 'Wer zitiert wen?—Zur Funktion von Zitaten bei der Herausbildung gemeineuropäischen Verfassungsrechts' (2006) *Juristenzeitung* 763; U Drobnig, 'The Use of Foreign Law by German Courts' in U Drobnig and S van Erp (eds), *The Use of Comparative Law by Courts* (The Hague, Kluwer Law International, 1999) 127.

[74] B-O Bryde, 'The Constitutional Judge and the International Constitutionalist Dialogue' in B Markesinis and J Fedtke (eds), *Judicial Recourse to Foreign Law* (London, UCL Press 2006) 295; W Hoffmann-Riem, 'Bundesverfassungsgericht (Constitutional Court) Germany' (2005) 3 *International Journal of Constitutional Law* 556.

[75] AM Cárdenas Paulsen, *Über die Rechtsvergleichung am Bundesverfassungsgericht* (Hamburg, Kovač, 2009) 6.

[76] A keyword scan only sees what the keywords can find. On the other hand, when 'manual' research is conducted by one person alone, weary eyes may overlook a word among the thousands of others they scan through. Moreover, counting by a person and not by a machine is susceptible to subjective evaluation. The decision BVerfGE 1, 97, 100 (1951), where the case law of the 'constitutional court (sic) of the United States' is mentioned, might serve as an example. The question is: does this count as a citation of foreign precedent?

[77] See Annual Statistics of the GFCC for the Fiscal Year of 2010, www.bverfg.de/organisation/gb2010/A-I-5.html. The yearly figure has risen to about 6,000 decisions.

[78] Approximately 85%, see www.bverfg.de/organisation/gb2010/A-I-5.html.

[79] § 31 paras 1 and 2 of the Rules of Procedure of the GFCC. It is stated in para 3 that important chamber decisions can be included in the collection: those will also form part of this study, since they have been selected as decisions of significance.

400 pages.[80] For reasons of manageability, this study will confine the search for empirical data to three decades of the jurisprudence of the GFCC: the formative period of the 1950s, the phase of governance optimism, political change and accusations of political intervention in the 1970s,[81] and finally the last 10 years of constitutional development. Furthermore, decisions relating to formal issues, such as (self-)recusation, are excluded from this analysis due to supposed irrelevance for the purposes of the overall project. Thus, this study is still able to capture almost half of the overall statistical universe considered relevant.[82]

B. Formal Analysis

Only a fairly small number of judgments of the GFCC actually cite foreign precedent, not surprisingly, though, since comparative reasoning counts as an auxiliary instrument in the toolkit of constitutional interpretation.[83] In only 32 of the 1,351 cases under review here can foreign jurisprudence be detected, which represents 2.4 per cent of all decisions. The ratio in the 1950s corresponds to the overall average of 2.4 per cent, declining to 1.5 per cent in the 1970s and finally climbing up to a remarkable 4.2 per cent in the 2000s (see Table 1).

Table 1: Ratio of Cases With and Without Foreign Precedent (1950s, 1970s, 2000s)

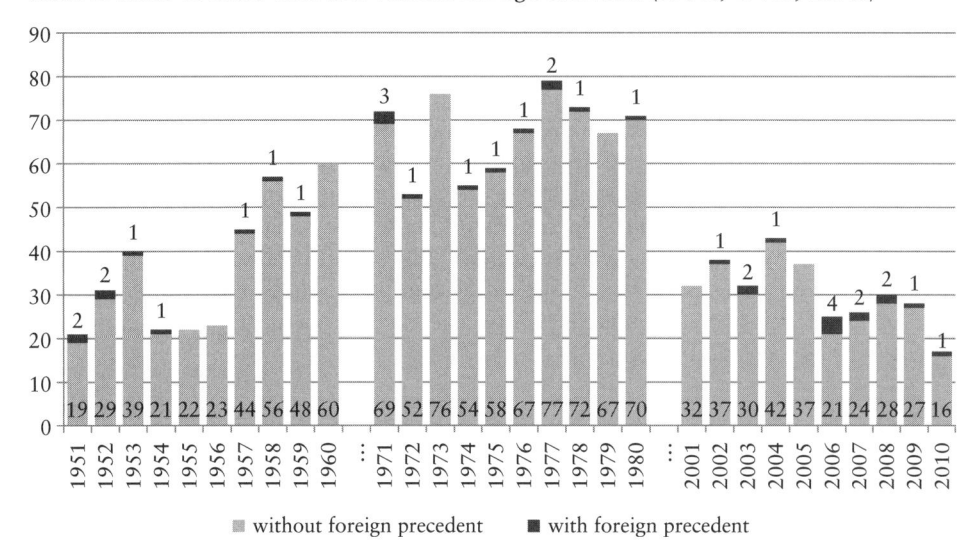

[80] This implies normatively that the decisions by the GFCC to exclude from resp. to include rulings in the official publication are generally trustworthy. The last decision covered by this inquiry was published on 21 July 2010.
[81] PE Quint, '60 Years of the Basic Law and its Interpretation: An American Perspective' (2009) 57 *Jahrbuch des öffentlichen Rechts der Gegenwart* 1, 7.
[82] 1,351 decisions are included in this study.
[83] U Drobnig, 'Rechtsvergleichung in der Deutschen Rechtsprechung' (1986) 50 *Rabels Zeitschrift für ausländisches und internationales Privatrecht* 610, 625, analysing the practice of German courts. For a wide panorama of uses of comparative law by courts see B Markesinis and J Fedtke, *Judicial Recourse to Foreign Law. A New Source of Inspiration?* (London, UCL Press, 2006) 109 ff.

i. The 'Bowl' Thesis

Two conclusions could follow from this account, the first being that one may prima facie legitimately call the GFCC a rather introverted court as far as the use of foreign precedent is concerned. Secondly, the three decades seem to epitomise evolutionary stages of 'Western' or, to be more precise, many European constitutional courts erected in the twentieth century. In the first phase of their existence, often after a dramatic change in the political system, young constitutional courts need to accumulate symbolic capital in their new and insecure institutional environment:[84] their task is to develop recognition, acceptance, and authority among and towards other political institutions and courts as well as the general public. Supporting one's own argument with established authority may be one way to help create a reputation in its own right. Another reason is a trite and pragmatic one: there simply exists a lack of the GFCC's own precedent which is able to answer constitutional questions at hand. Thus, it comes as no surprise that in the 1950s—also because other constitutional court siblings were yet to be founded—the GFCC mostly cites the Swiss Federal Court and the US Supreme Court (see Table 5), already at that time both courts with long traditions.[85]

After having established its own authority as well as convincing lines of precedent, the figures of foreign inspiration ought to drop, which they actually do in the case of the GFCC in the 1970s. Globally, the 1990s and especially the first decade of the twenty-first century are defined by an increasing transnationalisation of politics and law which is reflected in the jurisprudence of constitutional courts. Not only the national legal orders, but additionally the respective constitutional (and supreme) courts (need to) open up towards transnational legal matters. Accordingly, more international precedent is cited and considered, which also holds true for the GFCC: while no transnational sources at all can be found in the 1950s decisions considered, more than a tenth of the 2000s judgments includes international or European sources.[86] This tendency to transcend national borders spills over to the foreign figures. At least a moderate rise in the number of citations takes place: both absolutely and relatively.[87] Thus, the 'slope' thesis mentioned cannot be maintained but rather has to be adjusted.

ii. A More Differentiated Picture

The statistical 'bowl', a strong beginning, attenuation in the middle, and the overall long-term trend of rising willingness to consider foreign precedent, may also be

---

[84] For international courts see M Nunner, *Kooperation internationaler Gerichte* (Tübingen, Mohr Siebeck, 2009).

[85] B Markesinis and J Fedtke, *Judicial Recourse to Foreign Law. A New Source of Inspiration?* (London, UCL Press, 2006) 200 ff, suggest that many of the judges sitting back then were émigrés during the time of the Nazi rule and therefore brought back ideas inspired from abroad.

[86] 36 of 308. See also the openness towards international law (here: ECHR) in BVerfGE 74, 358, 370 (1987) and BVerfGE 92, 91 (1995).

[87] K-P Sommermann, 'Funktionen und Methoden der Grundrechtsvergleichung' in D Merten and H-J Papier (eds), *Handbuch der Grundrechte in Deutschland und Europa, vol 1: Entwicklung und Grundlagen* (Heidelberg, CF Müller, 2004) 631, para 86, thinks this development creates the main source of willingness to consider foreign law.

witnessed in principle when one looks at the annual citations by the GFCC prima facie (Table 2). Yet, looking closer, one gets a rather differentiated picture that is capable of contesting the two starting conclusions—the GFCC as an ignorant court and its citation practice reflecting the life phases of a typical European constitutional court. One might refrain from bluntly calling the GFCC an introverted court looking at the citation peaks in 1977 and 2006 and also taking into account its consideration of transnational and scholarly sources.

In addition, annual citations reveal that the GFCC does not steadily and regularly cite foreign case law as the long-term trend promises; instead, years of silence follow years of 'babel' talk (eg, 2003, 2004, and 2005). Some even get the impression that the GFCC cites foreign precedent rather coincidentally, depending on the qualities of the individual judge or the exigencies of the day.[88] However, one has to take into account that not every case at hand qualifies for comparison: the GFCC is dependent on the cases that are brought before it. Moreover, some peculiarities of German constitutional law, for example, established lines of case law or special proceedings such as forfeiture, do not lend themselves to outward experience automatically.[89] Furthermore, supposedly, other non-ordinary interpretative methods will vary as well.

It is harder to give explanations to a silent court—since it can be either the fault of unwillingness or inability—than to illuminate how the massive peaks in the 1970s and 2000s[90] came about. The latter is due to a proceeding pursuant to Art 100 para 2 BL in which the GFCC has the exclusive competence to identify rules of international law the task of which is fulfilled—in accordance with Art 38 para 1 lit d Statute of the ICJ—by not only looking at international case law, but also at other national precedent. Since international, not national, constitutional law is the trajectory of judicial argument here, one should not overestimate the importance of these statistical outliers of foreign national precedent.

Although the impression of a slowly but steadily rising long-term trend might be deceptive, the other two elements of the 'bowl' thesis cannot be rebuked that easily. In the 1950s, and especially in the opening year of the practice of the court, the GFCC looked abroad to help reduce the indeterminacy of German constitutional matters.[91] The above-mentioned international law proceedings before the GFCC and the unsolicited citations of foreign national case law in matters of European law[92] support the other half of the 'bowl' thesis in that the GFCC is bound to lift its constitutional curtain in transnational law contexts, in the aftermath of which a spill-over to citing foreign national precedent can be noticed. A by-product of the quest to see how other courts deal with similar transnational legal problems is the

---

[88] A Kaiser, 'Verfassungsvergleichung durch das Bundesverfassungsgericht' (2010) 18 *Journal für Rechtspolitik* 203, 204; B Markesinis and J Fedtke, *Judicial Recourse to Foreign Law. A New Source of Inspiration?* (London, UCL Press, 2006) 78.
[89] See also A Kaiser, 'Verfassungsvergleichung durch das Bundesverfassungsgericht' (2010) 18 *Journal für Rechtspolitik* 203, 206.
[90] BVerfGE 46, 342 (1977), BVerfGE 109, 13; 109, 38 (2003); BVerfGE 117, 141 (2006).
[91] BVerfGE 1, 97; 1, 44 (1950).
[92] BVerfGE 118, 79 (2007); BVerfGE 123, 267 (2009).

increasing respect for international cooperation acknowledging other players in the same game.[93]

Table 2: Number of Citations of Foreign Precedent by the GFCC (1950s, 1970s, 2000s)

— no of precedents cited
— no of total citations (including repeated citations of the same precedent)

iii. Distorted Ratios

Both human rights and institutional regulations, such as those concerning balance of power or issues of federalism, are suited for comparison since they are indeterminate in nature and appear in many other countries in more or less similar form.[94] By looking at the figures of how often the GFCC cites foreign case law in those areas, one might get a hint about the issues for which the GFCC holds comparative reasoning more appropriate. At first sight, human rights issues are more often turned to when looking across borders. However, blatantly in the 2000s, but also noticeable in the 1950s and 1970s, comparison takes place in comparatively more institutional cases compared to their percentage of the overall caseload (see Tables 3.1, 3.2, 3.3). While every fifth decision in the 2000s is mainly of institutional interest, institutional cases make up almost half of all decisions citing foreign precedent.[95] However, to my mind, this is not due to a shift of focus by the GFCC in the arena of comparative law. Many

---

[93] See also A von Arnauld, 'Public International Law and the Role of Federal Courts in Germany' in E Lagrange et al (eds), *The Practice of International Law in France and Germany—Les pratiques comparées du droit international en France et en Allemagne* (Leiden, Brill Publishers, 2012).

[94] L Pegoraro and P Damiani, Comparative Law in the Judgments of Constitutional Courts' in AM Rabello and A Zanotti (eds), *Developments in European, Italian and Israeli Law* (Milano, A Giuffrè, 2001) 131, 134 ff; A Barak, 'Comparison in Public Law' in B Markesinis and J Fedtke, *Judicial Recourse to Foreign Law. A New Source of Inspiration?* (London, UCL Press, 2006) 287, 290.

[95] 1950s: 80/370; 1970s: 66/673; 2000s: 60/308.

decisions dealing with fundamental rights are issued because they are necessary to protect individual spheres, not because they pose the most intriguing problems of constitutional law. If there already exists an established set of rules of constitutional law, comparative arguments tend not to be asked for. Institutional cases come up more rarely, but are often of a delicate nature because of their political background and because institutional matters are not as densely affected by legislation and thus are more open to interpretation, institutional cases leave space for backing comparative argument. Beyond that, disputes between bodies of government do not turn to matters of judicial conflict all the time; phases of conflict are replaced by calm times, which lead to ups and downs of institutional cases before constitutional courts.

Another plausible reason for the considerably high share of institutional cases is the phenomenon that low numbers—as in this case—distort ratios easily. In addition to that, the classified is heavily influenced by the subjective assessment of the classifier: in this case, I included disputes before the GFCC over the existence of rules of international law in the set of institutional cases. In the 2000s, a comparably high number of conflicts in this field reached the court; on top of that, once, two judgments with almost the same wording about a rule of international law were delivered the same day—both including foreign national precedent.[96] In conclusion, the numeric ratio of institutional and human rights cases can neither reveal which issue is significantly preferred by the GFCC nor which issue is more suitable for comparative reasoning.

Table 3.1: Number of Human Rights and Institutional Cases Citing Foreign Precedent in the 1950s

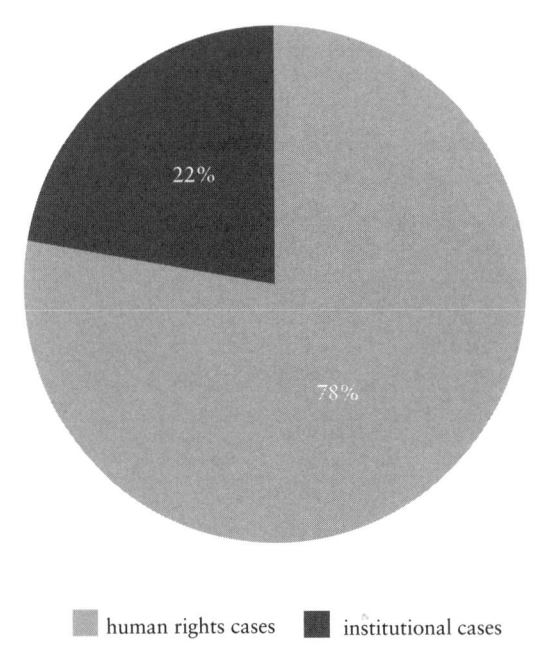

human rights cases 78%
institutional cases 22%

---

[96] BVerfGE 109, 13; 109, 38 (2003).

Table 3.2: Number of Human Rights and Institutional Cases Citing Foreign Precedent in the 1970s

■ human rights cases   ■ institutional cases

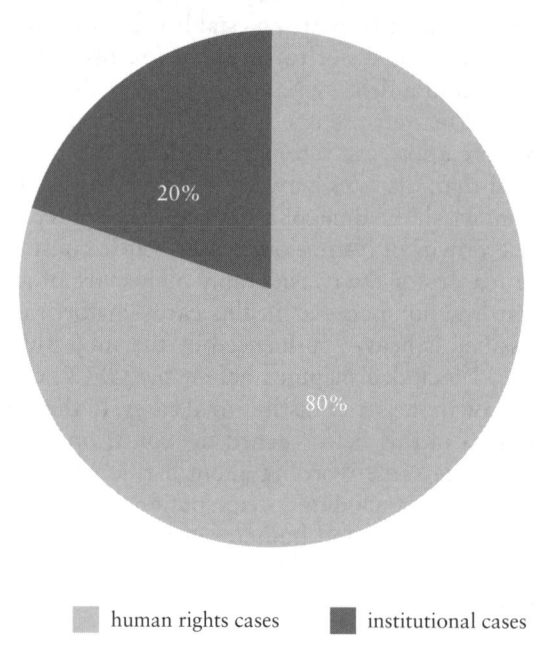

Table 3.3: Number of Human Rights and Institutional Cases Citing Foreign Precedent in the 2000s

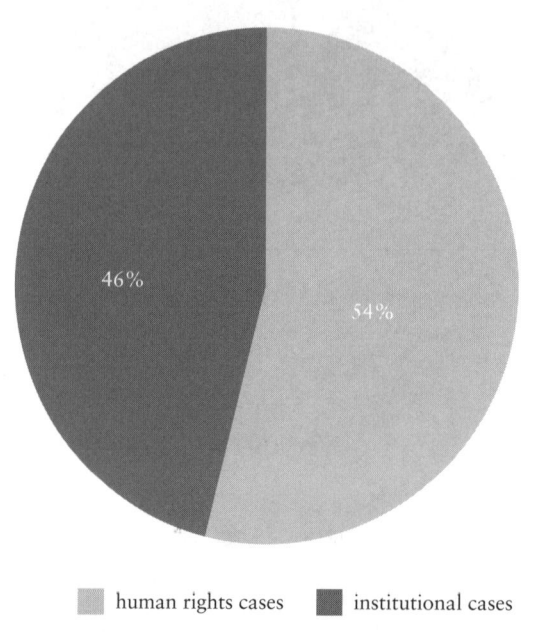

■ human rights cases   ■ institutional cases

iv. Authority and Liberty

Minor outliers in the history of comparative citations of the GFCC, especially at the beginning of the 1970s, can be traced to the then newly introduced separate opinions.[97] Although separate opinions do not belong to the authoritative part of the judgment, this anomaly does not warrant deducting the figures of separate opinions from statistical analysis. They may not entail direct legal consequences, but they reveal conflicts in the court most of which stay hidden behind the curtain of confidentiality of deliberation. One can draw the conclusion that the majority of the court had to defend its legal opinion against the separate opinion's arguments at least in the deliberations. Moreover, sometimes the position of a separate opinion may prevail in a later decision which thus partly adopts the argument of the former separate opinion. Separate opinions are opinions of the court.

The figures prompt the conclusion that separate opinions tend to be more open to citing foreign sources than the majority opinions of the court (see also Table 4) since the percentage of separate opinions' citations of all citations is almost double as high as the ratio of separate opinions to all the decisions considered (14.1 to 6.9%).[98] This result is plausible because the (partly) dissenting judges do not have to carry the consequences of the judgment on their shoulders the same way the latter do; they are freed from the constraints of authority being able to leave the official standards or argumentation behind.

The declining ratio of citations in separate opinions to all citations between the 1970s and the 2000s follows the fate of separate opinions in general. At the time of introducing the possibility of issuing separate opinions there seemed to be a pressing need to utter dissent after having suppressed it for 20 years. In recent years, a stronger push to consent can be noticed in the GFCC, also pushed by the authority of the chairs of the senates.

Table 4: Location of Citations

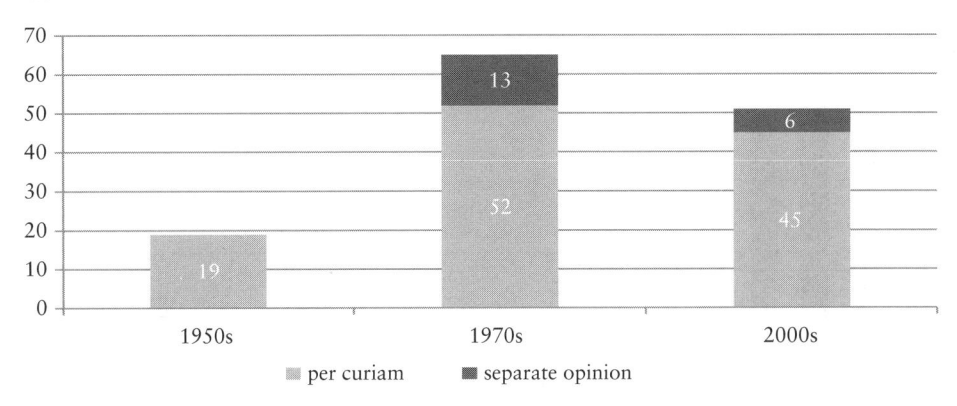

Decade	per curiam	separate opinion
1950s	19	
1970s	52	13
2000s	45	6

---

[97] BVerfGE 30, 173 (1971); BVerfGE 39, 1 (1975).
[98] 19/135 to 93/1351. Here, I include the reasons of those judges in a stalemate (4 to 4 or 3 to 3 decisions) that do not support the result of the decision, although, formally, they do not count as separate opinions. The percentage is even higher (18.1%) if one compares decisions with separate opinions with decisions without, of which all cite foreign precedent.

v. Euro-Atlantic Centrism

The selection of the relevant case law is the crucial point and also the Achilles' heel of any comparative endeavour in court.[99] By seeing who is cited the most by the GFCC one can find out which countries are held to be comparable enough to function as a general source of inspiration beyond the particularities of an individual case. Case law from six countries is cited more than five times by the GFCC in the three periods under review here: England, Austria, Italy, France, Switzerland and the United States.

Judgments from Switzerland and the United States have over time remained the leading citation countries, France, Italy and Austria catching up since the 1970s. The constitutional tribunals and courts of France and Italy have both been founded after the GFCC started issuing its decisions which explains the relatively belated consideration. The case law of these countries can fulfil two opposing functions. First, all of them share—with some variations, of course—similar constitutional

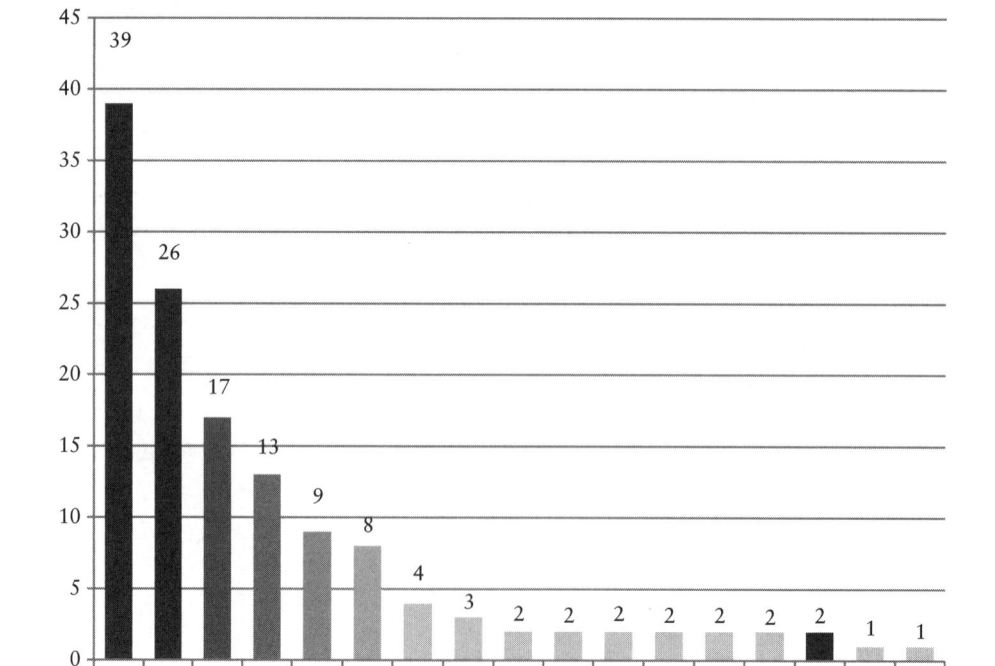

Table 5: Number of Citations per Country (1950s, 1970s, 2000s)

Country	Citations
USA	39
SUI	26
FRA	17
ITA	13
AUT	9
GBR	8
NED	4
CAN	3
NOR	2
CZE	2
SWE	2
JP	2
BEL	2
GRE	2
NONE	2
HUN	1
POL	1

---

[99] R Hirschl, 'The Question of Case Selection in Comparative Constitutional Law (2005) 53 *The American Journal of Comparative Law* 125; B Markesinis and J Fedtke, *Judicial Recourse to Foreign Law. A New Source of Inspiration?* (London, UCL Press, 2006) 165 ff.

values and ideologies,[100] which qualifies them for comparison. Secondly, they, some of them as mother countries, embody distinguishable patterns and pedigrees of constitutional thought and practice. Against their persuasive authority the GFCC is able to confront and defend its views. Between this range of commonality and difference, the GFCC obviously feels legally at home.

One can also look at the geographical allocation of citations from a negative viewpoint: apparently, the GFCC totally ignores constitutional developments outside the European realm (including the US and Canada). This limitation of sight does not do the global nature of constitutionalism justice. It seems that the use of foreign jurisprudence is governed by personal education, preferences and accessibility. Properly, though, the comparable and better, not the traditional, argument should count in constitutional jurisprudence.

C. Substantive Analysis

After viewing the decisions from the outside, it is also of interest to get to know how foreign precedent is handled within individual judgments. In many cases, the GFCC only cites the respective judgment in its reasoning[101] without indulging in any longer debate, an impression that is supported by the near congruence of the number of cited decisions and the total number of citations (Table 2). However, going into more detail, the picture is not totally monochromatic.

The biggest group of citations is used to affirm a constitutional result: an instructive example is the case of BVerfGE 32, 54 (1971) where the GFCC had to give meaning to the concept of 'home'. It supported its wide interpretation of the term by referring to decisions from Switzerland, Austria, Italy and the US because the wording of the Constitution those courts had to consider was close to that of the German Constitution.[102] In the incest between siblings case of BVerfGE 120, 224 (2008) the GFCC cites and even shortly describes the rulings of a couple of foreign decisions both of them in favour of penalising this form of incest on moral grounds, an argument it itself shared.

Rarely, foreign precedent is used to fill gaps in constitutional doctrine. In the famous *Lüth* case of BVerfGE 7, 198 (1958) freedom of opinion is determined with the additional help of a quote of Benjamin Cardozo stating that freedom of speech is the foundation of all other rights. A similar 'transfer' reference is made when experiences with the implementation of norms are taken from foreign judgments.[103]

Sometimes, foreign case law is used to illustrate and support own doctrine by contrasting it to foreign practice. In the remarkable decision of BVerfGE 1, 97 (1951) the easy admission procedure at the Swiss Federal Court is opined not to

---

[100] See, eg, for the comparability of US and German constitutional ideas H Steinberger, 'American Constitutionalism and German Constitutional Development' in L Henkin and AJ Rosenthal (eds), *Constitutionalism and Rights* (New York, Columbia University Press, 1990) 199, 216.
[101] There are exceptions: in BVerfGE 120, 378, 380 (2008), the Conseil Constitutionnel is cited to provide facts abroad.
[102] See also BVerfGE 30, 173, 225 (1971, separate opinion); BVerfGE 45, 187, 259 (1987); BVerfGE 104, 337, 349 (2002); BVerfGE 116, 69, 90 (2006).
[103] BVerfGE 116, 135, 146 (2006).

correspond to the purpose of the procedural requirements of the GFCC; because of its incomparability it should not be of any help construing German law. In the plenary decision of BVerfGE 2, 79 (1952) the GFCC distinguished itself as a specialised constitutional court from the Supreme Court which supposedly mainly acts as an appellate instance: since at least rhetorically, the GFCC was a more objective court than the US Supreme Court, it considered itself to be able to deliver advisory opinions (the competency of which does not exist anymore).

IV. IMPLICIT INFLUENCE OF FOREIGN PRECEDENT ON THE JURISPRUDENCE OF THE GFCC

Influences from foreign sources that are not identified by the courts themselves through citations are hard to find. Implicit influence can either work unconsciously through, for example, value patterns attained in foreign legal training, or consciously, but held back from the public. Since, at any rate, the GFCC will try to stay on its individual course of following precedent, both variants of implicit influence are hard to track.[104] However, it is very probable that those underlying connections really exist. As an insider claims, the citations of the GFCC are only the tip of the iceberg: 'the reader will have to take my word for it'.[105] Comparative material, he affirms, is used when the rapporteur is preparing the judgment if there is comparative German literature at hand.[106]

The rather recent *Wunsiedel* case[107] may serve as an example of implicit influence or even a silent dialogue between German and US constitutionalism. The somewhat paradoxical decision construed an unwritten exception to freedom of opinion (Art 5 BL) for actions glorifying Nazi rule on the one hand, while on the other limiting the possibilities of public authorities interfering in the marketplace of ideas in all other fields. The reasons justified the exception with the exceptional history of Germany; the liberal limitations, though, resemble the 'clear and present danger' test in US freedom of speech doctrine, one of the most liberal ones in the world.[108] Although no citation hints at the US Supreme Court's influence, either when explaining the German *Sonderweg* or when adhering to global values of freedom, the point of reference is in the air all the time through the course of the grounds.[109] The career of the rapporteur of the *Wunsiedel* case, Johannes Masing, supports this claim. He is known for his comparative teaching and appraised for his comparative research,

---

[104] See in general C Starck (ed), *Grundgesetz und deutsche Verfassungsrechtsprechung im Spiegel ausländischer Verfassungsentwicklung: Landesberichte und Generalbericht der Tagung für Rechtsvergleichung 1989 in Würzburg* (Baden-Baden, Nomos, 1990); A Nußberger, 'Wer zitiert wen?—Zur Funktion von Zitaten bei der Herausbildung eines gemeineuropäischen Verfassungsrechts' (2006) *Juristenzeitung* 763, 768, with examples of case law of Eastern European constitutional courts.

[105] B-O Bryde, 'The Constitutional Judge and the International Constitutionalist Dialogue' in B Markesinis and J Fedtke (eds), *Judicial Recourse to Foreign Law* (London, UCL Press 2006) 295, 297.

[106] Ibid, 295, 298.

[107] BVerfGE 124, 300 (2009).

[108] *Schenck v United States*, 249 US 47, 52 (1919) (Holmes). See S Martini, 'Diskriminierung (rechts) extremer Meinungen nach Art 5 Abs 2 GG. Überlegungen aus Anlass der Ausnahme-Entscheidung des Bundesverfassungsgerichts vom 4.11.2009' (2011) 59 *Jahrbuch des öffentlichen Rechts der Gegenwart* 279.

[109] Similarly, A Kaiser, 'Verfassungsvergleichung durch das Bundesverfassungsgericht' (2010) 18 *Journal für Rechtspolitik* 203 f.

though mainly on French law. One may only guess that a citation of the US Supreme Court case law was omitted because it would have endangered the obvious compromise in the first senate that tries to 'harmonise' two doctrinal counterparts: an illiberal as well as a liberal approach towards freedom of speech.

V. CONCLUSIONS

Over the decades, the GFCC appears to be a constitutional court that cites foreign sources rarely, which suits its systematic approach to German law (see II.D), but also does not shy away from citing foreign case law. The leading cases of the GFCC are among those which cite foreign precedent.[110] Although the majority of its cases—as is the case anywhere in the world—will pragmatically still be decided with the help of ordinary 'home-grown' arguments, the GFCC may in the future carefully draw more inspiration from foreign sources. Until now, it has—often erratically—used foreign precedent mostly in order to support its findings not giving too much weight to foreign sources.[111] In spite of the fact that it does not seem that the potential of this source of argument is exhausted, the GFCC is getting more and more used to it under the umbrella of European and international law as well as under the influence of other cases that are connected to foreign law. The decline of annual citations at the end of the first decade of the twenty-first century (Table 2) will probably not be permanent.

In addition, two other phenomena deserving further investigation may complete the picture that ultimately shows how introverted the GFCC is. The first development has to do with Germany's integration into European and international human rights law, adding further levels of jurisdiction to the German legal order and introducing new types of legal hierarchy. As an effect of that integration, remedies to the ECJ and the ECtHR put GFCC judgments at risk of being overruled. A more positive approach towards this institutional setting highlights the opportunities of fostering a dialogue between national as well as transnational 'constitutional' courts, the GFCC joining in with its—of course—rather national perspective.[112]

One might be able to, above all, reject the verdict that the GFCC closes its reasoning doors when including the consideration of foreign law in an inquiry. Quite frequently in the case law of the GFCC the discussion of foreign precedent is interrelated with the mentioning of foreign law material. A perfect example for this phenomenon is the abortion case of 1975.[113] Searching for foreign *case* law, one finds the separate opinion of judges Rupp-v Brünneck and Simon in which they stress the liberal commitment of the Basic Law also in respect of the free decision to abort a

---

[110] BVerfGE 1, 97 (1951); 7, 198 (1958); 30, 173 (1971); 37, 271 (1974); 39, 1 (1975); 45, 187 (1987); 123, 267 (2009).
[111] H Sauer, 'Verfassungsvergleichung durch das Bundesverfassungsgericht' (2010) 18 *Journal für Rechtspolitik* 194, 202.
[112] See, eg, A Voßkuhle, 'Multilevel Cooperation of the European Constitutional Courts' (2010) 6 *European Constitutional Law Review* 175; H Sauer, 'Verfassungsvergleichung durch das Bundesverfassungsgericht' (2010) 18 *Journal für Rechtspolitik* 194, 200 f; R Wahl, 'Das Bundesverfassungsgericht im europäischen und internationalen Umfeld' (B37-38/2001) *Aus Politik und Zeitgeschichte* 45, 51 ff.
[113] BVerfGE 39, 1 (1975).

child by backing their doctrinal position with the help of case law of the Austrian Constitutional Tribunal and the US Supreme Court. However, when also looking for foreign *law* one would not miss the line of thought of the majority court that takes exactly the opposite stance *without* referring to the US Supreme Court itself.[114] The majority rejects any argument in favour of deferring to international developments by—as in the *Wunsiedel* case—highlighting the particular legal standards of Germany, spoken roughly: the majority judges did not want to be responsible for the authorisation of killing unborn life on German grounds 30 years after the end of Nazi rule. In effect, they committed the legislator to protect unborn life and penalise abortion.

Compared to foreign law, the argumentation status of foreign case law seems to be higher as law can only be understood and then ultimately transferred into persuasive authority when its application is valued. Although application is regularly achieved and ultimately ensured by court decisions, citing foreign law may still prove to be an additional source of inspiration. The dialogue between courts does not correspond to a phone call in which partners (here: courts) simultaneously and spontaneously exchange arguments. The dialogue between legal orders is rather a distorted and delayed one, resulting in a series of monologues that are reacted to by other monologues. Legal orders send chain postcards to each other: on these are printed judgments as well as legal practice and provisions open to be read and used by willing communication partners. There is neither a flat rate nor a postcard monopoly on court decisions. Where a judgment is not available, a provision or legally determined practice may suffice for the sake of the argument.

The overall picture drawn here is thus a complex and multi-layered one. A seemingly inconsistent use of foreign case law may also be read as a useful case-by-case inspiration when the GFCC thinks it appropriate. Comparative method lends itself to constitutional interpretation especially when interpreting and applying constitutional norms or resolving complex socio-political problems shared by legal orders. Then, the legal argument may be enriched by foreign experiences. Those foreign sources are, moreover, more easily recognised when points of contact exist between legal orders: facts of the case, institutional relationships, legal duties to consider and to ascertain transnational law, in order to be able to apply transnational law to domestic contexts. Yet, whereas the GFCC has in its judgments discussed the status and role of transnational law, meta-reflection on foreign law and precedent is almost completely missing, probably because the GFCC tries to avoid the intriguing problem of legitimacy prominent in the opinions of US Supreme Court judges.[115] Another critique reveals a painful absence: observing the case law of the European and North American sphere the GFCC overlooks the rest. Finally, taking into account the findings of this paper and the moderate increase in citations of foreign case law over the last 60 years, the portrait of the GFCC as a legal hermit turns out to be but cartoonesque.

---

[114] Vice versa in BVerfGE 120, 224 (2008).
[115] See only A Kaiser, 'Verfassungsvergleichung durch das Bundesverfassungsgericht' (2010) 18 *Journal für Rechtspolitik* 203.

10

Hungary: Unsystematic and Incoherent Borrowing of Law. The Use of Foreign Judicial Precedents in the Jurisprudence of the Constitutional Court, 1999–2010

ZOLTÁN SZENTE[*]

TABLE OF CONTENTS

I. Constitutional Frameworks 254
II. The Court 256
III. Using Foreign Precedents in the Practice of the Constitutional
 Court—A Brief Quantitative Analysis 259
 A. The Relevant Judgments of the Constitutional Court
 and the Frequency of the Use of Foreign Precedents 259
 B. The Legal Areas of the Use of Foreign Judicial Practice 261
 C. Foreign Courts Referred to in the Constitutional Court's Jurisprudence 262
IV. Using Foreign Case Law in Context... 264
 A. Behind the Figures—The Practice of Reviewing Foreign Case Law 264
 B. Objectives and Goals of Using Foreign Judicial Cases in
 Constitutional Adjudication... 266
 C. Judicial Attitudes.. 269
 D. The Effects of the Use of Foreign Judicial Cases on
 Constitutional Review.. 271
V. Conclusions. The Main Characteristics of the Use of Foreign
 Judicial Cases in Hungarian Constitutional Review 271

WITHOUT DOUBT IF globalisation is a general phenomenon in the contemporary world, there is judicial globalisation too, which means the internationalisation of law, including the practices of the national courts. This tendency has numerous signs and several different reasons.

---

[*] Professor of Law, DSc, University of Széchenyi István, Faculty of Law, Department of Constitutional Law and Political Science, Győr.

In this study, I examine how the Hungarian Constitutional Court uses foreign judicial practices, doctrines and precedents in its jurisprudence.[**] In doing so, I will concentrate on the use of foreign cases from the jurisprudence of national constitutional and other high courts, without discussing how the experience of international and European tribunals is taken into account by Hungarian constitutional justices. Thus, the analysis and the statistical data relate only to foreign national courts. Nevertheless, I will make some references to citations of the practice of the European Court of Human Rights (ECtHR), for the purposes of comparison, or where there seems to be no alternative.

This work covers the period between 1999 and 2010, so it does not extend to the first decade of the Court, partly because it has already been discussed and analysed from a similar perspective[1] and partly because 1999 is a turning point in the life of the Constitutional Court, starting a new period after the so-called Sólyom-era. The scope of the analysis extends to the end of 2010, not only for technical reasons—that year brought about essential changes in the Court's life, as we will see. The Constitutional Court, owing to the overwhelming political change in the general elections of 2010, and the new Fundamental Law, has lost its institutional independence, and a substantial part of its earlier powers, and will not be the same as it was earlier.

In the absence of relevant official statistics, in this study, I use my own calculations and data in aggregating both the Court's decisions citing foreign precedents, and the cited foreign judicial cases. Some other data and conclusions, like the distribution of cases by subject, as well as the identification of the underlying objectives and goals of using foreign precedents, are results of my own qualitative analyses of the relevant cases.

I. CONSTITUTIONAL FRAMEWORKS

Until recently, Hungary was the only post-communist country in Central and East Europe where, after the defeat of Communist rule, no new Constitution was adopted. The transition to democracy or, as it is commonly named, the 'system change' in 1989–90 was achieved by a peaceful negotiating process producing an agreement between the ruling party (MSZMP) and the opposition parties and movements. The so-called 'National Roundtable' talks shaped a comprehensive political compromise not only on the schedule of the democratic transition from a Soviet-type, one-party authoritarian regime to a Western-like parliamentary democracy, but also on the rules of game, that is, the basic institutions and features of the new constitutional system. The results of this compromise were codified by the last one-party, Communist National Assembly, as a basic revision to the existing Constitution of 1949, which effectuated fundamental changes in Hungarian constitutional law. In fact, the general revision of the Constitution in 1989[2] changed

---

[**] I am grateful to Mihály Bihari (chairman of the Constitutional Court, 2005–2008, constitutional judge 1999–2008), Attila Harmathy (member of the Court, 1998–2007), István Kukorelli (constitutional judge, 1999–2008) and Péter Paczolay (chairman of the Constitutional Court, constitutional judge since 2006) who were interviewed for this study.

[1] C Dupré, *Importing the Law in Post-Communist Transitions. The Hungarian Constitutional Court and the Right to Human Dignity* (Oxford, Hart Publishing, 2003).

[2] Act No XXXI of 1989 on the amendment of the Constitution.

almost all the important parts of the basic law to such a degree that many refer to it as to 'a genuinely new' Constitution.[3] All references to the Communist ideology were exiled, and replaced by new values. For example, the Communist principle of democratic centralism was exchanged with the separation of powers and the rule of law, the centrally-planned economy with a 'social market' one, and a parliamentary government was established based on a multi-party political system and free elections. When the old Constitution was amended on 23 October 1989, all political actors believed that even the basically revised Constitution would only be a transitional one, as its preamble said, 'in order to facilitate a peaceful political transition to a constitutional state', the Parliament established the new text of the basic law, 'until the country's new Constitution is adopted'. Later in the 90s, some attempts were made to adopt a new text, but the fundamentally distinctive constitutional ideas and political efforts of the political parties, and the deep conflicts between them made it impossible. Nonetheless, the revised Constitution of 1949 operated well, and it proved to be fairly flexible: between 1989 and 2011 the Constitution was modified more than 30 times.

Nevertheless, when in the general elections of 2010 the conservative-right opposition gained a two-thirds majority in Parliament, which enabled the new coalition to make a new Constitution alone, the main argument for approving a new basic law was the unfortunate birth date (1949) of the Constitution. After a very rapid Constitution-making process, a completely new Constitution, the so-called Fundamental Law was adopted at Easter 2011,[4] only by the votes of the Government's MPs. It is the 58th new Constitution of the Continent since the end of the Second World War.

The new basic law has made only minor changes to the system of state organisation. The Fundamental Law refers *expressis verbis* to some principles which were missing in the old one, like the principle of separation of powers, and includes some innovations shaped by the Constitutional Court's jurisprudence in the preceding years. The republican form of state and parliamentary government have remained unchanged, even if new emphases and approaches appeared in the written text. The form of government is close to the German *Kanzlerdemokratie*,[5] with the 'constructive vote of non-confidence' as a special form of the political responsibility of the Government, providing great stability for the Executive. The head of state only has ceremonial functions, even if formally he/she is the chief commander of the army, or has some powers to dismiss the Parliament.

The general distrust between the political parties in 1989/1990 led to the establishment of various independent institutions to control the executive power. Thus, a strong Constitutional Court was founded, which has evolved a wide-ranging jurisprudence in constitutional matters. To keep the implementation of the state budget under control, a specialised supervising organ, the State Audit Office, was established and given great autonomy from daily politics. During the last two decades, no less than four ombudsmen were set up to watch over the rights of citizens, ethnic

---

[3] A Jakab, 'The Republic of Hungary. Commentary' in R Wolfrum, Rüdiger and R Grote (eds), *Constitutions of the Countries of the World* (New York, Oceana, 2008) 8.

[4] The Fundamental Law entered into force on 1 January 2012.

[5] A Körösényi, 'Das Politische Systems Ungarns' in W Ismayr (ed), *Die Politischen Systeme Osteuropas* (Opladen, Leske+Budrich, 2002) 321.

and national minorities, the interests of the 'generations of the future', and oversee the management of personal data. The institutional independence of the judiciary was strengthened by establishing its own autonomous organ for administering the courthouses.

Undoubtedly, the new Fundamental Law reduced the power of these controlling authorities; the range of responsibility of the Constitutional Court has been seriously restricted (see below); the number of ombudsmen has been decreased to one; and the judicial branch will probably lose its administrative autonomy. Some think that this series of changes means only the rationalisation of the exaggerations of the 'super rule of law', as it was established in 1989/1990, while others speak about the destruction of democracy and a turn towards a moderate autocracy.

The old Constitution needed a qualified (two-thirds) majority for more than 30 laws, requiring a wide-ranging consensus in legislation concerning the basic rights and separation of powers. The new basic law retained the frequently criticised type of 'cardinal laws' requiring a two-thirds majority for approval. Nevertheless, the subjects of these laws will partly change, since many policy-related regulations will need a qualified majority in the future. This can make effective governance much more difficult, because every time the Government does not have such an overwhelming majority, it will have to get support from the opposition. Thus, the management of national assets, the system of pensions and family support, tax allowances for raising children, or the maintenance of a voluntary reserve force can be regulated only by a two-thirds majority in the future.

The catalogue of basic rights was modelled after the Charter of Fundamental Rights of the European Union. The Charter was not completely incorporated into the text, but its pattern was tightly followed by the Constitution-makers.

The new Hungarian Fundamental Law is probably the most ideological basic law on the Continent; it refers in more places to God and Christianity, defines marriage as an alliance of a man and a woman, defends embryonic and foetal life 'from the moment of conception', and undertakes a continuity with the historic (and unwritten) Constitution whose 'achievement' is respected as an interpretative principle in constitutional matters.

Notably, it is an open question how the jurisprudence of the Constitutional Court connected to the old constitutional text will be handled. According to the Fundamental Law, all issues that are not dealt with in depth in it should be regulated in so-called 'cardinal laws'.

II. THE COURT

Before 1990, constitutional review had no traditions in Hungary. Although a so-called Council of Constitutional Law was set up in 1983, it had no power to annul unconstitutional legal rules. The Constitutional Court was one of the new institutions established by the constitutional amendment of 1989. During the Roundtable negotiations, both sides saw it as a guarantee for democracy, and, since then, the nomination process has always been complicated by political bargaining.

The political distrust between the negotiating parties during the transition period led to the establishment of an independent constitutional court with wide-ranging responsibilities. Basically, the Court was established on the pattern of the German Bundesverfassungsgericht,[6] establishing a 'European' or '*Kelsenian*' model of constitutional review, which embodies a centralised system of it:[7] the constitutional court has exclusionary power to examine the constitutionality of legal Acts, through abstract judicial review.

The main task of the Constitutional Court is the ex post judicial review of legal rules. Since everybody may submit any statutory Act to the Court for review (*actio popularis*), actually, all important laws land before the body. In certain areas, ex ante examination of the constitutionality of legal Acts (eg international treaties) falls also within the competence of the Constitutional Court, which is empowered also to investigate conflicts between international treaties and national law. The Court decides on individual constitutional complaints lodged against public authorities or courts violating rights guaranteed by the Constitution; but this function before 2013, differed from that of the 'real' constitutional complaints in some other European countries (eg, the *Verfassungsbeschwerde* in Germany), since practically, it is an abstract judicial review, because the Constitutional Court only had the power to intervene in an individual case if it found the Act on which the case had been decided unconstitutional. Another responsibility is to decide on the conflicts of competence between state organs. The function by which the Court may interpret the provisions of the Constitution without any individual legal dispute grants the Constitutional Court a primary political role, because in this respect the Court appears to be the final arbiter of discussions which usually have direct political implications.

The Court is a quasi-judicial organ, because, though it bears some characteristics of the judicial branch (like its structural independence or the irremovable status of the judges), other classic judicial principles and guarantees are missing (there is no contradictory procedure, for example).[8]

Until 2012, the Court consisted of 11 members who were elected by a qualified majority of MPs. Parliament elects members of the Constitutional Court from among learned theoretical jurists (university professors or academic doctors of legal science) and lawyers with at least 20 years of professional experience. Originally, they were elected for nine years, and could be re-elected once. Although there are strict conflict of interest rules, whose objective is to keep partisanship politics away from the Court,[9] the way of selecting its members brings the body close to politics.

The candidates are nominated by a parliamentary committee to which all factions delegate members. In theory, the Court is a well-balanced body from a political point of view, as both the government and the opposition are able to influence its composition, owing to the consensual election method of the judges. It can be

---

[6] G Halmai, 'Grundlagen und Grundzüge staatlichen Verfassungsrecht: Ungarn' in A von Bogdandy, P Cruz Villalón and PM Huber (eds), *Handbuch Ius Publicum Europaeum. Band I* (Heidelberg, CF Müller Verlag, 2007) 693.

[7] On the major characteristic of this model see L Favoreu, *Les Cours Constitutionnelles* (Paris, Presses Universitaires de France, 1986) 16–31 and L Sólyom and G Brunner, *Constitutional Judiciary in a New Democracy. The Hungarian Constitutional Court* (Michigan, University of Michigan Press, 2000).

[8] L Sólyom, *Az alkotmánybíráskodás kezdetei Magyarországon* (Budapest, Osiris Kiadó, 2001) 114–15.

[9] Eg the members of the Constitutional Court may not pursue political activities or make political statements, and can only be elected if they have not filled leading political or governmental positions in the previous four years.

justified empirically: in the last few years, only one candidate has been nominated by both sides.

Since 1990 (the court began work on 1 January of that year), the Constitutional Court has established rich and comprehensive jurisprudence; it has dealt with almost all the classic issues found in Western countries which have much longer constitutional traditions. Undoubtedly, the Court has reached a pre-eminent position in the Hungarian constitutional system, and accomplished much by elaborating on and standardising the living constitutional law.

It is a commonly shared view that the Court, in the first nine years of its operation (which period is generally called Sólyom Court after its first chairman) ran a strongly 'activist' practice.[10] There is good reason to think that this activism was, to a degree, unavoidable, as every attempt to make a new Constitution proved to be unsuccessful, the legislature was not able to fill its gaps, and it also failed to correct or modernise those basic institutions whose regulation demanded a qualified majority in Parliament. Thus, the Court was the only institution with enough power to solve the great constitutional (and, often, political) conflicts at a time when the institutional setting was paralysed.

To crystallise the results of the constitutional review, the Court made efforts to domesticate constitutional case law, whereas the Hungarian legal system has always belonged to the continental civil law tradition in which judicial precedents do not have any authoritative force vis-a-vis the statutory law. In fact, when the Court in its later decisions referred to its own earlier resolutions, sometimes it eliminated the problems coming from the poor textual ground of the arguments. Notwithstanding this, there is a wide-ranging consensus among scholars that after the very first years of its existence, the Court took up a much more moderate way of jurisdiction, which can be characterised by a more positivist constitutional interpretation.[11]

Nevertheless, particularly in the first years after the system change the Constitutional Court obviously gained some legitimacy for its own activism from this situation, when an 'unfinished', and, therefore, necessarily incomplete constitutional text in effect had a number of internal contradictions.

This role of the Court was not tolerated any more after a new coalition government was formed as a result of an overwhelming victory of the rightist opposition parties in the general elections in the summer of 2010. Since then, the Government has had a two-thirds majority in the Parliament, which enables the coalition parties to modify the Constitution as they wish. The Constitutional Court was for two decades the most effective and strongest counterbalance of the Executive. But just a few months after its formation, the new coalition government, using its two-thirds majority, transformed the process of nominating the justices of the Constitutional Court. Since then, membership of the parliamentary committee responsible for such

---

[10] G Halmai, 'The Hungarian Approach to Constitutional Review: The End of Activism? The First Decade of the Hungarian Constitutional Court' in W Sadurski (ed), *Constitutional Justice, East and West. Democratic Legitimacy and Constitutional Courts in Post-Communist Europe in a Comparative Perspective* (The Hague-London-New York, Kluwer International Law, 2002) 189–211; H Schwartz, *The Struggle for Constitutional Justice in Post-Communist Europe* (Chicago and London, The University of Chicago Press, 2000) 87–108.

[11] See, eg, G Halmai, 'Az aktivizmus vége? A Sólyom-bíróság kilenc éve' (1999) 2 *Fundamentum* 19–24.

nominations is not based on parity anymore, but reflects the party's strength in the National Assembly. Whereas the earlier regulation required a compromise between the parties to elect justices (because of the two-thirds majority requirement), since the autumn of 2010 the government parties have been able to elect their own nominees. The personal control of the Court was extended by the new Fundamental Law, empowering Parliament to elect the Head of the Court (who was, since 1990, elected by the justices themselves).

However, the possibility of changing the composition of the Court did not prove to be enough for the Government. When the Constitutional Court declared unconstitutional a law that imposed a 98 per cent tax on the extreme severance payment of public officials with retroactive effect, and annulled it, the government majority immediately curtailed the Court's most important power of constitutional review. Since then the Court has only been able to review and nullify the budgetary laws, the Acts on taxes, duties, pensions, customs or any kind of financial contributions to the state if they violate the right to life and human dignity, the right to the protection of personal data, freedom of thought, conscience and religion, and the rights related to Hungarian citizenship. The new Fundamental Law maintains this limitation, stipulating that the restriction of the Court's power will last as long as state debt exceeds half of the GDP. The Court has lost its monopoly of judicial review, because the legality of local government decrees are controlled by the Highest Court (*Curia*) from 2013.

Nevertheless, the Constitutional Court has been compensated for the loss of its fundamental power; the Fundamental Law, based on a German pattern, extends the institution of individual constitutional complaint. Although such a procedure has already been used, the Court could redress a violation of human rights only if the administrative or judicial decision objected to was based on an unconstitutional regulation. Now, it is enough if an individual decision itself violates the Fundamental Law. For handling the understandably growing workload, the number of justices rose from 11 to 15. The institution of the so-called *actio popularis* (ie everybody's right to turn to the Court for reviewing the constitutionality of a statutory Act without any personal interest) has ceased, as the Court itself has been proposing for several years.

III. USING FOREIGN PRECEDENTS IN THE PRACTICE OF THE CONSTITUTIONAL COURT—A BRIEF QUANTITATIVE ANALYSIS

A. The Relevant Judgments of the Constitutional Court and the Frequency of the Use of Foreign Precedents

In the period between 1999 and 2010, the Constitutional Court issued 1,016 decisions which were studied here.[12] Among these decisions, the Court cited 68 foreign precedents altogether in 19 cases (1.8 per cent). However, these data seem to be misleading for several different reasons. Firstly, in certain cases the Constitutional

---

[12] This study examines the decisions of the Constitutional Court in the area of constitutional review of statutory rules which have been promulgated in the Hungarian Official Gazette (*Magyar Közlöny*).

Court has never referred to foreign judicial practice. No less than 248 decisions were taken in so-called local government cases (reviewing local decrees), when the Court works in three-member-panels, and in which there was no reference at all. These decisions are published only when the Court nullifies a local government decree, but in these cases the body does not use any foreign judicial precedent. Another type of cases where 'law importation' is extremely rare, is that of the referendum cases, in which the body is actually an appeal court, reviewing the resolution of the National Election Board on the initiatives of national referendums. Although this task gave only a small workload to the Court for a long time, between 2006 and 2010, as a formal instrument of political protest against the unpopular government, the number of cases has grown. Nonetheless, among these 374 cases, the Court referred to a foreign judicial decision only once. All this means that if we ignore the local government as well as the referendum cases, in the remaining 622 cases, 3 per cent of all the decisions referred to at least one (but usually more) foreign judicial cases.

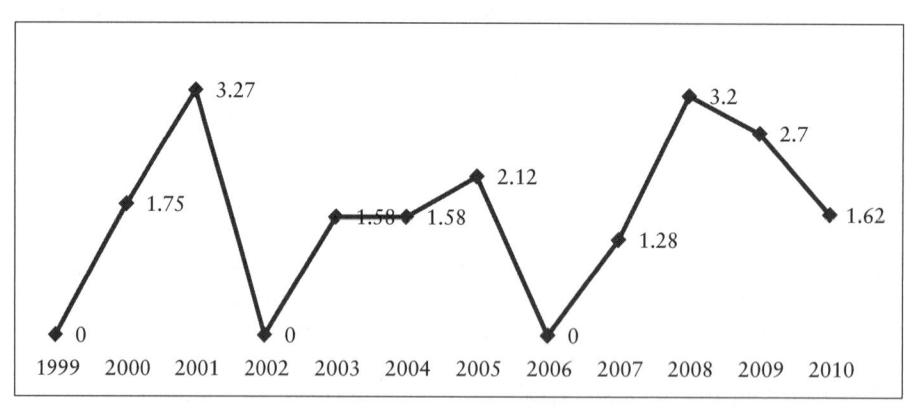

Figure 1: References to Foreign Precedents as a Percentage of All Decisions

Secondly, it is worth noting that although this study explores only the precedents of foreign national (mainly constitutional and supreme) courts, it makes sense that the Hungarian Constitutional Court cites cases of the ECtHR much more often than any other foreign court's cases.[13] Altogether, about 250 ECtHR precedents have been mentioned in 77 judgments of the Hungarian Constitutional Court.

When the Court uses precedents of foreign constitutional and other higher courts, it usually refers to one to four particular foreign judicial cases, but sometimes the decision reviews relevant foreign constitutional practice more widely, citing seven to 11 individual precedents. This has happened on some occasions in EU matters; when reviewing the constitutionality of the Lisbon Treaty of the European Union, for example, the Court referred to the relevant decisions of the German, Czech and Polish Constitutional Courts;[14] and while conducting a constitutional review of the European arrest warrant (EAW), the Court looked at

---

[13] Z Szente, 'A nemzetközi és külföldi bíróságok ítéleteinek felhasználása a magyar Alkotmánybíróság gyakorlatában 1999–2008 között' (2010) 2 *Jog, állam, politika* 47–72.

[14] See Decision No 143/2010 (VII 14) of the Constitutional Court.

Hungary 261

the precedents of seven continental constitutional tribunals.[15] Occasionally, the Court tries to sum up the legal developments of only one particular country, where the relevant issue has been discussed in detail.[16] Sometimes, the Court's decision contains only a general citation to the 'permanent jurisprudence' of a foreign constitutional court.

Although the frequency of the citations of the ECtHR's jurisprudence, as it was mentioned, exceeds that of national constitutional and other higher courts' precedents, there is no sound logic in deciding which judicial patterns are followed in particular cases. Actually, the Constitutional Court often selects references that back up its own conception or interpretative way. For example, whereas the Court referred only to the decisions of the ECtHR in a right-to-die case,[17] it conducted, surprisingly, a wide review of common law countries' relevant jurisprudence in its fundamental decision on passive euthanasia.[18] Sometimes the Constitutional Court compares American and European legal developments contrasting the jurisprudence of the US Supreme Court with that of the ECtHR, regarding the latter as representative of continental legal culture.[19]

B. The Legal Areas of the Use of Foreign Judicial Practice

For the analysis of these data on the basis of the concerned areas of law, it is rational to distinguish the human rights cases from those which relate to the separation of powers and to state institutions. Certainly, the relevant cases can be divided in different ways, but this method provides a more plausible analytical framework. It is to be noted that the citations relate only to some basic rights, even if sometimes the procedure of constitutional review affects a number of rights in the same cases. According to the primary subject of the relevant human right cases, citations have been used so far in matters as follows.

The other type of judicial review cases cited by the Constitutional Court are 'institutional matters', which relate to the organisational and procedural rules of state organs or other legal entities. It is quite rare for the Court to cite precedents of the European Court of Justice (ECJ), and this usually only happens in EU matters. Still, in decisions relating to the constitutionality of political parties' budgets, a family-based tax relief and the Lisbon Treaty, the Court referred to foreign constitutional courts' precedents. It is interesting that in some cases the justices used such references in their concurring or dissenting opinions, even if the majority decision did not mention any foreign judgments. Presumably, the minority judges tried to

---

[15] Decision No 32/2008 (III 12) of the Constitutional Court.
[16] As in the right-to-life (passive euthanasia) case, Decision No 22/2003 (IV 28) of the Constitutional Court, reviewing the practice of the US Supreme Court.
[17] Decision No 36/2000 (X 27) of the Constitutional Court (striking down a statute restraining the right of self-determination of persons having diminished mental capacity in the same way as of those who are not able behave in an autonomous way at all).
[18] Decision No 22/2003 (IV 28) of the Constitutional Court (declaring the right to bodily integrity as a constitutional right, involving the right to refuse life-sustaining medical treatment).
[19] See, eg, Decision No 57/2001 (XII 5) of the Constitutional Court (refusing the right to respond to a criticising newspaper article as a disproportionate restriction on the freedom of the press).

Table 1:

Subject area	Number of decisions citing foreign precedents	No. of cited foreign cases
Freedom of expression	4	16
Right to human dignity from this:	7	32
Right to die	(1)	(11)
Artificial sterilisation	(1)	(7)
Right to use personal name	(1)	(1)
Criminalisation of drug consumption	(1)	(1)
Gay and lesbian marriage	(2)	(5)
Compulsory vaccination	(1)	(7)
Freedom to move (European arrest warrant)	1	7
Freedom of religion	1	4
Right to assembly	1	2

open new dimensions of the dispute, or justify the raison d'être of their own views or arguments.

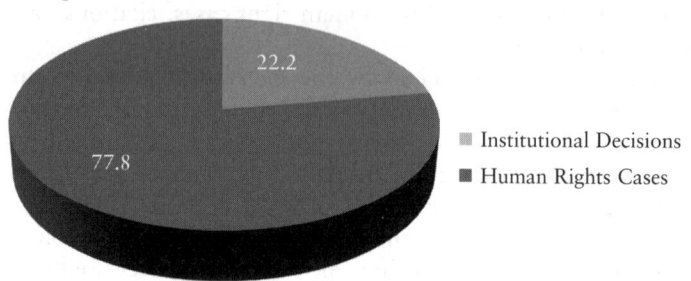

Figure 2: Percentage of Human Rights Cases and Institutional Decisions

C. Foreign Courts Referred to in the Constitutional Court's Jurisprudence

Apart from the European judicial tribunals, the Hungarian Constitutional Court refers most frequently to the jurisprudence of the German Federal Constitutional Court (German FCC), whose jurisprudence was cited 16 times in the examined period, referring to 20 decisions.[20] The German FCC was cited in both institu-

---

[20] BVerfGE 81, 278 (Bundesflagge) [1990]; BVerfGR 34, 269 (Soraya) [1973]; BVerfG, 1 BvR [1995/94]; BVerfGE 84, 9 (Ehenamen) [1991]; BVerfGE 1 BvL 83/86; 1 BvL 24/88 [1991]; BVerfGE 90, 145 (Cannabis) [1994]; BVerfGE 96, 375 [1997]; BVerfGE 1 BvF 1/01 [2002]; BVerfGE 2 BvR 1830/06 [2008]; BverfGE 93, 266 (Soldaten sind Mörder) [1995]; BVerfGE 73, 1 (Politische Stiftungen) [1986];

tional (eg taxation or retrospective legislation) and human rights cases, even where the case law of the ECtHR was not cited at all (although the ECtHR is the most frequently cited international court anyway). In some cases of civil liberties, the German Bundesverfassungsgericht was the only cited foreign court.[21] If we put aside the strict statistical figures, the achievement of this court is even more present in Hungarian constitutional jurisprudence, since in some cases its findings are mentioned only in general form,[22] or in a way that the original decision is not identified.[23]

The next most cited foreign court is the Supreme Court of the United States. Between 1999 and 2010, four decisions of the Hungarian Constitutional Court cited the Supreme Court's (and other federal courts') precedents. Although the citations occurred only in freedom of expression cases[24] and in the context of the right to self-determination,[25] 18 American cases appeared explicitly in the relevant four judgments.[26]

If we took into consideration the dissenting opinions, the French Conseil Constitutionnel would also be a more cited constitutional tribunal (in the context of the legislative process for the annual budget, EU law and election procedure).[27]

Since 1999 the Court has cited seven other national constitutional courts' precedents only in a few legal fields (right to privacy and right to assembly, EU law), altogether in nine judgments, referring to decisions of the Belgian,[28] Cypriot,[29] Czech,[30] Italian,[31] Polish,[32] Slovenian,[33] and Spanish[34] Constitutional Courts. The

---

BVerfEG 2 BvR 2236/04 [2005]; BVerfGE 33, 23 (Eidesverweigerung aus Glaubensgründen) [1972]; BVerfGE 78, 77, 84 [1988]; BVerfGE 2 BvL 42/93 [1998]; BVerfGE 102, 347, 359 (Schockwerbung) [2000]; BVerfG 1 BvR 1164/07 [2009]; BVerfGE 2 BvE 2/08 [2009]; BVerfGE 2 BvL 37/91 [1995]; BVerfGE 2 BvR 2194/99 [2006].

[21] As in cases concerning the right to a private name (BVerfGE 84, 9 [1991]) and the relation of the right to privacy and the prohibition of drug consumption (BVErfGE 90, 145 [1994]).

[22] Eg 'the jurisdiction of the German Constitutional Court as it has been proceeded since the 60s', or references to the doctrine of the 'living law' or 'mother law'.

[23] Cited only the date of the decision, or the journal where it was reviewed. Decision No 57/2001 (XII 5) of the Constitutional Court (actually referring to BVerfG, 1 BvR [1995/94]).

[24] *New York Times Co v Sullivan* [1964], *Red Lion Broadcasting Co v FCC* [1969], *The Miami Herald Publishing Company v Pat L Tornillo* [1974], *National Socialist Party v Village of Skokie* [1977], *Philadelphia Newspapers, Inc v Maurice S Hepps et al* [1986], *RAV v City of St Paul, Minnesota* [1992].

[25] *Skinner v Oklahoma* [1942], *Griswold v Connecticut* [1965], *Eisenstadt v Baird* [1972], *Cruzan v Director, Missouri Department of Health* [1990], *Quill v Vacco* [1997], *Washington v Glucksberg* [1997] were cited from the Supreme Court's practice, while *Murray v Vandevander*, Court of Appeals of Oklahoma [1974], *Compassion in Dying v State of Washington* [1995], and *Quill v Koppel* [1994] from the federal district courts' jurisprudence.

[26] In addition to the cases enumerated in n 24, these are: *Bigelow v Virginia* [1975], *Central Hudson Gas and Electricity Corporation v Public Service Commission* [1980]; one of them referred to a judgment of the Supreme Court of Virginia (*Virginia v Black* [2003]).

[27] Décision no 2001-48 DC [2001], Décision no 2005-530 [2005], Décision no 2004-496 DC [2004], Décision no 2006-540 DC [2006], Décision no 91–1141/1142/1143/1144 [1991], Décision no 93–1328/1487 [1993], Avis (CE) no 368.282 [2002].

[28] 128/2007, *Advocaten voor de Wereld* [2007].

[29] Ap 294/2005.

[30] ÚS 53/2000 (2000), ÚS 66/04 [2006]; ÚS 19/08 [2008]; ÚS 29/09 [2009]. The Czech Constitutional Court has been cited two times so far.

[31] Sentenza no 149/1995; Sentenza no 536/1995; Sentenza no 118/1996; Sentenza no 34/1996.

[32] P 1/05 [2005], K 21/05 [2006].

[33] U-I-367/96 [1996], U-I-127/01 [2004], U-I-14/06 [2006].

[34] ESP-1994-2-025.

latter's continuous practice was cited on another occasion, and 'a decision of the Spanish Constitutional Court in 1989' was also referred to.[35] (A dissenting opinion cited also a precedent of the Austrian Constitutional Court.[36])

The use of foreign judicial cases in constitutional adjudication is not confined to foreign national constitutional courts—occasionally, the Court uses foreign supreme and other court precedents as well. Certainly, it happens whenever the Court brings British judicial cases into consideration, since no constitutional court exists in Britain.[37] The euthanasia judgment of the Hungarian Constitutional Court—one of the decisions containing wide-ranging law comparison—cites a statement of the German Supreme Court,[38] and three other cases (from the Netherlands[39] and Canada[40]). The Spanish Supreme Court was also cited in a case where the subject of the constitutional dispute related to EU law.[41] In 2009, the Hungarian Constitutional Court, examining whether the official record of the voluntary reference to God in the oath of civil servants violates the Constitution, referred to a decision of the Belgian Cour d'Arbitrage.[42]

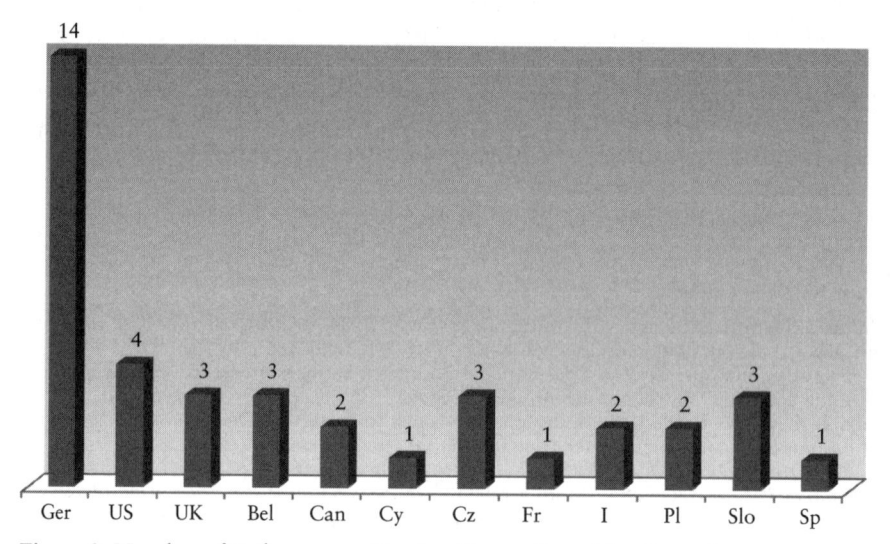

Figure 3: Number of References to Foreign Courts Sorted by Countries

---

[35] Decision No 57/2001 (XII 5) of the Constitutional Court (nullifying a statute that required the newspapers to publish rectifications for critical opinions).
[36] VfGh Beschluss V 136/94-10 [1995].
[37] In the euthanasia case (Decision No 22/2003 (IV 28) of the Constitutional Court) the Court referred to more British precedents not only from the House of Lords, but also from the courts of appeal: *Ms B v An NHS Hospital* [2002], *Re J* [1991] Fam 33 [1991], *Diane Pretty v DPP* [2001], *Eyre v Measday* [1986], *Gold v Haringey Health Authority* [1988]. Another British case (*DPP v Jones and anor* [1999]) was cited in a judgment dealing with the right to assembly.
[38] BGHSt 42, 305 [1996].
[39] Cited only as a 'decision of the Supreme Court taken in 1984'.
[40] *Rodriguez v the Attorney General of Canada* [1993]; *Irwin Toy v A-G of Quebec* [1989].
[41] *Sindicato de la Central Sindical Independiente y de Funcionarios (CSI-CSIF) c el Servicio Andaluz de Salud* [2003].
[42] Arrêt no 151/2002 de la Cour d'Arbitrage.

IV. USING FOREIGN CASE LAW IN CONTEXT

A. Behind the Figures—The Practice of Reviewing Foreign Case Law

As we said above, the quantitative features of studying the use of foreign precedents in constitutional review can be misleading, because these findings are based exclusively on published Court decisions, but the context of the decision-making process, and its circumstances, even if they might have great influence on the Court's decision, are ignored. Besides that, the quantitative data themselves do not tell us anything about the objectives of using foreign judicial cases in legal arguments or their effects on the final decisions.

Therefore, we have to widen the scope of the empirical study, and, secondly, we need to analyse the data in a qualitative way to identify the variables which affect the frequency and the way foreign judicial cases are used in Hungarian constitutional review.

According to the author's research, in practically all cases when an important matter is under consideration, a comparative review is made of the relevant regulation or the judicial practice of many foreign countries. Nevertheless, there is no standard content of such reviews, so neither formal nor informal rules guide these procedures. What is more, the presentation of some foreign examples might be an expectation, but it is not a compulsory part of the preparatory work. All these reviews are prepared by the staff of the constitutional judge who is the *rapporteur* of the case. It means that the Court does not have a specialised service which reports the relevant international judicial practices to the whole Court. Thus, although all the judges may bring foreign cases into the discussion, the use of foreign precedents basically depends on the judge who has been appointed to make a proposal for the Court's decision. Despite the fact that such a review—whatever its scope or quality—is made very frequently in landmark cases, it is often left out from the final version of the decision. The latter has no serious reason; many times, these references are accidentally put in, or left out from, the text. Certainly, if the argument of the Court does not have a steady textual basis or other consensual referential points, the chance of the appearance of such references grows. Similarly, when the Court has to decide highly controversial issues, it turns more readily to foreign examples to back up its view, whatever the constitutional text says.[43]

Sometimes the judgment refers to foreign judicial cases only in general, without specifying the relevant individual decisions. Such a reference may be formulated as a declaration that the interpretation of the Court is in harmony with that of the majority of the 'constitutional states',[44] or the Court may recall one of its earlier decisions in which it analysed the relevant foreign practices or precedents.

Another technique of referring to foreign judicial cases is to use specific and commonly shared concepts which embody or mediate themselves, the law doctrine or practice imported by the Constitutional Court at an earlier time. Thus, when the

---

[43] Eg in the case of the prohibition of the death penalty, or euthanasia. See Decision No 23/1990 (X 31) of the Constitutional Court.
[44] See, eg, Decision No 14/2000 (V 12) of the Constitutional Court.

Court refers to the 'clear and present danger' test in freedom of expression cases, to the 'general personal right' doctrine, or to the 'mother-law' approach, it does it without indicating the original (American and German) precedents, which are replaced with the earlier Constitutional Court's decisions that referred to these doctrines originally.

Finally it is worth noting that the frequency of citations in itself does not tell us much about the reasons and effects of the references, so it is extremely difficult to evaluate the character of the use of foreign judicial practices and cases.

B. Objectives and Goals of Using Foreign Judicial Cases in Constitutional Adjudication

Certainly, when analysing either the reasons for the use of foreign judicial practices, or the real effects of this 'law importation' on constitutional interpretation, we face practical and theoretical difficulties. Generally, the personal intentions and aims of the individual justices are not documented, or proved, so the motivations usually remain uncovered. Moreover, even the most reasoned presumptions cannot be tested or controlled; therefore their explanatory force is uncertain. Similarly, the real effects of using even a particular interpretative construction on the final result, or on constitutional law as a whole can hardly be estimated reliably. Nevertheless, we can get closer to understanding both the possible reasons and effects of the use of foreign case law by a qualitative analysis of this phenomenon, that is, by placing this argumentative practice in the context of constitutional adjudication.

We claim that the way of citing foreign judicial cases, and the use of these precedents in legal arguments, often informs us about the aims of their application.

i. Formal, Illustrative Citations

For an analytical framework, it is advisable to specify the possible reasons for citing foreign judicial cases. If we examine what role these references play in the legal reasoning of the respective cases, it can be said that in most cases they are mentioned only in a very formal way, without being used for establishing a view or an argument. That may explain why the preliminary review of relevant foreign judicial practice is left out of the final text in the end. Although all the interviewed constitutional judges confirmed, for example, that the ECtHR's decisions have a strong persuasive force in those human rights cases to which the European Convention of Human Rights is relevant, it is clear that judges do not attribute an authoritative role to the view of the ECtHR, or to any foreign constitutional court. Therefore, in general, foreign precedents are mentioned out of habit, in order to demonstrate that the Court took account of the most meaningful foreign law,[45] and to report that a comparative analysis in any given case was implemented. Another

---

[45] The Court often refers not only to the respective foreign judicial cases but also describes the relevant laws of some countries, usually Germany, France and Britain.

function of such a citation is to declare the harmony between the decision of the Constitutional Court with the most important foreign case law.

Among the relevant Constitutional Court's cases, this type of reference to foreign law, having only an illustrative function, is the most frequent use of foreign judicial precedents.

ii. Seeking Legitimacy by Using Foreign Judicial Precedents

From the functional point of view, it goes one step further when the Court refers to foreign cases to increase the legitimacy of its own decision. Sometimes the function of the citation is nothing other than to demonstrate the fact that the solution chosen by the Constitutional Court is not in contrast with European standards or tendencies. The jurisprudence of the ECtHR is primarily used for this legitimacy-seeking purpose but sometimes a wide-ranging review of the ruling precedents of the European national constitutional courts plays a similar role. On some occasions, the real function of the comparative analysis of foreign judicial practices is to demonstrate that continental legal development allows a wide-ranging discretionary power for states to decide what can be regarded as a necessary limitation in a democratic society. Sometimes the Court inserts a brief comparative analysis of the law of the European countries into the judgment, which is accompanied by references to foreign judicial precedents.

According to experience, constitutional judges turn to foreign judicial precedents and practices for building legitimacy for their own decisions mostly in cases in which there are deep moral or political cleavages between the different classes or groups of society. In doing so, the Constitutional Court tries to borrow the legitimacy of European standards for its own decisions. Moreover, where fewer grounds are found by the Court to justify its final decision, the more likely it will refer to proper foreign judicial precedents and practices. This was discernible in the euthanasia case,[46] and when the Court sustained the resolution of the National Election Board refusing a referendum on same-sex marriage.[47]

iii. The Use of Foreign Precedents to Support a Particular View

Another possible reason for applying foreign patterns is to support a particular viewpoint. One can call it a 'selective mode' of the use of judicial cases from other countries, which operates in fact as a 'law importation' for specified objectives. This judicial behaviour exploits the undoubtedly significant argumentative force of the foreign courts, particularly that of the ECtHR or the ECJ. The effectiveness of this method is also dubious—surely, these references in themselves are not enough to back up a special approach or to build a consensus around a particular compromise, in particular, when ECtHR case law is used to reduce the level of protection

---

[46] Decision No 22/2003 (IV 28) of the Constitutional Court.
[47] Decision No 65/2007 (X 18) of the Constitutional Court.

in human rights cases.[48] In these cases the selectivity of the citation method was observable, since the Constitutional Court referred only to those foreign examples which confirmed its own view.

This method of reference—which is also used sometimes by judges writing concurring or dissenting opinions—as a form of using foreign judicial precedents and practices is somewhere halfway between the illustrative and the authoritative application of them; although in itself the cases are not enough to justify a particular view, without them the reasoning would be less strong or convincing.

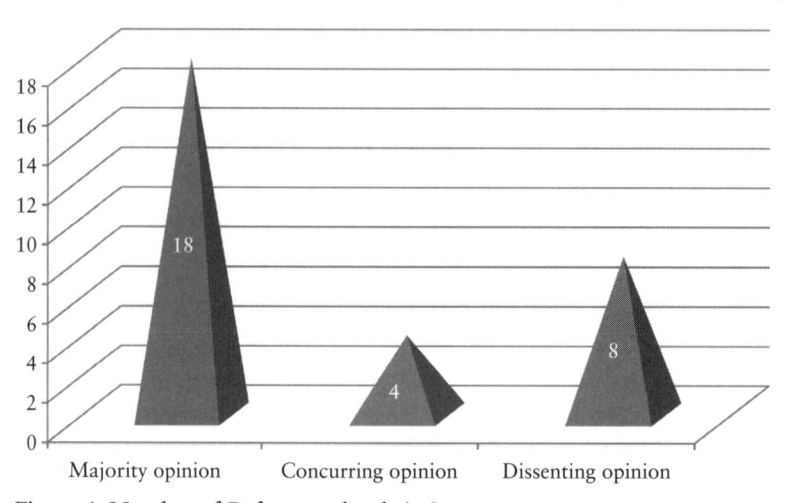

Figure 4: Number of References by their Source

iv. Source of New Ideas and Arguments

Although the Hungarian Constitutional Court, as I said above, has established a comprehensive jurisprudence in the last two decades, it can be regarded as a young constitutional tribunal which faces unprecedented legal problems from time to time. When the Court does not find any antecedents concerning a particular issue in its own practice, it is likely to borrow foreign legal patterns, constructions and particular solutions. Though theoretically this way of 'law borrowing' can be distinguished from the previous one; in particular cases it is very difficult to define whether a foreign construction inspired a specific way of thinking, or whether it was only cited to back up a well-established reasoning.

In recent years we can find some judgments which—citing foreign examples—applied unprecedented formulas to decide on issues raised only recently (eg the EAW),[49] sometimes changing the scope of a constitutional right (eg freedom of expression). This method of using foreign precedents—which takes place relatively rarely—does not raise the problem of legitimacy when the Court only 'learns' from

---

[48] Some scholars claim that the Constitutional Court in some of its recent decisions has narrowed the scope of freedom of expression in relation to the case law of the Sólyom Court in the 90s.
[49] Decision No 32/2008 (III 12) of the Constitutional Court.

other constitutional courts, or finds new ideas, but does not base its final decision solely on them.

v. The Adaptation of Complete Interpretative Doctrines or Legal Constructions

In theory, the most significant use of foreign judicial practices and precedents is adaptation of complete interpretative doctrines or legal constructions (possibly with minor changes). It is a commonly shared view that at the first stage of the existence of the Hungarian Constitutional Court, such foreign judicial practices were used in this way several times. Understandably, a new court, which must decide on basic constitutional issues, and solve sharp legal conflicts from the very first moment of its work, like the Hungarian one in the early 90s, needs patterns and 'good practices' used successfully in other places to follow. In the first period of its operation, the Hungarian Constitutional Court borrowed some whole interpretative constructions from abroad, like the doctrine of the 'living law', the concept of 'general personal right', the 'mother right' from Germany, and the construction of 'equal respect of human dignity' and 'positive discrimination' taken from Ronald Dworkin's theory.[50] This 'law importation' was extended not only to interpretative ways and doctrines, but also to the material scope of law, as happened in the case of human dignity.[51] Although sometimes the source of these borrowings was not indicated, similarities in the justification of these conceptions have often been described.[52]

However, as the jurisprudence of the Court was gradually extended, this complete adaptation of foreign judicial constructions began to decrease. In the period from 1999 to 2010, no such complete adaptation occurred.

C. Judicial Attitudes

Basically, the frequency of references to foreign courts' decisions depends to a great extent on the judges who take part in the decision-making. Under the working conditions of the Constitutional Court, the *rapporteur* of the case also has a particular role from this perspective. This judge prepares the draft resolution of the Court, conducts a review of relevant foreign regulations and judicial cases, and submits a report to the plenum of the body.

---

[50] This is the most famous case, since the first president of the Court, László Sólyom, confirmed it in an interview: 'A nehéz eseteknél' a bíró erkölcsi felfogása jut szerephez. Sólyom Lászlóval, az Alkotmánybíróság elnökével Tóth Gábor Attila beszélget (1997) 1 *Fundamentum*. Sólyom recognised also that the Court's concept of the rule of law reflects the German and the Anglo-Saxon approach of this concept. Sólyom, n 8 above, 142.

[51] See C Dupré, 'Importing Human Dignity from German Constitutional Case Law' in G Halmai (ed), *The Constitution Found? The First Nine Years of the Hungarian Constitutional Review on Fundamental Rights* (Budapest, INDOK, 2000) 215–21.

[52] Most constitutional judges claimed that some early judgments of the Court literally coincided with German precedents.

Although the relatively low number of constitutional judges[53] makes it problematic to classify them, we think that certain judicial attitudes which influence the judges' thoughts on the applicability of the foreign precedents can be identified. On account of the difficulties of these generalisations, some judicial-personality models can only be hypothetical at this time.[54] It is important to note that these speculative models do not exclude each other; since they lay stress on various kinds of attributes and attitudes, the same judge can be classified into more than one group.

The first model characterises the judges on their relevant judicial ideologies. The great majority of judges have a strong conviction emphasising the fact that the Constitutional Court's mission is to protect the national Constitution, which is the highest-ranking norm. From this position any international legal Act, or any foreign judicial practices connected to it, has only secondary significance. A review of relevant foreign judicial cases can have, at most, an illustrative role without any actual effect or influence. Certainly, the alternative view does not refuse the primacy of the Constitution, but its proponents suppose that the Constitution must be interpreted in accordance with international law, basically, with Community law.[55]

Another classification of judges is built on the various judicial attitudes coming from the specialities of their fields of interest. One possible cleavage is between the so-called 'civilists' (dealing with private law) and the public lawyers. Some claim that this attitudinal difference derives from the past when, before the democratic transitions, the comparative method was much more accepted in private law than in the more ideological public law. Therefore, those lawyers who had the opportunity to use foreign law in the past were more open to international examples and judicial practices than those lawyers dealing with constitutional or administrative law. Nevertheless, even if this characterisation is defensible, it can hardly be applied to younger generations who do not have to tackle such difficulties.

The different attitudinal models can probably be used for the 'practical' and the 'theoretical' lawyers as well. Although some evidence—mainly measuring references to foreign cases in individual concurring and dissenting opinions—shows that the former judges of ordinary courts use international examples much more rarely than the law professors, we must be careful not to generalise, since the overwhelming majority of constitutional judges have come from universities, not from courthouses.[56]

Anecdotal evidence points to another personality type, which can be—with an exaggeration—characterised as the 'prisoners of their legal branch'. Judges classified into this category are very strongly connected to their own area of law, and show

---

[53] Between 1999 and 2010, 22 judges in total served the Court, three of them as members of the earlier Sólyom Court (their mandates expired in July 1999). Since 1990, only four members of the Court were ordinary judges beforehand.

[54] For information on the professional careers of the judges see A Sereg, *Alkotmánybírák talár nélkül* (Budapest, KJK Kerszöv, 2005).

[55] The textual ground of this approach was in art 7, s (1) of the Constitution of 1949/1989 saying that '[t]he legal system of the Republic of Hungary accepts the generally recognized principles of international law, and shall harmonize the country's domestic law with the obligations assumed under international law'. Art 2/A of the text allowed a common exercise of 'certain constitutional powers' with EU institutions.

[56] Since 1990, only four former judges have been elected to be members of the Constitutional Court, and two other lawyers from practice.

an indifference towards any wide-ranging law comparison where it does not relate to their own field of interest.

Finally, lack of capacity can hinder the use of foreign judicial cases, and, conversely, language knowledge or former experience of comparative law can encourage judges to extend the scope of legal analysis also to foreign law.[57]

D. The Effects of the Use of Foreign Judicial Cases on Constitutional Review

As to the estimation of the effects of the use of foreign courts' decisions, although it is true that the objectives and goals of the references to foreign judicial cases often determine the effects of the foreign judicial precedents used, it is still extremely difficult to draw well-established conclusions about the influence of these foreign judicial patterns. It seems to be clear that, as a consequence of the formal citation, this kind of use of foreign precedents has produced only a very moderate effect on constitutional interpretation, or has not had any influence at all.

The use of foreign precedents to support a particular view is the next step towards influencing constitutional review but, since in this case references are sought only after establishing the opinion or the argument they are to support, they can only have minimal effect.

The use of other courts' decisions as sources of new ideas or arguments might have a slightly bigger influence on the jurisdiction of the Constitutional Court or, rather, on individual judges. Here there is also the problem of assessing to what extent the use of foreign judicial patterns increased the legitimacy of individual judgments. However, it can be claimed that the examples taken from foreign courts can persuade judges to choose a new direction or legal construction which would not have been followed otherwise.

Certainly, the adaptation of complete interpretative doctrines or legal constructions has the strongest influence on constitutional review. This is the case when the Constitutional Court, in its legal reasoning, follows the argument of a foreign court, adjusting national jurisprudence to international patterns.

V. CONCLUSIONS. THE MAIN CHARACTERISTICS OF THE USE OF FOREIGN JUDICIAL CASES IN HUNGARIAN CONSTITUTIONAL REVIEW

It is certain that the Hungarian Constitutional Court has not evolved a coherent theory on a way of using foreign judicial precedents and practices. It does not have a well-established practice of doing so either. It means that there is no consensual interpretative doctrine to determine in which cases an international comparison should be given and nor do general guidelines exist for choosing the method of comparison. Finally, it is not clear either what the legitimacy is of a pure reference

---

[57] The German orientation of some judges of the Sólyom Court was the main reason for borrowing from German legal doctrines in the early 90s. See Halmai, n 6 above, 693. Another example of the significance of individual influence is that the Court's judgments do not apply to a uniform indication of foreign precedents. For example, the ECtHR's cases are indicated in at least four various forms.

to foreign precedents in constitutional decision-making, that is, whether the citations themselves can be used as legitimate arguments in constitutional reasoning, or not (or, in other words, whether they can provide sufficient reason to choose a particular option among equally possible alternatives). There is no rule when and in which cases foreign precedents should be cited, as these references have no clear function in legal reasoning.

Maybe it would be an exaggeration to require the Court to establish such a coherent theory but, in the absence of it, there is no safeguard to defend judges from the selective or prejudiced citation of foreign law.

If we examine the practice of the Hungarian Constitutional Court in using foreign judicial precedents in constitutional review, we find that the intensity of constitutional 'law importation' has decreased since the first period of its operation. Once the Court had created the foundations of the constitutional structure, after the first years, during the 'consolidated' period, it only refined its case law, which did not need special dogmatic assistance from abroad. Moreover, those doctrines and concepts that were adapted in the early 90s were steadily built in this structure, and they are present in the constitutional jurisdiction even without any repeated reference to their original sources. Instead, the Court used to refer to its own earlier decisions as precedents, rather than citing the foreign cases on which these earlier cases were built. Thus, the doctrines of 'living law', the concept of the 'general personal right', and the 'mother-right' are persisting institutions of constitutional jurisprudence which do not need justification any more. This tendency illustrates the most important implicit impact of comparative constitutional law that influences Hungarian constitutional review constantly, even without explicit references.

Today, the Court refers most frequently to the ECtHR's case law. It means that the centre of interest has moved from the German FCC and the US Supreme Court to the ECtHR. Its obvious cause is Hungary's accession to the European institutions, and its ratification of the European Convention on Human Rights. Although this restructuring of the referential practice of the Court is apparently a conscious process, the appearance of most international references occurs incidentally, rather than in a well-designed procedure.

Another tendency is that the Court cites primarily foreign judicial precedents and practices in human rights cases. It seems that in other issues, such as cases relating to the separation of powers, the Hungarian Constitutional Court is more reluctant to refer to foreign patterns and bases its decision much more readily only on internal sources.

None of these findings tells us much about the future; after the transformation of the scope of responsibilities of the Court, and the occupation of the body by openly political appointees, a new era has probably begun in the life of the Constitutional Court, much closer to politics than ever. Thus, the question of the international judicial discourse will certainly not be a central issue in constitutional interpretation in Hungary for a long time.

11

A Gap between the Apparent and Hidden Attitudes of the Supreme Court of Japan towards Foreign Precedents

AKIKO EJIMA*

TABLE OF CONTENTS

I. Introduction 273
    A. The Purpose 273
    B. The Extent of Use of Foreign Precedents (Target) 274
    C. Working Method and Materials 275
II. Background 278
    A. History of Transplant of Foreign Legal Systems:
       Two Major Transplants from the Western Legal System 278
    B. Civil Law System or Mixed System? 279
    C. The Supreme Court of Japan 280
    D. Majority Opinions, Dissenting Opinions and Concurring Opinions
       of the Supreme Court 280
    E. Importance of the Law Clerk at the Supreme Court 281
    F. The Relationship between Constitutional Legal Scholarship and the Courts 281
III. Empirical Research 283
    A. Quantitative Approach 283
    B. Qualitative Approach 283
    C. Analysis 289
IV. Hidden Influences 290
    A. What Are 'Hidden Influences'? 290
    B. Some Examples 291
V. Conclusions 297

I. INTRODUCTION

A. The Purpose

THIS ARTICLE AIMS to examine the use of foreign precedents by the Supreme Court of Japan in constitutional cases by empirical method. It is difficult to deny that the Japanese national courts are influenced by foreign

---

* Professor, Law School, Meiji University, Tokyo, Japan. This paper revises the previous paper published in A Ejima, 'Enigmatic Attitude of the Supreme Court of Japan towards Foreign Precedents—Refusal at the Front Door and Admission at the Back Door—' *Meiji Law Journal* vol 16 (2009).

case law since some similarities between foreign case law and Japanese case law are sometimes observed. However, as the courts (particularly majority opinions of the Supreme Court of Japan) are very unlikely to refer to or cite foreign case law in a clear way, it is difficult to examine scientifically how and to what extent they are influenced in reality. On the other hand, constitutional academics often analyse and criticise the judgments of the Supreme Court of Japan by using foreign case law (particularly the case law of the Supreme Court of the United States) on the premise that the Court takes into account foreign case law. It is time to examine how and to what extent the Court takes into account foreign case law in order to make academic analysis and criticism effective and meaningful. In other words, it is time to examine the question of legitimacy and methodology of the use of foreign precedents.[1] Therefore, this article tries to draw a clear picture of how and to what extent the Supreme Court of Japan uses foreign precedents by using a quantitative approach (database searching) and a qualitative approach (analysis of specific judgments).

The article, combined with other comparative researches,[2] also aims to examine several constitutional and international legal questions by analysing the quantitative and qualitative research upon the judgments of the Supreme Court. First, to what extent is it possible to say that a transjudicial dialogue between courts exists in reality? Secondly, how and to what extent are the common law and civil law traditions converged? Thirdly, if the above questions can be answered in a positive way, does this contribute to admitting the universalism of human rights in reality? Since references to foreign law and case law in domestic courts are increasing in common law countries and some civil law countries, it is useful to consider the above questions from the new perspective of judicial practice in referring to or citing foreign precedents in an unselfconscious way or a self-conscious (and controversial) way.

B. The Extent of Use of Foreign Precedents (Target)

There is no constitutional court in Japan. However, 'the Supreme Court is the court of last resort with power to determine the constitutionality of any law, order, regulation or official act' (Article 81 of the Constitution of Japan). Moreover, it is accepted as an interpretation that all the courts have the same power.

There is an important difference between constitutional courts and supreme courts for the purpose of the research. In general it is appropriate to consider cases dealt with by constitutional courts as constitutional cases. On the contrary, cases dealt with by supreme courts are not necessarily constitutional cases. In fact the constitutional cases belong to a minority group, taking into account the fact that the Supreme Court of Japan receives around 10,000 cases per year. Therefore, in my research it was necessary to select cases which were relevant to the context of this

---

[1] Cf R Reed, 'Foreign Precedents and Judicial Reasoning: The American Debate and British Practice' (2005) 124 *LQR* 253; C Saunders, 'The Use and Misuse of Comparative Constitutional Law in the Courts' (2006) 13 *Indiana Journal of Global Legal Studies* 37; C Saunders, 'Comparative Constitutional Law in the Courts; Is there a Problem?' (2006) *CLP* 91.

[2] As to the details of other research, see other chapters of the book.

research. In this article I only deal with cases which refer to the provisions of the Constitution of Japan. In order to identify constitutional cases I use a function of the 'TKC' database (Database A, see below I.C.i.), which can search cases by statutes that are referred to in judgments or decisions.

It is also necessary to clarify the meaning of 'foreign precedents'. In this article foreign precedents means foreign precedents concerning constitutional issues such as human rights and constitutional (institutional) problems. Therefore I do not cover foreign precedents of non-constitutional issues although it is sometimes difficult to draw the line. The use of international case law is not included in the present article although it does not mean that I ignore its importance.

C. Working Method and Materials

i. Database

I used two databases. The first one is TKC (Database A).[3] The other is the official website of the Japanese judiciary (Database B).[4] Database A contains 15,885 judgments (*hanketsu*) and decisions (*kettei*) of the Supreme Court of Japan for the period between 5 November 1947[5] and 31 July 2008.[6] Database B has 8,101 judgments and decisions for the same period. In order to carry out the research as thoroughly as possible, I mainly used Database A because Database A contains more judgments than Database B. I used Database B as well as it provides English translations for selected judgments. It has to be noted that neither Database A nor B covers all judgments and decisions given by the Supreme Court of Japan but it can be safely said that together they cover the major constitutional cases.

ii. Time Period

This article covers the period between 1 January 1990 and 31 July 2008.[7] However, the additional research (see IV. below) is not restricted to this time period due to the purpose of the research which I shall explain later.

iii. Working Method

It is difficult to collect cases in which foreign precedents are used without omission because there is no official indication or sign which shows the existence of the use of foreign precedents. Empirically, it is recognised that the Supreme Court of Japan does not use foreign cases for its reasoning. Database A provides information regarding case analysis such as appellate history, significant cases cited, statutes

---

[3] www.tkclex.ne.jp.
[4] www.courts.go.jp.
[5] The Supreme Court of Japan was established in 1947 after the Constitution of Japan was promulgated on 3 November 1946 and took effect on 3 May 1947.
[6] This article is based on the search results I obtained on 31 July 2008.
[7] The period between 5 November 1947 and 31 December 1989 will be covered in future research.

cited and journal articles[8] in a searchable way[9] but it does not have a function to search for foreign precedents in Japanese case law. This shows the current situation of very weak usage (or even non-existence) of foreign precedents in a uniform way.

However, it is also admitted that the judges of the Supreme Court are at least aware of foreign case law from several jurisdictions where such case law is likely to be relevant in terms of similarities of the facts, or issues of the cases, since the reasoning of the judgment of the Court sometimes shows a resemblance to US case law (see IV. below). If I concluded that the Supreme Court of Japan is not interested in foreign case law or foreign law because there is no reference to or citation of foreign case law, this would fail to grasp the reality of hidden rather substantial influences of foreign case law on the Japanese Supreme Court.

In order to deal with the unclear and difficult situation, I adopted two approaches. First, I searched databases by Constitution-related words (such as the Constitution of the United States, constitutional court etc) on the presumption that a judgment is more likely to cite or refer to foreign case law if it cites or refers to foreign law or a name of a judicial institution. After I collected judgments and decisions where a foreign law or the name of a judicial institution was included, I read the whole text of the judgment or decision and checked whether it cited or referred to foreign case law. The problem I encountered here was how to choose search words. In order to have an accurate result, it was preferable to have as many as words possible. On the other hand, it was impossible to do a complete search since the possible search words are countless.

In order to cope with the problem, I temporarily limited the scope of search words on the basis of a hypothesis that countries on which Japanese legal scholars frequently do research as an object of comparative study are more likely to be consulted in judgments if any. The reason for the hypothesis was based on the legal history of Japan.[10] Since Japan transplanted the western legal system in the late nineteenth century, the comparative legal study of foreign countries (particularly Germany, the US, France and the UK) has been very influential. Therefore, if the Supreme Court (and counsel) referred to foreign cases, it was more likely that the Court would refer to the case law of the above countries. If it did not refer to any of them, it was very unlikely that the Supreme Court of Japan would refer to case law of countries not mentioned above. Some strong resemblances of reasoning and tests of constitutionality between the Japanese judgment and the US Supreme Court judgment underpin the assumption.[11]

Additionally, taking into account the popularity of comparative study in Japan, I also added some countries which are often chosen as an object of comparative study because of similarities of the situation or geographical proximity. The countries I searched were as follows: Italy, Spain, Belgium, the Netherlands, Sweden, Denmark, Austria, Switzerland, Canada, Australia, New Zealand, Russia, Poland, Hungary,

---

[8] They are mostly case comments written after the judgments.
[9] The extent of searchable words for Database B is limited.
[10] See II. below for details.
[11] See IV. below for details.

South Korea, People's Republic of China, Republic of China (Taiwan), Thailand, India, South Africa, Brazil and Costa Rica.

The search words I used can be classified into two groups. The first group is country-oriented: アメリカ憲法 *Amerika Kenpou* (American Constitution), 合衆国憲法 *Gasshuukoku Kenpou* (the Constitution of the United States), ドイツ憲法 *Doitsu Kenpou* (German Constitution), 基本法 / ボン憲法 *Kihon Ho/Bonn Kenpou* (Basic Law for the Federal Republic of Germany), ワイマール憲法 *Waimaru Kenpou* (Weimar Constitution), フランス憲法 *Furansu Kenpou* (French Constitution), 第5共和国憲法 *Dai5 Kyowakoku Kenpou* (the Constitution of the Fifth Republic of France), フランス人権宣言 *Furansu Jinken Sengen* (Declaration of the Rights of Man and of the Citizen of 26 August 1789), イギリス憲法 *Igirisu Kenpou* (British Constitution), 権利章典 *Kenri Shouten* (Bill of Rights), マグナ・カルタ *Maguna Karuta* (Magna Carta).

The second group is subject-oriented. I chose words which are likely to appear when foreign cases are referred: 憲法裁判所 *Kenpou Saibansho* (Constitutional Court), 最高裁判所 *Saikou Saibansho* (Supreme Court), 控訴裁判所 *Kouso Saibansho* (Court of Appeal), 地方裁判所 *Chihou Saibansho* (District Court), 連邦裁判所 *Renpou Saibansho* (Federal Court), 憲法院 *Kenpouin* (Conseil Constitutionnel), コンセイユ・デタ *Konseiyu Deta* (Conseil d'Etat), *Haki In* (Cour de Cassation), 貴族院 *Kizokuin* (House of Lords), 控訴院 *Kousoin* (Court of Appeal), 高等法院 *Koutouhouin* (High Court of Justice), EC 裁判所/ヨーロッパ司法裁判所 *EC saibansho/Yoroppa Shihou Saibansho* (European Court of Justice).

The second approach was the adoption of the word '*shogaikoku*' (foreign countries) as a search word on the presumption that the Supreme Court would use the word to generalise its comparative legal consideration instead of specifying which country it took into account. This choice can be legitimised by Japanese legal history where legal transplants and comparative legal studies have thrived (see II. below).

Although the above words do not cover all possible options, I am certain that this search was highly likely to uncover most of the relevant cases.

iv. Search Method

First, I extracted cases which referred to the Constitution of Japan by using a function of Database A to collect cases by statutes. I consider those cases as constitutional cases. Database A contains 234 judgments and decisions for constitutional cases for the period between 1 January 1990 and 31 July 2008. Secondly, I searched 234 judgments and decisions for the search words I set out above (see above I.C.iii). Thirdly, I checked where the search words appeared (majority opinion, dissenting opinion, and/or concurring opinion) in judgments and decisions. Fourthly, I counted the number of judgments where the search words appeared for the quantitative research (see III.A. below). Fifthly, I examined judgments and decisions where the search words appeared in order to evaluate the influence of foreign law or case law for the qualitative research (see III.B. below). Sixthly and lastly, I examined the 'hidden influences' of foreign case law in order to point out the characteristic attitude of the Supreme Court of Japan (see IV. below).

II. BACKGROUND

A. History of Transplant of Foreign Legal Systems: Two Major Transplants from the Western Legal System

Two points should be emphasised in order to understand the Japanese history of the transplantation of foreign legal systems and the significant position of comparative legal study in Japan.

First, long before even the modernisation of Japan which happened in the latter half of the nineteenth century, there was a well-established tradition of importing foreign law as a model: the most influential and long-lasting one was Chinese law from which ancient and medieval Japanese law received strong and direct influences.

Secondly, the co-existence of two different legal families (civil law and common law) in Japanese law is not an intentional or inherent result but rather an accidental and unavoidable one. The outcome of several transplants of different foreign laws is not an amalgam but a patchwork. The first fundamental legal reform occurred in the late nineteenth century. In the mid-nineteenth century when Japan opened itself to the outside world, the modernisation of law in a Western way was the most urgent and important priority in order to catch up with Western standards and revise the unequal treaties between Japan and Western countries since the reason for such unequal treaties was based on the argument that there had been no rule of law or democracy. The Japanese government (Meiji Government[12]) chose the Prussian constitutional system as a model for the Japanese Constitution after an aggressive debate on which country was suitable for Japan to follow as a model. The reason for the choice related to the similarities of the Japanese and Prussian situations. The latter had tried to catch up with other developed countries in order to modernise the country. The French model was refused since it was considered too radical for Japan.

The second thorough legal reform took place after World War II under the US occupation in order to make Japan more democratic and liberal. The result was that the strong influence of US law permeates practical and academic levels.

The major characteristics of the above two turning points were vividly reflected in the drafting process of two Japanese Constitutions. The first one, the Constitution of the Empire of Japan (大日本帝国憲法 *Dai Nippon Teikoku Kenpou*) was the first Western-model Constitution in the history of Japan. It was promulgated in 1889 and came into effect in 1890 in order to claim that Japan was a modernised country with a modern constitutional system. It was modelled on the Prussian Constitution because of the demand for a balance between modernisation and stability (tradition). Therefore, on the one hand, the Constitution was based on the principles of separation of powers and democracy. It included rights of Japanese subjects of the Emperor and an elected House (House of Representatives) as a democratic and constitutional aspect. On the other hand it kept a hereditary Emperor as an absolute

---

[12] The Edo Government (1603–1867) ruled by Tokugawa Shogun failed to achieve modernisation. It gave up the ruling power to the Meiji Government (1868–1912) ruled by Meiji Emperor after minor civil wars.

monarch who maintained full sovereignty; the Parliament legislated in the name of the Emperor, the Cabinet gave help and advice for the Emperor in order to govern and the courts gave justice in the name of the Emperor. Members of the House of Lords were not elected but nominated because of their hereditary aristocratic status. The House of Lords was expected to restrain the House of Representatives, that is, the people's power. The rights of subjects were easily curtailed by legislation and even by orders as there were no safeguards. Above all, the Constitution was prepared for appearance but not for substance (ie, not for the Japanese people). There is a famous anecdote that ordinary citizens did not understand what the Constitution (憲法 *kenpou*) was and misunderstood that they would receive silk cloth (絹布 *kenpu*) as a gift when they heard the news of the promulgation of the Constitution.

The present Constitution, the Constitution of Japan, was promulgated in 1946 and came into effect in 1947. The draft was prepared by the occupation army of the United States. An interesting aspect of this Constitution is that the draft itself is a hybrid of the Constitutions at that time. The Constitution adopts US-style judicial review; and the ordinary courts have a power to strike down statutes. It keeps a bicameral system of the legislature and Cabinet system although the House of Lords was replaced by the House of Councillors (an elected House). Rights of the people (not the subject) were enlarged by adding the equality principle and social rights. Moreover human rights are entrenched by the aforesaid judicial review. It should be emphasised that although the draft itself was prepared by the occupation authorities, it was discussed later at the new democratically elected House of Representatives.[13] The contemporary development of the Constitutions and Bills of Rights in the world influenced on a list of rights of the Constitution. Thus, the scope of the rights is wider than in the US Bill of Rights (the Japanese one has clauses on equality between men and women and social rights[14]). The US judicial model is codified into the Constitution. It is also noteworthy that the birth and development of the Constitution of Japan coincide with the development of international human rights law. Therefore, in theory, it is easier to find more connections between the Japanese Constitution and international human rights treaties. However, in practice, international human rights law has played an extremely limited role in Japanese case law.

B. Civil Law System or Mixed System?

As the historical background shows, in general Japanese law is based on a civil law system. However, because of the accumulation of case law and addition of judicial review, the importance of case law has been increasing in the long run. Especially in the field of constitutional law, the case law of constitutional law has become increasingly important because of the newly-adopted judicial review system. Moreover, taking into account the total absence of amendment of the Constitution

---

[13] For the first time Japanese women over 20 years of age participated in the election.
[14] Art 25 on social rights was added following the proposal of a socialist member of the Diet (Japanese Parliament) at the deliberation of the draft.

since it was enacted, the interpretation of the Constitution by reference to case law is significant.

C. The Supreme Court of Japan

The Supreme Court consists of a Chief Judge and 14 judges. The judges, save for the Chief Judge, are appointed by the Cabinet (Article 79 of the Constitution). The Emperor appoints the Chief Judge of the Supreme Court as designated by the Cabinet (Article 6). Three major groups from which judges are selected are judges, prosecutors and counsel (barristers). There is no law to specify the allocation but since the 1970s it has been the case that six judges are selected from judges, four are selected from counsel and two are selected from prosecutors, based on a custom of filling a vacant post by a person who has the same background of a retiring judge. The Court has also recruited a law professor, an ex-diplomat and an ex-minister in order to obtain judges with wider knowledge and experience. A female judge was appointed in 1994 for the first time. Since then the Court had kept the one-female-judge situation until 2010 when the Court appointed a female judge, that increased the number of the female judges to two. At present there are two female judges. Moreover, it was the first time the Court had a female judge whose background was as a professional judge and law school professor since the previous female judges were all ex-ministers of the Ministry of Labour or the Ministry of Health, Labour and Wealth.[15]

The appointment of the judges of the Supreme Court must be reviewed by the people at the first general election of members of the House of Representatives following their appointment, and must be reviewed again at the first general election of members of the House of Representatives after a lapse of 10 years, and in the same manner thereafter. In the cases mentioned in the foregoing paragraph, when the majority of the voters favours the dismissal of a judge, the judge is dismissed. The judges of the Supreme Court must retire at 70 years old. They receive, at regular stated intervals, an adequate salary which must not be decreased during their terms of office (Article 79).

D. Majority Opinions, Dissenting Opinions and Concurring Opinions of the Supreme Court

The judgment of the Supreme Court is given by one of three Benches[16] (each Bench consists of four or five judges) or by the Grand Bench (15 judges). Any of the Benches can transfer a case to the Grand Bench when it finds that the case in question includes a possibility of unconstitutionality or change of the precedent of the Supreme Court. The opinion of the majority is shown as one opinion. The names of the judges who agree with the majority opinion are shown. The judges who disagree

---

[15] The former was replaced by the latter due to the organisational reform of government.
[16] They are called the First Bench, the Second Bench and the Third Bench.

with the majority opinion, or wish to complement the majority opinion, can write dissenting or concurring opinions. In general the judges are more likely to agree with the majority opinion, without expressing their own view. However, in some controversial cases judges tend to write either dissenting or concurring opinions. For example, in judgments about the constitutionality of the electoral system, a few judges expressed an opinion on democracy and the role of the parliament (see III.B.ii. below). A propensity towards the citation of foreign law or foreign case law by the courts is weak in general.

E. Importance of the Law Clerk at the Supreme Court

It is necessary to mention the important role of the law clerk at the Supreme Court. They are judges of the lower courts and they are nominated as law clerks of the Supreme Court, keeping their status as judges.[17] They are relatively young judges who have worked as a judge for about 15 years before their appointment as a law clerk.[18] Law clerks read case records and submit reports to the judges in order to help judges screen cases (options are dismissal, return to the previous court, or acceptance as a Bench case or a Grand Bench case). Taking into account the present workload of the Supreme Court (it receives around 7,000 cases per year) and the number of judges (15 judges), the role of law clerks is important. There is speculation that law clerks may play a more substantial role in deciding whether an appeal should be accepted or not and in writing a draft of judgments than they are legitimately expected to do. Some law clerks regularly publish case comments on judgments of the Supreme Court in legal journals. Moreover, the Supreme Court of Japan itself has a legal library which covers comparative legal materials including case reports of foreign countries.

F. The Relationship between Constitutional Legal Scholarship and the Courts

Constitutional legal scholars have shown a strong interest in foreign law and case law. It is still quite common that when young scholars enter academic life, they choose one of the Western countries as an object of a thorough comparative study (the country becomes a 'model country' for them). There are advantages and disadvantages. The great advantage is that even when they examine purely Japanese issues, they consciously or subconsciously look at issues from the perspective of their model country. Therefore, it is likely that their discussion can contain a comparative analysis simultaneously. One of the serious disadvantages is that, since specialisation and ramifications in law have gone deeper and further, it is now very difficult to become a specialist of more than one country. Scholars therefore tend to concentrate on one specific foreign country for a comparative study. Therefore their comparison is more likely to become a unilateral comparison than a multilateral

---

[17] They are different from clerks at the lower courts who are not judges and are recruited following a specific examination.
[18] In 2006 there were 34 law clerks.

comparison. When comprehensive comparative research covering major relevant countries is necessary, it has to be performed by a group of scholars. The problem they encounter is that it is extremely difficult to agree on definitions and concepts as each scholar has his/her own definitions and concepts based on his/her model country.

The discussion concerning the introduction of a constitutional court in Japan is a good example to explain the above difficult situation. Scholars who support the introduction of a constitutional court in Japan as a solution to change the passive Supreme Court often refer to constitutional courts in Europe, particularly the German Constitutional Court. It is often the case that their model countries are continental European countries that have constitutional courts. On the other hand scholars who study the US Constitution are more sceptical about having a constitutional court.

The concept of human rights is also heavily influenced by model countries. Ironically it can happen that the definition and concept which Professor A uses (assume that Professor A's model country is Germany) is difficult to understand for Professor B whose model country is the UK which was historically reluctant to codify human rights into a general abstract document. Therefore the Europeanisation of law, if it exists, is a very interesting (and probably helpful) phenomenon for Japanese scholars.

The link between the legal scholarship of constitutional law and the courts has been weak. There are several reasons. Firstly, the Japanese system of nomination and promotion of judges is so bureaucratic that it encourages judges to stay in the circle of judges, but not outside.[19] The Supreme Court always has one academic judge. However, while they are judges at the Supreme Court, they are likely to maintain the status quo rather than propose a reform which they would have supported as academics.[20] The judges whose backgrounds were as judges and prosecutors (they consist of the majority at the Supreme Court with eight out of 15 in total) are more likely to be traditional and conservative-minded.

Secondly, judges are very careful not to show their political viewpoint in order to be seen as neutral or independent. Constitutional matters are often political and controversial. Therefore it is difficult for them to discuss issues in public.[21]

Thirdly, the academic comparative study is very country-oriented, as I explained earlier, so it is not so easy to evaluate its value from a wider perspective. This is the problem that legal academics need to rethink.

The weak link between constitutional scholars and judges is related to the restrained attitude of judges towards foreign law. Constitutional academics have criticised the

---

[19] Supreme Court (Grand Chamber, hereinafter GB), judgment of 1 December 1998 (Judiciary Disciplinary Action case, see below III.B.i.a.), *Saikou Saibansho Minji Hanreishu* (the official case law report published by the Supreme Court, hereinafter *Minshu*) 52-9-1761.

[20] A professor of Anglo-American and Constitutional Law confessed in his book which he published after he retired from the Supreme Court that his views as an academic and his views as a judge of the Supreme Court were different due to the task and role of the judge of the Supreme Court. M Ito, *Saibankan to Gakusha no Aida* [Between the Judge and the Academic] (Yuhikaku, 1993). His opinion as a judge in several controversial cases disappointed other academics who expected to see more radical judgments as he, as an academic judge, was considered to be liberal and a strong supporter of freedom of expression.

[21] Ibid.

Supreme Court on two points from a perspective of comparative study. First, it is inappropriate that the Supreme Court does not refer to or take into account US case law in a clearer way despite the similarities of the issues and contexts. Secondly, how the Supreme Court uses US case law (in a hidden way (see IV. below) is misleading. In my view, foreign case law (particularly US case law) sometimes plays a crucial role in deducing legal reasoning and constitutionality tests 'from a back door'. I shall try to show some examples later (see IV. below). On the other hand the comparative study of foreign case law as well as international human rights law has been a useful source for appellants who bring constitutional cases to the courts.

III. EMPIRICAL RESEARCH

A. Quantitative Approach

There is no explicit citation of foreign case law or foreign law in the majority opinion of the judgments and decisions. In this article an explicit citation means a full case citation including the name of the case; the published sources in which it may be found, if any; the name of the court; and the year of the decision or judgment. There is one case in which a dissenting opinion refers to foreign case law (see III.B.ii.f. below). Moreover, there are six cases in which dissenting opinions refer to foreign law (see III.B.ii. below). There are four cases in which concurring (supplementary) opinions refer to foreign law (see III.B.iii. below).

These results appear to show that the Supreme Court of Japan is not interested in foreign case law. The following qualitative analysis, however, reveals a different story in that the Supreme Court has paid attention to foreign law or case law. Therefore, I include cases where foreign law is referred to in my research in order to highlight the hidden interest of the Supreme Court.

There is no systematic method of citation or reference to foreign law or case law in the case law of the Supreme Court. Therefore, I describe how foreign law or case law is mentioned in each case in the qualitative analysis. There are two interesting examples in the majority opinions of the Supreme Court in which the word *shogaikoku* is used without clarifying which countries they meant. The details are explained in III.B.i.

B. Qualitative Approach

i. Majority Opinion

        a. Judicial Disciplinary Action (1 December 1998)[22]

This case concerns disciplinary action against a judge who participated in a symposium concerning a controversial Communication Interception Bill (which became the Communication Interception Law later)[23] The majority opinion held that legal

---

[22] Supreme Court (GB), judgment of 1 December 1998, *Minshu* 52-9-161.
[23] The organiser of the symposium dealt with the Bill from a critical viewpoint and the judge in question had sent a letter to a newspaper to raise a question against the Bill.

restrictions and practices in 'foreign countries' which adopt a more relaxed attitude towards individual activities of judges can be referable but it is not appropriate to apply them directly to the Japanese context.

b. Nationality Law (4 June 2008)[24]

In this case the words 'foreign countries' are used by both sides: in the majority opinion and the dissenting opinion. This case concerns the legal status (nationality) of a child who was born out of wedlock between a Philippine mother and a Japanese father who legally admitted that he was the father of the child. The Minister of Justice had refused the application for Japanese nationality for the child. The majority opinion held that the child was entitled to acquire Japanese nationality according to the constitutional interpretation of the Nationality Law, mentioning the existence of law reforms in 'foreign countries' abolishing the unequal status between legitimate and illegitimate children.

On the contrary, the dissenting opinion (Judges Yokoo, Tsuno and Furuta) disagreed with the majority opinion on this point. It argued that it was not appropriate to take into account the trend in Western countries, particularly European countries, since there were more international marriages because of the geographical and historical situation and that regional integration was intensified by the development of the EU.

ii. Dissenting Opinion

a. Illegitimate Child (Inheritance) (5 July 1995)[25]

This case concerns the constitutionality of the Japanese Civil Law which prescribes different treatment for a legitimate child and a child born out of wedlock (defined as an 'illegitimate child' in the Civil Law) as to the legal allocation of an inheritance when the deceased person does not leave a testament or there is a disagreement concerning the allocation of the inheritance. The law provides that an 'illegitimate' child is entitled to inherit half of the allocation of the inheritance to which a legitimate child is entitled.

The majority opinion denied unconstitutionality by admitting a wide discretion to the legislature. However, it was a controversial case as the Tokyo High Court had struck down the legislation as unconstitutional in the same case and the Supreme Court judgment itself accompanied five dissenting opinions and five concurring (supplementary) opinions.

Interestingly, both of the dissenting opinions and concurring opinions mentioned foreign law. For example, Judge Kabe's concurring opinion even included the following:

> What is at issue in the present case is not the appropriateness of the legislation which denies, as can be seen in *the often quoted US cases*, the right of the illegitimate child (extra-marital child) as the child of the deceased, but the appropriateness of the shares of

---

[24] Supreme Court (GB), judgment of 4 June 2008, *Hanrei Jiho* 2002-13.
[25] Supreme Court (GB), judgment of 5 July 1995, *Minshu* 49-17-89.

inheritance based upon the premise that the extra-marital child should naturally be one of the heirs (emphasis added).

It is not clear what 'the often quoted US cases' are since he did not give any citations or any hints as to what they might be.

What he wants to emphasise is that the issue in question was not the propriety of the legislation denying the entitlement of an illegitimate child to be an heir as the American legislation in question does, but the propriety of the allocation of the inheritance on the premise that an illegitimate child can be one of the heirs. His usage of foreign law and case law can be classified as 'an example not to be followed (*a contrario*)' in a broader sense.

Judge Onishi's concurring opinion also mentioned the legal reform of European countries in abolishing the unequal status of illegitimate children but he denied the unconstitutionality of the law by emphasising the necessity of a delicate balance between private parties' interests protected by the Civil Law.

On the contrary, the dissenting opinion of five judges strengthened their reasoning by pointing out that it was a general trend in 'foreign countries' that the legal distinction between a legitimate child and an illegitimate child became to be considered as unreasonable and legal reform in order to treat them equally has occurred since the 1960s.

b. Election (House of Councillors) (2 September 1998)[26]

This case concerns the constitutionality of the disparity of value of votes among constituencies of the Election of the House of Councillors from the viewpoint of the equality principle (Article 14 of the Constitution). Due to the rapid urbanisation more and more people moved to the city from rural areas. Consequently, the actual value of one vote varies depending on where electors live. The maximum disparity between an urban constituency and a rural constituency reached 1:4.99.

The majority opinion accepted the constitutionality of the Election Law, admitting a wide discretion to the legislature. However, five dissenting opinions were expressed. The dissenting opinions of Judge Ozaki and Fukuda argued that the acceptable disparity had to be between 10 per cent and 20 per cent (therefore the present disparity was unconstitutional), referring to the situations of the US, the UK, Germany and France and US lawsuits concerning the acceptable disparity. His reference to US lawsuits had no specific citations but referred only to the year of the rulings, which only helps the reader guess what they could be. Therefore, I don't consider it to be a citation or reference. Interestingly the dissenting opinion also referred to academic writings that are rarely referred to in the Supreme Court.

c. Election (House of Representatives) (10 November 1999) I[27]

This case concerns the constitutionality of the disparity (1:2.309) of the value of votes among constituencies of the Election of the House of Representatives. The

---

[26] Supreme Court (GB), judgment of 2 September 1998, *Minshu* 52-6-1373.
[27] Supreme Court (GB), judgment of 10 November 1999, *Minshu* 53-8-1441.

majority opinion held it constitutional but it was a controversial judgment as five dissenting opinions accompanied it.

The dissenting opinion of Judge Fukuda interestingly stated that

> it is impossible to adopt an argument that the interpretation of the Constitution of Japan has to be done according to the case law accumulated by the Japanese judiciary and it is not necessary to consider experiences in foreign countries.

Then, he expanded the number of countries held up for comparison from the US, the UK, France and Germany to which he had referred in the judgment of 2 September 1998 (see above III.B.ii.b) to Italy and Canada which also managed to maintain a disparity of less than 25 per cent. Consequently, he claimed that the examples of other countries were extremely helpful to see how lightly the principle of equality of the Japanese Constitution was taken in the election of Parliament and to what extent it was possible to amend the current situation in order to achieve the goal (1:1) as closely as possible.

d. Election (House of Representatives) (10 November 1999) II [28]

This case concerns the constitutionality of the newly reformed electoral system as the majority system.[29] This was also a controversial case as five judges wrote dissenting opinions. Judge Fukuda repeated what he had said in his dissenting opinion in III.B.ii.c.

e. Election (House of Councillors) (6 September 2000)[30]

This case concerns the constitutionality of the disparity (1:4.99) of the value of votes among constituencies of the House of Councillors. The majority held it constitutional, admitting a wide discretion of Parliament, but five dissenting opinions were expressed.

The dissenting opinion of Judge Fukuda emphasised the importance of judicial review as a mechanism to examine whether legislation made by the legislature based on consideration of policies was constitutionally incompatible or not, mentioning the role of judicial review in other countries. He pointed out the necessity of changes in the precedent.

f. Election (House of Councillors) (14 January 2004)[31]

This case concerns the constitutionality of the disparity (1:5.06) of the value of votes among constituencies of the House of Councillors. The majority held it constitutional, admitting a wide discretion of Parliament. However the content of the

---

[28] Supreme Court (GB), judgment of 10 November 1999, *Minshu* 53-8-1704.
[29] After the political scandal and upheaval, political reform took place in 1994. One of the measures for reform was to change the electoral system from a medium-sized constituency system to a mixed mechanism combining a majority system (300 seats) and a proportional representative system (200 seats, later reduced to 180 seats).
[30] Supreme Court (GB), judgment of 6 September 2000, *Minshu* 54-7-1997.
[31] Supreme Court (GB), judgment of 14 January 2004, *Minshu* 58-1-56.

judgment became more complicated than the judgment of 6 September 2000 (see above III.B.ii.e.) since six judges expressed dissenting opinions and nine judges who agreed with the majority opinion wrote concurring opinions.

The dissenting opinion of Judge Fukuda strongly argued for the need for a judgment admitting the unconstitutionality of the present disparity existing at the constituencies of the House of Councillors. He emphasised that disparity of vote values was taken seriously in the US, Germany and Italy as he did in previous cases (see above III.B.ii.c.–e.), referring to judgments of the US Supreme Court as the 'judgment of 1962' and the 'judgment of 1983'. Although he did not give the citation detail we know that by the 'judgment of 1962' he is referring to *Baker v Carr* (1962) as he described the content of this American judgment. Therefore, this is the only example of a dissenting opinion referring to foreign case law.

Moreover he suggested that if the Court continued to avoid declaring the present disparity as unconstitutional, it would trigger an argument for a constitutional court and the Court would lose the power of judicial review since the Court might be considered to be useless at protecting a democratic government whose healthy condition was fundamentally guaranteed by judicial review.

The dissenting opinion of Judge Kajtani also mentioned that the equality principle of vote values was rigorously protected in Western democratic countries. Particularly he pointed out the fact that the US Supreme Court held that the 'one person one vote' principle had to be applied in elections and that since 1963 the principle has been rigorously applied. It should be noted that Judge Kajitani referred to the dissenting opinion of the judgment of 2 September 1998 (see above III.B.ii.b.).

g. Nationality Law (4 June 2008)[32]

See above III.B.i.b.

iii. Concurring (Supplementary) Opinion

a. Illegitimate Child (Inheritance) (5 July 1995)[33]

See above III.B.ii.a.

b. Separation of Government and Religion (Laïcité) (2 April 1997)[34]

This case concerns the constitutionality of an act of local government which paid the fee for offerings to the Yasukuni shrine, a principal Shinto shrine in Japan. The Constitution of Japan provides for freedom of religion (Article 20) and the separation of government and religion in order to ensure religious liberty (Articles 20 and 89). The issue is whether the local government's payment is considered to be a religious act which is prohibited under the Constitution or a social custom which

---

[32] Supreme Court (GB), judgment of 4 June 2008, *Hanrei Jiho* 2002-13.
[33] Supreme Court (GB), judgment of 5 July 1995, *Minshu* 49-17-89.
[34] Supreme Court (GB), judgment of 2 April 1997, *Minshu* 51-4-1673.

the Japanese people may expect the local government to practise. The historical background to the case is that before and during World War II the Yasukuni shrine played an important spiritual and religious role in maintaining government policy which was undemocratic and militaristic, and often suppressed freedom of other religions.

It is noteworthy that the Supreme Court previously established a constitutionality test (purpose–effect test) concerning the principle of separation of government and religion in its judgment of 13 July 1977 (see IV.B.iii.). It is widely considered that the Court applied the 'Lemon' test of the US Supreme Court although the citation was not found in the judgment. In the judgment of 13 July 1977 the Court held that local government did not breach the Constitution as a result of the application of the test. The conclusion and the test itself were severely criticised by academics. They claimed that the test (or how the test was applied) was so broad and ambiguous that it could not control government activity in order to guarantee the protection of freedom of religion. On the contrary, in the 1997 judgment, the Court ruled that local government had breached the Constitution. Therefore, it is interesting to see whether the Supreme Court maintained the previous test (but reached a different conclusion on the facts) or developed the previous precedent into a different test.

The concurring opinions of Judge Takahashi and Ozaki are noteworthy on this point. They criticised the purpose–effect test as too obscure to decide the extent of a constitutionally-permissible relationship between government and religion. Judge Takahashi supported the absolute separation of government and religion and proposed a new test to the effect that it was not permissible for the government to be involved with any religion unless complete separation was impossible or inappropriate.

Judge Ozaki, who shared the same view (absolute separation) with Judge Takahashi, pointed out an interesting comparison. He stated that it was wrong to adopt the purpose–effect test just because of apparent similarities of Amendment Clause 1 of the US Constitution and Article 20 of the Constitution of Japan. In his view the US Constitution sets out what is prohibited under the Constitution (he cited the words of the US Constitution). Therefore it is necessary to make it clear what is prohibited and to establish a test for that purpose. On the contrary the Japanese Constitution prohibits all religious acts of government. Therefore, it is logical to prescribe narrowly what is permissible as an exception under the Constitution on the premise that all religious acts are prohibited. In his words, government must not be involved with an act whose religious nature is suspected unless there is clearly a highly legal interest which would permit an exception to the separation principle. How he used the US Constitution can be classified as 'an example not to be followed (*a contrario*)' in a broader sense.

c. Illegitimate Child (Inheritance) (27 January 2000) I[35]

This case concerns the constitutionality of the Japanese Civil Law as mentioned above. The concurring opinion of Judge Fujii generally mentioned the trend of

---

[35] Supreme Court, judgment of 27 January 2000, *Hanrei Jiho* 1260-6.

legislation in 'foreign countries' and ratification of international human rights treaties in the context of analysing the background of influential opinions which were sceptical towards the law. He, however, dealt with it more discreetly and gave a wider discretion to the legislature.

d. Illegitimate Child (Inheritance) (27 January 2000) II[36]

The issue is the same as in III.B.iii.c. Judge Fujii repeated the same concurring opinion.

C. Analysis

Despite the fact that appellants often cite or refer to foreign law or case law which reinforces their arguments and submit academic papers as evidence, it is very unlikely that foreign law or case law influences judgments of the Supreme Court in an explicit way.

There are, however, some exceptions. First, when the gaps between Japanese law and foreign law are very wide, a comparison between them catches the attention of judges who disagree with the majority opinion. Good examples are the cases concerning disparity of vote values (see above III.B.ii.b.–f.) among constituencies and cases concerning the legal distinction of a legitimate child and an illegitimate child (see above III.B.ii.a. and g.).

In the former example, dissenting opinions of the Supreme Court strongly claimed the unconstitutionality of the Election Law by widely referring to foreign law and case law, such as that of the US, the UK, Germany, France, Italy and Canada in order to show the fact that permissible disparities in Western democratic countries were far narrower than in Japan.

In the latter example, the dissenting opinion also referred to the general trend in foreign countries of abolishing the legal distinction between a legitimate and an illegitimate child and supported the appellants' claim of unconstitutionality.

Interestingly, not only the dissenting opinion but also the majority opinion mentioned the legal trend in foreign countries to strengthen the conclusion of unconstitutionality in the Nationality Law case (see above III.B.i.b.).

Secondly, although there is a gap between Japanese law and foreign law and although that gap is enormous, some judges felt obliged to emphasise that it was important to respect the differences between Japan and foreign countries (see above III.B.iii.a., c. and d.).

It can be pointed out that dissenting opinions are more likely to refer to foreign law or case law than majority opinions or concurring opinions. The reason for this is presumably that it is helpful for a dissenting opinion to rely on foreign law, or case law of foreign countries, which has formed the basis of Japanese law when the foreign law or case law supports the dissenting opinion. On the contrary, because of the minimalistic attitude of the Supreme Court of Japan, if the Court can derive

---

[36] Supreme Court, judgment of 27 January 2000, *Katei Saibansho Geppo* 52-7-78.

a conclusion from Japanese law and the case law of the Supreme Court of Japan and the conclusion is compatible with foreign law and case law, then the Court can feel it is enough to rely on its own case law and not necessary to cite the foreign law or case law.

IV. HIDDEN INFLUENCES

A. What are 'Hidden Influences'?

In this section I discuss cases where the majority opinions do not cite or refer to foreign case law or foreign law in an explicit way but where the reasoning and/or test (standard) of constitutionality is so similar to existing foreign case law that it is difficult to deny the existence of influences. In other words, the similarities are so strong that it could have been classified as a direct influence if the Court had added a formal citation.

In order to cover the most appropriate examples of hidden influences and depict interesting characteristics of case law of the Supreme Court, in this section I enlarge the time period to include earlier cases. Examples are not exhaustive.

Presently I can think of three sources of hidden influences. First, appellants often cite or refer to foreign case law or foreign law to reinforce their argument although it is unlikely that judges adopt their argument based on foreign legal authorities.

Secondly, some judges whose backgrounds are academic tend to have more comparative legal knowledge. A good example is Judge Ito who was formerly an Anglo-American law professor at Tokyo University before he was appointed as a judge of the Supreme Court. Therefore his reasoning, and even tests of constitutionality, is strongly influenced by his study of US case law (see below IV.B.iv.).

Lastly, it can be presumed that law clerks may prepare some comparative law materials including foreign law and case law which are relevant to the particular case in question. It is even possible to speculate that when law clerks support a drafting process of judgments, their knowledge of foreign case law, particularly US case law, might have an indirect influence on the process. It looks more likely when it is taken into account that law clerks are in their late 30s to early 40s many of whom have studied constitutional law by using textbooks influenced by US constitutional case law. The best example is a textbook written by Professor Ashibe of Tokyo University who was keen on activating the role of the Supreme Court as a guardian of the Constitution and human rights after his comparative study in the United States.[37]

It should be noted that in the 1980s the theme of judicial review became very popular among scholars and a thorough comparative study of US case law has continued since then. Particularly, the aforementioned Professor Ashibe played an important role in familiarising the judiciary with a uniform way of adjudicating constitutional cases, by suggesting various tests (standards) of constitutionality

---

[37] N Ashibe, *Constitutional Law*, 5th edn (Iwanami, 2011) is a bestselling constitutional law textbook in Japan.

which he learned from US case law. Direct influence (whether his efforts were successful) was limited and difficult to evaluate as the Supreme Court does not adopt the same tests of constitutionality as Professor Ashibe advocated. However, if I compare the judgments of the earlier period and the current judgments, differences exist. The reasoning of judgments became clearer and some constitutionality tests can be recognised although constitutional legal scholars still criticise the ambiguity of the reasoning and the inappropriateness of the constitutionality test.

Judges are more concerned with the harmony and consistency of judgments and the constitutional role of judges as a last resort to protect human rights. Because of an accumulation of judgments they put themselves in a situation where they are not only required to give an answer to the case in question but also required to deliver consistent and persuasive precedents. Although judicial change takes more time to emerge and is subtle in the Japanese context, it does happen in my view.[38] The next section will show some examples.

B. Some Examples

i. *Pharmacies' Location Regulation (30 April 1975)*[39]: *Level of Scrutiny and Footnote Four of Carolene Products*

This case concerns legal regulation on locations of pharmacies by the Pharmaceutical Affairs Law. At the beginning of the judgment, the majority opinion emphasised the difference between freedom to choose an occupation and freedom of mental activities (freedom of conscience, religion and expression).

Indeed, because an occupation is in essence a social and, moreover, principally an economic activity, and by its nature something in which mutual social relations are important, in comparison to other constitutionally guaranteed freedoms, especially the so-called 'mental' freedoms, the demand for regulation by a public authority is stronger. Thus, we can see that Article 22, paragraph 1 of the Constitution on freedom of occupational choice, with the reservation 'to the extent that it does not interfere with the public welfare', may be considered to derive from an intent to emphasise this point in particular.[40]

Academic scholars understood the judgment in the sense that the Court admitted the supremacy of freedom of expression and therefore, when the Court examines the constitutionality of restrictions upon freedom of expression, it does so more carefully by using stricter tests. Therefore, they claimed that the Supreme Court of Japan accepted the idea of there being a level of judicial scrutiny depending on the characters of rights as the US Supreme Court did. As I explained before, efforts of Japanese constitutional scholars introduced the idea of a level of scrutiny into Japanese constitutional legal study. However, it is not certain whether the Supreme Court was aware of footnote four of the case of *United States v Carolene Products*

---

[38] In September 2008, a judge of the Supreme Court who was born after World War II was appointed for the first time.
[39] Supreme Court (GB), judgment of 30 April 1975, *Minshu* 29-4-572.
[40] www.courts.go.jp/english/judgments/text/1975.04.30-1968-Gyo-Tsu-No.120.html.

Company[41] but it is likely that the Court (or young legal clerks) knew the idea of a level of judicial scrutiny in the US.

> There may be narrower scope for operation of the presumption of constitutionality when legislation appears on its face to be within a specific prohibition of the Constitution, such as those of the first ten amendments, which are deemed equally specific when held to be embraced within the Fourteenth...
>
> It is unnecessary to consider now whether legislation which restricts those political processes which can ordinarily be expected to bring about repeal of undesirable legislation, is to be subjected to more exacting judicial scrutiny under the general prohibitions of the Fourteenth Amendment than are most other types of legislation. Nor need we enquire whether similar considerations enter into the review of statutes directed at particular religious ... or national ... or racial minorities ...: whether prejudice against discrete and insular minorities may be a special condition, which tends seriously to curtail the operation of those political processes ordinarily to be relied upon to protect minorities, and which may call for a correspondingly more searching judicial inquiry.[42]

Ironically, the Japanese Supreme Court has never admitted a violation of Article 21 which guarantees freedom of expression. The level of scrutiny for freedom of expression cases which the Court adopted has been often criticised on the basis that it was not strict enough to protect freedom of expression.

ii. Public Safety Ordinance (10 September 1975)[43]

This case concerns the group parades and demonstrations which violated the Public Safety Ordinance of Tokushima City and the Road Traffic Law. The appellants claimed that the legislation violated Article 31 of the Constitutional Law as it was not clearly written.

This case showed characteristics of the opinions of the Supreme Court which I clarified in section III. Firstly, the majority opinion did not refer to or cite any foreign case law. Secondly, one of the concurring opinions showed a strong affinity to US Supreme Court case law. Judge Kishi referred to historical vicissitudes of the clear and present danger test of US case law in order to show the extent of the doctrine.

> The judicial precedents of the United States Supreme Court apply the principle of 'clear and present danger' in deciding continuality [sic][44] because the purpose of regulations is to control the expressions as they are, and it is striving to decide the constitutionality of such regulations by a strict standard. The principle was originally used for deciding the constitutionality of punishing the acts such as instigation or agitation of the acts that cause a substantial harmful effect that may be constitutionally prevented by the nation. The grounds for the control can be seen in the idea that those expressions that may cause imminent danger of a substantial harmful effect can be regarded as an action causing such a harmful effect, therefore, there is no time to wait for a natural control by exchange of free expressions. The said principle has been applied widely especially since the 1930s and in deciding the control over the acts of freedom to be unconstitutional, the phrase

---

[41] *United States v Carolene Products Company*, 304 US 144 (1938).
[42] Ibid, fn 4.
[43] Supreme Court (GB), judgment of 10 September 1975, *Saikou Saibansho Keiji Hanreishu* (hereinafter *Keishu*) 29-8-489.
[44] The original Japanese text says 'constitutionality'.

has appeared like a cliche, however, consideration has been accumulated on the scope of its application, and in 1950, it has become clarified that the principle does not apply to every case, as it does not apply to the case where the purpose of control is to prevent the critical and harmful effect caused by the action. In 1951, it was pointed out that the principle had been widely applied to cases where guaranteed interests are insignificant and are not sufficient to regard the control as constitutional. Even for the control that intends to prevent the harmful effect of expressions themselves, when the interests to be guaranteed are extremely important, the range of control can be expanded and with respect to the application of the principle, it has become evident that the consideration is required by means of weighing up the advantages and disadvantages. In 1965, it was decided that the acts of parades and gatherings are a mixture of action and expression, therefore, in order to prevent a substantial harmful effect caused by the phase of action, to punish a demonstration in the neighborhood of the courts is constitutional. In 1968, with respect to a case of a symbolic action, that is the act of burning a draft card in public, when an act of speech and non-speech are combined to one action and a sufficient national interests [sic] can be seen in controlling the phase of non-speech, it is not unconstitutional to restrict the freedom of expression that was accompanied by the restriction. Further, in the judicial precedent in 1973, which decided that prohibition of political action by public officials is constitutional, an important consideration was given to the distinction between a genuine speech and a speech with action.

It goes without saying that I do not doctrinally follow the judicial precedents in the U.S. Among the said summarized judicial precedents, there are opposing opinions which are worth listening to, however, some of the cases have a different nature of content from those in question in Japan. Nevertheless, the reason for having cited them, I think it is worthwhile paying attention to the change of application of the principle in the above judicial precedents. That is, I think it is important to consider that the change of its application was not deducted by mere logic, but as a result of induction based on experience, the emphasis is placed on the choice of rational values in the judicial procedure, and even if there was an age of expanding the application of the principle, these days, it has been consciously used as a standard for deciding the constitutionality of the control over expressions.[45]

Thirdly, the reason Judge Kishi invoked US case law was not for admitting a violation of the Constitution, but to limit the extent of protection of freedom of expression. The same attitude can be observed in other cases (see above III.B.iii.).

iii. Separation of Government and Religion (Laïcité) (13 July 1977)[46]: Purpose–effect Test and Lemon Test

The case concerns the constitutionality of the local government act which presided over a ceremony in a Shinto style (Jichinsai[47]). Such ceremonies are often performed before the construction of buildings in Japan to pray for safety. The issue is whether the ceremony is a religious activity which the government is prohibited from practising under the Constitution (Articles 20 and 89) or a social custom which the people expect the local government to carry out to ensure the safety of construction work.

---

[45] www.courts.go.jp/english/judgments/text/1975.09.10-1973-A-.No.910.html.
[46] Supreme Court (GB), judgment of 13 July 1977, *Minshu* 31-4-533.
[47] A religious ceremony to pray to a god of earth that the construction work would not disturb the god.

The court used a test to decide whether the act in question was constitutional or not:

> 'religious activity' should not be taken to mean all activities of the State and its organs which bring them into contact with religion, but only those which bring about contact exceeding the aforesaid reasonable limits and which have a religiously significant *purpose*, or the *effect* of which is to promote, subsidise, or, conversely, interfere with or oppose religion. The prime example of such activities is the propagation or dissemination of religion, such as religious education, which is explicitly prohibited in Article 20, Paragraph 3; but other religious activities like celebrations, rites, and ceremonies are not automatically excluded if their purpose and effects are as stated above. Thus, in determining whether a particular act constitutes proscribed religious activity, external aspects such as whether a religious figure officiates or whether the proceedings follow a religiously prescribed form should not be the only factors considered. The totality of the circumstances, including the place of the activity, whether the average person views it as a religious act, the actor's intent, purpose, and degree (if any) of religious consciousness, and the effects on the average person, should be taken into consideration to reach an objective judgment based on socially accepted ideas (emphasis added).[48]

The stark similarities (using the same words such as purpose and effect) between the above purpose–effect test and the Lemon test of the US Supreme Court was pointed out by Japanese scholars although the Court did not cite *Lemon v Kurtzman*.[49]

> Every analysis in this area must begin with consideration of the cumulative criteria developed by the Court over many years. Three such tests may be gleaned from our cases. First, the statute must have a secular legislative *purpose*; second, its principal or primary *effect* must be one that neither advances nor inhibits religion, Board of Education v Allen, 392 US 236, 243 (1968); [403 US 602, 613] finally, the statute must not foster 'an excessive government entanglement with religion'. Walz, supra, at 674 (emphasis added).[50]

Taking into account the fact that the Court had no previous experience of how to interpret the separation clause, it can easily be imagined that the Court consulted the case law of the US Supreme Court since some clauses of the Japanese Constitution are largely modelled on the US Bill of Rights and, in particular, Article 20 of the Japanese Constitution is considered to be influenced by the First Amendment of the US Constitution. The latter point was raised by the dissenting opinion of Judge Fujibayashi. Moreover, the introduction of the principle of separation of government and religion was one of the principal policies of the occupation period. Moreover, Japanese judicial review was considered to be modelled on US judicial review. Therefore, it is difficult to say that the Court has not been influenced by US case law.

If the purpose–effect test and the Lemon test are observed carefully, there are significant differences. Before analysing the differences, the important difference between the original Japanese text and the translated English text which I use in my

---

[48] www.courts.go.jp/english/judgments/text/1977.7.13-1971.-Gyo-Tsu-.No..69.html.
[49] *Lemon v Kurtzman*, 403 US 602 (1971).
[50] Ibid.

article has to be pointed out. The latter translated the important part of the judgment from which the purpose–effect test was drawn as

> 'religious activity' should not be taken to mean all activities of the State and its organs which bring them into contact with religion, but only those which bring about contact exceeding the aforesaid reasonable limits and which have a religiously significant purpose, *or* the effect of which is to promote, subsidize, or, conversely, interfere with or oppose religion (emphasis added).

This means that if the religious activity has (a) a religiously significant purpose, or (b) the effect of it is to promote, subsidise, interfere or oppose religion, the activity is unconstitutional. However, in the original Japanese version, it is not clear whether it is necessary to satisfy (a) or (b), or (a) and (b) in order to recognise the activity as unconstitutional. Probably, according to ordinary Japanese usage, it is more natural to interpret the Japanese original text as (a) and (b).[51] However, as I took the English text from the official website of the Supreme Court, in this article I stick with the English text on the premise that (a) or (b) is the official view.

The Lemon test requires the government to fulfil all three conditions in order to be accepted as constitutional. If any of these three conditions are violated, the government act is considered to be unconstitutional. On the other hand, according to the Japanese test if the government act has a religiously significant purpose, or the effect of the act is to promote, subsidise, or, conversely, interfere with or oppose religion, the act is deemed unconstitutional. Moreover, the Japanese test does not include the third requirement of the Lemon test ('an excessive government entanglement with religion'). Therefore, the judgment was criticised on the basis that the Supreme Court of Japan softened the Lemon test in order to allow the government to carry out questionable religious activities.

The advantage of not officially citing foreign case law may be to protect the Court from criticism.[52] After all, the Court did not cite the US case law. Therefore, criticism about the Lemon test is not directly applicable to the Japanese Court. However, if this was an academic work, it would be called plagiarism or, at least, misquotation.

Probably the problem of hidden influence (not disclosing the source) is that there is no clear explanation why the purpose–effect test can draw a line between a prohibited religious act and a permissible religious act. On the contrary, the US Supreme Court established the test by consideration of the cumulative criteria developed by the Court over many years. The legitimacy and rationality of the US test is supported by fact and experience.

The purpose–effect test was so influential that courts never failed to use the test in cases concerning the principle of separation of government and religion (see above III.B.iii.b.) since the 1977 judgment. However, some scholars point out that

---

[51] The requirement for (a) and (b) makes the extent of unconstitutional religious activity narrower.
[52] In the United States, the use of foreign precedents has been controversial and the media have criticised Justices of the Supreme Court who have cited foreign law. See Reed, n 1 above at 253. cf Ginsburg, 'A Decent Respect to the Opinions of [Human] Kind: The Value of a Comparative Perspective in Constitutional Adjudication' (2005) 64 *CLJ* 575.

the purpose–effect test is not applicable and adequate for all cases concerning the separation principle. If the origin of the Japanese purpose–effect test is US case law, then it is more productive to disclose the origin and examine to what extent US case law is relevant, taking into account the differences of fact and background. A thorough and exhaustive comparison of Japanese and US cases (including similarities and differences of cultural and historical background) helps to clarify the range of the purpose–effect test. If the origin of the test is not US case law, it is important to analyse all the cases concerning separation of government and religion in order to re-examine the extent of the purpose–effect test. In 2010 the Court dealt with a case concerning the separation principle without using the purpose-effect. A new academic discussion on the purpose-effect test started.

iv. Prohibition on Leaflet Distribution (18 December 1984)[53]:
   Public Forum Doctrine

This case concerns freedom of expression in relation to the distribution of a political leaflet at a railway station run by a private railway company. The appellants claimed that criminalising their act of distribution was unconstitutional. The majority opinion simply denied the appellants' claim. The majority admitted that Article 21 did not guarantee absolute freedom of expression and permitted necessary and reasonable restraint on freedom of expression. It did not show any specific test to judge constitutionality or adopt stricter scrutiny. This is an example of the fact that the Court has not introduced any stricter scrutiny or a stricter test for freedom of expression (see above IV.B.i.).[54]

The interesting characteristic of this case is the concurring opinion of Judge Ito who was an Anglo-American law professor before he joined the Court. In his opinion, he introduced the concept of a 'Public Forum' where freedom of expression has to be guaranteed as carefully as possible in order to secure a place (public forum) where people can communicate their opinion to other people in an effective way. The English words 'public forum' were not translated but written as 'puburikku fouramu'[55] (パブリック・フォーラム). Therefore it is very clear that the concept is imported from outside, that is, from US case law. However, he did not cite any US case law concerning the public forum doctrine. It is interesting to consider why he mentioned the public forum doctrine despite the fact that he joined the majority opinion and stated that the place in question did not have the strong nature of a public forum.

---

[53] Supreme Court (Third Bench), judgment of 18 December 1984, *Keishu* 38-12-3026.

[54] It should be recalled that the judgment was given not by the Grand Bench but by the Third Bench.

[55] In Japan foreign words are often written or spoken as they sound in Katakana. Katakana (one of three characters of Japanese) is used to make people notice that they are foreign words. The advantage of this usage is that they don't need to translate them. The disadvantage is that they accept the words without thinking what they mean in reality. Moreover, it is very likely that how to read the words is greatly influenced by the Japanese language, eg, public forum is pronounced pu-bu-ri-kku fo-u-ra-mu.

v. Use of City Hall (7 March 1995)[56]: Clear and Present Danger Test

This case concerns the refusal of a permit to use a city hall for a political meeting (a political campaign of the leftist group against a newly planned airport). The organiser of the meeting claimed that the refusal by the city council violated the right to freedom of expression and association (Article 21 of the Constitution) and that the refusal was censorship which the Constitution prohibited (Article 21). The Court ruled that the refusal was constitutional (one concurring opinion).

I choose this as the last case because it includes points I raised. Moreover, it shows a typical situation of case-law building by the Supreme Court of Japan. First, the principal issue of the case is freedom of expression. The Court has never found a violation of the Constitution and it did not in the case in question.

Secondly, similarities in the wording of the scrutiny test between Japanese and US case law can be found. The Court required the city council to foresee a clear and present danger in order to refuse the permit of the city hall. *Schenk v United States* established the test in 1919 but there is no citation of it by Japan.

> The question in every case is whether the words used are used in such circumstances and are of such a nature as to create a clear and present danger that they will bring about the substantive evils that the United States Congress has a right to prevent. It is a question of proximity and degree. When a nation is at war, many things that might be said in time of peace are such a hindrance to its effort that their utterance will not be endured so long as men fight, and that no Court could regard them as protected by any constitutional right.[57]

Thirdly, because of the accumulation of Japanese case law it seems that the Court becomes less likely to mention the case law of foreign countries. Instead, the Court cites its own case law. However, there are some problems from a perspective of case-law building. For example, the Court referred to the judgment of 23 December 1953 which was not ratio decidendi but obiter dictum on the matter in question.[58] The Court also referred to the judgment of 11 June 1986[59] in which the facts and context are different from the case in question. Similar problems are widely recognised in other cases. The concept and principle of the precedent is relatively ambiguous and loose.

V. CONCLUSIONS

In my view, the influence of foreign law or case law at the Supreme Court of Japan seems relatively bigger than scholars have empirically thought if hidden influences are taken into account. Majority opinions of the Supreme Court have received hidden influences from foreign case law, particularly the case law of the US Supreme Court. One of the judges of the Supreme Court of Japan clearly stated that it was

---

[56] Supreme Court (Third Bench), judgment of 7 March 1995, *Minshu* 49-3-687.
[57] *Schenck v United States*, 249 US 47 (1919).
[58] The judgment of 23 December 1953 dismissed the appeal because it did not find a legal interest to be protected. The 1953 judgment, however, added a supplementary opinion on the constitutionality of the refusal of the permit as a matter of further elaboration, to which the 1995 judgment referred.
[59] It concerned an injunction to prevent defamation against an electoral candidate by a journalist.

not acceptable to deny the importance of foreign experiences although it was in his dissenting opinion.

The problematic aspect is, however, that foreign case law is rather randomly and arbitrarily utilised when it is convenient for judges to use it in order to reinforce their reasoning or argument. Besides, since judges do not show citations of foreign case law when they mention it or indirectly utilise it, it is often difficult to identify cases considered. After all the present methodology for citation of precedents of Japanese case law itself is problematic as it does not show which page or paragraph of a judgment or decision the Court is citing. This is a great difference between the Japanese jurisdiction and common law jurisdictions which acknowledge precedents in a methodological way.

I conclude the article with an attempt to answer further constitutional and international legal questions which I raised in the beginning. Firstly, as to the existence of trans-judicial dialogue between courts, the phrase 'trans-judicial dialogue' needs to be clarified in order to have a productive and substantial discussion. If 'trans-judicial dialogue' means a situation where a court of country A refers to or cites country B's case law and vice versa, then the Japanese situation is not a dialogue but a one-sided import. Justice Ginsburg once wrote:

> If US experience and decisions can be instructive to systems that have more recently instituted or invigorated judicial review for constitutionality, so we can learn from others now engaged in measuring ordinary laws and executive action against charters securing basic rights.[60]

Her argument is suggestive and encouraging for 'others' although her position is controversial in the United States. On the other hand, the growing interest in comparative law in the US and Europe will support the development of such dialogue in a positive way. In the Japanese context more attention should be given to the necessity for legitimacy to include a methodology of using foreign precedents in order to avoid misuse of foreign precedents and achieve consistent and productive use of foreign precedents. I also would like to emphasise the possibility that the existence of the European Court of Human Rights (ECtHR) greatly promotes 'trans-judicial dialogue' by the accumulation of the case law of the ECtHR in the European context. The case law of the ECtHR can be recognised as semi-constitutional cases since many of the cases are dealt with either by the constitutional courts or supreme courts before they go to Strasbourg and the ECtHR takes into account domestic judgments.

Secondly, as to the convergence of the common law and civil law traditions, it is necessary to do a more detailed and wider analysis by widening the scope of research to include civil and criminal laws since Japan has transplanted civil law and common law. In general there is a convergence of the common law and civil law tradition in Japan in a generally unselfconscious but interesting way. The present research shows that Japan does not distinguish between common law case law and civil law case law.

---

[60] Ginsburg, n 52 above, 576.

Lastly, it can safely be said that the Supreme Court of Japan has accepted the universalism of human rights as an ideal or a principle which is crucial in terms of how human rights are implemented in Japan. Particularly from a perspective of the judicial implementation of human rights, there are many practical and theoretical issues to be tackled. I suppose that foreign precedent is a source of knowledge to explore how the wording of general and abstract human rights clauses can be interpreted. The experiences of other constitutional courts and supreme courts should be more widely and thoroughly examined to encourage jurisprudential fertilisation.

12
Mexico: Struggling For an Open View In Constitutional Adjudication

EDUARDO FERRER MAC-GREGOR* AND RUBÉN SÁNCHEZ GIL**

TABLE OF CONTENTS

I. The Mexican Constitutional Tradition 301
   A. Historical Notes 301
   B. The New Mexican Judicial Review System 304
   C. Mexico and the Inter-American Court of Human Rights 306
II. Foreign Precedents in Mexico 307
III. Foreign Judicial Doctrines Adopted by Mexican Courts 311
   A. Proportionality and Balancing 311
   B. 'Heightened' Equal Protection 312
   C. German '*Existenzminimum*' 312
   D. 'Political Questions' 313
   E. Supporting Quotations of Foreign Precedents 315
   F. The 'Same-Sex Marriage' Case 316
IV. Foreign Precedents in Separate Opinions 318
V. Conclusions 319

I. THE MEXICAN CONSTITUTIONAL TRADITION

A. Historical Notes

DUE TO ITS Spanish heritage, the Mexican legal system is attached to the civil-law tradition. Following civil-law guidelines and combining them with the principles of the French revolution, it can be concluded that the system's main element is the written law enacted by a legislature representative of the people. Therefore, and in broad terms, the bench's role in Mexico has traditionally never been very important; nevertheless, we have to consider certain political and historical elements.

---

* JD (University of Navarra, Spain). Researcher at the Institute of Legal Research of the National Autonomous University of Mexico ('UNAM'; Universidad Nacional Autónoma de México).
** JD (UNAM).
The authors would like to thank Édgar Caballero González, LLB, for his work on the analysis of the Mexican Supreme Court judgments and separate opinions referred to herein, and the graphs depicting the results of our research.

It was not until the *juicio de amparo* (protection trial)[1] was established in the Mexican Federal Constitution in 1847[2] that the judges' work began to gain some attention, although not that much. Considering the Constitution just as a mere 'political program' and not a 'higher law', for a long time judges did not apply the constitutional regulation of *amparo* because of its lack of secondary legislation. This handicap was overcome when in 1849 judge Pedro Sámano granted an *amparo* by applying constitutional provisions directly.[3]

Afterwards, the *amparo* was extremely active until it was increasingly restricted by the Supreme Court. It was the time when Porfirio Díaz was President of Mexico—more or less for 30 years—and Ignacio Vallarta a *ministro*[4] of the Supreme Court. The latter was the one who figured out the present technicality of the Mexican *amparo*. However, in that time and due to Vallarta's labour and his admiration for the American judicial system, two important institutions were established relevant to this topic: the use of a precedent system in judicial activity and reference to foreign precedents as a tool for constitutional adjudication.

Regarding the first one, Vallarta exposed his ideas on judicial precedents in a very innovative comparative work on both institutions.[5] According to him, *amparo* judgments have the 'highest' function of 'fixing public law', which is 'the greatest of their effects', because they represent the 'supreme, definitive, final interpretation of the Constitution'. Also, he emphasised that due to the idea that 'constitutional questions' are only solved through 'legislative acts', the judges themselves did not give importance to the doctrinal aspect of judicial opinions, which has meant that even 'after a hundred, a thousand judgments that have repeated its unconstitutionality, a legislative act remain[s]'. Vallarta's ideas on the use of a precedent system finally came into legislation: sections 34 and 70 of the Amparo Act of 1882 settled down the duty of inferior judges to obey the constitutional interpretation laid down by the Supreme Court in five judgments in a row. For a long time this was the main way for the Mexican bench to establish '*jurisprudencia*',[6] a precedent which must be observed by lower courts,[7] but nowadays the Supreme Court can set binding precedents through procedures other than *amparo* (which for a very long time was the

---

[1] *Amparo* stands for 'protection'. The name of this process goes back to medieval injunctions issued by Spanish Justices (*Justicia*). Although the proposed translation indicates the English meaning of the word, it is almost impossible to deliver the exact sense of it, and especially the almost poetic nuance of this term in our language.

[2] The *amparo* trial was created in the 1841 Constitution of the present State of Yucatan, which during that time was politically separated from Mexico. The federal Constitution did not establish *amparo* until the mentioned year.

[3] See H Aldasoro, *La primera sentencia de amparo dictada a nivel federal* (San Luis Potosí, UASLP, 1999).

[4] Mexican Supreme Court judge, as named by the third para of Constitution 1917 s 94.

[5] I Vallarta, *El juicio de amparo y el writ of habeas corpus* (Mexico City, FcoDíaz de León, 1881) 316–22.

[6] This term points to judicial precedents, unlike the sense that 'jurisprudence' has in English, referring to legal philosophy or theory.

[7] We have to distinguish between '*jurisprudencia*' and '*tesis aislada*' (isolated thesis). The first one is compelling due to the circumstances of its creation (repeating judgments, number of votes, etc), the second one is not, at least at first sight. Discussion in Mexico over stare decisis has not even begun, but we could say that regarding the equality (*igualdad*) constitutional principle, even the *tesis aisladas* has a minimal compelling force.

only one with effective life): constitutional controversy, unconstitutionality action and solving the contradiction between its own Chambers or lower courts.

As said, Mexican comparative tradition could be traced to Vallarta's judicial opinions. In them, this jurist displayed his wide knowledge of legal culture and American constitutional law. The classic example on this matter is his opinion regarding the *amparo* filed by a textile factory against a tax; in it Vallarta precisely cited classic American precedents established by Marshall,[8] and supported their use with these words:

> Without doctrines, precedents and judgments among us, these serious questions at the same time have a complete novelty and undisputable importance. Delicate and difficult as its resolution is, I did not want to trust my own reasoning but I have occurred to the sources of our constitutional law,[9] the American precedents, in search of doctrines to illustrate my opinion, requiring grounds for the vote that I am about to cast.[10]

A new era of Mexican precedents began in 1917 when our present Constitution was enacted after the Revolution that triumphed over Porfirio Díaz. It is amazing that without our modern communications the Supreme Court said that 'applying a foreign doctrine to solve a case, is not [illegal] if the judgment is based on national laws that explicitly apply to it'.[11] Although the Court was talking about theories and not about precedents, its latter opinion shows that there was an open orientation to comparative legal knowledge. This orientation ceased regarding the Constitution for a very long time; the fundamental law became a matter of political speech and a (practically) overwhelmingly empowered presidency left no room for constitutional judges to develop the implications of its text; if a case were about 'political' issues it was impossible for judges to enforce constitutional rules fully.[12]

Mexican democratic transition led to the constitutional amendment of 1994 which brought very important changes to the *role* and *powers* of the Supreme Court. Afterwards, a new constitutional change was enacted in 1996 allowing the constitutional challenge of electoral laws and Acts. We could say that nowadays the unconstitutionality of almost any act—except for certain 'political questions' (in a legal sense)—can be challenged. In addition, a disruption in the political regime allowed the Supreme Court to act much more freely. For almost the last two decades

---

[8] *McCulloch v Maryland*, 17 US (4 Wheaton) 316, 428, 430 (1819) and *Providence Bank v Billings*, 29 US (4 Peters) 514, 563 (1830).

[9] Mexican public law has always been inspired by foreign institutions. It was objected to that the first Mexican Constitution (1824) was simply an 'extralogical imitation (*imitación extralógica*)'—a phrase that has endured through all these centuries, and is very easily used against any proposal that seems influenced by foreign thought—of the American one (see I Burgoa, *Derecho constitucional mexicano*, 11th edn (Mexico City, Porrúa, 1997) 421). Even up to this date we preserve clear American constitutional souvenirs: the text of s 133 of the Mexican Constitution is basically the same as the text of art VI of the American Constitution. Furthermore, it is perfectly settled that the *juicio de amparo* is inspired by American judicial review, clearly influenced by Tocqueville's *De la démocratie en Amérique*; and the latest constitutional developments in our country are inspired by European 'Neoconstitutionalism'.

[10] Vallarta, *Amparo y Habeas Corpus*, 16, 22, 27 and 28.

[11] Ruling issued on 26 August 1939 (*SJF* (5th epoch, vol LXI) 3543).

[12] See JR Cossío, *La teoría constitucional de la Suprema Corte de Justicia* (Mexico City, Fontamara, 2002) 116–17. For instance in 1982–83 a renowned attorney and legal scholar filed an *amparo* suit to obtain information about the federal public debt that caused the worst economic crisis in Mexican history, using the freedom of information right contained in art 6 of the Constitution; the Court affirmed that this provision grants no right to citizens, but establishes an information system for political parties (*SJF* (August 1992) 44).

the Court has had enormous weight in the Mexican political system and often speaks the final word on important national issues.

During the reign of 'constitutional minimalism'—as justice José Ramón Cossío Díaz called it—before the democratic transition, the Constitution and the *amparo* trial were sort of 'fetish objects' of political speech.[13] We could say in broad terms that two opposing tendencies were present: one considering the Constitution and the *amparo* as national creations that had to be preserved from foreign influence; and the other thinking that Mexican constitutional order—particularly the *amparo* trial—should turn to foreign experience and knowledge for improvement. For many decades the first option was the most 'popular' and gave birth to the orthodox theory of the *amparo* trial.

Generally speaking, Mexican legal methodology still keeps a nineteenth-century approach, in which adjudication is regarded only as a syllogistic operation in which the exact correlation between legal and factual grounds of a decision is a requirement for its validity.[14] The teaching of constitutional law has been based on this model too, and it has had additional problems: it keeps a traditional conception of constitutional law (ie disregarding the study of international law of human rights and constitutional procedures different from the *amparo* trial); most of the traditional constitutional-law handbooks are obsolete, since they were drafted in the mid-twentieth century and there is not a great number of specialised constitutional journals and scholarly commentaries on the subject, though the latter has changed during the last 10 years due to the importance of some Supreme Court opinions.[15]

B. The New Mexican Judicial Review System

In 2011 the Mexican judicial review system became very, very complex.

Constitutional review in Mexico has traditionally relied on a 'semi concentrated' judicial system in which not every court has had constitutional jurisdiction as in the United States. Notwithstanding section 133 of the Mexican Constitution,[16] in 1999 the Supreme Court stated that only Federal Courts, acting in certain (constitutional) procedures (*amparo*, constitutional controversy, action of unconstitutionality, etc) have the power to enforce constitutional provisions.[17] Doing so, the highest bench put an end to a long-term discussion about the authority of judges acting only with ordinary powers to disregard unconstitutional laws.

However, on 23 November 2009, the Inter-American Court of Human Rights issued a judgment against Mexico in which it stated:

> With regard to judicial practices, this Tribunal has established, in its jurisprudence, that it is aware that the domestic judges and tribunals are subject to the rule of law and that,

---

[13] See JR Cossío Díaz, *La teoría constitucional de la Suprema Corte de Justicia*, ibid, 61, 116–17.
[14] See *SJF* (*Semanario Judicial de la Federación*; Federal Judicial Journal) *Appendix* (2000), vol VI, 166.
[15] See M Carbonell, 'Reflexiones sobre la enseñanza del derecho constitucional' (2003) 5–7 *Cauces* 12–18.
[16] Which is basically the same as art VI of the American Constitution, and thus the founding provision for a diffuse judicial review in which every court has the power to strike down unconstitutional laws.
[17] *SJF Appendix* (2000) vol I, 196.

therefore, they are compelled to apply the regulations in force within the legal system. But once a State has ratified an international treaty such as the American Convention, its judges, as part of the State's apparatus, are also submitted to it, which compels them to make sure that the provisions of the Convention are not affected by the application of laws contrary to its object and purpose, and that they do not lack legal effects from their creation. In other words, the Judiciary shall exercise a 'control of conventionality' *ex officio* between domestic regulations and the American Convention, evidently within the framework of its respective competences and the corresponding procedural regulations. Within this task, the Judiciary shall take into consideration not only the treaty but also the interpretation [of] the Inter-American Court, final interpreter of the American Convention, has made of it.[18]

After a series of discussions regarding this international judgment, the Mexican Supreme Court overruled its former precedent that banned a diffuse control of constitutionality. In the Supreme Court's view, the '*ex officio* control of conventionality' ordered by the Inter-American bench,[19] understood as a power that *every* court must exercise in order to enforce the provisions of international human-rights treaties, is incompatible with the traditional exclusiveness of Mexican constitutional review. On the other hand, the new section 1 of the Mexican Constitution orders that *every* state agent should 'promote, respect, protect and guarantee' all human rights established in the Constitution and international treaties signed by Mexico, which confirms that *no* judge should apply legal provisions that oppose constitutional or international human rights.[20]

Since this Supreme Court opinion, besides traditional constitutional procedures (*amparo* and others) Mexico has a *diffuse* judicial review system as in the United States. Due to the recent issuing of the said opinion, legal scholars and legislative and judicial authorities have not yet realised all of the problems that will arise from this *hybrid* system, and all of the consequences that it might have, especially in order to separate clearly the duties and tasks of constitutional and ordinary jurisdictions.

The Supreme Court is not the only one with constitutional jurisdiction: Federal Circuit Courts and the Electoral Federal Court (*Tribunal Electoral del Poder Judicial de la Federación*, TEPJF), *grosso modo*, also have the power to declare the unconstitutionality of legislation and administrative resolutions, notwithstanding that nowadays every Mexican judge is allowed to avoid the application of unconstitutional laws in actual cases. But of course the Supreme Court has the final word on constitutional construction, and can be regarded as the ultimate interpreter of the 'supreme law of our land'. For this reason, we focus our study on decisions issued by the Supreme Court,[21] though considering some important opinions of other benches.

---

[18] *Radilla-Pacheco v Mexico* (English version), para 339, bit.ly/AtncNt.
[19] See E Ferrer Mac-Gregor, 'El control difuso de convencionalidad en el Estado constitucional' in H Fix-Zamudio and D Valadés, *Formación y perspectiva del Estado mexicano* (Mexico City, El Colegio Nacional-UNAM, 2010) 151–88.
[20] Varios 912/2010, 14 July 2011, paras 23–30 (*SJFG*(*Semanario Judicial de la Federación y su Gaceta*; Federal Judicial Journal and its Gazette) (October 2011) 313).
[21] According to s 94 of the Constitution, the Mexican Supreme Court 'shall be composed of eleven justices (*ministro*) and shall sit as a Plenary Bench (*Pleno*) or as Chambers (*Sala*)'. Before 1995 the Court had up to five different Chambers. Today the Mexican Supreme Court has a First Chamber (*Primera*

C. Mexico and the Inter-American Court of Human Rights

Mexico is a member of the Inter-American Human Rights system. Our country signed its founding treaty, the American Convention on Human Rights (*Convención Americana sobre Derechos Humanos* or '*Pacto de San José*') in 1981, and recognised in 1999 the jurisdiction of its *ad hoc* Court established in San José, Costa Rica.

However, for a long time Mexican lawyers—courts included—did not pay attention to the opinions of the Inter-American Court of Human Rights (IACHR); this situation has changed. In our opinion, the Mexican Supreme Court's recent friendly position towards Inter-American precedents has even led our judges to turn to the judgments of the European Court of Human Rights (ECtHR), whose influence in Inter-American opinions is evident; this constitutes a very interesting comparative practice, as we will show later.[22]

The Supreme Court has increasingly quoted opinions of the ECtHR, especially since 2005, in majority opinions and in separate opinions. Finally, in 2011 the Mexican Court acknowledged that the IACHR's case law is binding to some extent, which is a great step towards the enforcement of human rights in Mexico.

In 2008 the 7th Civil Court of the First Judicial Circuit laid down that precedents of the IACHR are 'guiding (*orientador*) criteria' for the interpretation of human-rights provisions.[23] Some years later, the Second Chamber of the Supreme Court ruled—but not in a binding precedent—that international judgments are 'part of Mexican positive law'.[24]

Whether Mexican courts should comply with the IACHR's case law is still a disputed issue. Regarding the binding nature of the *Radilla* judgment of that international bench for Mexican judicial authorities, the Supreme Court considered two different kinds of IACHR 'precedents': (i) opinions issued on cases in which Mexico was a party and that are *binding* (*obligatorio*) on all domestic authorities, especially those of the judicial branch; and (ii) opinions issued on cases in which Mexico was not a party and that are only guidance (*orientador*) for national judges. Notwithstanding this, the Court established that Mexican courts 'should (*deber*)' take 'guiding' international precedents into account and apply them if their opinion protects human rights with a wider range.[25]

From our point of view, in this opinion the Mexican Supreme Court did not take Inter-American precedents as merely persuasive case law but as binding. A precedent is binding if it *must* be considered in legal adjudication, even if finally it does not prevail

---

Sala) and a Second one (*Segunda Sala*), both of them composed of five justices and presided over by one of their members. Before 1995 the Court had up to five different Chambers. Compelling precedents laid down by the Plenary Bench are binding on both Chambers.

[22] Although the use of international precedents is not a target of this research, these facts are very meaningful in the Mexican context. There has been, among judges and lawyers, an intense rejection of the influence of international courts, even the IACHR; because of this situation it is important that the Supreme Court has at least interrupted this way of thinking by referring to international human rights precedents. On the other hand, it must be taken into account that since Mexico is not (obviously) a party to the European human rights system, the quoting by the Supreme Court of Strasbourg precedents could be considered as a reference to foreign judicial opinions; Mexico is indeed under the jurisdiction of the IACHR, and the *Pacto de San José* is an element of its domestic legal system.

[23] *SJFG* (December 2008) 1052.
[24] *SJFG* (August 2010) 463.
[25] Varios 912/2010, 14 July 2011, paras 19–21 (*SJFG* (October 2011) 313).

because there is another case-law rule that is more suitable to solve the case. We believe that the Supreme Court tried to affirm the absolute binding effect of international judgments that directly address Mexico's legal situation, that is, the consequences of the *res judicata*, and not to set boundaries to the stare decisis principle regarding international precedents. However, we see labelling Inter-American case-law as 'guiding (*orientador*)' and not as 'binding (*obligatorio*)' as a reflection of the traditional approach to judicial precedents in Mexico,[26] and that the Supreme Court wrongly allowed that those precedents could be not acknowledged as a basic source of law.

II. FOREIGN PRECEDENTS IN MEXICO

We believe that a modern view of the Constitution and the *amparo* trial has recently gained an increasing number of followers, due to an intense scholar exchange between Mexico and other countries (especially Spain). An essential part of this new standpoint is the comparative judicial experience: it seems to us that Mexican judges have turned to foreign decisions to find new constitutional 'strategies' or have tried to apply in the Mexican legal system those with good outcomes in other countries.

However, according to orthodox practice, Mexican Courts have tried not to cite explicitly those foreign precedents upon which they have based their decisions. This makes it very difficult to assess when and how a Mexican court has based its decision upon a foreign judgment.

Our study focused on a period of 16 years (1995–2010) in which the Mexican Supreme Court—Plenary Bench, 1st and 2nd Chambers—issued 65,403 judgments.[27] We took as a sample 5,452 majority decisions and 1,171 separate opinions by the Supreme Court *ministros*. These items are relevant because they were published in the *SJFG*, the official case report of the Mexican Federal Courts, during the said period.[28] Not every federal judgment is published in Mexico, even if it was issued by the Supreme Court, though they are available in some way.[29] Only certain decisions and their concomitant separate opinions are published because: (1) they have decided upon the unconstitutionality of a law, (2) they fulfill the requirements to become binding, and/or (3) they are important for special reasons. One can say that any published decision is prima facie important.[30]

Many other judicial decisions are published in the form of a '*tesis*' (thesis). These are meant to be an abstract of a case's ratio decidendi.[31] We used them in our

---

[26] See above n 7.
[27] According to its annual reports (*Informe de labores*) drafted by its Presidency, which are available on bit.ly/UCFIc7.
[28] The *SJFG* database is called 'IUS'. Its compilation is edited on a semestral basis. This monthly-updated database can be found on the following internet site: ius.scjn.gob.mx, but it is only available in Spanish.
[29] The Mexican Supreme Court website (scjn.gob.mx) has a database from which one can get the Court's opinions. One can also file a public information request in order to get a copy of not-so-easily-available judicial decisions.
[30] For instance, the judgment cited above n 21, regarding the diffuse judicial review system and its corresponding powers for all Mexican Courts. This opinion has not decided upon the validity of any law and nor is it binding. However, it is very important since it has opened the door in Mexico for the said kind of judicial review.
[31] See General Agreements 5/2003 and 12/2011 of the Plenary Bench of the Mexican Supreme Court.

research for the next section of this paper, in which we refer to the implicit influence of foreign precedents on Mexican judicial decisions.

The only judgment that we did not analyse from the *SJFG* was the one delivered for the constitutional controversy (140/2006 on 'political questions') that we will refer to in the next section of this paper. This case was only reported through a *tesis*, an official abstract of its *ratio decidendi*, without any reference to a foreign precedent, but having learned the contents of this opinion, we could see that an important American precedent was cited in it, as we will see later.

Our search was primarily based on finding keywords related to several countries, which allowed us to detect explicit references to foreign precedents, and then on reading the said judgments and separate opinions of the Mexican Supreme Court. The graphs presented in this section are based on this procedure.

Among the 5,452 cases that we analysed, only 28 have an explicit citation of a foreign precedent;[32] this means that in 0.5136 per cent of the said cases there has been a reference to comparative law. The following graphs depict the number of *explicit citations of foreign precedents*, and not those of cases, judgments or separate opinions in which such citations were inserted. Considering the meagre citation of foreign precedents by the Mexican Supreme Court, we believe that by doing so we can provide clearer information about the Mexican approach to foreign precedents.

Our first graph shows the number of citations of foreign precedents in Mexican Supreme Court decisions.

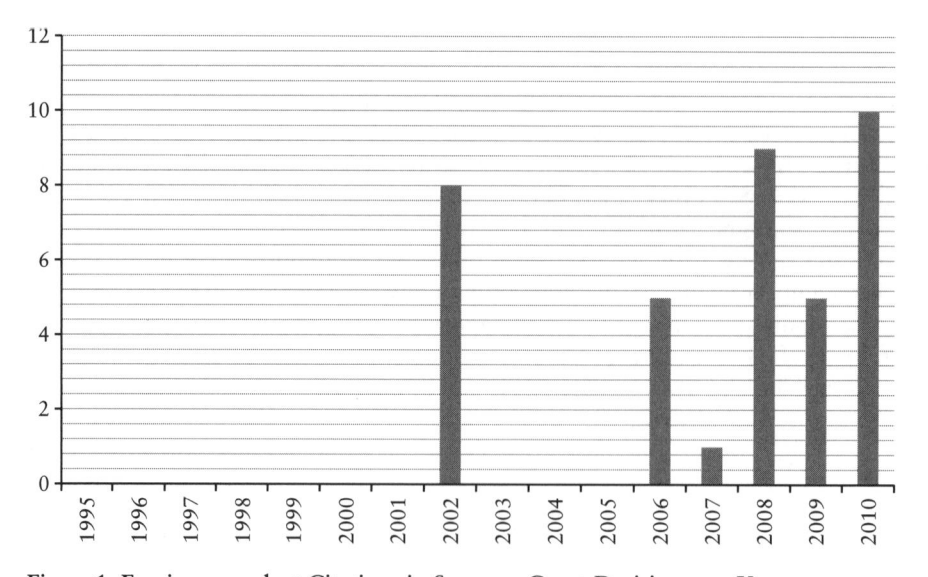

Figure 1: Foreign-precedent Citations in Supreme Court Decisions per Year

It is remarkable that the number of the said citations practically goes unnoticed among the more than 5,000 judgments that we have analysed—there are only 38.

The number of citations of foreign precedents in separate opinions is also very tiny—34 citations among a sample of 1,171 items—as depicted in our second graph.

---

[32] We are talking about 'cases' which comprises both majority and separate opinions, because the latter are only published as an attachment to the corresponding majority opinion.

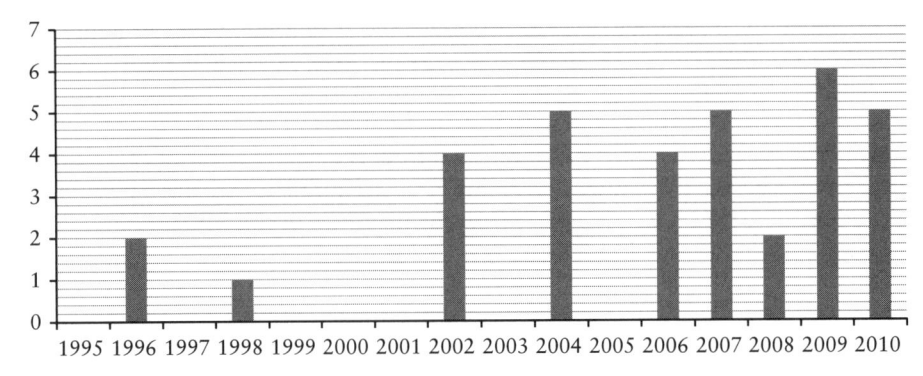

Figure 2: Foreign-precedent Citations in Supreme Court Separate Opinions per Year

However, comparing the percentage of these references in both fields, we noticed a significant difference. The incidence of the citation of foreign precedents in majority opinions is 0.6970 per cent, while in separate opinions it rises to 2.9035 per cent,[33] a surplus of a little more than 316 per cent. This situation suggests that dissenting judges seek support for their opinions in other jurisdictions in order to demonstrate the correctness of their view, an argumentative force that majority opinions do not need.

On the other hand, it is remarkable that the citation of foreign precedents took place in separate opinions years before it did so in majority opinions. The latter suggests that to turn to other jurisdictions was a practice that the *ministros* personally found suitable, and it was later adopted by the Court.

It is also interesting that according to our survey the ECtHR is the most cited 'foreign' jurisdiction in the Supreme Court's majority opinions, as Figure 3 shows.

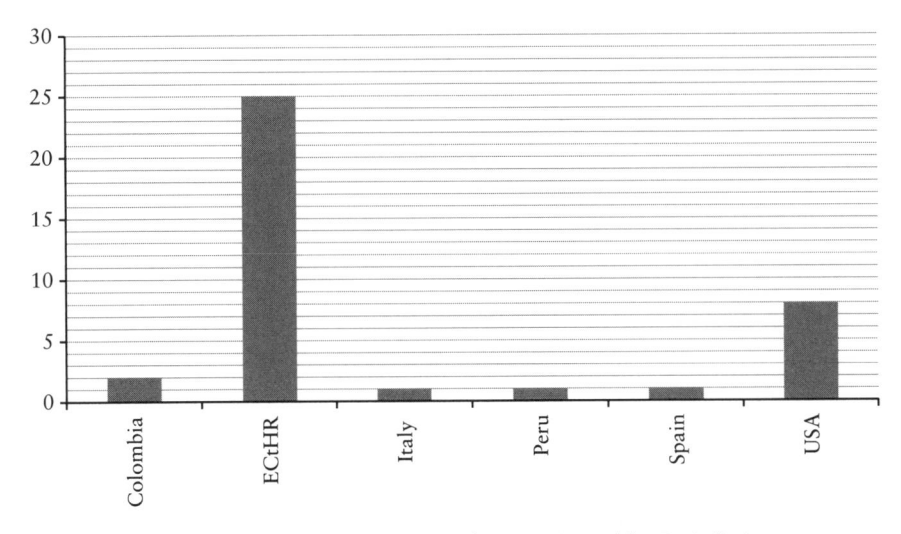

Figure 3: Foreign-precedent Citations in Judgments Sorted by Jurisdiction

---

[33] Assuming that in each majority or separate opinion only a single foreign-precedent citation was made. Actually, these opinions often cite more than one foreign precedent so the said percentages must be even lower.

This reference to the European bench does not mean that the Mexican Supreme Court indeed considers it more than other jurisdictions, since it does not often acknowledge foreign influence. It is possible that the American, German or Spanish Constitutional Courts are more influential than the Court of Strasbourg, though in an implicit way, as shown by the cases referred to in the next section of this study.

Another remarkable fact shown by Figure 4 is the influence of the Colombian Constitutional Court on separate opinions of the members of the Mexican Supreme Court.

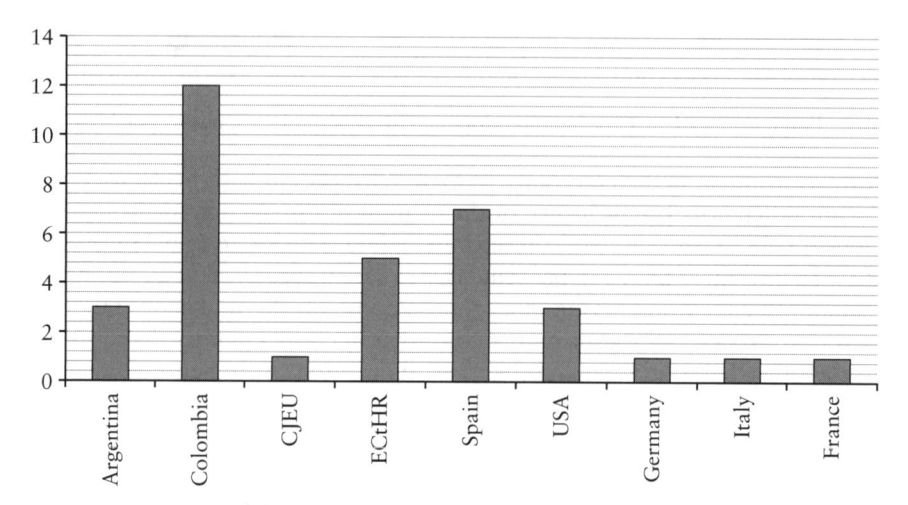

Figure 4: Foreign-precedent Citations in Separate Opinions Sorted by Jurisdiction

Colombia has a leading role in Latin America regarding constitutional theory and practice. This bench's prestigious position is reflected by the attention paid by the *ministros* to the opinions of the Colombian Constitutional Court.

Finally, Figure 5 shows the distribution of the references to foreign judgments by the Mexican Supreme Court according to the matter of the case—human rights or institutional issues.

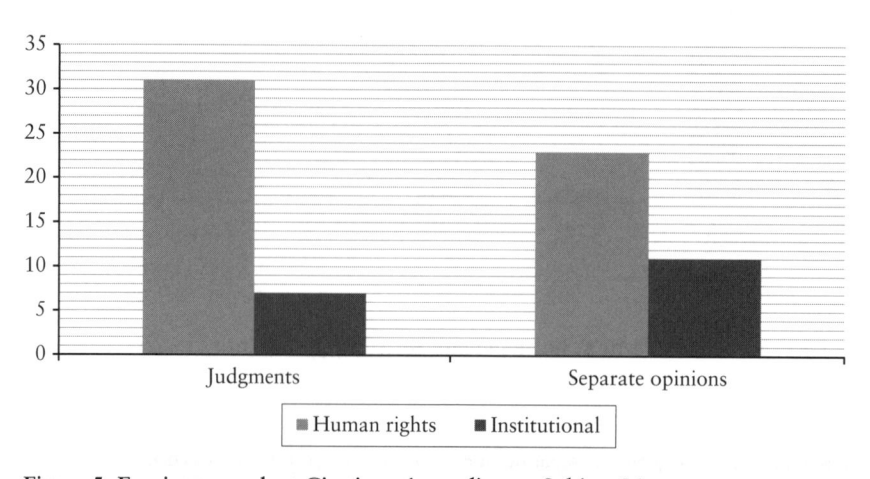

Figure 5: Foreign-precedent Citations According to Subject Matter

According to this table, the Mexican Supreme Court—as well as its *ministros*—mostly refers to foreign precedents when it comes to solving matters regarding human rights. That could indicate that the Mexican constitutional judges look for guidance in other jurisdictions that have solved 'universal' matters, while the rules of the political system that they are also meant to decide upon are considered more as a 'domestic' issue in which foreign opinions would be of little or no help. Notwithstanding this, the *ministros'* personal opinions consider foreign precedents more often than majority opinions in connection with institutional issues, which could confirm the theory that the minority looks for sound arguments in foreign precedents.

It is even possible to notice some *very clear* cases in which Mexican courts have been influenced by foreign judicial doctrines. We will refer to them in the next section of this chapter.

Moreover, in a later section, we will consider the use of foreign precedents in separate opinions by judges of the Mexican Supreme Court. Although they are not binding, these opinions can show the state of the art of specific topics in the Mexican legal discussion.

III. FOREIGN JUDICIAL DOCTRINES ADOPTED BY MEXICAN COURTS

A. Proportionality and Balancing

It could be said that the so-called 'principle of proportionality' in its primal German construction[34] has been embraced by the Mexican courts, thanks to their inspiration from Spanish constitutional judgments.[35] This principle is a very comprehensive tool used to set the limits and range of constitutional rights and other legal principles, composed of three sub-principles: suitability, necessity and proportionality in the narrow sense, whose subject is the famous balancing test.[36]

According to our research, the Supreme Court was the first one to imply the use of the idea of proportionality, regarding the judicial test on tax equity.[37] Copying a well-known Spanish precedent,[38] but without saying it was doing so, the Mexican Supreme Court introduced to the Mexican legal system in 1996 a 'balancing judgment (*juicio de equilibrio*)' between means and purposes as standard to determine the fairness, and therefore the validity, of a legislative classification.[39] Unfortunately, the said transcription was incomplete and thus it lost a good deal of the Spanish Constitutional Court's clarity, and the idea was not understood by Mexican courts and lawyers.

---

[34] See BVerfGE 19, 342 (348–49).
[35] AAlvez, '*¿Made in Mexico?* El principio de proporcionalidad adoptado por la Suprema Corte de Justicia de la Nación ¿La migración de un mecanismo constitucional?'(2010) 253 *Revista de la Facultad de Derecho de la UNAM*, 381, 387.
[36] R Alexy, 'Constitutional Rights, Balancing, and Rationality' (2003) 2 *Ratio Juris* 135–36.
[37] 'Tax equity' is just a mode of the equality principle. The latter has mostly been developed in Mexico through precedents regarding the former, and we think of it as a consequence of the 'constitutional minimalism' mentioned before.
[38] STC 76/1990, FJ 9, A).
[39] *SJF Appendix* (2000) vol I, 240.

'Lower' benches, such as several Circuit Courts and the Electoral Court (TEPJF), established important precedents tending to lay down the principle of proportionality and the balancing test in the Mexican legal system; they did not cite specific foreign or international judgments, but it could be seen that they were clearly inspired by the European (German and Spanish) doctrine of proportionality[40] and balancing.[41]

As we have said, the only domestic court competent to fix the interpretation of Mexican fundamental law is the Supreme Court. Others like those mentioned above are competent for the adjudication of certain constitutional issues, but in broad terms such courts' constitutional construction is not binding and should not be considered as a precedent—nonetheless it could be persuasive in some degree and taken as a 'mere' illustrative example.[42]

The Supreme Court continued to develop the proportionality standard, especially regarding the analysis of legislative classifications.[43] Finally, in 2007 it laid down that the three steps of this reasonableness test must be displayed by the constitutional judge in the setting of fundamental rights' ranges and limits, and that it has textual support in Article 16 of the Constitution and its prohibition of arbitrariness.[44]

B. 'Heightened' Equal Protection

Clearly inspired by the American constitutional doctrine of a 'heightened equal protection scrutiny',[45] the Mexican Supreme Court recognised the need for a 'strict' analysis of legislative classifications relating to explicit constitutional prohibitions of discrimination,[46] which uses higher standards for its validity.[47] This precedent was laid down by the First Chamber of the said highest court, but was recently adopted by the Second one which talked about a 'special intensity' of such 'careful scrutiny', but without the statutory required votes to be considered a binding precedent.[48]

C. German *'Existenzminimum'*

The Mexican Supreme Court has followed the doctrine of a 'vital minimum (*mínimo vital*)'. The summaries of the judgments that laid down this doctrine in Mexican constitutional law—which will be cited later—do not explicitly cite any foreign precedent. Nevertheless, since this doctrine has been soundly established in Spanish

---

[40] *TEPJF Compilation* (2005) 235 and *SJFG* (September 2005) 1579 (explicitly referring to Alexy's 'theory of principles').
[41] *SJFG* (November 2003) 955 and *SJFG* (March 2003) 1709 (also copying another very influential Spanish constitutional judgment: 171/1990, FF.JJ. 4–5).
[42] See Supreme Court Provision 5/2003, s IV(I)(11).
[43] *SJFG* (September 2006) 75 and *SJFG* (March 2007) 334.
[44] *SJFG* (December 2007) 8.
[45] See *Romer v Evans*, 517 US 620 (1996).
[46] Gender, preferences, health, etc. See Constitution 1917 s 1.
[47] *SJFG* (April 2008) 175.
[48] *SJFG* (June 2008) 439.

and especially German constitutional case law, we could say that this doctrine was very likely to have been taken from such jurisdictions.[49]

The First Chamber of the Mexican Supreme Court has laid down that human dignity requires minimal conditions for the very existence of human beings. Therefore, the legislator is not allowed to tax the minimum wage, because it is the necessary income for the survival of individuals, and if taxes were imposed on it people who receive this minimum amount would not be able to provide for their 'elementary needs', and so they would be subject to the will of others, losing their autonomy and their democratic participation.[50] It is remarkable that the Court based this concept on the Kantian definition of 'human dignity', which has been used by the German Federal Constitutional Court (German FCC),[51] in order to enforce the *mínimo vital* in the Mexican constitutional system.

This precedent was implicitly followed by the Second Chamber of the Mexican Supreme Court. In several decisions from 2007, the said Chamber has invoked section 123 of the Mexican Constitution which forbids any seizure or taking of minimum wages, in order 'to prevent that a worker gets a lower income', thus prohibiting the legislator from imposing any taxation on it; however, the ultimate ground for this opinion was to promote 'human dignity and liberty referred [as a general principle] in article 25, first paragraph, of the Constitution', which is part of the economic chapter of the Mexican fundamental law.[52] Unlike the precedents on this matter issued by the First Chamber, and due to the number of cases in which it was used as ratio decidendi,[53] the mentioned ruling of the Second Chamber has a binding effect on every Mexican court, which is especially important regarding the constitutional interpretation it holds and the effective enforcement of constitutional principles.

As far as we are aware, up to the time this paper was finished there has been no other precedent on this issue that highlights the boundaries of the '*mínimo vital*' or that points out more of its implications and consequences.

D. 'Political Questions'

On 15 August 2007, the First Chamber of the Mexican Supreme Court decided constitutional controversy 140/2006. This case stands out from Mexican precedents based upon foreign decisions or merely relying on them, because the Court's judgment was directly influenced—at least, it seems so—by a precedent of the American Supreme Court explicitly cited by the Mexican bench.

---

[49] STC 113/1989, FJ 3 and BVerfGE 82, 60 (85–86). Among the reasons that point to a European origin of the doctrine of the 'vital minimum' laid down by the Mexican Supreme Court, we must consider that it gave to this doctrine the name used by the Spanish Constitutional Court, which has had a notorious influence from German constitutional law (for the latter assessment, see FJ Ezquiaga Ganuzas, *La argumentación en la justicia constitucional y otros problemas de aplicación e interpretación del derecho* (Mexico City, TEPJF, 2006) 341).
[50] *SJFG* (May 2007) 792; *SJFG* (May 2007) 793; and *SJFG* (January 2009) 547.
[51] See BVerfGE 30, 1 (25–26).
[52] *SJFG* (September 2007) 553.
[53] Amparo Act (*Ley de Amparo*) (1936) s 192.

In this controversy the Governor of the Mexican State of Oaxaca challenged a resolution (*punto de acuerdo*) by the Chamber of Representatives (*Cámara de Diputados*) of the Federal Congress, in which the latter exhorted him to resign his office, due to the disorder that had taken place in the mentioned State.[54] This suit was initially admitted,[55] but in the end was rejected because its matter was a non-justiciable 'political question'.

The opinion of the Mexican Court was based on the assumption that 'purely political questions' cannot be judicially reviewed. The Court took this for granted saying that constitutional theory has unsuccessfully tried to define what a 'political question' is, and so it is very hard to define this concept in abstract terms. As an example, the Court cited the *locus classicus* of the opinion of the American Supreme Court in *Baker v Carr*:

> It is apparent that several formulations which vary slightly according to the settings in which the questions arise may describe a political question, although each has one or more elements which identify it as essentially a function of the separation of powers. Prominent on the surface of any case held to involve a political question is found a textually demonstrable constitutional commitment of the issue to a coordinate political department; or a lack of judicially discoverable and manageable standards for resolving it; or the impossibility of deciding without an initial policy determination of a kind clearly for non judicial discretion; or the impossibility of a court's undertaking independent resolution without expressing lack of the respect due coordinate branches of government; or an unusual need for unquestioning adherence to a political decision already made; or the potentiality of embarrassment from multifarious pronouncements by various departments on one question.[56]

It is generally accepted that *Baker v Carr* is the leading case on the 'political question' doctrine of the American Supreme Court.[57] Its reference in the Mexican case that we are now commenting on leads to the conclusion that our Highest Bench thought that this doctrine was an undisputed and well-established one. However, the Mexican Court failed to follow the *'golden rule' of comparative law*; in Marie-Claire Ponthoreau's words: *'il faut avoir une connaissance des concepts juridiques dans leurs propres contextes pour éviter précisément des erreurs d'interprétation* (one has to learn legal concepts in their own contexts, just in order to prevent interpretative mistakes)'.[58]

---

[54] On those days, teachers of Oaxaca held several demonstrations to fight for better work conditions, to which local government did not agree. Many organisations joined the teachers, and afterwards their movement proposed larger requirements and protested against all kinds of social problems. The city of Oaxaca was virtually occupied by demonstrators, and this situation caused a lot of social, political and economic difficulties—for instance, tourism went down 75%.

[55] See the related precedent laid down in *SJFG* (February 2007) 1396.

[56] *Baker v Carr*, 369 US 186, 217 (1962).

[57] Cf J Nowak and R Rotunda, *Constitutional Law*, 8th edn (St Paul, West, 2010) 127; and L Tribe, *American Constitutional Law*, 3th edn (New York, Foundation Press, 2000) 375.

[58] M-C Ponthoreau, *La circulation judiciaire de 'l'argument de droit compare' Quelques problems théoriques et techniques à propos du recours aux precedents étrangers par le juge constitutionnel* (according to our knowledge, this work has not been published in French—a Spanish translation will appear in 14 *Revista Iberoamericana de Derecho Procesal Constitucional*—, since it is a continued version of the author's work included in F Mélin-Soucramanien (ed), *L'interprétation constitutionnelle* (Paris, Dalloz, 2005) 167–84.

The American jurisdiction gave birth indeed to the 'political-question' doctrine, but there is no such thing as a 'transnational political-question doctrine', settled down as a 'universal' principle of constitutional procedural law. For instance, the German FCC has not developed a 'political-question' doctrine, because of the 'ubiquity' of constitutional law which does not allow courts to avoid any matter from a constitutional point of view, but tends to rule every question. This understanding of constitutional law turns constitutional courts into a 'King Midas', because under it judges are able to turn every question into 'constitutional-law gold'.[59]

On the other hand, with a careful reading of *Baker v Carr* the Mexican Court would have noticed that this precedent advanced the idea that a 'political question' is really unusual, since several tacit norms underlie the Constitution and they must be taken into account to consider whether there are 'judicially discoverable and manageable standards' that rule the case. In *Baker*, the American Supreme Court reversed the challenged judgment that denied standing to the appellants on the grounds that the matter of their original petition was allegedly a 'political question', applying as a principle the 'equal protection clause', regulated by '[j]udicial standards [that] are well developed and familiar'.[60] In addition, Tribe reports 'only two cases since *Baker v Carr* in which the Supreme Court has invoked the political-question doctrine to hold an issue nonjusticiable', and that this doctrine is considered precisely to admit the justiciability of the question posed to the Court.[61]

In the American constitutional system, the 'political questions doctrine' is more related to the ability of the Courts to find 'enforceable rights from constitutional provisions' and to 'creat[e] judicially manageable standards', than to the 'assumption that there are certain constitutional questions that are *inherently* non-justiciable' (emphasis added).[62] The Mexican Supreme Court should have considered the original context of the doctrine that it upheld, seeking the correct application of it; thus, the constitutional controversy 140/2006 stands as a *very important lesson* for future experiences regarding the use of foreign precedents in Mexico.

E. Supporting Quotations of Foreign Precedents

The Supreme Court and also the Federal Electoral Court have cited foreign precedents in order merely to support their opinions, especially about fundamental and human rights.

The First Chamber of the Supreme Court has laid down two remarkable precedents in criminal matters. In the first one, regarding some cautionary measures

---

[59] See K von Beyme, 'Génesis de la revisión constitucional en los sistemas parlamentarios' in *Tribunales constitucionales y democracia*, 2nd edn (Mexico City, SCJN, 2008) 277; Tribe, *American Constitutional Law*, 367; and R Wahl, 'Lüth und die Folgen. Ein Urteil als Weichenstellung für die Rechtsentwicklung' in T Henne and A Riedlinger (eds), *Das Lüth-Urteil aus (rechts-) historischer Sicht. Die Konflikte um Veit Harlan und die Grundrechtsjudikatur des Bundesverfassungsgerichts* (Berlin, BWV, 2005) 389.
[60] Above n 56.
[61] Above n 31 at 376 and 383. The mentioned cases are: *Gilligan v Morgan*, 413 US 1 (1973) and *Goldwater v Carter*, 444 US 996 (1979).
[62] Cf Tribe, *American Constitutional Law*, 367, 371 and Nowak and Rotunda, *Constitutional Law*, 137.

in an *amparo* trial, it used a judgment of the ECtHR—as well as another of the IACHR—to rule that any restriction to personal liberty should be allowed by the constitutional text itself.[63] Regarding the effectiveness of defence rights in criminal matters, it has quoted some precedents of the said international courts and of the German FCC.[64]

The comparative activity of the Federal Electoral Court has been more intensive. Though we have not observed that this bench has directly and explicitly based its decisions upon foreign precedents, it has invoked them to support its advanced points of view in important issues: the limitations of the passive right to vote,[65] freedom of speech as a cornerstone of a democratic society and its possible restrictions,[66] the 'spot-war' cases of the fierce presidential campaign of 2006,[67] political rights and their limitation due to criminal verdicts,[68] and its opinion for the Supreme Court regarding independent candidates.[69]

The mentioned opinions do not use foreign precedents as the foundation of their majority opinions, but only to support some basic and very general views about human rights involved in the corresponding case. Nevertheless, their importance is evidently a very clear indication of an opening in the way of legal thinking and reasoning in the Mexican legal system.

Finally, on the other hand, we can expect more references to European precedents—and to those from 'foreign' human-rights protection systems—because of the 'conventionality review' acknowledged by the Mexican Supreme Court.[70]

F. The 'Same-Sex Marriage' Case

One significant example regarding the use of foreign precedents in Mexican constitutional adjudication is the so-called *Same-Sex Marriage* case. The final judgment of the Mexican Supreme Court did not include any reference to foreign judicial opinions, despite the original draft doing so. However, it raised important methodological questions regarding the orientation that foreign precedents could give, and how to use them in domestic judicial opinions.

On 29 December 2009, the local legislative power of Mexico City issued a series of reformed provisions of its Civil Code. These new provisions: (i) allowed marriage between persons of the same sex, and (ii) gave these married couples the right to adopt children. Of course, these legal changes were very controversial.

---

[63] Explicitly citing *Baranowski v Poland*: SJFG (March 2007) 151.
[64] Explicitly citing *Kamasinski v Austria, Stanford v United Kingdom, Tripodi v Italy*; BVerfGE 9, 89 (95); and *SJFG* (May 2007) 104 ff.
[65] SUP-JDC-037/2001 (quoting the ECtHR and the Spanish Constitutional Court).
[66] SUP-JDC-393/2005 (referring to the *Handyside* case of the European Court, the American Supreme Court in *Murdock v Pennsylvania*—and the preferred position of that freedom—and *New York Times v Sullivan*, and judgment 12/1982 of the Spanish Constitutional Court).
[67] SUP-RAP-31/2006 (quoting European cases *Oberschlick* and *Lingens*, as well as the American precedents cited above n 67).
[68] SUP-JDC-20/2007 (referring to the *Hirst* case of the ECtHR and constitutional precedents from Canada, Israel and South Africa).
[69] SUP-AG-2/2007 (European case *Refah Partisi (Parti de la Prospérité)etautres c Turquie*).
[70] Above n 20.

In January 2010, the conservative federal government, through the Federal General Attorney (*Procurador General de la República*), filed an unconstitutionality action against these legal reforms. This lawsuit basically claimed that they violated the concept of 'family' set out in Article 4 of the Constitution, since they neither comprised same-sex marriage nor parenthood. The Supreme Court finally upheld the challenged provisions and ruled that they were not unconstitutional, because 'the Federal Constitution does not refer, nor is limited, to a specific kind of family'.[71]

Ministro Sergio Valls was entrusted with the drafting of the Court's opinion on this matter.[72] The original draft mentioned several legal provisions and foreign precedents favourable to same-sex marriages, and concluded that 'there is a world tendency to acknowledge the marriage between persons of the same sex, or at least to extend the benefits and liabilities derived from marriage to homosexual unions'.[73] This comparative-law analysis was excluded from the final draft of the judgment.

The first objection to references to foreign law came from *ministro* Sergio Aguirre. This judge opposed them for the following reasons:[74]

— It is groundless to say that there is a 'world tendency' in favour of same-sex marriages, since only a 'minority' of countries have accepted it;
— The situation of countries like 'Holland, Belgium, Spain, Norway and Sweden' is very different to Mexico's, hence it is 'difficult' to take it as a point of reference; and
— If these comparative-law citations were kept, in order to have a 'complete knowledge' of the matter, it would be 'important' to add references to countries—like Germany—that do not designate same-sex unions as 'marriages' but give them another name, and to stress that not every nation that has acknowledged homosexual marriages, accepts that they are allowed to adopt children. In this judge's opinion, the lack of a 'complete view' of the problem meant that the judgment did not reflect an 'objective note' of the issue.

Furthermore, *ministro* José Ramón Cossío said that although the references to foreign law included in the said draft were 'very interesting, very enlightening', he did not see their connection to the merits (*fondo*) of the case. He concludes therefore that these foreign references are expendable in order to avoid unnecessary arguments, and that there is no need to include them in the final draft of the judgment, especially because it is difficult to ascertain their binding effect. *Ministros* Fernando Franco and Arturo Zaldívar, shared Cossío's opinion despite the reasons expressed by Luis Aguilar and Olga Sánchez Cordero.[75]

Finally, *ministro* Valls agreed to exclude all references to foreign (case) law in the final draft of the Court's opinion, although they were intended to determine the context of the case. The exclusion of the comparative-law section of the draft was decided by a 6–5 vote, in which *ministra* Margarita Luna Ramos had the final word during

---

[71] *SJFG* (August 2011) 878.
[72] References to the text of this draft and to the thoughts of other *ministros* were taken from the minutes of the plenary session of the Supreme Court held on 3 August 2010, available on bit.ly/IgBPGS.
[73] Ibid 7.
[74] Ibid 8 f.
[75] Ibid 11 ff.

a later plenary session;[76] she considered that the arguments of the lawsuit should be answered specifically, and not with abstract references to comparative law.[77]

The objections raised by *ministro* Aguirre against the references to foreign precedents in this case are the bottom line of legal comparison in (constitutional) adjudication. Nowadays, it is not difficult to encounter foreign law regarding almost any legal matter; we can browse the internet and find the opinions of several important jurisdictions, or we can even buy academic books on foreign law through well-known e-commerce sites. The issue with comparative law today concerns the principles that rule the 'import' of foreign solutions to domestic adjudication.

There are several questions on this subject that are still waiting for an answer, especially in Mexico as *ministro* Aguirre highlighted with regard to the *Same-Sex Marriage* case: (i) when can we speak of a 'world trend' or at least of a 'model solution' in comparative law?, in other words, does one swallow (or two or three) make a summer?; (ii) why should Holland, Belgium, Spain, the USA, Germany or any other jurisdiction be a constitutional 'role model', leaving us compelled to follow their legal solutions?; and (iii) what criteria should be used to distinguish between a biased 'trend' and an 'objective' and 'comprehensive' comparative conclusion?—one could be that legal comparison should be a 'dialectic' confrontation between both sides of the problem, but this only puts off the determination of these criteria.[78]

Although the *Same-Sex Marriage* case is not a model of legal comparison, since it was not (explicitly) decided upon a comparative trend,[79] we can hold it as a remarkable example of the problems of comparative law, especially for constitutional adjudication.

IV. FOREIGN PRECEDENTS IN SEPARATE OPINIONS

Just as in the United States, Germany and other countries, Mexican *ministros*—and other judges—can add a personal opinion to a judgment, in order to expose their reasons for dissenting from the majority opinion or their reasons why a different judgment should have been reached. Indeed, as an immediate reflection of the *ministros*' personality and legal culture, there can be found in these separate opinions (*voto particular*) a clear citation of foreign precedents; not so long ago one of them was even calling for the Supreme Court—extensible to any other legal operator—to be open-minded to comparative exercises in Mexican constitutional adjudication:

> [F]rom my point of view, today the precedents of international or regional courts, *as well as the ones of other countries of the free world*, cannot be still alien to us or barely appear as a little atoll in our judgments. Aside that some [international] jurisdictions have been accepted by Mexico and, in that sense, [their precedents] are binding to us, as the Inter-American Court of Human Rights', the essence of fundamental rights is universal.
>
> In order to prevent the isolation of this Court, we must take part of the international case-law dialogue (coloquio jurisprudencial), and make of [legal] comparison a method

---

[76] Held on 9 August 2010. See the minute of this session on bit.ly/Ic4z4s.
[77] Ibid 8 and 14–15.
[78] See Ponthoreau, *L'argument de droit comparé*, above n 58.
[79] We can only guess if the international 'tendency' in favour of same-sex marriage and parenthood influenced the approach of the original draft of the judgment, and thus somehow determined the solution that was finally given to this issue.

of constitutional interpretation. What has been advanced in other countries is a part of humanity's patrimony that we must avail of. (emphasis added).[80]

The importance of the transcribed phrases is not only their contents but also the situation in which *ministro* Genaro Góngora Pimentel has expressed them. They came from his separate opinion in the so-called *Media Act* (*Ley de Medios*) *case*, one of the most important Mexican constitutional issues in the last 20 years, regarding (judicially tackled-down) legal reforms that benefited powerful media corporations against national and even governmental interests.[81] In the same personal opinion, Góngora Pimentel practised what he preached, and in order to support his point of view he cited constitutional precedents from Germany,[82] Italy[83] and France,[84] relating them to the opinion of the IACHR which he acknowledged as binding on Mexican courts.[85]

A mere obiter dictum reference to foreign precedents took place in the debate over another very important issue: the *Budget Veto case*. This judgment has been one of the most controversial cases of the Supreme Court to date, since it ruled that the President has the right to oppose legislative decisions on the federal budget, but without a clear constitutional text that grants him this power. In his personal opinion regarding this case, *ministro* Góngora Pimentel[86] again invoked a foreign precedent: the *Line Item Veto II* American case,[87] to show that the Mexican Supreme Court should have followed the example of the Washington bench, and not granted to the President the 'exorbitant power' of practically eliminating congressional powers.

V. CONCLUSIONS

The *first issue* with the use of foreign precedents in Mexican constitutional adjudication is to establish comparative perspectives as a necessary, not only useful, technical tool. We could say that there is a silent but increasing struggle in Mexico between a traditional isolating approach on constitutional adjudication and a comparative one, although comparative law was an important tool in the early days of our constitutional life. Due to the not so long ago rooted nationalist tendency of Mexican legal thought, the comparative effort was taken as an activity that should be rejected; but nowadays the table has turned thanks to new generations' perspectives and the impelling reality of our 'global village': young judges and legal scholars are influenced by foreign modes of legal reasoning and the Mexican Supreme Court

---

[80] Unconstitutionality action 26/2006 (dissenting opinion), *Diario Oficial de la Federación*, 20 August 2007, section III, 80.
[81] On the complexity of this judgment and its contents, see E Ferrer Mac-Gregor and R Sánchez Gil, *Efectos y contenidos en las sentencias de acción de inconstitucionalidad. Análisis teórico referido al caso 'Ley de Medios'* (México, UNAM, 2009) (available on: bibliojuridica.org).
[82] BVerfGE 73, 118.
[83] Constitutional Court, Judgment 420/94.
[84] Constitutional Council, Decision of October 10th and 11th 1984.
[85] Above n 34 at 99.
[86] This judge used to cite foreign precedents regularly in his separate opinions, but we ought to say that his colleague José Ramón Cossío Díaz was the author of the leading Court opinions in which foreign doctrines mentioned in the latter sections (proportionality, 'heightened' equal protection and *Existenzminimum*) were acknowledged in Mexico.
[87] *Clinton v City of New York*, 524 US 417 (1998).

has finally acknowledged the importance and usefulness of foreign human-rights and constitutional precedents.

The *second issue* is that despite the slight advances of the comparative point of view in Mexican constitutional adjudication, our courts are still reluctant to make a explicit citation of the foreign precedents they took inspiration from. When they refer or quote one of them, it is generally only as a mere support for a previously established opinion. *We cannot say that a Mexican constitutional judgment has been explicitly based upon a certain foreign precedent.*

The inconvenience of omitting the explicit citations of the foreign precedents that have determined the decisions of Mexican courts is very evident, as it especially shows the 'import' of the principle of proportionality from Spanish precedents. It denies people (trial parties, legal scholars and citizens in general) the opportunity to know the origin of the standards or procedures taken by Mexican courts, and thus to review whether they are using them correctly and accordingly to their nature.[88] This lack of citation also diminishes the transparency of Mexican constitutional adjudication: judges must make evident which are the ultimate grounds of their decisions, so the 'community' can control their reasoning.[89]

The *third obstacle* that Mexican constitutional adjudication must overcome in order to develop comparative reasoning is of a methodological kind. As a consequence of the unpaid attention to the importance of the use of foreign precedents and its implications, a broad debate over this matter has not taken place in Mexico. Our judges and scholars must discuss, at least, the following issues: (i) when to look for foreign precedents to solve domestic legal questions, (ii) which jurisdictions should be taken as a 'model' and why,[90] (iii) which criteria must be satisfied before accepting a foreign precedent as a 'soft source'—a kind of 'soft law' for national adjudication—, and (iv) how validly to make up a 'standard procedure' to rely on a foreign solution to solve a national problem (considering which elements are meant to be taken into account—especially the inherent differences between the common-law and civil-law systems—and how judges should build their arguments).[91]

Nevertheless, *there are some foreign judicial doctrines that the Mexican Supreme Court and other benches of our country have recently adopted*, and we can conclude in this regard that their adoption was caused by an increasing comparative influence in our legal theory and adjudication. This influence is causing the *ministros* and other judges to take into account more often the international *status quaestionis* of the issues they have to settle in their judgments, at least in a general manner, especially when fundamental rights are at stake. Hopefully, this stream will increase its strength and influence other courts—even ordinary ones which now have constitutional review powers—, to provide Mexican constitutional law with a broader horizon, because legal science is a universal one.[92]

---

[88] Alvez, *Made in Mexico?*, 387.
[89] See R Dworkin, *Freedom's Law. The Moral Reading of the American Constitution*, 3rd edn (Cambridge, Harvard University Press, 1999) 31.
[90] For several reasons, we suggest that this list must include (mentioned in a kind of 'order of appearance'): the United States, Germany, Spain, Colombia and South Africa, among national courts, and Strasbourg and Luxembourg among international ones.
[91] Above n 72.
[92] R David and C Jauffret-Spinosi, *Los grandes sistemas jurídicos contemporáneos*, 11th edn, translation by Jorge Sánchez Cordero (Mexico City, UNAM-CMDU-FLDM, 2010) 11.

13
Romania: Analogical Reasoning as a Dialectical Instrument

ELENA SIMINA TANASESCU[*] AND STEFAN DEACONU[**]

TABLE OF CONTENTS

I. The Context 324
   A. The Constitution and the Legal System 324
   B. The Judicial System and Other Courts (Constitutional Court of Romania) 325
   C. Legal Scholarship 328
II. The Empirical Research 329
   A. Implicit Citations of Foreign Case Law 330
   B. Explicit Citations of Foreign Case Law 330
III. Conclusion.. 344

THE CONTEMPORARY DEBATE over constitutionalism and its comparative potential and/or appetite will not be over soon. Arguments in favour and against the use of the comparative method in constitutional matters have been thoroughly pondered. History and traditions, or national identity and legal particularism, have been confronted with the universalism inherent in an increasingly globalising world. Comparisons have been attempted with various Constitutions and normative standards, various state authorities and institutional designs and, indeed, different constitutional adjudications and methods of legal reasoning. The use of foreign precedents by constitutional judges is part and parcel of this ongoing discussion and has to be considered within the context of what has lately become known as judicial dialogue. However, current research on the use of foreign precedent in constitutional adjudication does not refer to all possible applications of the comparative method in constitutional law, but concentrates only on referrals by constitutional judges to case law of their peers. This leaves out various other forms of judicial (trans- or inter-national) dialogue and applications of legal comparison. By focusing only on the use of constitutional foreign precedents (and not on foreign law, international standards or international case law) this research

---

[*] Professor, University of Bucharest.
[**] Associate Professor, University of Bucharest.

attempts to test the hypothesis of the existence of judicial cross-fertilisation at a constitutional level in general, and in Romania in particular.[1]

Narrowing down the purpose of this paper only to the use of foreign precedents by constitutional judges does not equate with reducing the ardour of the debate, rather the contrary. It would be difficult to summarise here all arguments invoked in favour of or against the use of foreign precedent in constitutional adjudication.[2] On the one hand, acknowledging that common issues require common solutions seems a mere truism nowadays, whereas supporters of the comparative and analogical method have always underlined the informative added value residing in the knowledge of other legal systems and precedents, putting forward the fact that recognising differences allows for a better understanding of one's own legal culture. On the other hand the fear of legal hegemony and the claim for the distinctiveness of a given human and legal community, as well as the issue of responsibility (towards the people) generated by the legitimacy of one's legal standards coupled with the potential for manipulation inherent to the analogical argument[3] have been invoked in order to defend a more cautious approach with regard to the use of foreign precedent in constitutional adjudication.

To be sure, analogy and dialectical reasoning are the very tools of any judge. Having that in mind, transnational legal analogy can be facilitated by cultural and/or legal proximity, common legal standards and instruments due to a common legal space or a community in the broad meaning of the word (eg European Union or EU), cultural or educational background of judges, scholarship favourable to comparativism or even easily accessible databases.[4] However, the use of analogy in the area of judicial reasoning may require an adequate methodology and special attention to the way in which arguments are articulated[5] because justice not only has to be done, but also has to be seen to be done. In order legitimately to fulfil the judicial function, judicial decisions have to be based on reasons acceptable not only

---

[1] S Deaconu, 'Utilizarea jurisprudenței constituționale a altor state de către judecătorul constituțional român', *Perspectivele constituționalismului în România* (Monitorul Oficial, București, 2010) p 24.

[2] For an overview of literature dedicated to this over the last 15 years see the annotated list established under the coordination of Tania Groppi by researchers of the Centre for European and Comparative Public Law (DIPEC), University of Siena at www.unisi.it/dipec/en/interestgroup.php.

[3] From a purely logical perspective, an analogy presupposes a calculus of similitude between two objects, based on a double abstraction (through a simplification–generalisation of both the source-object and the target-object) coupled with two inductions (in the first stage, when setting the basis for the comparison) and a deduction (in the second stage, that of attributing to the target-object the characteristics of the source-object), while all these logical operations have as a starting point partial similarities (ie a relation of proportionality between the source-object and the target-object) and not identity (ie full equality between the two objects of the comparison). Therefore, the analogical argument may lead to conclusions of total similarity based on partial similarity thus producing plausible and not certain arguments; or, in other words, 'it could allow a judge to "reach the result he wants to reach" with no restrictions'. cf M Minow, 'The Controversial Status of International and Comparative Law in the United States' (2010) 52 *Harvard International Law Journal Online* 8.

[4] D Mauss, 'Le recours aux précédents étrangers et le dialogue des cours constitutionnelles' (2009) *Revue française de droit constitutionnel* 275 ff.

[5] C Saunders, 'Comparative Constitutional Law in the Courts: Is There a Problem?' (2006) 13 *Current Legal Problems* 37.

to those directly involved, but also to others[6] and in this respect analogy may prove to be a double-edged sword.

Indeed, there is a clear connection between the nature of comparative judicial reasoning and the questions it may raise with regard to legitimacy and methodology.[7] Counter-intuitive as it may seem, relativism and universalism—both determined by globalisation—can be argued against with the very tool of analogy of legal reasoning in constitutional adjudication. Relativism and legal particularism can be countered through the dialogical value of using foreign precedent in constitutional adjudication: the three steps it (logically) involves—identification, justification and choice of the foreign precedent to be referred to—allow for any outcome of the intended comparison and thus diminish the methodological importance of the comparison. Universalism relies so heavily on the generalisation of similarities that it questions the rational demonstrative value of its own argument and ends up being valid only for a highly limited type of matters (basically, fundamental rights). Thus, judicially, constitutional cross-fertilisation may also serve rather to demolish than to reinforce both relativism and universalism. The use of foreign precedents by constitutional judges may be a 'sign of current times' and could serve as an indicator of preferences shown by constitutional judges for rational or dialectical instruments, but, in the end, it is only a tool for the quest of an interpretative pattern that might legitimise them and their judicial function.

The case of Romania could be a good example of the paradoxical situation where a general context extremely favourable to comparative law combines with a scarce use of foreign precedent by constitutional judges. The Romanian Constitution, which came into force in 1991, created a Constitutional Court according to the European model of judicial review, thus breaking with tradition. This was not the first attempt to modernise or democratise the Romanian state through import/transplant of political institutions and legal standards. However, once created, such institutions live their own life and—more often than not—tend to adapt to local culture, while creating a fertile environment for comparisons and analogies. The wariness of the Romanian Constitutional Court towards the use of foreign precedents must take into consideration the fact that analogical judicial reasoning produces plausible arguments that hold a degree of probability while not giving any certainty and could be viewed as a preference for rational demonstrative tools rather than dialectical instruments if it was not more the expression of a judicial self-restraint that tends to become loose over time.

This research is based on all decisions rendered by the Romanian Constitutional Court since its creation in June 1991 until 31 December 2011. Only 14 out of a total of (roughly) 13,250 rulings display a clear reference to foreign precedent, thus questioning the very concept of judicial cross-fertilisation.

---

[6] And perceptions may vary a lot. Posner holds that increasing use of foreign precedent consolidates the tendency of the Supreme Court of the United States to behave as a moral vanguard and a cosmopolitan court searching for international legal consensus, which he interprets as 'aggressively political approaches covered by a veneer of legal reasoning'. EA Posner, 'Transnational Legal Process and the Supreme Court's 2003–2004 Term: Some Skeptical Observations' (2004) 12 *Tulane Journal of Comparative & International Law* 23.

[7] SK Harding, 'Comparative Reasoning and Judicial Review' (2003) 28 *The Yale Journal of International Law* 409.

I. THE CONTEXT

A. The Constitution and the Legal System

In order to understand the current legal system of Romania and the various influences that foreign law had on it, a brief historical reminder of the process of the Romanian state- and nation-building may prove useful. Following attempts at national revolutions in 1848, the Romanian Principalities of Moldova and Wallachia united in 1859 and adopted a modern and democratic (for those times) Constitution in 1866, partly inspired by the Belgian Constitution of 1831. After the First World War, in 1918, the Romanian Kingdom united with former Habsburg provinces (Transylvania, Banat and Bukovina) and the former Tsarist province of Bessarabia to become what is commonly known as Great Romania. The Constitution adopted in 1923 drew heavily on the previous one, only with minor alterations needed in order to accommodate a larger population on a larger territory and a greater diversity of legal norms. This democratic state lasted until 1938 when, under pressure from two sides (Germany and Russia), Romania lost Bessarabia and part of Bukovina to Russia, parts of Transylvania to Hungary and fell under the rule of various right extremists. The Constitution adopted in 1938, partly inspired by its German counterpart, was to be suspended in 1940. After the Second World War, and until 1989, Romania was governed by communists, who emphasised a nationalistic discourse under a totalitarian political regime. The three Constitutions adopted during this period were inspired by Soviet models; however, this foreign source of inspiration almost disappeared with the last one, adopted in 1965, which represented the beginning of a strong emphasis put on nationalistic values in Romania. After what it has become customary to describe as 'the events of December 1989', democracy was restored and the Romanian state started afresh, within legal boundaries that were to be drafted from scratch once more.

The Constitution of Romania currently in force was adopted in 1991, relatively soon after the change of the political regime and, according to its 'founding fathers',[8] was founded upon Romanian constitutional traditions as well as other Constitutions, in particular those of France, Spain and Italy.[9] It was drafted by a special (partly extra-) parliamentary commission, made up of specialists in public law and university professors. In the first phase, the commission issued basic principles and sketched a structure for the future draft of the Constitution; these documents were widely circulated for several months, including in national newspapers, under the label 'thesis of the Constitution'. Following this large consultation and upon further circulation of the document to various international bodies and experts, basic principles were adopted by the Constituent Assembly. In a second phase the commission proceeded to draft the text of the Constitution, which was then debated and amended over a bit more than a year. Finally, the Constitution was

---

[8] For a detailed explanation see A Iorgovan, *Odiseea elaborării Constituției* (Editura Uniunii Vatra Românească, Târgu Mures, 1998). Also see I Muraru and M Constantinescu, *Studii constituționale* (Actami, București, 1995).

[9] I Vida, 'Bătălia pentru Curtea Constituțională' in *Despre constituție și constituționalism—liber amicorum Ioan Muraru* (Hamangiu, București, 2006) 238–40.

adopted by the Constituent Assembly on 21 November 1991 and passed through a national referendum on 8 December 1991. In 2003 the Constitution was revised with the declared aim of making Romania's accession to the European Union possible and enhancing the efficiency of state apparatus.

Various analyses have been made with regard to the text of the Constitution and possible foreign influences on it, without, however, a final or decisive conclusion being made. Some authors[10] have underlined the strong influence of the French institutional setting, mainly with regard to the political (semi-presidential) regime and the general design of the office of the President of Romania, while others[11] have noticed punctual similarities with other foreign fundamental laws (eg those between the Romanian Advocate of the People and the Spanish *Defensor del Pueblo*). The list of fundamental rights is a syncretic collection of Romanian traditions (right to petition or the right of the person damaged by a public authority in its rights or legitimate interests to the acknowledgement of its right, invalidation of a legal Act and the reparation of the damage suffered) and more recent influences (right to information or freedom of movement). However, the grand design of state authorities and the general structure of the fundamental law belong to national, rather than universal, constitutionalism.[12]

Following the coming into force of the Constitution in 1991 the entire legal system went through a massive process of adaptation. Three causes have contributed to the incredible quantitative augmentation (inflation) of the Romanian legal system: political and economic transition, accession to the EU, and the need to implement a new Constitution in parallel with the construction of a state governed by the rule of law. An already positivist legal doctrine and practice has been made comfortable in its approach towards a civil law legal system that started to show its deficiencies or inner contradictions sooner rather than later.

B. The Judicial System and Other Courts (Constitutional Court of Romania)

Against this background, and from the very beginning, the new Constitution granted functional independence to judges, although they continued to be considered in charge only of the implementation of the law and not the creation of legal standards. Judges enjoy independence in ruling over cases presented in front of them; at the same time, they are held responsible for judicial errors and for all activities rendered in the administration of justice. One isolated voice[13] pleaded for the absolute independence of judges, holding that they are the institutional guarantee for the

---

[10] T Drăganu, *Drept constituțional și instituții politice. Tratat elementar*, vol II (Lumina LEX, București, 1998) 224 ff.

[11] I Muraru, 'Reflectarea drepturilor omului în noua Constituție a României' in I Muraru and M Constantinescu, 172–73.

[12] For one of several possible definitions of concepts see J Tully, 'The Imperialism of Modern Constitutional Democracy' in M Laughlin and N Walker (eds), *The Paradox of Constitutionalism. Constituent Power and Constitutional Form* (Oxford University Press, 2007) 315.

[13] I Deleanu, *Instituții și proceduri constituționale—în dreptul român și în dreptul comparat* (CH Beck, București, 2006) 11–126.

responsibility of the rest of state authorities. The majority of authors[14] agree with the dominant opinion in comparative law[15] that irresponsibility could be viewed as the price paid by the community for the independence of judges but, with the absolute meaning mentioned above, this price would become much too high. In a democratic system of government, functioning in accordance with the principle of checks and balances, a power should never remain without control and the authority invested with a right of oversight over all the others should never be uncontrollable and, thus, deprived of liability.

Misused or misunderstood, functional independence of judges combined with a more and more complex legal system brought diversity and uneven case law, which was found to be counterproductive and against the very principles of a state governed by the rule of law. Thus, lately, unification of legal practice and case law has become one of the main targets of Romanian authorities, particularly in a context where the European Court of Human Rights (ECtHR) (*Păduraru v Romania*, 2005, among others) and the European Court of Justice (ECJ) (*Jipa v Ministry of Administration and Interior*, 2008) started to highlight the malfunctioning of the Romanian judicial system. In this context, the use of precedent is not a common feature in Romania, despite a natural tendency of judges to get inspired and/or continue well-established practices at the level of their respective courts. However, across the state, this phenomenon does not translate into a greater coherence of case law or, indeed, of the judicial system itself.

Moreover, judicial (civil and criminal) procedures allow for separate opinions (which are not qualified by legislation, but in practice tend to be qualified by judges themselves as rather dissident), but the use of this facility is relatively rare in lower courts. The judges of higher courts and particularly those of the Constitutional Court tend to use this feature relatively often, mainly with the purpose of presenting dissenting opinions. However, it is not a rare occurrence for constitutional judges to reach a decision with a majority of votes, but separate opinions are not issued. Mention has to be made here that all separate opinions, be they dissenting or concurring, have only doctrinal value and are not binding in any way.

As for judicial review, a long (since the famous 'tramways of Bucharest' case in 1912[16]) but not very strong tradition of diffuse and concrete control of the constitutionality of laws opposed—rather seriously and for quite some time[17]— regular judges being appointed to the newly created Constitutional Court. Despite accusations that the Romanian Court was merely copying the French Conseil Constitutionnel, the 'Kelsenian model' of judicial review has been transplanted into Romania according to the German model, slightly adapted to the specificities of Eastern Europe. Thus, the Romanian Constitutional Court checks for the

---

[14] CE Alexe, *Judecătorul în procesul civil, între rol activ și arbitrar*, vol 1 (CH Beck, București, 2008) 269; CE Alexe, 'Răspunderea judecătorilor, garanție a independenței justiției' (2004) 1 *Pandectele Române* 215; A Boar, 'Judecătorul-putere și răspundere' (1998) 1 *Dreptul* 25.

[15] M Cappelletti, *Le pouvoir des juges* (Economica, Presses Universitaires d'Aix Marseille, 1990) 176.

[16] G Jeze, 'Pouvoir et devoir des tribunaux en général et des tribunaux roumains en particulier de vérifier la constitutionnalité des lois à l'occasion des procès portés devant eux' (1912) *RDP* 138.

[17] And this opposition is perceived as still ongoing by I Vida, n 9 above, 240.

constitutionality of laws and treaties ratified by Romania before[18] and after[19] their coming into force, rules on legal disputes of a constitutional nature between public authorities, decides upon challenges to the constitutionality of political parties, and is the electoral judge for presidential elections. In Romania the Constitutional Court has a special jurisdiction and is not part of the general/common judicial system. Judges at the Constitutional Court have a status assimilated to the one of regular judges, but they are not part and parcel of the judiciary. The Constitutional Court of Romania was created in June 1992 and since then it has accumulated more than 13,000 decisions and a few hundred court rulings.

On a different note, unlike other ex-communist states, Romania has managed to preserve its Civil Code of 1865—heavily inspired by the Napoleonic Code of 1801—albeit with dramatic revisions until the autumn of 2011. Article 3 of the former corresponded to Article 4 of the latter and provided for miscarriage of justice (*déni de justice*) as a potential infringement of the very function of a judge if he or she claims the law would be incomplete or unclear. A long and well-established tradition among Romanian scholars, be they specialists in civil law or in the theory of law, holds that this provision allowed, and even required, the analogy of law to be used whenever the judge found himself in a difficult situation. Thus, knowledge of comparative law becomes not only interesting, but also bears potential practical consequences; therefore, the potential use of legal reasoning via comparison with similarities existing in other legal systems comes as a natural fact of life to many generations of Romanian lawyers. Despite this, foreign precedents are never used in Romanian legal practice, partly due to the general context of a civil law system which allows for the analogy of law to be used only when the alternative would be a legal vacuum or a highly positivistic legal doctrine and practice.

The ratification in 1994 of the ECHR brought about an important change in the attitude of judges, who started more and more to use not only international standards for the protection of human rights in their judgments, but also relevant international (mainly ECtHR) case law. The Constitutional Court did not escape this general trend.[20] The same applies to EU law and the case law of the ECJ once Romania became a member of the European Union (1 January 2007).

---

[18] Through an abstract and a priori judicial review, initiated by a complaint stemming from: 50 deputies, 25 senators, any of the presidents of the two houses of Parliament, the President of Romania, the Government, the highest court of the land, or the ombudsman. In such cases the Constitutional Court may issue an 'objection of unconstitutionality' which obliges Parliament or the government to review the law or delegate legislation as to make it compliant with the decision of the Constitutional Court.

[19] Through a concrete and a posteriori judicial review (improperly) called an 'exception of unconstitutionality', which can be initiated by the ombudsman or by the parties or the judge in a trial in front of regular courts or in front of commercial arbitration. In such cases the proceedings in front of the court or the commercial arbitration may continue even after the exception of unconstitutionality has been raised, but if the provision upon which the case has been ruled is found unconstitutional it should be reopened based on an extraordinary way of appeal.

[20] Particularly after 2000, see www.ccr.ro/default.aspx?page=decisions/default.

C. Legal Scholarship

The influence of legal scholarship on the activity and decisions of the Constitutional Court of Romania is hard to assess.

Seven of the first nine judges appointed to the Constitutional Court in 1992 were law professors from various universities across the country. Later on, this composition was to be severely altered, so that in some of the recent renewals of constitutional judges none of the appointed persons had connections with legal scholarship. The trend was somewhat reversed in June 2010, but the impact of this on case law could not be assessed within the timeframe set for this analysis.

Ties between constitutional judges and legal scholarship depend a lot on individual personalities and tend to vary over time. The same can be said with regard to the participation of Romanian constitutional judges in the international fora available to them. Thus, specific judges may have the habit of consulting law professors when they feel additional substance to their line of argument is needed, but this is utterly informal and always has to remain secret, no trace of 'external' consultation being identifiable in any of the Court's decisions. Several discussions and interviews conducted with current and previous incumbents of such a position have strongly confirmed this conclusion. Similarly, participation in bilateral or multilateral gatherings or conferences depends a lot not only on the availability of specific judges, but also on the propensity towards international cooperation of the specific president of the Court.[21] However, mention has to be made here with regard to the constant participation of the Constitutional Court of Romania, ever since its creation, in all international organisations and conferences relevant for institutions dealing with judicial review,[22] as well as with regard to its bilateral relations with similar institutions all over the world. These can be considered as opportunities for judges to get acquainted with foreign case law directly from the source, without the interference of any legal doctrine.

In spite of the quasi-absence of direct and/or visible contact with legal scholars from Romania or abroad, contact via the library and internet still remains available. The Constitutional Court displays a broad collection of books and publications, internet subscriptions included, relevant to its activity, and magistrate-assistants who support judges tend to make use of all resources at hand. Also, whenever the subjects of cases and timeframes allow, comparative law files and files with relevant case law of international jurisdictions or other constitutional courts are made available to constitutional judges. Although foreign law and jurisprudence are quite rarely mentioned in constitutional decisions, several interviews conducted with

---

[21] This is most noticeable when having a look at the frequency of the so-called 'Franco-Romanian constitutional days': held, in principle every second year since 1992, once in Paris and once in Bucharest, the last one goes back to 2003, when the Romanian delegation to Paris also included a law professor from the University of Bucharest, while previous meetings in Bucharest have always included a strong delegation of French professors of constitutional law (see www.ccr.ro/default.aspx?page=events/constitutionaldays). As for the 'German-Romanian constitutional days' they only took place once in Bucharest and even then only one law professor was invited. No trace of these last ones can be found on the website of the Romanian jurisdiction.

[22] Notably the European Commission for Democracy through Law (Venice Commission), the Conference of European Constitutional Courts or the Association of Constitutional Courts Having in Common the Partial Use of French.

judges of the Romanian Constitutional Court have confirmed that, usually, they are or may be aware of similar cases ruled on in other courts or other relevant information that could support a decision-making process in the case at stake for them.

However, foreign case law does not enjoy a large place in general scholarly debate in Romania. Apart from cases against Romania before the ECHR and ECJ, and unless highly important or reverberating cases are decided by international courts, pure foreign case law is not commonly debated in Romanian academic fora. Niche law reviews, such as scientific publications of the three traditional law faculties in Bucharest,[23] Iassy and Cluj rarely happen to include excerpts of or comments on foreign case law and the only law review (*Pandectele Române*) which boasts such a section in fact fills it with case law from international courts or jurisdictions.

II. THE EMPIRICAL RESEARCH

Over 20 years of existence the Constitutional Court of Romania has issued more than 13,000 decisions. This analysis has taken into account all rulings of the Romanian Constitutional Court since its creation on 1 June 1992 until 31 December 2011 through careful reading of each and every decision. Constitutional judges directly mentioned or alluded to foreign case law in only 14 of these, that is, foreign precedent is present in a percentage of 0.1 per cent of the case law of the Constitutional Court of Romania. The figure is very close to the margin of error of any statistical data and quite difficult to show in a graph. Within the scope of the comparative study that made this publication possible, this places Romania in the group of countries where foreign case law is very rarely used.

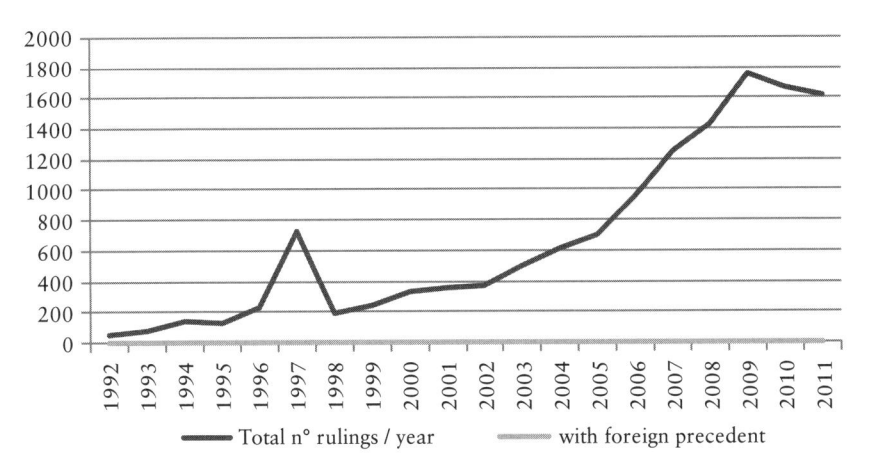

Figure 1.

---

[23] Eg, www.drept.unibuc.ro/Partea-I-s287-ro.htm.

330 *Elena Simina Tanasescu and Stefan Deaconu*

A. Implicit Citations of Foreign Case Law

Brief mention has to be made here with regard to the implicit[24] influence of foreign precedent, which is difficult to assess accurately. A broad and general reference was made to foreign precedent in only six cases: decision n°115/1996 refers to 'practise of other constitutional jurisdictions' as an additional argument for the constitutionality of the Labour code, decisions n°22/2000 and n°34/2000 quote the 'constant constitutional practise in other states' in applying the principle of equality, while decisions n°121/2000 and n°295/2002 vaguely mention 'constitutional case law in other countries' to further support their main argument. A bit more specific, but without clearly quoting a foreign precedent, a separate opinion to decision n°53/2011 refers to

> the Report of the Constitutional Court of Bulgaria presented at the XIIth Congress of the Conference of Constitutional Courts in Europe which mentions that acts provided for by article 149 para.1 point 2 of the Bulgarian Constitution may be either individual acts or normative acts

in order to stress that a discussion on the legal nature of acts submitted to the control of the Romanian Constitutional Court in the case at hand could have followed the same pattern. However, several interviews or private conversations held with judges and clerks at the Constitutional Court could not help to identify the specific foreign precedent referred to, although all of them overtly 'confess' to an awareness of foreign case law. These six decisions were not taken into account in this research since they do not seem to bear any significant consequences for the outcome of this specific research.

B. Explicit Citations of Foreign Case Law

i. Quantitative Approach

The table below presents the evolution in time of the explicit use made by the Constitutional Court of Romania of foreign precedent.

Table 1

Year	Total no rulings per year	No of rulings referring to foreign precedent	Case of the Constitutional Court of Romania	Cases quoted or referred to
1992	49		–	
1993	71		–	
1994	141		–	
1995	131		–	

(continued)

---

[24] Apart from those very rare situations where judges at the Constitutional Court give interviews and deliberately mention being aware of existing foreign precedent there is no trace of potential influence. Even in such cases the great majority of their decisions do not bear any trace of foreign precedent.

Year	Total no rulings per year	No of rulings referring to foreign precedent	Case of the Constitutional Court of Romania	Cases quoted or referred to
1996	225	2	Decision n°107/1995 Decision n°140/1996	Decision n°1/28.01.1987 **Germany** Decision n°12.568/1990 **Austria** Decision n°36/1994 **Hungary**
1997	716		–	
1998	188		–	
1999	239	2	Decision n°113/1999 Decision n°203/1999	Decision n°99-412 **France** Decision n°10/22.09.1999 **Bulgaria**
2000	326		–	
2001	354	1	Decision n°124/2001	Miranda v Arizona (1966) **USA**
2002	363		–	
2003	494		–	
2004	602		–	
2005	701		–	
2006	953	1	Decision n°478/2006	In re St Nazaire Co (1879) of Court of Appeal of **England** Case n°A-463-90 of 1991 of Federal Court of Appeal of **Canada**
2007	1,246	1	Decision n°334/2007	Miranda v Arizona (1966) of **USA** Dickerson v United States (2000) of **USA**
2008	1,416		–	
2009	1,751	1	Decision n°1415/2009	Decision n°89-269 **France**
2010	1,659	3	Decision n°872/2010 Decision n°874/2010 Decision n°873/2010	Decision n°455/B/1995 and n°277/B/1997 and n°39/1999 (XII.21) **Hungary** Decision n°2009-43-01 of 21.12.2009 **Latvia** Decision of 18.01.2010 **Latvia** Decision of 12.07.2001 **Lithuania**

(continued)

Year	Total no rulings per year	No of rulings referring to foreign precedent	Case of the Constitutional Court of Romania	Cases quoted or referred to
2011	1,609	3	Decision n°766/2011 Decision n°1470/2011 Decision n°1533/2011	Decision of 14.07.2005 **Czech Republic** Decision of 10.01.2001 **Czech Republic** Decision n°10-16 **France** Decision 33/06 of 27.03.2009 **Lithuania** Decision n°2/2009 (I.12) **Hungary** Decision n°2004-492 **France** Decision n°2 BvR 987/7.09.2011 **Germany**
	13,234	14		

It is interesting to note that 11 foreign countries have been considered relevant by the Romanian Constitutional Court and the frequency of citation cannot be considered to point to any specific preference. A brief summary of these 14 decisions follows.

a. Equality between Men and Women regarding the Minimum Age of Retirement

Decision n°107/1995 relates to an 'exception of unconstitutionality' concerning Law n°3/1977 on retirement and social assistance (concerns fundamental rights; references foreign precedent in the text of the decision as brought up by the parties in the constitutional case).

The parties invoking the unconstitutionality (as opposed to the principle of equality) of the legal provision stating that women can retire at 60 years and should retire at 62 years while men can retire at 65 years and should retire at 67 years attached to the documents filed with the Court the rulings of the Constitutional Court of Germany and of the Constitutional Court of Austria.

In its general reasoning, as an additional argument to those already stated in favour of the constitutionality of the difference in the retirement age, the Constitutional Court of Romania summed up (in no more than three lines) the two decisions brought by the parties and mentioned the correspondence it had with those very courts in order to clarify the issue and concluded that social and professional realities make it such that, for the time being, the difference relating to the age of retirement has to be maintained in Romania.

> Even in cases like Austria, where the Constitutional Court ruled that the principle of gender equality imposes the same retirement age, the legislative authority has not currently accepted this point of view. In Germany, according to the decision put with the file, based on social and professional realities confirmed in a large social poll, the Karlsruhe Court decided that, for the time being, a difference in the age of retirement is justified.

b. Freedom of Expression v Libel against Public Authorities

Decision n°140/1996 relates to an 'exception of unconstitutionality' regarding the criminal punishment of 'libel against a public office' (concerns fundamental rights; references foreign precedent in the text of the decision as brought up by the parties).

The parties invoking the unconstitutionality of this particular form of libel as contrary to freedom of expression filed with the Constitutional Court a ruling of the Constitutional Court of Hungary, where a similar provision of the Hungarian Criminal Code had been found unconstitutional.

After explaining why this particular form of libel was not unconstitutional, judges stated that 'the decision of the Constitutional Court of Hungary cannot be considered as an argument for the current proceeding and the reasoning made there cannot be examined by the Constitutional Court of Romania'.

c. The Right of Persons Belonging to National Minorities to Preserve their Cultural Identity

Decision n°113/1999 relates to an 'objection of unconstitutionality' regarding the legislative delegation granted by Parliament to Government on 1 July 1999 (concerns state institutions—parliamentary procedures; references foreign precedent in a separate opinion as brought up by the constitutional judge).

The decision concerned the a priori control of the legislative delegation which ended with the ratification by Romania of the European Charter of Regional or Minority Languages. In a separate opinion one judge (I Muraru) argued, inter alia, that Articles 1, 6, 13, 114 and 148 of the Romanian Constitution (pertaining, respectively, to the characteristics of the Romanian state, the constitutional protection granted to national minorities, the official language of Romania, the legislative delegation and the revision of the Constitution) were of 'European inspiration, particularly French'. The President of the French Republic had asked the Constitutional Council to determine whether the ratification of this European Charter had to be preceded by a revision of the Constitution, given the interpretative declaration made by France and the engagements that were to be taken according to the third part of this convention. And judge Muraru continued

> the European Charter of Regional and Minority Languages is a problem common to the States of the Council of Europe. That is why, maybe less as a purely legal argument for our Constitutional Court, it worth mentioning some documents existing in other countries. In that sense, we consider that we may reference the Decision n°99-412 DC of June 15th, 1999 of the French Constitutional Council ... The Constitutional Council decided that it contains provisions contrary to the Constitution.

d. Access to Information of Public Interest

Decision n°203/1999 relates to an 'objection of unconstitutionality' regarding the Law on access to one's own personal file and the disclosure of 'Securitate' as the political police (concerns fundamental rights; references foreign precedent (final decision) in the text of the decision as invoked by the Constitutional Court).

The MPs which notified the Court argued that limiting the number of persons on which one might inquire about with the state agency in charge of the archives of 'Securitate' on their possible status as 'agent of Securitate' infringed the right to free access to information as granted by Article 31 of the Constitution. The Constitutional Court rejected the claim and referenced the entire documentation it had consulted, which included similar laws in Germany, Hungary and Bulgaria, including a relevant ruling of the Constitutional Court of Bulgaria.

The foreign case law referenced was not used by the Constitutional Court of Romania in its reasoning, but merely referred to as an additional document which could be corroborated with all other facts in that case in order to allow the Court to reach its decision that the Romanian law was constitutional.

e. The Right to Defence

Decision n°124/2001 relates to an 'exception of unconstitutionality' regarding the Criminal Procedural Code (concerns fundamental rights; references foreign precedent in a separate opinion as brought up by the constitutional judges).

The parties claimed that specific provisions of the Criminal Procedural Code infringed upon the constitutional right to a defence (as protected by Article 24 of the Constitution) as they prevented the chosen lawyer from being present at all phases of the criminal procedure, including when facts were gathered by the prosecutors, and allowed for legal counselling only during the criminal trial, that is, only after the defendant had been informed of a criminal action being started against him/her.

The Constitutional Court, with a majority of five to four votes, rejected the claim. However, in a separate opinion four judges (I Muraru, N Popa, L Mihai and RP Vonica) referenced the famous precedent *Miranda v Arizona* (1966) of the Supreme Court of the United States. According to them

> the legislation of States with a democratic tradition provides—under specific forms—for a system of a general guarantee of the right to defence, including by using the prerogative of legal counselling and assistance by a lawyer. Thus, in the United States of America, through a decision ruled in 1966 in the case Miranda v Arizona, the Federal Supreme Court established, among others, that people enjoy the right to defence from the very beginning of the criminal procedure. State authorities may not use the declarations made by people without the respect of the due process of law, among which the right to legal counselling and assistance by a lawyer. In case a person does not have a lawyer, State authorities must prove that that person had been previously informed on his rights, including the one to legal assistance, prior to answer any question, so that the person has given up his right to defence fully aware. When the suspect requires consulting a qualified lawyer prior to making any statement he or she cannot be asked questions. The simple fact that the suspect has answered some questions or that he has voluntarily made declarations does not lead to the conclusion that he gave up to his right not to answer following questions. He may decide at any moment to consult a lawyer and only afterwards to answer the questions.

f. The Principle of *res judicata*

Decision n°478/2006 relates to an 'exception of unconstitutionality' regarding the Civil Procedural Code (concerns fundamental rights; references foreign precedent in the text of the decision as invoked by the Constitutional Court).

The Constitutional Court rejected the claim arguing that the principle *res judicata* was fully protected by the legal provisions deferred to it. It also added that

> this fundamental principle of civil procedure, which is recognised in numerous countries of Romano-Germanic law, is also known in the Anglo-Saxon law under the name of *functus officio*, which means that after ruling a case the court can no longer decide upon it, the only possibility of changing or correcting the solution being the legal reformation remedies (eg the decision of the Court of Appeal of England In re St Nazaire Co of 1879 or the more recent case low of the Federal Court of Appeal of Canada, as, for instance, in case n°A-463-90 of 1991).

g. Presumption of Innocence and the Right of the Person not to Self-incriminate

Decision n°334/2007 relates to an 'exception of unconstitutionality' regarding the Criminal Procedural Code (concerns fundamental rights; references foreign precedent in the text of the decision as invoked by the Constitutional Court).

The suspect claimed that the Criminal Procedural Code was unconstitutional only to the extent that any declaration made by any suspect could only be used against him/her.

The Constitutional Court rejected the argument. In its reasoning it stated, inter alia, that

> with regard to the right of the person not to accuse him/herself, the Supreme Court of the United States ruled in the case Miranda v Arizona of 1966 that any confession of a suspect cannot be received by the court unless the suspect is previously informed about those 'Miranda rights'. Thus, before the interrogation takes place, the suspect must be informed that he or she may remain silent, that any declaration he or she makes may be used against him or her and that he or she has the right to be assisted by a lawyer, and if he does not have sufficient material resources a lawyer ex officio will be appointed. These procedural guarantees effectively ensure that the suspect will not accuse him/herself. In another case Dickerson v United States of 2000 the Court re-affirmed this principle—the right to remain silent—as having [a] constitutional nature, even if it is not expressly mentioned in the Constitution.

h. Government Assuming Responsibility in Front of Parliament

Decision n°1415/2009 relates to an 'objection of unconstitutionality' regarding a law on a uniform salary system for employees in the public sector (concerns state institutions—parliamentary procedure; references foreign precedent in a separate opinion as invoked by the constitutional judges).

Members of the parliamentary group which notified the Court argued that Government could not assume its political responsibility in front of Parliament three times during the same day on three different draft laws and qualified this attitude as abuse and an attempt to substitute the executive for the legislature.

The Constitutional Court rejected the argument. In a separate opinion to this decision three judges (A Cojocaru, T Toader and V Zoltan Puskas) considered that laws thus adopted by the Government were unconstitutional. The separate opinion considered that the Government could not assume responsibility in the same parliamentary session, and particularly during the same day, without the effect of diminishing the role of Parliament, which the Constitution declared to be the sole legislative authority. The separate opinion continued by invoking the example of France:

> the interpretation is also in agreement with the French example, where, after the executive used this procedure 39 times in the ninth term, the French Constitutional Council (Decision n°89-269 of January the 22nd 1990) noticed that this procedure 'de facto deprives the National Assembly of its essential functions'. Following the revision of the Constitution on the 23rd of July 2008 the French constituent power explicitly mentioned that Government may assume its responsibility on the law on state budget and the law on the social security budget and that 'Government may assume its responsibility on a draft law only once during one term'. The revision of the French Constitution came into force on the 1st of March 2009.

i. Government Assuming Responsibility in Front of Parliament

Decision n°872/2010 and **Decision n°874/2010** relate to 'objections of unconstitutionality' regarding a law needed to re-establish a balanced state budget and which de facto diminished salaries in the public sector by 25 per cent and public pensions by 15 per cent (concerns fundamental rights; references foreign precedent in the text of the decision as invoked by the Constitutional Court).

Constitutional judges decided that the reduction of pensions by 15 per cent was unconstitutional because 'the right to a state pension is a fundamental right pre-constituted since the active period of life of any individual', which creates 'the correlative obligation of the state to pay a pension based on the principle of contributivity [sic] during the passive part of the life of any individual'.

In order to underline this idea, the Court noticed

> some considerations made by other Constitutional Courts with regard to the right to [a] pension. Thus, the Constitutional Court of Hungary, in its decision n°455/B/1995 ruled that the pension calculated according to the rules of the state social security cannot be restricted and through its decision n°277/B/1997 ruled that unilaterally changing the quantum of pensions is unconstitutional, directly referring to the impossibility for the legislator to diminish big pensions in order to increase small pensions. Likewise, the same constitutional jurisdiction decided that the contributively [sic] pension is an 'acquis' right to such an extent that to change its nominal quantum is unconstitutional. As a matter of fact, similar considerations are to be found also in the Decision n°2009-43-01 of the 21st of December 2009 of the Constitutional Court of Latvia.

j. Government Assuming Responsibility in Front of Parliament

Decision n°873/2010 relates to an 'objection of unconstitutionality' regarding a law to establish certain measures in the area of state pensions which aimed at the elimination of the special pensions of magistrates (concerns fundamental rights; references foreign precedent in the text of the decision as invoked by the Constitutional Court).

Constitutional judges decided that a reduction of the special (bigger) pensions that magistrates enjoy would have the significance of a limitation of the independence of judges.

The Romanian Constitutional Court invoked a similar situation presented in front of the Constitutional Court of Latvia which,

> in its ruling of the 18th of January 2010 declared unconstitutional and inapplicable specific provisions of the Law on the judicial authority noticing they contradict the principle of the independence of judges. Given the financial situation of Latvia and international commitments it has taken Parliament decided to recalculate the salaries of judges with the aim of reducing them. The Constitutional Court noticed that the concept of independence of judges includes an adequate remuneration, comparable to the prestige and the responsibility of their profession.

> The Constitutional Court of Lithuania, in its ruling of the 12th of July 2001, declared that democratic states accept the fact that judges must have not only high professional qualifications and a perfect reputation, but also need material independence and security with regard to their future. The state has the obligation to establish such salaries for judges as to compensate for their status, functions and responsibilities, and maintaining the salaries of judges is one of the guarantees of their independence.

> The Constitutional Court of the Czech Republic in its ruling of the 14th of July 2005 noticed that in democratic states financial security is clearly recognised as one of the essential elements than ensure the independence of judges.

k. Judicial Review of Laws No Longer in Force

Decision n°766/2011 relates to an 'exception of unconstitutionality' referring to the article which allows the judicial system and the Constitutional Court itself to filter exceptions of unconstitutionality on the ground that 'the law is no longer in force' (concerns state institutions; references foreign precedent in the text of the decision as invoked by the Constitutional Court).

The Constitutional Court of Romania has consistently over a long period of time decided that exceptions of unconstitutionality which refer to legal provisions that are no longer in force at the point when the Court decision is rendered should be disregarded not on their merits, but on procedural grounds, as being irrelevant for general compliance of the normative system with the requirements of the fundamental law. However, in this particular case, the defendant insisted and explained in detail why he found this position not to be accurate and the Constitutional Court decided to depart from its well-established precedent. As an additional argument, it specifically referred to case law of foreign constitutional courts:

> In the case of judicial review, European constitutional courts have accepted as part of their jurisdiction the control of legal norms which are no longer in force, but which remain applicable to the specific case that raises the exception of unconstitutionality at hand. Thus, based on internal regulation or tendencies in their own case law, the German, Italian, Hungarian, Czech, Polish or French constitutional jurisdictions have considered [it] more important to analyse the substance of such legal provisions in order to eliminate those that do not correspond to constitutional requirements, than to establish a purely formal criteria [sic] of procedure that would lead to the end of the constitutional case. Highly illustrative is the situation of the Czech Republic, where the Constitutional Court has ruled in its decision of January the 10th 2001 (the Constitutional Court had been notified on June the 29th 2000 with an exception of unconstitutionality of a law that had been revised on June the 13th 2000 and which revision should have come into force on July the 1st 2000) that an

exception of unconstitutionality referring to a legal text that was no longer in force will not be rejected as non-admissible for procedural grounds, but will be examined on its merits because common judges have the obligation to apply the law and do not enjoy the possibility to consider a law unconstitutional and thus not apply it. When a common judge considers that the law which needs to be applied is unconstitutional he or she has to notify the constitutional court otherwise, by applying such a law, he or she would be infringing the Constitution. Likewise, the Constitutional Council of France declared that the exception of unconstitutionality may also refer to a legal text no longer in force. Decision n°2010—16 of July 23rd 2010, published in the Official Journal of July 27th 2010, expressly mentioned that alteration or ulterior abrogation of the contested legal provision does not have as legal effect the disappearance of the potential infringement of freedoms and rights guaranteed by the Constitution. Another example is offered by the Constitutional Court of Lithuania which, through its decision rendered on March the 27th 2009 (file n°33/06) ruled that when the legal text criticised for unconstitutionality has been modified in its essence, the constitutional court has the obligation to check the legal norm with which it has been notified, irrespective of it still being into force or not. On the other hand, the Constitutional Court of Hungary controls the constitutionality of the legal norm with which it has been notified in its version prior to the modification, abrogation or revoking in case it may still be applicable in a case pending in front of the judge a quo. To this effect, article 44 para 1 of the Procedural Rules in front of the Constitutional Court of Hungary, approved through the Decision of the Constitutional Court n°2/2009 (I.12) published in the Official Journal of the Constitutional Court, year XVIII, n°1/January 2009, provides that, 'according to the procedure foreseen by article 38 of the Law on the organisation and functioning of the Constitutional Court, its decision may find a legal norm which is no longer in force unconstitutional if in the concrete case at hand this legal norm is still applicable'.

1. Presumption of Innocence

Decision n°1470/2011 relates to an 'exception of unconstitutionality' referring to Article 320 of the Criminal Procedure Code providing for the possibility of the defendant admitting his/her own guilt (concerns fundamental rights; references foreign precedent in a separate opinion).

A major change of civil and criminal codes occurred in Romania towards the end of 2010 in order to allow for the speeding-up of judicial procedures to make the total length of trials more predictable. However, the majority of constitutional judges decided that some of the novelties introduced mainly in the Criminal Procedure Code infringed the Constitution. In particular, the acceleration of criminal trials via the settlement of guilt based upon an admittance of guilt coming from a defendant prior to the start of any criminal procedures was found to breach the most favoured principle of criminal law and the presumption of innocence.

In a separate opinion one judge considered that the settlement of guilt did not infringe upon the presumption of innocence:

> Regarding the incidence of the presumption of innocence within a procedure of preliminary admitting of guilt, similar to the one foreseen by article 320[1] of the Romanian Criminal procedure code, one has to mention the Decision n° 2004-492 DC of March the 2nd 2004 of the French Constitutional Council which ruled that—during the procedure called 'reconnaissance préalable de culpabilité'—the judge cannot be held by the preliminary admitting of guilt made by the defendant, but on the contrary, 'is obliged to make sure that the defendant admitted freely and sincerely that he/she is the author of the facts and to check upon

their reality'. In the same decision, the French Constitutional Council stated that 'the judge must determine not only the reality of the consent given by that person, but also his/her sincerity' whenever issuing an ordinance to ratify the agreement on the settlement of guilt.

m. Margin of Appreciation of Parliament when Balancing Fundamental Rights and State Institutions

Decision n°1533/2011 relates to an 'objection of unconstitutionality' referring to the Law for the Approval of the Emergency Ordinance of the Government n°71/2009 regarding the payment of certain amounts of money pertaining to the salaries of employees in the public sector (concerns fundamental rights; references foreign precedent in the text of the decision as invoked by the Constitutional Court).

From 2007 to 2009 some categories of employees in the public sector have won court cases through which the Romanian state was obliged to pay compensation of a significant amount to a large number of persons. Faced with the global economic crisis which hit Romania only towards the end of 2009, the state decided to schedule payments and spread them out over an interval of five years. Upon the adoption of the law imposing such temporising measures, the opposition contested the very idea of paying in instalments and invoked formal arguments pertaining to the procedure of adoption of the respective law, as well as arguments referring to the potential infringement of the constitutional right to salary.

Considering that compensation won in court is different in kind and has nothing in common with a salary, the Constitutional Court nevertheless invoked the principle of proportionality with regard to the action of Parliament in temporising payments towards public employees. Noting that more than 27,700 final court decisions pending on 31 December 2010 obliged the state to pay over eight billion ROL in total, which represented 1.4 per cent of Romania's estimated GDP for 2012, constitutional judges held that the state also had 'the obligation to protect national interest in the economic and financial activity', according to Article 135 of the fundamental law. Therefore, Parliament had to have control over fundamental decisions in the area of budget policy and enjoyed a certain margin of appreciation while balancing the stability of the state budget and the economic performance of the state.

> The Constitutional Court must respect this margin of appreciation, its control being limited to the obvious infringements of the constitutional texts (also see the Decision of the German Constitutional Court 2 BvR 987/10 of September the 7th 2011 on complaints of unconstitutionality against the package of measures on the financial aid granted to Greece and funds made available for saving the Euro).

ii. Qualitative Approach

Although the number of decisions of the Constitutional Court of Romania where foreign precedent is mentioned is very low, the figures can still be interpreted.

The most common distinction which can be made among these few decisions is the one pertaining to the *area of constitutional law* they are addressing. 11 out of the total 14 decisions refer to the protection of fundamental rights. In eight out of these 11 decisions dealing with fundamental rights, the foreign case law quotation is made within the very reasoning of the Constitutional Court, while in only three cases foreign precedent is referenced in separate opinions. Also, in three out of those 11 decisions foreign case law is referenced only for the argument to be rejected, while in the majority of cases foreign precedent is used as an additional argument to support the reasoning of the constitutional judges (the three separate opinions are included in this last category). However, the overwhelming majority of decisions that deal with the protection of fundamental rights tend to reinforce the general idea that, at least in Romania, judicial dialogue finds more favourable conditions in the area of universal values, such as fundamental rights, and seems less appealing for subjects relating to state functioning, despite possible parallels or analogies of law.

Only three decisions out of 14 separate opinions refer to issues pertaining to institutional arrangements; in all cases specific decisions adopted by the French Conseil Constitutionnel are quoted in order to highlight the similarity of arguments that could be made with regard to procedures in front of the Romanian Parliament. In one case (1415/2009) the justification might be that the Government assuming responsibility in front of Parliament is a procedure that the Romanian and French Constitutions have in common and the analogy of law might have stirred the parallel on legal reasoning. In another one (766/2011) a broad similarity of context can be noticed (judicial review pertaining to abrogated laws), while in the last one (113/1999) there was no similarity of legal or political institutions, but rather of context and situation. Although three in more than 13,000 cases over 20 years can, only with difficulty, be considered as a figure on which conclusions can be based, it seems safe to infer from the scarcity of decisions pertaining to institutional arrangements that this area is much less prone to the use of foreign precedent. Moreover, since in two cases foreign case law has only been mentioned as an additional argument in separate (dissenting) opinions and even the judges quoting it underlined that it should not be considered as 'a purely legal argument' rather as 'a document' to be known, one may safely deduce that analogy of legal reasoning finds its natural limits in the area of political institutions. While fundamental rights can be considered an expression of universal values, institutional arrangements of given States do remain specific and difficult to compare.

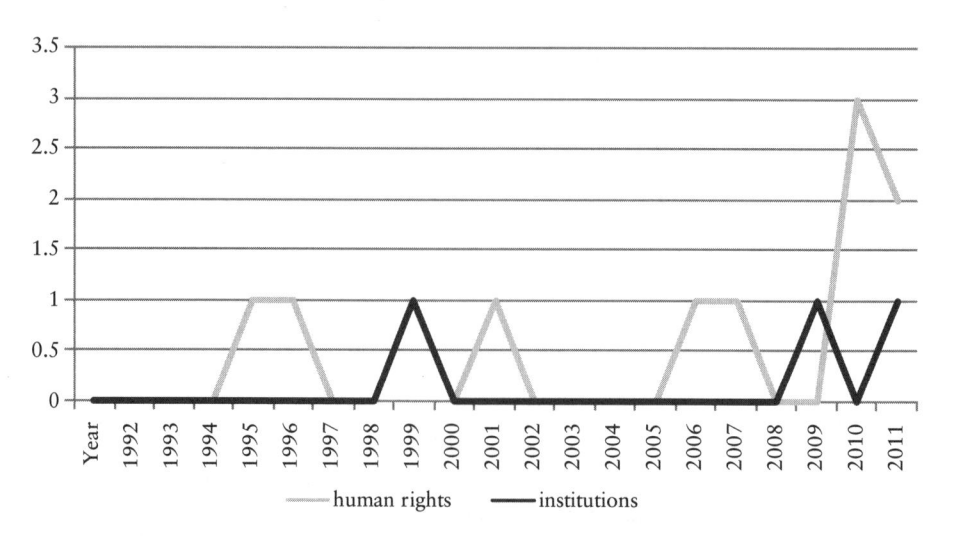

Figure 2.

Over time (particularly during the last two years) the number and variety of quoted foreign precedents with regard to fundamental rights seem to have increased. In addition, factual observation and interviews with concerned parties point to the fact that there is no pattern of quotation related to the personal educational or professional backgrounds of constitutional judges. Foreign precedent is rather hand-picked, on a random basis. Referrals are made according to available information; various conversations with constitutional judges and clerks have shown that one of the main sources of information is the Venice Commission and its dedicated website, as well as various networks which exist among constitutional courts or judges.

Another common criterion for a quantitative analysis could be the *judicial review procedure* used to reach the decision where the foreign precedent is quoted. So far this statistic seems slightly unbalanced, six such decisions being the result of an a priori control and eight the result of a so-called 'exception of unconstitutionality'. This is to say that judges tend to use the instrument of legal reasoning analogy irrespective of the way in which they have been addressed or the type of procedure they are confronted with. However, this partial conclusion could be reversed in the near future, as the past two years have shown a tendency towards judges using foreign precedent more in abstract review than in exceptions of unconstitutionality. This may be caused by another interesting trend which points to the fact that foreign precedent is increasingly used by constitutional judges *ex officio* in cases with a potentially important political and social impact; such cases tend to be dealt with, in the specific Romanian context, in abstract rather than in concrete constitutional review.

A general criterion for any such analysis is the *part of the decision* where foreign precedent is mentioned. In only four cases the explicit quotation of clearly identifiable foreign precedent belongs to judges drafting separate opinions and, out of these, two are cases pertaining to the functioning of Parliament. As expected, in such situations foreign precedent is mentioned in order to underline that 'even there' constitutional judges proceeded in similar ways to the ones considered by the separate opinion and that the majority opinion did not want to take into account. However, this relatively small number of separate opinions quoting foreign precedent displays a lack of interest of judges in arguing against their colleagues based on comparative grounds as if this kind of legal reasoning was not solid or convincing enough. One of the judges explicitly declares (113/1999) that 'although this could not be held as a purely legal argument in front of the Romanian Constitutional Court' he nevertheless dares also to mention a foreign precedent in order to support his line of argument. As a contrast, in 10 cases it is the Constitutional Court in its majority opinion which raises a legal argument following a comparison with foreign case law. It is interesting to note that (with one exception—decision n°1533/2011) in these 10 cases there was no separate opinion, as if case law analogy is a safer argument when used in a consensual manner by all judges rather than as an argument *a contrario*. Moreover, in nine of these cases the decision was reached with the favourable votes of all present judges (unanimity)[25] as a sign that foreign precedents can serve as an

---

[25] According to arts 51 and 52 of Law 47/1992 pertaining to the organisation and the functioning of the Constitutional Court of Romania decisions can be reached with the majority of votes of present judges, but, according to art 59 of the same law, those who vote against the majority do not have to draft a separate opinion. In practice it quite often happens that decisions are adopted by a majority (special

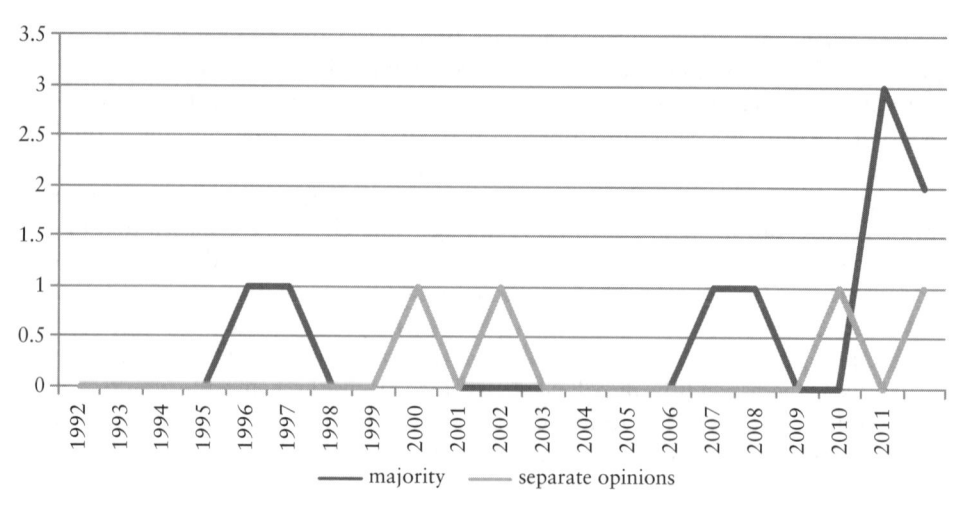

Figure 3.

additional argument ('also there') only when a broad consensus is reached and not in controversial situations. However, mention has to be made that over the last five to six years the Constitutional Court has used foreign precedents increasingly in what have been perceived as difficult cases with high political impact, in order to offer additional justification for the position it held. Particularly relevant for this situation are the decisions adopted during 2010 and, to a lesser extent those of 2011, where also the largest number of foreign precedents is quoted.

If we take a look at how foreign precedent has come to the attention of the Constitutional Court we notice that only in five cases was it initially invoked by the parties and constitutional judges merely responded to it. None of the cases displays a situation where the judge *ad quem* raised comparative legal reasoning, and the same applies for all the rest of the claimants able to bring cases in front of the Constitutional Court. In the early years of the Court, it was referral parties that started to mention foreign precedent, only to forget this kind of comparative reasoning later on. Over time, constitutional judges started to see the benefits of such a method and switched their attitude with regard to foreign precedent from pure reluctance to what one may call reserved interest.

The *geographic source* of foreign precedent referred to by the Constitutional Court of Romania boasts a broad diversity of countries: from Germany, Austria and France in Western Europe, to Canada and the US in North America and also Bulgaria, the Czech Republic, Hungary, Latvia and Lithuania in Eastern Europe. It is interesting to note that countries which could be considered to be faced with similar legal or factual situations such as those in Eastern Europe are more numerous, while those which might have been taken previously as 'raw models' are less

---

mention is made in the *corpus* of the decision just before the final conclusion), but no separate opinion follows. During the first 10 to 12 years of its existence the Constitutional Court used to adopt decisions based on consensus and with unanimity. Lately this practice has been put aside and a growing number of decisions are adopted with a majority; some also have separate opinions.

frequently quoted. Thus, out of the five East European countries mentioned in the case law of the Romanian Constitutional Court, Hungary stands out with four quotations, France, generally perceived as the great source of legal inspiration of the Romanian legal system, achieves parity with four quotations, while Latvia and Germany, with three quotations each, come before Lithuania, the Czech Republic and the US with two quotations each.

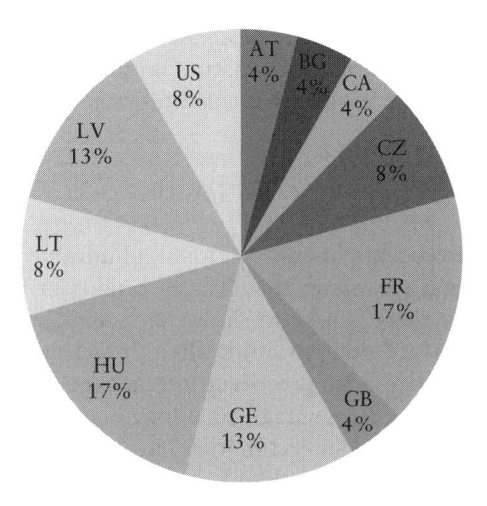

Figure 4.

However, indeed, the most interesting analysis—which draws on both quantitative and qualitative criteria—relates to the actual *use in the decision-making process* of foreign precedent by the constitutional judges. The first time (1996) a party ran an argument based on foreign precedent the Constitutional Court managed to interpret it in such a way that it changed the meaning which was given to it by the party which referred to it, while the second time (1996) it simply dismissed it. Only after 2000 (and the end of the first complete term that the first ever appointed judges had) did the Constitutional Court start to use foreign precedent not only as additional information but actually as useful additional argument. Over time, foreign precedent became a tool used more by the constitutional judges than by the parties, even in cases where the protection of fundamental rights was at stake. Moreover, lately, the use of foreign precedent has become standard for constitutional judges in an abstract procedure as opposed to the beginnings of the Constitutional Court, when foreign precedent was invoked rather by the parties in exceptions of unconstitutionality. In case a relation has to be established between appointments at the Romanian Constitutional Court and the use of foreign precedents one may assert that when judges started no longer to have academic backgrounds or activities the frequency, importance and number of citations of foreign precedent increased. A possible conclusion might be that judges who do not have an academic background feel the need to support their reasoning with comparative material in an attempt to prove that 'even there' similar conclusions can or were reached. The passage in the use of foreign precedent from 'not applicable' to 'even there in a specific case' and to 'also there in several cases' could reflect a potential evolution in the way of reasoning of constitutional judges; this could be speculated to be either a tendency of weakening self-assurance of constitutional judges or as a greater openness towards judicial dialogue and cross-fertilisation.

If anything, a trend with regard to the use of foreign precedent by the Romanian Constitutional Court would show that the parties started to mention it as contextual information and even additional argument, separate opinions took it over as additional argument against majority decisions and then constitutional judges started to refer to it as contextual information until they discovered an interest in having additional arguments for abstract constitutional review.

III. CONCLUSION

Referring to foreign precedents in constitutional adjudication means using a comparative method in legal reasoning that has its origins in legal analogy. In pure (mathematical) logic, analogy is used to show that a similarity exists in some characteristics of things that are otherwise not alike. In a legal argument, analogy of law may be used when there is no precedent in point (be it legal principles or even prior case law close in facts). Reasoning by analogy involves referring to a case that concerns a somewhat unrelated subject matter, but is governed by the same general principles, and applying those principles to the case at hand. Analogy of legal reasoning by referring to foreign precedents involves a double analogy, concerning both the merits and relevant legal principles on one hand and the way to use these elements in a distinct legal argument. According to this method, a partial similarity of either of the two elements already mentioned may give way to a conclusion of total similarity and thus induce conclusions which are only possible and not necessary (in mathematical terms). In other words, reasoning by analogy produces plausible arguments that hold a degree of probability but do not give any certainty. This makes analogical reasoning a dialectical instrument but not a rational demonstrative tool.

Keeping in mind these rather abstract and general conclusions, when dealing with the use of foreign precedent in constitutional adjudication one has to remember that a Constitution is the supreme law of the land and any analogy in this area has its natural limits. Romanian constitutional judges, who only started their activity in 1992, seemed to be well aware of this basic fact and rarely used analogical reasoning in their arguments. Despite exposure to direct judicial interaction and against a general scholarly trend favourable to judicial cross-fertilisation the first judges of the Romanian Constitutional Court seemed to be endowed with a solid theoretical background and only used foreign precedent parsimoniously. This did not prevent them from maintaining a vivid dialogue with colleagues of all practices and directions. However, over the second decade of existence of the Romanian Constitutional Court the trend seems to have been reversed and two parallel and paradoxical phenomena can be noticed: while direct international exposure of constitutional judges has been rather more limited, the use of foreign precedents as additional arguments in the court's reasoning started to increase. If put back into the general context of Romanian constitutional case law, this tendency should not be of concern: the number of decisions quoting foreign precedents is so low when compared to the total number of decisions issued by that court that, even if further increased, the rhythm of foreign quotation will not alter the line of reasoning of the Court. But the passage from mere 'non applicable' to 'also there and everywhere' meaning 'in all the rest of the world' clearly has a significance that should not be ignored.

At a more general level, the highly limited number of cases where Romanian constitutional judges quoted foreign precedents does not seem to confirm either the thesis of the convergence of common law and civil law, or of judicial dialogue among peer judges or courts (constitutional ones in addition). Having in mind the limited reliability of such statistical figures as those offered by the case law of the Romanian Constitutional Court in using foreign precedents, the only trend which seems to be confirmed refers to the universal value of fundamental rights. However, even this assertion comes with a caveat due to the particular situation of the Romanian Constitutional Court; since 2000 the Court started to quote and directly apply the European Convention on Human Rights and the relevant case law of the European Court of Human Rights, as well as other international legal instruments pertaining to the protection of human rights. In a context which made it possible for the court to allocate greater importance to the issue of fundamental rights it should not come as a surprise that its sensitivity encompasses not only international jurisdictions but also peers. Seen from this perspective, even the thesis of the universal value of fundamental right gathers a strong subjective dimension and no longer remains an invariable framework for all kinds of (constitutional) adjudication.

14

Russia: Foreign Transplants in the Russian Constitution and Invisible Foreign Precedents in Decisions of the Russian Constitutional Court

SERGEY BELOV[*]

TABLE OF CONTENTS

I. The Russian Constitution, its Cultural and Historical Origins and
    Foreign Influences on the Text 348
    A. History of Reforms in 1980–90s 348
    B. Constitution Convention in 1993. The Role of Foreign Experts and
        the Use of Foreign Law Arguments in Discussions 352
II. The Judicial System in Russia and Techniques of Judicial Reasoning 356
    A. The Russian Legal System and the Role of the Courts 356
    B. The Constitutional Court: Competence, Structure, Procedure 358
    C. Decisions of the Constitutional Court: Types and Role in the Legal System,
        Structure (Dissenting Opinions), Legal Positions and Significance of the
        Reasoning of the Decision 359
    D. Using Foreign Law in General. The Framework of Using Judicial Precedents.
        Refraining from the Use of Non-binding Sources of Law in the
        Reasoning of Decisions 363
        i. Russian Legal Scholarship and its Attention to the Influence
            of Foreign Case Law 366
III. Empirical Research on Using Foreign Precedents by the Russian
    Constitutional Court 367
    A. Explicit Citations of Foreign Case Law 367
        i. Quantitative Research 367
        ii. Qualitative Research 368
    B. Implicit Influence of Foreign Precedents 370
IV. Conclusion 371

---

[*] PhD, Associate Professor at St Petersburg State University, Law Faculty (St Petersburg, Russia).

I. THE RUSSIAN CONSTITUTION, ITS CULTURAL AND HISTORICAL ORIGINS AND FOREIGN INFLUENCES ON THE TEXT

A. History of Reforms in 1980–90s

THE CURRENT RUSSIAN Constitution was adopted in 1993 as a result of reforming of the Soviet state and legal systems in the late 1980s to early 1990s. The main direction of these reforms was the destruction of the Soviet system and the introduction of the principles of the 'Western-European and American' type of democracy, as it was called in Russia. This kind of democracy was opposed to the 'people's democracies' of the Soviet states (the USSR, the countries of Eastern Europe, China, Cuba and others).

The Soviet democracy of the USSR—established in and developed since the Great October Revolution of 1917 until the mid-1980s—was more prepared to 'export' than to 'import' legal principles, rules and jurisprudence. Soviet legal scholars insisted on the advantages and peculiarities of the Soviet system compared to the 'bourgeois' legal systems of Europe, the USA and other 'capitalist' states of their kind. The political union of the Soviet states ('states of the Warsaw Pact') demanded law and state systems in these states to be organised according to the model of the USSR, especially in the period immediately after the end of World War II.[1] By the 1980s, the governmental and legal systems in Soviet states differed in details while preserving the main principles of the Soviet model. Some countries, like China, parted from developments in the USSR system. Inside the USSR, however, no one was ready to follow the Chinese or other examples—let alone to implement even more distant foreign experience. State authorities (both legislative and judicial) did not attempt to look abroad.

The particularities of the Soviet system are found in the major principles of the state and the law.

As distinct from the principle of the separation of powers, the Soviet state was based on the principle of 'democratic centralism', which meant subordination of all state authorities to the Soviets of different levels (the only 'state power' bodies). This principle was grounded in the idea of the supremacy of the representative bodies, which could control other state bodies. Functions were distributed among them (Soviets [*sovety*] enacted laws and common directives, executive committees administered them, and courts and the militia [police] enforced the laws), but there was no institutional independence in exercising their powers.

The 'rule of law' (*gospodstvo prava*) principle was refused in favour of the principle of 'legality' (*zakonnost*), which demanded precise adherence to statutory rules and left much less discretion to courts in resolving legal disputes (because the policy of regulating social relations ought to be defined by the Soviets, not by the courts). Then and now, statutes are interpreted in Russia in a very literal way; courts carry out a textual analysis of statutes rather than taking into consideration their aims and principles.[2]

---

[1] While in Eastern Europe civil law evolved independently from the USSR legal system, independence was not allowed for the constitutional law system—see G Ajani, 'By Chance and Prestige: Legal Transplants in Russia and Eastern Europe' (1995) 43 *American Journal of Comparative Law* 100–01.

[2] This problem is discussed in contemporary literature concerning not only Russia, but other former socialist states as well—see Z Kühn, 'Worlds Apart: Western and Central European Judicial Culture at the Onset of the European Enlargement' (2004) 52 *American Journal of Comparative Law* 531–67. In Russia

At the same time, Soviet private law was very similar in its structure, and some of its institutions, to the law of the major continental European states, especially Germany. The specifics of the economic system resulted in the absence of institutions such as the law of private corporations, private entrepreneurs, etc. The structure of the RSFSR[3] Civil Code adopted in the 1960s (which remained in force until 1994–96) was similar to the 1900 German *Burgergezetzbuch* (*BGB*).[4] This statutory regulation played a major role in the development of Soviet private law, while court practice was only of minor significance.

These facts permit us to state that the general features of the Soviet legal system followed the German style, while the constitutional principles of the organisation of the USSR state retained Soviet-era peculiarities.

The nature of the Soviet system began to change radically in the process of the great reforms, started in 1985 by Mikhail Gorbachev and known as '*Perestroyka*' ('rearrangement' or 'transformation'). The causes and sources of these reforms are still a topic of public discussion; one can find economic as well as political and cultural roots for these reforms. Defects in the Soviet economic, political and legal systems became evident during the 1970s to 1980s—a period which was called 'the era of stagnation' (*Epoha Zastoya*),—and stimulated modernisation.

The first stage of these reforms concerned mainly the political system. Reforms affecting the Soviet economic and legal system began to be introduced in the late 1980s. In 1989–91, the principles of the state began to change. In these same years, the legal system of the Russian Federation also began to develop independently from that of the USSR. For example, while in the USSR the Committee of Constitutional Control (similar to the French Conseil Constitutionnel) was organised in 1991 to supervise the constitutionality of statutes, in the Russian Federation a separate law on the constitutional court was adopted in 1991, and in 1992 the Russian Constitutional Court came into being.

The last RSFSR Constitution of 1978 was amended several times in the period from 1990–93. These amendments were precursors to the adoption of new principles of a democratic state, which began with the promulgation of a new Constitution in 1993. In 1991, the principle of the separation of powers was adopted. The same year, a constitutional amendment—made on the basis of a referendum—introduced a new institution: the post of President, elected by the people. These changes started the political struggle between the presidential and parliamentary models of government, which ended in the political crisis of October 1993, when President Boris Yeltsin used military forces to dissolve the Parliament (*Verhovnyj Sovet*) and take control over the elaboration of the draft of a new Constitution for the Russian Federation.

Adopting both the principle of the separation of powers and institutions like a presidency were the beginning of borrowing foreign legal institutions in Russia.

---

it started to be discussed only recently with reference to the practice of the ECHR. Practice of this court is becoming the focus of political debates also as to 'different' legal traditions being implemented in Russia—see IB Borisov and DA Ivailovskiy, 'Sootnosheniye otdel'nyh poziciy Evropeyskogo suda po pravam cheloveka s nacional'nym izbiratel'nym zakonodatel'stvom' (Correlation of Some Positions of the European Court of Human Rights with National Election Legislation) (2009) 3 *Constitucionnoe i Municipal'noe Pravo* 25–29 (in Russian). Hereinafter, unless otherwise stated, all Russian materials have been translated by the author.

[3] Russian Soviet Federative Socialist Republic—name of the Russian Federation (RF) in 1936–91.

[4] B Rudden, 'Civil Law, Civil Society and the Russian Constitution' (1994) 110 *The Law Quarterly Review* 56, 61.

The tendency to adopt foreign principles prevailed also in the process of preparing a new Constitution in the years 1990–93. Basic principles of the Soviet state were renounced and principles of a democratic state previously rejected began to be adopted: in addition to the doctrines of the separation of powers and the rule of law (in its German version, '*Rechtsstaat*'; '*pravovoe gosudarstvo*' in Russian) they are: human rights as the primary value of the state, a liberal economy, a social state, and a federal structure. These 'legal transplants' have been called 'one of the most extensive transfers of legal ideas in the modern history of law'.[5] This reception could be evaluated as implicit foreign influence; yet, at the same time, it was not the influence of any particular state but, rather, that of a summarised and generalised model of a Western European/North American state plus inspiration from international law documents.

The form of government can be taken as an example. In Russia, it is the President who appoints ministers (the Prime Minister is appointed with the consent of the State Duma—the lower chamber of parliament). Ministers are responsible to the President: in the case of a vote of no confidence to the Government in the State Duma, the Russian Federation President decides either to dismiss the Government or to dissolve Parliament. Unlike in the US, there is a Prime Minister in Russia and the President is not designated as the chief of the executive power. The Russian President is the head of state; he determines state policy and coordinates the activity of other state bodies, as does the French President.[6] Neither the American nor French form of government was consistently transplanted in the Russian Constitution.

Recent foreign literature reveals the discussions about the degree of foreign law influence on the Russian Constitution.[7] In Russia, this question has not yet been the subject of any special research,[8] not even in materials published upon the occasion of the fifteenth anniversary of the Russian Federation Constitution.[9] An evaluation of the degree of foreign influence is a matter for separate research; thus, we shall attempt only briefly to trace foreign influences as reflected in the materials of the Constitutional Convention, which was convened in June 1993 for preparing the draft of the new Constitution and worked until November 1993. This review will be prefaced by two remarks.

---

[5] RS Sharlet, 'Legal Transplants and Political Mutations: The Reception of Constitutional Law in Russia and the Newly Independent States' (1998) 7 *Eastern European Constitutional Review* 107.

[6] This similarity was underlined by one of the foreign experts who worked with members of the Constitutional Convention, the French Professor Michel Lesage—see M Lesage, (*interview*) 'Amerikanskaya model' ne dlya Rossii' (American model is not for Russia) (2003) *Rossiyskaya gazeta* 11 December (in Russian).

[7] RS Sharlet, n 5 above; G Ajani, n 1 above; V Schwartz, 'The Influences of the West on the 1993 Russian Constitution' (2009) 32, No 1 *Hastings International and Comparative Law Review* 101–54.

[8] A Medushevskiy, 'Rossiysakya model' konstitucionnyh preobrazovaniy v sravnitel'noy perspektive' (The Russian Model of the Constitutional Transformations in Comparative Perspective) (2003) 2 (43) *Konstitucionnoe Pravo: Vostochno-Evropeyskoe Obozrenie* 148–66 (in Russian).

[9] The most detailed history of the Constitutional Convention can be found in O Rumjancev, (*Senior Secretary of the Constitutional Convention in 1993*) 'Iz istorii sozdaniya Konstitucii Rossiyskoy Federacii: o rabote konstitucionnoy komissii, 1990–1993' (From the History of Creation of the Constitution of the Russian Federation: About the Work of the Constitutional Commission, 1990–1993) (2008) *Gosudarstvo i Pravo* No 9: 5–12, No 10: 5–13, No 11: 5–13, No 12: 5–14 (in Russian); O Rumjancev, 'Iz istorii sozdaniya Konstitucii Rossiyskoy Federacii: sostyazatel'nyi konstitucionnyi process. Dva proekta konstitucii (may–avgust 1993)' (From the History of Creation of the Constitution of the Russian Federation: Adversarial Constitutional Proceedings. Two Drafts of the Constitution, May–August 1993) (2008) *Constitutional and Municipal Law* No 23: 10–18, No 24: 2–7 (in Russian).

Russian politicians and scholars would be reluctant to acknowledge that the new Russian Federation Constitution was adopted based on legal principles, institutions and specific rules originating from Germany, France, the United States and others of the oldest democracies.[10] The main obstacle to such recognition we believe is of a psychological nature: Great Russia must (be seen to) act independently, preserving its national uniqueness;[11] it could use the ideas but not the practice of foreign states. The prevailing political rhetoric in Russian holds that its historical and political courses are independent. Publically revealing foreign influence would not be in the general line of this patriotic discourse.[12]

> The difficulty was that most US advisers were innocent of the history and circumstances, not to mention the languages, of the countries in which the new constitutions were being drafted. As a consequence, much of the advice took on an abstract, heuristic, and ethnocentric tone and, hence, fell on deaf ears on the other side of the constitutional and national divide ...
>
> In contrast to the controlled receptions of the Imperial and Soviet periods of Russian legal history, the reception process in the post-Soviet states has been relatively chaotic. Drawing from national and multinational sources of Western law, as well as occasionally spontaneous transfers based on the 'accident of personal relationships'.[13]

Patriotism nevertheless did not become an insurmountable obstacle for the adoption of *international* law rules and the recognition of their legal influence in Russia; in this case there were no threats to national sovereignty and uniqueness.[14] Human rights and freedoms in the text of the Russian Constitution had their clear origins in the norms of international law.

Moreover, Article 15(4) of the 1993 Russian Federation Constitution provides for the incorporation of rules of international law directly into the Russian legal system; international treaties of the Russian Federation are deemed to be superior to Russian Federation federal laws. Article 17 provides that:

> In the RF, the rights and freedoms of man and citizen are recognized and guaranteed according to the generally recognized principles and norms of international law and in conformity with this Constitution.[15]

---

[10] The recent publications of Russian authors accented that the role of foreign experts is exaggerated—see MA Mitjukov (member of Verhovny Sovet, member of the Constitutional Commission from 1991–93) 'K istorii Konstitucii Rossiyskoy Federacii 1993' (To the history of the Constitution of the Russian Federation 1993) (2005) 4 *Pravo i Politika* 112–20 (in Russian).

[11] '... the new Russia is not a vanquished postwar Japan waiting for a Western-style constitution to be imposed upon it'—V Schwartz, n 7 above, 116.

[12] In a discussion on the Constitution Convention the chairman (Vladimir Shumejko, Deputy Prime Minister) says: 'I previously talked to Fidel Castro and he said: everybody suggested the Chinese variant of the reform, but there would never be the Chinese variant, because we did not have Chinese in Cuba. We don't need to be compared with anybody. We are working out the Constitution of the Russian Federation. Let us think about the Russian Federation': '*Konstitucionnoe Soveschanie: stenogrammy, materialy, dokumenty*' (*Constitutional Convention: verbatim transcripts, materials, documents*) vol 3 (Moscow, Yuridicheskaya Literatura, 1995) 387 (in Russian)—hereinafter referred to as '*Constitutional Convention: verbatim transcripts, materials, documents*'.

[13] RS Sharlet, n 5 above, 115.

[14] One of the members of the Constitution Convention said: 'We are writing the Constitution of a great country and it needs to correlate the highest standards of the international law'—see *Constitutional Convention: verbatim transcripts, materials, documents*, vol 4, 126 (in Russian).

[15] Translation from: GP van den Berg, 'Russia's Constitutional Court: A Decade of Legal Reforms. Part 2, The Constitution of the Russian Federation Annotated' 28 *Review of Central and East European Law* 2002–03 No 3/4.

This provision of the Russian Constitution has influenced the Constitutional Court of the Russian Federation, which has also been more ready to use international law materials (treaties and international court precedents) than those of the courts of foreign jurisdictions.[16] Legal research has also paid attention to the use of international law, rather than foreign law and precedents, by the Russian Constitutional Court.[17]

B. Constitution Convention in 1993. The Role of Foreign Experts and the Use of Foreign Law Arguments in Discussions

The Convention preparing the draft of a new Russian Constitution began its work in June 1993 and materials of this Convention are readily accessible (verbatim reports of its sessions, written opinions and expert opinions). Thus, we are in a position to attempt to evaluate the degree (at least in part) of foreign influence on the text and legal institutions of the new Russian Federation Constitution.

Expert opinions were sent to Russia from various countries (the United States, Germany, France, Italy, Spain, Austria, Japan, Norway, Finland, Luxembourg, and others) as well as from international organisations. Some experts (the late Professors Michel Lesage—University Paris-I Pantheon Sorbonne—, Albert P Blaustein—Rutgers (the State University of New Jersey) School of Law—, and Professor Stephen Holmes—University of Chicago (1985–97) now of NYU) worked regularly with the Constitutional Convention. A special consolidated report of the Venice Commission of the Council of Europe[18] was prepared by the chairman of this Commission—the late Professor Antonio Mario La Pergola (Advocate-General and judge of the Court of Justice of the European Communities (1994–2006) and also justice of the Italian Constitutional Court), while some experts' opinions were sent individually.

Not much of this expert advice, however, was reflected in the final draft text. The Constitution text did not include provisions granting to the Constitutional Court the power to examine the conformity of the law of the Russian Federation with international law, as had been suggested by foreign experts.[19] Rules permitting

---

[16] See also A Trochev, 'Russia's Constitutional Spirit: Judge-Made Principles in Theory and Practice' in BS Gordon and R Sharlet (eds), *Russia and its Constitution: Promise and Political Reality (Law in Eastern Europe)* (Leiden, Martinus Nijhoff Publishers, 2008) 56–60.

[17] See, eg, OI Tiunov, (Justice of the Russian Constitutional Court, retired) 'Resheniya Konstitucionnogo Suda Rossiyskoy Federacii i Mezhdunarodnoe Pravo' (Decisions of the Russian Constitutional Court and International Law) (2001) 10 *Rossiyskaya Justicia* 14–16 (in Russian); G Danilenko, 'Primenenie mezhdunarodnogo prava vo vnutrenney pravovoy systeme Rossii: praktika Konstitucionnogo Suda' (Applying International Law in the Internal Legal System of Russia: The Practice of the Russian Constitutional Court) (1995) 11 *Gosudarstvo i Pravo* 115–25 (in Russian).

[18] The Report of the Venice Commission was published in O Rumyancev (ed), *Iz istorii sozdaniya Konstitucii Rossiyskoy Federacii (From the History of Creation of the Constitution of the Russian Federation)* (Moscow, Wolters Kluwer, 2008) vol 3, book 3, 974–84 (in Russian), hereinafter referred to as *From the History of Creation of the Constitution of the Russian Federation*. See also www.venice.coe.int.

[19] Suggestion in the Report of the Venice Commission, ibid.

the holding of dual citizenship, which were opposed by experts,[20] were retained. The form of government, mentioned above, contrary to experts' opinions,[21] was preserved, etc.

Nevertheless, some institutions were adopted. In a letter dated 3 April 1992, Professor La Pergola noted that expert commentaries concerned not so much the draft text rather evaluated the legal form of the constitutional institutions transplanted from western countries. La Pergola used the example of the ombudsman, which had never existed in Russia and was later incorporated into the final text of the Constitution. Experts annotated examples of constitutional review systems to make choices from among the alternatives available,[22] sent examples of legislative regulations of some institutions (eg the state of emergency legislation in Spain), giving the Russian draftspersons the possibility of elaborating on the specific rules and regulations based on foreign experience.

Occasionally, members of the Constitutional Convention voted against proposals of foreign experts; but, later, the same provisions appeared in the final text. The proposals of Professor Lessage are one example. The Convention voted to reject all of his suggestions, including the idea of the separation of local self-government from the state.[23] Yet, these principles were later included in the Constitution.

Several seminars were held in which foreign experts participated in the framework of the Constitution Convention. For example, a Russian-French seminar 'The Draft of the New Russian Constitution and Democratic Processes in Russia' took place in Moscow in March, 1992. Discussions of the seminar resulted in corrections to the draft: on the one hand, the individual responsibility of members of the Government which had been proposed was withdrawn from the text while, on the other hand, the power of the President to dissolve the Parliament appeared.[24]

Arguments about foreign law and legal doctrine were used in the discussions of the Constitutional Convention in different ways. Methods of forming the upper chamber of the Parliament (equal representation of regions v proportional representation of the regional population) as well as the national character of subjects of the federation (comparing to universal states or *Länder*) were discussed and compared to the respective principles of Germany, the United States and other federations. In both cases, foreign experience was rejected in favour of Russian specificities.[25]

Arguments for including the President in the system of executive power were rejected on the ground that Russia cannot 'blindly' copy foreign models and that consequent implementation of the separation of powers is something not acceptable for Russia. It was stated that the separation of powers would lead these powers to 'mutual devouring' (*vzaimnoe pozhiraniye*), while the President was the only state authority which reconciled them. The other argument was that there is no system of

---

[20] See the dissenting opinion of Professor Helgesen (University of Oslo) to the Report of the Venice Commission, n 18 above.
[21] n 18 above.
[22] Report of Professor Steinberger, n 18 above.
[23] *Constitutional Convention: verbatim transcripts, materials, documents*, vol 5, 189.
[24] See *From the History of Creation of the Constitution of the Russian Federation*, vol 3, book 3, 1001 ff (in Russian).
[25] *Constitutional Convention: verbatim transcripts, materials, documents*, vol 2, 69, 376 and others.

political parties in Russia which could provide a political balance to the President, the Government and parliamentary powers.[26]

Thus, we can see that Russian political specificities prevail and form obstacles for the consistent reception of foreign models in the Constitution.

A similar approach can be found in the regulations governing Russian citizenship. A proposal to include in the Constitution the principle *jus soli* for acquiring citizenship encountered active opposition from among those who insisted that the Russian legal tradition was closer to the 'European' *jus sanguinis* than the 'American' *jus soli*.[27] The final text became neutral on this question, delegating the choice to the legislator. At the same time, the Convention totally ignored opinions of foreign experts[28] and arguments of foreign experience[29] in this question, including the possibility of dual citizenship in the final text. These rules were later corrected in the legislation, establishing limits of rights for those Russian citizens who had other citizenship (in addition to Russian citizenship). These persons are banned from holding state positions and cannot be candidates for any elected bodies, etc.[30]

Only a few foreign state institutions (of minor importance) were adopted in virtually the same form as they existed in the state of their origin. Some examples are: the procedure for amending the Constitution—approval by a vote of two-thirds of the subjects of the federation (after the US Constitution[31]) and the institution of a parliamentary ombudsman (making reference to Sweden and Denmark).[32]

Concerning the Bill of Rights (the second chapter of the Constitution—'Rights and Liberties of Man and the Citizen'), foreign influence is less evident than that of international law. Nevertheless, we can find the traces of foreign law in several provisions.

The provision establishing the equal status of man and woman was supported with reference to one of the amendments to the US Constitution.[33] Referring to foreign practice, members of the Constitution Convention included a right to strike in the text;[34] the necessity of a judicial search warrant was added by reference to the 'old American Constitution' and Article 35 of the Japanese Constitution;[35] and the possible limitation of the freedom of free enterprise was established by referring to the Swiss legal limits for land use.[36]

Some foreign experts have claimed that the wording of the Bill of Rights followed their expert opinion.[37] For example, a number of rights in the Constitution

---

[26] *Constitutional Convention: verbatim transcripts, materials, documents*, vol 3, 256–57.
[27] *Constitutional Convention: verbatim transcripts, materials, documents*, vol 4, 32–33.
[28] Expert opinion of Yan Helgesen, University of Oslo in *From the History of Creation of the Constitution of the Russian Federation* (Moscow, Wolters Kluwer, 2008), vol 3, book 3, 986.
[29] *Constitutional Convention: verbatim transcripts, materials, documents*, vol 4, 48.
[30] Federal law of 25 July 2006, amending the Federal law 'On Basic Guarantees of Electoral Rights and Right of Participation in Referendum of Citizens of the Russian Federation' No 67–FZ of 12 June 2002.
[31] See the proposal in *Constitutional Convention: verbatim transcripts, materials, documents*, vol 5, 30.
[32] *Constitutional Convention: verbatim transcripts, materials, documents*, vol 5, 298.
[33] *Constitutional Convention: verbatim transcripts, materials, documents*, vol 3, 286.
[34] *Constitutional Convention: verbatim transcripts, materials, documents*, vol 3, 30.
[35] *Constitutional Convention: verbatim transcripts, materials, documents*, vol 2, 337.
[36] *Constitutional Convention: verbatim transcripts, materials, documents*, vol 2, 363.
[37] Andrzej Rapaczynski's materials—see Schwartz, n 7 above, 146–51.

were granted not to citizens, but to 'every person'; capital punishment remained in the Constitution 'until its abolition',[38] and freedom of labour (but not the right to employment) was guaranteed.

'Russian specificities' were also discussed as regards social rights. The guarantees of free medical care and state assistance to house indigents were incorporated in the Constitution. However, foreign experts cautioned against including too many unenforceable rights in the Constitution text,[39] and there were heated discussions among members of the Constitutional Convention about the disadvantages of state social support. They cited social payments and free housing as leading to social parasitism in Germany[40] and the United States.[41] These provisions remained in the Constitution text in rather broad wording,[42] reflecting[43] the post-Soviet specifics and the political situation at the time of adopting the Constitution.

Other provisions of the constitutional Bill of Rights were formulated based on international law; thus, rights (mostly personal and political rights, freedoms and guarantees) were constructed very closely in wording and in breadth to the International Bill of Rights[44] and to the European Convention on Human Rights.[45] These circumstances allowed the Constitutional Court to remark, in one of its decisions from 2010,[46] that human rights are understood to be the same in the Russian Constitution and in Acts of international law. We can view this opinion as the first step of the Court to an explicit openness to *from-abroad* materials in its practice, though it is still only international, but not foreign, constitutional sources.

---

[38] This wording led the Constitutional Court to interpret the intent of the Constitutional authors as looking at the death penalty as a temporary measure; see Ruling of the Constitutional Court of 19 November 2009 No 1344-O-R. Rulings (*opredeleniya*) of the Russian Constituional Court are types of decisions made on questions arising in judicial procedure (accepting or refusing a case for consideration, interpreting the final decision, etc). Final decisions solving a case are named Judgments (*postanovleniya*).

[39] Schwartz, n 7 above, 144–45.

[40] *Constitutional Convention: verbatim transcripts, materials, documents*, vol 4, 318.

[41] *Constitutional Convention: verbatim transcripts, materials, documents*, vol 3, 386–87.

[42] The Russian Constitution 1993 text—*art 39*: 'Everyone is guaranteed social security on the basis of age, in the case of sickness, disability, or loss of the breadwinner, for the upbringing of children, and in other cases established by a law'; *art 40 (1)*: 'Everyone has the right to housing. No one may arbitrarily be deprived of a dwelling', *art 40(3)*: 'A dwelling is provided free of charge or at affordable rate from state, municipal, and other housing funds in accordance with norms established by a law to low-income and other citizens, mentioned in a law who are in need of housing'; *art 41*: 'Everyone has the right to health protection and medical aid. Medical aid in state and municipal health-care institutions is provided to citizens free of charge, at the expense of funds of the relevant budget, insurance contributions, and other revenues'.

[43] Together with certain economic provisions—eg 'equal protection of all forms of ownership': private, state, municipal and others (art 8).

[44] The international covenants on civil and political rights and on social, cultural and economic rights of 1966 came into force for the USSR in 1976 and were inherited as binding by the RF. They were republished in *Bulleten' Verhovnogo Suda Rossiyskoy Federacii* No 12, 1994.

[45] The RF ratified the main part of the Convention (text of the Convention and Protocol Nos 1, 4, 7, 9, 10 and 11) with Federal law of 30 March, 1998 No 54-FZ.

[46] Judgment of the Russian Constitutional Court 26 February 2010 No 4-P.

II. THE JUDICIAL SYSTEM IN RUSSIA AND TECHNIQUES OF JUDICIAL REASONING

A. The Russian Legal System and the Role of the Courts

Every law student in a Russian university is taught that Russia belongs to the civil law system and that it is especially close to Germany. Statutes are supposed to be the main source of law; judicial precedent is not binding. The Constitution (Article 120) establishes that judges are independent and obey the law only.

These approaches go back to the Soviet legal system, which was completely incompatible with judicial precedent because of the principles of 'democratic centralism' and 'legality' mentioned above.

At the same time, courts needed help with the interpretation of statutes; therefore, they sought to study previous practice of resolving cases of the same kind in other courts. The Supreme Court attempted to ensure conformity of the practice of different courts. Thus, the Supreme Court would prepare Resolutions (*Postanovleniya*) of the Supreme Court Plenum. These Resolutions summarised court practice and interpreted statutory provisions according to opinions of the Supreme Court.

The legal nature of Supreme Court Plenum Resolutions was a matter discussed from time to time in Soviet legal literature. A number of scholars argued that this was a form of judicial law-making. In making law, the Supreme Court was acting ultra vires and the place of these Resolutions in the system of the sources of law was too indefinite.[47] Others insisted that they were nothing more than a form of statutory interpretation and that they should be considered as secondary legal materials and not be treated as a source of law.[48]

At the same time, judges were forced to take these Resolutions into consideration, since their decision could be reviewed by the next instance if they were to follow their own interpretation of the law ignoring the opinion of the Supreme Court.

Apart from Resolutions of the Plenum, the Supreme Court also published Reviews of judicial practice (*obzor sudebnoy praktiki*), consisting mainly of decisions of the Supreme Court which revised decisions of lower courts. In this form, the practice of the Supreme Court influenced the practice of statutory interpretation; it was studied by law students and thus actually played a significant role in the Russian legal system.

In the post-Soviet era, the system of judicial interpretation of statutes has been preserved, although new principles of the state and the legal system have

---

[47] A Mad'yarova, *Raz'yasneniya Verhovnogo Suda Rossiyskoy Federacii v mehanizme ugolovno-pravovogo regulirovaniya* (Clarification of the Supreme Court of the Russian Federation in the Mechanism of Criminal Law Regulation) (St Petersburg, Juridicheskiy centr press, 2002) (in Russian).

[48] See A Cherdancev, *Voprosy tolkovaniya sovetskogo prava* (Questions of Interpretation of Soviet Law) (Sverdlovsk, 1972) 38–39 (in Russian); S Bratus', 'Pravovaya priroda sudebnoy praktiki v SSSR' (Legal Nature of the Courts Practice in the USSR) (1975) 6 *Sovetskoe Gosudarsto i Pravo* 13–21 (in Russian); O Tyomushkin, 'Tolkovanie zakona Plenumom Verhovnogo Suda SSSR' (The Interpretation of a Law by the Plenum of the Supreme Court of the USSR) (1976) 3 *Sovetskoe Gosudarsto i Pravo* 4–40 (in Russian); A Pigolkin, 'Tolkovanie norm prava i pravotvorchestvo, problemy sootnosheniya' (The Interpretation of Norms of Law and Law-making, Problems of Correlation) in A Pigolkin (ed), *The Law, Creation and Interpretation* (Moscow, Spark, 1998) 70 (in Russian).

stimulated new discussions about the role and significance of judicial practice.[49] As conservative jurists insist, the new principle of the separation of powers does not allow judicial law-making, because this is solely within the competence of the legislator. Court decisions can be studied as examples of how law is applied but not considered as a source of law.[50] Others, including judges of the Russian Supreme Court, argue that these guides and interpretations by the Supreme Court are practically necessary for lower courts and for legal practice in general.[51] One can find in this line of argument that practical necessity prevails over legal principles.

Under the 1993 Constitution and the 1996 Federal Constitutional Law 'On the Judicial System', the Russian judicial system consists of three branches (subsystems): (1) courts of common jurisdiction, resolving most civil, administrative and all criminal cases, (2) state arbitration courts, resolving economic disputes among entrepreneurs and among entrepreneurs and state agencies, and (3) constitutional courts: the Constitutional Court of the Russian Federation and constitutional (charter—*ustavnye*[52]) courts of the subjects of the Russian Federation.

The legislative framework of using court practice began to change in the late 1990s and the role of court decisions in the legal system has begun to grow. This process concerns mainly state arbitration courts. These courts have become more technically and politically advanced as compared to the more conservative courts of common jurisdiction (*sudy obschey yurisdikcii*). In 2002, the binding force of Resolutions of the Plenum of the Highest Arbitration Court was established by a federal law.[53] A few years later the Highest Arbitration Court required lower courts 'to take into consideration' the practice of the Highest Arbitration Court in resolving each particular case.[54] This Resolution led to a wide discussion in the legal literature.[55] In 2010, the Chief Justice of the Highest Arbitration Court, Anton Ivanov, confirmed the intention of the Court to transplant the idea of judicial precedent into the system of state arbitration courts.[56]

---

[49] *Sudebnaya praktika kak istochnik prava* (Court Practice as a Source of Law) (Moscow, Institute of State and Law of the Russian Academy of Science, 1997) (in Russian); *Sudebnaya praktika kak istochnik prava* (Court Practice as a Source of Law*)*: collected articles by B Topornin, E Servern, K Gunter and ors (Moscow, Jurist, 2000) (in Russian).

[50] VS Nersesyanc, 'Sud ne zakonodatel'stvuet i ne upravlyaet, a primenyaet pravo' (The Court does not make the Law and does not Administer, but Enforces the Law) in *Court Practice as a Source of Law* (1997) 21–38 (in Russian).

[51] V Zhuykov, 'K voprosu o sudebnoy praktike kak istochnike prava' (To the question on the Courts' Practice as a Source of Law) in *Court Practice as a Source of Law* (2000) 78–90 (in Russian).

[52] Republics, one of the five subjects of the RF, have Constitutions; others (kray, oblast', city of federal significance, autonomous okrug and autonomous oblast') have charters as the main Act of their regional legal systems.

[53] Art 170(4) of the Arbitration Procedure Code of 24 July 2002.

[54] Resolution of Highest Arbitration Court, 14 February 2008, No 14.

[55] E Trikoz, 'Novoe postanovlenie VAS RF N14: vvedenie precedenta ili raspredelenie sudebnoy nagruzki?' (New Resolution of the Highest Arbitration Court No 14: Implementation of Precedent or Distribution of Courts' Loading?) (2008) 4 *Arbitrazhnoe Pravosudie v Rossii* (in Russian).

[56] See the text of the speech at www.arbitr.ru/press-centr/news/speeches/27369.html (in Russian).

B. The Constitutional Court: Competence, Structure, Procedure

The Constitutional Court of the Russian Federation was organised in 1991 as a body of constitutional control to examine the constitutionality of federal laws and certain other normative Acts. In 1993, the Court played a major role in the political conflict between the President and the Parliament, supporting the latter. Its activity was suspended by a presidential edict. The place of the Constitutional Court in the court system was vehemently discussed in the framework of drafting the new Constitution. Two alternatives were discussed: either to reorganise it as a constitutional chamber of the Supreme Court or to preserve its position as an independent body and the only one controlling constitutionality.

The second option was chosen and included in the Constitution, but the status of the Constitutional Court was reformed: it lost some powers, for example, the power to evaluate the constitutionality of the application of legislation which had been deemed as being too wide and too vague.[57] The Court was no longer allowed to hear a case on its own initiative and so now has less authority to interfere in political disputes. The new status of the Constitutional Court is set forth in the Constitution and in the 1994 Federal Constitutional Law 'On the Constitutional Court of the Russian Federation'.

The Constitutional Court today has jurisdiction to hear five kinds of cases.

(1) The first category is for cases dealing with the constitutionality of federal Acts and Acts of subjects of the Federation, but only those of a normative character; these cases can be initiated by: (a) authorised state bodies irrespective of a specific case ('abstract control' of constitutionality); (b) a judge applying the law while hearing a case; or (c) a person, in whose case the law has been applied and who alleges violations of her/his constitutional rights ('concrete' control). This type of case, especially concrete control, comprises the majority of cases heard by the Constitutional Court since 1994 (11,350 out of 11,975).[58]

In practice, the Russian Constitutional Court has extended its jurisdiction by rendering decisions on revealing the constitutional sense of the law. While refraining from declaring that a law violates the Constitution, the Constitutional Court restricts the application of such law. In some cases the Constitutional Court under the guise of revealing the constitutional sense added brand new rules to the law.[59]

Other kinds of cases are: (2) official interpretations of the Constitution (12 final decisions since 1995), (3) those resolving jurisdictional disputes among state bodies (two final decisions since 1995), (4) findings on the procedural compliance

---

[57] See NV Vitruk, (Justice of the Russian Constitutional Court, retired) *Konstitucionnaya yusticiya v Rossii, 1991–2001: ocherki teorii i praktiki* (*Constituional Justice in Russia, 1991–2001*: Essays of Theory and Practice) (Moscow, Gorodetz-izdat, 2001) (in Russian).

[58] Legal databases (eg www.consultant.ru, accessible in Russian only) and the website of the Russian Constitutional Court (www.ksrf.ru) today include approx 12,000 decisions of the Constitutional Court made since it resumed its work in 1995.

[59] In its Decision of 20 February 2006, the Russian Constitutional Court revealed the constitutional sense of art 336 of the Civil Procedure Code. This article allowed only parties of a court case to appeal against the court decision. The Constitutional Court decided that, according to the constitutional sense of this article, persons whose rights and obligations were touched by the court decision could also appeal against the part of a decision which concerned them.

of an impeachment of the President (no decisions) and (5) those controlling the constitutionality of questions proposed for a federal referendum (no decisions).

Until February 2011, the Constitutional Court heard cases in three different panels: in plenary sessions in the presence of all 19 judges and in chambers of 10 or of nine judges. Only plenary sessions could accept a complaint for further proceedings and hear the most important cases (official interpretation of the Constitution, cases of constitutionality of the Constitutions and charters of the subjects of the Russian Federation, etc), but final decisions of the chambers in the frameworks of their jurisdiction were deemed to be decisions of the Constitutional Court and cannot be revised by a plenary session. Since February 2011 the Constitutional Court hears cases only in plenary sessions, as the chambers structure was abolished by a federal law in November 2010.[60]

The procedure is organised rather like the procedure of ordinary courts although the principles of adversarial proceedings and of oral hearings are limited in the Constitutional Court. The case file is prepared for the hearing by the judge who reports the case. This judge has broad powers to demand submission of evidence: documents, expert opinions, etc. The same judge prepares a draft decision. The court hearing includes oral discussion of the parties in the case (the body which has promulgated the challenged Act and the claimant), although the hearing is much less important than in an ordinary court procedure: not all evidence is presented in the courtroom and, as established in the Law 'On the Constitutional Court of the RF' (Article 74), the Court may decide a case without being limited to the arguments presented by the parties. The active role of the Court is explained in the literature by reference to the protection of the public interest which cannot depend on the activity and skillfulness of the persons who put a case in front of the court. Thus, the Court is empowered to conduct its own investigation, to discover arguments pro and contra about the constitutionality of the challenged Act and to resolve the case on its own opinions and arguments.

C. Decisions of the Constitutional Court: Types and Role in the Legal System, Structure (Dissenting Opinions), Legal Positions and Significance of the Reasoning of the Decision

As we have noted above, the Constitutional Court first appeared in Russia only in 1991, and during the first decade of its activity Russian scholars discussed the nature of its decisions and their place in the legal system. The range of positions was quite wide.

One group of scholars[61] argued that the Constitutional Court was no more than a court; so, it was a body that applied the law but not one which made law and its decisions were no more than legal acts, proclaiming the correlation between a norm of the Constitution and the law. According to this opinion (which is close to the

---

[60] Federal constitutional law of 3 November 2010 No 7-FKZ.
[61] Two main supporters of this position are Russian legal philosopher Vladik Nersesyanc (Institute of State and Law in the Russian Academy of Science) and constitutionalist Oleg Kutafin (Moscow State Law Academy): see, eg, V Nersesyanc, n 51 above.

position of 'originalism' in US constitutional law), the Constitutional Court must follow the literal wording of the Constitution, interpreting the will of its authors, and has no discretion to interpret the sense of constitutional norms.

The Constitutional Court itself and its judges in their scholarly articles have sought to disclaim this approach, underscoring rather broader discretion and therefore the significance of Constitutional Court decisions. The Constitutional Court held in a 1998 decision that its acts had the same sphere of action in time, space and persons as normative Acts have.[62] The Chief Justice of the Constitutional Court, Valery Zor'kin, has referred to decisions of the Court as 'precedents',[63] basing his position on the idea of the binding force of the 'legal position of the Court' (*pravovye posicii suda*).

Provisions of the Law 'On the Constitutional Court of the Russian Federation' provide for the nullification not only of the Act which has been declared non-constitutional by the Constitutional Court, but also of those Acts which have the same or similar provisions.

This rule gives more significance to arguments and conclusions made by the Court. The Constitutional Court saw here the ground for a new phenomenon of the Russian legal system: the so-called 'legal position' of the Constitutional Court.[64] To summarise the meaning of this phenomenon by scholars and judges of the Constitutional Court, one could say that a legal position is the interpretation of the Constitutional provisions on any particular question as resolved by the Court.[65] The binding force of the legal position has become universal, because all bodies which apply and enforce the law body as well as the legislator are bound by legal positions in implementing statutes in force and in elaborating new statutes. Decisions of the Constitutional Court could thus be treated not as 'classic' judicial precedent, but, rather, as precedent for interpreting Constitutional rules, determining their understanding in legal practice later on.

The nature and properties of the legal position are one of the key points in the use of foreign law and foreign precedent by the Russian Constitutional Court. Since the Court claims that its interpretation of the Constitution is binding upon all, it pays great attention to the motives and arguments on which its decisions are based. Almost every idea which is included in the rationale of a decision is supposed to be of potential significance for future legal practice.

While the constitutional provisions which are interpreted by the Constitutional Court appear indefinite (as constitutional principles), the Constitutional Court has wide discretion in their interpretation. Viewed from afar, these powers seem to encompass an absolutely unlimited degree of discretion and the Court should be

---

[62] Decision of the Constitutional Court of the RF, 16 June 1998, about interpretation of arts 125, 126 and 127 of the Constitution.

[63] VD Zor'kin, 'Precedentnyi kharakter resheniy Konstitucionnogo Suda Rossiyskoy Federacii' (The Precedential Character of Decisions of the Russian Constitutional Court) (2004) 2 *Journal Zhurnal Rossiyskogo Prava* 3–9 (in Russian).

[64] LV Lazarev, *Pravovye pozicii Konstitucionnogo Suda Rossii* (Legal Positions of the Constitutional Court of Russia) (Moscow, Gorodets, 2003) 38–99 (in Russian).

[65] Ibid.

described not only as 'a negative legislator',[66] but a law-making body. A judge of the Constitutional Court, Nikolay Bondar', finds in the decisions of the Constitutional Court not only new legal rules, but also a way to develop legal doctrine.[67]

This wide discretion is reflected in a legal instrument which has been used by the Constitutional Court since 2002 for resolving constitutional cases:[68] the resolution of disputes being a process of balancing constitutional values (*balansa konstitucionnyh cennostey*). This in fact is the Russian variant of the 'proportionality principle', though the Russian Constitutional Court and Russian legal doctrine do not use the term 'proportionality'. The core of this approach is to examine the manner in which the main constitutional values—individual rights and public interests—are coordinated. The Court makes a determination of whether the legislator has given priority to either of the two competing values and defines what the balance between them needs to be. Of course, this approach lies in the field of substantial judicial activism. The Constitutional Court sometimes examines the political decisions of the legislator accessing the balance of constitutional values in a legislator's decision. This practice appears to be interference with the Parliament's powers. At the same time, the balance of constitutional values estimation approach is fruitful for research analysing the Constitutional Court's decisions. In considering the convergence and divergence of decisions of the Russian and foreign constitutional courts, one can see the significance and essence of certain constitutional principles as well as the way they are balanced against each other in Russia compared to other jurisdictions.

The judicial activism of the Russian Constitutional Court concerns not only the essence of constitutional interpretation, but also the range of its powers and the character of its decisions, which is a more practical problem than the theoretical evaluation of Constitutional Court decisions as a source of law.

Deciding cases under its competence, as defined above, according to the Law 'On the Constitutional Court of the Russian Federation', the Court uses three forms of decisions. Final decisions in a case heard by the Constitutional Court are either Conclusions (*Zaklyucheniya*—only in cases of control of the procedural compliance of impeaching the President, which has never occurred) or Judgments (*Postanovleniya*—in all other types of cases). Other decisions, rendered for procedural purposes (as mentioned above),[69] are called Rulings (*Opredeleniya*).

Rulings were originally used for procedural purposes exclusively. Legal positions interpreting the Constitution were supposed to appear only in Judgments. The Russian Constitutional Court extended the role and significance of its Rulings, and in doing so also expanded its own jurisdiction. In 2000, the Constitutional Court began to issue so-called 'Rulings with positive content' (*opredeleniya s pozitivnym soderzhaniem*).

---

[66] EV Kolesnikov, 'Resheniya konstitucionnyh sudov kak istochnik rossiyskogo konstitucionnogo prava' (Decisions of the Constitutional Courts as a Source of Russian Constitutional Law) (2001) 2 *Pravovedenie* 32–53 (in Russian).

[67] NS Bondar', 'Normativno-doktrinal'naya priroda resheniy Konstitucionnogo Rossiskoi Federacii kak istochnik prava' (Normative-doctrinal nature of decisions of the Russian Constitutional Court as a Source of Law) (2007) 4 *Zhurnal Rossiyskogo Prava* 75–85 (in Russian).

[68] One of the first decisions, based on this kind of constitutional analysis, was the Judgment of the Constitutional Court 2 April 2002 No 7-P.

[69] See n 38 above.

These later Rulings were taken in those cases where a final decision in the form of a judgment was not needed. From its formal description as provided by judges and scholars,[70] Rulings with positive content could be made when the question being deliberated was not new for the Court. When the Constitutional Court had formulated its legal position in one of its previous cases, it repeated this position in a Ruling with positive content. At the same time, if the Constitutional Court saw that the problem was not of great significance and that it was only a matter of the claimant's case being decided incorrectly, it might not proceed with a formal hearing. In such a case, the Constitutional Court considered the case in a plenary session, but without the parties and their representatives. These proceedings were in written form and not oral. The Court could issue a finding to the claimant that her/his case had been decided incorrectly although the law itself did not violate the Constitution. In fact, the Constitutional Court was confirming that although the law was applied unconstitutionally in the claimant's case that did not disclaim the constitutionality of the law itself. Thus, the Constitutional Court tried to revise decisions of other courts with these Rulings although formally it does not have such powers. Courts of common jurisdiction and state arbitration courts argue that the Constitutional Court rendered such Rulings ultra vires as it had no jurisdiction to revise particular cases. Just a few cases were revised according to the opinion of the Constitutional Court by the Supreme Court or the Highest Arbitration courts. The Constitutional Court insists that all its decisions have to be enforced and that all cases have to be revised.[71]

Amendments to the Law on the Constitutional Court, adopted in November 2010, revised the practice of Rulings with positive content. These amendments granted to the Court the power to make Judgments in a written order, not hearing cases in oral proceedings. As a result, some Judgments establishing a new legal position are still made following a complete oral procedure, but some Judgments, reproducing existing legal positions, are made following a written procedure.

All decisions of the Constitutional Court are rendered as a consolidated document, prepared by the judge-reporter of the case and supported by the majority of the judges having voted for the final text. The decision has four parts: (i) *introduction (vvodnaya chast')* (who has brought the complaint to the court, which judges have decided the case, who are the representatives of the parties, witnesses, experts, etc, what was the matter and the ground for the case), (ii) *descriptive (opisatel'naya chast')* (how the challenged law was applied to the claimant, what is the nature of the problem raised before the Constitutional Court), (iii) *motivational (motivirovochnaya chast')* (the argument of the Court, including the interpretation of the

---

[70] See A Trochev, *Judging Russia: The Role of the Constitutional Court in Russian Politics 1990–2006* (Cambridge University Press, 2008) 124.

[71] A case heard by the Constitutional Court in November 2008 can be used as an example. The Deputy Chairman of the Russian Supreme Court initiated the revision of a civil case on his own initiative without any request from the parties to the case. One party appealed to the Constitutional Court, insisting that this 'supervision' of civil cases contradicts constitutional principles of judicial procedure. The Constitutional Court satisfied the complaint, and the person went back to the Supreme Court. But the Supreme Court argued that the unconstitutionality of the rule would act *ex nunc*, and the case of the claimant would not be revised and furthermore that the revision was right in core (in the essence of the case), regardless of an unconstitutional procedure rule being applied.

Constitution of the matter of the case; this is called the legal position (*pravovye pozicii*) of the Court) and (iv) the *conclusion (rezolyutivnaya chast')*. Constitutional Court practice differs from that of other Russian courts in the way in which it recounts the parties' position. In the descriptive part of the decision the Russian Constitutional Court retells in its own words the core of the claim, but does not quote the positions of the parties. Thus, if a claimant has referred to foreign court practice, this will not be reflected in the text of the decision.

Although the name of the judge-reporter is indicated in the introductory part, the decision is considered to be the result of all judges' intellectual activity. The final decision is made *in camera*; therefore, no one but the judges themselves is in a position to evaluate the contribution of each judge to the final text. The law establishes only that the decision is made by a vote of all the judges (no judge who has heard the case can abstain from voting; the chairman votes last) and that a judge who does not agree with the decision or with the argument can submit a separate opinion. This opinion is not proclaimed in the courtroom but, rather, published together with the decision. The law does not distinguish dissenting from concurring opinions, and they are not named differently; only the text of the opinion reveals what the special view of the judge is.

Separate opinions are used in all Russian courts although the meaning is not the same. In courts of common jurisdiction or in state arbitration courts, a separate opinion shows to the appellate court that the decision was not unanimous in the trial court. The appellate court would take this opinion into its consideration, and the arguments contained in this opinion can become a ground for revision of the trial court's decision. In the Constitutional Court, the decisions of which are not subject to appeal, a separate opinion is the only way for the judge to show his or her position. This opinion can have political but not legal effect.

D. Using Foreign Law in General. The Framework of Using Judicial Precedents. Refraining from the Use of Non-binding Sources of Law in the Reasoning of Decisions

The use of foreign law or legal precedent is not a usual phenomenon for courts in the Russian Federation in general or for the Russian Constitutional Court in particular. A number of reasons for this can be posited.

Most Russian judges look at the Russian legal system as a sealed vessel. The legal principles and the legal system are regarded as being self-sufficient. Moreover, legal formalism prompts judges to think (mostly if not exclusively) about the wording of norms, not about substantive legal institutions, principles and concepts. Many judges think that they cannot cite foreign precedents in their decisions because they are not binding in the Russian legal system. The motivation of any court decision is made exclusively with Russian sources of law: statutes and the practice of their implementation in the upper court(s). Appellate courts consider that a judge making a decision has to reflect in its text every argument that s/he takes into consideration. If the argument is based on a source which is not binding, this becomes (one more) ground for doubting the correctness of the decision.

Although Russian legal doctrine (mainly in the area of private law) often looks abroad to analyse and to adopt (transform) foreign experience,[72] legal practice is a long way away from using precedent from foreign jurisdictions in support of judicial decisions. This can be viewed as both legal isolation and legal patriotism. While scholars find the roots of Russian law institutions and compare them to similar institutions abroad, courts research at most principles and the nature of legal institutions in the Russian legal system. Courts usually do not look to the foreign law roots of any Russian legislation.

The Russian Constitutional Court is not overly formalistic, but it pays a great deal of attention to the arguments of a decision, so there is no way to support a decision with non-binding sources of law. As it sets forth the court's legal position, which has binding force, the legal position must be based only on binding norms. Any allusion to foreign law or foreign judicial decisions would be treated as an intrusion into the Russian legal system, and since the Constitution does not allow this, the decision of the Constitutional Court would be weakened in the eyes of most Russian lawyers.

As a result, all references to foreign law (both to normative Acts and precedent), found in the practice of the Constitutional Court have been made only in separate opinions. Since these are not treated as binding, the judges writing them feel freer to refer to materials outside the normal scope of judicial inquiry than they would if they were not authoring a separate opinion.

In only six cases heard by the Constitutional Court during the course of its post-1991 history (over 11,000) were there references to foreign law; all of these were made in separate opinions. Citations of foreign laws were given to illustrate the position of a judge who authored the separate opinion. In all these opinions an overview of foreign case law was presented. In one case foreign laws were supposed to illustrate the wide discretion of the legislator on that particular question (acceptability of contingency fees for advocates).[73] In another opinion, foreign practice was summarised to provide examples of prohibitions against worsening sentences during appeal from the legislation of France, Germany and Spain.[74]

In a case concerning the interpretation of the Russian tax statute the Russian legal tradition of using legal terms in the same sense in all branches of the law (eg, the understanding of 'common ownership' should be the same in family law and in tax law) was contrasted with that of the British Commonwealth.[75] In interpreting the tax-law phrase 'in the ownership of the taxpayer', the courts of general jurisdiction had failed to pay attention to the rules of family legislation which contained rules and regulations governing common property. Thus, foreign practice here was presented *a contrario*, considering that Russian decisions should be different to those made abroad.

---

[72] See G Ajani, n 8 above.
[73] Separate opinion of Justice Nikolay Bondar' to Judgment 23 January 2001 No 1-P. Foreign practice was presented relating to Belgium and Lithuania (ban on contingency fees); the UK, the USA, Canada, and Australia (common permission of contingency fees) and Germany, Austria, Spain, Portugal, Switzerland (conditional permission of contingency fees).
[74] Separate opinion of Justice Sergey Kazancev to Judgment 16 May 2007 No 6-P.
[75] Separate opinion of Justice Gadis Gadgiev to Ruling 2 November 2006 No 444-O.

Two dissenting opinions, concerning questions of election law, referred to foreign law (in one case, to that of the USA; in another, to that of the UK), although the reference to UK law was made through a decision of the European Court of Human Rights. The Justice, Anatoliy Kononov, argued that the ban on non-candidates carrying out election propaganda was unconstitutional because such a rule was not found in foreign democracies.[76] US law (referring to decisions of US courts) was also used in the same matter in the dissenting opinion of Justice Gadis Gadgiev.[77]

The last reference made to foreign law during the period of our examination from 1991 to 2011 was the reference to a 1999 case on the resignation of three judges of the Supreme Court of Panama. The Russian Constitutional Court needed to evaluate the constitutionality of a law establishing an age limit for sitting judges before it had entered into force. The Court confirmed the constitutionality of the law. In a dissenting opinion, Justice Vladimir Yaroslavcev referred to the Panamanian case, by referring to a 1999 report of the International Commission of Jurists (although he did not cite the decision of the Panamanian Supreme Court itself).[78]

The Justices of the Russian Constitutional Court in their publications insisted on the independence of the Court in constructing its positions and rejected the idea of the Court borrowing these positions from abroad. If there is similarity between the position of the Russian Constitutional Court and the position of foreign courts, it is explained as 'the same approach' or a 'parallel way of thinking' but not as 'following' foreign precedent.

Justice Nikolay Bondar' in his book 'Konstitucionalizaciya social'no-ekonomicheskogo razvitiya rossiyskoy gosudarstvennosti' (Constitutionalisation of Socio-Economical Development of the Russian Statehood) pointed out the similar principles of regulating and protecting social rights in the practice of the Russian and German Constitutional Courts.

> In the framework of this approach [considering that the Constitution demands the state to provide social support at such level as to ensure human dignity will be protected] the Russian Constitutional Court essentially followed the understanding of the nature and normative content of 'personal dignity', inherent for German constitutional law doctrine and practice, which presumes that personal dignity covers, *inter alia*, equality of people and social responsibility of the state to a person.
>
> The Federal Constitutional Court of Germany, relying on the principle of *socialstaat* in the aggregate with the inviolability of human dignity (art 1(1) of the German Grundgezetz) concluded that all state bodies are obliged to respect and protect human dignity with the guarantee of a living wage for everybody (eg BverfG E 40, 121 (133), BverfG E48, 346 (361), BverfG E 75, 348 (360), BverfG E 82, 60 (80, 85), BverfG E 89, 346 (353).[79]

Following this approach to social rights protection—similar to that of the Federal Constitutional Court of Germany, the Russian Constitutional Court held, in 2005, that personal dignity defined the minimum level of social claims to the state, which

---

[76] Separate opinion of Justice Anatoliy Kononov to Judgment 16 June 2006 No 7-P.
[77] Separate opinion of Justice Gadis Gadgiev to Judgment 14 November 2005 No 10-P.
[78] Separate opinion of Justice Vladimir Yaroslavcev to Ruling 15 February 2005 No 1-O.
[79] NS Bondar', *Konstitucionalizaciya social'no-economicheskogo razvitiya rossiyskoy gosudarstvennosti* (Constitutionalisation of Socio-Economical Development of the Russian Statehood) (Moscow, Vikor-Media, 2006) 182 (in Russian).

had to provide conditions for satisfying needs of persons and for the realisation of personal constitutional rights.[80]

Justice Bondar' has also referred to foreign case law and legislation on the question of the limits upon legislative discretion in reducing social guarantees. The Russian Constitutional Court held that lowering the level of social protection can only be carried out by fulfilling the principle of legal certainty, named by the court as 'the principle of supporting confidence of people to the state', claiming reasonable stability of legal regulation, inadmissibility of arbitrary changing and giving to the people the possibility of adapting to the new conditions.[81] This position, in Bondar's view, correlates with the decisions of the constitutional courts of Germany (4 July 1995), Lithuania (3 December 1997) and Croatia (4 March 1998 and 12 May 1998).[82]

This 'dignity and confidence' approach of both the Russian and German constitutional courts reflects the balance of constitutional values based on certain legal criteria. The idea of regulating social rights in the Russian Constitution was quite different: social rights were so vague in the level of their protection that they looked more like state policies than legal norms. The apprehensions of foreign experts that widely and indefinitely guaranteed social rights in the Constitution would cause their unenforceability[83] were not confirmed by this practice of the Russian Constitutional Court.

i. Russian Legal Scholarship and its Attention to the Influence of Foreign Case Law

Legal scholarship played a significant role in the development of judicial practice in the Soviet state. Judges were required to undergo regular training in universities and special academies and, also, to take part in seminars with professors of law.

In the post-Soviet era, regular training for judges came to an end and was replaced with others influence of legal scholarship on the judicial practice. Many courts have expert institutions attached to them—special scholarship-consulting councils, with legal professors as experts. Difficulties of statutory interpretation are discussed in these councils which give optional recommendations to judges from the doctrinal point of view.

Russian legal literature includes some books aimed at helping judges in their work. They are primarily commentaries on the main codes of law and statutes as well as reference books concerning particular categories of cases heard by the courts. All these materials still use only Russian law sources and usually do not refer to any foreign case law.

We could not find *any* legal research[84] discussing the use of foreign precedents in the Russian courts and only managed to find two articles dealing with the influence

---

[80] Ruling of the Constitutional Court 15 February 2005 No 17-O.
[81] See, eg, Judgment of the Constitutional Court 24 May 2001.
[82] NS Bondar', n 79 above, p 188.
[83] See V Schwartz, n 7 above, 144–45.
[84] This research is based on analysis of electronic catalogues of the main Russian libraries, including those of the Russian National Library and the Russian State Library. It covers only Russian-language literature; foreign literature would have less influence on legal practice mainly because few judges can read in other languages.

of contemporary foreign law (in addition to a few more works about the influence of Roman law[85]) on Russian law. One of these articles concerns family law issues;[86] the other, constitutional justice.[87] The latter deals with principles of the organisation of the Constitutional Court and the model of constitutional control used in Russia. The authors conclude that using the German model of constitutional court in Russian regions faces a number of difficulties and that copying this model has failed in Russia. Their suggestion is to combine the German model of constitutional control with models from other jurisdictions (the US model, *amparo* procedure, etc).

III. EMPIRICAL RESEARCH ON USING FOREIGN PRECEDENTS BY THE RUSSIAN CONSTITUTIONAL COURT

A. Explicit Citations of Foreign Case Law

i. Quantitative Research

From 1991 until now, the Russian Constitutional Court has made only six references to foreign court precedents, out of over 11,000 decisions.[88] As we said, all these references have been made in 'separate' (dissenting) opinions (*osoboe mnenie*)[89] of Constitutional Court justices, all concerning human rights. Three of the six references were made by Justice Anatoliy Kononov.

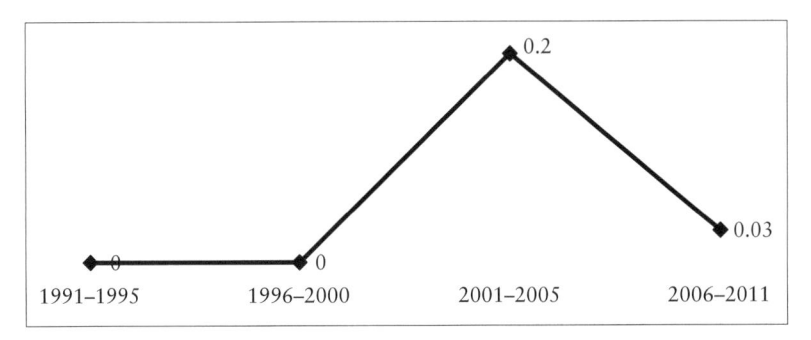

Figure 1: References to Foreign Precedents as a Percentage of All Decisions

---

[85] See, eg, SY Kritskaya, 'Recepciya rimskogo prava v rossiyskom ugolovnom prave' (Reception of Roman Law in Russian Criminal Law) (2004) 1 *Leningradskiy Yuridicheskiy Journal* 46–47 (in Russian).

[86] LY Grudcyna, 'Vliyanie zarubezhnogo opyta na reformirovanie nasledstvennogo prava v Rossii' (Influence of Foreign Experience on Reforming Inheritance Law in Russia) (2005) 6 *Sovremennoe Pravo* 60–66 (in Russian).

[87] SV Taradonov and DS Petrenko, 'Nekotorye aspekty mezhdunarodnogo i zarubezhnogo vliyaniya na konstitucionnoe pravosudie v Rossii' (Some Aspects of International and Foreign Influence on Constitutional Justice of the Russian Federation) (2007) 3 *Gosudarstvo i Pravo* 57–69 (in Russian).

[88] These facts were found out both by interviewing the judges and the staff experts of the Constitutional Court and searching the legal database of the Russian legislature (Consultant Plus), which includes decisions of the Russian Constitutional Court, with the keywords 'foreign', 'USA', 'Germany', 'Spain', 'Italy', 'Czech', 'Ukraine', 'Hungary', 'Bulgaria', 'Constitutional Court (but Constitutional Court of Russia)', 'Supreme Court (but Supreme Court of Russia)', 'Constitutional Council', 'Constitutional Tribunal'.

[89] As we said, in Russian judicial practice separate opinions do not differ in form whether they are dissenting or concurring. Mostly frequently their role is to disagree, thus most of them are dissenting.

368 Sergey Belov

The first reference was made in 2001 and concerned a conflict between a witness with immunity from prosecution and the statutory obligation of the witness to report a traffic accident to the police, to stay at the scene of the accident and to assist the police in investigating the accident. In his dissenting opinion, Kononov referred to a number of decisions rendered by constitutional courts in foreign democracies and mentioned, in particular, that similar cases had been heard by the constitutional courts of five countries as well as by the Canadian Supreme Court.[90]

Next, in opinions on election-law matters (limitations on freedom of information within the framework of election campaign), citations were made by Justice Kononov to a decision (the same one in two cases) of the Slovakia Constitutional Court,[91] and by Justice Gadis Gadzhiev to decisions of the US Supreme Court and the United States Court of Appeals, Seventh Circuit.[92]

In 2005 Justice Gadgiev also referred to a decision of the German Constitutional Court on the conflict between legal certainty and fairness in his opinion on tax law liability.[93]

The sixth and last citation to foreign case law was made in the separate opinion of Justice Sergey Kazantsev where he referred to a decision of the Spanish Constitutional Court dealing with the possibility of appealing (and revising) a judgment of acquittal.[94]

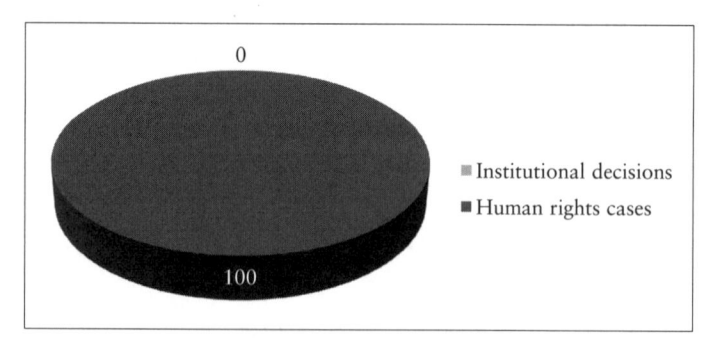

Figure 2: Percentage of Human Rights Cases and Institutional Decisions

ii. Qualitative Research

Foreign decisions were related (their essentials were summarised by the judges of the Russian Constitutional Court in a few phrases, without quoting or translation) in four opinions. Furthermore, the dissenting opinion of Justice Kazantsev mentioned the Spanish Constitutional Court's decision without specifying the date or the precise number; the dissenting opinion of Justice Kononov, which

---

[90] Separate opinion of Justice Anatoliy Kononov to Judgment 25 April 2001 No 6-P.
[91] Separate opinions of Justice Anatoliy Kononov to Judgment 30 October 2003 No 15-P and Judgment 16 June 2006 No 7-P.
[92] Separate opinion of Justice Gadis Gadgiev to Judgment 14 November 2005 No 10-P.
[93] Separate opinion of Justice Gadis Gadgiev to Judgment 14 July 2005 No 9-P.
[94] Separate opinion of Justice Sergey Kazancev to Judgment 16 May 2007 No 6-P.

related decisions of the constitutional courts of Korea, Spain and Germany and the Canadian Supreme Court, referenced these decisions with the date of issue only (without the publication source or title of the case).[95] Justice Gadzhiev once made full proper references to decisions of the US courts[96] in one of his dissenting opinions; in another he referred only to the date of the German Constitutional Court judgment.[97]

Two dissenting opinions (both by Justice Kononov) contained direct quotations from a judgment of the Constitutional Court of Slovakia[98] identified only with the year in which it had been rendered (1999).

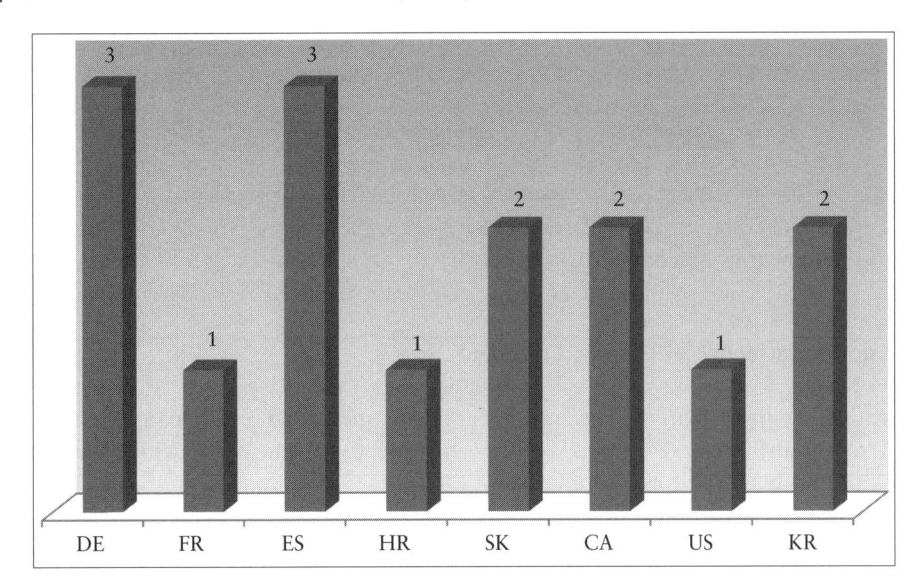

Figure 3: Number of References to Foreign Courts Sorted by Countries

In all six cases with references to foreign decisions the manner of quoting was predetermined by the style of the dissenting opinion. A justice—the author of the dissenting opinion—tried to strengthen his own position and looked for arguments abroad. It was not a kind of 'even there' a certain measure had been adopted argument; rather, it was: 'Look, you missed these arguments from abroad which sound very convincing'. In five cases, the arguments used referred to a single foreign jurisdiction: the US, Spain and Germany (once each); and Slovakia (twice). In the sixth case, reference was made to decisions of a group of democracies: the constitutional courts of Spain, Germany, France and Croatia. Korea and the Supreme Court of Canada had also resolved similar cases.

---

[95] Decisions of constitutional courts: Korean, of 27 August 1990; Spanish, of 23 December 1995; German, of 16 November 1998; and the Canadian Supreme Court decision of 10 June 1999.
[96] US Supreme Court decision *McConnell v Federal Election Commission* 540 US 93 (2003) and the United States Court of Appeals, Seventh Circuit case of *Brian Majors v Marsha Abell* 361 F3d 349 (2004).
[97] 14 March 1963.
[98] Both opinions quoted the same paragraph, and one of them quoted one more paragraph.

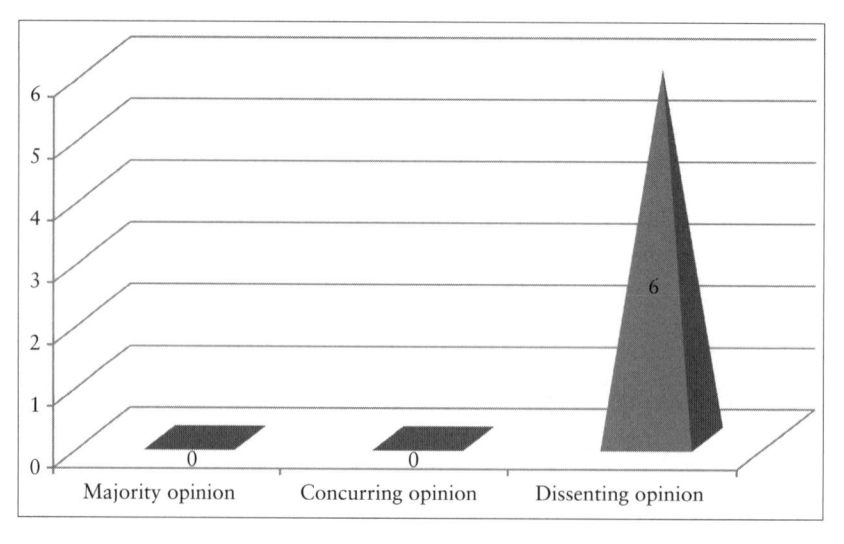

[Chart: Majority opinion 0, Concurring opinion 0, Dissenting opinion 6]

Figure 4: Number of References by their Source

B. Implicit Influence of Foreign Precedents

The influence of the foreign precedents cannot be measured in the manner normally used for quantitative research. We can only use two indicators, which indirectly show the influence of foreign practice.

The *first indicator* is the acquaintance of the Justices of the Constitutional Court with foreign practice. Direct references in the separate opinions, shown above, allow us to assume that the Justices are seeking to acquaint themselves with foreign practice and, thereby, to compare the ways for solving similar problems abroad with solutions proposed for the Russian Constitutional Court.

This familiarity is systematic enough.

There is a special department of international relations, research and analysis of judicial foreign practice within the Russian Constitutional Court. It has compiled a database of translations of foreign Constitutions, statutes regulating the activity of constitutional courts and decisions of constitutional courts and other courts in constitutional law matters. This database includes a complete set of the decisions of the constitutional courts from CIS (Commonwealth of Independent States) countries, as there is regular exchange of the full texts of all the decisions between these courts and the Russian Constitutional Court.

Using this database and the database of the Venice Commission of the Council of Europe (CODICES) as well as occasionally the decisions of foreign courts which may be available through the Internet, the Russian Federation Constitutional Court's special department has compiled more than 100 reviews of the practice of foreign courts concerning particular questions submitted at the request of the Chairman of the Constitutional Court and justices reporting the case on the panel. These reviews include analyses, citations from international law Acts, extracts from foreign Constitutions, and occasionally statutes and short summaries of decisions on a question significant for the Russian Constitutional Court. The references to foreign law and practice in the dissenting opinions referred to above are based mainly on these reviews. Summaries of foreign practice, classifications of foreign models,[99] references to foreign statutes and court precedents[100] considered in the opinions referred to above have also been taken from these reviews.

Even in those cases where they have submitted a dissenting opinion, Justices may still be acquainted with foreign court practice but have decided not to include this form of argument in the final text of the decision.

The *second indicator* is a comparison of the approaches to the resolution of constitutional conflicts of the Russian Constitutional Court on the one hand and foreign constitutional courts on the other. Such a comparison does not directly reveal the influence of foreign judicial practice. Nevertheless, it allows one to evaluate whether or not the Russian Constitutional Court has taken on board the manner of argument usual for those old democracies, the legal constitutional principles of which were transplanted in Russia during the constitutional reforms of the last decade of the twentieth century. Analysis of this kind does not fit the scope of this research.

IV. CONCLUSION

Summing up, there are several serious obstacles to using foreign precedents by the Russian Constitutional Court. Some of these obstacles lie in the field of the specificities of the Russian political system and Russian political culture. Legal patriotism and social as well as political circumstances prevent the Russian Constitutional Court from widely and frequently using foreign precedents. Foreign practice appears rather divergent in different jurisdictions (as shown in the overviews of the Court's special department), and this allows the Court to follow its own logic at the end of the day, using other practice by way of discretion. In choosing a precedent to follow, the Russian Constitutional Court would have more grounds to follow decisions from CIS countries, which are closer in a political and social context, than old democracies of Western Europe and the US, though it addresses the practice of courts in old democracies.

Another obstacle lies in the nature and structure of Russian Constitutional Court decisions. While these decisions are interpreted as binding in all their parts, legal formalism does not allow references to foreign law, which is not binding in Russia. As mentioned above, any argument made by the Russian Constitutional Court could be used for interpreting the Court's position, its understanding of the Constitution, for applying the considered law or statutes, or reproducing the law, by other courts. Due to these circumstances the Constitutional Court uses any non-binding sources very carefully and does not show any foreign precedents in the text of the decisions, even though they are obviously known to it.

---

[99] In the opinion of Justice Bondar' to Judgment 23 January 2007 No 1-P.
[100] In the opinion of Justice Kononov to n 90 above.

15

Judges as Discursive Agent: The Use of Foreign Precedents by the Constitutional Court of Taiwan

WEN-CHEN CHANG AND JIUNN-RONG YEH[*]

TABLE OF CONTENTS

I. Introduction 373
II. The Development of Constitutionalism, Judicial Review and Legal Culture 374
   A. The Development of Constitutionalism and Democracy 374
   B. The Creation, Functions and Jurisdictions of the Constitutional Court 376
   C. Legal Culture of Strong Foreign Influence 379
III. Explicit Citations of Foreign Precedents 380
   A. Quantitative Analysis 381
   B. Qualitative Analysis 386
IV. Implicit Influences of Foreign Precedents 389
V. Conclusion 391

I. INTRODUCTION

ONE OF THE most vibrant constitutional democracies in East Asia, Taiwan has developed strong constitutionalism and judicial review since the late 1980s.[1] The Constitutional Court (also known as the Council of Grand Justices[2]) was created in 1948, and has become one of the oldest constitutional

---

[*] Wen-Chen Chang, Associate Professor, College of Law, National Taiwan University; Jiunn-rong Yeh, Distinguished Professor, College of Law, National Taiwan University College of Law. We would like to express our deepest gratitude to Dr Wen-Chieh Wu for his invaluable assistance in the empirical method, and to Mr Daniel Yen-Chung Chen and Ms Shao-Man Lee for their superb research assistance. Also, this research would not have been possible without the grants we received from the National Science Council in Taiwan.

[1] Tom Ginsburg, *Judicial Review in New Democracies: Constitutional Courts in Asian Cases* (New York, Cambridge University Press, 2003).

[2] The Court was known as the Council of Grand Justices under the 1958 Act Regarding the Council of Grand Justices. But, in 1993, with the passage of the Constitutional Interpretation Procedure Act, the Court was rechristened the Constitutional Court. For a brief introduction to the Court and the content of the Constitutional Interpretation Procedure Act, see *Judicial Yuan—Relevant Statutes*, Justices of the Constitutional Court, www.judicial.gov.tw/constitutionalcourt/en/p07_2.asp?lawno=73.

courts in East Asia and even beyond.[3] The Court has provided effective checks and balances with the exercise of legislative and executive powers, and been praised as a successful guardian of individual rights and freedoms.[4] Each year the Court renders about 20 to 30 decisions (also known as interpretations), half of which are invalidations of statutes or regulations found inconsistent with the Constitution.[5] In 2000, the Court even made a decision in which constitutional amendments were declared unconstitutional and rendered null and void.[6]

Despite an active and longstanding judiciary, Taiwan's Constitutional Court has not often relied on or directly referred to foreign legal authorities in its own decisions. Interestingly however, beginning in the late 1980s, foreign or even international legal sources became more and more visible in its decisions, and especially so in the separate opinions issued by individual justices.[7] This study is thus aimed at analysing empirically the use of foreign precedents by Taiwan's Constitutional Court from its first decision in January 1949 to July 2010.

Aside from this introduction, section II discusses relevant contexts relating to the development of constitutionalism, judicial review and legal culture in Taiwan. The complete empirical results are presented and discussed in the subsequent two sections. Section III analyses the explicit citations of foreign precedents including both quantitative and qualitative discussions. Section IV represents an attempt at discerning the implicit influence of foreign precedent citations in the separate opinions upon the majority reasoning. Section V concludes.

II. THE DEVELOPMENT OF CONSTITUTIONALISM, JUDICIAL REVIEW AND LEGAL CULTURE

A. The Development of Constitutionalism and Democracy

Taiwan was ceded to Japan in 1895 by the Ch'ing Dynasty of China as part of the price for losing the Sino-Japanese War. After the Japanese government surrendered in World War II, the nationalist government of the Republic of China (ROC) regained Taiwan and made it into one province of China in 1945. The ROC Constitution was made in 1946 and came into effect in 1947 amidst the civil war between the nationalist party that controlled the ROC government and the rising communist party. The nationalist government eventually lost the civil war and retreated to Taiwan in 1949. As a result, the People's Republic of China was established by the

---

[3] Ginsburg, *Judicial Review* (2003) 120 f; Wen-Chen Chang, 'The Role of Judicial Review in Consolidating Democracy: The Case of Taiwan' (2005) 2(2) *Asia Law Review* 73, 74 ff.

[4] Ginsburg, *Judicial Review* (2003) 125 f, 144 ff. See also J Yeh and WC Chang, 'The Emergence of East Asian Constitutionalism: Features in Comparison' (2011) 59 *American Journal of Comparative Law* 805, 806 ff.

[5] Chang, 'The Role of Judicial Review' 85 f.

[6] JY Interpretation No 499 (24 April 2000). An English translation is available at www.judicial.gov.tw/constitutionalcourt/en/p03_01.asp?expno=499.

[7] Ginsburg, *Judicial Review* (2003) 139; WC Chang, 'The Convergence of Constitutions and International Human Rights: Taiwan and South Korea in Comparison' (2011) 36 *North Carolina Journal of International Law and Commercial Regulation* 593, 602 f.

communist party on the mainland while the nationalist party relocated the ROC government to Taiwan.

Due to the ensuing conflicts with the communist party on the mainland, the initial rule of the ROC government in Taiwan was not in accordance with democratic constitutionalism. The martial law decree was imposed in 1949, and the temporary provisions were passed to supersede parts of the ROC Constitution in order to expand the powers of the president and to freeze representative elections.[8] Political liberalisation and democratisation eventually started in the late 1980s. The opposition party was formed in 1986, and the martial law decree was lifted in 1987. Constitutional revisions were undertaken to pave the way for groundbreaking political reforms, altogether seven times between 1991 and 2005.[9] As a result, the first parliamentary election was held in 1990 and the first presidential election in 1996. The nationalist party lost the presidential election in 2000, marking the first peaceful regime change in Taiwan.

The ROC Constitution was a product of both autochthonous efforts and foreign influences. On the one hand, the national government was divided into five branches—the Executive, Legislative, Judicial, Control and Examination Yuans—a five-power scheme devised from Chinese culture and tradition by Sun Yat-sen in addition to the National Assembly, representing the sovereignty of the people.[10] On the other hand, the separation of powers as well as checks and balances between these five powers were considerably modelled on pre-World War II German and Japanese Constitutions. The design of the Judicial Yuan, the highest judicial organ in the exercise of judicial powers, was initially inspired by the Federal Supreme Court of the United States.[11] The chapter on fundamental rights and freedoms in the ROC Constitution was reflective of civil and political rights that were generally recognised after World War II; in addition there was a chapter on fundamental national policies that addressed social and economic policies.[12]

The revisions of the ROC Constitution in the 1990s were mainly on the arrangements of government institutions to suit the needs of democratic developments in Taiwan. The five-power scheme stipulated by Sun Yat-sen was replaced by institutional arrangements modelled on a semi-presidential system with a directly elected president, a prime minister heading the Executive Yuan answerable to the Legislative Yuan, the only representative body of the people. The Control and Examination Yuans—while kept intact—have become subsidiary, independent institutions, aside from the Judicial Yuan.[13]

---

[8] Ginsburg, *Judicial Review* (2003) 113 f.
[9] JR Yeh, 'Constitutional Reform and Democratization in Taiwan: 1945–2000' in P Chow (ed), *Taiwan's Modernization in Global Perspective* (Westport, USA, Praeger Publishers, 2002).
[10] Ginsburg, *Judicial Review* (2003) 112f.
[11] Ibid, 116. See also L Shao-Liang Liu, 'Judicial Review and Emerging Constitutionalism: The Uneasy Case of the Republic of China on Taiwan' (1991) 39 *American Journal of Comparative Law* 509 ff.
[12] An English translation of the ROC Constitution is available at english.president.gov.tw/Default.aspx?tabid=1107.
[13] Ginsburg, *Judicial Review* (2003) 116 f; Yeh and Chang, 'East Asian Constitutionalism' (2011) 822 f.

B. The Creation, Functions and Jurisdictions of the Constitutional Court

The Council of Grand Justices, later renamed the Constitutional Court, was created in 1948 and relocated to Taiwan in 1949 with reappointed justices. The Court had about 17 justices who were appointed with a renewable term of nine years by the president, with the consent of the representative bodies.[14] The constitutional revision of 2000, however, stipulated that the Court would be composed of 15 justices with non-renewable terms of eight years, to be appointed in a staggered way.[15] Between 1948 and 2003, the Court had six terms of justices, each with a term of nine years. In 2003, there were eight justices appointed for four years and seven appointed for eight years, and the staggered appointments have continued ever since.

The qualifications of justices were specified to enable the recruitment of a mixture of legal scholars, career judges, legislators, and persons with a combination of scholarly and political experience.[16] In practice, however, the vast majority of those appointed have either been law professors or career judges with prior experience from the highest courts of various jurisdictions or as judicial officials in the Judicial Yuan or the Ministry of Justice. In the past, more career lawyers were appointed than law professors. Since the 1990s, however, at least half or more justices appointed have been law professors. Currently, the Court consists of nine law professors, five career judges, and only one former private attorney.[17] Partly due to the strong representation of former academics in the Court, justices have possessed impressive educational credentials and considerable training in foreign law. For instance, in the present Court, among 15 justices, eight of them have doctorates from Germany, one from the United States, and one has a Masters from Japan and one a Masters from the United States. Only four justices have no foreign law degrees, and among these four, three have a local doctorate.

The Constitutional Court has, since 1948, exercised an exclusive power to review and invalidate laws and rules which contravene the Constitution. A centralised

---

[14] Before the 1990s, the confirmation was provided by the Control Yuan. After the 1992 constitutional revision changed the status of the Control Yuan from a representative body to a semi-judicial one, the confirmation power was shifted to the National Assembly. In 2005, the constitutional revision abolished the National Assembly and the power to confirm judicial appointments was transferred to the Legislative Yuan, now the only representative body. English translations of all constitutional revisions are available at english.president.gov.tw/Default.aspx?tabid=435.

[15] See art 5 of the Additional Articles of the ROC Constitution. An English translation is available at english.president.gov.tw/Default.aspx?tabid=1036#05.

[16] The Organic Act of the Judicial Yuan sets forth five categories of people who are eligible for appointment, and no single category is supposed to comprise more than one third of the Court. These five categories include a candidate who 1) has served as a Justice of the Supreme Court for more than 10 years with a distinguished record; 2) has served as a Member of the Legislative Yuan for more than nine years with distinguished contributions; 3) has been a professor of a major field of law at a university for more than 10 years and has authored publications in a specialised field; 4) has served at the International Court of Justice, or has published authoritative works in the field of public or comparative law; or 5) is a person highly reputed in the field of legal research who has political experience. See also Ginsburg, *Judicial Review* (2003) 120 f; Chang, 'The Role of Judicial Review' 85 f.

[17] The list of current justices (and their CVs) is available at www.judicial.gov.tw/constitutionalcourt/en/p01_03.asp.

system of judicial review has been in place for more than 60 years. However, as indicated in the previous discussion, the drafters of the ROC Constitution initially envisaged the Judicial Yuan being composed of grand justices and modelled on the US Supreme Court,[18] a final court of appeal in possession of all jurisdictions over civil, criminal, and administrative cases as well as constitutional review.[19] A decentralised system of judicial review with the Judicial Yuan as the final resort was what had been planned.[20] Due in part to the prior establishment of the Supreme Court of civil and criminal jurisdictions and the Administrative Court, and in part to the strong influence of the civil law tradition, the decentralised system has never been crystallised. From the very beginning, justices of the Constitutional Court have sat separately from other final courts of appeal, and exercised an exclusive power of judicial review. This practice was institutionalised by subsequently enacted laws regarding the jurisdictions of the Court[21] and a constitutional interpretation by the Court itself: JY Interpretation No 371, where the Court reiterated its exclusive power of judicial review and allowed lower courts only a referral power in cases where the constitutionality of laws or regulations is at issue.[22]

The jurisdictions of the Constitutional Court in Taiwan are similar to other specialised constitutional courts in Europe and elsewhere. The Court has jurisdiction over constitutional questions raised by individual petitions referred by the lower courts, or petitioned by government agencies, or one third of legislators, and over jurisdictional conflicts between government branches or agencies. These two jurisdictions occupy the majority, if not all, of the Court's entire docket.[23] The Court also has jurisdiction over the adjudication of presidential impeachment and the dissolution of unconstitutional political parties, but it has not yet received any cases in these areas.[24] Otherwise, the Constitutional Court has from the beginning been responsible for issuing uniform interpretations of statutes and regulations in situations where the final courts of various jurisdictions such as the Supreme Court or Supreme Administrative Court arrive at conflicting interpretations.[25] This jurisdiction over unified interpretations constitutes only two per cent of the Court's caseload, down from approximately 20 per cent in the 1960s and 1970s and 50 per cent in the 1950s.[26]

It should be noted that unlike other constitutional courts, the Constitutional Court in Taiwan can only review 'in abstract' the constitutionality of laws and regulations even when the request for review is brought up by individuals whose

---

[18] See n 11 above.
[19] See ch VII of the ROC Constitution, english.president.gov.tw/Default.aspx?tabid=1114.
[20] Ginsburg, *Judicial Review* (2003) 116.
[21] The 1958 Act Regarding the Council of Grand Justices, which was subsequently replaced by the 1993 Constitutional Interpretation Procedural Act, www.judicial.gov.tw/constitutionalcourt/en/p07_2.asp?lawno=73.
[22] JY Interpretation No 371 (20 January 1995). An English translation is available at www.judicial.gov.tw/constitutionalcourt/en/p03_01.asp?expno=371.
[23] Chang, 'The Role of Judicial Review' 76 f.
[24] Ibid at 77.
[25] Ibid. See also Ginsburg, *Judicial Review* (2003) 123 ff.
[26] See Chang, 'The Role of Judicial Review' (n 3) 77 (Table 1).

cases have exhausted all available judicial proceedings. The Court cannot issue a direct remedy even for these cases. This is very different from the power of other constitutional courts, such as the German Constitutional Court, in deciding individual constitutional complaints where the Court may provide direct remedies.[27] Given this constraint, in 1984, in order to provide incentives for individuals to file constitutional applications, the Court issued *Interpretation No 185*, asserting that if laws or regulations applied in final judgments were declared as unconstitutional, individuals who filed such constitutional applications would be entitled to a retrial or an extraordinary appeal.[28] This has since increased individual applications to the Court's docket.[29]

Constitutional petitions to the Court are first sent to a panel of three justices for an initial review, which panel makes suggestions for dismissal or acceptance. Final decisions of dismissal or acceptance, however, still require a majority vote.[30] A two-thirds quorum is required for the justices of the Constitutional Court to render decisions regarding the constitutionality of statutes while a simple majority is sufficient in deciding the constitutionality of administrative regulations or judicial precedents and in rendering unified interpretations.[31] In the first term of the Court (1948–58), the majority decisions were written in one or two paragraphs of rulings without detailed reasoning being given. No concurring or dissenting opinions were allowed to be issued at this time. From the second term that started in 1958 to the beginning of the fifth term in 1987, 'dissenting opinions' signed by individual justices could be issued separately. However, 'dissenting opinions' at this time actually included both those dissenting with the ruling and those dissenting with the reasoning, the latter of which should have been characterised as concurring opinions. Only after 1987 was the issuance of concurring and dissenting opinions institutionalised.[32] Since the 1980s, not only has the issuing of separate opinions increased steadily (Table 1), the length of majority opinions, particularly the reasoning part, has also expanded considerably.

Before 1993, the Constitutional Court adjudicated cases without any oral arguments being held. It relied only on written submissions by petitioners or relevant parties or government agencies. The 1993 Constitutional Interpretation Procedural Act permitted the Court to hold oral hearings if found necessary.

---

[27] DP Kommers, *The Constitutional Jurisprudence of the Federal Republic of Germany*, 2nd edn (Durham and London, Duke University Press, 1997) 15.

[28] JY Interpretation No 185 (27 January 1984). An English translation is available at www.judicial.gov.tw/constitutionalcourt/en/p03_01.asp?expno=185.

[29] Ginsburg, *Judicial Review* (2003) 136. The Court had already hinted at this position in an earlier decision, JY Interpretation No 177 (5 November 1982). An English translation is available at www.judicial.gov.tw/constitutionalcourt/en/p03_01.asp?expno=177.

[30] See art 10 of the 1993 Constitutional Interpretation Procedural Act, www.judicial.gov.tw/constitutionalcourt/en/p07_2.asp?lawno=73.

[31] See art 14 of the 1993 Constitutional Interpretation Procedural Act, www.judicial.gov.tw/constitutionalcourt/en/p07_2.asp?lawno=73. This was reduced from three-quarters in deciding the constitutionality of statutes and two-thirds in deciding the constitutionality of administrative rules and judicial precedents and in rendering unified interpretations, stipulated by the 1958 Act Regarding the Council of Grand Justices.

[32] Ginsburg, *Judicial Review* (2003) 128 (Table 5.4).

The Court has since only held oral hearings in seven cases.[33] Upon the request of petitioners or justices, the Court may order the petitioners, relevant parties or government agencies to brief the Court.[34] On occasion, the Court may convene an unofficial session to invite academics to discuss issues in pending cases and provide the judges with relevant legal analyses including foreign jurisprudence.[35]

C. Legal Culture of Strong Foreign Influence

Taiwan's traditional legal system was modernised during the colonial rule of Japan between 1895 and 1945. The modern legal codes that Japan borrowed from Europe—primarily Germany, Switzerland and France—were introduced to Taiwan's legal system and education. At the same time, the Ch'ing Dynasty of China and the ROC government that succeeded it also began to modernise the traditional Chinese legal system by borrowing legal codes from Japan and Europe. As a result, when the Japanese government left in 1945, the legal system in Taiwan was already modelled on the civil law system and experienced no significant change with the subsequent rule of the ROC government.[36]

Because of the borrowed legal system, the legal culture in Taiwan has been extremely receptive to foreign influences. Most evident is the requirement for legal teaching. While a doctorate is a prerequisite for teaching in any universities in Taiwan, teaching law often requires a doctorate from abroad. Take for example the current law faculty composition of the National Taiwan University College of Law, the top law school in Taiwan. At present, there are 43 full-time law professors including associate and assistant professors. Among them, 18 have a doctorate from Germany, 12 from the United States, seven from Japan, four from England, and one from France. Only one full-time professor is locally trained.[37] The dominance of foreign-trained law faculties is indicative of strong foreign influence in Taiwan's legal system.

This emphasis on foreign-trained legal talent is also found in the judicial circle. For example, the first President of the Judicial Yuan (in 1928), Wang Chung-Hui,

---

[33] These include JY Interpretation No 334 (14 January 1994), JY Interpretation No 392 (22 December 1995), JY Interpretation No 419 (31 December 1996), JY Interpretation No 445 (23 January 1998), JY Interpretation No 585 (15 December 2004), JY Interpretation No 603 (28 September 2005), and JY Interpretation No 689 (29 July 2011).

[34] See art 13 of the 1993 Constitutional Interpretation Procedural Act, www.judicial.gov.tw/constitutionalcourt/en/p07_2.asp?lawno=73.

[35] Once or twice per year, the Court may also invite scholars from overseas to deliver speeches or lectures on the topics of its own interests or concerns.

[36] See generally TS Wang, *Legal Reform in Taiwan under Japanese Colonial Rule (1895–1945): The Reception of Western Law* (Seattle, University of Washington Press, 2000); T Fu Chen, 'Transplant of Civil Code in Japan, Taiwan and China: With the Focus of Legal Evolution' (2011) 6 *National Taiwan University Law Review* 389 ff.

[37] For a list of faculty members and their CVs, see www.law.ntu.edu.tw/english/full_time_professors.html.

had a doctorate from Yale Law School in 1905,[38] the Vice-President had a doctorate from France,[39] and the first native Taiwanese justice on the first-term Constitutional Court, Tsai Chang-Lin, had a Masters in law from Tokyo Imperial University and served as a judge in Japan for 10 years.[40] In subsequent terms of the Court, there were always a few justices with foreign law degrees from Germany, Japan, the United States, France and Britain appointed, and the number has increased steadily over time. In the current Court, 11 out of 15 justices either have a doctorate or a Masters from abroad. While justices holding foreign law degrees are predominantly those appointed from legal academia, most career judges also have at least a Masters of law from abroad.

Interestingly however, notwithstanding the strong influence of foreign law, judicial decisions of both ordinary courts and the Constitutional Court have not included a great deal of foreign law references or citations. This is in part due to the customs of a civil law system in which judicial decisions often do not include references or citations, and in part due to the fact that domestic laws and legal scholarship have already been influenced by foreign law and there is thus no need for courts to refer to foreign law. By relying on domestic laws or legal scholarship, courts and their decisions are certainly influenced by foreign law. This may also explain why courts in Taiwan also do not often refer to international legal authorities in their decisions. However the failure to make international legal references may also be due to the international isolation of Taiwan due to its perplexing relationship with the PRC on the mainland.[41]

III. EXPLICIT CITATIONS OF FOREIGN PRECEDENTS

The Constitutional Court of Taiwan issued its first decision in January 1949. By the end of July 2010, the Court had altogether rendered 680 interpretations. This section examines empirically the explicit citations of foreign precedents in the majority and separate opinions of all these decisions.[42] Both a quantitative approach and a quality-based approach are adopted to analyse interpretations explicitly citing foreign precedents.

In the quantitative research, we collect judicial opinions rendered by the Constitutional Court of Taiwan from JY Interpretation No 1 to JY Interpretation No 680, available on the website of the Judicial Yuan.[43] We code each citation of foreign precedent by types of opinion where it is cited (including rulings, reasoning, concurring or dissenting opinions), date of issue, issues concerned (institutions

---

[38] See *Archive of Grand Justices' Interpreting Constitution* (The Secretariat of the Grand Justices ed 1998) 11 ff (in Chinese).
[39] Ibid.
[40] Ibid at 115 f.
[41] See Chang, 'The Convergence of Constitutions' (n 7) 593 f.
[42] Only a very small fraction of these decisions were unified interpretations. As some of these unified interpretations were still related to constitutional provisions, this study does not separate unified interpretations but instead includes all interpretations issued by the Constitutional Court in its analysis.
[43] Interpretations of the Justices of the Constitutional Court, Judicial Yuan, www.judicial.gov.tw/ConstitutionalCourt/p03.asp.

or human rights), and the background of justices (having scholarly backgrounds or career lawyer backgrounds).[44] We also code cited foreign precedents by the original countries of courts.[45] As expected, explicit citations of foreign precedent in the majority opinions are scant: they appear in only four majority opinions. However, there has been a sharp increase in explicit foreign law citations in the concurring and dissenting opinions (Table 1 and Figure 1).[46] This trend has since continued. By the end of 2011, there was still no additional citation of foreign precedents found in majority opinions, but explicit references in separate opinions continued to rise.

In the quality-based approach, four cases directly citing foreign precedents are analysed in detail. These decisions include JY Interpretation No 165, JY Interpretation No 342, JY Interpretation No 392, and JY Interpretation No 499.

A. Quantitative Analysis

In the 680 interpretations issued by the Constitutional Court, only four interpretations (0.59%) explicitly cited foreign decisions in their majority opinions.[47] If explicit citations in concurring and dissenting opinions are included, then there are 66 out of 680 interpretations (9.7%) that explicitly cited foreign precedents. In those four decisions whose majority opinions explicitly cited foreign precedents, three were concerned with institutional issues and only one was concerned with fundamental rights. With regard to their results, two decisions declared the challenged laws (including both statutes and constitutional amendments) unconstitutional, one held the challenged statute constitutional, and one involved a constitutional clarification. These four decisions altogether cited 11 foreign precedents, including three decisions of the US Supreme Court, two decisions of the Japanese Supreme Court, two decisions of the German Constitutional Court, two decisions of the Turkish Constitutional Court, one decision of the Italian Constitutional Court, and one decision of the European Court of Human Rights (ECtHR). The majority of the foreign decisions, namely six out of the 11, were cited in JY Interpretation No 499, a landmark

---

[44] Justices with scholarly backgrounds means those working as law professors before their appointments. Justices with career lawyer backgrounds are primarily those serving as judges at separate supreme courts or lower courts and those serving as government officials such as Attorney-General or Secretary-General of the Judicial Yuan.

[45] One citation is defined as one foreign case citation within one paragraph.

[46] Up to 25 February 2012, there have been 696 interpretations made by the Constitutional Court of Taiwan. The Court did not cite foreign precedents directly in majority opinions after JY Interpretation No 680. On the other hand, the increase in explicit foreign law citations in the concurring and dissenting opinions can still be found.

[47] They include: JY Interpretation No 165 (concerning institutional issues, involving constitutional clarification), JY Interpretation No 342 (concerning institutional issues, sustaining challenged statutes), JY Interpretation No 392 (concerning fundamental rights, declaring challenged statutes unconstitutional), and JY Interpretation No 499 (concerning institutional issues, declaring constitutional amendments unconstitutional).

decision where the Court unprecedentedly declared constitutional amendments unconstitutional.[48]

Rarely seen in majority opinions, however, foreign precedents were primarily cited in separate concurring and dissenting opinions. In all 680 interpretations, 685 separate opinions were issued by individual justices. Among them, 108 separate opinions (15.8%) cited foreign precedents. Interestingly, foreign precedents were more likely to be cited in concurring opinions (22.7%) than in dissenting opinions (11.5%) (Figure 2).[49] Moreover, while foreign precedents occurred more often in majority opinions concerning institutional issues than in those concerning rights protection, they were more likely to be cited in separate opinions concerning rights protection (6.1%) than in those concerning institutional issues (3.9%) (Figure 3).

Altogether in majority and separate opinions, foreign precedents appeared 508 times, and 423 foreign precedents were cited indicating that a number of foreign precedents were relied upon more than once. Foreign precedents were mostly from Germany (291 times/238 precedents), the United States (120 times/97 precedents), Japan (52 times/47 precedents), the European Court of Justice and the ECtHR (23 times/20 precedents). They might also have come from France, Austria, Turkey, Canada, Hungary, Italy, Switzerland, the Philippines and South Korea[50] (Table 2).

Majority opinions never include any footnotes. The citations of foreign precedents in the majority opinions are placed in quotations. Interestingly, however, references to foreign precedents in separate opinions were largely covered in footnotes (nearly 80%) rather than in quotations. We also find that justices from scholarly backgrounds were more likely to refer to foreign precedents in footnotes than in quotations. In contrast, justices with backgrounds as career judges placed foreign precedents rather equally in footnotes and in quotations. Regardless of whether they were in footnotes or in quotations, foreign precedents were rarely discussed in detail in separate opinions, nor were any lengthy paragraphs quoted for detailed discussion. Also noteworthy is that references to foreign precedents in the majority opinions were, without exception, used for supporting the Court's reasoning. While greater varieties existed in ways of referencing foreign precedents in separate opinions, the predominant use was for supporting the arguments made by individual justices. Citations used *a contrario* have been scarce.

The most important finding of our empirical study is the relationship between justices' backgrounds and the frequency of their foreign precedent citations. More citations of foreign precedents were provided by justices from scholarly

---

[48] JY Interpretation No 499 (24 April 2000). An English translation is available at www.judicial.gov.tw/constitutionalcourt/en/p03_01.asp?expno=499.

[49] Concurring opinions include full concurring opinions and those concurring in part, while dissenting opinions include full dissenting opinions and those dissenting in part. Those 'concurring in part and dissenting in part' were included in neither category.

[50] They were from France (3 times/3 precedents), Austria (3 times/3 precedents), Turkey (2 times/2 precedents), Canada (1 time/1 precedent), Hungary (1 time/1 precedent), Italy (1 time/1 precedent), Switzerland (1 time/1 precedent), the Philippines (1 time/1 precedent) and South Korea (1 time/1 precedent).

backgrounds (390 times) than justices who were career judges (184 times), namely *twice as many* (Figure 4).[51] A predominant number of foreign precedents cited by justices who studied in Germany for Masters or doctorates were from German courts, representing 74.8 per cent (258 out of 345 times). For justices who had learning experiences in the United States, 65.5 per cent (74 out of 113 times) of their references to foreign precedents were from American courts, mostly the United States Supreme Court. Interestingly however, justices who had learning experiences in Japan were still more likely to refer to German precedents (70.4%, 38 out of 54 times) than to refer to Japanese precedents (18.5%, 10 out of 54 times). It should be noted that justices from scholarly backgrounds cited a wider variety of foreign precedents. Foreign precedents outside the most-cited jurisdictions—Germany, the United States and Japan—were almost exclusively provided by justices from scholarly backgrounds.

A final interesting observation may be on the tendency of the Court to use foreign precedents over time. Table 1 clearly shows that there has been no increase or decrease in the Court's use of foreign precedents in majority opinions. The Court has consistently been restrained from directly referring to foreign precedents in majority opinions. By referring to foreign precedents in two majority opinions, this put the sixth term ahead in terms of considering foreign precedents the most often. In sharp contrast, however, there has been a steady increase in referring to foreign precedents in separate concurring or dissenting opinions, from 1.6 per cent in the fifth term, 3.5 per cent in the sixth term, to 15.8 per cent in the current Court term. The number of times that foreign precedents have been cited has sharply increased from 14 in the fifth term, 63 in the sixth term, to 413 in the current Court term.

In addition, Table 1 shows a clear change over time with regard to most-cited jurisdictions. Before the 1980s, the most-cited jurisdiction was Japan, mostly the Japanese Supreme Court. However, in the fifth term of the Court, the most-cited jurisdiction became the United States. Yet very soon after that, the most-cited jurisdiction changed to Germany (in the sixth term) which has been maintained ever since. This may be explained by the scholarly composition of the Court. The fifth term of the Court had about five justices with scholarly backgrounds, and two of them obtained a doctorate from the United States, one from Germany, and one from Japan. Moreover, in the fifth term, three justices appointed from career lawyers also had advanced law degrees from the United States. Thus, it was not surprising that the most-cited jurisdiction in the fifth term of the Court was the United States. But in the sixth term, among six justices with scholarly backgrounds, three obtained doctoral degrees from Germany, two from Austria, and one from Japan. With this composition in justices' backgrounds, the most-cited jurisdiction shifted to Germany. For the current Court, among 15 justices, eight of them have a doctorate from Germany, one from the United States, one has a Masters from Japan and one from the United States. Expectedly, Germany has remained as the most-cited jurisdiction.

---

[51] See n 44 above.

Table 1: The Number of Foreign Precedents (FP) Cited in Interpretations

	1st Term 1948–58	2nd Term 1958–67	3rd Term 1967–76	4th Term 1976–85	5th Term 1985–94	6th Term 1994–2003	Since 2003–07/2010
Interpretations	79	43	24	53	167	200	114
Interpretation with FP in majority opinions	0 (0.0%)	0 (0.0%)	0 (0.0%)	1 (1.9%)	1 (0.6%)	2 (1%)	0 (0.0%)
Number of majority and separate opinions	79	121	86	162	441	593	468
Number of majority and separate opinions citing FP	0	4 (3.3%)	2 (2.3%)	4 (2.5%)	7 (1.6%)	21 (3.5%)	74 (15.8%)
Number of FP cited (times/precedents)	0	8 (8)	5 (5)	5 (4)	14 (13)	63 (55)	413 (351)
Mostly cited jurisdictions (times/precedents)	0	Japan: 5 (5) France: 3 (3)	Japan: 5(5)	Japan: 5 (4)	US: 7 (6) Japan: 4 (4) Germany: 3(3)	Germany: 27 (23) US: 14 (11) Japan: 12	Germany: 261 (219) US: 98 (85) Japan: 21 (17)

Source: by authors

Table 2: Jurisdictions of Foreign Precedents (FP) Cited in Interpretations

	Germany	US	Japan	European Courts	France	Austria	Others
No of FP citations in majority and separate opinions	291	120	52	23	3	3	16
No of FP cited in majority and separate opinions	238	97	47	20	3	3	15

* European Courts include the European Court of Justice and the European Court of Human Rights
* Others includes Turkey, Canada, Hungary, Italy, Switzerland, the Philippines and South Korea
Source: by authors

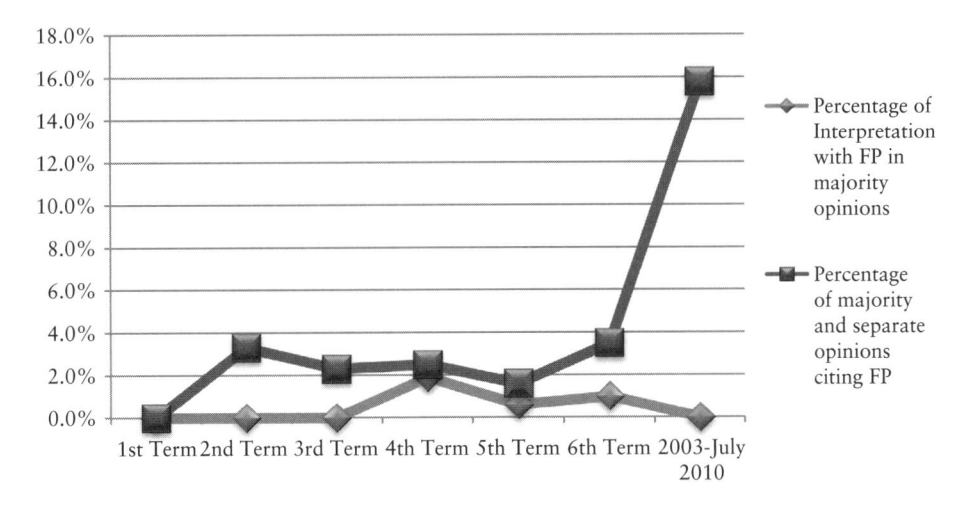

Figure 1: Frequency of JY Interpretations Citing Foreign Precedents

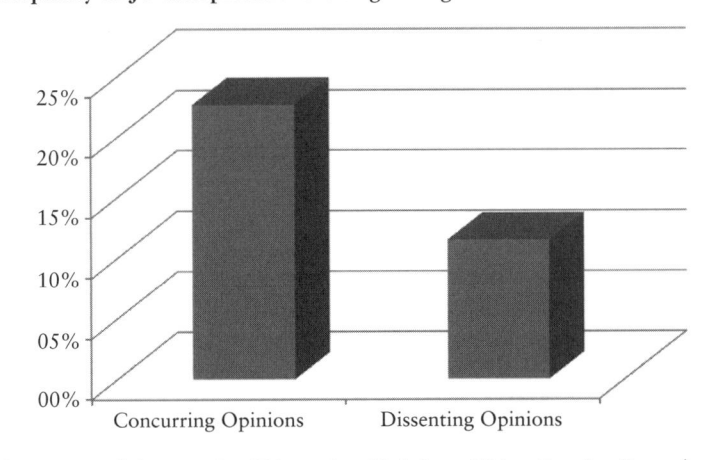

Figure 2: Frequency of Concurring/Dissenting Opinions Citing Foreign Precedents

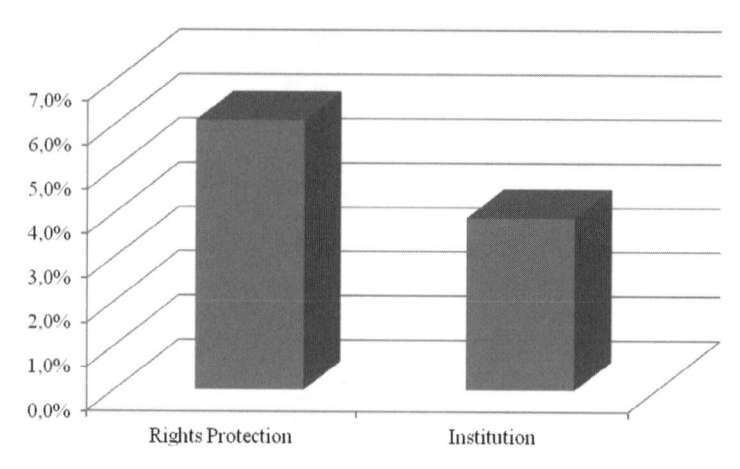

Figure 3: Frequency of Issue Concerned and Separate Opinions Citing Foreign Precedents

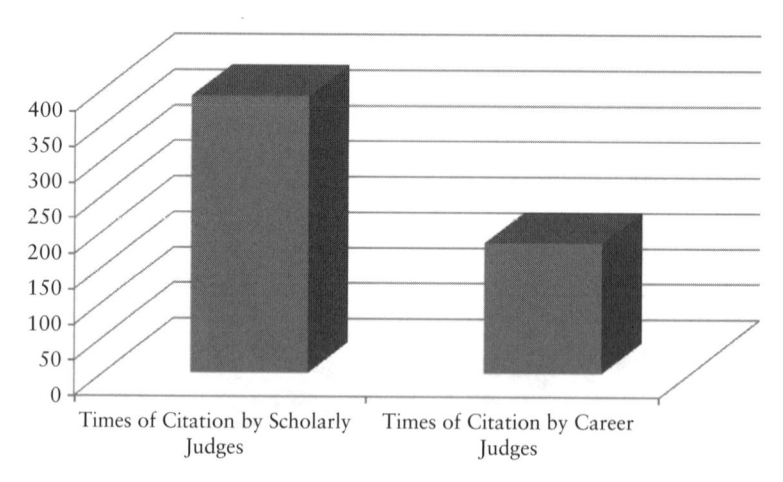

Figure 4: Citation of Foreign Precedents and Scholarly Backgrounds of Judges

B. Qualitative Analysis

In addition to the preceding quantitative analysis, the following examines qualitatively the ways that foreign precedents were referred to in the majority and separate opinions.

The first time the Court directly cited foreign precedents in the majority opinion was in JY Interpretation No 165.[52] The Court cited a Japanese Supreme Court case

---

[52] JY Interpretation No 165 (12 September 1980). An English translation is available at www.judicial.gov.tw/constitutionalcourt/en/p03_01.asp?expno=165. The decision provided no immunity protection for local representatives. The Court reasoned that '[t]he Constitution does not ... expressly extend such protection to local representatives of the people, nor do the Constitutions of other countries. Among them, some, such as that of Japan, do not extend such protection to local representatives (See the decision by the Grand Tribunal of the Supreme Court of Japan on May 24, 1967)...'.

to support its decision to extend less immunity to local councilors given the silent nature of the Constitution.[53] That year was 1980, 35 years after the suspension of Japanese colonial rule and 10 years before the dawn of democratic and constitutional reforms in the late 1980s. The Court's first use of foreign precedents generated no controversy at all. It is interesting to note that the applicant in this case referred to a decision of the US Supreme Court which obtained no attention from the Court.[54]

The second case in which the Court directly referred to foreign precedents was JY Interpretation No 342.[55] 14 years had passed after the first time the Court cited a foreign decision,[56] and political and social contexts had changed dramatically. Now, the Court—since its unprecedented decision to order a new election for national representatives in JY Interpretation No 261—assumed an important role in resolving constitutional disputes during the initial process of democratic and constitutional reforms.[57] In this case, the Court was requested to decide whether three controversial Bills concerning national security organs were passed despite the chaotic voting situation with bloody filibusters.[58] Although the applications did not mention any foreign precedents, the Court on its own initiative referred to three foreign precedents: one from the US Supreme Court,[59] another from the Japanese Supreme Court,[60] and the other from the German Federal Constitutional Court.[61]

---

[53] Although the Constitution expressly extends immunity to national representatives, it remains silent regarding local councillors. This is similar to the way that the Japanese Constitution deals with local councillors' immunity. The Court argues that the silent nature of the Constitution justifies less, if not no, constitutional immunity for local councillors and cited a Japanese Supreme Court decision that rendered the same argument.

[54] The applicant was the Control Yuan, a functional equivalent to the Ombudsman.

[55] JY Interpretation No 342 (8 April 1994). An English translation is available at www.judicial.gov.tw/constitutionalcourt/en/p03_01.asp?expno=342. The decision held the challenged statutes constitutional.

[56] During this time, there were only about 10 interpretations whose separate opinions referred to foreign legal authorities.

[57] JY Interpretation No 261 (21 June 1990). An English translation is available at www.judicial.gov.tw/constitutionalcourt/en/p03_01.asp?expno=261.

[58] Starting in 1993, one third of legislators may petition the Court if in their exercise of constitutional functions they have doubts about the proper application of relevant constitutional provisions or have doubts about the constitutionality of relevant laws. *Interpretation No 342* was the result of such petitions.

[59] In its reasoning, the Court wrote: '... The judgment of the United States Federal Supreme Court in 1890 states that bills of act which have been signed by the leaders of both houses and which have been submitted to the President for approval and delivered to the State Secretary shall be considered passed in the state council without having to refer to the meeting minutes or the relevant documents of the two houses. This is based on the principle of separation of powers in that each department is equal and there is mutual respect amongst the departments. As such, the review power of the judiciary authorities with respect to these matters shall be subject to constraints (See Field v Clark, 143 US 649)'.

[60] In its reasoning, the Court wrote: '... A judgment of the Japan Supreme Court in 1962 states that since the Amendment to the Police Act has been resolved by both houses and has been promulgated in accordance with the legal procedures, the court shall respect the self-regulating nature of the two houses and shall not adjudicate the facts pertaining to the stipulation of the rules of assembly which are referred to in the notion of appeal in determining the validity or invalidity thereof (Judgment of the Japan Supreme Court, March 7, 1962)'.

[61] In its reasoning, the Court wrote: '... The judgment of the German Federal Constitutional Court in 1977 also states that unless the rules of assembly are in violation of the Constitution, matters relating to the progress of the meeting and the discipline thereof shall fall within the domain of the self-regulation of the state council. If during the review process there is participation by members from different parties and there is no fundamental dispute at the time of the voting, and, at the time of the voting, irrespective

The majority opinion discussed each of these cases in detail to support its arguments for parliamentary autonomy. It argued that based upon the separation of powers, any judgment concerning the legislative process should be left for the legislature. As a result, the constitutionality of three controversial legislative enactments was sustained.

Unlike the first time, however, the Court's lengthy and detailed discussions of foreign precedents invited strong disagreement. A concurring opinion delivered by Justice Herbert HP Ma, who has a doctorate from Harvard Law School, criticised the majority opinion's direct quotation of foreign precedents. Justice Ma argued that the Court had to render decisions and establish its own dignity and authority based upon interpretative powers vested in it by the domestic Constitution and relevant laws. He stressed that it would be unwise for the Court to rely upon external sources including foreign precedents when rendering decisions. However, Justice Ma stressed that if there was any need to refer to foreign precedents to reinforce or support judicial reasoning, it must be done in quotations or footnotes but not in the main text. In his view, two things must be distinguished: *a mental process* by which the Court consulted internal or external legal sources for reaching its conclusion and *a decision-making process* in the form of *reasoning* whose authority must be confined within the normative parameters of the Constitution. Despite his discord with direct references to foreign precedents, Justice Ma made no objection to indirect references of foreign sources in quotations or footnotes. For him, while the Court's decision and reasoning must be confined within endogenous legal sources, exogenous sources would still be allowed insofar as they were referred to indirectly in quotations or footnotes.

Since Justice Ma's disagreement with referencing foreign precedents in JY Interpretation No 342, references to foreign precedents became rare in majority opinions. The third time one appeared was in JY Interpretation No 392, where foreign precedents were provided and argued by applicants as well as by government officials in oral arguments heard by the Court. In this case, the Court ruled unconstitutional the relevant provisions of the criminal procedural code that authorised prosecutorial powers to detain criminal suspects.[62] Citing German and Japanese criminal procedures, the Court argued that the power to detain criminal suspects was part of judicial power and this was made express in the Constitution. However, in the defence made by the Ministry of Justices, the prosecutorial power of detention was supported by relevant provisions in the International Covenant on Civil and Political Rights and the European Convention on Human Rights. In response,

---

of the number of persons in attendance, if no more than five members raise any objections thus confirming that there is no support for a resolution, then the effect of the resolution would not be affected (BverfGe 44, 308ff)'.

[62] JY Interpretation No 392 (22 December 1995). An English translation is available at www.judicial.gov.tw/constitutionalcourt/en/p03_01.asp?expno=392. The decision held the challenged statutory provisions unconstitutional. The Court reasoned that '... the judgment rendered by the European Human Rights Court in the Pauwels Case (1988) indicated that, if the law confers the authority of criminal investigation and indictment on the same officer, even though the officer exercises powers independently, his neutrality in carrying out his duties should be considered highly suspect, hence, it violates the provision "other officer authorised by law to exercise judicial power" referred to in Article 5, Paragraph 3, of said Convention'.

however, the Court referred directly to a 1988 decision by the ECtHR to support a narrower reading of such provision, thus forbidding prosecutors from exercising any detention powers.

The most recent direct reference to foreign precedents in a majority opinion was in JY Interpretation No 499.[63] In this case, the Court reviewed the constitutionality of constitutional amendments and struck them down. To support its power in scrutinising procedurally and substantially the constitutionality of constitutional amendments, the Court referred to German, Italian and even Turkish constitutional courts' decisions. It discussed two US Supreme Court decisions[64] and argued that despite the political question doctrine, the US Supreme Court was never prevented entirely from the scrutiny of unconstitutional constitutional amendments. Similar to JY Interpretation No 392, foreign precedents were provided by both parties in their petition to the Court. However, the cases cited in the majority opinions were from the justices themselves. Our interview with one of the justices who obtained a doctorate from Austria and participated in this case reveals how this justice was able to find the two precedents of the Italian and Turkish Constitutional Courts by reading a German legal magazine.

IV. IMPLICIT INFLUENCES OF FOREIGN PRECEDENTS

Given the minimal explicit citations of foreign precedent, in this part we try to find ways to measure empirically implicit influences of foreign precedents on Taiwan's Constitutional Court. As discussed earlier, the Court's explicit citations of foreign precedents in majority opinions were sparse but explicit citations of foreign precedents in separate opinions have been on a steady climb.

If individual justices are influenced by foreign precedents and clearly state so in their separate opinions, it is reasonable to assume that majority opinions are also influenced—at least indirectly or implicitly—by foreign precedents. Hence, an empirically feasible way to discern implicit influences of foreign precedents

---

[63] JY Interpretation No 499 (24 April 2000). An English translation is available at www.judicial.gov.tw/constitutionalcourt/en/p03_01.asp?expno=499. The Decision held that the challenged constitutional amendments were unconstitutional. The Court reasoned that '... Among judicial precedents in several countries, cases have shown that their constitutional courts not only take on procedural matters, but also conduct review on substantive matters; for example, the German Bundesverfassungsgericht (Federal Court of Constitution, or BVG) ... the Italian Corte Constituzionale (Court of Constitution) decision ... and the Turkish Court of Constitution Judgment ... [However, for countries that place] differences on both the institution and the process of the constitutional amendment and legislative enactment (such as the United States), diverse viewpoints do exist. Citing the U.S. Supreme Court's opinion on Coleman v. Miller, 307 US 433 (1939), the Related Institution claimed that Congress has complete and exclusive power in deciding the process of amending the Constitution without subjecting itself to judicial review ... However, the Coleman holding that the court lacks jurisdiction because ratification of a constitutional amendment is a "political question" has not achieved the status of majority opinion in the United States. In a 1984 case involving a California citizens' initiative to amend the Constitution, Justice William Rehnquist, writing on behalf of that court, held that Coleman cannot be read expansively to conclude that the process of amending the Constitution is a matter of "political question," thereby exempt from judicial review (Uhler v the American Federation of Labor-Congress of Industrial Organizations, 468 US 1310 (1984))...'.

[64] *Coleman v Miller*, 307 US 433 (1939); *Uhler v AFLCIO*, 468 US 1310 (1984).

is to examine the use of foreign precedents in separate opinions, thus assuming their influences upon majority opinions. As this study has shown, in Taiwan's Constitutional Court, concurring opinions are more likely to cite foreign precedents than dissenting opinions. While justices have been extremely cautious about explicitly citing foreign precedents in majority opinions, separate opinions faced no such criticism and justices enjoyed much greater freedom in opinion writing.

This study screens the concurring and dissenting opinions that cited foreign precedents to examine if there could be any assumed linkage between the cited foreign precedents and the reasoning of the majority opinions. The standard instances include—but are not limited to—citations in separate opinions to illustrate further standards of review, balancing tests, key factors of consideration and unenumerated rights. In considering dissenting opinions, this study includes those with clear contentions of majority opinions. The result is shown in Table 3.

From January 1949 to June 2008, there are 29 interpretations (out of a total of 644 interpretations) that can reasonably be found to be influenced by foreign precedents cited in their separate concurring or dissenting opinions. The ratio is 5.1 per cent, which is considerably higher than the ratio of explicit citations in majority opinions (0.62 per cent) but barely elevates the Court to the category of courts that frequently cites foreign precedents. It is no surprise that implicit influences are found in most concentrations of recent interpretations that have a higher ratio of foreign

Table 3: Explicit and Implicit Influence of Foreign Precedents on JY Interpretations

	Until 06/2008 03–10)	1st term (48–58)	2nd term (58–67)	3rd term (67–76)	4th term (76–85)	5th term (85–94)	6th term (94–03)
Interpretations with Explicit Foreign Precedent Citations	0	0	0	1	0	1	2
Interpretations with Implicit Influence of Foreign Precedent Citations in Separate Opinions	21	0	0	1	0	0	7
Interpretations with Separate Opinions Citing Foreign Precedents	28	0	4	2	3	7	18
Total Number of Interpretations	78	79	43	24	53	167	200

Source: by author

precedent citations in separate opinions. With the rise of foreign precedent citations in separate opinions, a greater degree of implicit influence of foreign precedents cited in separate opinions can reasonably be linked to the reasoning provided by majority opinions.

Having only implicit influences on majority opinions, foreign precedents cited in separate, particularly concurring, opinions are typically those leading precedents that enjoy paramount or even canonical jurisprudential importance in foreign jurisdictions, such as free speech and due process of law cases from the US, or German case law on human dignity or proportionality. For instance, in 29 interpretations, most implicit influences by US precedents are concerned with free speech, religious freedom, the right of privacy and independent agency. At the same time, most influences from German case law are involved with human dignity, occupational freedom (the pharmacist decision), judicial review, the principle of legal trust and constitutional organs' royal duty to the Constitution. In one case where the case law of the ECtHR has an implicit influence as exhibited from the citation in the separate opinion, it concerns the rights of criminal defendants, the core of European human rights jurisprudence. Hence, although these foreign precedents were explicitly cited in the separate opinions but not in the majority opinions, their influence on the majority opinions can be fairly inferred particularly given their paramount or even canonical jurisprudential importance in their respective foreign jurisdictions.

V. CONCLUSION

As one of the oldest constitutional courts in the world, Taiwan's Constitutional Court has rarely referred to foreign precedents in majority opinions. Our study found only four cases where the Court directly quoted foreign precedents in majority opinions. Despite this reservation, however, the referencing of foreign precedents in separate opinions was on a steady rise, and 13.4 per cent of separate opinions directly referred to foreign precedents.

Most citations of foreign precedents were provided by justices from scholarly backgrounds rather than justices with backgrounds as career lawyers. Our study finds an apparent linkage between justices' foreign educational backgrounds and the jurisdictional preference of their foreign precedents. The predominant number of German precedents were cited by justices who studied in Germany for Masters or doctoral degrees. Similarly, most American cases were cited by justices with American educational connections. Thus, the change in the composition of justices' backgrounds would also affect the most-cited jurisdictions. Justices with scholarly backgrounds are the primary agents introducing foreign precedents to the Court. No other factors would have a similar influence upon the Court's use of foreign sources.

16

United States of America: First Cautious Attempts of Judicial Use of Foreign Precedents in the Supreme Court's Jurisprudence

ANGIOLETTA SPERTI[*]

TABLE OF CONTENTS

I. Introduction: The Context 393
II. Some Remarks on the Method of Research 394
III. Short Account of the Scholarly Debate 398
IV. Results and Conclusions of the Empirical Analysis 403
    A. The Early Cases 403
    B. The More Recent Cases 404
    C. Other Cases of Great Interest 408
V. Conclusions 409

I. INTRODUCTION: THE CONTEXT

ALTHOUGH THE CULTURAL and historical origins of the US Constitution reveal deep lines of influence between the Framers and some of the most respected European authorities, American constitutional law appeared until a few years ago 'especially insular and inward looking'.[1] The United States was mostly an *exporter* of constitutional principles and—as Judge Calabresi put into evidence[2]—'if a doctrine was not tried in the United States there was no place else to look'. In the past some American scholars have criticised the insularity of American courts and scholarship.[3] Such insularity was due mostly to the lack of comparative

---

[*] Researcher in Law, University of Pisa, Department of Public Law, Pisa, Italy; LLM University of California, Los Angeles (USA); PhD Scuola Superiore S Anna, Pisa, Italy.
  The author wishes to thank Prof Paolo G Carozza (University of Notre Dame, Law School) for his valuable comments and suggestions.
[1] R Schlesinger, HB Baade, PE Herzog and EM Wise, *Comparative Law. Cases, Text, Materials* (New York, Foundation Press, 1998) p 7.
[2] *United States v Then*, 56 F3d 464 (1995) at 468–69, Calabresi dissenting.
[3] Schlesinger, Baade, Herzog and Wise, *Comparative Law*, n 1 above, p 7.

law courses in the law schools' curricula and to the difficulties arising from poor knowledge of the less widespread foreign languages.[4]

The wide diffusion of judicial review worldwide, even in common law countries, and the greater attention paid by American scholars to comparative law, finally forced changes in the federal courts and at the level of the Supreme Court. The first Supreme Court case showing greater attention to foreign law—*Lawrence v Texas*[5]—and the publication of the first handbooks of comparative constitutional law where cases by foreign constitutional courts were translated into English and commented on revealed a change of perspective in constitutional law.

In the last few years a complex and articulate debate on the opportunity of using foreign case law in US courts (especially the US Supreme Court) and foreign courts arose: in no other country has the citation of foreign cases received similar attention by scholars or stirred such a heated debate as in the United States.

The debate also involved the political branches of government whose hostility to foreign law seemed stronger than that of some Supreme Court Justices. Furthermore,

> what is critical to the divergence ... is that while the Supreme Court's use of international and foreign law has been primarily confined to domestic law, Congress and the Executive have cast suspicion on international jurisprudence at both the domestic and international levels.[6]

Several resolutions[7] and Bills[8] have been introduced in Congress since 2003 in order to prohibit American courts from relying upon foreign materials but none of them has been passed or come up for a full vote.

II. SOME REMARKS ON THE METHOD OF RESEARCH

Following on from this background, this report aims to show that, although in the United States the use of foreign citations is not so extensive as it is in other common

---

[4] See especially N Dorsen, M Rosenfeld, A Sajó and S Baer, *Comparative Constitutionalism. Cases and Materials* (St Paul, Thomson West, 2003); V Jackson and M Tushnet, *Comparative Constitutional Law* (New York, Foundation Press, 1999).

[5] *Lawrence v Texas*, 539 US 558 (2003).

[6] See, eg, DT Hutt and LK Parshall, 'Divergent Views on the Use of International and Foreign Law: Congress and the Executive Versus the Court' (2007) 33 *Ohio Northern University Law Review* 113, 124.

[7] HR Res 468, 108th Cong (2003); HR Res 446, 108th Cong (2003); HR Res 568, 108th Cong (2004); HR Res 568 108th Cong (2004); H Res 97, 109th Cong 3 (2005); S Res 92, 109th Cong (2005); HR Res 97, 109th Cong (2005).

[8] Constitution Restoration Act of 2004, HR 3799, 108th Cong (2004); American Justice for American Citizens Act, HR 4118, 108th Cong (2004); S 2082, 108th Cong (2004); S 520, 109th Cong (2005); HR 1070, 109th Cong (2005); 112th Cong. To amend title 28, United States Code, to prevent the misuse of foreign law in Federal courts, and for other purposes. (Introduced in House—IH) [HR 973 IH]; [111th] Proposing an amendment to the Constitution of the United States relating to the use of foreign law as authority in Federal courts. (Introduced in House—IH)[HJ.RES.106.IH]; [111th] To prevent the undermining of the judgments of courts of the United States by foreign courts, and for other purposes. (Introduced in Senate—IS)[S.580.IS] S.3394 [110th] To prevent the undermining of the judgments of courts of the United States by foreign courts, and for other purposes. (Introduced in Senate—IS.)

law countries, recent developments in jurisprudence and scholarly debate should be considered novel and of great interest.

First of all it is important to note the following premises which underlie the research:

(a) For the purposes of this report, only references to foreign cases have been taken into consideration. Such citations—unlike other citations we will mention in the following paragraphs—often reveal the emergence of a dialogue among constitutional courts and the use of comparative law as an aid to constitutional interpretation.[9]

(b) We thought it useful to divide the relevant cases into two groups: a) the first group[10] includes the cases which are the most relevant ones for the purpose of the research as they actually contain explicit foreign citations; b) the second group[11] includes cases that cite foreign jurisprudence but that were decided in the early phases of the US Supreme Court's activity. Although they refer to foreign cases, in the early years citations were mostly due—as we will clarify later on—to the lack of American case law on the topic or due to a particular area of law being taken into consideration (ie admiralty law issues). Finally, c) the third group[12] comprises a few cases which *do not* explicitly cite foreign precedents but could provide useful information on the perspectives of Supreme Court Justices on the use of foreign jurisprudence and on the opportunity for a dialogue among constitutional/supreme courts.

(c) In our opinion, generic references to English law (such as those frequently occurring in the first Supreme Court case law) should be considered neither as a form of dialogue among courts, nor as a proper use of foreign law for constitutional interpretation.[13] In the formative era of American law, references to English law were usually useful to emphasise differences and analogies between the new American system of government and the English tradition.

---

[9] The empirical research was performed through keyword searches on the Lexis-Nexis databases.
[10] See below at § IV.B.
[11] See below at § IV.A.
[12] See below at § IV.C.
[13] See eg, *United States v Wilson*, 32 US (7 Pet) 150, 162 (1833) (pardons); *Ex parte McNiel*, 80 US (13 Wall) 236 (1871) at 239 (maritime law; pilots of vessels); *Wilkerson v Utah* 99 US 130, 134 (1879) ('At common law, neither the mode of executing the prisoner nor the time or place of execution was necessarily embodied in the sentence. Directions in regard to the former were usually given by the judge in the calendar of capital cases prepared by the clerk at the close of the term'); *Hurtado v California*, 110 US 516 (1884) 530–31 (containing a long digression on the English notion of due process of law where the Bonham's case was also cited); *Campbell v Holt*, 115 US 620 (1885) at 622 (on the doctrine of prescription); *Geer v Connecticut*, 161 US 519 at 527 (1896); *Duncan v Louisiana*, 391 US 145, 151–52 (1968) (on the origins of the trial by jury); *Cunnius v Reading Sch Dist*, 198 US 458, 469–70 (1905) (on 'the general power of government to provide for the administration of the estates of absentees'); *Twining v New Jersey*, 211 US 78, 110–11 (1908) (exemption from self-incrimination); *Poe v Ullman*, 367 US 497, 548 (1961); *Banco Nacional de Cuba v Sabbatino*, 376 US 398, 421 n 21 (1964) (on the origins of the act of state doctrine); *Neb Press Ass'n v Stuart*, 427 US 539, 566 n 10 (1976); *Smith v California*, 361 US 147, 160–67 (1959) (where Justice Frankfurter mentions two English cases in order to clarify that 'the publication of obscene printed matter was clearly established as a common-law offense in England in 1727'); *Adamson v California*, 332 US 46 (1947) at 64, 68 and 87 (mentioning the 'canons of decency and fairness which express the notions of justice of English-speaking peoples even toward those charged with the most heinous offenses'); *Rochin v California*, 342 US 165 (1952) (on the same topic).

(d) Furthermore, we did not take into consideration citations pertaining to international law, maritime law and international commercial law. For these fields of law, for instance, references to civil law materials were very frequent and required in the absence of American and English studies.[14] At the end of the nineteenth century, in fact, when the United States had developed its own case law, reliance on comparative materials subsided.[15]

(e) At the same time, in the context of this research, generic references to rule of law principles, common law traditions, or the historical roots of a principle, may reflect the purpose of the Court to enliven her arguments instead of an actual use of comparative materials.

(f) For the same reason we also did not take into account generic references to the views of the international community on similar issues.[16]

(g) References to foreign legislation—although important in the general context of the use of comparative law—should be distinguished from references to foreign constitutional cases.[17] Although some methods of interpretation could also be adopted for the interpretation of statutes, we hold that comparing statutory texts sometimes has a different aim such as the evaluation of the consequences of legislative solutions which have been adopted in other countries.[18] In this

---

[14] See generally, R Pound, *The Formative Era of American Law* (New York, Little, Brown and Company, 1938).

[15] See DS Clark, 'The Use of Comparative Law by American Courts' in U Drobnig and S van Erp (eds), *The Use of Comparative Law by Courts* (Kluwer Law International, 1997) 297.

[16] *Grutter v Bollinger*, 539 US 309, 344 (2003) ('The Court's observation that race-conscious programs "must have a logical end point," according with the international understanding of the office of affirmative action'); *Thompson v Oklahoma*, 487 US 815, 830–31 (1988) (plurality opinion) (on the issue of the death penalty for juveniles); *Enmund v Florida*, 458 US 782, 796–97 n 22 (1982) (noting the 'climate of international opinion concerning the acceptability of a particular punishment' and in particular the doctrine of felony murder); *Coker v Georgia*, 433 US 584, 592 (1977) fn 4 ('in almost all of the States and in most of the countries around the world, it would be difficult to support a claim that the death penalty for rape is an indispensable part of the States' criminal justice system'); *Trop v Dulles*, 356 US 86, 102 (1958), referring to the climate of international opinion concerning the acceptability of a particular punishment and in particular to a United Nations survey pertaining to the death penalty in rape cases); *Betts v Brady*, 316 US 455, 462 (1942) ('universal sense of justice'); *Knowlton v Moore*, 178 US 41 (1900) 47–78 (death duties).

[17] See *McCreary County v ACLU*, 125 S Ct 2722, 2748 (2005) (on separation between church and state); *Locke v Davey*, 540 US 712, 734 (2004); *Raines v Byrd*, 521 US 811, 828 (1997) (comparing the US Supreme Court with other constitutional courts on standing to sue); *Burson v Freeman*, 504 US 191, 206 (1992) (showing that most States had incorporated the paper ballot into their electoral system); *McIntyre v Ohio Elections Commission*, 514 US 334, 381–82 (1995) (citing England, Australia, and Canada as foreign democracies that prohibit anonymous campaigning); *Palko v Connecticut*, 302 US 319, 423 (1937) (stating that '[c]ompulsory self incrimination is part of the established procedure in the law of Continental Europe'); *Lochner v New York*, 198 US 45, 71 (1905) (Harlan, J, dissenting) (mentioning that the number of hours a labourer should work continuously was a matter of serious concern among 'civilized peoples' of other nations); *Arver v US*, 245 US 366, 378–79 (1918) (citing foreign legislation on military service); *Cubbins v Mississippi River Commission*, 241 US 351 (1916) (interruption of the natural flow of a river); *United States v Perkins*, 163 US 625 (1896) 627–28 (foreign legislation on inheritance tax); *Knox v Lee*, 79 US 457, 458 (1870) 569.

[18] See, eg, *Miranda v Arizona*, 384 US 436, 486 (1966) (arguing that '[t]he experience in some other countries also suggests that the danger to law enforcement in curbs on interrogation is overplayed. The English procedure since 1912 under the Judges' Rules is significant'); *Muller v Oregon*, 208 US 412, 419 (1907), quoting the 'Brandeis brief' where legislation of seven European countries (imposing a restriction upon the hours of labour that may be required of women) are mentioned; *New York v United States*, 326 US 572, 584 (1946) ('Attempts along similar lines to solve kindred problems arising under the Canadian and Australian Constitutions have also proved a barren process'); *McGowan v Maryland*, 366 US 1101

report, we take into consideration the use of comparative law for the purpose of constitutional interpretation.

(h) Reliance on international case law, treaties or custom is not relevant for the purposes of this research and therefore this report does not take into consideration references to the 'law of nations' during the early days of American history or other cases mentioning the views of the international community on similar issues.[19] Furthermore, we did not take into consideration cases concerning the interpretation of an international treaty.[20]

International law should not be considered equal to foreign law as 'international law and international agreements of the United States are law of the United States and supreme over the law of the several States'.[21] Although there are different perspectives on the relationship between international and domestic law (as, in particular, some support a 'monistic' or internationalist approach while others support a 'dualistic' approach[22]), international law should not be treated as foreign law for the purposes of constitutional interpretation. Instead, in the scholarly debate on the use of foreign case law—not only in the United States—these materials have frequently been taken into consideration

---

(1961); *Poe v Ullman*, n 13 above, 555, Harlan dissenting, fn 16 (mentioned the 'unqualified disapproval of contraception' implicit in the laws of several European countries).

[19] See *Talbot v Jansen*, 3 US (3 Dall) 133 (1795) (law of nations); *Ware v Hylton*, 3 US (3 Dall) 199, 216, 230–31 (1796) (law of nations on confiscation of property); *Murray v Schooner Charming Betsy*, 6 US (2 Cranch) 64, 118 (1804) (holding that congressional statutes should not be construed so as to violate the law of nations); *The Rapid*, 12 US (8 Cranch) 155 (1814) at 159–60 (law of nations); *Worcester v Georgia*, 31 US (6 Pet) 515, 560–61 (1832) (relying on the doctrine of the law of nations); *Columbian Insurance Co of Alexandria v Ashby*, 38 US (13 Pet) 331 (1839) pt 337 (citing Roman law and foreign authorities on piracy); *Jackson v The Magnolia*, 61 US (20 How) 296, 302 (1857) (admiralty law); *The Head Money Cases*, 112 US 580, 597–99 (1884) (interpretation of Act of congress according to a treaty); *Whitney v Robertson*, 124 US 190, 194 (1888) (interpretation of a treaty); *The Chinese Exclusion Case*, 130 US 581, 600, 602–03 (1889) (interpretation of a treaty); *Hilton v Guyot*, 159 US 113, 163 (1895) (this case cites English cases in order to conclude that 'the comity of the United States did not require the court to give conclusive effect to the judgments of the courts of France'); *Jones v United States*, 137 US 202 (1890) (the Court observed that dominion could be acquired by discovery and occupation under the law of nations 'recognized by all civilized States'); *The Paquete Habana*, 175 US 677, 700 and 708 (1900) (relying extensively on international law practice and theory and concluding that '[t]his review of the precedents and authorities on the subject appears to us abundantly to demonstrate that at the present day, by the general consent of the civilized nations of the world, and independently of any express treaty or other public act, it is an established rule of international law, founded on considerations of humanity to a poor and industrious order of men, and of the mutual convenience of belligerent States, that coast fishing vessels, with their implements and supplies, cargoes and crews, unarmed, and honestly pursuing their peaceful calling of catching and bringing in fresh fish, are exempt from capture as prize of war'). See also *Zadvydas v Davis*, 533 US 678, 721 (2001). For a detailed account and analysis of these cases, see SG Calabresi and S Dotson Zimdahl, 'The Supreme Court and Foreign Sources of Law: Two Hundred Years of Practice and the Juvenile Death Penalty Decision' (2005) 47 *William and Mary Law Review* 743, 757 ff.

[20] See, eg, the recent case *Abbott v Abbott*, No 08-645 (US May 17, 2010) where the United States Supreme Court resolved an important issue about the scope of the Hague Convention on Civil Aspects of International Child Abduction (Child Abduction Convention) and for this purpose cited several foreign decisions concerning the interpretation of the Convention's clauses.

[21] Restatement (third) of the Foreign Relations Law of the US: International Law and Agreements as Law of the United States § 111.

[22] On this debate, see JC Yoo, 'Globalism and the Constitution: Treaties, Non-Self-Execution, and the Original Understanding' (1999) 99 *Columbia Law Review* 1955, 1959.

in order to show that the openness of American courts towards foreign law is not novel.

No scholar, as far as we know, has suggested that foreign law might be treated as a source of law in the United States.[23] Justice Breyer emphasised this point arguing that 'comparative use of foreign constitutional decisions will not lead us blindly to follow the foreign court. As I have said before—we are interpreting our own Constitution, not those of other nations'.[24] However, often there is not such a clear assessment of the role of international law in connection with the role of international law within (and in relation to) the American sources of law system.

(i) The empirical research was performed through a keyword search and took into account the Supreme Court's case law from its earliest beginnings. However, Chart 1 refers only to the Rehnquist Court (1986–2004) and the Roberts Court (2004–10 only) in order to show the number of relevant cases out of the total number of cases. This choice was due to the impossibility of drawing a diagram taking into account the total number of US Supreme Court cases since 1789. Furthermore, as we will clarify in the following pages, we consider the use of foreign law as an aid to constitutional interpretation in the United States mostly as a recent development.

(j) However we also took into consideration five cases (decided between 1908 and 2010) although they do not actually cite foreign case law but mostly refer to 'the opinion of the world community' on similar issues, or to foreign legislation. These cases are taken into account in Charts 2, 3 and 4 and discussed in detail in section IV.C.

(k) Finally, in this report citations of foreign cases in the main text of the opinion of the Court have been distinguished from citations in footnotes or in concurring and dissenting opinions. From this point of view, the Supreme Court's decision in *Lawrence v Texas*,[25] where a case of the European Court of Human Rights (ECtHR) is cited in the opinion of the Court, but the use of foreign case law is also discussed in a dissenting opinion, is particularly important in the context of this research.[26]

III. SHORT ACCOUNT OF THE SCHOLARLY DEBATE

In the wide debate on the use of foreign law by American courts, some prominent American scholars support the need to study foreign legal materials and have

---

[23] See, eg, M Tushnet, 'Referring to Foreign Law To Express American Nationhood' (2006) 69 *Albany Law Review* 809, distinguishing between 'uses' and 'references'.

[24] Justice Breyer, 'Keynote Address Before the Ninety-Seventh Annual Meeting of the American Society of International Law (Apr 4, 2003)' (2003) 97 *American Society of International Law Proceedings* 265, 266.

[25] n 5 above.

[26] See, for a similar conclusion, DM Amman, '"Raise The Flag and Let It Talk": On the Use of External Norms in Constitutional Decision Making' in (2004) 4 *International Journal of Constitutional Law (Icon)* 597; MA Case, 'Of "This" and "That" in *Lawrence v Texas*" (2003) *Supreme Court Review* 75; WE Eskridge, '*Lawrence v Texas* and the Imperative of Comparative Constitutionalism?' (2004) 2 *International Journal of Constitutional Law (Icon)* 555.

described the benefits of comparative constitutional law.[27] Anne-Marie Slaughter[28] for instance observed that

> for [Supreme Court Justices], looking abroad simply helps them do a better job at home, in the sense that they can approach a particular problem more creatively or with greater insight. Foreign authority is persuasive because it teaches them something they did not know or helps them see an issue in a different and more tractable light ...

Vicki C Jackson[29] argued that 'approaches taken in other countries may provide helpful empirical information' in interpreting the US Constitution, that 'comparisons can shed light on the distinctive functioning of one's own system' and 'foreign or international legal sources may illuminate "suprapositive" dimensions of constitutional rights' as 'many modern constitutions include individual rights that protect similar values at an abstract level, often inspired by human rights texts'. These rights 'have "universal" aspects, reflecting "the inescapable ubiquity of human beings as a central concern" for any legal system and widespread (though not universal) aspirations for law to constrain government treatment of individuals'.

Michel Rosenfeld has justified the importance of foreign law emphasising the need for the Supreme Court to pursue 'fairness above predictability' and Mark Tushnet described the advantages of a process of judicial 'bricolage'.[30]

However, most scholars do not declare themselves entirely open to the adoption of foreign solutions in constitutional interpretation: even those who support the importance of looking abroad for the purpose of interpreting the American Constitution held that this should be done cautiously in order to avoid mistakes or erroneous interpretations. As Michelman wrote, most law review articles on this topic 'repeat a standard set of arguments that misrepresent the claims made by those who sometimes refer to, or defend the occasional reference to, non-US law in constitutional interpretation'.[31] We share this opinion and we argue that some of

---

[27] See B Ackerman, 'The Rise of World Constitutionalism' (1997) 83 *Vanderbilt Law Review* 771; VC Jackson, 'Constitutional Comparison: Convergence, Resistance, Engagement' (2005) 119 *Harvard Law Review* 109; VC Jackson, 'Comparative Constitutional Federalism and Transnational Judicial Discourse' (2004) 2 *International Journal of Constitutional Law (Icon)* 91; VC Jackson, 'Constitutional Dialogue and Human Dignity: States and Transnational Constitutional Discourse' (2004) 65 *Montana Law Review* 15; VC Jackson, 'Narratives of Federalism: Of Continuities and Comparative Constitutional Experience' (2001) 51 *Duke Law Journal* 223; HH Koh, 'International Law as Part of Our Law' (2004) 98 *American Journal of International Law* 43, 44; HH Koh, 'On American Exceptionalism' (2003) 55 *Stanford Law Review* 1479; HH Koh, 'Paying "Decent Respect" to World Opinion on the Death Penalty' (2002) 35 *University of California at Davis Law Review* 1085; P McFadden, 'Provincialism in United States Courts' (1995) 81 *Cornell Law Review* 4; FI Michelman, 'Reflection' (2004) 82 *Texas Law Review* 1737; M Rosenfeld, 'Constitutional Adjudication in Europe and the United States: Paradoxes and Contrasts' (2004) 2 *International Journal of Constitutional Law* 633, 649; AM Slaughter, 'A Global Community of Courts' (2003) 44 *Harvard International Law Journal* 191; E Stein, 'Uses, Misuses and Nonuses of Comparative Law' (1977) 72 *Northwestern University Law Review* 198; M Tushnet, 'The Possibilities of Comparative Constitutional Law' (1999) 108 *Yale Law Journal* 1225.
[28] Slaughter, 'A Global Community of Courts', n 27 above, 201–02.
[29] Jackson, 'Constitutional Comparisons: Convergence, Resistance, Engagement', n 27 above, 116–18.
[30] M Rosenfeld, 'Constitutional Adjudication in Europe and the United States: Paradoxes and Contrasts', n 25 above, 649; M Tushnet, 'The Possibilities of Comparative Constitutional Law', n 27 above, 1300.
[31] M Tushnet, 'When is Knowing Less Better Than Knowing More? Unpacking the Controversy over Supreme Court Reference to Non-US Law' (2006) 90 *Minnesota Law Review* 1275, 1276.

the arguments which have been advanced against the use of comparative law for the purpose of constitutional interpretation do not properly concern constitutional interpretation: some of these objections in fact pertain to the role of the courts in more general terms and other objections pertain to the risks and the difficulties which all comparative law studies have to face. On the basis of the similarities with the debate—which occurred in the past—on the advantages of comparison from a more general perspective we hold that some of the issues concerning the dialogue among the courts should therefore be discussed from a different point of view.[32]

Furthermore, we think that, especially in the United States, some of the objections arise from an overvaluation of the importance of foreign material in constitutional cases.

However, recent law review articles have set the terms of the debate and described the most discussed objections to the use of foreign law.[33] The 'recurring themes' of the debate concern: a) the use of comparative materials as a threat to democracy and sovereignty; b) the 'technical' difficulties arising from researching the materials and c) the risk of an improper or incorrect use of foreign law due mainly to differences in the social, cultural or economic context.[34]

The first critique—described as 'an American objection'[35]—was advanced by those who believe that the use of foreign materials allocates decision-making power to foreign bodies who lack democratic legitimacy in the United States.[36] This argument is related to the idea that citing foreign law undermines judicial legitimacy by impermissibly expanding judicial discretion. Justice Scalia, for example, moving from an originalistic approach to constitutional interpretation, argues that the judiciary is an undemocratic institution within a political system whose legitimacy is derived from the consent of the governed. On the basis of this assumption, courts should enforce only what was enacted by the elected representatives of the people; unelected judges taking any initiative or exercising any discretion would be behaving in an undemocratic manner. It follows that relying on foreign materials implies an undemocratic exercise of judicial discretion and improper policymaking by the courts.[37] This interpretation also implies that a Court should adhere closely to the text and the original intent of those upon whose authority the legitimacy of the text rests.[38]

---

[32] A Sperti, 'Le difficoltà connesse al ricorso alla comparazione a fini interpretativi nella giurisprudenza costituzionale nel contesto dell'attuale dibattito sull'interpretazione' (2008) 2 *Rivista di Diritto Pubblico Comparato ed Europeo (DPCE)* 1033.

[33] See M Radhert, 'Comparative Constitutional Advocacy' (2007) 56 *American University Law Review* 553 but see also for a detailed analysis and comment, B Markesinis and J Fedtke, 'The Judge as a Comparatist' (2005) 80 *Tulane Law Review* 11, 20; AL Parrish, 'Storm in a Teacup: The US Supreme Court's Use of Foreign Law' (2007) *University of Illinois Law Review* 637.

[34] Although this objection should be properly distinguished from the general 'countermajoritarian objection', in the scholarly debate the former is often combined with the latter to strengthen the arguments questioning the legitimacy of courts.

[35] Markesinis and Fedtke, 'The Judge as a Comparatist', n 33 above, 132.

[36] See especially RA Posner, 'The Supreme Court, 2004 Term: Foreword: A Political Court' (2005) 119 *Harvard Law Review* 31, 84–90; RA Posner, 'No Thanks, We Already Have Our Own Laws: The Court Should Never View a Foreign Legal Decision as a Precedent in Any Way' (2004) 7/8 *Legal Affairs*, also available at legalaffairs.org/issues/July-August-2004/featureposnerjulaug04.msp.

[37] See KI Kersch, 'The New Legal Transnationalism, the Globalized Judiciary, and the Rule of Law' (2005) 4 *Washington University Global Studies Law Review* 345, 346.

[38] For a similar approach see also A Aleinikoff, 'Thinking Outside the Sovereignty Box: Transnational Law and the US Constitution' (2004) 82 *Texas Law Review* 1989, 1993 (who argues that 'sovereignty

On the basis of these arguments, scholars have also described comparative constitutional law in the judicial review context as opportunistic and haphazard.[39] Anderson, for instance, argues that citing foreign law makes it possible for 'judges to troll deeply ... in the world's corpus juris' to reach a politically preferred outcome'[40] an argument that has been also advanced by Chief Justice Roberts in his confirmation hearings and by Richard Posner who talked about the 'promiscuous opportunities' offered by comparative law.[41]

The sovereignty objection therefore also implies a critique concerning the discretionary selection of foreign material, a 'cherry picking' selection where courts will surely succeed in selecting a foreign case that best supports their position and suits the case before them. Ramsey, for instance, has addressed this issue by suggesting guidelines to follow in order to ensure more systematic references to foreign law.[42]

The second objection relates to the practical and more 'technical' difficulties which might arise from the use of foreign law. This argument has been also debated in the past in the context of the difficulties which, in general, comparison between legal systems must face.[43] Difficulties in particular might arise in searching for the material, especially in countries where electronic databases do not exist or are not accessible by foreign scholars and courts. Furthermore, it might be difficult to make sure that the information is up to date[44] and a further limit might be researchers' limited knowledge of foreign languages.[45]

The third objection concerns the risks of improper or incorrect use of foreign law due mainly to differences in the social, cultural and economic context between the borrowing country and the country whose foreign solutions are 'imported'.

---

functions in two senses here: as the supreme legal authority within the nation's territory, and as self-rule. On this account, foreign norms are doubly troubling because they threaten US "sovereignty" by subjecting the nation to the will of other nations and because they conflict with the democratic norm that the people choose the rulers and the rules that govern them. To impose foreign law in the United States is, in effect, to enfranchise nonresident noncitizens. It is lawmaking outside the box'). RH Bork, 'Whose Constitution Is It, Anyway?' (2003) *National Review*, Dec 8, 37; DE Childress III, 'Using Comparative Constitutional Law to Resolve Domestic Federal Questions' (2003) 53 *Duke Law Journal* 193; PW Kahn, 'Interpretation and Authority in State Constitutionalism' (1993) 106 *Harvard Law Review* 1147, 1154; DJ Kochan, 'Sovereignty and the American Courts at the Cocktail Party of International Law: The Dangers of Domestic Judicial Invocations of Foreign and International Law' (2006) 29 *Fordham International Law Journal* 507.

[39] See especially RP Alford, 'The United States Constitution and International Law: Misusing International Sources to Interpret the Constitution' (2004) 98 *American Journal International Law* 57, but see also Parrish, 'Storm in a Teacup' n 33 above, 651.

[40] K Anderson, 'Foreign Law and the US Constitution' (2005) 6/7 *Policy Review* 33, 34.

[41] See Parrish, n 33 above, 661 ff.

[42] MD Ramsey, 'International Materials and Domestic Rights: Reflections on Atkins and Lawrence' (2004) 98 *American Journal of International Law* 69.

[43] See generally, K Zweigert and H Kötz, *Introduzione al diritto comparato* (Milano, Giuffrè, 1992) 34 ff and, regarding the Italian scholarly debate, R Sacco (ed), *L'apporto della comparazione alla scienza giuridica* (Milano, Giuffrè, 1980) (in particular the essays by G Bognetti, A Pizzorusso, G Zagrebelsky and V Denti).

[44] On these objections, see especially Markesinis and Fedtke, n 33 above, 112 ff and R Hirschl, 'The Question of Case Selection in Comparative Constitutional Law' in (2005) 53 *American Journal of Comparative Law* 125.

[45] Posner, 'The Supreme Court, 2004 Term: Foreword: A Political Court', n 36 above, but see also EA Young, 'Foreign Law and the Denominator Problem' (2005) 119 *Harvard Law Review* 148, 165, who describes the risks of decision costs and error costs when courts use comparative materials lacking international legal training as well as adequate knowledge of foreign languages.

The so-called 'cultural objection' is also related to the presumption that the adoption of solutions which have been accepted in other countries, in particular in the context of the protection of human rights, may lead to the emergence of universal values or to a universal 'common core' of human rights[46] therefore involving the risk of disregarding the (social, cultural, etc) peculiarities of each legal system.[47] From an opposite point of view, other scholars held instead that 'without regard to whether problems and solutions are essentially similar across different constitutional systems, one can maintain that there is a significant degree of congruence between problems and their possible solutions across the spectrum of contemporary constitutional democracy'.[48]

Scholars have analysed deeply the reasons why Americans regard the United States as fundamentally different from all other nations and its Constitution as unique among world Constitutions.[49] According to Steven Calabresi

> the ferocious battles we have over the meaning of the Constitution and the confirmation of Supreme Court Justices can be explained by the fact that Americans see the Constitution as a quasi-religious creed that explicates America's exceptional mission. The Constitution is not merely a law; for us, it is our state written book of common prayer. To control the meaning of the Constitution is nothing less than to control America's exceptional mission in the world.[50]

Sujit Choudhry has described this 'legal particularism' as a doctrine which emphasises that 'legal norms and institutions generally ... emerge from and reflect particular national circumstances, most centrally a nation's history and political culture'.[51] Moving from this assumption, he argues, some scholars emphasise the importance of the reliance on internal sources of law and on cultural and political history, while others consider the importance of the structure of legal argument, or the 'rhetoric and consciousness' of persons in a given society.[52]

---

[46] See especially DS Law, 'Generic Constitutional Law' (2005) 89 *Minnesota Law Review* 652 and Posner, 'The Supreme Court, 2004 Term: Foreword: A Political Court', n 36 above.

[47] See also JO McGinnis, 'Foreign to Our Constitution' (2006) 100 *Northwestern University Law Review* 303, 308; CF Rosenkrantz, 'Against Constitutional Borrowings and Other Nonauthoritative Uses of Foreign Law' (2003) 1 *International Journal of Constitutional Law (ICON)* 269, 294 (arguing that 'borrowing and dialogic uses of foreign constitutional norms by courts are problematic'). The cultural objection has been advanced also by those who also criticised the reference to foreign materials as 'undemocratic'. See above, fns 38 and 37 and corresponding text.

[48] See Dorsen, Rosenfeld, Sajò and Baer, *Comparative Constitutionalism*, n 4 above, 8 (who also argue that 'if there were a universal ideal of "constitutionalism," then all constitutions could be evaluated according to the same criteria. Moreover, consistent with the prescriptions of constitutionalism, one could determine in what respects all constitutions ought to be alike and in what respects they could legitimately differ'. For an overview of the debate see Markesinis and Fedtke, n 33 above, 119 ff; Radhert, n 33 above, 592 ff.

[49] See SG Calabresi, 'American Exceptionalism and the Supreme Court's Practice of Relying on Foreign Law' (2006) 86 *Boston University Law Review* 1335 who analyses the American ideological tradition of proclaiming and believing that the United States is an exceptional country, different from every other country in the world and traces this popular tradition of American exceptionalism from its European and Puritan roots to the present day; M Tushnet, *Taking the Constitution Away from the Courts* (Princeton, Princeton University Press, 1999) 181–82, 188–93.

[50] Calabresi, 'American Exceptionalism', n 49 above, 1340.

[51] S Choudhry, 'Globalization in Search of Justification: Toward a Theory of Comparative Constitutional Interpretation' (1999) 74 *Indiana Law Journal* 819, 830–32.

[52] For an account of this debate, see Choudhry, n 4 above, 831, quoting WP Alford, 'On the Limits of "Grand Theory" in Comparative Law' (1986) 61 *Washington Law Review* 945 (1986); F Schauer, 'Free Speech and the Cultural Contingency of Constitutional Categories' (1993) 14 *Cardozo Law Review* 865 and GP Fletcher, 'Constitutional Identity' (1993) 14 *Cardozo Law Review* 737.

This objection has been also taken into consideration by Supreme Court Justices: in a well-known opinion in *Thompson v Oklahoma*,[53] Justice Scalia wrote that 'we must never forget that it is a Constitution for the United States of America that we are expounding' and in *Printz v United States*, argued that 'comparative analysis [is] inappropriate to the task of interpreting a constitution.'[54]

Answering this objection Justice Breyer wrote that

> of course, we are interpreting our own Constitution, not those of other nations, and there may be relevant political and structural differences between their systems and our own ... But their experience may nonetheless cast an empirical light on the consequences of different solutions to a common legal problem.[55]

IV. RESULTS AND CONCLUSIONS OF THE EMPIRICAL ANALYSIS

A. The Early Cases

Although the United States Supreme Court has made extensive use of foreign materials (case law and legislation) since her early period of activityfrom early on, the use of foreign law as an aid to constitutional interpretation (or as a means of dialogue among constitutional courts) should be considered a recent development.[56]

The empirical analysis showed 19 cases which explicitly referred to foreign jurisprudence in the early period of American history.[57] In particular, most of the early citations of foreign cases occurred in the first 50 years of activity of the US Supreme Court when, in some fields of the law, no national jurisprudence had yet been developed. Furthermore, most of the cases dealt with admiralty law issues (especially piracy) or with slavery (sale or capture of slaves), two fields of the law which involved relationships with foreign nations and where the development of customary practices (in particular through judicial decisions) was particularly relevant for the solution of the American cases.

It should also be noted that some of the early cases reveal the intention of the Supreme Court to underline differences and analogies with the English tradition: for instance, the Court clarifies that English cases are mentioned as Justices are more familiar with them. In *Rose v Himely*,[58] for instance, Chief Justice Marshall wrote:

---

[53] *Thompson v Oklahoma*, n 16 above, 868, fn 4.
[54] *Printz v United States*, 521 US 898, 921 fn 11 (1997).
[55] *Printz v United States*, n 54 above, 977 (Breyer, dissenting).
[56] The development occurred mostly during the Rehnquist Court and the Roberts Court. For this reason in Chart 1 we show the number of references as a percentage of all decisions taking into consideration these two periods.
[57] *Chisholm v Georgia*, 2 US (2 Dall) 419 (1793); *Calder v Bull*, 3 US (3 Dall) 386, 391 (1798); *Ex parte Bollman*, 8 US (4 Cranch) 75 (1807); *Rose v Himely*, 8 US (4 Cranch) 241, 270–71 (1808); *Brown v United States*, 12 US (8 Cranch) 110, 143–44 (1814); *M'Coul v Lekamp's Administratrix*, 15 US (2 Wheat) 111, 117 n 1 (1817); *United States v Smith*, 18 US (5 Wheat) 153, 163 (1820); *Johnson v McIntosh*, 21 US (8 Wheat) 543, 572–84 (1823); *The Antelope*, 23 US (10 Wheat) 66, 116–18 (1825); *Ogden v Saunders*, 25 US (12 Wheat) 213, 223 (1827); *Ker v Illinois*, 119 US 436 (1886) at 444; *Dred Scott v Sandford*, 60 US (19 How) 393 (1856); *Osborn v Nicholson*, 80 US (13 Wall) 654 (1871) 660; *Reynolds v United States*, 98 US 145 (1878) at 158; *Juilliard v Greenman*, 110 US 421 (1884) 447; *Place v Norwich & New York Transportation Co*, 118 US 468 (1886) at 494; *Bram v United States*, 168 US 532 (1897) 545; *Hovey v Elliott*, 167 US 409 (1897) at 420–23.
[58] *Rose v Himely*, n 57 above, 270–71.

We find, that in the courts of England, whose decisions are particularly mentioned, because *we are best acquainted with them*, and because, as is believed, *they give to foreign sentences as full effect as are given to them in any part of the civilized world*, the position that the sentence of a foreign court is conclusive with respect to what it professes to decide, is uniformly qualified with the limitation that it has, in the given case, jurisdiction of the subject-matter (emphasis added).[59]

In other cases citations aim to demonstrate the similarities with England, or long-established common law traditions, on fundamental principles (ie habeas corpus). Other cases, conversely, show the Framers' intent to distinguish the newly-established nation from her mother country.

For these reasons, although the early cases provide useful indications about the importance of citations of foreign cases in the first years of the Court's activity, they should be treated carefully and considered comparable to the cases where the use of international materials or customary international practices are involved or where 'the views of the international community' are taken into consideration by the Supreme Court. In fact, some of the cases also refer to 'the law of nations' and international materials. Furthermore, most of the early cases frequently relied heavily on admiralty law writings and on international law handbooks by European scholars.

B. The More Recent Cases

Since 1900, the most relevant case for the purposes of this research is *Lawrence v Texas*,[60] where the Supreme Court addressed the validity of a Texas statute making it a crime for two persons of the same sex to engage in certain intimate sexual conduct. Writing for the Court, Justice Kennedy traced the history of American sodomy laws from colonial times. He concluded that the historical grounds relied upon in *Bowers v Hardwick*[61]—a 17-year-old controlling case which addressed a similar issue—were actually 'more complex than the majority opinion and the concurring opinion by Chief Justice Burger indicate'. In order to support the overruling of *Bowers*, Justice Kennedy also mentioned an ECtHR case, *Dudgeon v United Kingdom*,[62] and clarified that this decision was at odds with the premise of *Bowers*.

Lawrence is very important as the citation of a foreign case is not only explicit but also expressed in the text of the opinion of the Court. This makes it possible to distinguish *Lawrence* from the 13 cases decided since the end of the nineteenth century and mentioning foreign precedents and from other cases relevant for the purpose of the research (as shown in Chart 4). In particular, before *Lawrence*, cases mostly contained foreign citations in a footnote (seven cases) or in a concurring or dissenting opinion (three cases). 11 cases contained citations in the majority opinion.

The prominent position of the citation in the main argument of the Court's opinion was deeply criticised by Justice Scalia who, in his dissent (joined by Chief Justice Rehnquist and Justice Thomas) argued that

---

[59] Ibid.
[60] *Lawrence*, n 5 above at 576–7.
[61] *Bowers v Hardwick*, 478 US 186 (1986).
[62] 45 Eur Ct H R (1981) at 52.

[c]onstitutional entitlements do not spring into existence ... because foreign nations decriminalize conduct ... Court's discussion of these foreign views (ignoring, of course, the many countries that have retained criminal prohibitions on sodomy) is therefore meaningless dicta. Dangerous dicta, however, since 'this Court ... should not impose foreign moods, fads, or fashions on Americans'.[63]

If we take into account the Supreme Court cases since the end of the nineteenth century, only two other cases gave similar relevance to foreign citations: *Roe v Wade*,[64] on abortion, and *Wolf v Colorado*,[65] on illegal search and seizure. In *Roe* the Supreme Court quoted the 1939 English case of *Rex v Bourne*, which held that an abortion performed to save the life of the mother was exempted from the criminal penalties of the Offences Against the Person Act of 1861.[66] In *Wolf*, the Court cited several English and commonwealth cases which held admissible evidence obtained by illegal search and seizure.[67] However, it should be noted that in both cases citations were due to the lack of Supreme Court jurisprudence on the topics, whereas in *Lawrence* foreign citations aimed to support the majority's overruling of *Bowers*.

The other Supreme Court cases mentioning foreign precedents are very limited. We are aware of two cases with explicit citations of foreign decisions in the dissenting or concurring opinions[68] and of five cases containing an explicit citation in the footnotes[69] out of a total of nine recent cases containing explicit citations. References to foreign precedents as a percentage of all decisions (during the Rehnquist Court) were approximately 0.3 per cent of all decisions (as shown in Chart 1). No case contains an explicit citation of a foreign case during the Roberts Court, in particular from 2004 until 2010, although this period will be taken into consideration in section IV.C for some cases of great interest from a comparative point of view.

Most of the cases (Chart 2) dealt with human rights and the death penalty (nine cases, ie approximately 72 per cent out of a total of 13 cases) although it should be noted that this number refers also to five other cases that we considered relevant for the purpose of the research and these will be discussed in section IV.C). Only three cases are related to due process of law or to other fair trial guarantees. In Chart 2 we show that cases pertaining to these issues represent approximately 28 per cent of the total number of cases (13) containing foreign citations.

If we take into consideration the purpose of the citations, it is possible to infer from the citations that they are usually due to the Supreme Court wishing to show how similar issues have been addressed elsewhere. This purpose is stated explicitly by the Supreme Court in the above-mentioned *Lawrence* case but *Knight v California* is also worth a mention, because Justice Breyer stated that a 'growing number of courts outside the United States—courts that accept or assume the lawfulness of the

---

[63] *Lawrence*, n 5 above, Scalia dissenting 710.
[64] *Roe v Wade*, 410 US 113 (1973).
[65] *Wolf v Colorado*, 338 US 25 (1949).
[66] *Roe*, n 64 above, 135–38.
[67] *Wolf*, n 65 above, 30, 39.
[68] *Knight v Florida*, 528 US 990, 997–98 (1999) and *Smith v California*, n 13 above, 160–67.
[69] Washington v Glucksberg, 521 US 702 (1997) 718 fn 16 (but see also fn 8); *Miranda v Arizona*, n 18 above, 486–89 (fns 46 and 59); *Smith v California*, n 13 above, 164 fn 1; *New York v United States*, n 18 above, 580 fn 4, 583 fn 5; *O'Malley v Woodrough*, 307 US 277, 281 fn 8 (1939).

death penalty—have held that lengthy delay in administering a lawful death penalty renders ultimate execution inhuman, degrading, or unusually cruel'.[70]

Furthermore, *Lawrence* should be distinguished by other cases mentioning foreign decisions as the opinion really enters into a discussion of the reasons supporting the different conclusions reached by foreign courts. In other cases—such as the death penalty cases—citations aim to 'acknowledge the overwhelming weight of international opinion against the juvenile death penalty' or to emphasise the general disapproval against the death penalty but there is no substantial analysis of foreign law.[71]

Some other cases use foreign citations in order to emphasise the values the United States shares with other countries, mostly common law countries (first of all England, but also South Africa, New Zealand, Canada and India, with a total of 12 single citations in seven cases).[72] In particular, as shown in Chart 3, citations often remember the long-established English tradition on the protection of fundamental rights. A very limited space is instead usually given to other European countries or to South America (two cases with a total of six citations),[73] Asia (one case with one citation) and Africa (two cases with one citation each).[74]

References to foreign precedents as percentage of all decisions

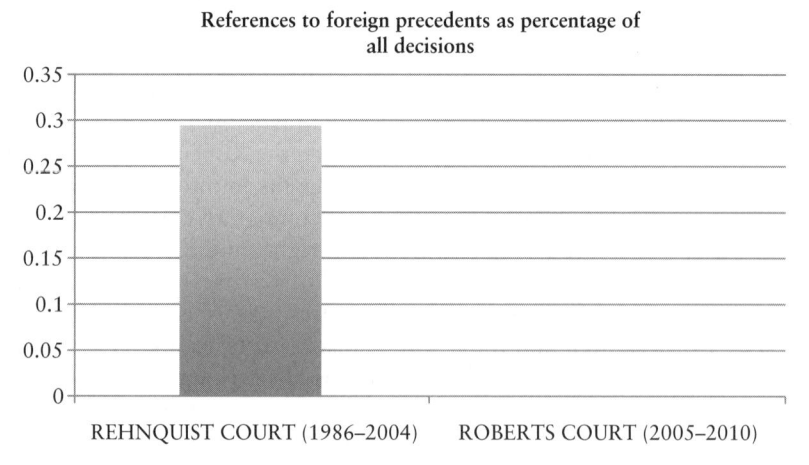

	REHNQUIST COURT (1986–2004)	ROBERTS COURT (2005–2010)
	~0.29	0

Chart 1

---

[70] *Knight*, n 68 above, 990. Justice Breyer also cites jurisprudence from the Privy Council, the Supreme Court of India, the Supreme Court of Zimbabwe and the ECtHR.

[71] See, ie, *Roper v Simmons*, 543 US 551 (2004) at 577 and *Atkins v Virginia*, 536 US 304 (2002) at 317.

[72] See *O'Malley v Woodrough*, n 69 above, 281, fn 8 (mentioning a Supreme Court of South Africa case); *Miranda v Arizona*, n 18 above, 135 (where the Court extensively refers to foreign legislation in particular laws of England, Scotland and India as well as English case law); *Smith v California*, n 13 above, 165 fn 1 (mentioning two English cases in order to clarify that 'the publication of obscene printed matter was clearly established as a common-law offense in England in 1727'); *Washington v Glucksberg*, n 69 above, 718 fn 16 (quoting several commonwealth cases on assisted suicide and referring to New Zealand and Australian legislation); *Knight v Florida*, n 68 above, 997–98 (mentioning jurisprudence from the Privy Council, the Supreme Court of India, the Supreme Court of Zimbabwe and the ECtHR).

[73] See *Washington v Glucksberg*, n 69 above, 718 fn 16 (quoting also a 1997 case of Colombia's Constitutional Court which legalised voluntary euthanasia for terminally ill people); *New York v United States*, n 18 above, 583 fn 5 (mentioning five Brazilian cases on similar issues).

[74] See *Knight v Florida*, n 68 above, 997–98 (mentioning the Supreme Court of India and a Supreme Court of Zimbabwe case); *O'Malley v Woodrough*, n 69 above, 281 fn 8 (mentioning a Supreme Court of South Africa case).

Percentage of human right cases and institutional decisions

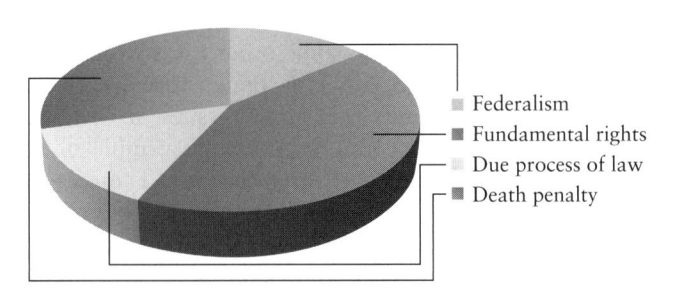

- Federalism
- Fundamental rights
- Due process of law
- Death penalty

Chart 2

Number of references to foreign courts sorted by countries

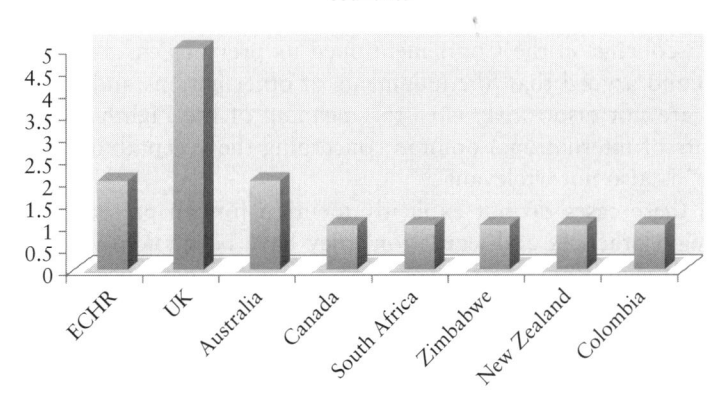

ECHR: 2
UK: 5
Australia: 2
Canada: 1
South Africa: 1
Zimbabwe: 1
New Zealand: 1
Colombia: 1

Chart 3

Number of reference by their source

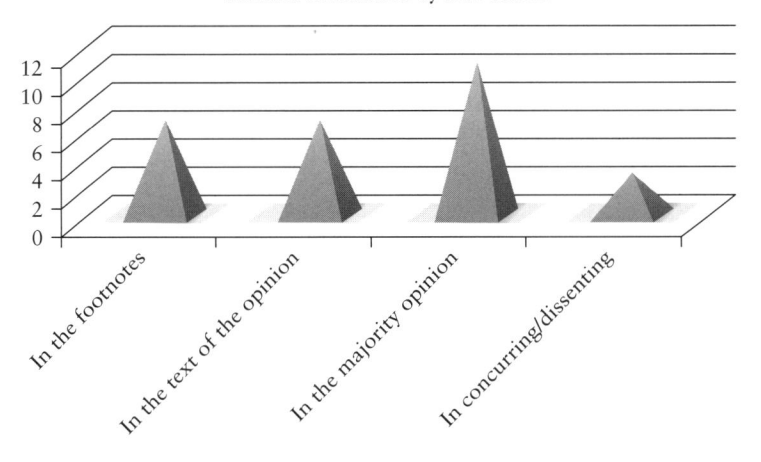

In the footnotes: 8
In the text of the opinion: 8
In the majority opinion: 12
In concurring/dissenting: 4

Chart 4

C. Other Cases of Great Interest

The above-mentioned cases are the most interesting ones for the purposes of the research but it is also worth mentioning some other cases which should be considered useful although they do not actually cite foreign case law but mostly refer to 'the opinion of the world community' on similar issues or to foreign legislation. The more recent cases also refer to *Lawrence* as an example of the comparison with foreign constitutional/supreme court jurisprudence. These cases are: *Roper v Simmons*,[75] on the juvenile death penalty where the Justices engaged in a very interesting discussion on the relevance of international opinion on the use of foreign materials; *Atkins v Virginia*;[76] *Printz v United States*;[77] and *Muller v Oregon*[78] where Justice Brewer remembered the Brandeis' brief quoting foreign legislation on a similar issue.[79]

Finally, in 2010, the Supreme Court released its decision in *Graham v Florida*.[80] The Court held that a juvenile offender's sentence of life imprisonment without possibility of parole for a non-homicide crime violated the Federal Constitution's Eighth Amendment prohibition against cruel and unusual punishment. In order to reach such a conclusion the Court mentioned its previous cases (in particular, the *Roper* case) and argued that 'the judgments of other nations and the international community are not dispositive as to the meaning of the Eighth Amendment. But "[t]he climate of international opinion concerning the acceptability of a particular punishment" is also not irrelevant'.[81]

Although these cases do not explicitly mention foreign precedents (but mostly refer to foreign practices and legislation) they have been taken into consideration with the more significant cases mentioned above and have been included in the charts. They should be taken into great account as they address the importance of foreign materials for the solution of national cases and clarify the main objections which have been suggested against the use of foreign constitutional case law.

The cases also reveal the different perspectives of the US Supreme Court's Justices on the use of foreign jurisprudence. In his dissenting opinion in *Printz*, for instance, Justice Breyer clarified why a comparison with other experiences can be useful to the courts: he argued that

> of course, we are interpreting our own Constitution, not those of other nations, and there may be relevant political and structural differences between their systems and our own. But their experience may nonetheless cast an empirical light on the consequences of different solutions to a common legal problem—in this case the problem of reconciling central

---

[75] *Roper v Simmons*, n 71 above, 577.
[76] *Atkins v Virginia*, n 71 above, 317.
[77] *Printz v United States*, n 54 above, 976.
[78] *Muller v Oregon*, n 18 above, 420.
[79] This case is often cited by scholars as an example of the attention paid in the past by the Supreme Court to foreign experiences.
[80] *Graham v Florida*, 130 S Ct 2011, 2033 but see also Thomas, dissenting, 2053, fn 11 (addressing the issue concerning the use of foreign materials in Supreme Court cases).
[81] *Graham*, n 80 above, 2033.

authority with the need to preserve the liberty-enhancing autonomy of a smaller constituent governmental entity.[82]

In *Roper*, Justice O'Connor's and Justice Scalia's interesting remarks on the relevance of foreign materials in their respective dissenting opinions exemplify the different perspectives in the Supreme Court. Justice O'Connor argued in favour of the dialogue with foreign countries as America's 'evolving understanding of human dignity certainly is neither wholly isolated from, nor inherently at odds with, the values prevailing in other countries'. She held that American Courts

> should not be surprised to find congruence between domestic and international values, especially where the international community has reached clear agreement—expressed in international law or in the domestic laws of individual countries—that a particular form of punishment is inconsistent with fundamental human rights. At least, the existence of an international consensus of this nature can serve to confirm the reasonableness of a consonant and genuine American consensus.

From a different perspective, Justice Scalia firmly rejected

> the basic premise of the Court's argument—that American law should conform to the laws of the rest of the world—ought to be ... I do not believe that approval by 'other nations and peoples' should buttress our commitment to American principles any more than (what should logically follow) disapproval by 'other nations and peoples' should weaken that commitment.

This short account of the American cases dealing with the opportunity of a comparison with foreign jurisprudence, makes it necessary to mention Judge Calabresi's dissenting opinion in *United States v Then*[83] who suggested that

> in exercising restraint American courts might nonetheless take note of what the Constitutional Courts of some cognate countries have done in like situations. Both the Constitutional Courts of Germany and Italy have addressed the problem of laws that were rational when enacted, but which, over time, have become increasingly dubious.

Judge Calabresi also addressed the issue concerning the importance of dialogue with other constitutional courts concluding that 'wise parents do not hesitate to learn from their children'.[84]

V. CONCLUSIONS

On the basis of the results of the empirical analysis, we are able to conclude that although in the United States the use of foreign citation is not so extensive as it is in

---

[82] *Printz*, n 54 above, 976.
[83] *United States v Then*, n 2 above.
[84] 'At one time, America had a virtual monopoly on constitutional judicial review, and if a doctrine or approach was not tried out here, there was no place else to look. That situation no longer holds. Since World War II, many countries have adopted forms of judicial review, which—though different from ours in many particulars—unmistakably draw their origin and inspiration from American constitutional theory and practice. See generally M Cappelletti, *The Judicial Process in Comparative Perspective* (1989). These countries are our "constitutional offspring" and how they have dealt with problems analogous to ours can be very useful to us when we face difficult constitutional issues. Wise parents do not hesitate to learn from their children'.

other common law countries, the few cases containing explicit citations of foreign cases or addressing the issue of the dialogue among constitutional courts make the United States one of the most important countries in the landscape concerning cross-fertilisation among constitutional courts.

This is due also to the circumstance that in the United States the concurring and dissenting opinions made it possible for the Justices of the Supreme Court to express thoroughly their position on the use of foreign materials whereas in other countries (like France and Italy) the structure of the constitutional case and the absence of dissenting or concurring opinions do not allow to the Justices to engage in a similar exchange of opinions.

Furthermore, as we mentioned above, the importance of the United States is due to the great attention which in this country has been paid by scholars to the issue of constitutional borrowing.

Conclusion
The Use of Foreign Precedents by Constitutional Judges: A Limited Practice, An Uncertain Future

TANIA GROPPI AND MARIE-CLAIRE PONTHOREAU

TABLE OF CONTENTS

I. The Results of the Research: A Limited Practice 411
   A. Quantitative Data Considerations 411
   B. Qualitative Considerations 422
II. Perspectives: An Uncertain Future 428

I. THE RESULTS OF THE RESEARCH: A LIMITED PRACTICE

A. Quantitative Data Considerations

i. Two Groups of Countries

THE RESEARCH HAS been conducted by the authors according to different techniques. Most of them initially resorted to searchable databases provided by the courts, employing relevant keywords in order to retrieve constitutional cases (when necessary) and citations of foreign precedents; others, according to the number of decisions, opted for a less filtered and more direct analysis of the texts of the decisions, through 'manual' research.

During the second stage, the citations (all of them or just a selection) were directly examined to understand how precedents had been used and for what purpose.

Although we are aware that an important margin of error may exist in the discretionary choice of the keywords, in the potential incompleteness of electronic databases and, finally, in human fallibility, we believe that the results may be considered representative of the use of foreign case law by the courts herein examined.

The quantitative research underlined the existence of two 'categories' of courts, presented in the two parts of the book.

The differences between the two groups are significant. In the first group we find countries like Namibia, where 93 per cent of the decisions of the Supreme Court in the entire time of its existence refer to foreign cases, or South Africa, where 52 per cent of the decisions of the Constitutional Court, since the beginning of its activity, cite foreign cases. Just to provide an example, the case of *S v Makwanyane* contains 220 citations of foreign cases. Another relevant example is provided by Ireland: since 1937, 396 decisions of the Supreme Court on constitutional cases out of 902 (43.9 per cent) cite foreign precedents. In India, since 1950, out of 1908 constitutional cases, 179 (9.3 per cent) quote foreign precedents.

Even in those case studies in which it was not possible to collect data for all the period of activity of the court, the results are impressive. During the period from 2000 to 2008, the High Court of Australia cited foreign case law in 99 out of 193 constitutional cases (51.3 per cent). From 1982 to 2010 the Supreme Court of Canada cited foreign precedents in a total of 377 constitutional cases out of the 949 decided (39.7 per cent). From 1994 to 2010 the Supreme Court of Israel quoted foreign case law in 121 cases out of 431 constitutional cases, representing 28 per cent of the total, with a peak of 54 per cent in 1995, the year when the landmark decision *Bank Hamizrahi*,[1] that introduced the judicial review of legislation in Israel, was released. This decision alone refers to 35 foreign precedents.

In the second group, the Taiwanese case is more nuanced: since the beginning of the Court's activity in 1949, 66 decisions out of 680 (9.7 per cent) quote foreign precedents, but most of the citations are located in dissenting opinions (only four majority opinions refer to foreign cases). In Mexico only 11 majority decisions and 18 separate opinions citing foreign cases have been detected. In Romania only 14 out of the total of (roughly) 13,250 rulings rendered by the Constitutional Court since its establishment display a clear reference to foreign precedent (0.1 per cent). Even less, almost negligible, is the number in Russia (6 out of 11,000, all in separate opinions), the jurisdiction that seems to be the most hostile to the practice of citing foreign precedents among those presented in the book.

In Austria, out of 13,251 cases decided between 1980 and 2010, the Constitutional Court's decision included explicit references to foreign precedents in only 60 cases (0.45 per cent), although the Constitutional Court itself mentioned a foreign precedent in its reasoning in only 16 out of the 60 cases, whereas, in all other cases, the quotation was only made by one of the parties. In Germany, out of a sample of 1,351 decisions (selected by analysing the decades of the 1950s, 1970s and 2000s), only 32 of them cite foreign cases (2.4 per cent). In Hungary, between 1999 and 2010, out of 1016 decisions, 19 cited foreign cases (1.8 per cent). In Japan, in the period analysed (1990–2008), the report found one explicit citation (out of 234 constitutional cases) in a dissenting opinion, although there are some non-specific citations and, more importantly, strong implicit influences, as is underlined in the report. In the US, the report shows that during the years of the Rehnquist Court (1986–2004) only 0.3 per cent of cases cite foreign case law and citations are almost absent in the years of the Roberts Court (2005–10).

ii. The Influence of the Legal Tradition

There is an almost perfect correlation between the two groups of courts as presented in the book and the legal tradition the courts belong to: on the one hand, the common

---

[1] *Hamizrahi Bank v Migdal* delivered in 1995 (CA 6821/93 United Mizrahi Bank Ltd v Migdal Cooperative Village, 49 (4) PD 221).

law (or mixed) tradition and, on the other, the civil law tradition, with the notable exception of the US Supreme Court, a common law jurisdiction where the practice of explicit citation of foreign case law is rather limited or absent.[2]

This conclusion is reached despite some structural features of constitutional review which might emphasise and encourage a convergence among the two legal traditions. Constitutional courts, in those civil law countries where a concentrated system of judicial review has been established, are different from ordinary courts: members of these courts are appointed according to a special procedure that normally involves political institutions; these members are often scholars and not professional judges; constitutional adjudication often admits separate opinions and constitutional courts do not have, normally, an overburdening docket. In addition, constitutional interpretation favours legal reasoning based on general principles and is thus less formalistic, leaving more room for discursive argument.

The force of the tradition seems to prevail over the special structural features of constitutional adjudication.

As the Australian report points out, in the first group of courts the willingness to resort to foreign case law is a direct product of the 'openness' of these legal systems, which finds its origin, in turn, in the joint legacy of common law methodology and the evolution of states within the British constitutional tradition.

In these countries a continuum exists in the attitude of the supreme and the ordinary courts towards the citation of foreign case law,[3] to the point that in the case of supreme courts there is no relevant difference between citations in constitutional cases and in other cases, as mentioned in the Australian, Canadian, Irish and Israeli reports.

Certain features of the common law methodology of adjudication assist in explaining the relative willingness of common law courts to cite authorities from other jurisdictions:[4] the typically inductive mode of reasoning, often by way of analogy; the discursive form that written reasons take; and the adversarial process in which the respective parties may refer to foreign precedents in support of their argument.

Those features do not exist, or exist only to a limited extent, in the civil law tradition, constitutional courts included.

Sometimes, as in Austria, a strictly positivistic approach to constitutional interpretation may explain the diffidence towards non-binding sources of law. However, even in those countries where constitutional interpretation is not completely formalistic, such as Germany, Hungary or Russia, citations of foreign cases are rare or inexistent. On the other hand, the 'legalistic' approach to constitutional interpretation

---

[2] Some other common law jurisdictions (Singapore and Malaysia) not represented in the book have shown signs of 'discomfort' with the quotation of foreign precedents: C Saunders, 'Judicial Engagement with Comparative Law' in T Ginsburg and R Dixon (eds), *Comparative Constitutional Law* (Northampton, E Elgar, 2011) 574; A Thiruvengadam, 'The Use of Foreign Law in Constitutional Cases in India and Singapore: Empirical Trends and Theoretical Concerns', Working Paper at the VII World Congress of the International Association of Constitutional Law, 2010 (Mexico).

[3] The different attitude of the ordinary courts in common (and mixed) law systems and in civil law systems has already been pointed out by previous studies, especially by the essays contained in U Drobnig and S van Erp (eds), *The Use of Comparative Law by Courts* (The Hague, Kluwer, 1999).

[4] C Saunders 'Judicial Engagement with Comparative Law', n 2 above, 571.

dominant in Australia did not prevent the High Court from extensively citing foreign case law.

Another important feature presented in the first group of countries, and pointed out especially in the report on India, is the openness of the legal culture of jurists, characterising not only countries of the Commonwealth area, but also some mixed systems, such as those in South Africa, Israel and Namibia: in those jurisdictions law has never been merely a 'national' matter, as it has been, until very recently, in most civil law countries. For young legal scholars, completion of their studies in a foreign country has always been a significant component of legal education, a phenomenon that continued even after their home countries achieved independence. This legal culture played an important role not only for those judges that were educated in this context, but also for lawyers, who share this approach: in India very often foreign precedents are introduced in the case file and submitted to the Court by the parties appearing before the Court in order to support their claims and views.

A strong tradition of importation of foreign law, a legal culture open to comparative studies, and a legal education normally completed abroad could also be found in some countries in the second group, but in that case, these elements have not been sufficient to integrate and increase explicit citations in judicial reasoning, as the examples of Japan and Taiwan point out very well. If in Japan a weak connection between constitutional scholars and judges may in part account for the low rate of citations of foreign precedents, in Taiwan the situation appears different, since most of the judges have a strong academic profile that in more recent years has determined a sharp increase in citations of foreign cases in separate opinions: citations, however, remain almost absent from majority opinions.

Other factors, such as a choice in favour of a diffuse or concentrated review, are not relevant in order to explain differences in dealing with foreign precedents. The Mexican example, and even more clearly that of the Supreme Court of Japan, confirms that a legal system inspired by the civil law tradition is a more relevant factor in determining a court's attitude towards the citation of foreign precedents.

In this respect, even the existence of an adversarial procedure does not seem to play an important role, as the report on Austria clearly shows: this country's Constitutional Court is not at all prone to cite foreign precedents on its own account and hardly ever takes notice of foreign precedents when they are cited by one of the parties.

Not even linguistic barriers seem to influence a court's openness to foreign case law: for example, in Austria, even German case law, thoroughly known by Austrian constitutional judges, has been cited only in a few cases (even though much more often than other foreign precedents).

The same can be said for the style of reasoning. The German Constitutional Court, as other constitutional courts, uses a doctrinal and solemn style. Its decisions run to hundreds of pages, filled with social and political theories and doctrinal sources (amounting to an average of 10 citations per decision). Nonetheless, citations of foreign cases are extremely rare.

Finally, individual qualities of judges are a key factor in explaining the practice in both groups of countries. The research confirms that judges with an academic background are more interested in comparative law and foreign precedents than career judges, and that there is a close link between individual views on interpretative methods (as expressed in extrajudicial speeches and publications) and explicit citations of foreign case law.

iii. The Diachronic Analysis

The data does not provide clear evidence that the use of foreign precedents dramatically decreases once a court has established its legitimacy and its set of precedents, as seemed obvious to most of the scholarship.

What is clear is that the enactment of a new Constitution, or of a new Bill of Rights, could encourage openness towards foreign precedents, especially if the cultural context is favourable. This happened in the US in the early years of its foundation, when foreign case law was often quoted, and it was evident in Ireland soon after the enactment of the 1937 Constitution and in India after 1950. Analogously, the enactment of the Canadian Charter of Rights and Freedoms (Canadian *Charter*) or of the Israeli Basic Laws on Human Rights supplemented the already existing tendency to cite foreign law case determining an increase in the number of citations.

In South Africa the novelty of the Constitution joined forces with an additional element: that country's eagerness to become part of the international democratic community again after the apartheid regime had been abolished; consideration of foreign precedents became a logical consequence of such desire. Similar considerations may be extended to Namibia, a context where we can find not only a new democratic Constitution, but also strong international and foreign influences in the Constitution-making.

In *S v Makwanyane*[5] Justice Chaskalson pointed out that foreign law is important in the early stages of transition when there is 'no developed indigenous [rights] jurisprudence on which to draw', but one should 'appreciate that this will not necessarily offer a safe guide to the interpretation' of the Bill of Rights.

With the passing of time, in some countries we found a slight decrease in the citation rate: this was the case for Canada, Ireland and South Africa, but not Australia, Israel or Namibia. This decrease is more significant in India.

In general, in the countries mentioned above, openness to foreign case law remains unchanged. The case of South Africa should be noted, where after a slight decline since 1995, the rate increased again in 2004 and has since remained more or less consistent, except for 2010, when it declined again, possibly due to the appointment of a number of new judges to the Constitutional Court, according to the South African report. In Ireland, the Supreme Court has progressively decreased the number of foreign citations and quotations due to the consolidation of its constitutional jurisprudence and authority, limiting the use of foreign case law to when new constitutional issues—not yet addressed in domestic jurisprudence—are brought before the Court.

On the other hand, the enactment of new Constitutions in countries where a tradition of citation of foreign cases was not present did not necessarily result in the citation of foreign precedents, as the Hungarian, Romanian and Russian reports point out. Traces of an early (relatively) higher propensity to give citations may be

---

[5] *S v Makwanyane* [1995] 3 SA 391 (CC) 37.

found in Germany: the citation rate was indeed higher in the 1950s, and dropped after the Constitutional Court established its own authority and a significant line of precedents. However, the report shows a slight increase in the number of citations in the last decade.

In Russia the tendency remains unchanged (near to zero). In this case nationalism represents the main obstacle to foreign influences. The report refers to a psychological resistance: according to the dominant political rhetoric 'Great Russia must (be seen to) act independently, preserving its national uniqueness'.

In Hungary, in the early years, there was a strong implicit influence of German case law that decreased later, also as a consequence of the growing reference to the ECtHR's case law. In Romania, although the practice remains extremely limited, more recent years show a trend of slow but continuous increment.

Taiwan shows a tendency towards an increase in citations: while this may be linked, on the one hand, to the recent transition to democracy, what seems more influential is the increase in the use of separate opinions, where almost all the explicit citations are found.

The diachronic analysis underlines again the importance of a country's legal tradition: a tendency to openness could be encouraged by the enactment of a new Constitution but it is not discouraged by the passing of time since the Constitution-making process.

iv. What Type of Issues?

The research clearly shows that citations of foreign case law prevail in both groups of countries in human rights decisions, whereas they appear less frequently in institutional decisions.

'Human rights decisions' covered all cases patently dealing with the protection of human rights; conversely, 'institutional decisions' were understood as judgments dealing with issues concerning the parliament and its members, the government, the president, decentralisation (especially in federal States) and the courts. A clear division among these matters has not always been possible and was ultimately left to the discretion of the authors, some of whom decided to introduce a third category, such as 'other issues'. This distinction was not possible in Australia, where the Constitution does not include a Bill of Rights, thus all the cases are qualified as 'institutional cases'.

Sometimes the reason for the prevalence of foreign citations in human rights cases can be related to the constitutional text itself: thus, section 39 of the South African Constitution explicitly refers to the interpretation of the Bill of Rights. In addition the role played by the limitation clauses contained in several Constitutions—referring to a 'free and democratic society'—should also be underlined. Indeed, as the Canadian report points out, determining what limitations are justified in a 'free and democratic society', requires some degree of comparison, since the words 'free and democratic' imply a contrast with societies that are not, and, conversely, commonality with others sharing the same features.

Beyond these specific provisions, an explanation of frequent references to foreign precedents in this field is probably given by the universal character of human rights. This concept has been underlined by many courts, and summarised appropriately by Justice Strydom of the Supreme Court of Namibia, who, in *Alexander v Minister of Justice and Others*, wrote:

> Because of the international character of human rights, a study of comparable provisions in other jurisdictions, as well as the interpretation thereof, is not only relevant but provides this Court with valuable material which may assist this Court in its own interpretation.[6]

Despite this prevalence, citations are not completely absent in institutional decisions.

The Irish report points out that institutional features, like the form of government, are usually peculiar to each country, thus an especially careful approach in the selection of materials is needed. For example, Irish decisions dealing with the prerogatives of the Parliament not to be subjected to the interference of the executive branch and the judiciary quote several precedents from similar countries like the UK, the US and Australia.

Especially relevant in this respect is the case of Israel, where US precedents play an important role not only in human rights but also in institutional cases. The Israeli report points out that the Israeli government system is inherently different from that of the US. The Israeli parliamentary system, the multiplicity of parties, the election method, and the structure of the government and its branches are much closer to the typical governmental structure of several European countries than to the American model. Thus, one would theoretically have expected references to countries such as the UK and other EU members to be more extensive. The limited number of references to continental courts is even more surprising in view of the fact that several constitutional–institutional issues dealt with by the Israeli Supreme Court are addressed also by European countries.

In the second group of countries as well, the few explicit citations mostly refer to human rights cases, as the Austrian, Hungarian and Romanian reports underline. The Hungarian report shows that on some occasions the Court refers to foreign cases in EU matters, such as in reviewing the constitutionality of the European Union's Lisbon Treaty or the constitutionality of the European arrest warrant.

In Germany, the rare citations are more likely in institutional cases (compared to their percentage of the overall caseload). The report indicates that while institutional cases are brought before the Court more rarely and are often of a delicate nature because of their political background, at the same time institutional matters are not as densely affected by legislation and are thus more open to interpretation, leaving more space for a comparative argument.

Finally, in most of those countries foreign precedents are used in cases concerning very controversial or new issues (such as abortion or bioethics) or issues with a potentially important political and social impact. Actually, as emerged from many reports, proportionality stands out as fertile ground for the flourishing of citations of foreign precedents, confirming what a prominent scholar of comparative law (who as a judge played an important role in the cross-judicial dialogue), Aharon Barak, argued in a recent book.[7]

---

[6] *Alexander v Minister of Justice and ors*, 2010 (1) NR 328 (SC).
[7] A Barak, *Proportionality: Constitutional Rights and their Limitations* (Cambridge Studies in Constitutional Law) 2012, 181 ff (and figures at 182) for the migration of proportionality.

v. Which Countries?

Recent studies on the declining influence of US constitutionalism[8] could lead us to assume a corresponding decline in the US Supreme Court's influence.[9]

Undoubtedly, the research shows that, besides the US Supreme Court, other courts are increasingly cited, such as the Supreme Court of Canada, the Constitutional Court of South Africa and, to a lesser degree, the German Constitutional Court. However, the US Supreme Court remains the landmark reference for almost all other courts worldwide, especially those in the first group.[10]

There are many different reasons that drive the courts, in different countries, to express a preference for US case law. A linguistic barrier is probably the first factor to be considered: it excludes non-English speaking courts from the 'competition' for primacy. As the Israeli report aptly points out, this barrier prevents the 'migration' of legal concepts and decisions from certain European countries such as Germany, France, Italy, and Spain. It is not by chance that the only country where a considerable number of references of French cases is present, is bilingual Canada.

Despite the growing practice of English translation of foreign decisions, for example, access to German cases is still difficult for many judges around the world, and sometimes German citations are made indirectly, by way of reference to the contributions of German scholars.[11] In South Africa an interesting debate developed on this point, which also found room in a decision where a judge polemically wrote: 'The German jurisprudence on this subject is not by any means easy to summarise, especially for one who does not read German'.[12] In that Court, German citations were closely linked to one specific judge at the Court, and they dramatically decreased after he retired.[13]

Other reasons may help to explain the primacy of the US Supreme Court over other English-speaking courts. Only in a handful of countries, like Australia, Ireland and India may the explanation be found in the similarities between the

---

[8] D Law and M Versteeg, 'The Declining Influence of the United States Constitution' (2012) 87 *New York University Law Review* 762.

[9] This was the finding, 15 years ago, of C L'Heureux-Dubé, 'The Importance of Dialogue: Globalization and the International Impact of the Rehnquist Court' (1998) 34 *Tulsa Law Journal* 15. See also A Barak, 'A Judge on Judging: The Role of a Supreme Court in a Democracy', 116 *Harvard Law Review* 16 (2002) 114.

[10] The reports do not provide evidence regarding which eras of the US Supreme Court—and corresponding decisions issued therein—are more prone to be cited. Thus it is not possible to verify the validity of those remarks, very common in scholarship, indicating that 'the [US] Supreme Court has undermined the global appeal of its own jurisprudence by failing to acknowledge the relevant intellectual contributions of foreign courts on questions of common concern and by pursuing interpretive approaches that lack acceptance elsewhere': D Law and M Versteeg, 'The Declining Influence of the United States Constitution', n 8 above, 852. See also V Jackson and J Greene, 'Constitutional Interpretation in Comparative Perspective: Comparing Judges or Courts?' in T Ginsburg and R Dixon (eds), *Comparative Constitutional Law* (Northampton, E Elgar, 2011) 599 at 607.

[11] Especially popular among English speaking judges is the book of DP Kommers, *The Constitutional Jurisprudence of the Federal Republic of Germany* (Durham, Duke University Press, 1997).

[12] This remark was made by Kriegler J in *Du Plessis v De Klerk* [1996] 3 SA 850 (CC) 39.

[13] On the influence of Justice Ackerman on the German citations by the South African Constitutional Court, see C Rautenbach and L du Plessis, 'In the Name of Comparative Constitutional Jurisprudence: The Consideration of German Precedents by South African Constitutional Judges' forthcoming in *German Law Journal*.

national Constitutions and the US Constitution, since other countries' fundamental documents significantly differ from that of the US.[14]

In most countries the reason is linked to the obvious considerations of the age and prominence of the US Supreme Court or, more generally, to the influence of US legal culture on legal education.

This is especially evident in Israel, where the 'Americanization' of the Israeli law schools[15] has also had an impact on case law. The Israeli Supreme Court referred to US citations also in several constitutional–institutional issues in which Israeli law is completely different from that of the US. An in-depth review of these issues reveals, according to the Israeli report, that in several cases citations of US precedents were used without a discussion on the appropriate sources of comparative law.

Taking into account US case law does not automatically imply its endorsement. In many cases citations could be 'aversive' or 'negative'. This is especially evident in Canada, where US precedents are cited in human rights decisions, mainly in the early years of the interpretation of the Canadian *Charter*, although very often results achieved by US courts have not been followed.[16] The different structure of the *Charter*, especially with regard to its general limitation clause (s 1), represented a starting point for the development of a distinctively Canadian jurisprudence.

UK courts are still frequently quoted in Commonwealth countries, to the point that they still rank first in Australia and Ireland and still hold an important place in Canada. Together with the UK, other Commonwealth courts are also quoted in those countries, such as Indian or New Zealand courts.

Other courts are growing in influence, such as the Constitutional Court of South Africa and the Supreme Court of Canada.

The Constitutional Court of South Africa represents, quite obviously, a model for the Namibian judges, but it is extensively quoted also by the Canadian Supreme Court and, occasionally, by other courts, such as the Supreme Court of Israel and the High Court of Australia.

The Supreme Court of Canada is popular among others courts in the first group[17] and it is the most quoted by the Constitutional Court of South Africa. As the South African report points out, the popularity of Canadian precedents comes as no surprise and can be attributed mainly to the huge influence that the Canadian *Charter*

---

[14] Especially those established after the Second World War and even more those of the more recent wave of constitutionalism: L Weinrib, 'The Post War Paradigm and the American Exceptionalism' in S Choudhry (ed), *The Migration of Constitutional Ideas* (Cambridge, Cambridge University Press, 2006) 84. The fact that at the turn of the twenty-first century 'the constitutions of the world's democracies are, on average, less similar to the US Constitution now than they were at the end of World War II' has been extensively pointed out by D Law and M Versteeg, 'The Declining Influence of the United States Constitution', n 8 above, 762.

[15] S Haim, 'Legal Colonialism—Americanization of Legal Education in Israel' (June 8, 2010) *Global Jurist* 10.2 (2012), available at SSRN: ssrn.com/abstract=2034386.

[16] With regard to the outcome of the cases, between 1982 and 2010, out of 268 constitutional cases with citations of US precedents, US solutions were followed in only 15% of the cases, while being distinguished in 29% of them. The remaining cases (56%) present merely informative references to US precedents (neither followed, nor distinguished).

[17] Empirical evidence on the influence of the Supreme Court of Canada on other jurisdictions had already been provided in T Groppi, 'A User-friendly Court. The Influence of Supreme Court of Canada Decisions Since 1982 on Court Decisions in Other Liberal Democracies' (2007) 36 *Supreme Court Law Review* 337.

had upon the drafters of the South African Bill of Rights. An analogous explanation may be found in Israel, where Canadian cases are often cited. As noted, the Israeli basic laws on human rights include a limitation clause similar to the one in the Canadian *Charter*. Among Canadian precedents, especially popular is *R v Oakes*,[18] devising the proportionality test for that country's limitation clause.

Finally, decisions of the European Court of Human Rights (ECtHR) are experiencing an increasing influence, as the reports on Australia, Canada, South Africa and Mexico, in particular, have pointed out. In this latter jurisdiction, the influence exerted by the ECtHR's case law on the Inter-American Court of Human Rights (IACHR) is the main explanation for the growing practice. Also, the US Supreme Court, in the very controversial case of *Lawrence v Texas*,[19] quoted a case decided by the ECtHR. The many reasons explaining this phenomenon have been touched on by the reports, and include the accessibility for English-speaking countries of the ECtHR's decisions and the fact that human rights are a more fertile ground for foreign citations.

In the second group of countries, the rare citations are much more articulated: various countries are represented, although some reports point out a preference for closer jurisdictions.

In Romania, although only 14 decisions in total refer to foreign cases, 11 different countries are cited, ranging from the US to Latvia. The few citations included in the separate opinions of the Constitutional Court of Russia as well, refer to a vast set of countries, ranging from the US to Slovakia. In Mexico, many different jurisdictions are quoted, although, besides the ECtHR, a primary role is played by the Constitutional Court of Colombia. In Germany the US Supreme Court remains the most cited, followed by Switzerland and other European courts, to the point that the author labelled this attitude as Euro-Atlantic centrism.

The Constitutional Courts of Austria and Hungary prefer to quote the German Constitutional Court, and even implicit influences are derived from that Court.

In Taiwan, a close link has been pointed out between the legal education of the judges and the jurisdictions cited; a link that is easily recognisable since foreign precedents are cited almost only in separate opinions. The German precedents are the most cited, since most of the judges have a doctorate from a German university; the US follows, then Japan, according to the legal education of the judges. The report points out that these data could change in the future with changes in the composition of the Court.

It should be pointed out that in Hungary the Constitutional Court sometimes compares American and European legal development patterns, contrasting the jurisprudence of the US Supreme Court with that of the ECtHR, referring to the latter as representative of continental legal culture.

In conclusion, the research shows the absence of explicit transjudicial communication. Not only are there few countries where explicit citations are used, but the number of countries quoted is limited as well. An explicit circulation does exist

---

[18] *R v Oakes*, 1 SCR 103 (1986).
[19] *Lawrence v Texas*, 539 US 558 (2003).

within a circumscribed area, which coincides with some English-speaking countries citing each other.

One could argue that this is the result of a correct contextualisation of citations, consciously limited to countries with similar cultural and legal features. However, this consideration does not dispel doubts that often English-speaking courts may wilfully disregard cases originating from non-English-speaking jurisdictions, not for reasons lying in the special features of these countries' legal systems (a fact that would still allow 'a contrario' citations) but, more likely, due to the presence of a linguistic and cultural barrier, as clearly shown by the case of Israel.

vi. Which Opinions?

Foreign precedents are present in all different types of opinion (majority—that in most of the jurisdictions coincide with the opinion of the court—, concurring and/ or dissenting).

In some cases this use cannot be clearly identified: for example in Austria separate opinions are not allowed, in Ireland the one-judgment rule is mandatory in most constitutional cases, in Namibia dissenting opinions are not frequent and in Australia there is no practice in the High Court of clearly identifying the majority reasons as the opinion of the Court.

In general, in the first group of courts the number of citations seems linked to the level of disagreement on a specific issue and the number of opinions filed, as the Canadian, South African and Israeli reports point out. In Canada, for example, the highest numbers of citations of foreign precedents are found in majority and dissenting opinions, and not in the 'per curiam' opinions. However, the Israeli report also underlines that the majority (over 70 per cent) of foreign citations is made by judges in the majority opinion because the main function of the use of foreign precedents is to support the decision.

In the case of South Africa, where a very sophisticated use of foreign precedents is normal practice, quite often judges refer to separate opinions in foreign precedents whilst the same foreign case is sometimes considered by both the judges delivering the majority opinion and those filing dissenting or concurring opinions, within the same decision.

In the second group of countries, it is more likely to find foreign cases' citations in separate opinions, as the reports on Japan, Mexico and Taiwan show.

Taiwan deserves a special mention, as there are only four citations of foreign precedents in the majority opinions between 1949 and 2010. However, out of a total of 680 decisions, 108 separate opinions quote foreign precedents. There is a close link between the scholarly background of justices and the frequency of their foreign precedent citations: most citations of foreign precedents were provided by justices with academic backgrounds (390 times), as opposed to justices with professional backgrounds (career judges) (184 times), namely twice as many.

The only other report that provides weighted data on separate opinions (by considering the ratio of separate opinions out of the total number of decisions), the German one, shows that judges giving separate opinions tend to be more open to quoting foreign sources than those delivering majority opinions: the author argues that dissenting judges do not have to carry the consequences of the judgment on their shoulders the same way the latter do; they are freed from the constraints of authority being able to leave the official standards or argument behind.

In Russia all the—extremely rare—foreign citations have been made in separate opinions. The report points out that, since the majority opinions are considered binding in all their parts, even in obiter dicta, non-binding materials, such as foreign cases, are not allowed. Instead, as separate opinions are not considered binding, the judges writing them feel more free to refer to foreign cases.

B. Qualitative Considerations

i. Are Judges Comparatists?

The reports tend to underline that courts of the first group are perfectly conscious of the issues raised by the use of foreign precedents. They also point out that courts are cautious in this practice. This caution is for two key reasons.

First of all, courts tend to contextualise citations according to the different constitutional and legal system they are from and they do not hesitate to distinguish the case before them from the foreign authority when this is necessary in light of the domestic context. This happens especially in Canada and South Africa.

Secondly, courts are well aware of the difficulty of good contextualisation and refer to foreign precedents only to find assistance and enlightenment in developing domestic constitutional interpretation and not merely to import foreign solutions.

Mistakes in understanding or citing foreign cases are unreported. If one considers cherry-picking—ie citing only foreign decisions supporting the preferred result—as a form of misuse,[20] the research shows that courts cherry pick all the time: they normally avoid justifying their case selection.

Many statements may be found in the decisions quoted by the reports to testify the awareness of the risks of citing foreign precedents.[21]

What is not clear is the methodology followed by the courts in the selection of cases to be cited. We referred earlier to the Israeli report on institutional cases, where the Supreme Court of Israel quoted US instead of European precedents which, according to the author, would have been much more suitable.

In this vein, it is important to underline the objection of one of the judges of the Mexican Supreme Court to references to foreign precedents in the 'same-sex

---

[20] We can quote the Judge of the Constitutional Court of South Africa, Albie Sachs, cited by U Bentele, 'Mining for Gold: The Constitutional Court of South Africa's Experience with Comparative Constitutional Law' (2009) 37 *Georgia Journal of International and Comparative Law* 219, 239: 'yes, we cherry pick all the time when we use authorities, foreign or domestic ... it's got to be a cherry that fits'.

[21] The opinion of Justice Breyer of the Supreme Court of the US in *Printz v United States*, 521 US 898, 976 is well known. See also, eg, the opinion of Justice Ackermann of the Constitutional Court of South Africa in *National Coalition for Gay and Lesbian Equality v Minister of Justice* [1999] 1 SA 6 (CC) 48 or the opinion of Justice O'Regan, of the same Court, warning against the risks of 'shallow comparativism': *Fose v Minister of Safety and Security* [1997] 3 SA 786 (CC) 35. See also the opinion of Justice Macken, of the Supreme Court of Ireland, *Pól O Murchú v An Taoiseach* (2010) IEHC 26, or of Justice Wilson, of the Supreme Court of Canada in *Lavigne v Ontario Public Service Employees Union* [1991] 2 SCR 211.

marriage case':[22] why cite foreign precedents or laws in favour of same-sex marriage and not add references to countries that do not designate same-sex unions as 'marriages'? The very point about citation of foreign authorities was highly controversial in that case and an important debate on the legitimacy of the practice was raised: the exclusion of references to foreign law from the final text was eventually decided by a 6-5 vote, with the prevailing argument that the issues raised by the lawsuit should be answered specifically, and 'not with abstract references to comparative law'.

Finally, very few statements may be found against the practice, besides the well-known opinions of some Justices of the US Supreme Court. In *Thompson v Oklahoma*,[23] Justice Scalia wrote that 'we must never forget that it is a Constitution for the United States of America that we are expounding', while in *Printz v United States*, he argued that 'comparative analysis [is] inappropriate to the task of interpreting a constitution'.[24]

In addition, some opinions of the Australian High Court can be reported, although they are rather isolated and seem influenced by the American debate (such as the opinion of Justice Heydon in the Roach case, according to which 'our law does not permit recourse to these materials').[25] Also, one opinion of a Judge of the Constitutional Court of Taiwan, in one of the few cases where the majority used foreign citations, can be quoted (Justice Herbert HP Ma, with a doctorate from Harvard Law School, argued that 'it would be unwise for the Court to rely upon external sources including foreign precedents when rendering decisions').[26]

In the second group of countries the main issues are the reasons that prevent the courts from making explicit reference to foreign cases. The only report that addresses this aspect in depth is the Japanese one. According to the author, there is an 'advantage' for courts in avoiding explicit citations of foreign case law: this way they may freely manipulate foreign precedents, without incurring criticism of the doctrine.

Although we agree with some commentators that 'bricolage is probably the only performance we can reasonably expect from judges',[27] and that a systematic use of foreign precedents would be a Herculean task, we believe that if judges engage in this practice (a practice that is completely optional) they should be careful in the selection of appropriate cases and in the understanding of the context for judicial cross-fertilisation. Dangers, coming in the form of potential loss of legitimacy for courts, of approximate comparisons etc, are well known and do not need to be reiterated here.[28]

---

[22] SJFG (August 2011) 878.
[23] *Thompson v Oklahoma*, 487 US 815, 868, fn 4 (1988).
[24] *Printz v United States*, 521 US 898, 921, fn 11 (1997).
[25] *Roach v Electoral Commissioner* (2007) 233 CLR 1 at 224–25.
[26] JY Interpretation No 261 (21 June 1990). An English translation is available at www.judicial.gov.tw/constitutionalcourt/en/p03_01.asp?expno=261.
[27] V Ferreres Comella, 'Comparative Modesty' (2011) 7 *European Constitutional Law Review* 517, 526, referring to the 'modesty' of V Jackson, *Judicial Engagement in a Transnational Era* (2009) 189. The word 'bricolage' was referred to as introduced by M Tushnet, 'The Possibilities of Comparative Constitutional Law' (1999) *Yale Law Journal* 1225.
[28] U Drobnig and S van Erp (eds), *The Use of Comparative Law by Courts* (The Hague, Kluwer, 1999) 16.

ii. The Roles of the Use of Foreign Precedents

a. To Provide a Guiding Horizon

In most of the countries in the first group, the citation of foreign precedents has primarily (but not exclusively) had the function of providing a guiding horizon. The motto of the court could be: 'First let's look around, then we will decide.' The foreign case law is cited at the very beginning of the interpretative process, to find sources of inspiration. In this case, courts tend to refer concisely to decisions from many different jurisdictions, without deeply discussing or analysing foreign precedents.

This is the most common usage in South Africa, on which the author of that country's report underlines that approximately 2,534 foreign citations are used at the very first stage of the interpretative process, when reasoning must be oriented.

The Irish report points out that the Supreme Court prefers to refer to its own precedents; however, when a new sensitive issue arises and there are no domestic precedents (for example, in the case concerning withdrawal of medical and feeding treatments),[29] it looks at how the issue has been addressed elsewhere before engaging in the interpretation of the national Constitution.

The Hungarian report labels this function as 'illustrative' and points out that this is the most frequent use of foreign judicial precedents in Hungary.

b. A Probative Argument

In many cases, judges quote specific foreign precedents in order to support their decision. This is known as a 'probative argument', in which the court accepts and applies a constitutional principle or a specific interpretation of a constitutional clause from another jurisdiction.

'Probative comparison' takes place in two different ways.

When referring to all liberal democracies, the approach is very similar to the definition of a 'guiding horizon', although the comparison happens at a different stage of the decision-making process, in which the interpretative reading has already been selected and must only be made persuasive. In these cases, courts refer to foreign arguments by making synthetic references, or without quoting specific precedents at all.

Conversely, in the first group of countries, when a single legal order and its case law is referred to, precedents, often selected from a previously established 'guiding horizon', are extensively cited and discussed, both in majority and minority opinions, and very often these countries refer to foreign minority opinions.

The Indian report provides interesting data: most of the decisions quoting foreign cases make reference to more than five foreign judgments. The author of that country's report points out that when judges decide to look at another jurisdiction, they try to delve deeply into the point of view of foreign judges and the evolution of the jurisprudence of those countries. In a context less inclined to citation, an analogous

---

[29] *In re a Ward of Court (Withholding Medical Treatment) (No 2)* (1996) 1IR 79.

remark (citation of more than one foreign case at a time, sometimes more than seven) is pointed out by the Hungarian report.

The Irish report shows that in 'probative arguments' the court makes a more careful selection of the countries and refers only to precedents coming from the UK, the US, Australia and Canada. The most evident example is represented by the proportionality test defined by the Supreme Court of Canada in *R v Oakes*,[30] which has been substantially 'transplanted' into Irish law by the Supreme Court.[31]

According to the Canadian report, judges seem to feel compelled to cite a higher number of precedents not only to overcome opposition from colleagues but also to make their decisions more acceptable to their audience. In particular, Canadian judges appear to cite foreign precedents more frequently when they overturn government action than when they uphold it.

In Israel most foreign decisions (over 70 per cent) were meant to establish the 'even there' claim. Namely, they were meant to bolster the Israeli Supreme Court by referring to a set of laws that supports the Court's decision. Where constitutional judges wish to establish their rulings on foreign case law, among other things, the fact that countries with similar judicial values support their judicial conclusions further legitimises their decisions.

This is the main role played by explicit references to foreign cases in the second group of jurisdictions, both in majority and (more often) separate opinions: the rare citations are always aimed at supporting the preferred result, as pointed out by the reports on Austria, Germany, Hungary, Romania, Russia, Mexico and Taiwan.

This is also the case with the US Supreme Court, where the few recent citations (such as in *Lawrence v Texas*)[32] have been used to support the decision. In the US, in cases such as those relating to the death penalty, citations more often aim at 'acknowledge[ing] the overwhelming weight of international opinion against the juvenile death penalty' or at emphasising general disapproval against the death penalty but without a substantial analysis of foreign law.[33]

c. *A Contrario* Argument or Aversive Argument

In some cases, judges quote specific foreign decisions to distinguish the case and their final decision from them. This approach seems confined to just a few jurisdictions, all included in the first group.

The South African report is the only one that presents numerical data on this issue. It accounts for only 22 citations in this category out of a total of 2,742 citations of foreign cases.

In other jurisdictions, such as Ireland, when courts want to underline the 'uniqueness' of the national legal order (for example, in judgments on the rights of the unborn), they prefer to ignore foreign case law, although, referring to one of the most cited foreign courts, the Supreme Court of Ireland 'has emphasised that, given

---

[30] *R v Oakes* (1986) 1 SCR 103.
[31] *Heaney v Ireland* (1994) 3 IR 593.
[32] *Lawrence v Texas*, 539 US 558 (2003).
[33] See, ie, *Roper v Simmons*, 543 US 551 (2004) at 577 and *Atkins v Virginia*, 536 US 304 (2002) at 317.

the difference in some constitutional provisions between the two States, the United States Supreme Court decisions must be used with care'.[34]

The same considerations apply to Israel, where in a recent case on the unconstitutionality of a constitutional amendment[35] many foreign cases (mainly from India and Turkey and, for the first time, a decision of the Czech Constitutional Court) were cited, to point out that the situation in Israel is different from the customs in the countries whose cases were cited because the doctrine of unconstitutional constitutional amendment assumes the existence of a complete Constitution and an amendment made to it, while the Israeli constitutional process is as yet incomplete.

India and Canada deserve a special mention in this regard. In India judges often engage in a detailed discussion of foreign cases to conclude that the 'Indian Constitution is unique and the American or other foreign precedents cannot be of much assistance'.[36] In Canada the research points out that, while there are, certainly, a few instances of endorsement of US interpretations of the *Bill of Right*'s provisions, in the majority of cases, results achieved by US courts have not been followed. This is consistent with the view that engagement with foreign law is first and foremost an exercise in self-understanding, which leads to identifying the distinguishing elements of Canadian society. As a result, consideration of US precedents by the Supreme Court of Canada is mainly '*a contrario*'. Thus, the research shows that the Court is willing to be receptive to foreign solutions only when they are compatible with the principles informing Canadian society and its legal system.

iii. Implicit Influences

Influence by foreign sources that are not identified by the courts themselves through citations is hard to identify. Implicit influences can either work unconsciously through, for example, value patterns developed during foreign legal training, or, conversely, consciously, but held back from the public.

However, in today's globalised world, implicit influences are very likely, irrespective of the attitude of a single court to quoting foreign precedents explicitly. In most of the courts that do not cite foreign precedents special departments of international relations and research exist providing judges with full information about, and translations of, foreign cases. This happens in Russia, for example, where that department has compiled more than 100 reviews of the practice of foreign courts concerning particular questions submitted at the request of the Chairman of the Constitutional Court and of the reporting judge.

Only a few authors had the opportunity to assess those influences by way of interviews with members of the courts or law clerks. When they did, as in the Austrian and Hungarian reports, the result was a long list of cases where the influence of foreign precedents (German precedents in both countries) was relevant. The interview carried out by the author of the Hungarian report points out that in practically

---

[34] See *O'B v S* (1984) IR 316.
[35] HC 4908/10 *Knesset Member Bar-On v Israel's Knesset* (not yet published, rendered 7 April 2011).
[36] *Golak Nath v State of Punjab*, 1967 SCR (2) 762.

all cases when an important matter is under consideration, a comparative review is made by the staff of the constitutional judge who acts as the *rapporteur* of the case (as the Court does not have a specialised service). Despite the fact that such a review is usually carried out for landmark cases, it is often left out from the final version of the decision. The interview with judges and law clerks of the Romanian Constitutional Court confirmed an analogous attitude: they are perfectly aware of existing foreign law (the main source of information being the Venice Commission and its dedicated website,[37] as well as various networks established among constitutional courts or judges),[38] but they do not quote it.

In the Mexican report many implicit influences (mainly of German or Spanish origin), such as the proportionality and balancing tests, and the vital minimum doctrine have been detected through a careful examination of the case law.

Many implicit influences, all originating from US case law, have been detected by the Japanese report: the Supreme Court of Japan is a strong importer of US Supreme Court decisions, but always in a non-express fashion. This circumstance has determined instances of misuse of foreign cases, which, quite often, have been 'manipulated' by the Japanese judges (the author labels this phenomenon as 'plagiarism or misquotation'). A very good example is freedom of expression, a field in which, although the Japanese Supreme Court finds evident inspiration in US cases, the Court never declared a violation of the Constitution and always showed, as in the vast majority of its case law, a very deferential attitude towards the government.

Very often, a vehicle for implicit influences is reference to academic literature (at least in those courts that admit this possibility), as the German report underlines, by quoting the words of a former judge: 'Comparative material', he indicates, 'is used when the rapporteur is preparing the judgment if there is comparative German literature at hand'.[39] The Indian report points out that in recent years the quotation of academic literature seemed to be the *escamotage* to consider foreign elements in a decision without explicitly relying on them.

The report on Japan identifies three sources of hidden influences: first, the role of appellants who cite foreign precedent or foreign law in their briefs in order to reinforce their arguments; second, the backgrounds of some judges who are academics with a legal education obtained outside their country, and lastly the role of law clerks who may conduct research and make available to the judges some comparative law materials.

The Taiwanese report also maintains that the citations included in separate opinions could be considered as sources of implicit influences: according to the authors, there is good reason to assume that the reasoning provided in majority opinions is influenced by the foreign precedents cited in separate opinions and they also tried to measure the level of implicit influences in majority opinions.

Finally, most of the reports concerning courts in Europe identify Europeanisation as a source of implicit influence. In other words, there are common principles

---

[37] See CODICES website at www.codices.coe.int.
[38] On the role played by those networks see, eg, V Jackson, *Constitutional Engagement in a Transnational Era* (Oxford, Oxford University Press, 2009) 100.
[39] B-O Bryde, 'The Constitutional Judge and the International Constitutionalist Dialogue' in B Markesinis and J Fedtke (eds), *Judicial Recourse to Foreign Law* (London, UCL Press, 2006) 295, 298.

that circulate by way of the ECtHR's (and in minor measure the CJEU's (Court of Justice of the European Union)) case law. The best example is, again, the principle of proportionality.

The lack of consensus on the use of foreign precedents could explain why some courts prefer to refer to the ECtHR rather than to foreign courts. In the Hungarian case, for example, references have moved from German Federal Constitutional Court and US Supreme Court precedents to the ECtHR's case law.

Comparing the aforementioned extensive implicit influences to the pattern of rare explicit citations which emerged in the analysis of the second group of countries, one can only speculate about the reasons for this prevalent approach. Considering that the main (and often exclusive) audience of any court is almost always represented by one or more domestic actors (be they other institutions, the government and/or the public at large), one could be drawn to assume that courts prioritise legal arguments that are more likely to persuade their learned audience (and also indirectly preserve the legitimacy and acceptance of the institution).[40]

Thus, the presence or absence of explicit citations of foreign case law could provide an (admittedly, rather approximate) indicator of the arguments that each court's domestic audience is more likely to prefer and accept, or, more precisely, of the arguments that each court 'supposes' are most likely to enhance the acceptance of its decisions by the domestic audience. If one endorses such a perspective, the propensity of courts towards the use of foreign citations could provide information not only on a country's legal tradition, but also on its general degree of openness towards 'foreign' influences. It is our view that further, in-depth exploration of the attitude of each court's audience could shed more light on the practice of the judicial use of foreign case law, especially with regard to the second group of jurisdictions.

II. PERSPECTIVES: AN UNCERTAIN FUTURE

The findings of the research show that the 16 courts examined in this book do not share the same attitude towards the citation of foreign precedents.

While some courts are eager to quote foreign case law explicitly and extensively in numerous decisions, others are reluctant to embrace this practice.

The two groups of courts coincide—except for the notable and well-known 'exception' of the resistance of the US Supreme Court to the use of foreign cases—with the divide between countries with a common law (or mixed) tradition, on the one hand, and countries belonging to the civil law tradition, on the other. Other factors, often pointed out by scholars, such as the propensity of more recent courts, without a strong line of precedents, to look at case law of older and better established courts, especially during their formative periods, do not seem to be decisive.

The gap between the two groups not only concerns 'how much' courts quote foreign precedents: important differences can also be found in the quality of citations.

Courts in the first group do not resort to foreign cases just to support their decisions. Sometimes they also engage in a dialectical conversation with foreign

---

[40] MC Ponthoreau, 'L'argument fondé sur la comparaison dans le raisonnement juridique' in P Legrand (ed), *Comparer les droits résolument* (Paris, PUF, 2009) 537–60.

courts, distinguishing the case before them from these decisions' reasoning, and ending up with 'aversive' or 'negative' use (especially Canada and South Africa). They are shown to be aware of the high level of risk involved in referring to foreign cases and display a cautious and conscious attitude. However, not even these courts (exactly as the courts included in the second group) succeed in explaining their foreign case selection, especially with regard to the jurisdictions cited. With the remarkable exception of the Constitutional Court of South Africa, these courts seem to neglect cases originating in non-English-speaking jurisdictions, an attitude that seems more the consequence of a linguistic and cultural barrier, rather than an effort of correct contextualisation. Our suspicion is that this practice of citation, more than contributing to the enhancement of 'legal cosmopolitanism', actually promotes the creation of a 'closed circle', from which most of the non-English speaking countries are left outside in the cold.[41]

Courts in the second group, when explicitly referring to foreign precedents, neither discuss the cases in depth, nor try to explore the context. Citations, often mere passing references, are always aimed at supporting the (already determined) decision or the separate opinions. In fact, most citations are indeed included in separate opinions, a practice resulting mainly from the personality and background of the single judges drafting them, much more than in the first group of courts. A vast array of countries is cited from different legal and constitutional traditions, although quite often references to closer jurisdictions tend to prevail.

In this group, courts are perfectly aware of foreign case law. They are active members of networks of constitutional judges, very often have specially-dedicated departments and can even count on the work of foreign law clerks. Also, frequently judges are prominent constitutional law scholars, with important international experience. What happens, therefore, is that they simply decide not to cite foreign precedents expressly. At the same time important implicit influences are present. While they certainly do not need to 'expand their horizon', what is missing here is a more transparent, verifiable motivation, to avoid mistakes and manipulations.[42]

In spite of these basic differences, some common features exist between the two groups.

1) The research did not show any case to be decided relying on the mere 'importation' of a foreign decision: citations of foreign precedents, at best, provide additional arguments in support of a court's or a judge's previously-developed position.
2) Courts do not explain or justify the case selection, nor the jurisdictions selected: in this sense, it would be fair to say that they 'cherry pick' all the time.
3) Citations of foreign case law are prominent in both groups of courts in human rights cases, whereas they are less frequent in institutional ones. Proportionality results to be a fertile ground worldwide for the flourishing of the citation of foreign precedents.

---

[41] This finding shows assonances with that of Law and Versteeg, according to which '[t]he evolution of global constitutionalism is characterized by a combination of *intra*-group convergence and *inter*-group divergence': D Law and M Versteeg, n 8 above, 821.
[42] V Ferreres Comella, 'Comparative Modesty' (2011) 7 *European Constitutional Law Review* 517, 526.

4) Citations are more likely to occur in new and complex cases, or, at any rate, in cases dealing with issues with a potentially important political and social impact.
5) The number of citations is directly related to the level of disagreement: the more separate opinions are filed, the more references to foreign case law are present.
6) The US Supreme Court still remains a landmark reference for almost all the other courts examined, especially for those in the first group, although undoubtedly other courts are gaining in influence, such as the South Africa Constitutional Court, the Supreme Court of Canada and the ECtHR.

At the conclusion of this extensive project, very few doubts are left regarding the existence of growing horizontal communication between the various constitutional systems[43] or on the role constitutional judges are playing in this communication.

What the research has shown is that, among the 16 countries examined, the practice of explicit citation of foreign case law is rather circumscribed and belongs to a limited 'family' of courts.

At present, no signs lead us to think that this ultimate divide will change, at least not in the near future. However, the research detected some recent trends, which could indicate a route towards future developments and eventually guide comparative constitutional law scholars keen to engage in more empirical research.

In the first group, the increasing availability of English translations of foreign constitutional decisions and the increase in comparative studies have not yet determined clear moves in the direction of a more open attitude towards non-English-speaking jurisdictions. It is fair to assume that, due to this increased communication and friendlier atmosphere, sooner or later this may happen. This is a serious assumption, although no clear evidence in this sense has been detected, except for an increase in citations of the ECtHR's cases. We believe that special attention should be paid to the role that ECtHR case law is playing worldwide due to its being considered representative of continental legal culture.

In the second group, despite frequent requests on the part of scholars for constitutional courts to use foreign cases more explicitly, to date no evidence exists that their reluctant attitude is going to change. The research pointed out a growing preference of courts to give explicit citations of case law of international regional courts: this is especially evident in Europe, with regard to the ECtHR, but also in Mexico with respect to the IACHR. One can only guess if international case law is going to serve the aims of transnational constitutionalism, and thus claims in favour of a transparent use of foreign case law would soon become outdated. We believe that this issue, raised by prominent scholars,[44] should be explored in depth, also by way of comparative empirical research.

In conclusion, evidence exists that both groups of countries are evolving towards forms of transjudicial communication not focused on the use of foreign precedents, or at least not on precedents of other *national* jurisdictions. This can be seen

---

[43] See G Halmai, 'The Use of Foreign Law in Constitutional Interpretation' in M Rosenfeld and A Sajò *The Oxford Handbook of Constitutional Comparative Law* (Oxford, Oxford University Press, 2012).

[44] E Benvenisti, 'Reclaiming Democracy: The Strategic Use of Foreign and International Law by National Courts' (2008) 102 *The American Journal of International Law* 241.

especially in the area where foreign case law has been more influential, that is, human rights: horizontal and vertical circulation could find a suitable cohabitation, or the arrival of relevant competitors could narrow the space available to foreign case law.

As we already warned in the foregoing, some relevant countries have not been included in the book, and thus, the generalisations and conclusions hereby presented should be taken with an extra dose of prudence.

Despite this caveat we believe that, by introducing some original empirical data and materials in the theoretical debate on transjudicial communication, this book may help pour 'new wine into new wineskins'.